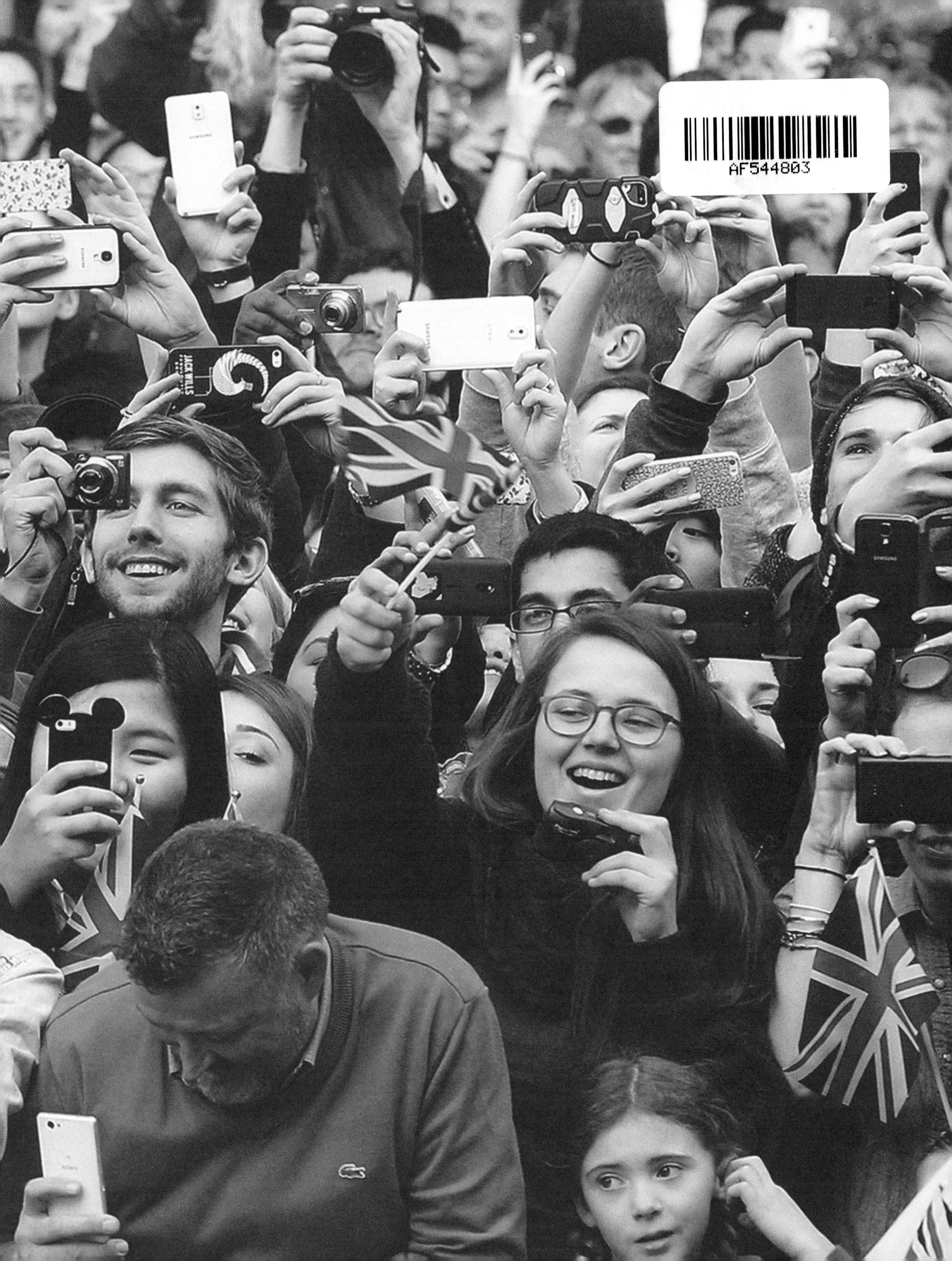
JACK WILLS

MODERN MONARCHY

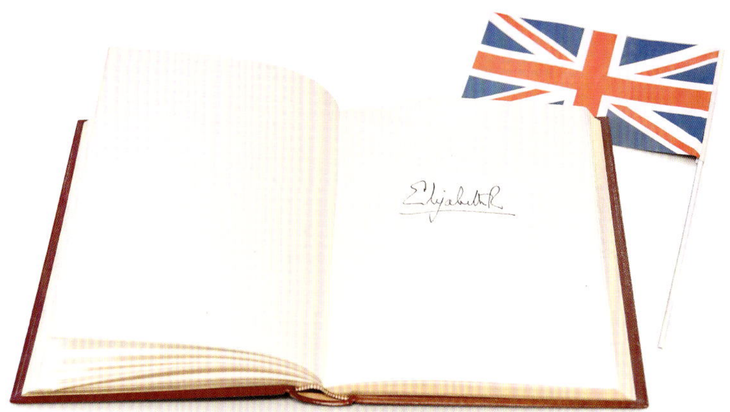

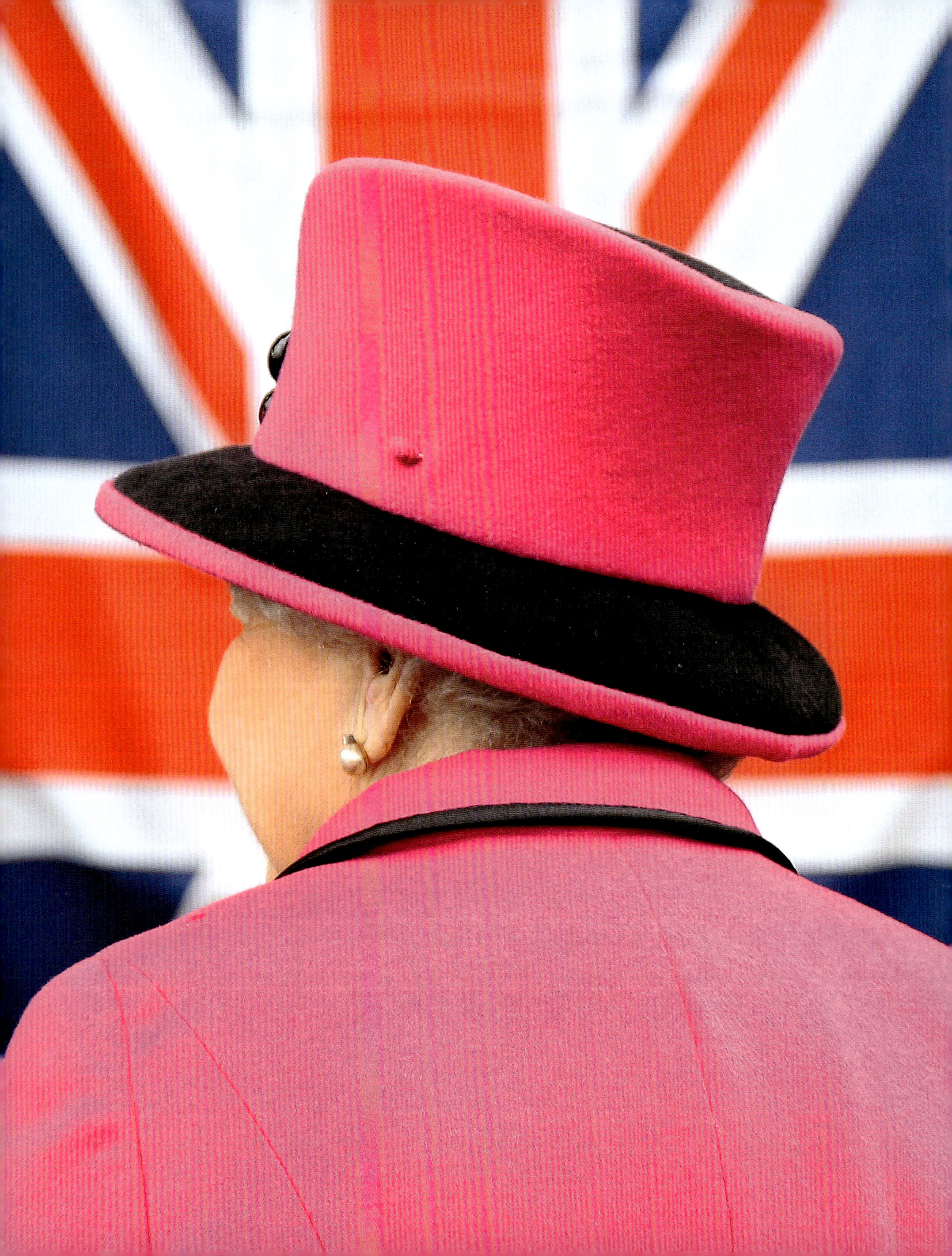

MODERN MONARCHY

THE BRITISH ROYAL FAMILY TODAY

FOREWORD BY MICHAEL PRITCHARD
PHOTOGRAPHY AND TEXT BY CHRIS JACKSON

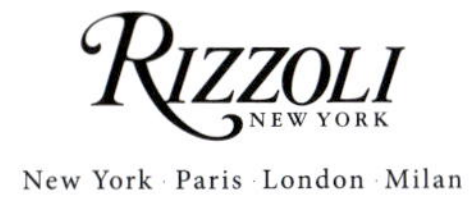
RIZZOLI NEW YORK
New York · Paris · London · Milan

gettyimages

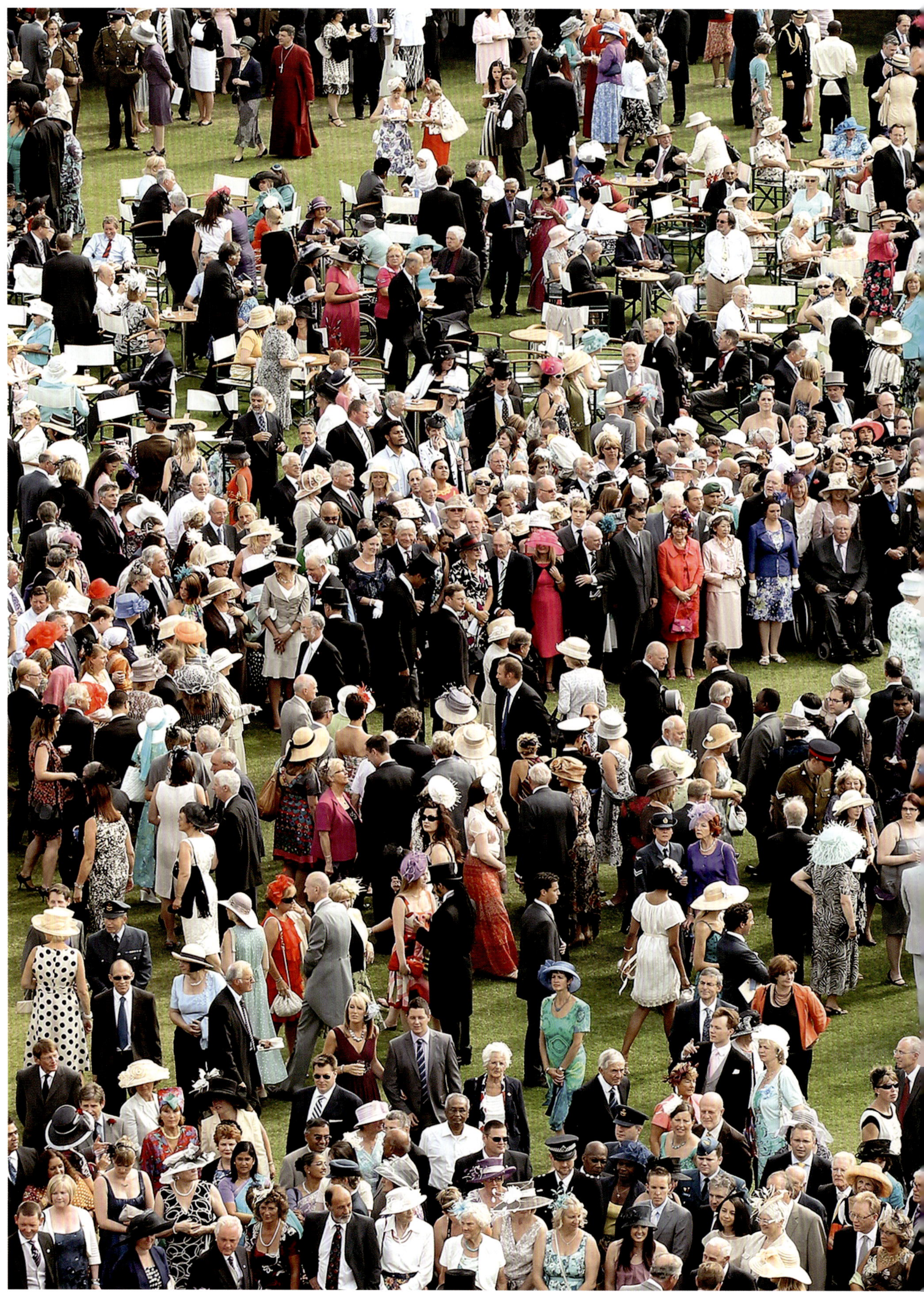

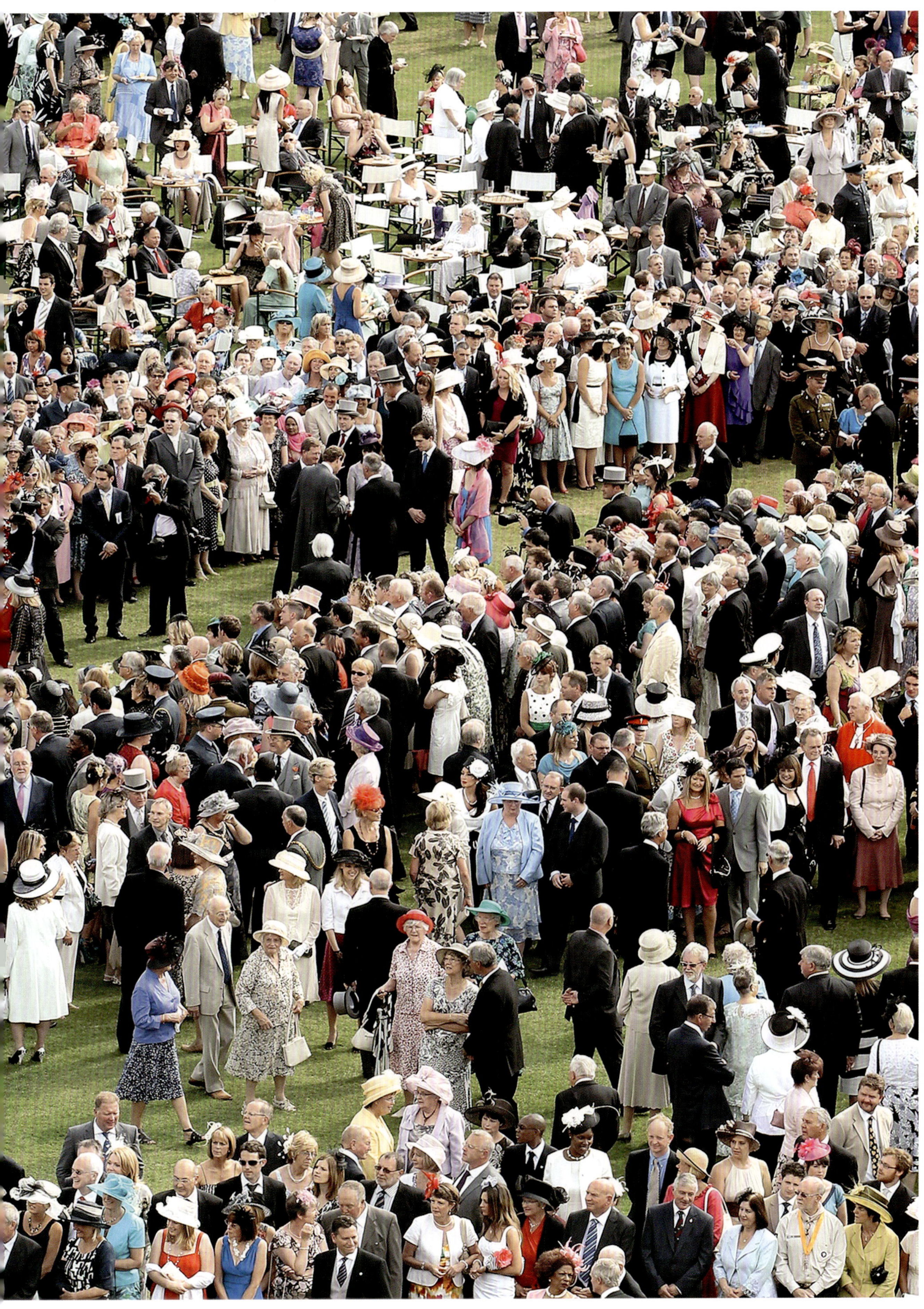

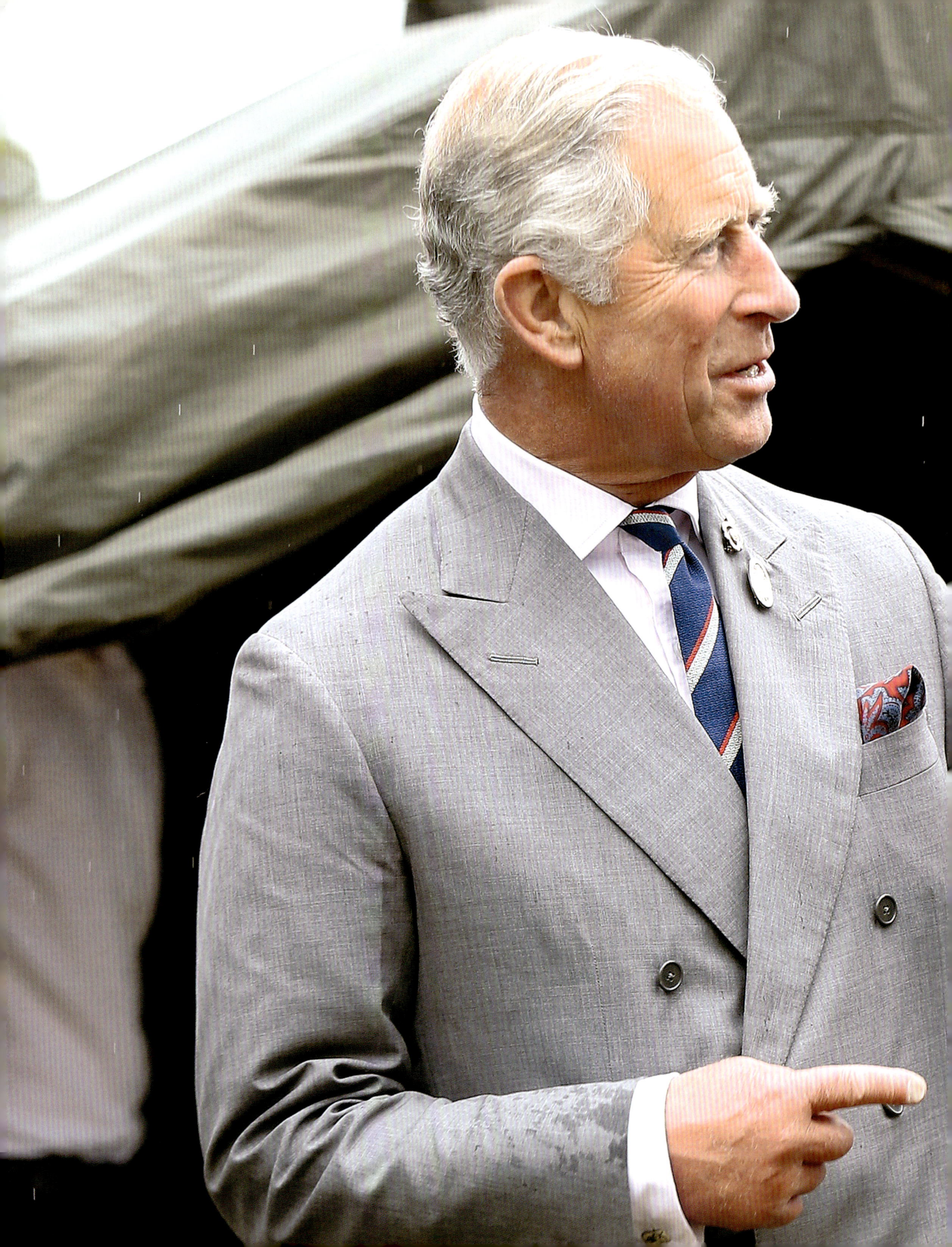

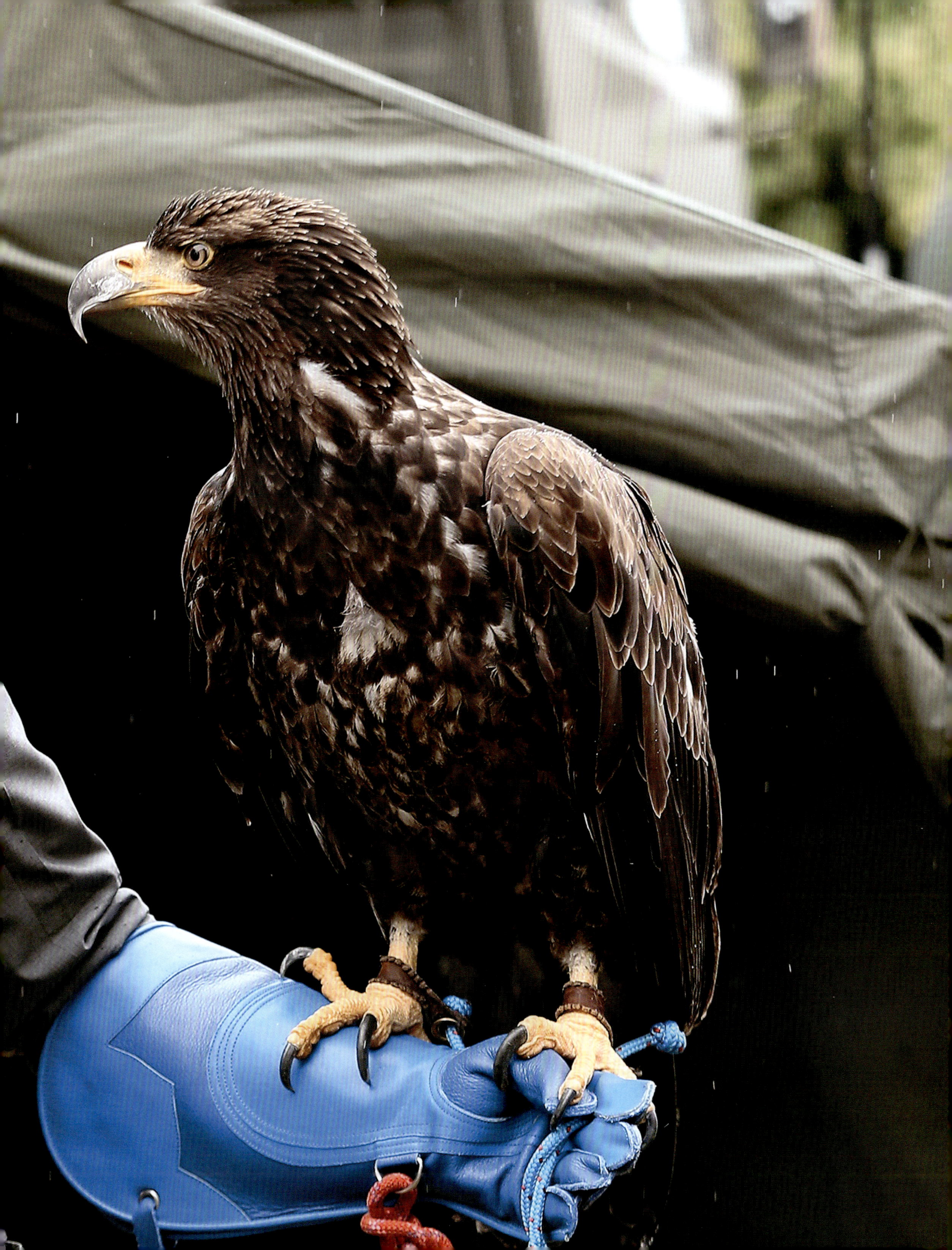

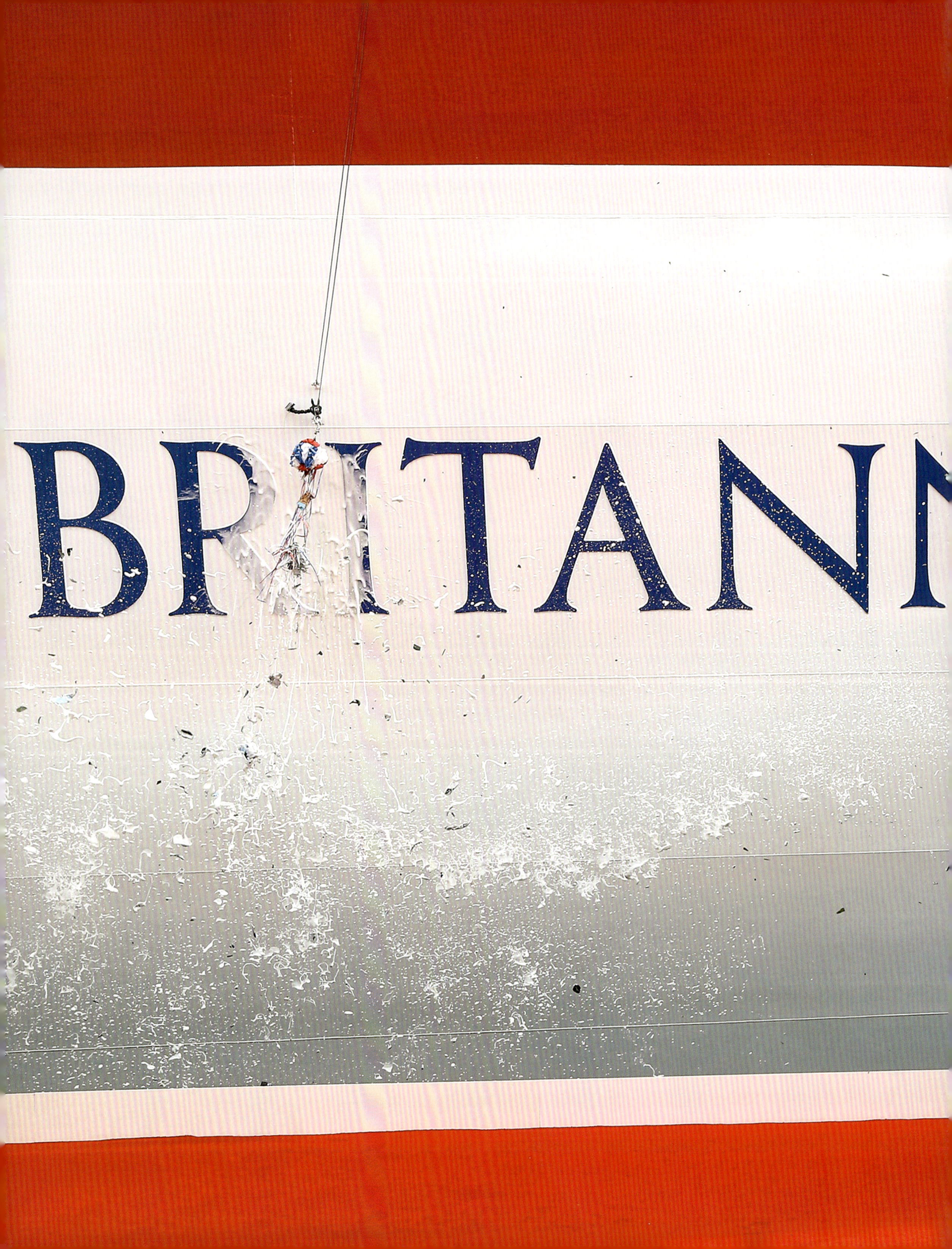

BRITANN

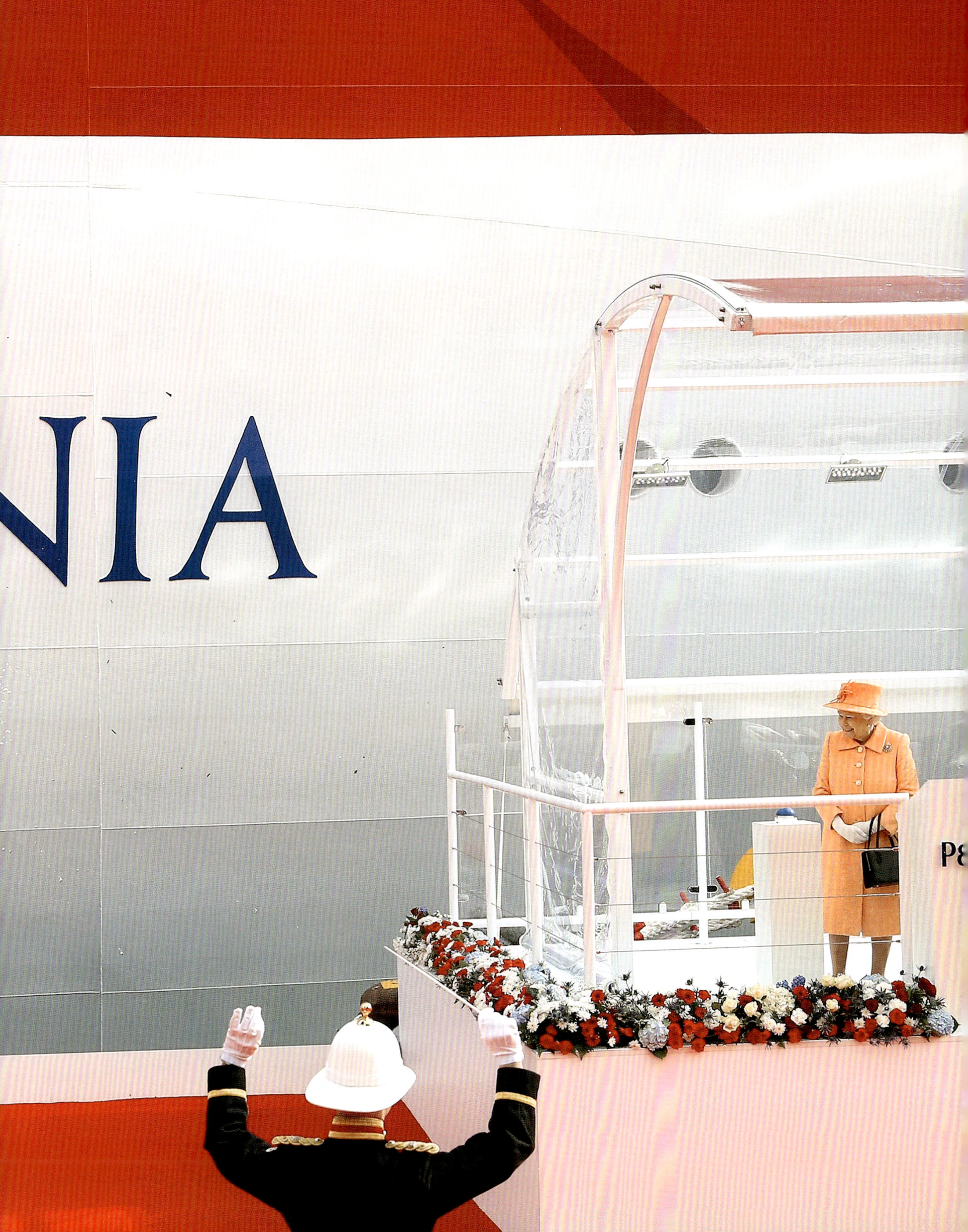
NIA

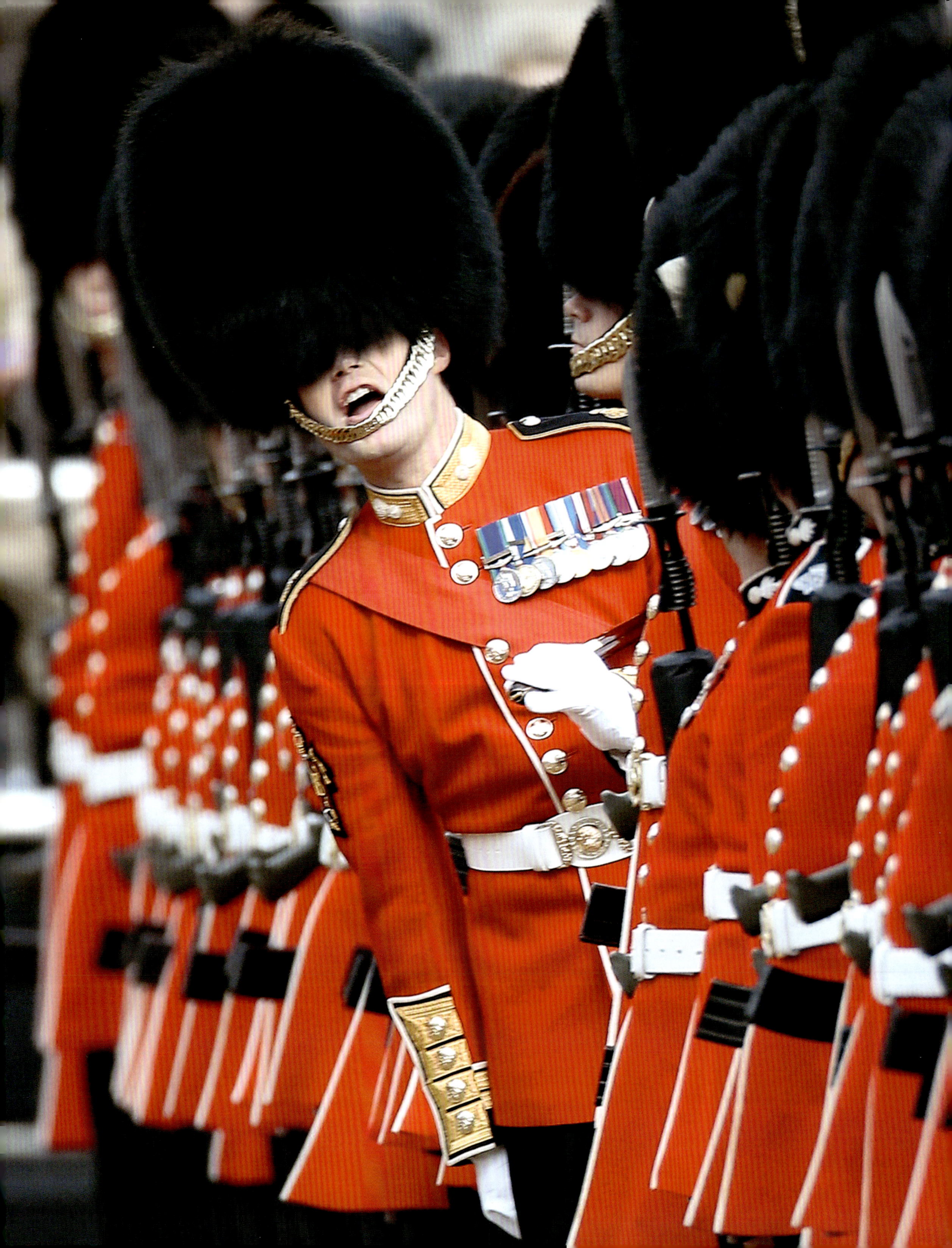

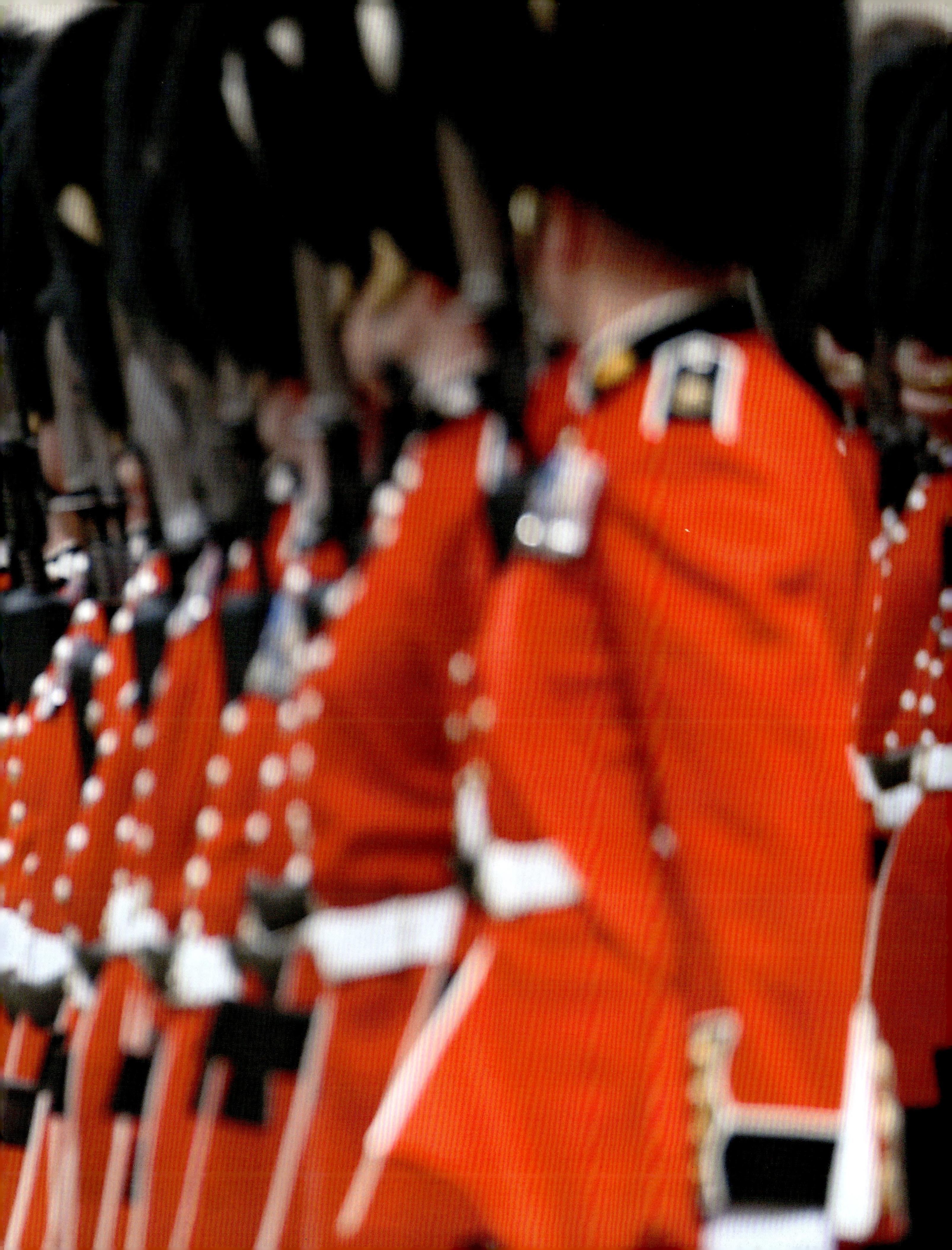

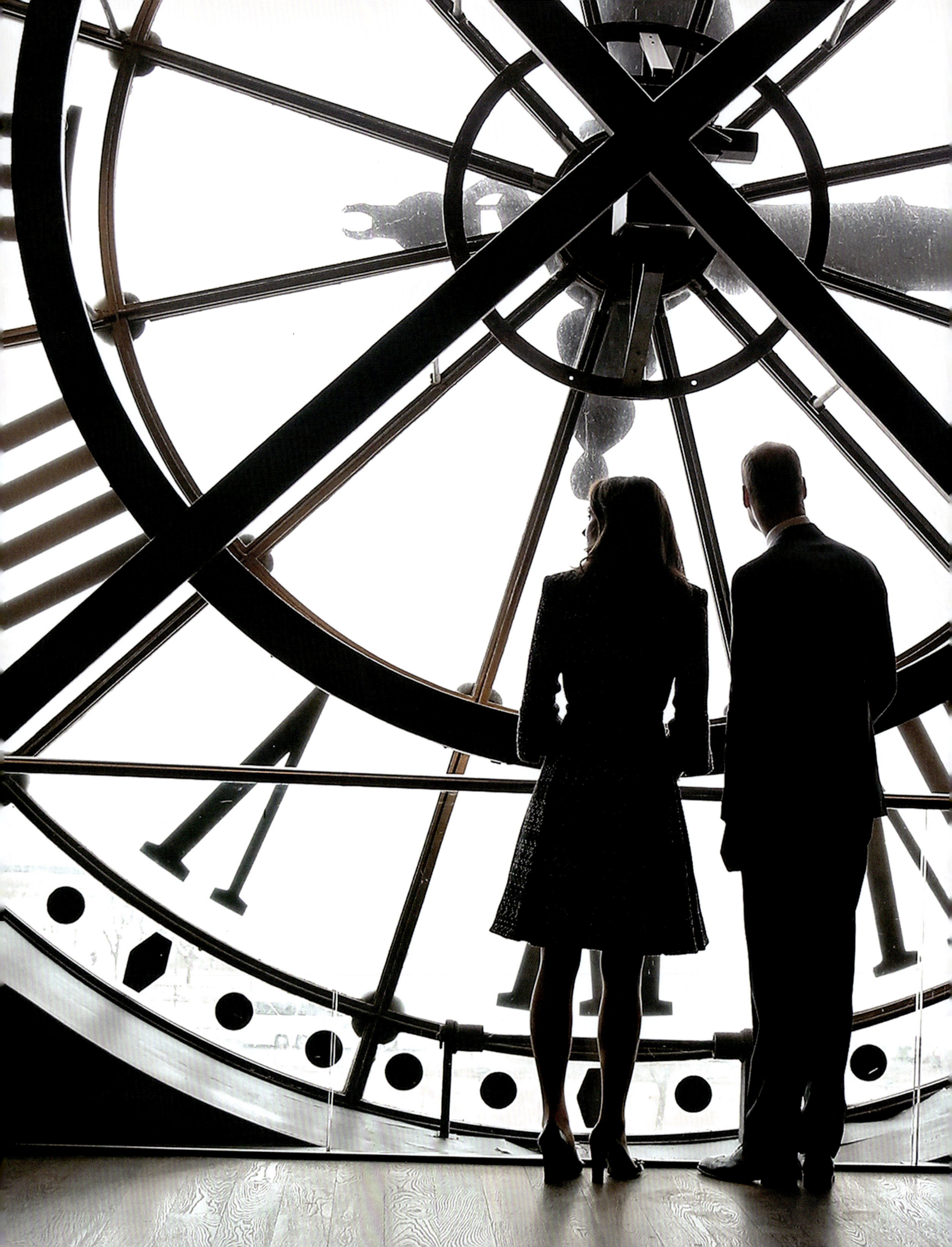

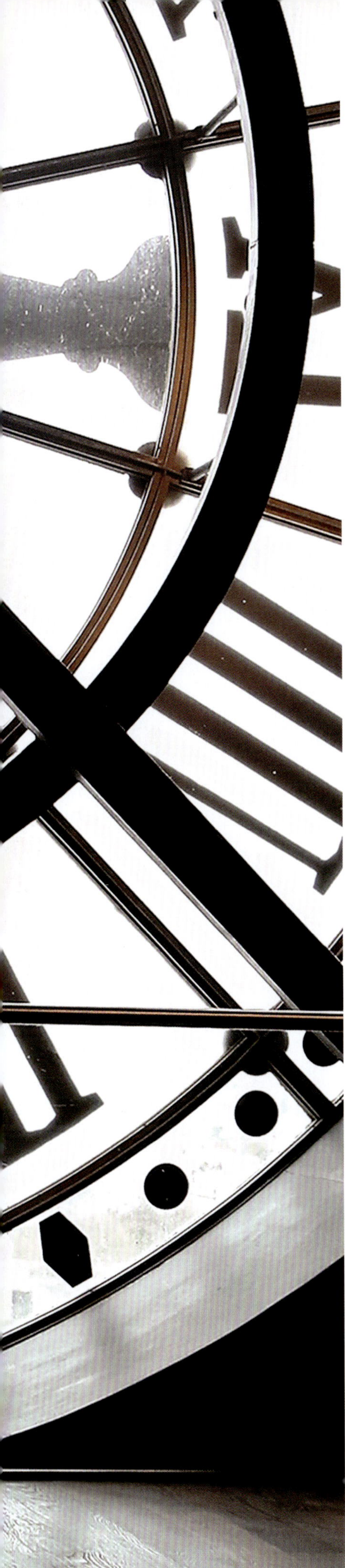

Contents

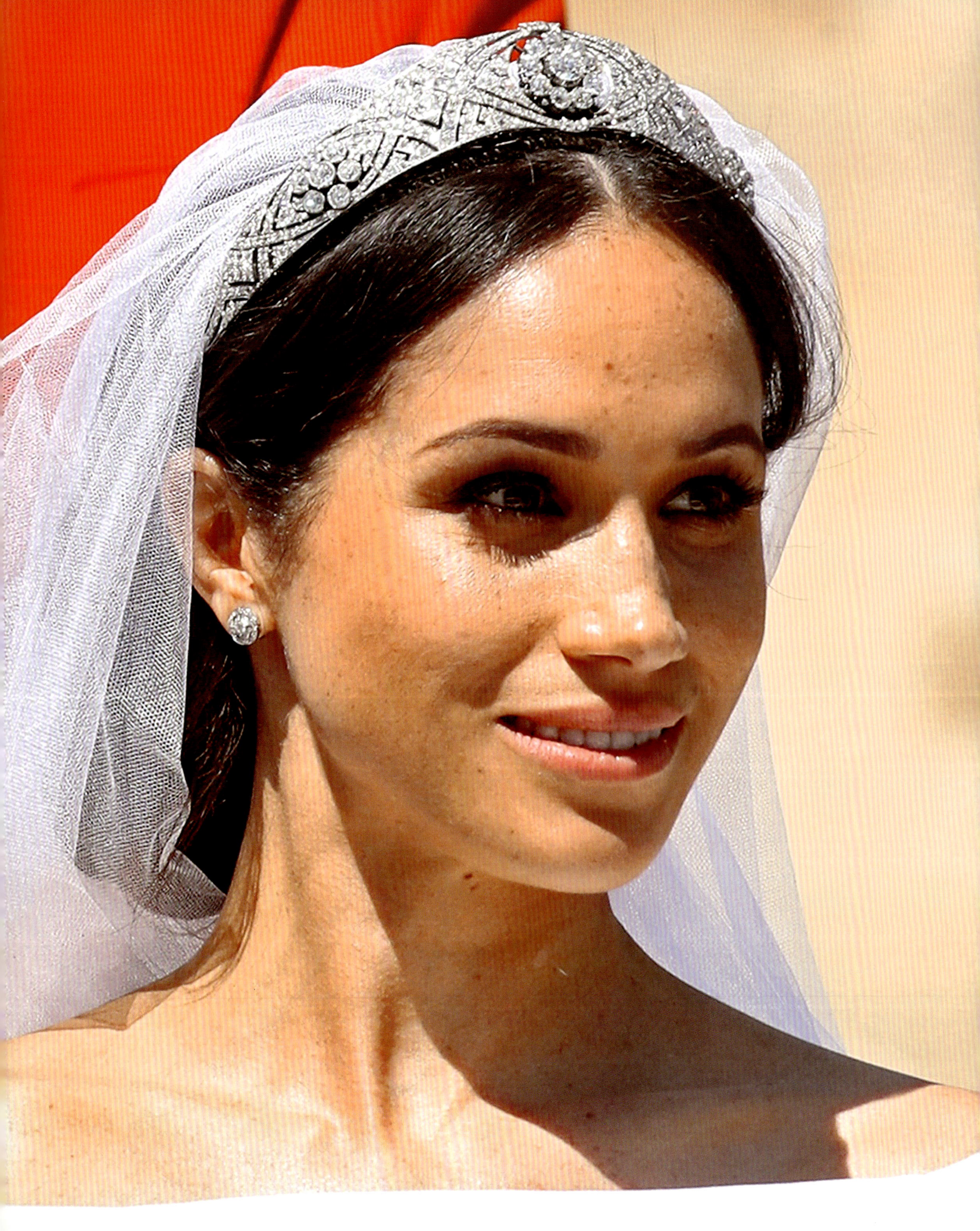

Royalty, Photography, and the Royal Photographic Society

MICHAEL PRITCHARD

There has been a long association between royalty, photography, and the Royal Photographic Society, starting in the 1850s and continuing today through the work of Chris Jackson, a photographer who has had unique access to the royal family at public events and more informal occasions.

Soon after photography was invented in 1839, the royal family began their involvement with the medium, purchasing photographs and forming their own collection of art photography. Much of this interest was channelled through the Photographic Society, later the Royal Photographic Society. A relationship was established with Roger Fenton, my predecessor as the Society's secretary, who photographed the royal family informally and relaxed, a far cry from the portraits that were made available to the public.

Queen Victoria recognised the importance that photography could play in presenting the monarchy to the public. The monarch, her consort, and the wider royal family were the subjects of professional photographers anxious to take their portraits and sell them to a public hungry for images. The craze for cartes de visite beginning in the late 1850s meant that anyone could purchase a portrait of royalty to add to their family album.

Today's images of the royal family are less directed, and access and style of royal photography can vary a great deal. Chris Jackson's work is distinguised by its relaxed intimacy. His photographs are respectful, but continue to engage and present new perspectives on a much photographed family.

Back in the 1870s, photography of state occasions was limited by restrictions imposed by the photography itself. By the early 1890s there was a burgeoning demand for photographs, and an ability to reproduce photographs directly in newspapers and magazines. The era of the press photographer, able to capture royalty at formal events, had arrived. Alongside this came rapid growth of amateur photography—it was now possible for a snapshotter or press photographer to capture a photograph or an unguarded moment from the street or, in a more limited way, pictures inside a building. The control of her public image that Victoria had exerted earlier in her reign was relegated to formal state portraits and events.

Opposite The Duchess of Sussex, wearing the Queen Mary Diamond Bandeau tiara, smiles from the Ascot Landau carriage on the day of her wedding to Prince Harry, Duke of Sussex, on May 19, 2018.

Move forward 130 years and the demands of Instagram and social media mean that today's photographers, the printed press, and the royal family have new international audiences to engage with, far in excess of their Victorian forebears. The new Kodak camera of 1888 and an enthusiasm for photography on the part of Princess—later Queen—Alexandra, encouraged members of the royal family to take their own photographs. Alexandra regularly took family photographs, just as any well-to-do person might have done, and in 1908 a group of 136 of her photographs were published as *Queen Alexandra's Christmas Gift Book*. More than thirty charities benefited from its large sale.

The British monarchy has continued to take photographs and to support photography. Queen Elizabeth II is a photographer and her sister, Princess Margaret, regularly attended RPS exhibitions and opened the Society's Bath photography centre in 1980. More recently, the Duchess of Cambridge has shown herself to be an accomplished photographer, releasing her own photographs of her three children to the press. She, too, now has honorary membership of the Royal Photographic Society.

The role of the royal photographer remains essential in presenting the royal family to the public. Chris Jackson, perhaps the best known, has had greater access to the royal family than most. He has accompanied members of the royal family on tours and state visits. With the younger generation of royals, he has documented their charitable endeavours, and shown them engaging with the public with a distinctive warmth. His photography has presented them in a new, informal, way—a distant cry from those early Victorian photographs. By gaining the confidence of those he photographs and returning each year to the regular "diary" events, Chris has developed an unrivalled knowledge of where to be and when to get his photograph.

Looking back over the past 170 years, there is continuity that continues to bind royalty with photography, through their own photography, to their engagement with those who photograph them, and with the Royal Photographic Society, which brings all three together. The global interest in royalty, which was present in the 1850s, remains stronger than ever, and it relies on people like Chris to document the pageantry, events, activities and, on occasion, personal moments that continue to enchant the world. This book showcases the best of this work through the photography of Chris Jackson.

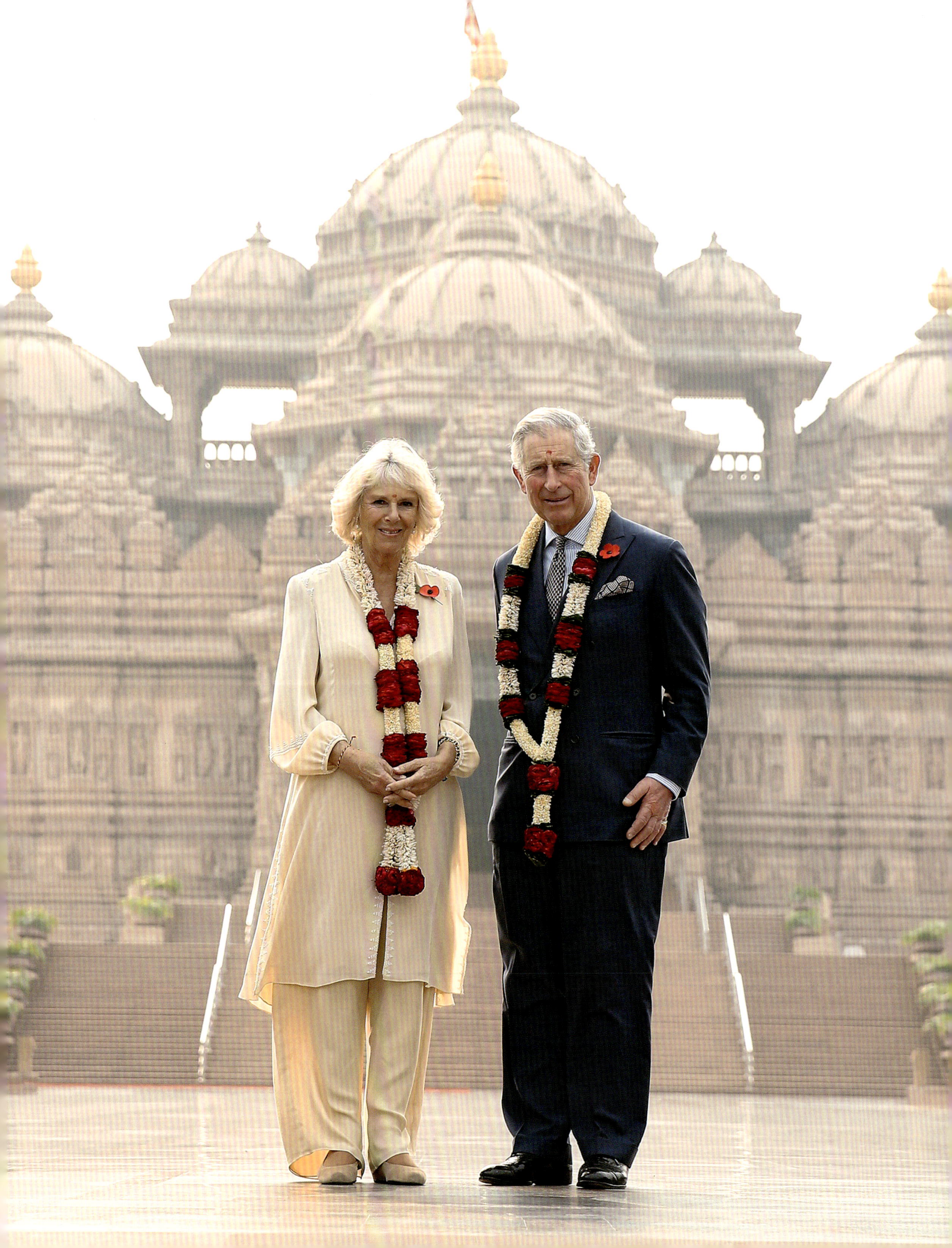

Introduction

CHRIS JACKSON

The modern British royal family has continuously adapted to face the many challenges of changing times, to stay relevant whilst maintaining the tradition and ceremony that are at the very core of what makes them so unique and has been key to their lasting appeal. It's an exciting time to document the royals. Weddings, births, and christenings remain positive celebrations embraced by the nation and broadcast to millions globally. The enduring respect Her Majesty Queen Elizabeth garners around the world has remained a constant for decades and an anchor for the royal family. In 2015 she became Britain's longest reigning monarch and in 2017 the world's longest—an incredible achievement. It is this stalwart omnipresence that has made her the unique leader we see today. As head of the Commonwealth and its realms she is the figurehead of a "family" encompassing fifty-three nations, including some of the richest and poorest on earth, the largest, India, to the smallest, the tiny Pacific island of Tuvalu. This tremendous responsibility cannot be shouldered indefinitely and as the Queen transitions many of her patronages and responsibilities to younger members of the family, we look to the future. These young and dynamic royals embrace their privileged position as a tool to change things for the better, respect the experience of their elders, and bring a dynamic, relevant, and "Modern Monarchy" to a whole new generation.

There is no job description for the modern royal. Diplomacy, enthusiasm, patience, compassion, and loyalty must all feature highly in the brief. Above all, a sense of energy is essential. I often find myself endeavouring to keep up with the hectic schedule of the Prince of Wales on a royal tour as he skips lunch, often completing eight or more official engagements in a day. Over the course of 2017, the Prince of Wales completed 546 engagements both at home and abroad. This incredible work ethic was beaten in the United Kingdom only by one of the hardest working royals, Princess Anne, who attended 455 engagements domestically. This commitment to serving the country runs deep across all members of the royal family. My job as a photographer is to create a record of the historic moments that define our nation, to capture the deeply personal passions the royals have for their charity work, patronages, and responsibilities, and to create images that give insight into the personalities of some of the most well known and photographed faces in the world. For a country and monarchy in a constant state of flux, it is an exciting time to be doing my job, one I consider to be an incredible privilege.

Over the following chapters I aim to give insight into the many facets of life as a modern royal, from travel and life on a royal tour, to the diplomatic challenges of dressing for the occasion. I look at the power the royals have as ambassadors for Britain around the world, shining a spotlight on issues as diverse as conservation and mental health, distilling fifteen years of photographing the royals into my favourite moments of tradition, ceremony, emotion, warmth, and humour. Every image in this book is a moment, and every moment captured—no matter how big or small—has played a part in the history of the British royal family. Together, they form a compelling picture of a very "Modern Monarchy."

Opposite The Prince of Wales and the Duchess of Cornwall visit the Akshardham Temple in Delhi during an official visit to India in 2013.

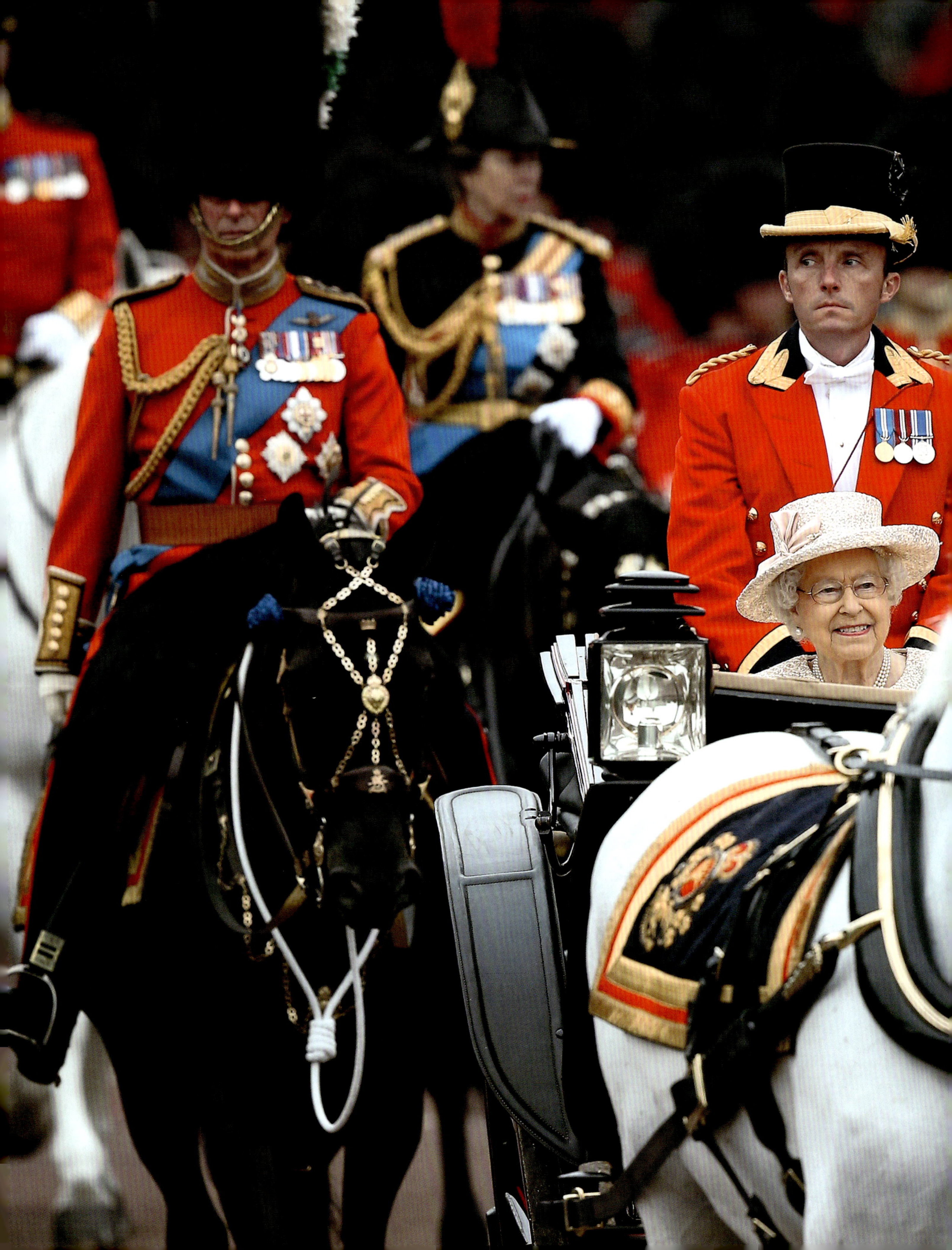

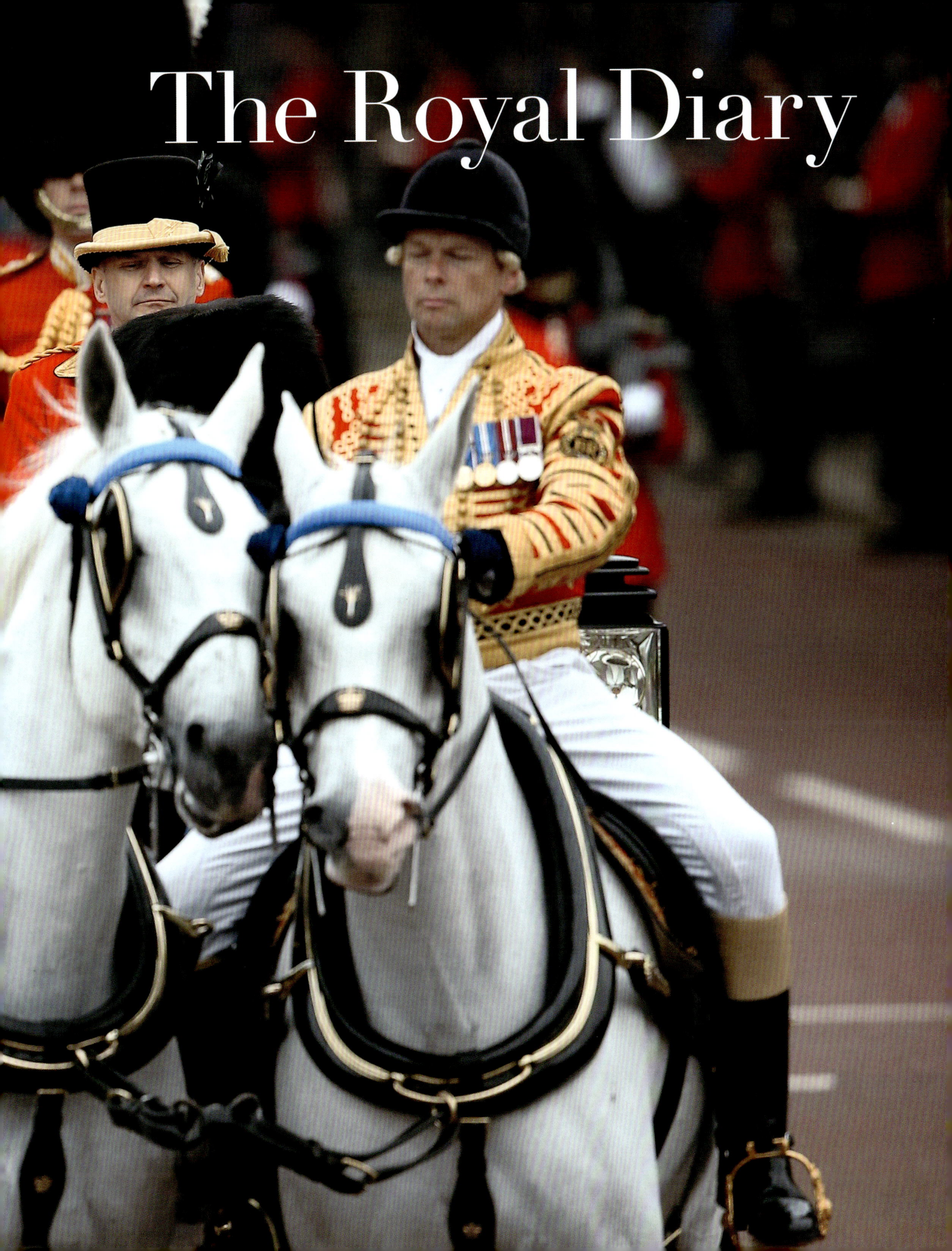
The Royal Diary

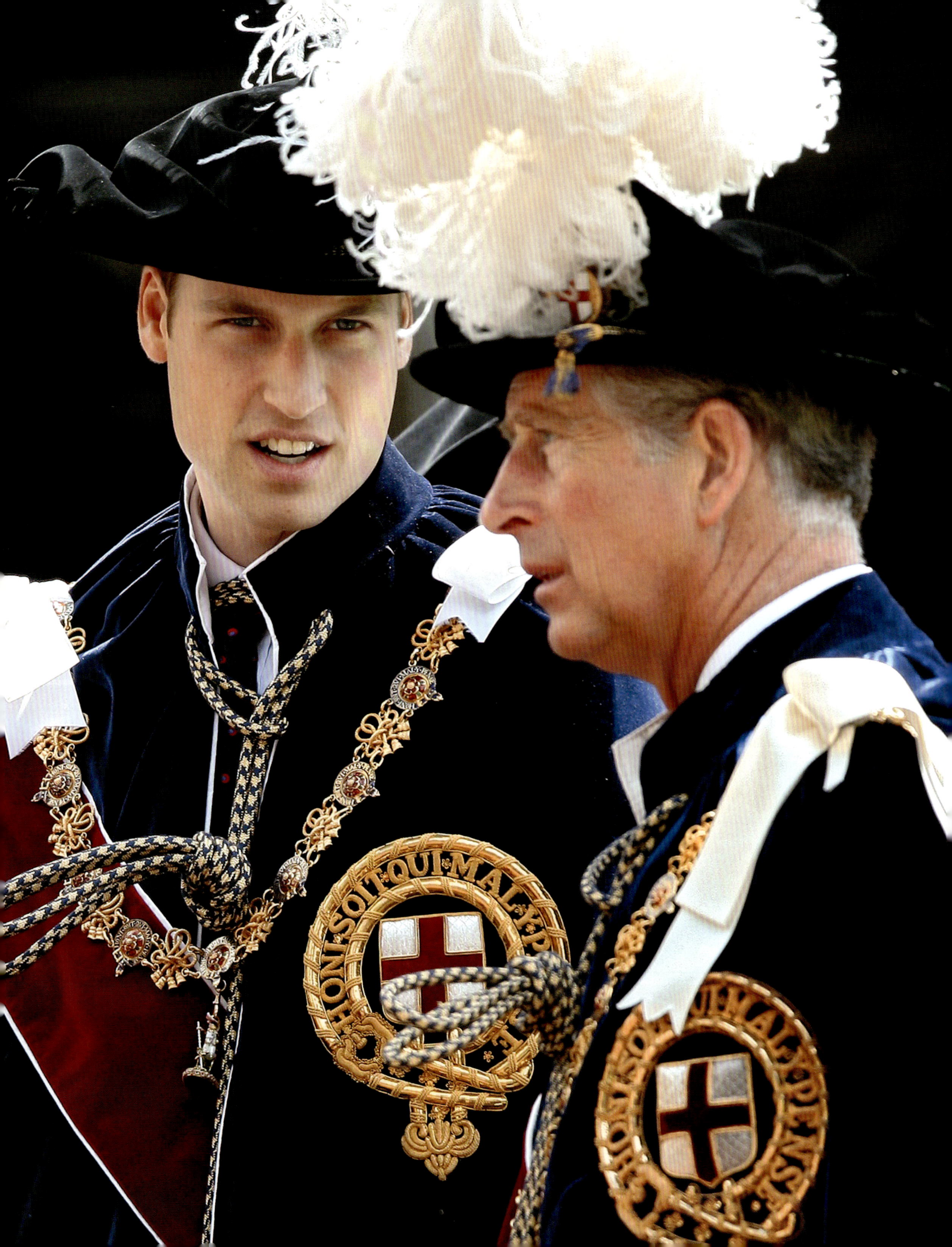
HONI SOIT QUI MAL Y P
QUI MAL Y PENSE

Throughout the year the royal diary is structured around regular events, many of which have occurred for centuries. Royal Ascot, the Garter and Thistle ceremonies, Buckingham Palace summer garden parties, the State Opening of Parliament, and Trooping the Colour are just some of the more well-known occasions. These formal dates are punctuated by numerous one-off occurrences—royal christenings, births, weddings, and memorials. Tradition plays an integral part in the planning of the diary, and its events form the backbone of a complex and constantly evolving schedule that also must take into account current world issues and affairs. Whilst many of these annual moments are part of working life, others cross into private life. Polo has been played by the royal family in the summer season for centuries and is a favourite pastime of Princes William and Harry. Matches are generally held to support their favourite charities and over the years they have raised millions for good causes whilst providing a glamorous backdrop for affluent philanthropists to mingle with the great and the good.

Staying on top of this hectic diary can certainly be a struggle. For someone who documents the official activities of the royal family, trying to determine coverage can be a huge challenge. Different members of the family embark on their own royal tours and trying to document everything and everyone inevitably results in numerous nights away from home and racks up the air miles. Missing events can be challenging. Ultimately, you simply have to be there to record something, and can't be in two places at once. A photographer learns the finer points of each occasion. Over the years you develop intuition for how to get the best images, where to stand, what will happen and when. Things don't always go according to plan, but accruing experience reduces your dependence on luck, which is helpful in a situation where you often have limited control. This familiarity is a welcome aspect of my job and makes me feel as though the term is starting or finishing. Christmas at Sandringham House traditionally marks the end of the royal callendar, and the Sandringham Flower Show signals the start of "summer break." It is this regularity that provides a framework for the royal year and a context to look back on past years and see the generational changes.

Preceding pages The Queen smiles from the state carriage as she processes during Trooping the Colour. Since 1748, this annual event has marked the sovereign's official birthday. During the colourful proceedings, troops of the Household Division pay tribute to the monarch with much pomp and ceremony.

Opposite On June 15, 2009, Prince William became the 1,000th Knight of the Garter. The Order of the Garter is the oldest British order of chivalry, founded by Edward III in 1348. The ceremony is watched by large crowds on the grounds of Windsor Castle.

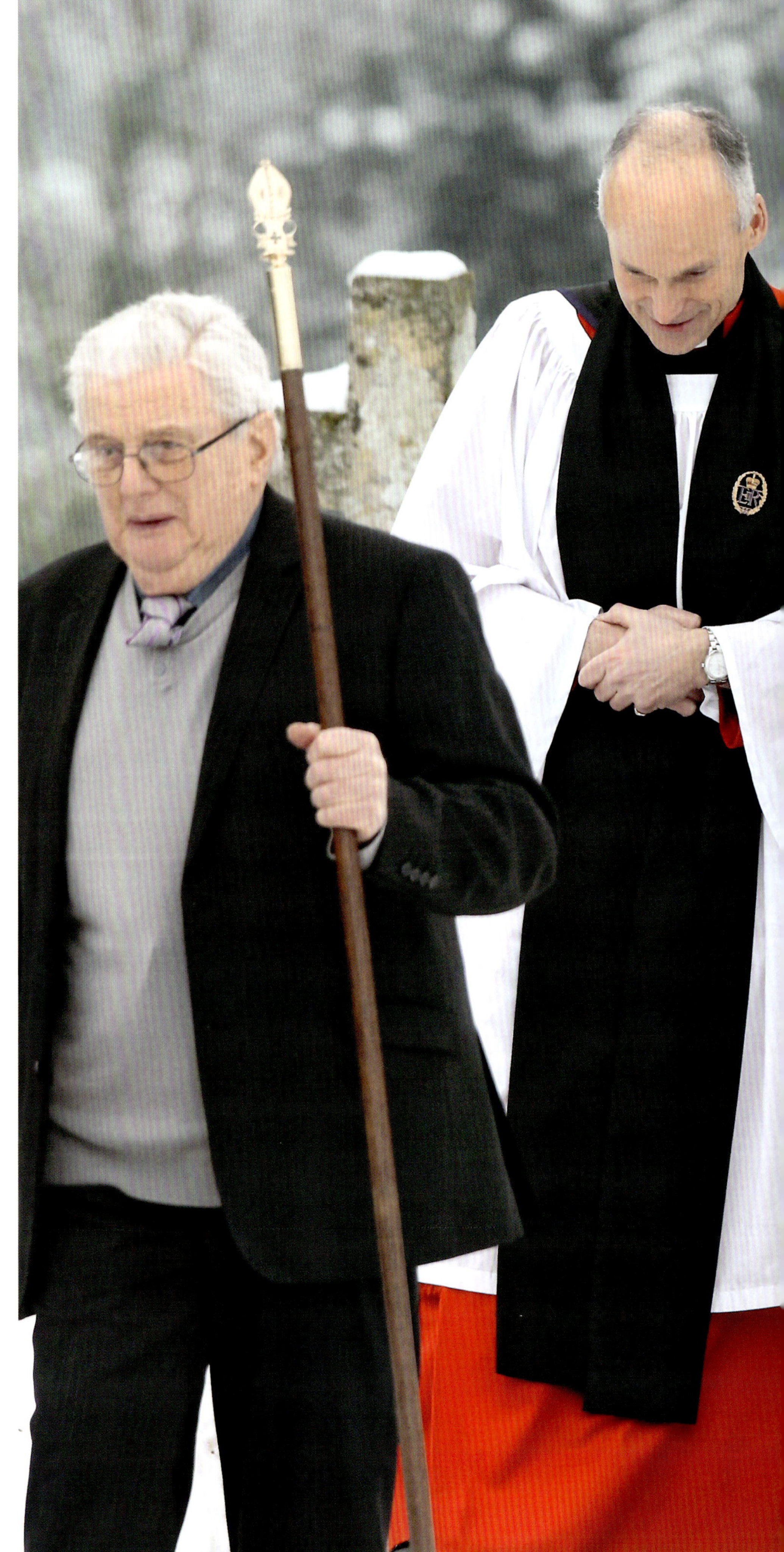

The Queen and the Duke of Edinburgh walk through the snow to West Newton Church for Sunday service. The Queen and Duke remain at their Norfolk residence, Sandringham House, through the Christmas season and until early February. Whilst in Norfolk they usually attend the Sunday service at one of the churches on the estate.

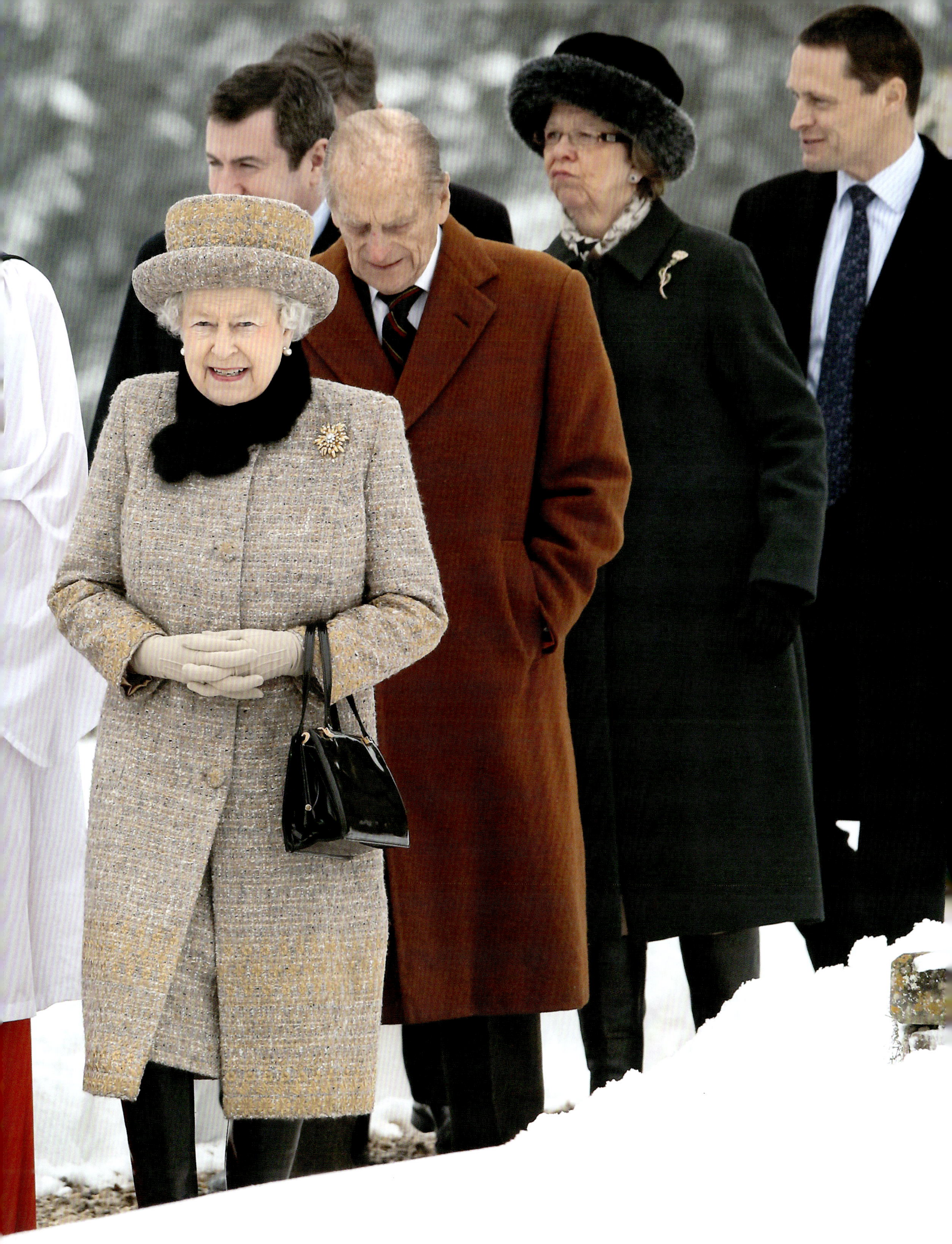

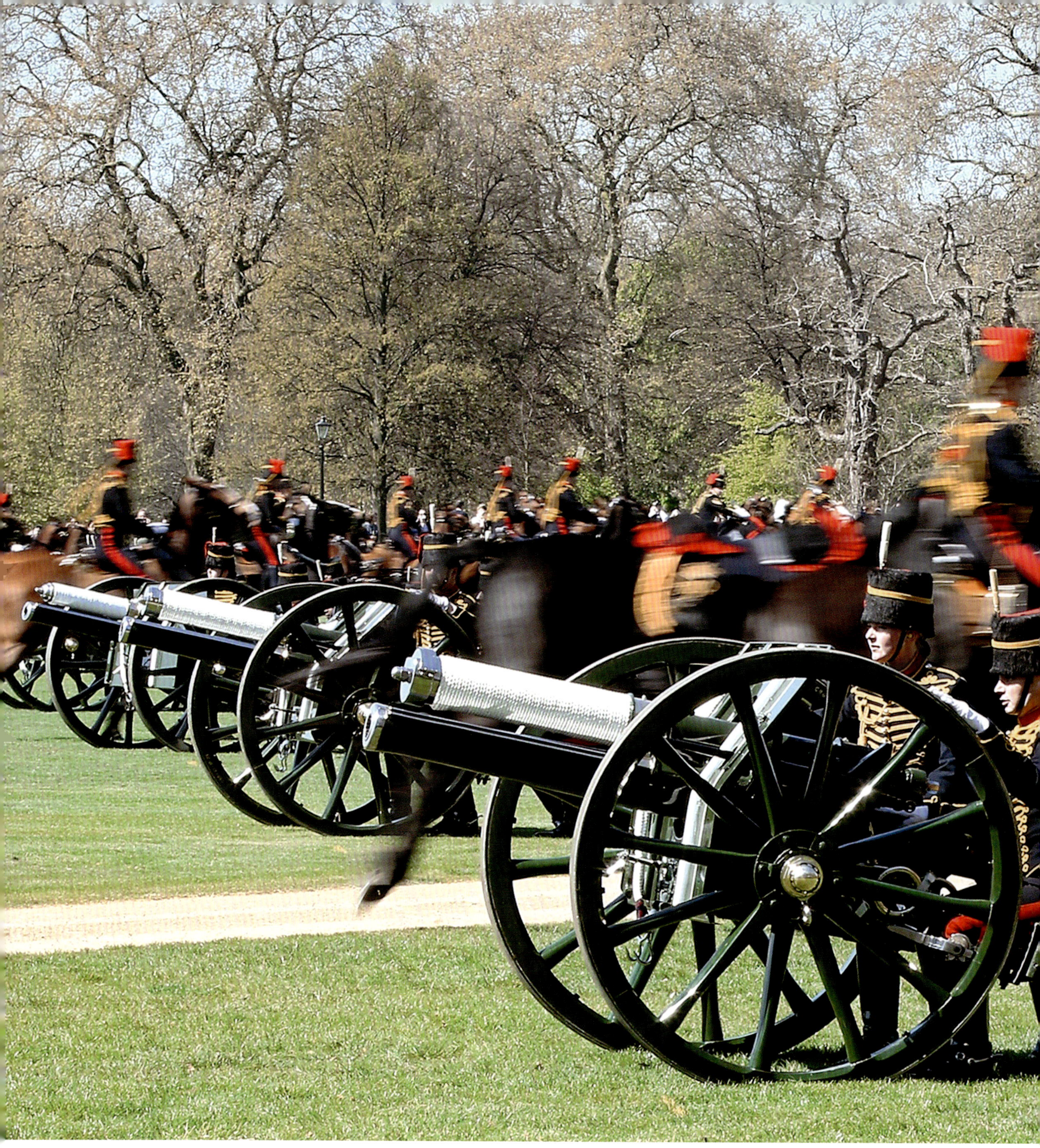

Whilst Trooping the Colour marks the Queen's official birthday, her actual birthday, on April 21st, is marked by a gun salute. Here soldiers of the King's Troop Royal Horse Artillery mark the Queen's eighty-ninth birthday with a forty-one-gun salute in Hyde Park on April 21, 2015.

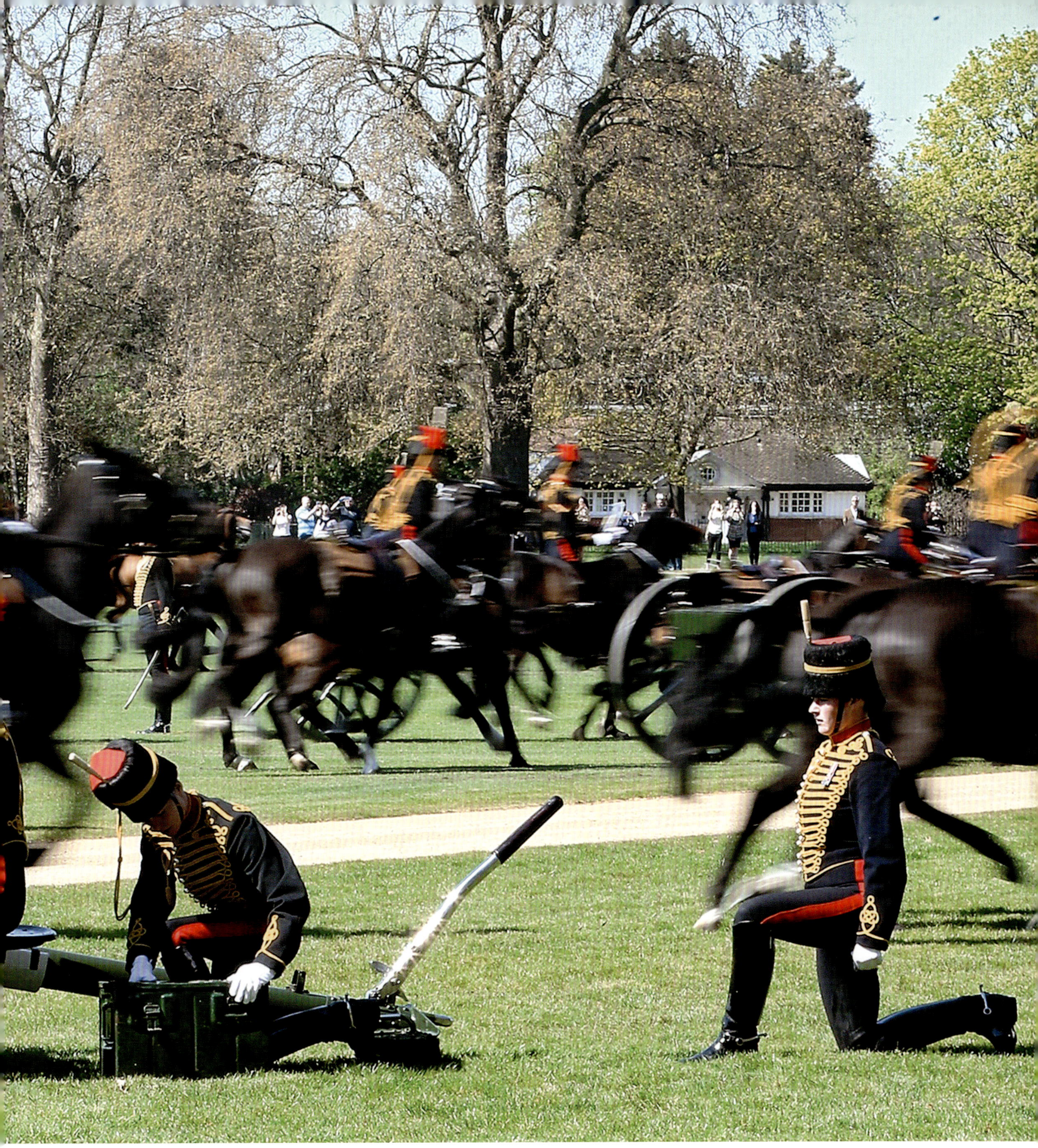

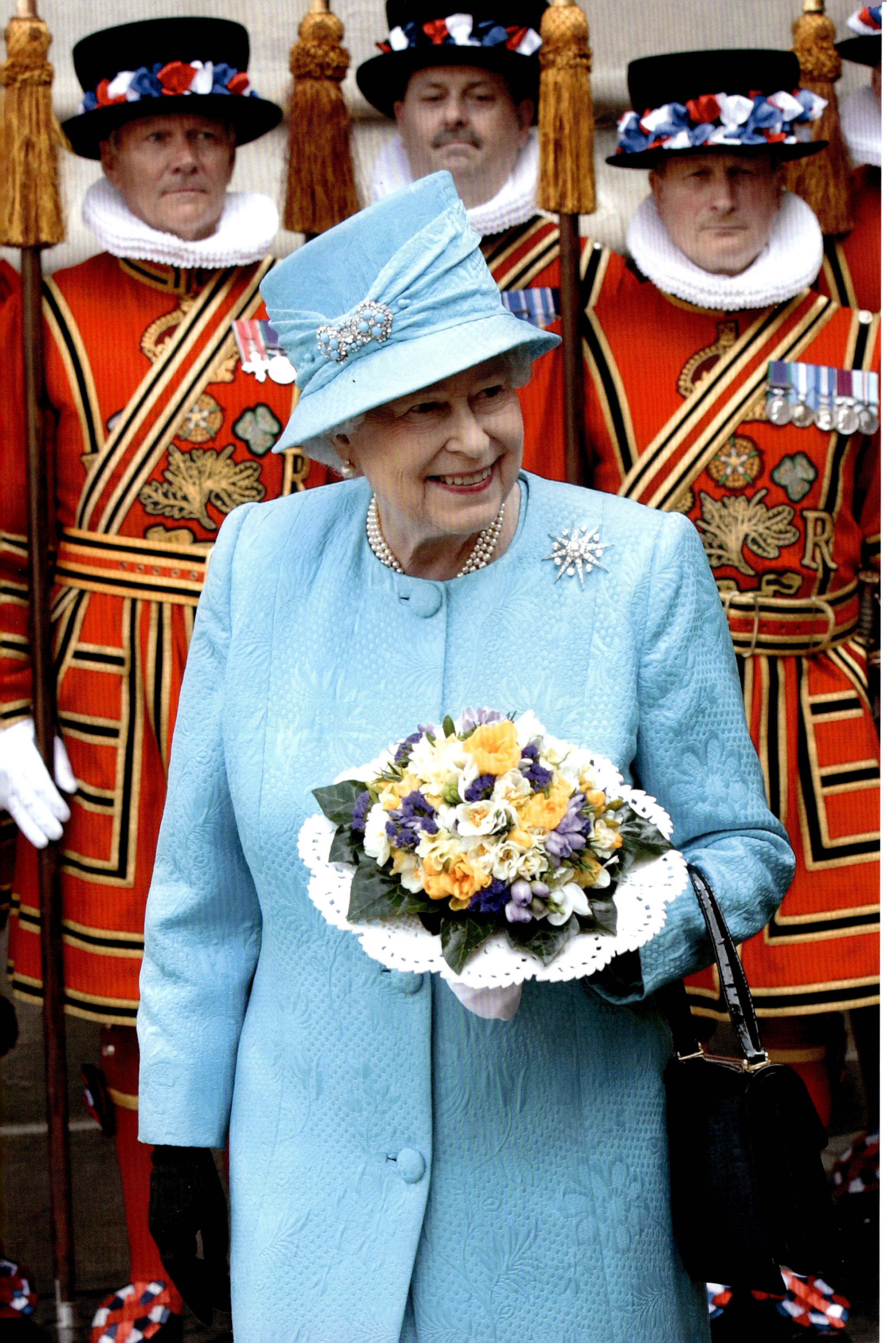

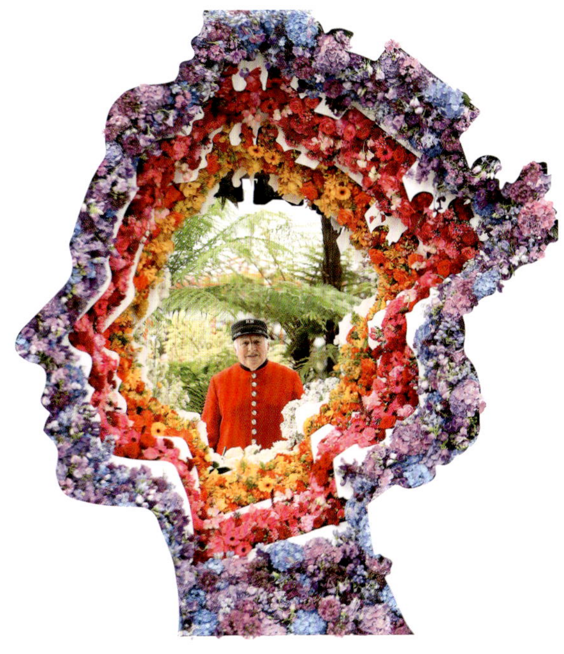

Opposite Ahead of Easter Sunday, the Queen marks Maundy Thursday by visiting a cathedral in the United Kingdom. By 2018, the Queen had attended a Maundy service at every cathedral in the country, so she returned home to St. George's Chapel in Windsor Castle. Here she holds a traditional nosegay bouquet during the Maundy service at Westminster Abbey.

Left The Chelsea Flower Show is a floral spectacular that has been a part of the royal diary since Queen Alexandra opened it in 1913. The displays often have a royal theme. Here a Chelsea pensioner looks out through a colourful display depicting the monarch titled "Behind Every Great Florist."

Below Prince Harry meets Basotho singers from Lesotho in the garden of Sentebale, the charity he founded. Designed by Matt Keightley, the Hope In Vulnerability Garden was created to raise awareness of Sentebale's work providing healthcare and education to Lesotho's most vulnerable.

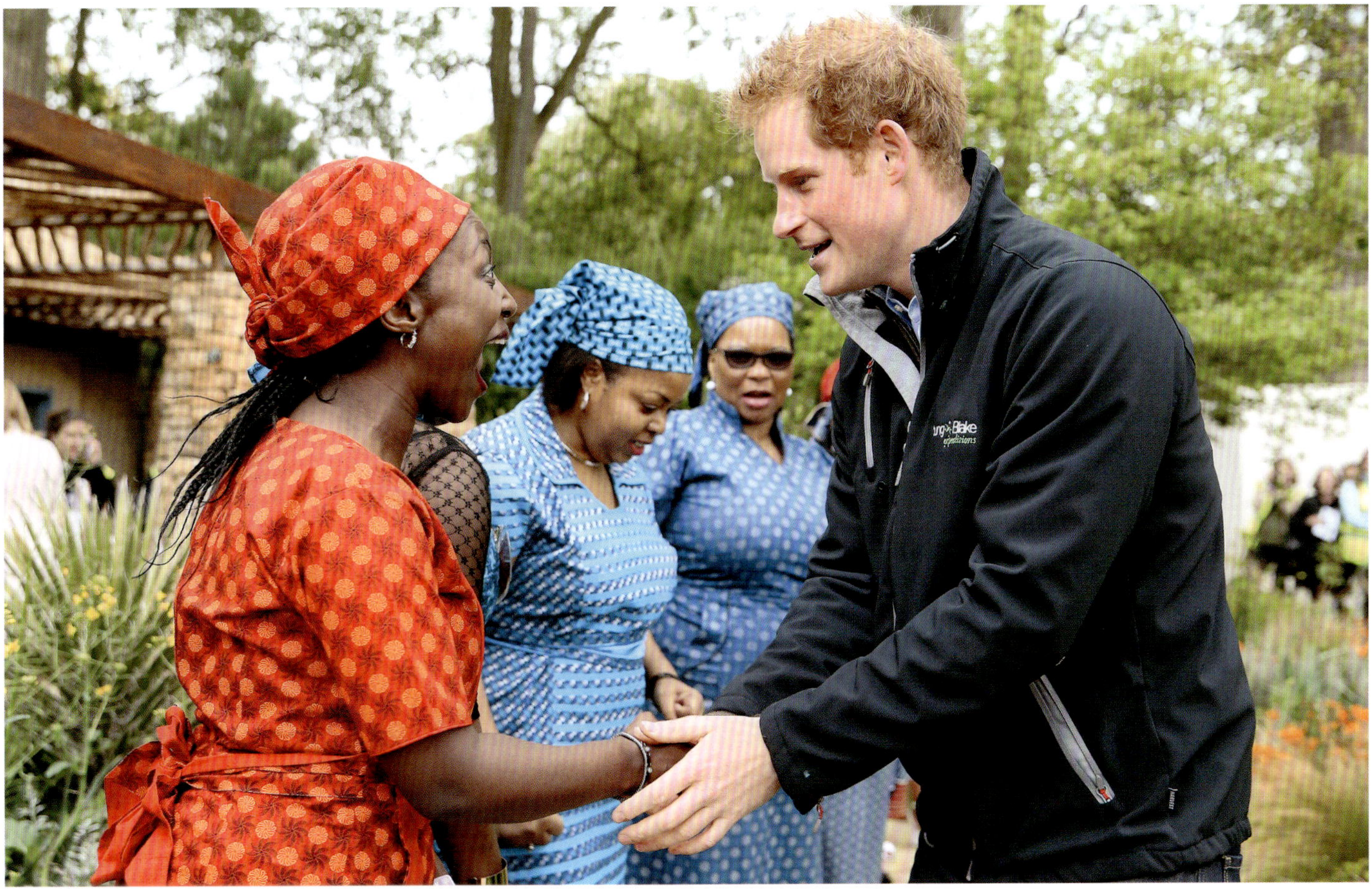

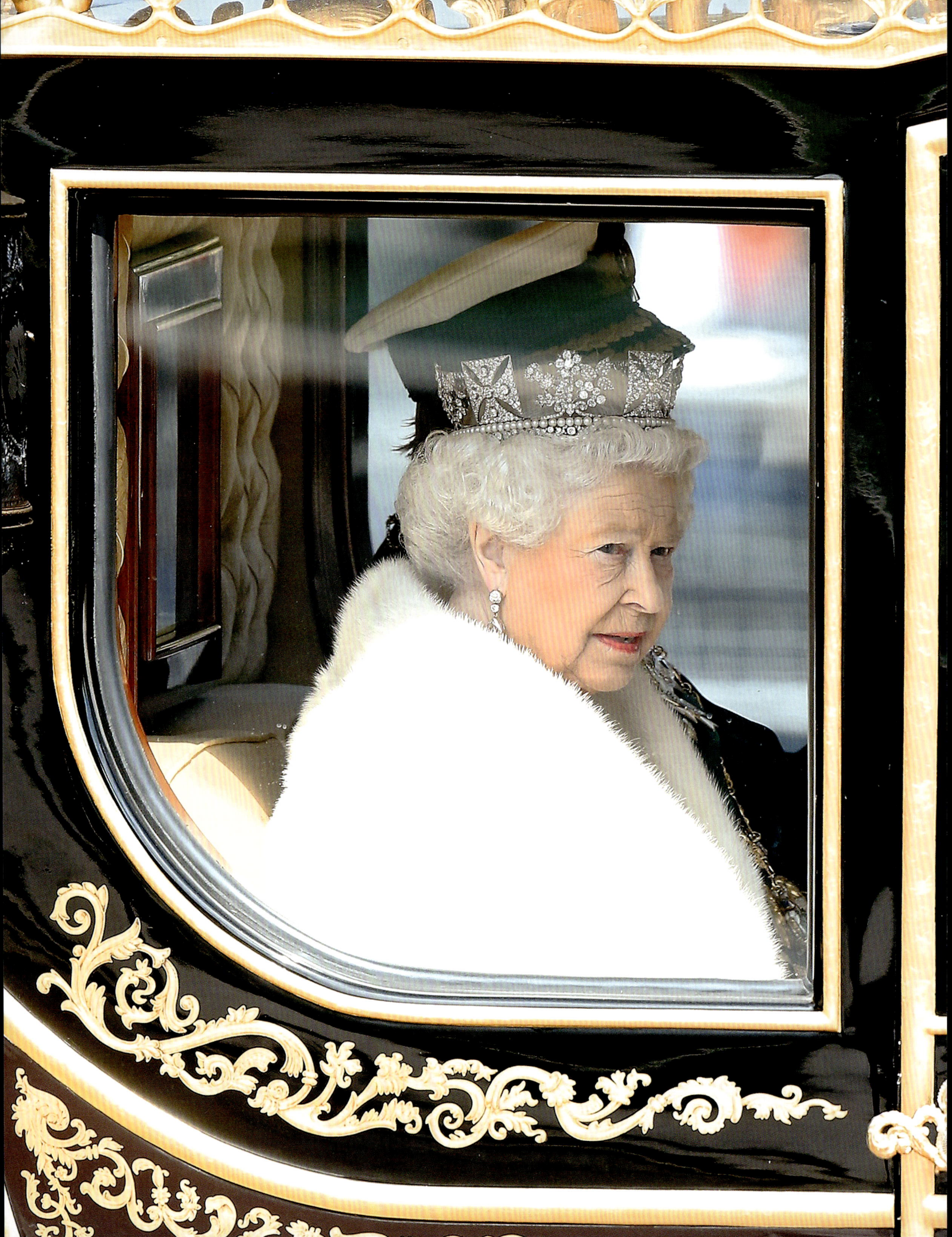

Opposite The Queen looks out from the Diamond Jubilee state coach as she leaves Buckingham Palace and heads to the Houses of Parliament during the State Opening. The Queen has opened almost every session of Parliament since being crowned.

Right The Imperial State Crown is transported from Buckingham Palace to the Houses of Parliament ahead of the Queen's arrival.

Below The Yeomen of the Guard walk through the Peers' Lobby in the Houses of Parliament after carrying out the ceremonial search ahead of the State Opening.

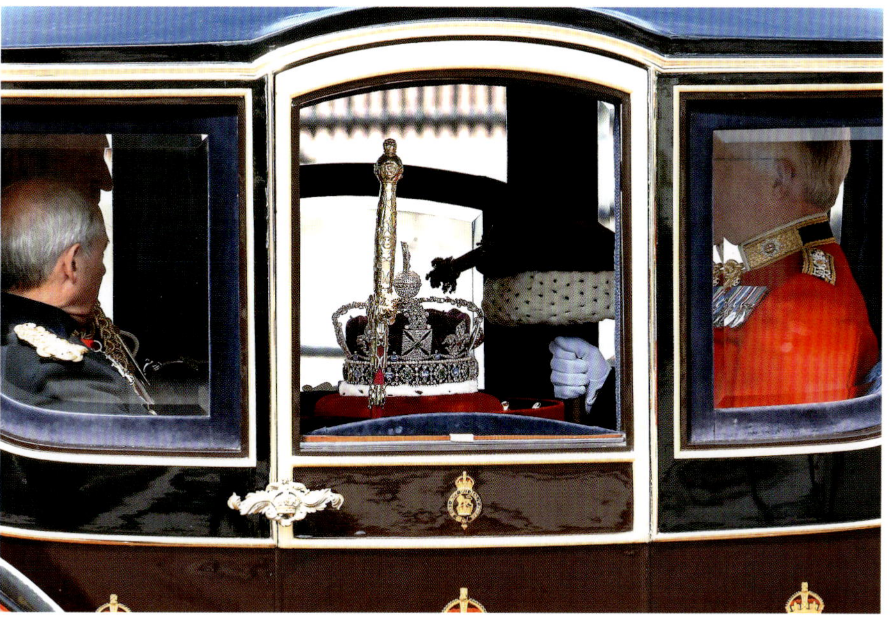

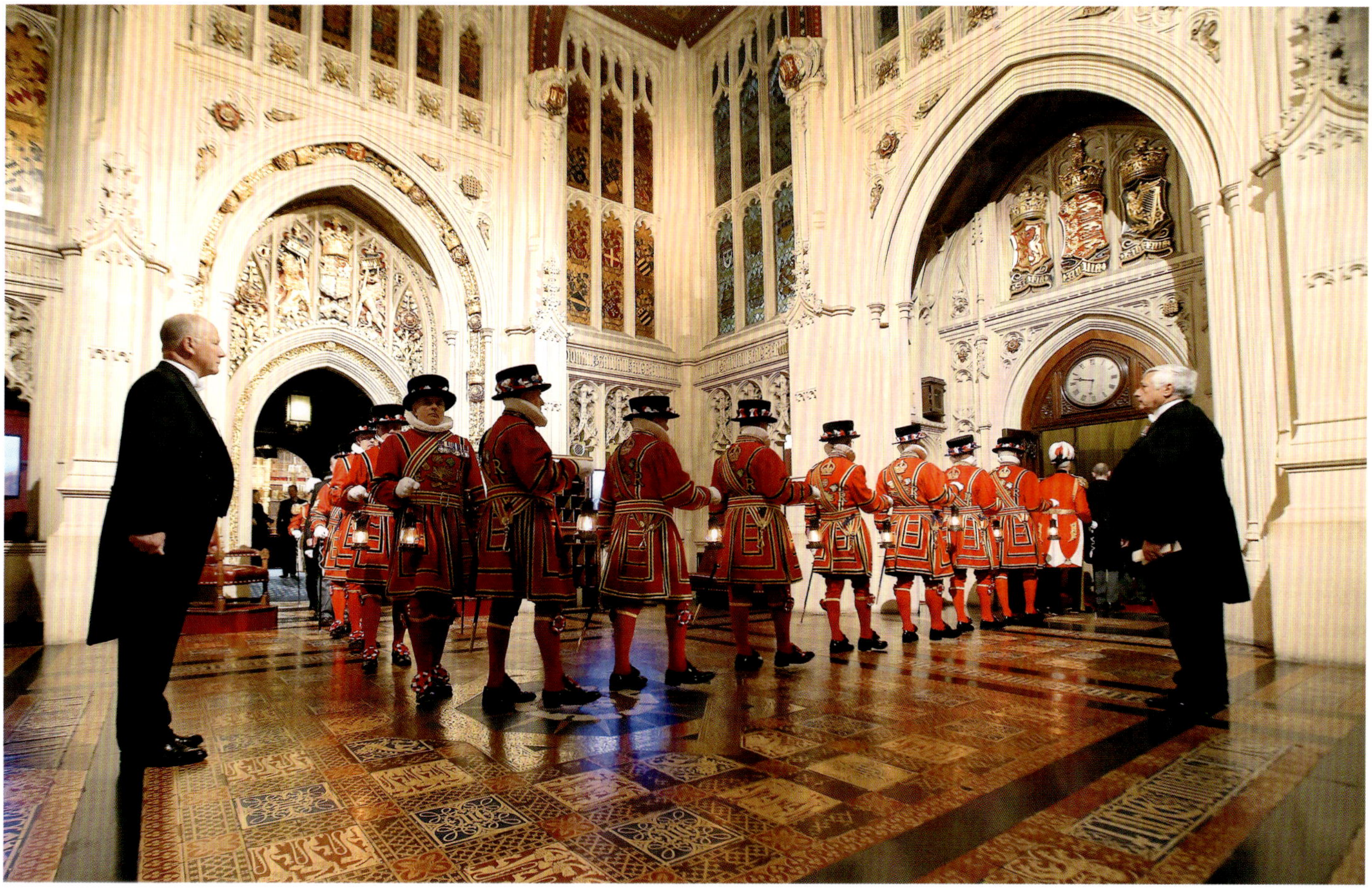

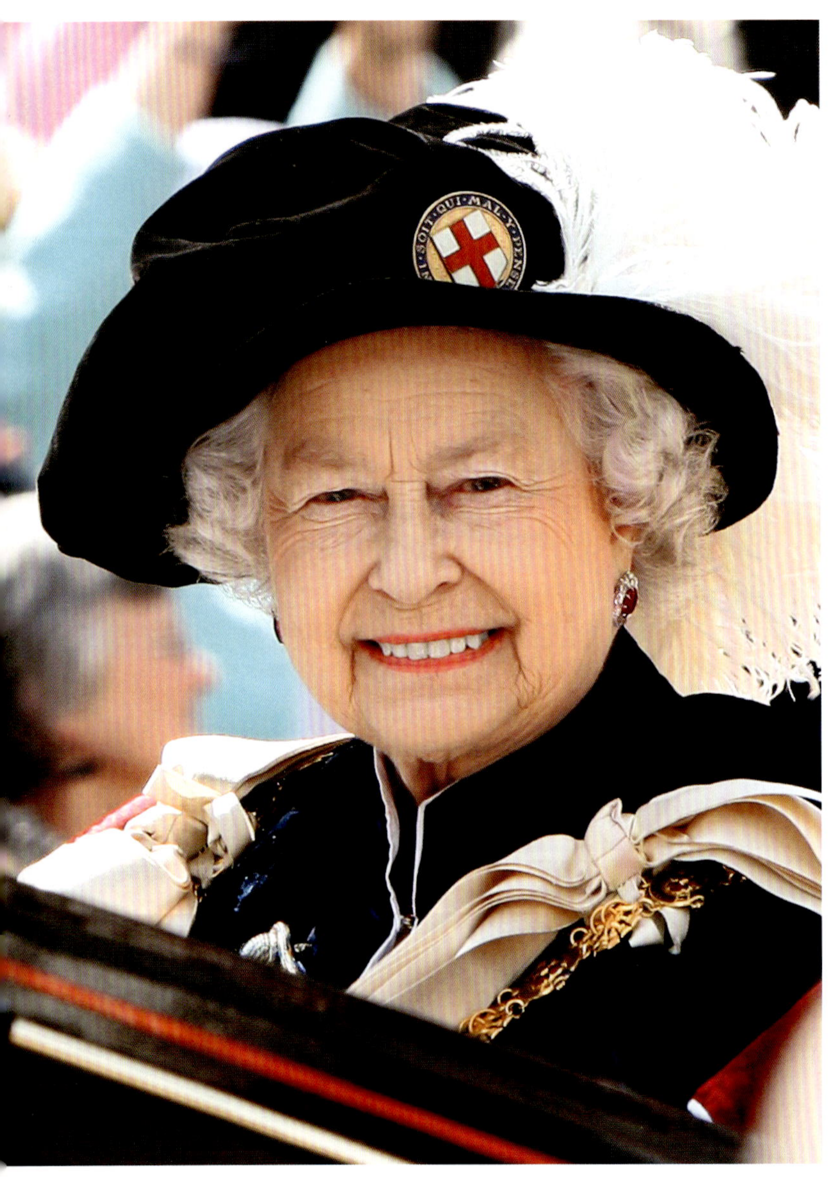

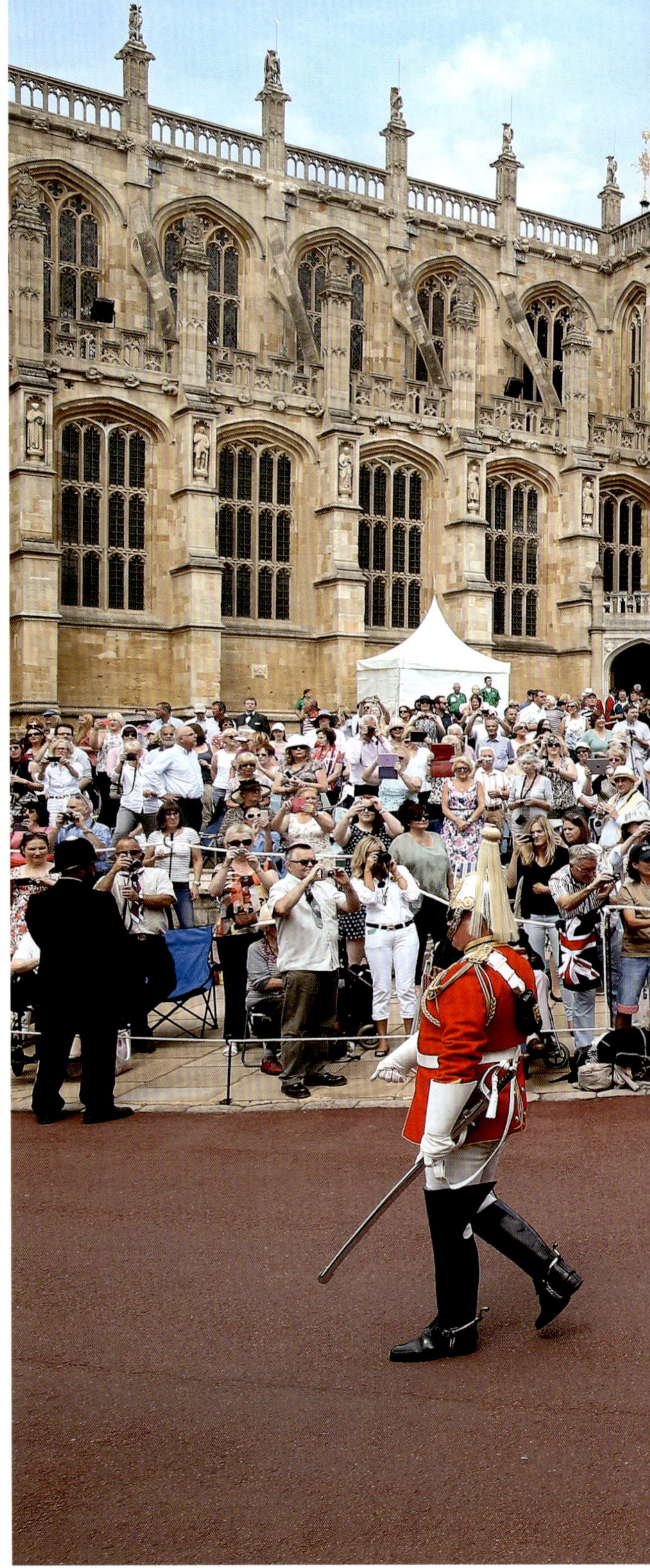

Above The Queen leaves St. George's Chapel during the Order of the Garter ceremony, the 660th anniversary service on June 16, 2008.

Opposite Members of a Household Cavalry band lead the staircase party formed by the Life Guards and the Blues and Royals as they process to St. George's Chapel during the Order of the Garter ceremony at Windsor Castle.

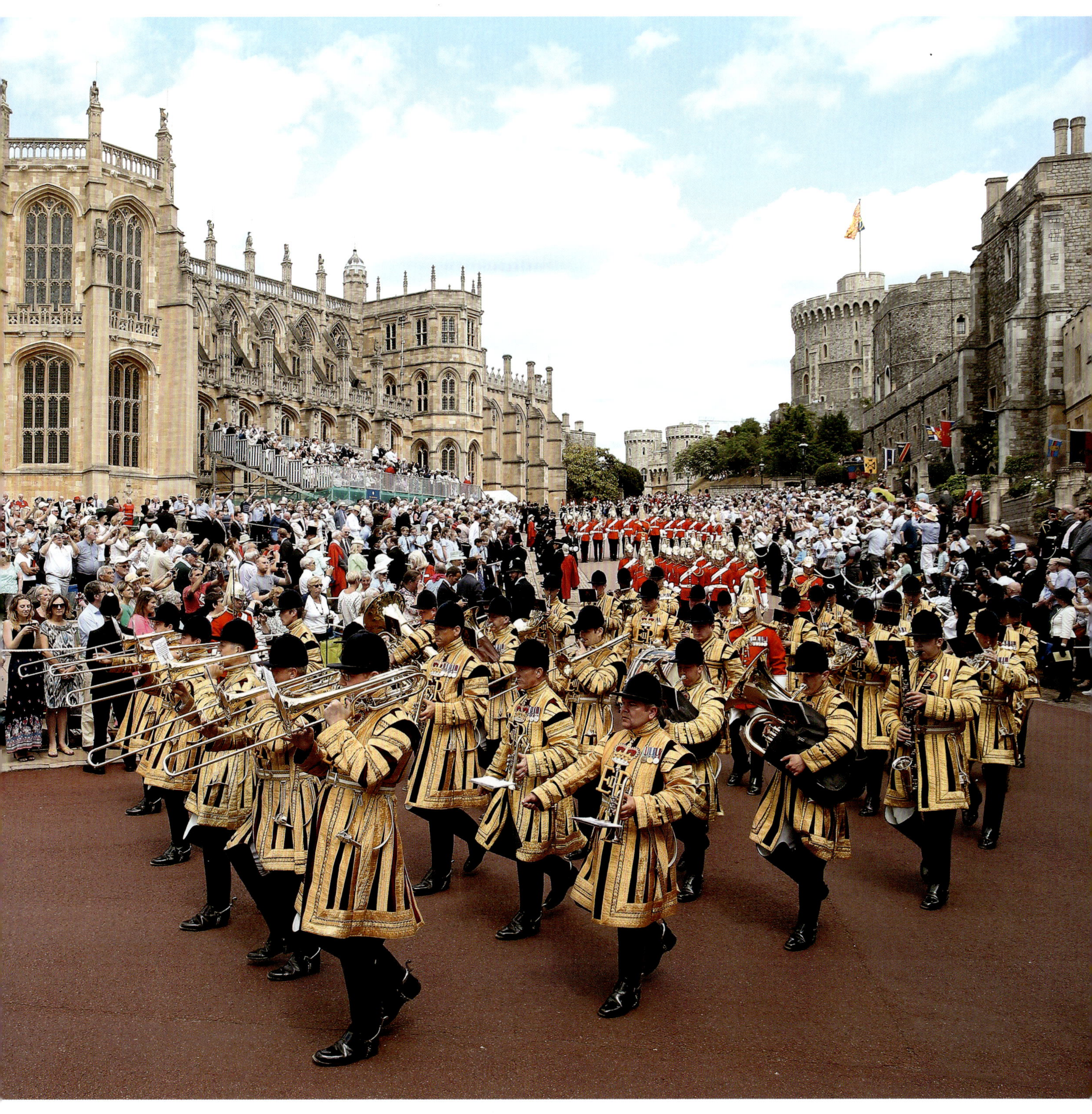

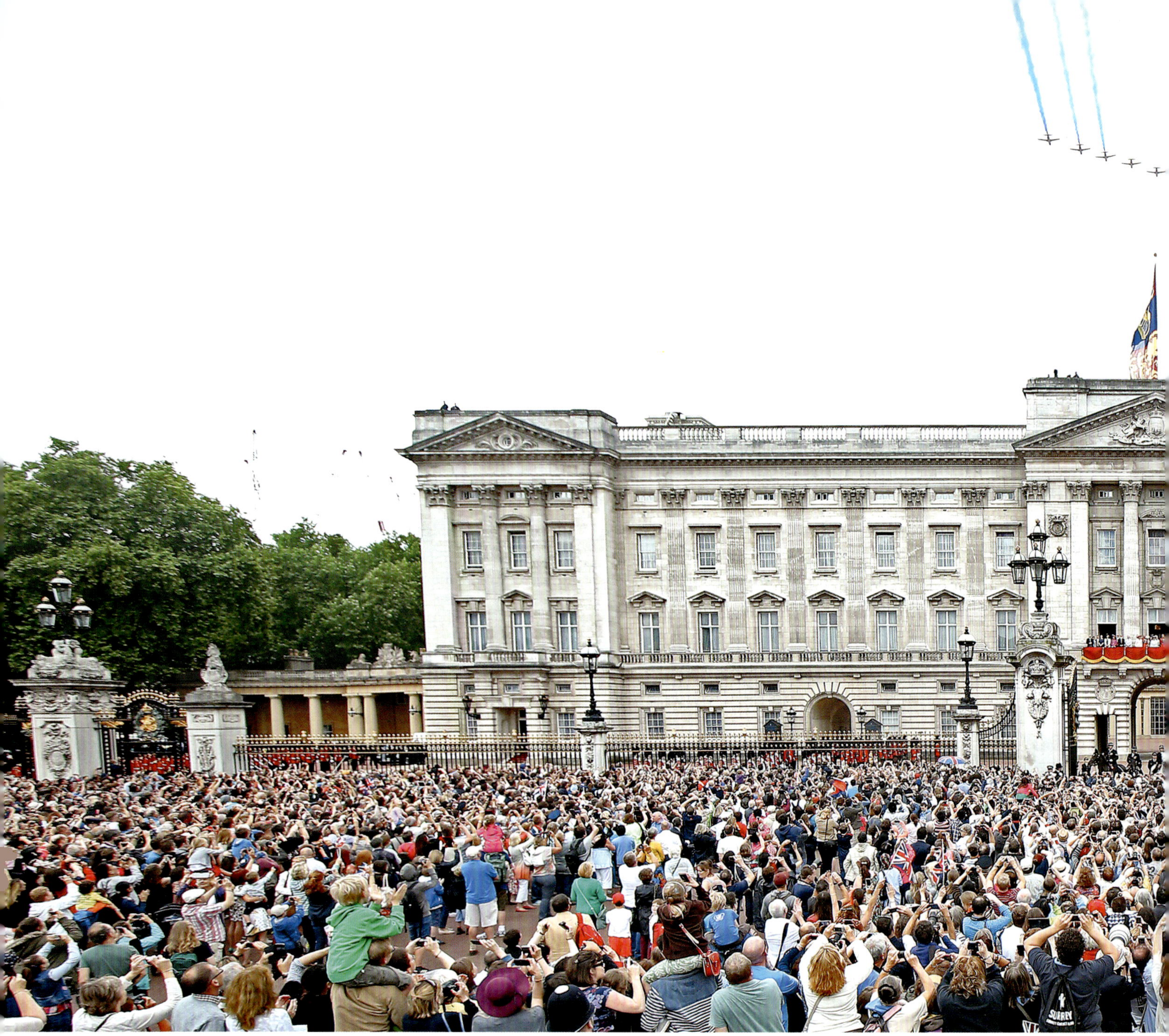

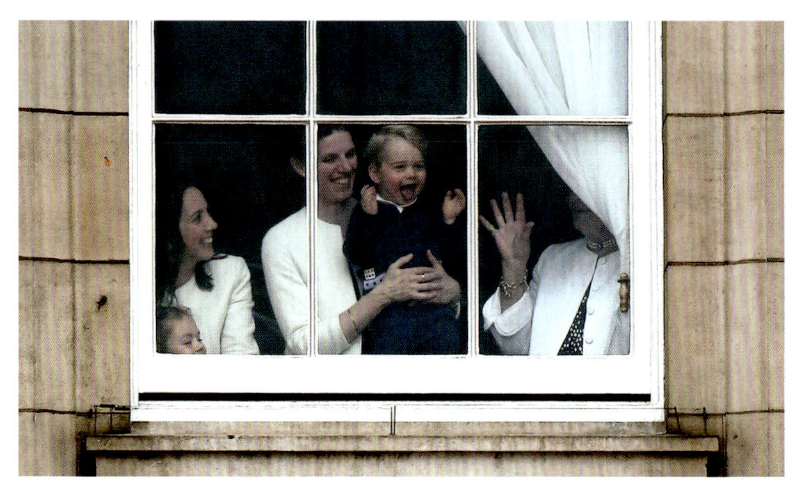

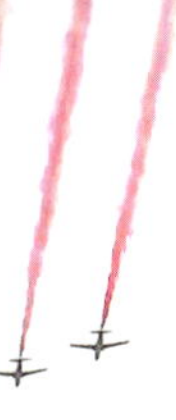

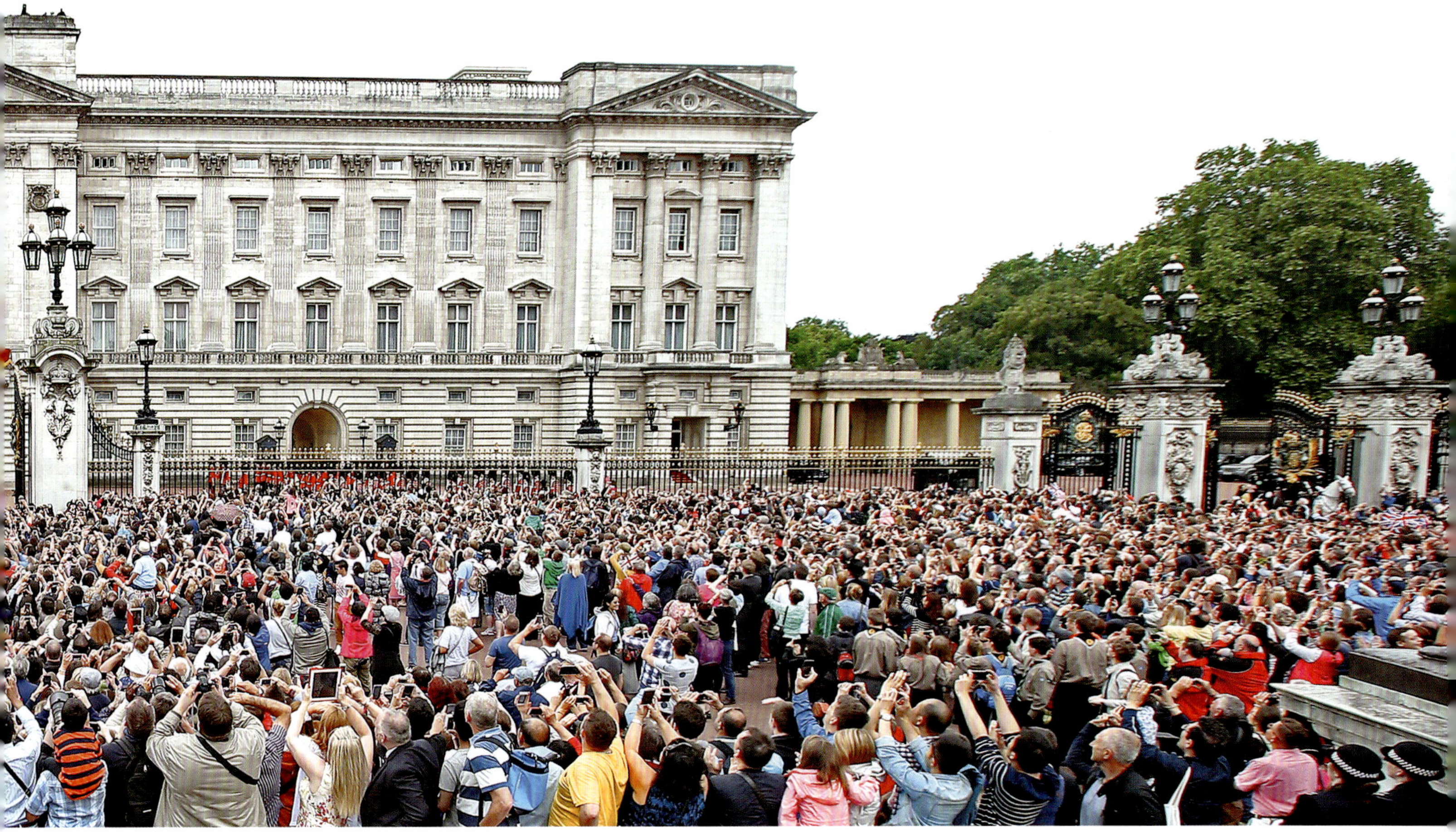

Above The Royal Air Force Aerobatic Team, known as the Red Arrows, flies over Buckingham Palace during the Queen's official birthday celebration, Trooping the Colour.

Left On June 13, 2015, Prince George is held by his nanny, Maria Teresa Turrion Borrallo, as he waves from the window of Buckingham Palace at his father. The Duke of Cambridge is riding out on horseback in the Trooping the Colour ceremonial procession.

Following pages The Trooping the Colour procession makes its way down the Mall to Buckingham Palace from the Horse Guards Parade.

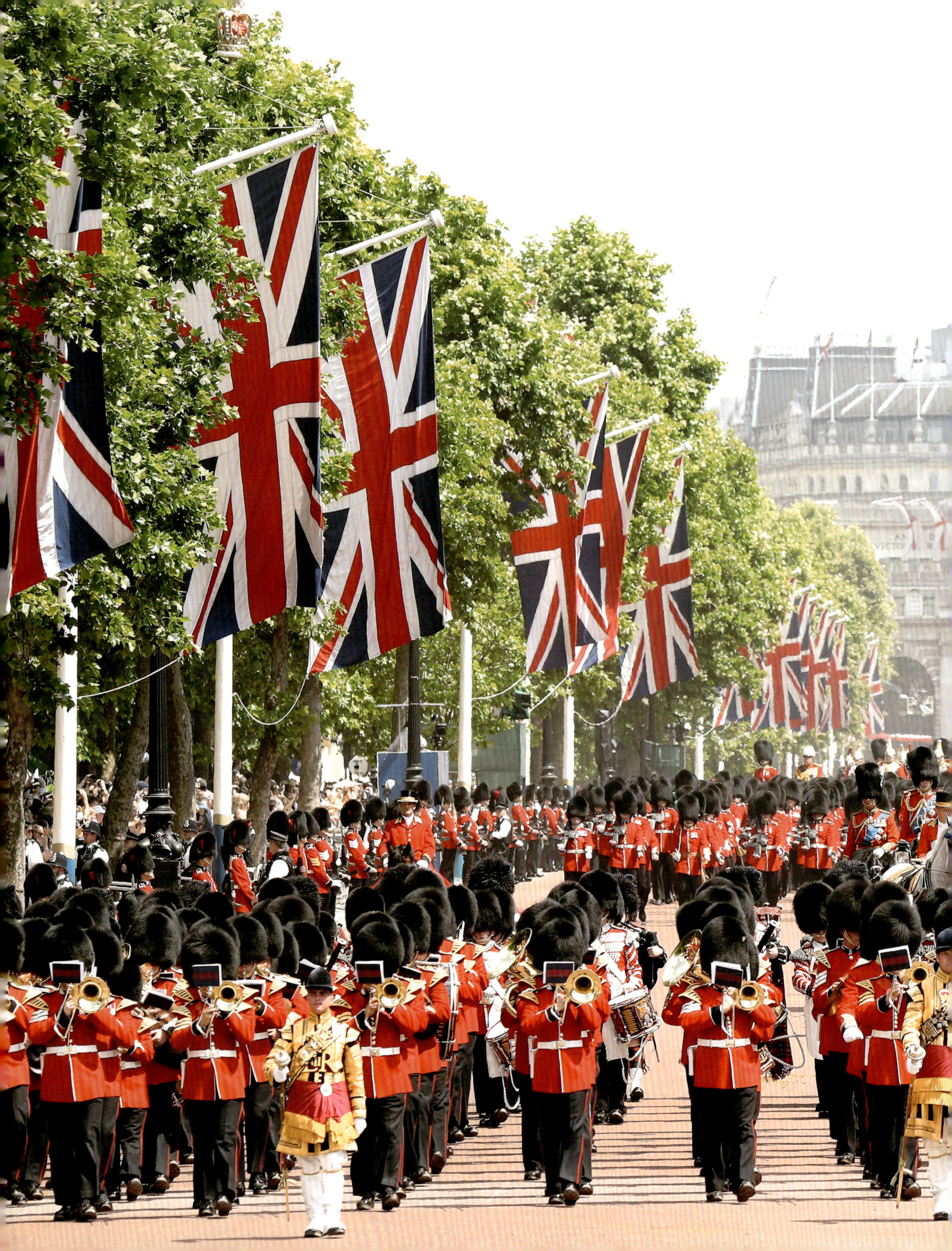

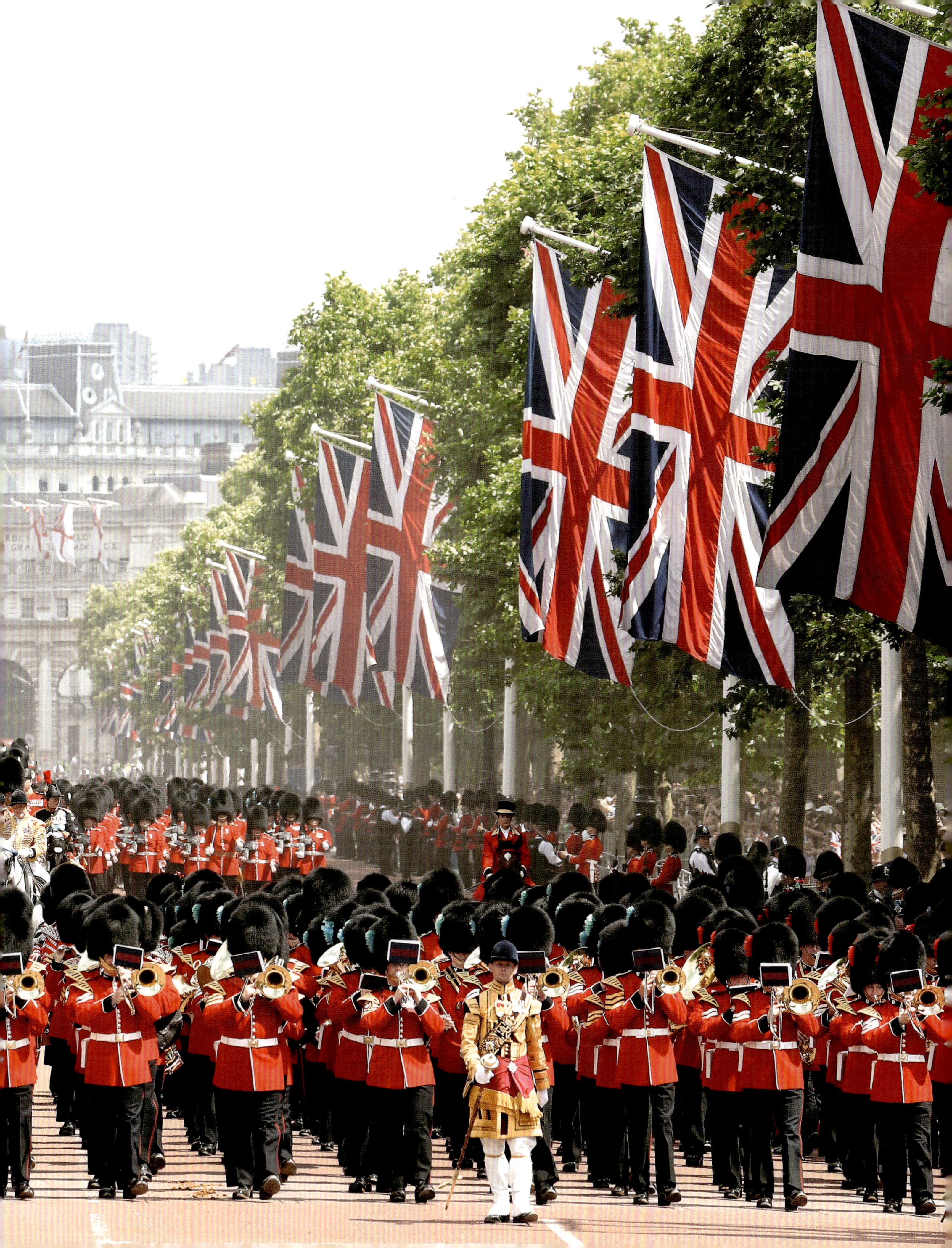

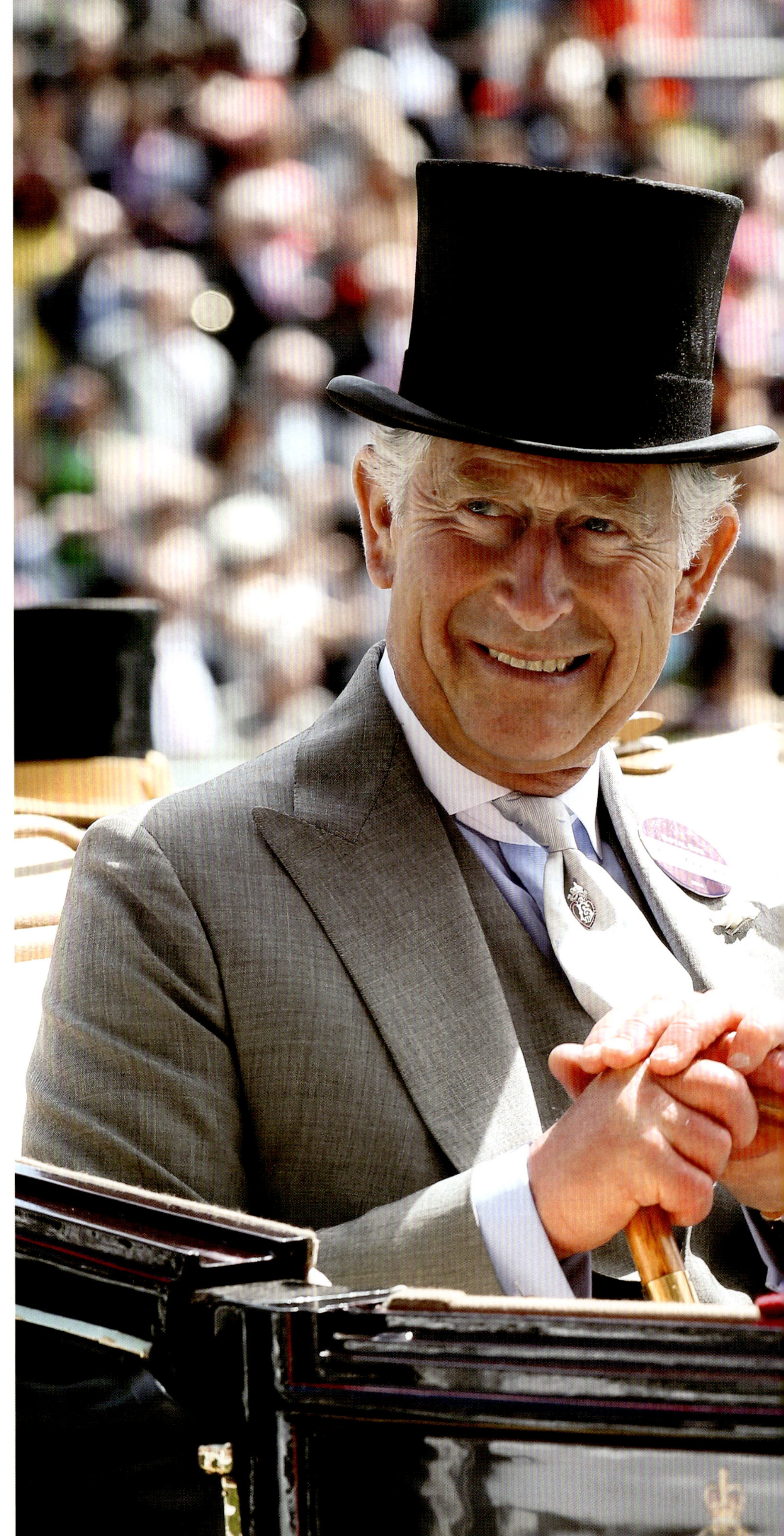

Royal Ascot is a quintessentially British event held every June. The royal family forms an integral part of the ceremony and tradition of this colourful and fashion-oriented horse racing event. Each day of the festival the Queen and the Duke of Edinburgh head up the carriages that process into the parade ring in front of morning-suit-clad racegoers.

Opposite The Prince of Wales and Duchess of Cornwall are greeted by crowds as they enter the ring, whilst on the **following pages** the Queen waves from the leading carriage in front of the iconic Ascot stand.

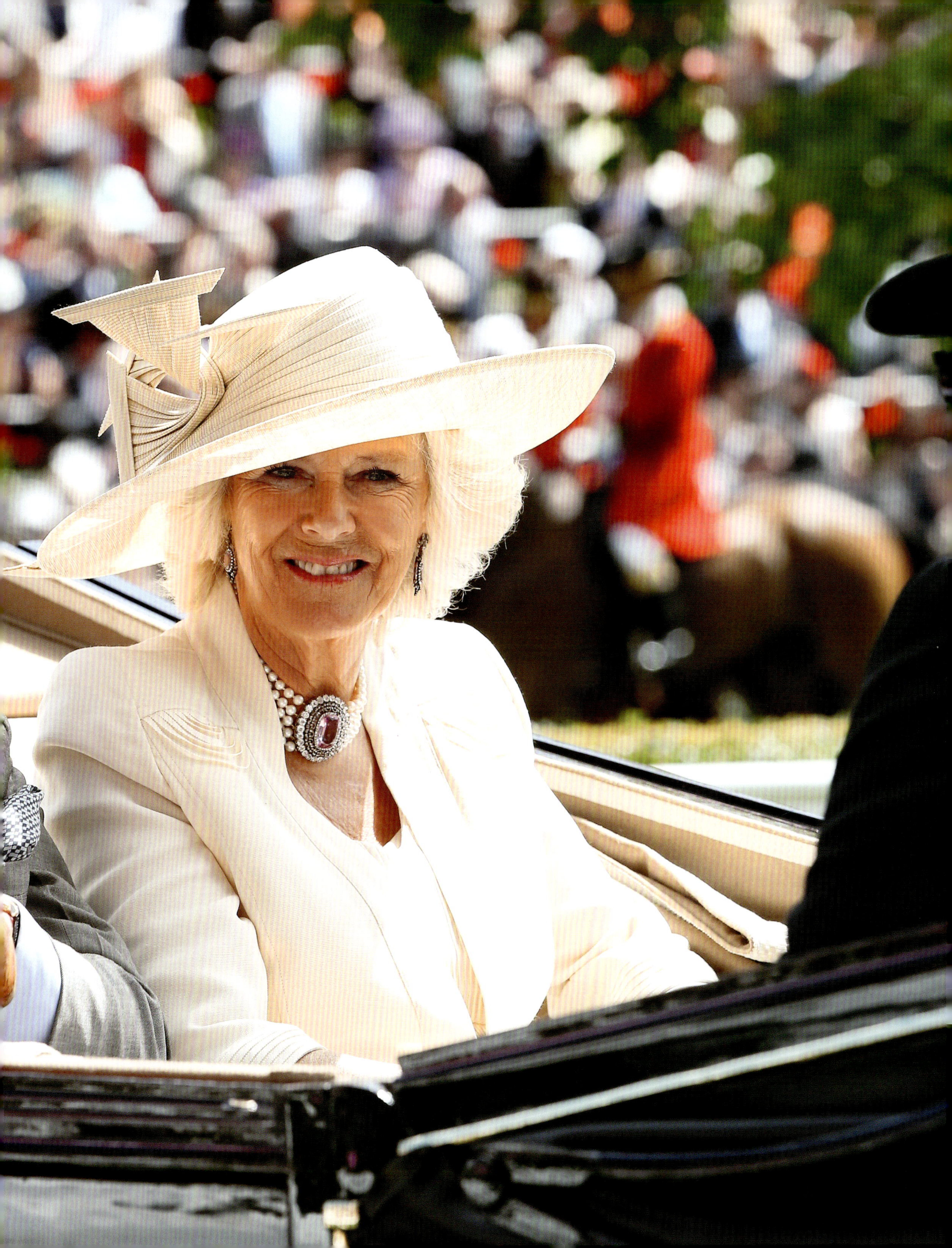

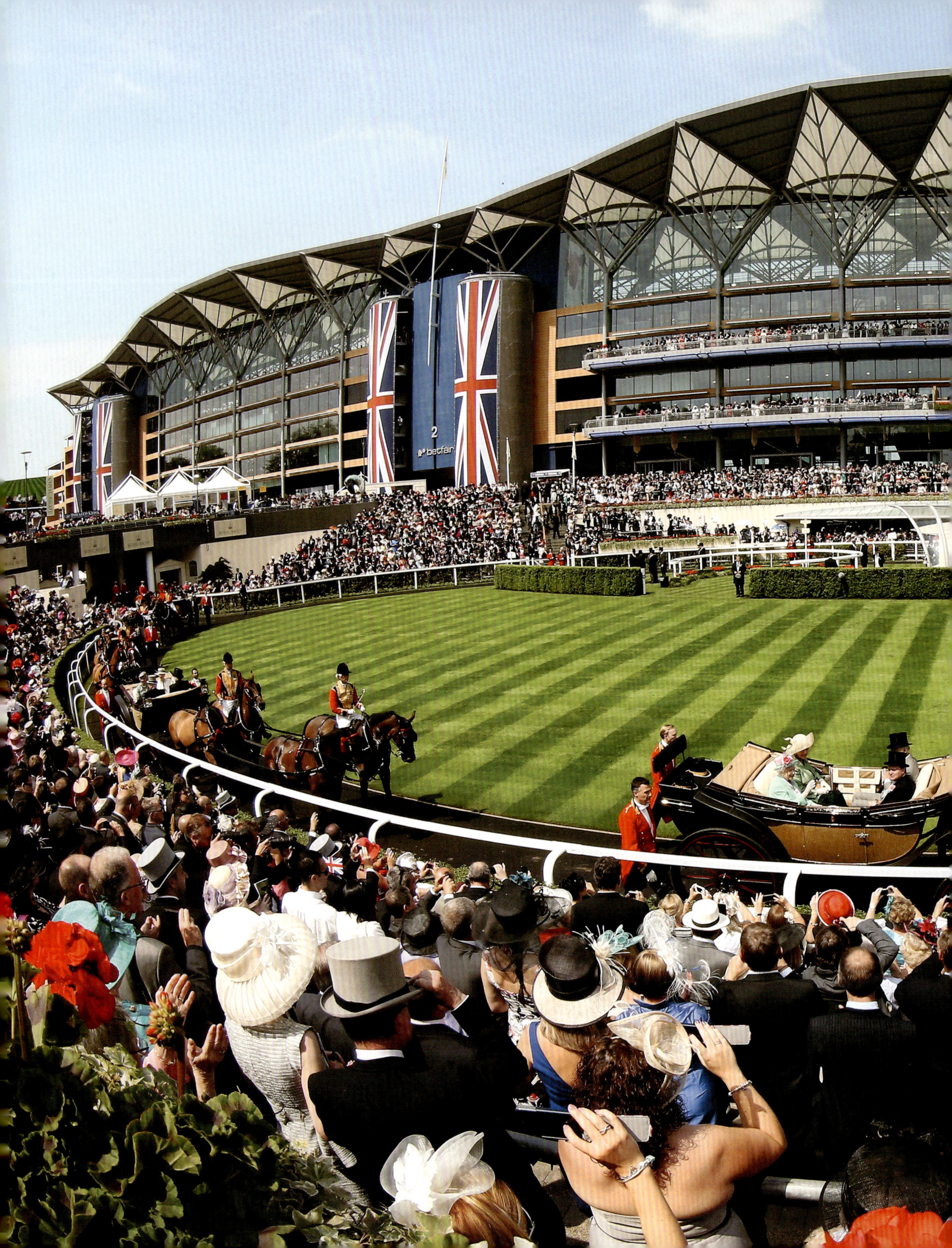
betfair

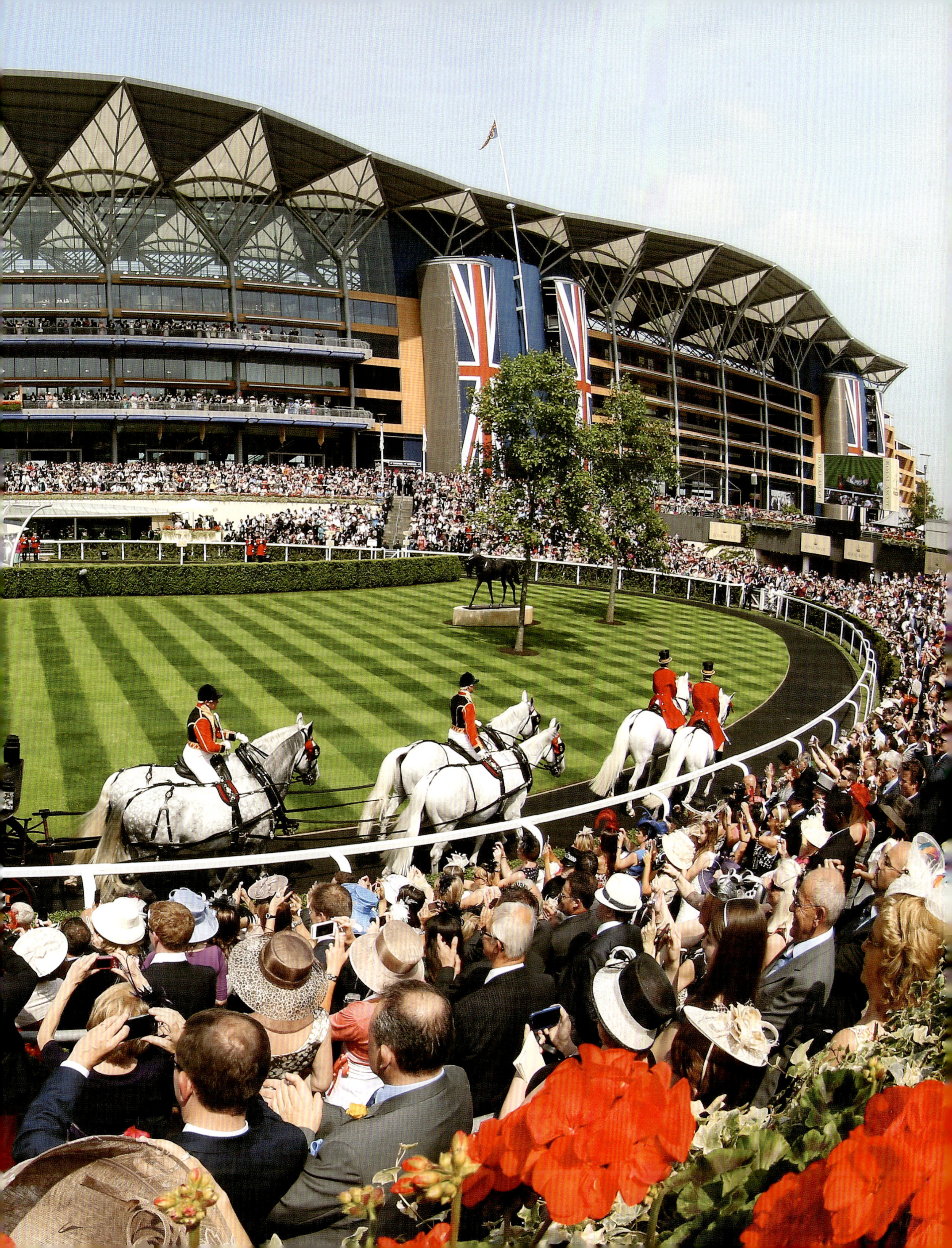

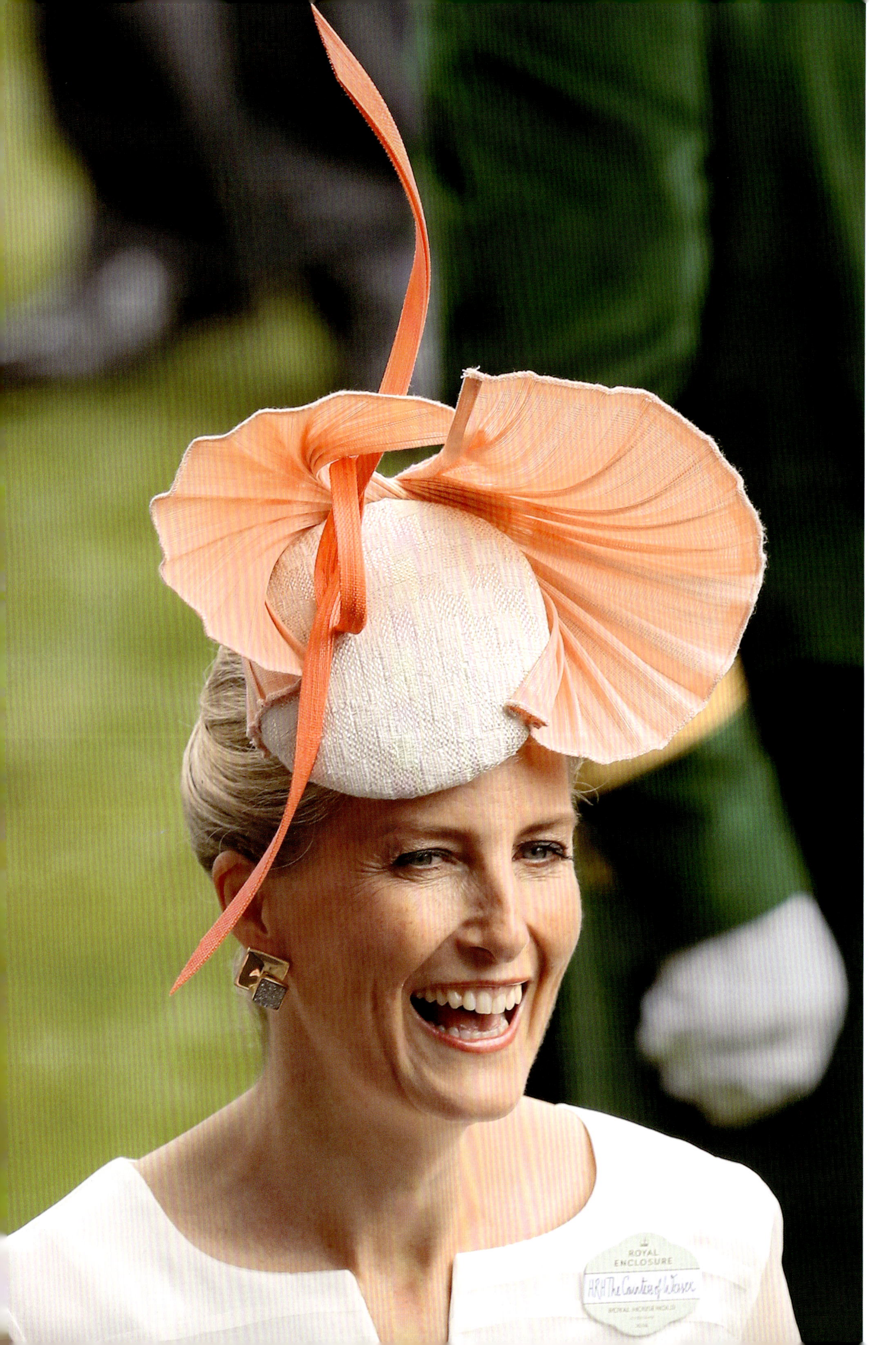
ROYAL ENCLOSURE
HRH The Countess of Wessex

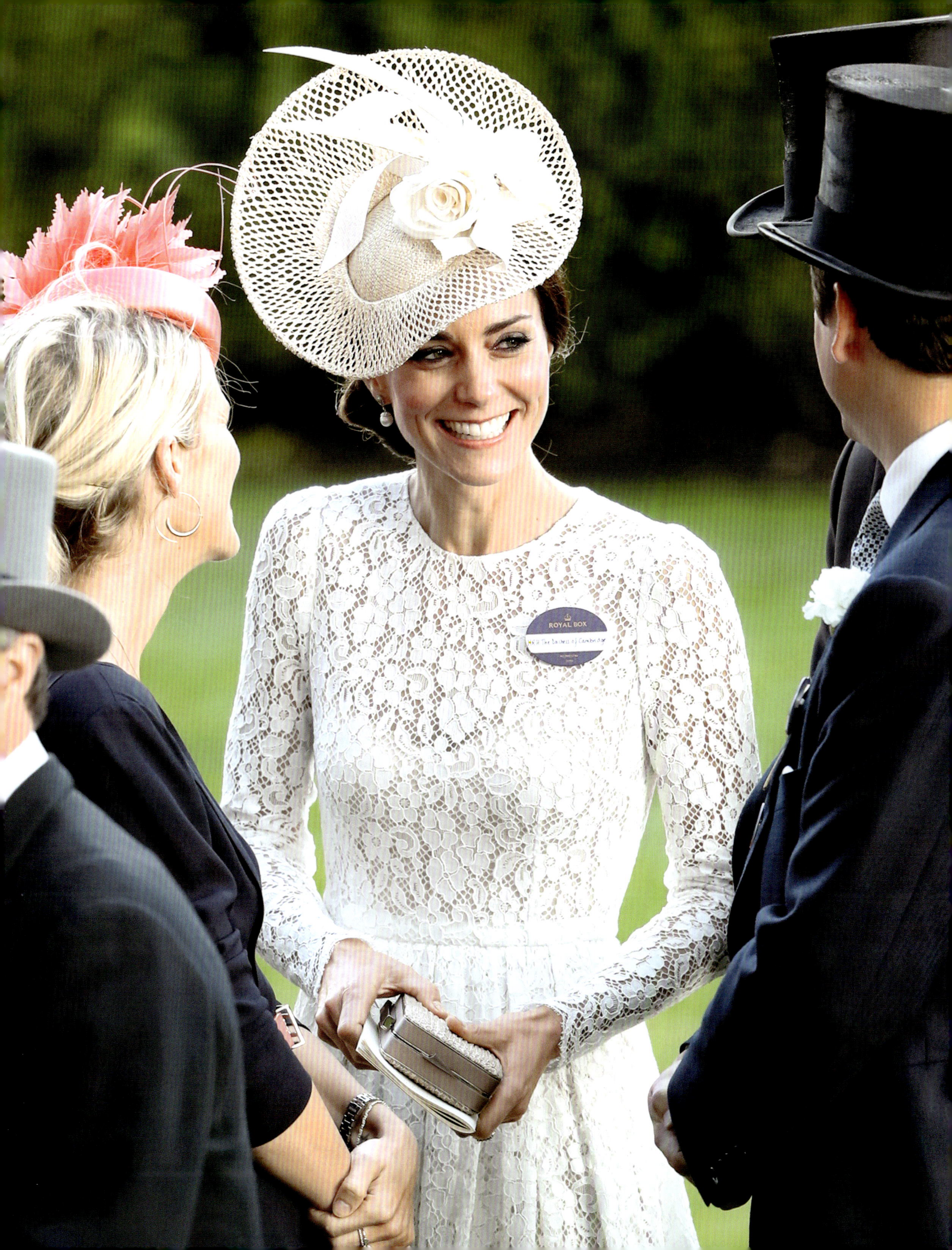
ROYAL BOX

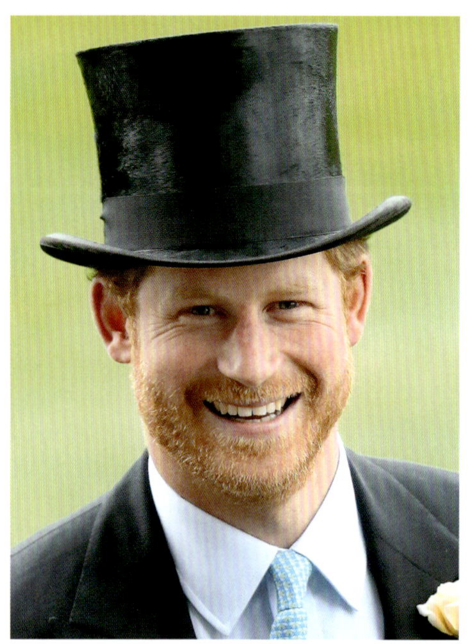

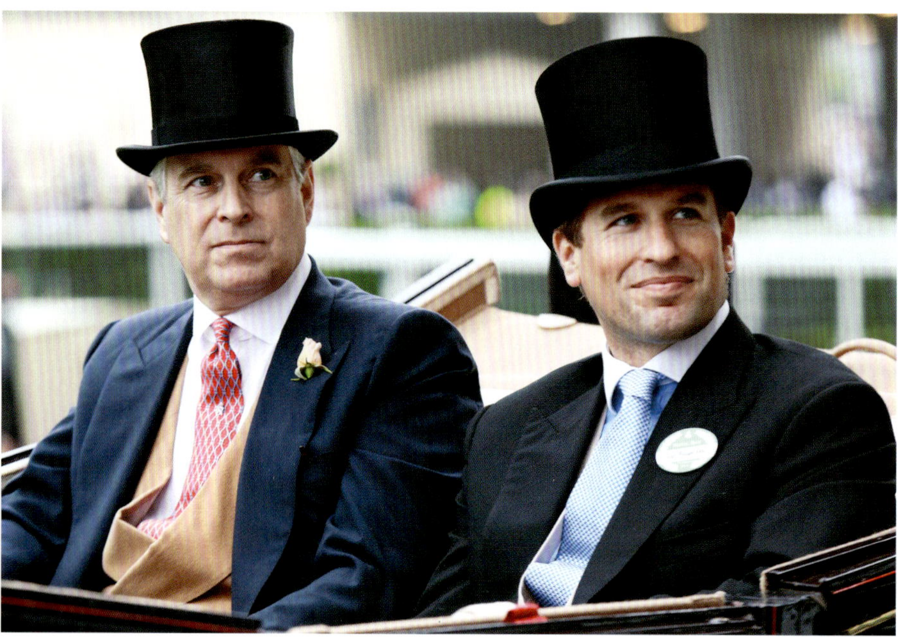

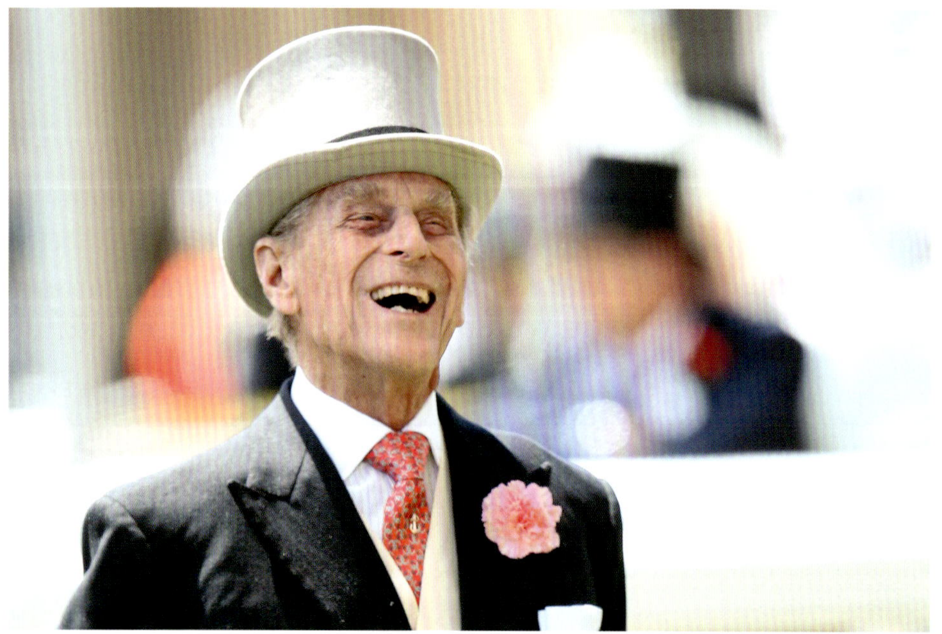

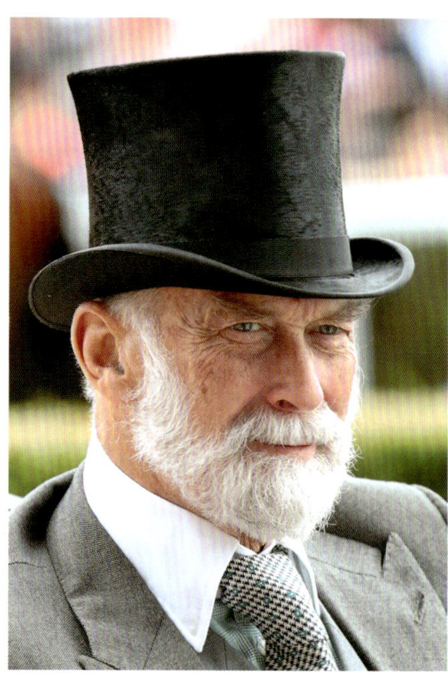

Preceding pages Flamboyant headwear is the order of the day at Royal Ascot. The Countess of Wessex (left) and the Duchess of Cambridge (right) both cut glamorous figures as they enjoy the proceedings in the parade ring.

Above Men are traditionally required to wear morning dress to Royal Ascot. For those in the royal enclosure, a top hat is essential. Generations of the royal family, from Prince Harry, Prince Andrew, Peter Phillips, and Prince Michael of Kent to the Duke of Edinburgh, have enjoyed the event and male members normally sport colourful ties or waistcoats.

Opposite Princess Beatrice (right) and Princess Eugenie (left) clearly relish supporting their grandmother, the Queen, as she enjoys one of her great passions, horse racing.

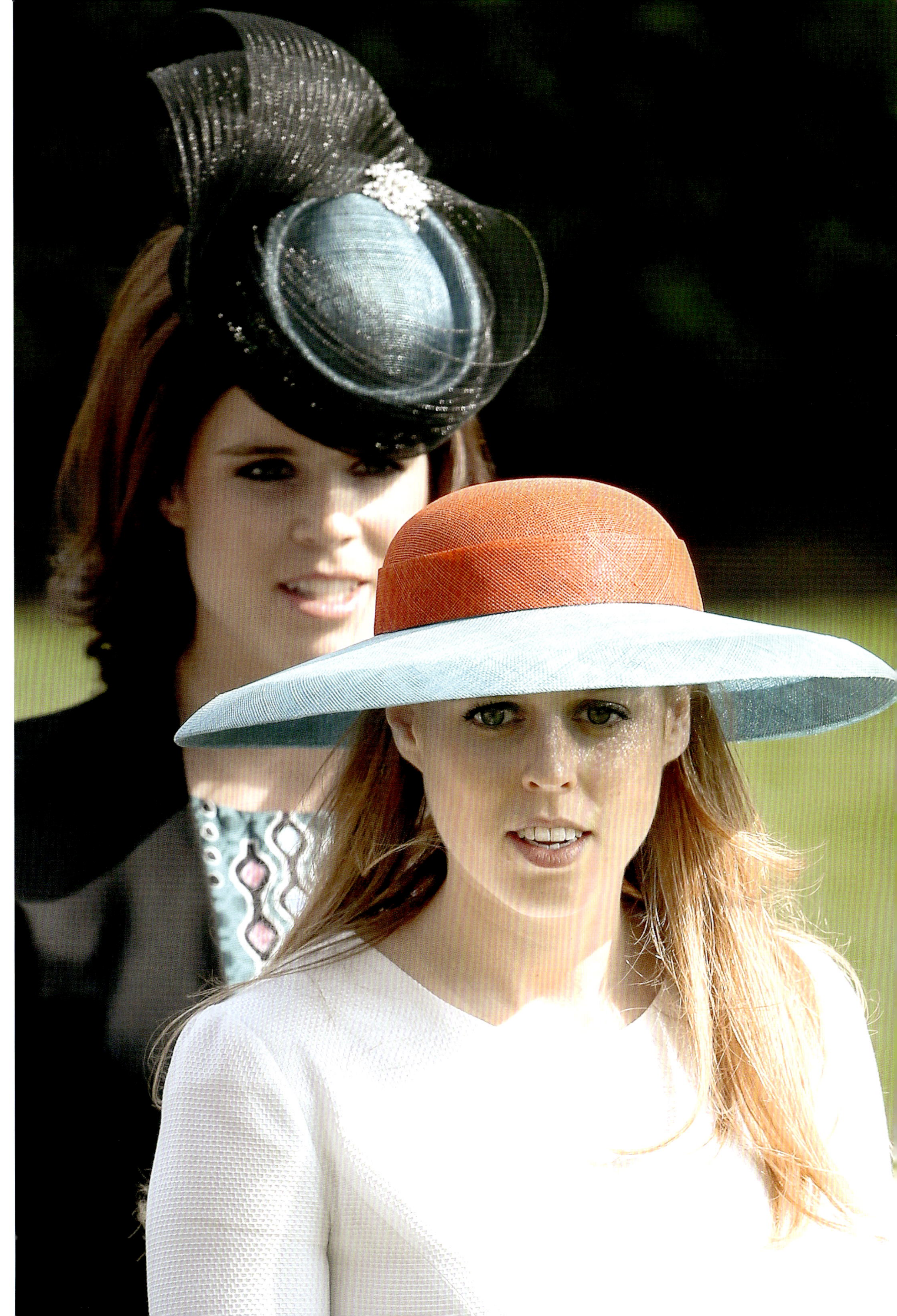

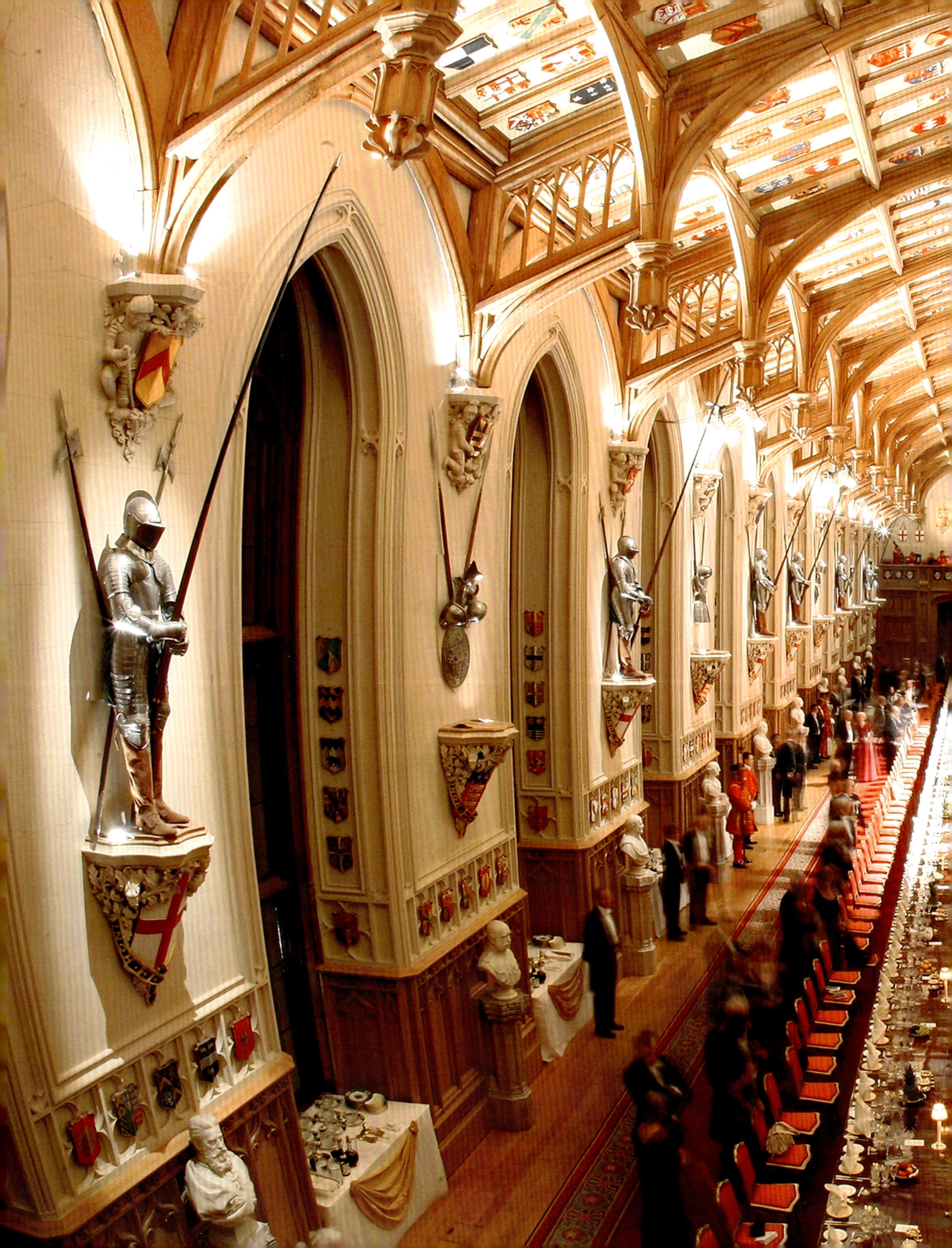

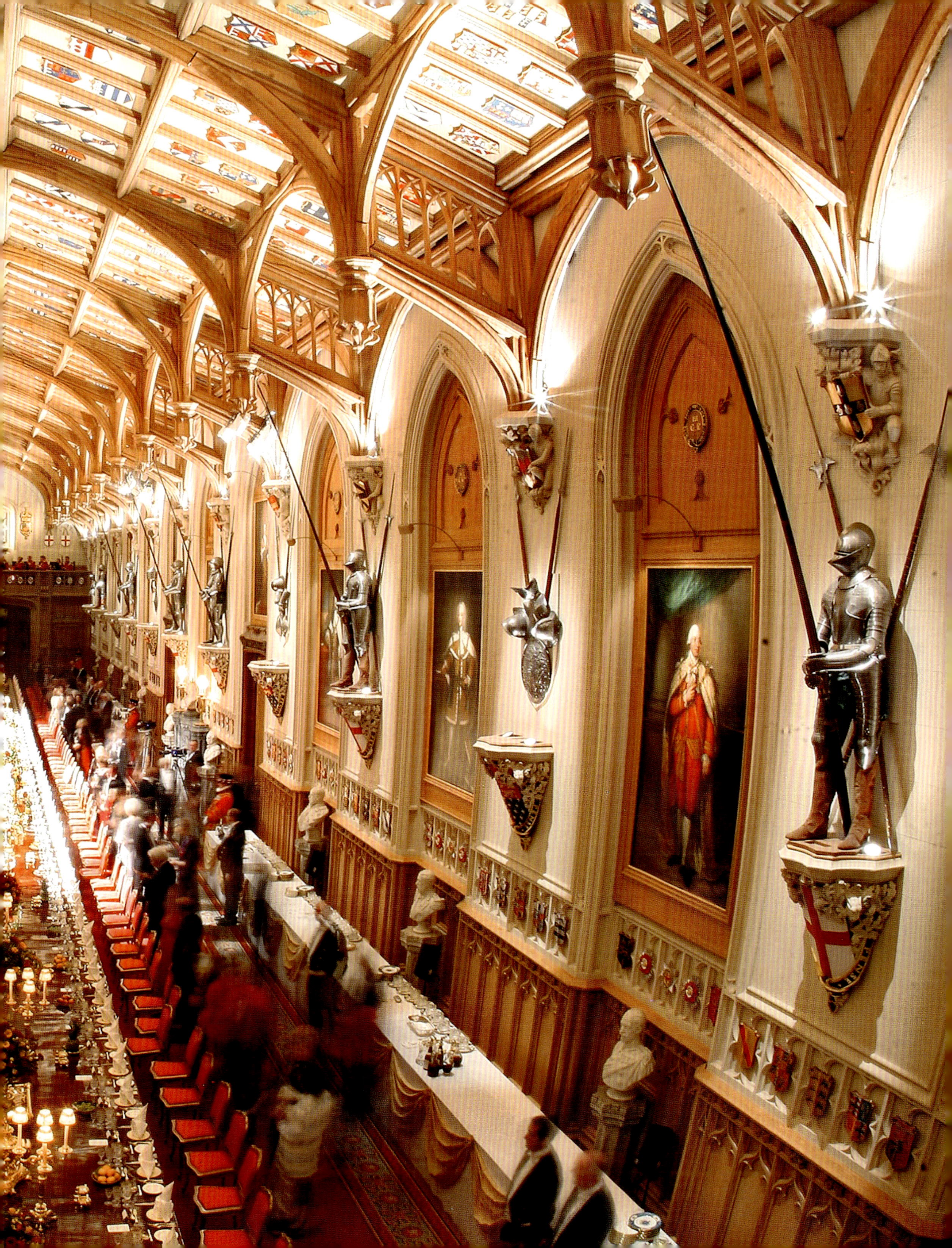

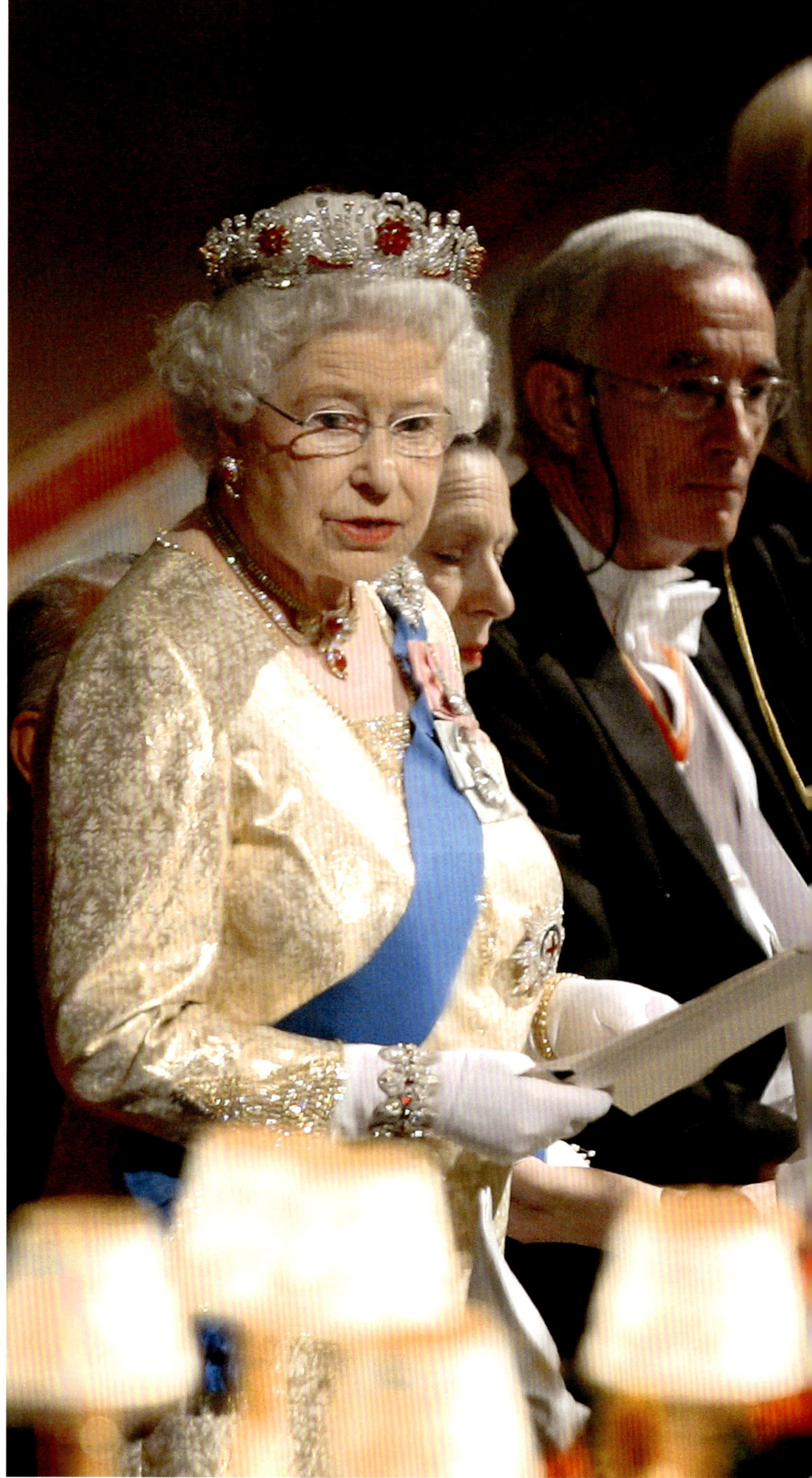

Preceding pages State visits play an important role in developing and maintaining Britain's relationships with countries around the world. Prime ministers, presidents, and foreign monarchs are invited to visit the United Kingdom on the advice of the British Foreign and Commonwealth offices. Visitors typically are afforded a ceremonial welcome and a full state banquet. This banquet was set up for Pratibha Patil, President of the Republic of India, in the 180-foot St. George's Hall in Windsor Castle.

Right The Queen delivers a speech in Windsor Castle during the same visit.

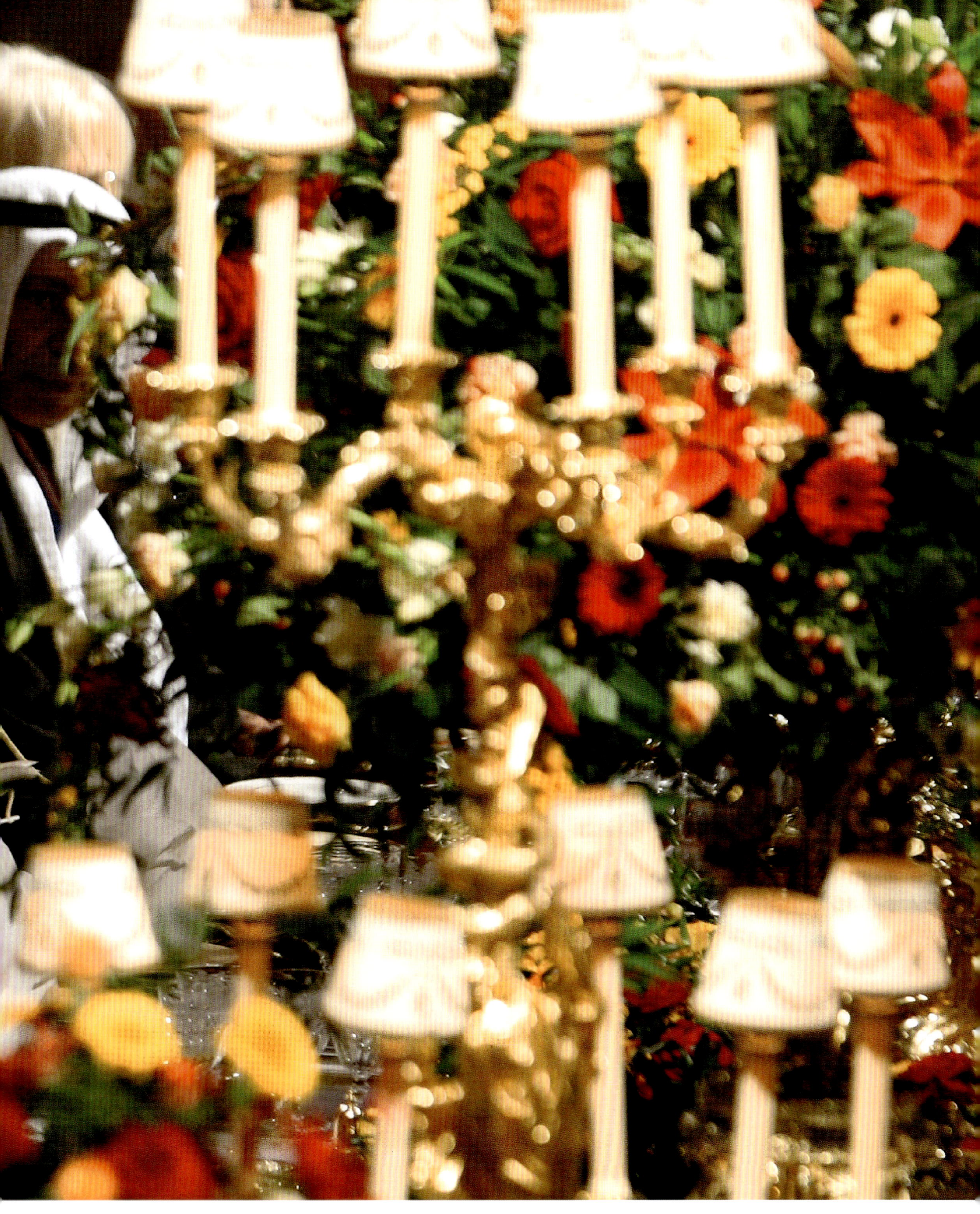

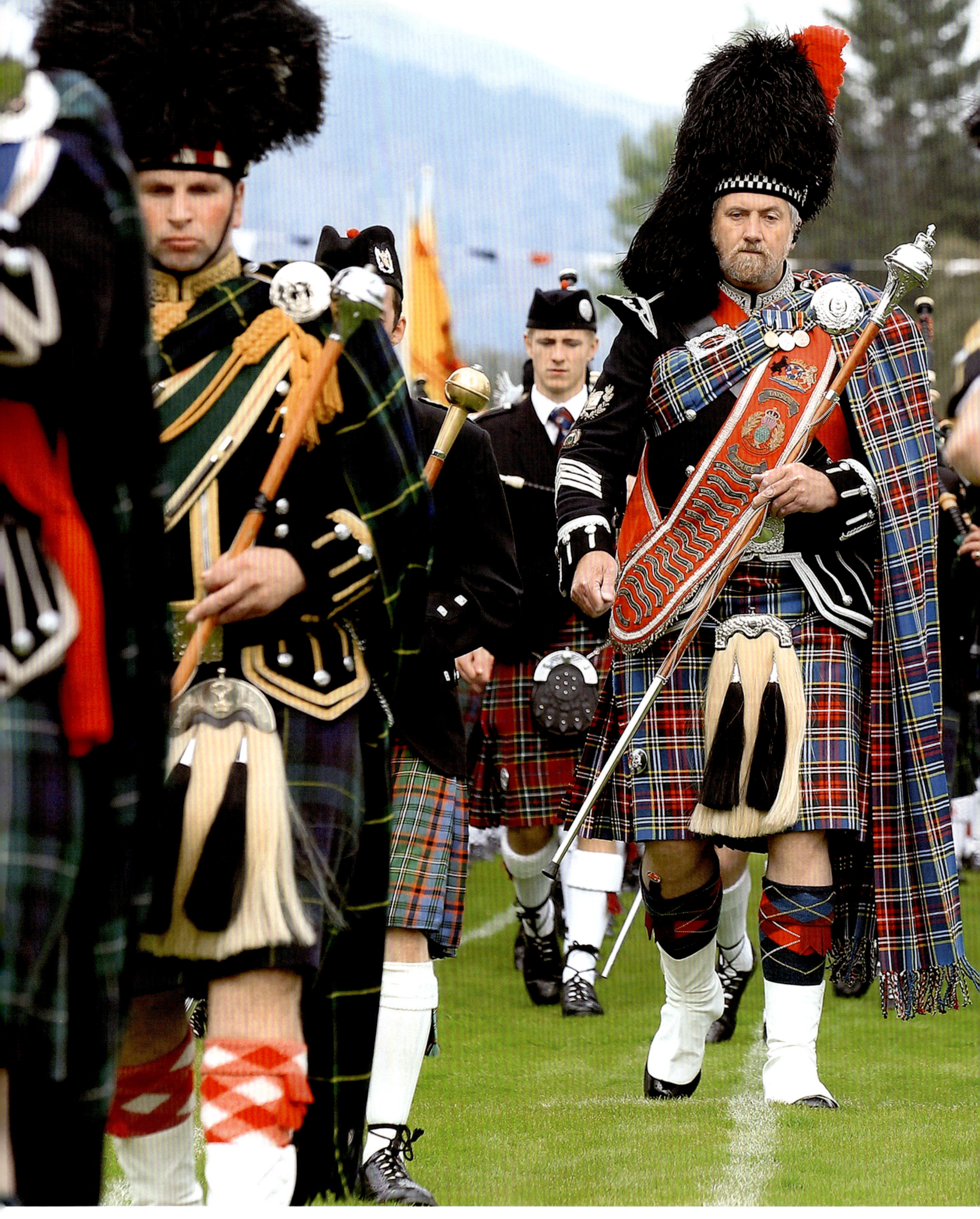

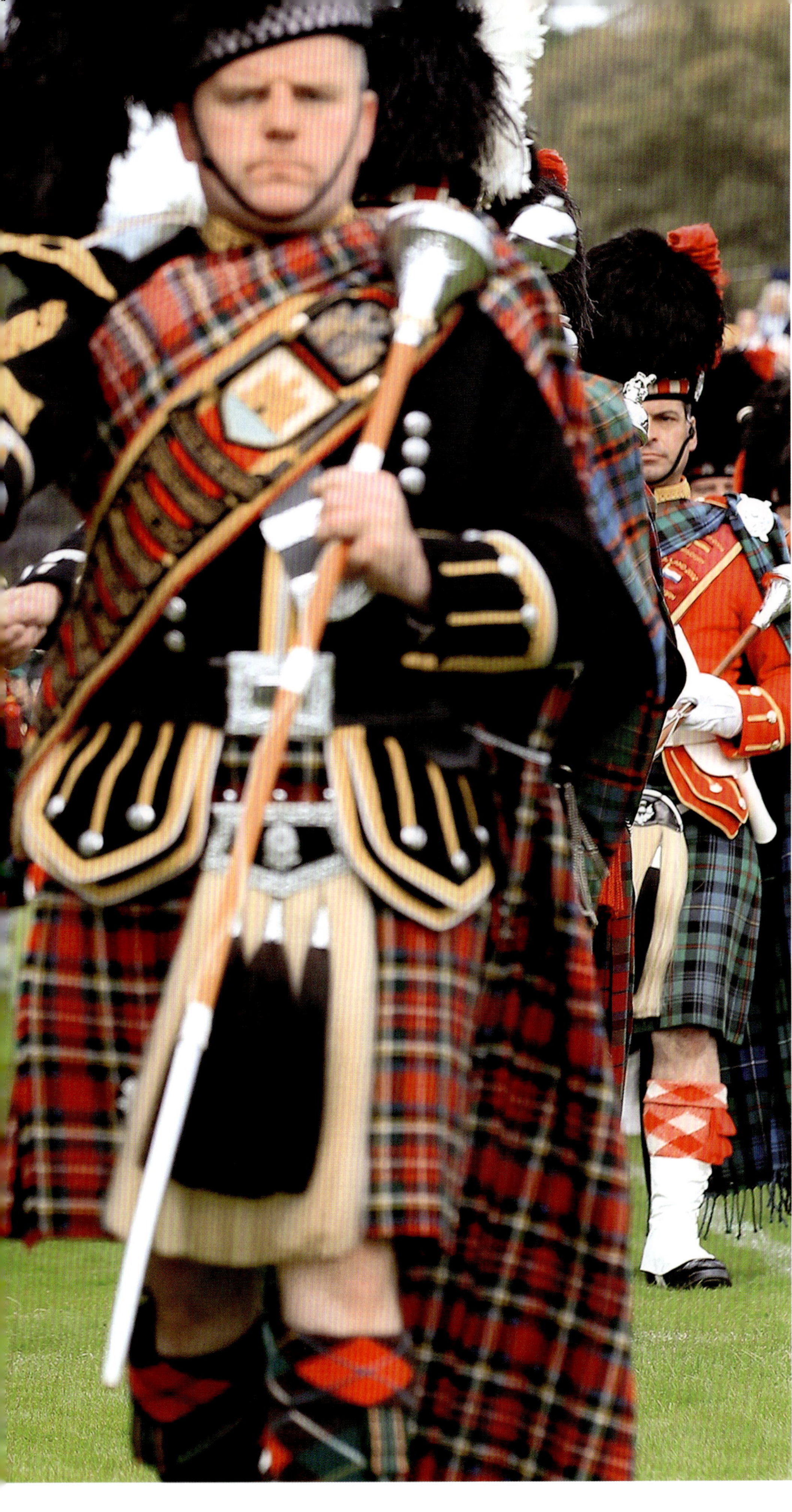

One of my favourite events of the year to photograph occurs on the first Saturday of September. The Braemar Gathering is probably the most famous of the Scottish Highland Games and has existed in its current form since 1832. A celebration of Scottish and Celtic culture, the games feature an array of traditional activities from dancing to tossing the caber and tug-o-war. The games are staged at the Princess Royal and Duke of Fife Memorial Park in Braemar not far from the Queen's summer retreat, Balmoral Castle. Here Scottish tartans are on display during the traditional parade.

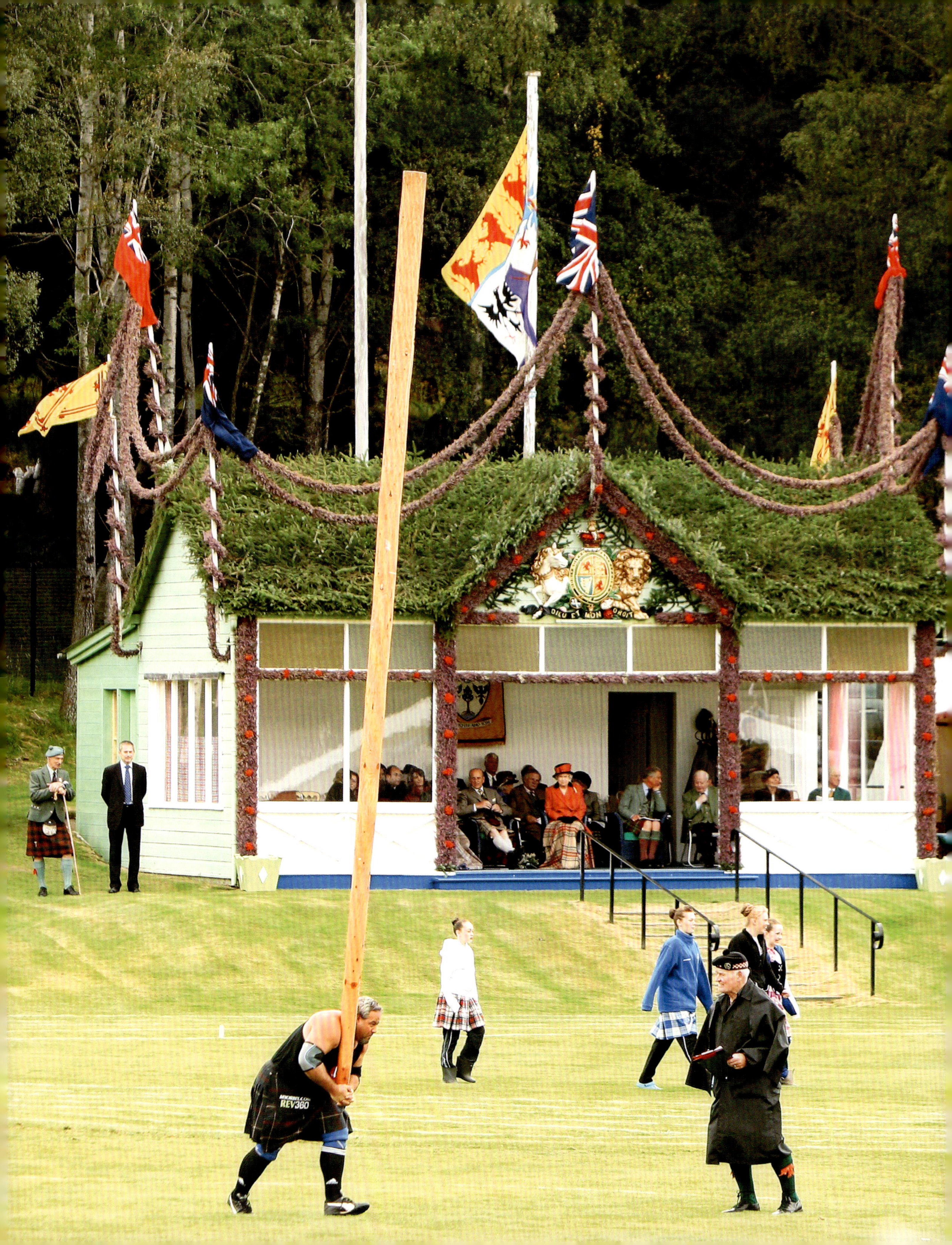
REV380

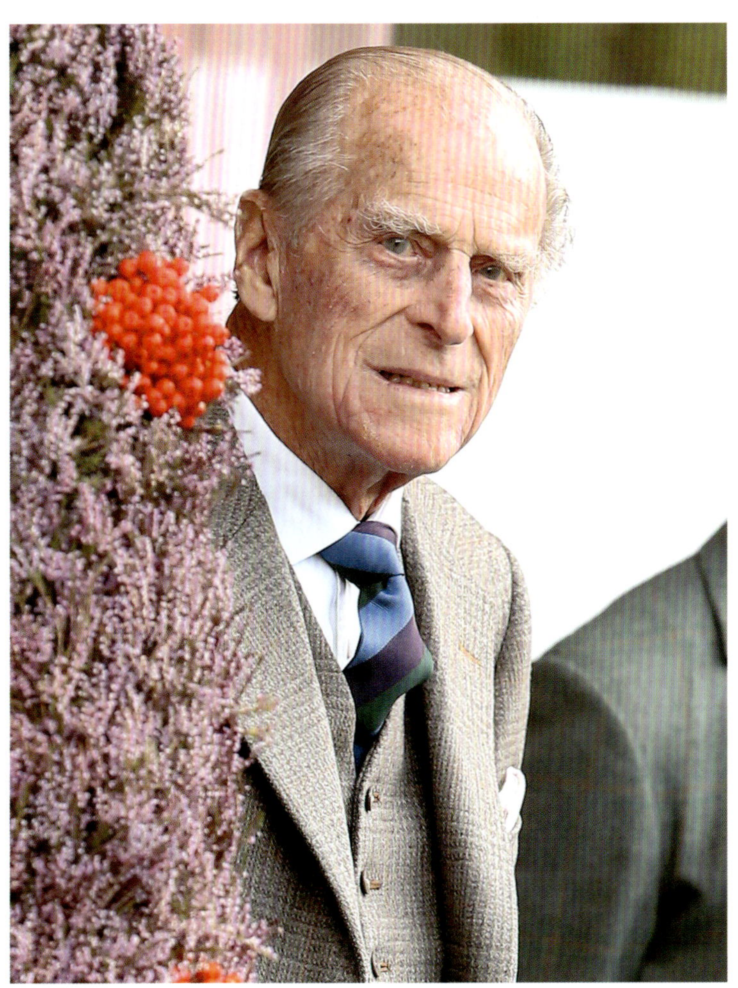

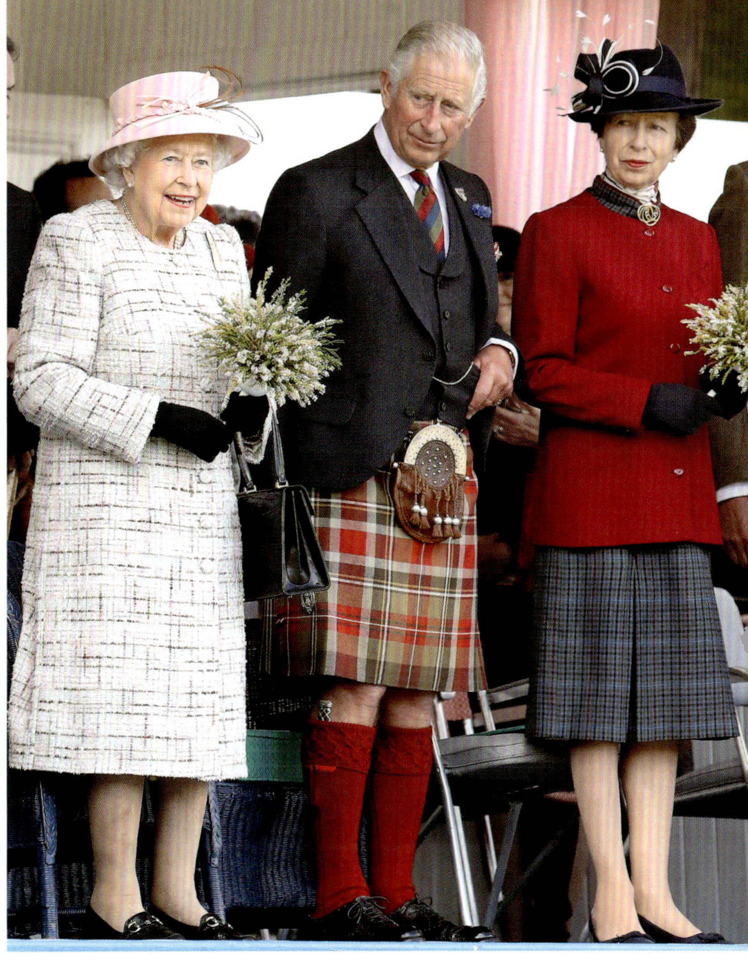

Opposite The royal party watches the games from a wonderfully adorned royal box. The large arena, approximately the size of a soccer pitch, is a frenetic scene of various competitions. Probably the most iconic is the caber toss, where competitors from all over the world test their mettle by thrusting an almost twenty-foot caber into the air.

Top left The Duke of Edinburgh peers around the edge of the vibrant heather that borders the elaborately decorated royal enclosure.

Top right The Highland Games are very much a family affair. Here the Prince of Wales and his sister, Princess Anne, accompany a smiling Queen.

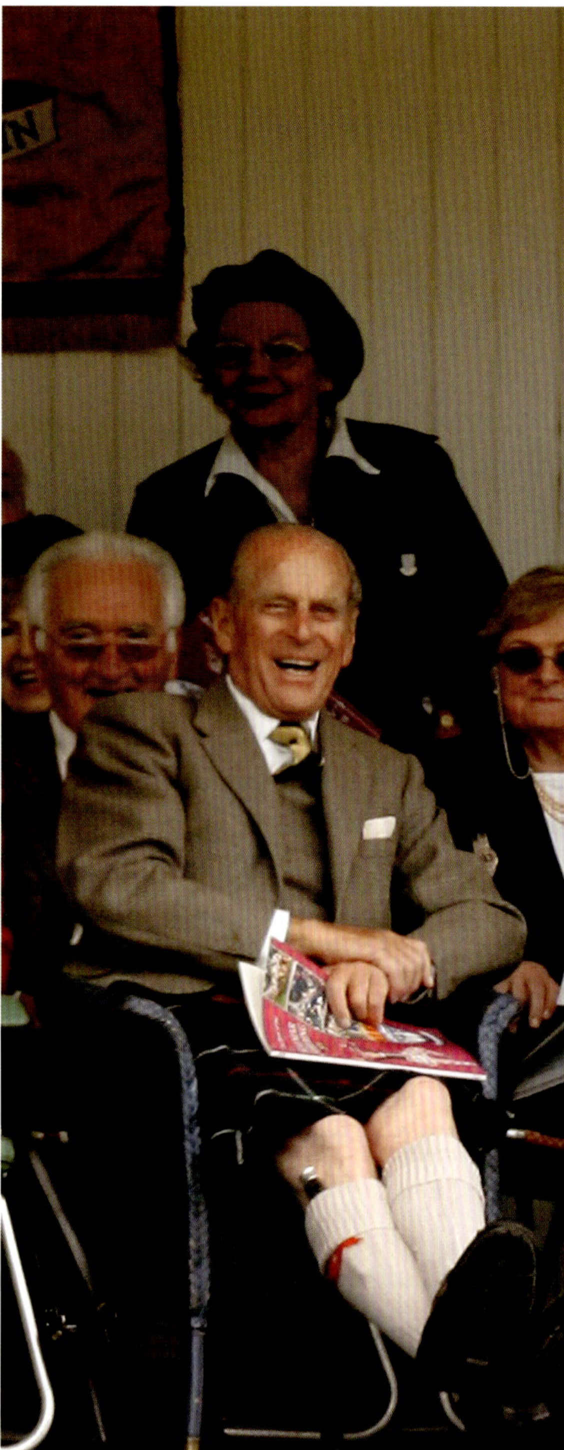

This scene from 2006 is one of my all-time favourite moments at the Highland Games. The royal party generally spends about one hour watching the action and you certainly have to be on the ball to capture a good shot. In this photo, the children's sack race has the family in hysterics. It's great to be able to record such candid and relaxed moments when the family is together—a million miles from the formality of most royal events.

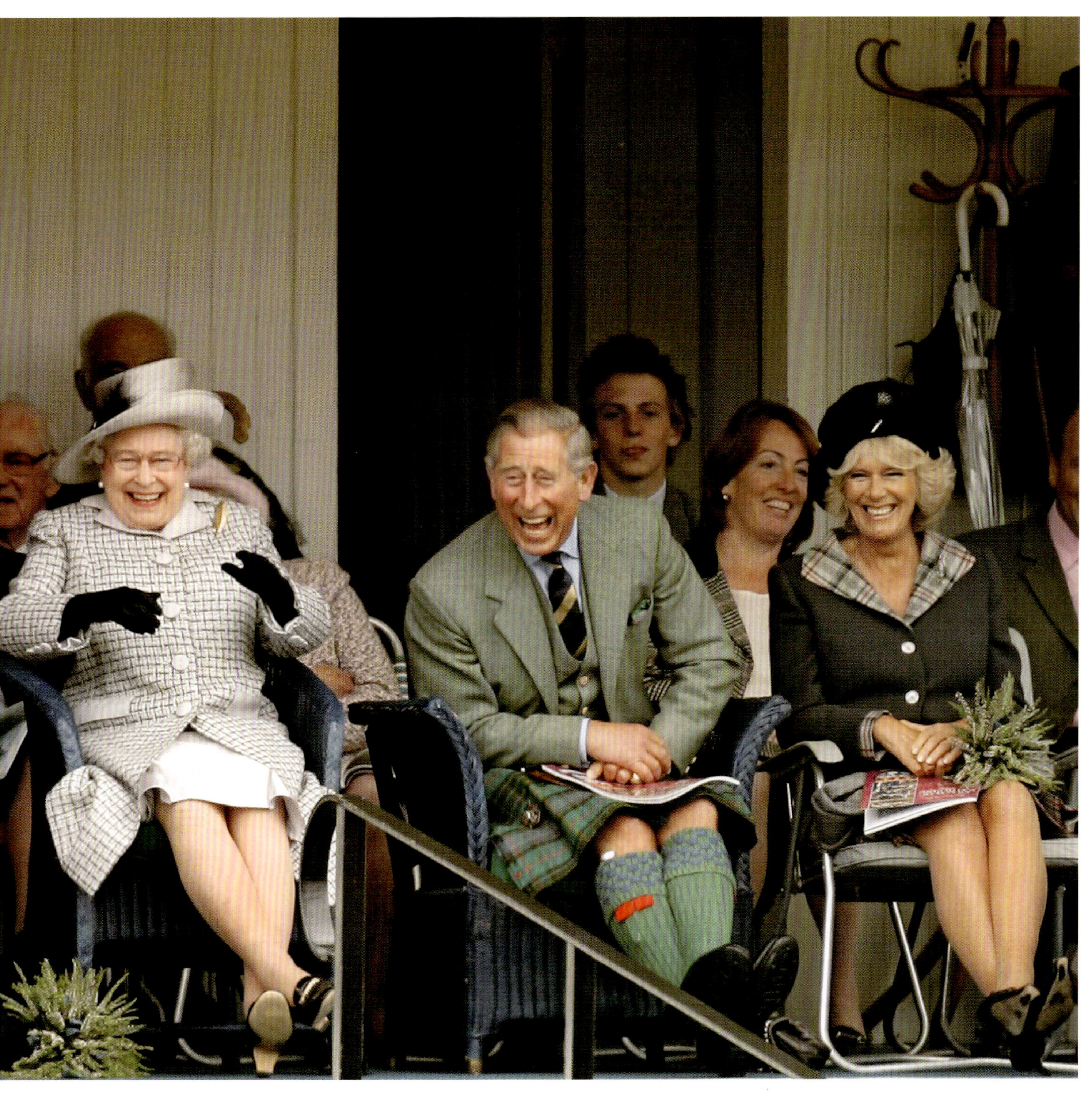

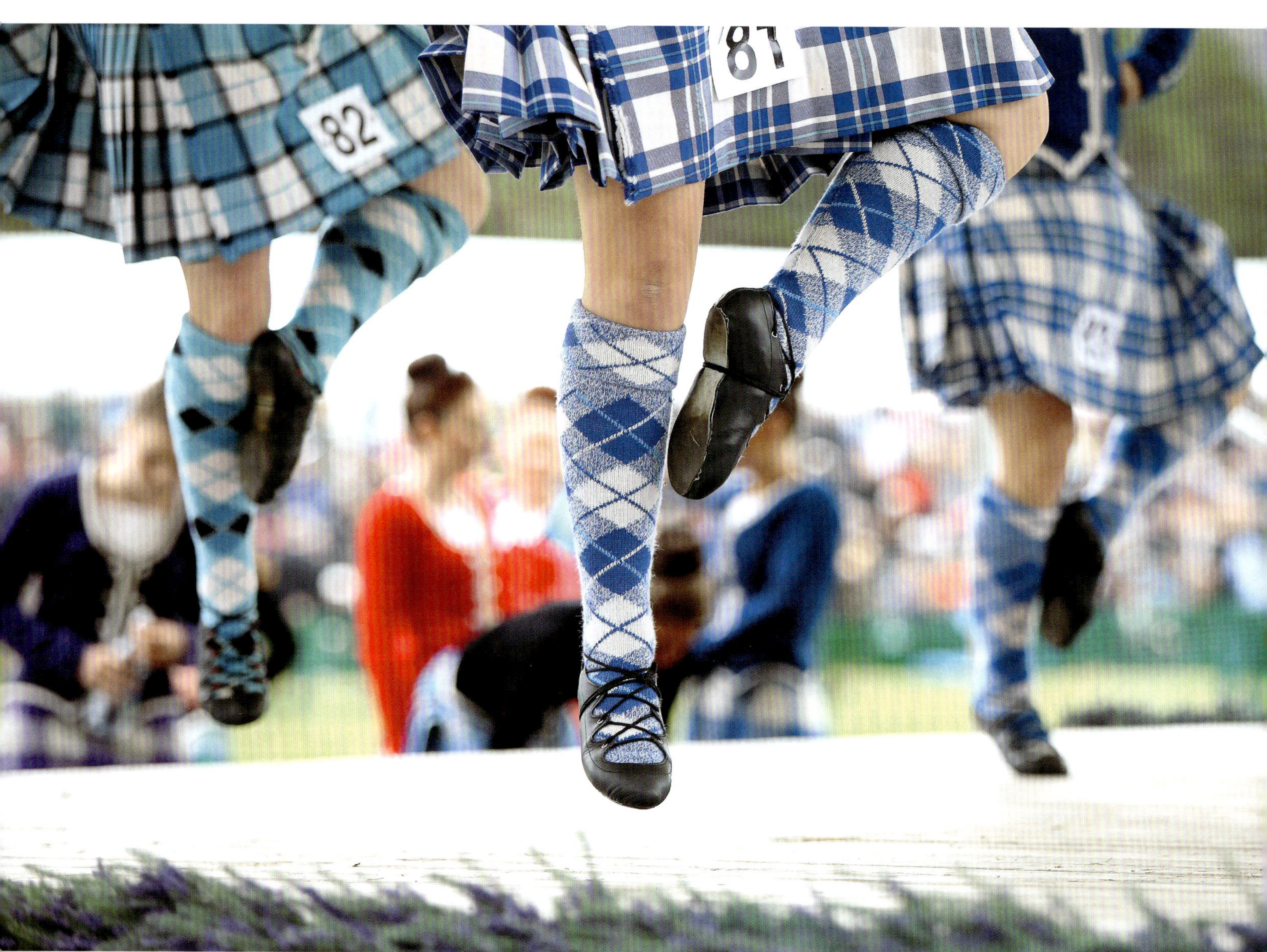

Above and opposite Much of the beauty is in the detail at an event like the Highland Games. Highland dancing, also known as the Highland Reel, is a transfixing and energetic part of the games and is accompanied by bagpipe music. Dancers wear special shoes called ghillies and tweed and tartan are de rigueur.

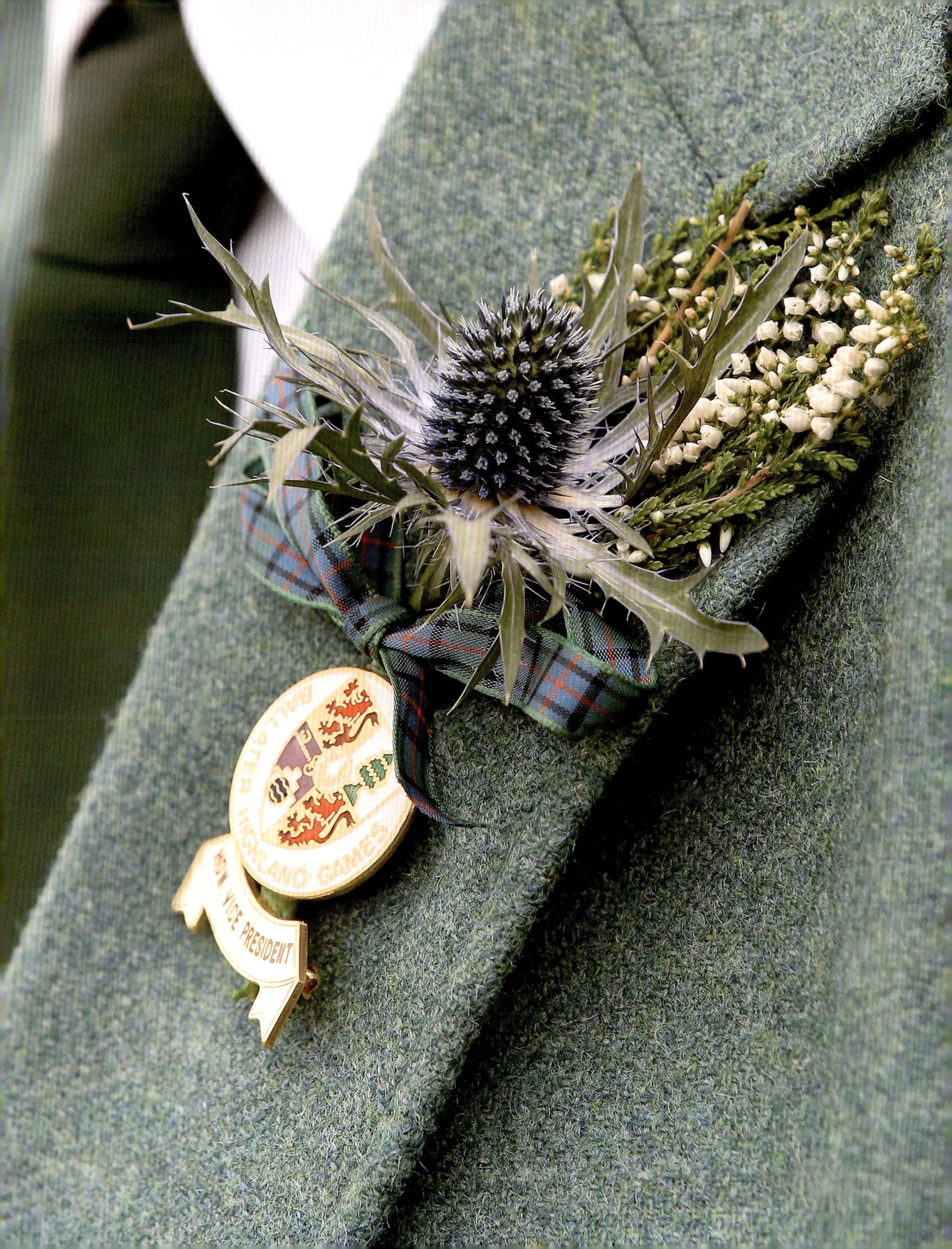
BALLATER HIGHLAND GAMES
HON. VICE PRESIDENT

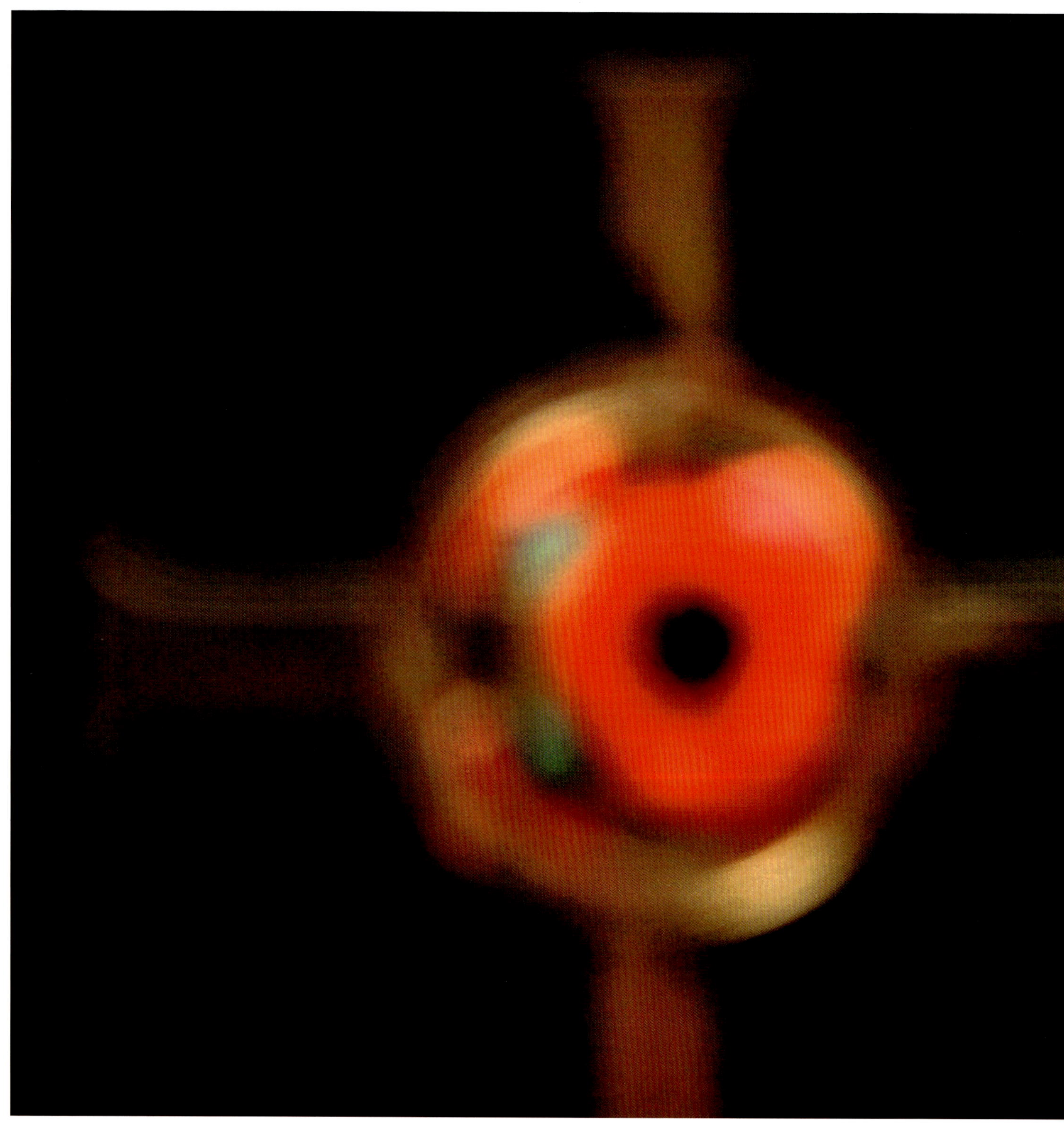

Commemorated on the second Sunday in November, Armistice Day, or Remembrance Sunday, provides a poignant reminder of the important role the royal family plays in remembering those who have made the ultimate sacrifice. In 2017, for the first time, the Prince of Wales laid a wreath at the Cenotaph on behalf of the Queen, who watched from the balcony with the Duke of Edinburgh. Here on November 9, 2008, the Queen pays her respects to mark the ninetieth anniversary of the end of the First World War.

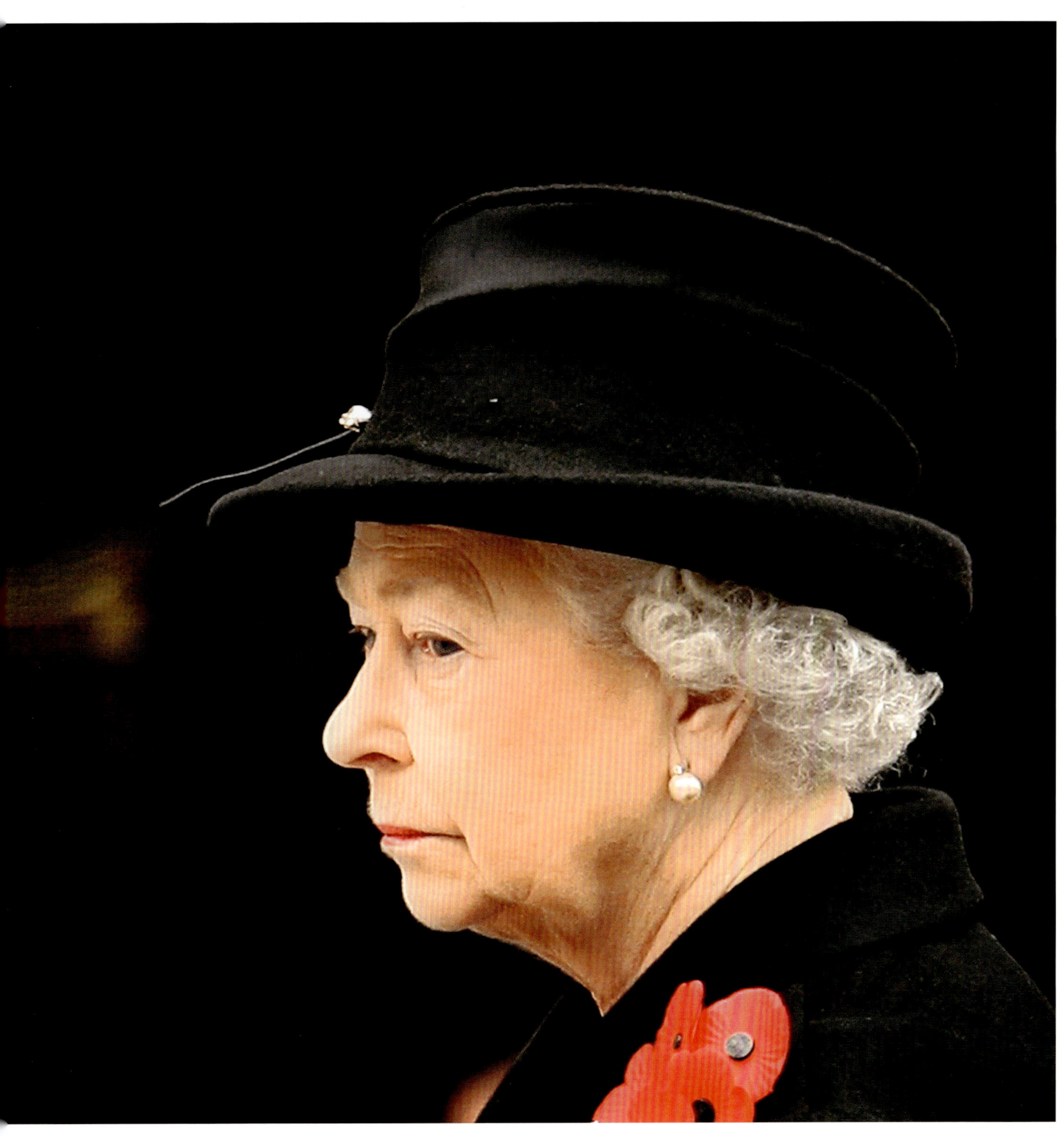

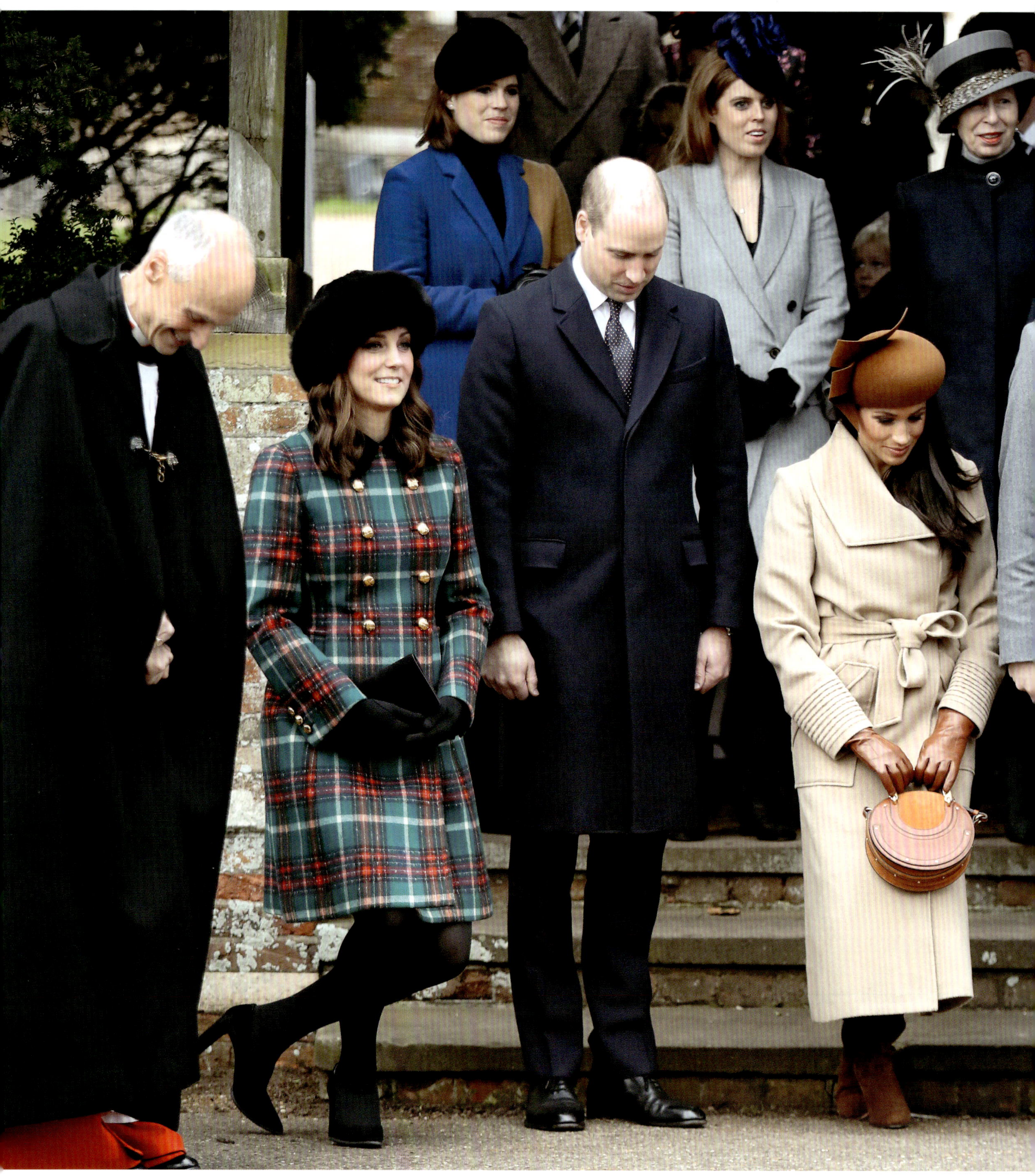

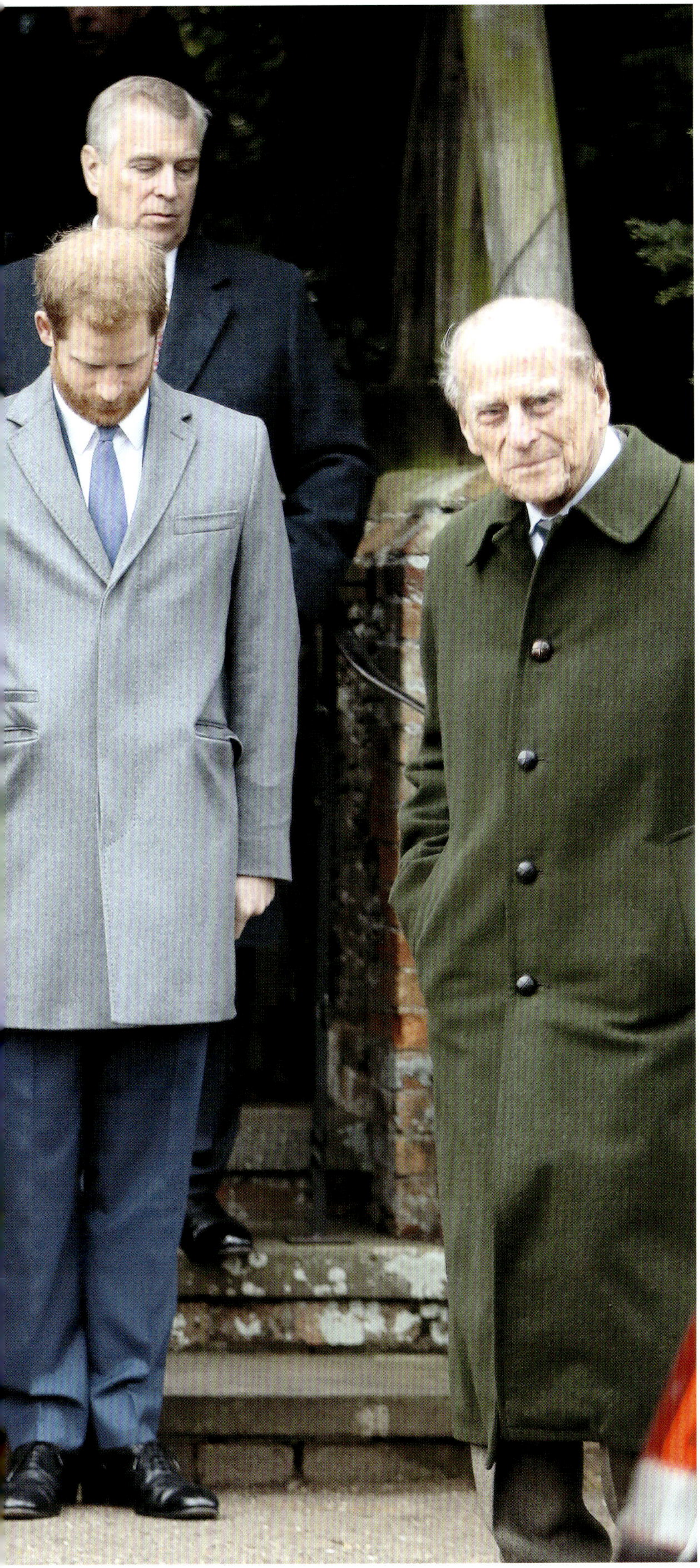

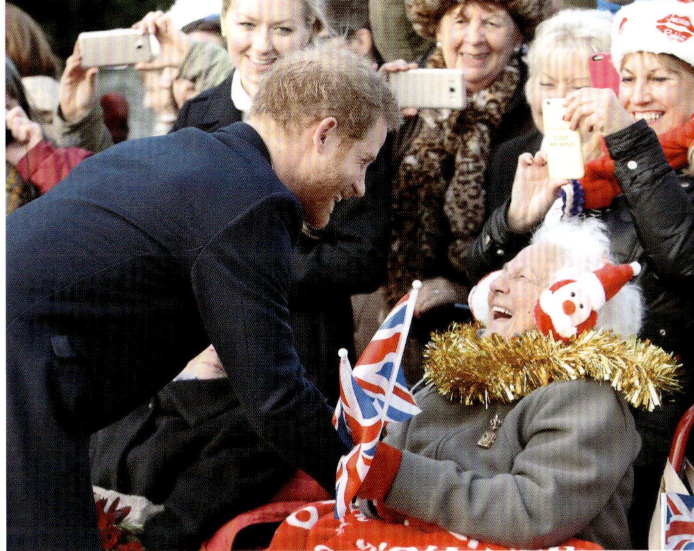

Opposite Members of the royal family traditionally spend the Christmas period at the Queen's Norfolk residence, Sandringham House. The public element of this period remains the church service in Sandringham on Christmas Day. This is one of the few events where the royal family gathers in a more informal environment. Christmas 2017 was Meghan Markle's first with the family. As the Queen departed, the younger royals curtsied and bowed in unison.

Above Many of the public who gather outside the church in Sandringham on Christmas Day have been doing so for years, and the atmosphere is always one of happiness and relaxed festivity. You can rely on Prince Harry to inject some fun into the proceedings, as he did when he met some cheery Norfolk ladies.

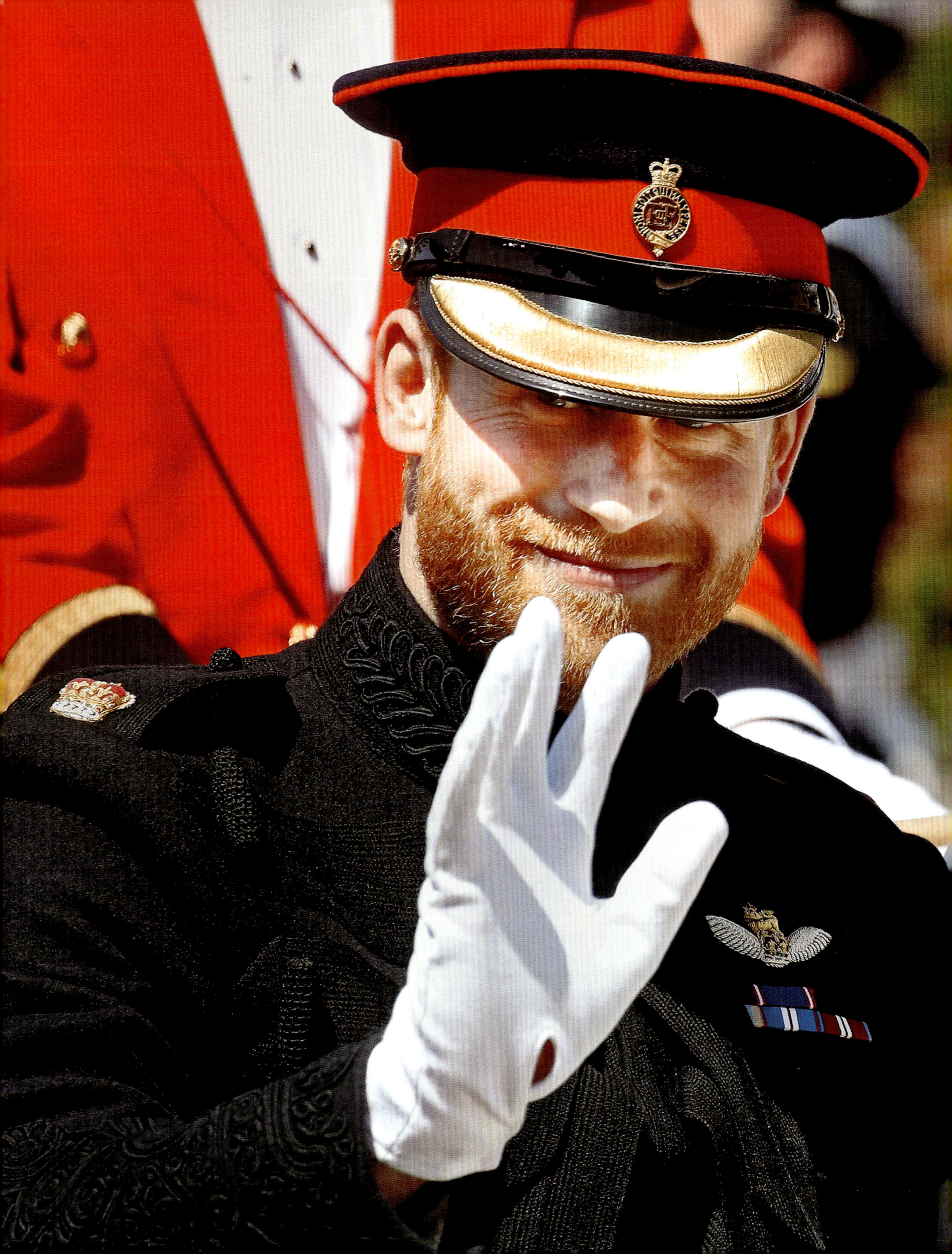

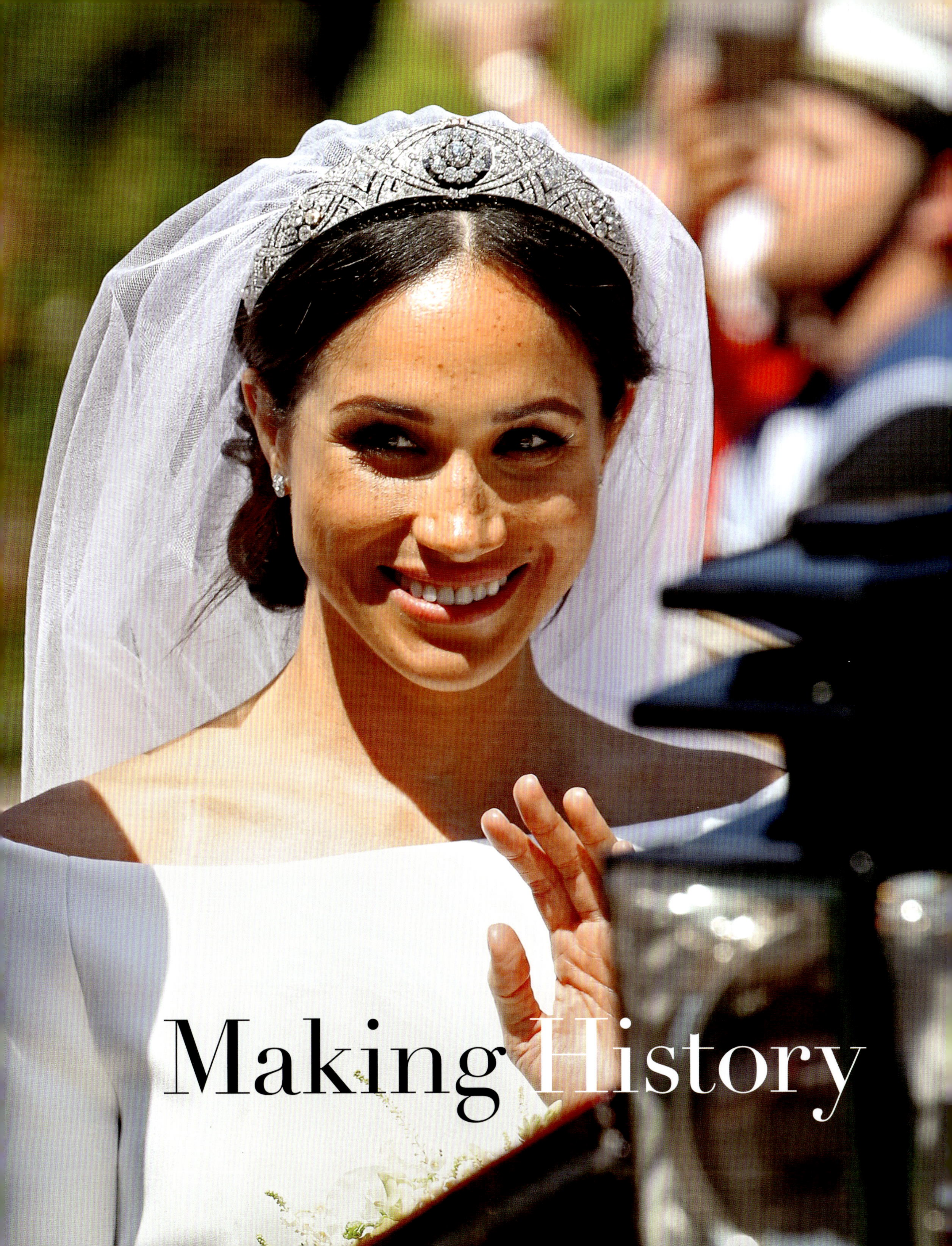

Making History

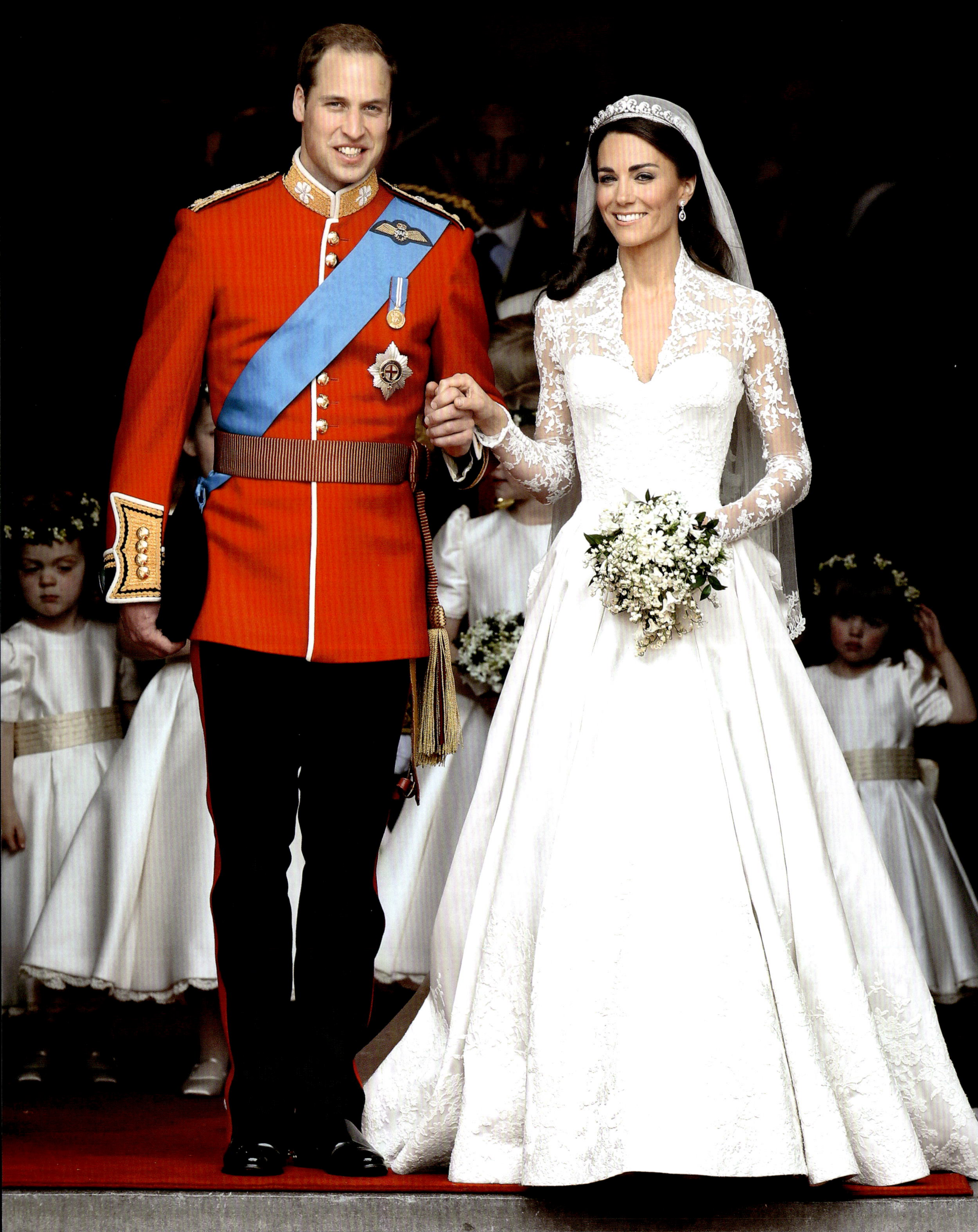

Documenting the British royal family allows me a privileged front-row seat to historic moments. Defining periods of national celebration come only a handful of times in a royal photographer's career. The moments that live on in history may only last for a few seconds, but images of those instances are seared into the national psyche for decades and even centuries: The roar of the crowd and the chorus of shutters as the Duke and Duchess of Cambridge stepped out of Westminster Abbey in their first moments as a married couple, and the more contemplative but nonetheless important moment when Prince George stood on tiptoes to check on his little sister in her pram at her christening. The Queen waving from the *Gloriana* during the Thames Diamond Jubilee Pageant celebrations or the Prince of Wales and Duchess of Cornwall stepping off a plane to a traditional welcome in Papua New Guinea as the evening light turned to glorious Technicolor. All are indelibly printed on my memory. The images I capture are shared around the world within minutes through the Getty Images wire services, which supplies global media outlets with content. It still gives me the same thrill as seeing my photographs published in my Cardiff student newspaper twenty years ago.

The diversity of characters and personalities across the royal family keeps me on my toes. I strive to capture everything from the children's refreshing and enchanting appearances to the power and aura of Her Majesty Queen Elizabeth II. I am required to be nimble as I capture both Prince Harry's passionate and relaxed approach and the powerful presence of the Duke and Duchess of Cambridge, whose global brand can affect change in a wide array of areas, from mental health awareness to anti-poaching initiatives. The excitement of documenting Meghan Markle's first official appearance with Prince Harry at the Invictus Games in Toronto and their subsequent engagement filled me with optimism for a positive new dynamic in the royal family. The thrill of capturing something new is counterbalanced by experience built over the years with in-depth knowledge of my subjects, their nuances and mannerisms, how they may behave in certain situations, and what to expect.

The images I create form part of the incredibly colourful patchwork of British history, documenting moments that are then forever recorded as part of what makes Great Britain great is an absolute honour. You only have to peruse the selection of royal images in the Getty Images Archive, home to over ninety million images, to get an idea of the importance of royalty in the collection.

Preceding pages Prince Harry, now the Duke of Sussex, and Meghan Markle, the new Duchess of Sussex, leave the Horseshoe Cloister on the grounds of Windsor Castle travelling in the Ascot Landau carriage after their marriage ceremony at St. George's Chapel, Windsor Castle, on May 19, 2018. The event was one of great celebration for the nation and broadcast to a global audience of millions. The day could not have panned out more perfectly: the weather, the crowds, the colour, and the festive atmosphere all came together for the newly wedded couple. This was an incredibly special event for all involved and to capture those first moments of the married couple radiating happiness was thrilling.

Opposite The Duke and Duchess of Cambridge depart Westminster Abbey on their wedding day, April 29, 2011.

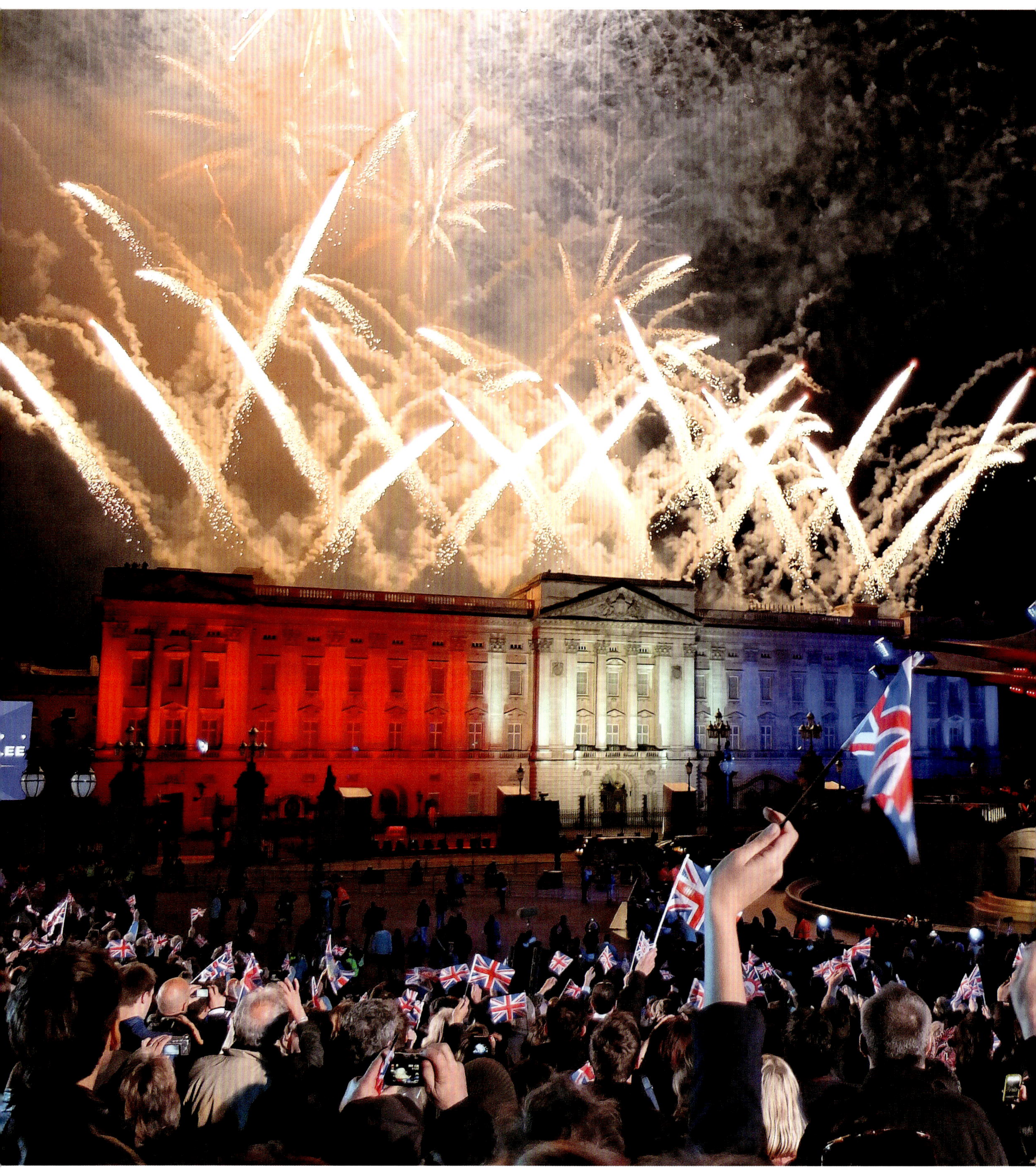

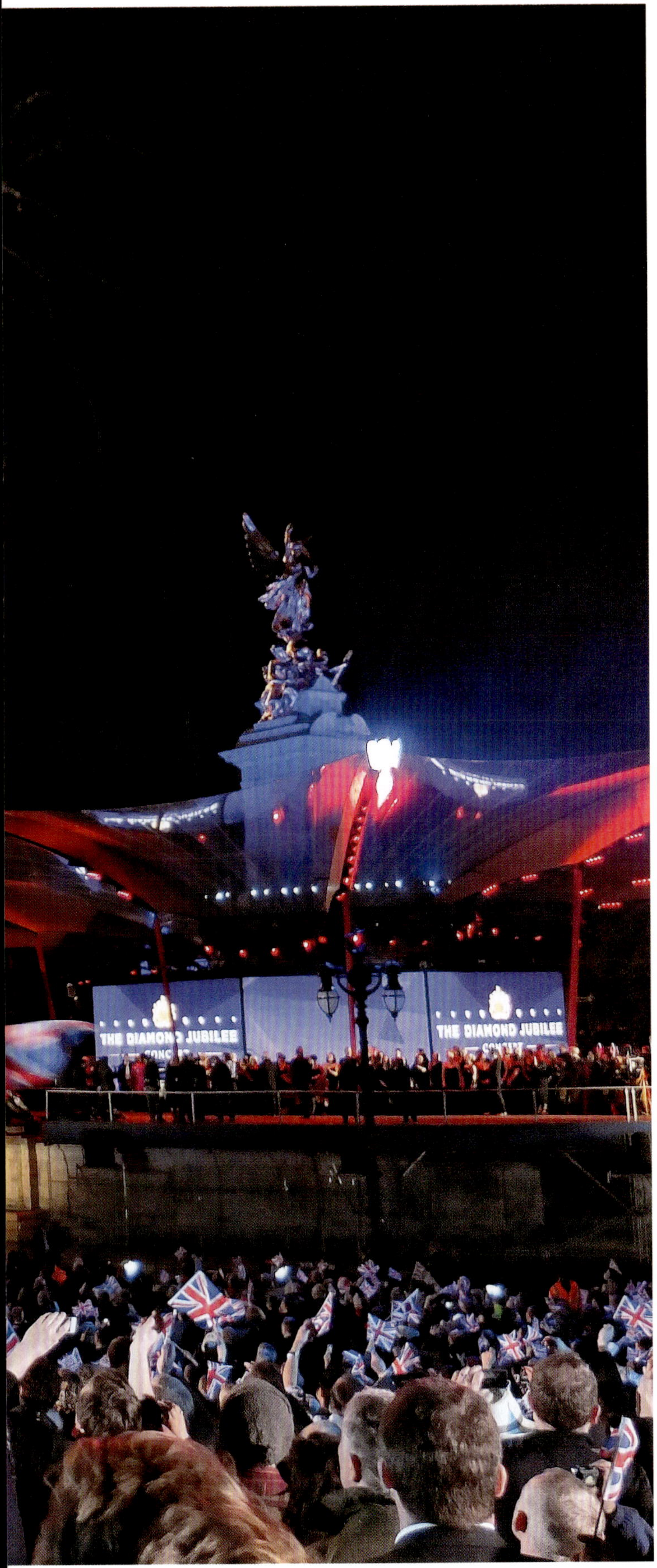

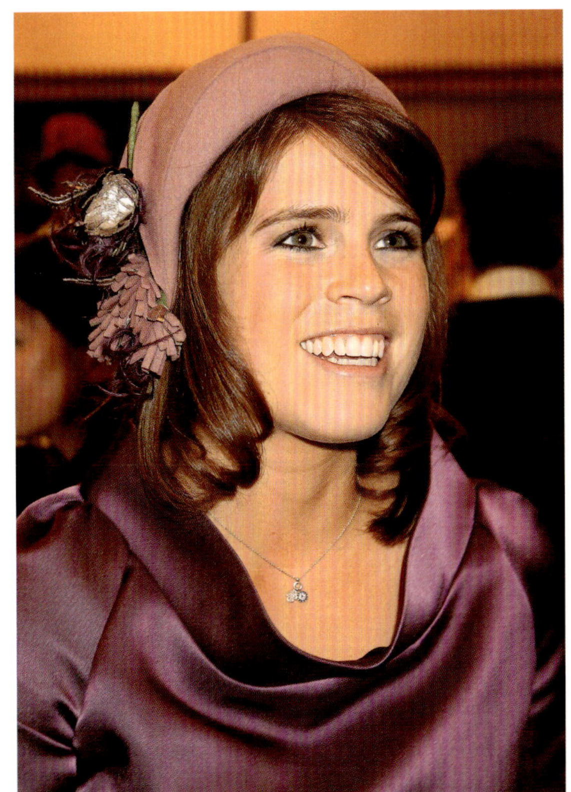

Opposite Fireworks illuminate Buckingham Palace during the Diamond Jubilee concert on June 4, 2012 in London. The Diamond Jubilee marked only the second time in history the United Kingdom has celebrated such a milestone. Thousands of well-wishers from around the world flocked to London to witness the spectacle as the country celebrated the sixtieth anniversary of the Queen's ascension to the throne.

Princess Eugenie (above) shows off her Union Jack-themed nail varnish (below) during a Diamond Jubilee reception at the Guildhall in London.

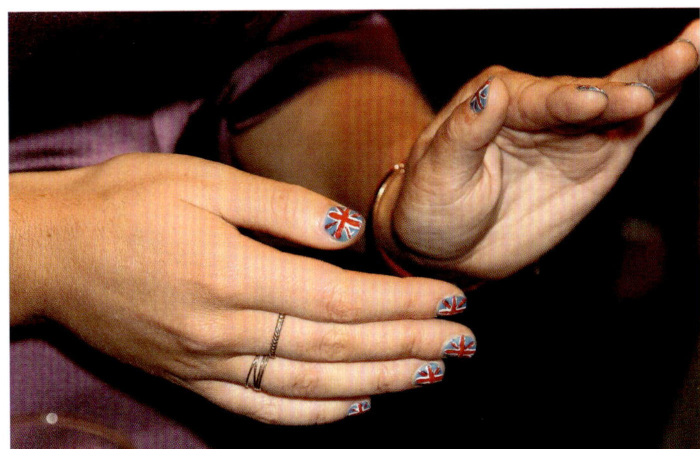

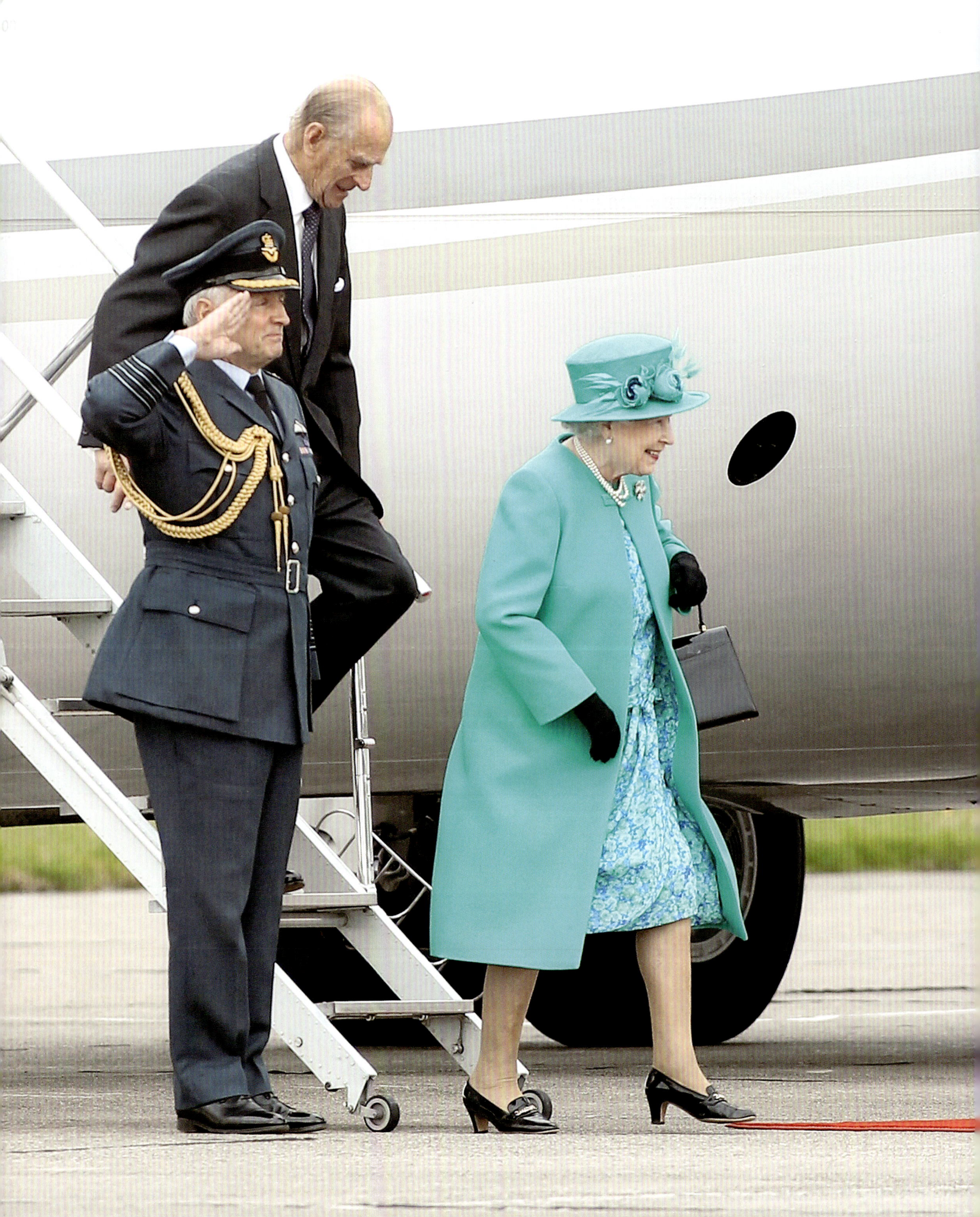

Opposite May 17, 2011, the Queen steps onto Irish soil for the first time as she disembarks the royal flight on arrival in Dublin. This moment marked the beginning of a historic first visit to Ireland with the Duke of Edinburgh. The visit, at the invitation of the president of Ireland, Mary McAleese, was significant as it signalled the first visit to Ireland by a monarch since 1911.

Below During a historic walkabout in the city of Cork in southwest Ireland, the Queen shares a joke with fishmonger Pat O'Connell at the English Market.

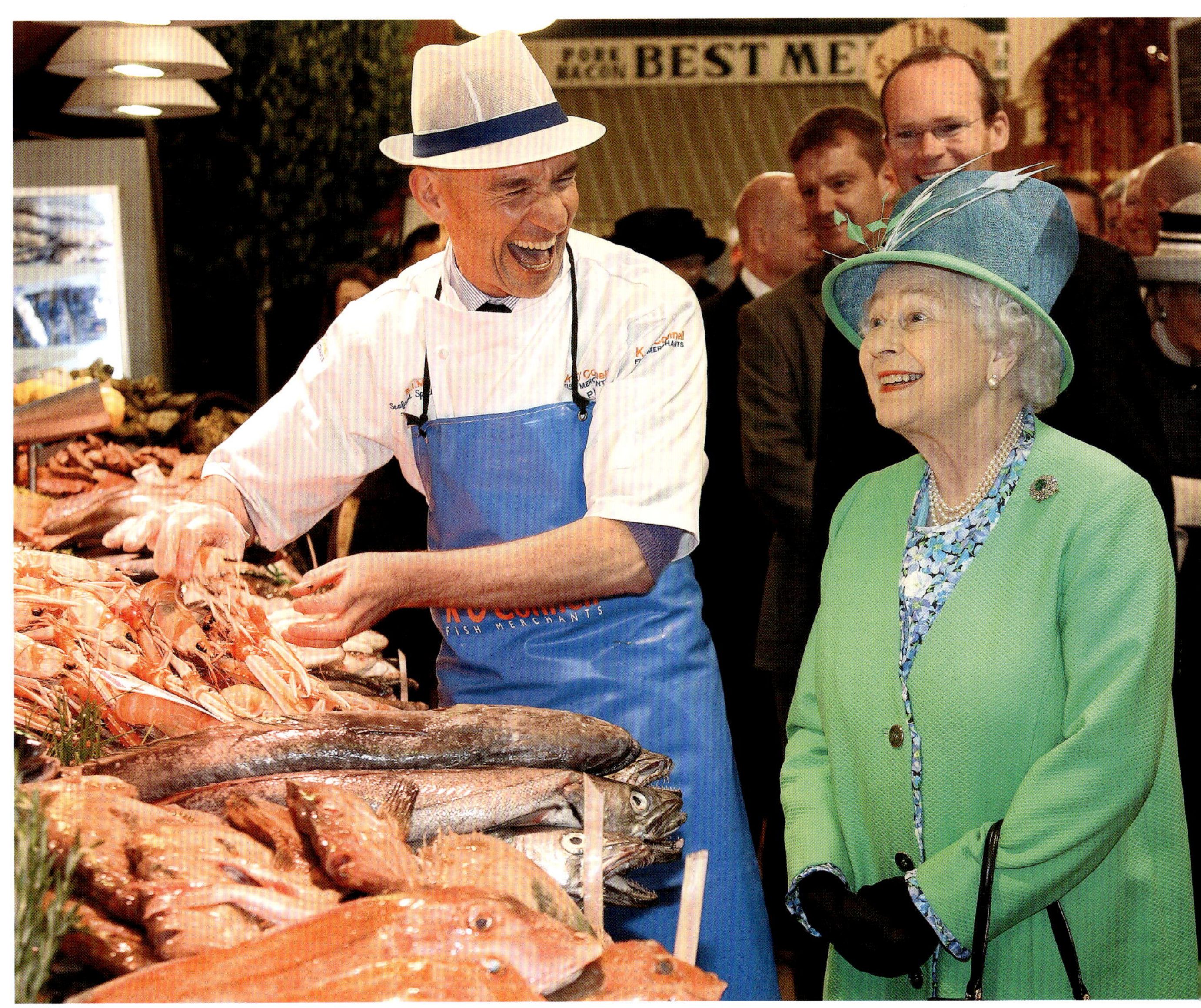

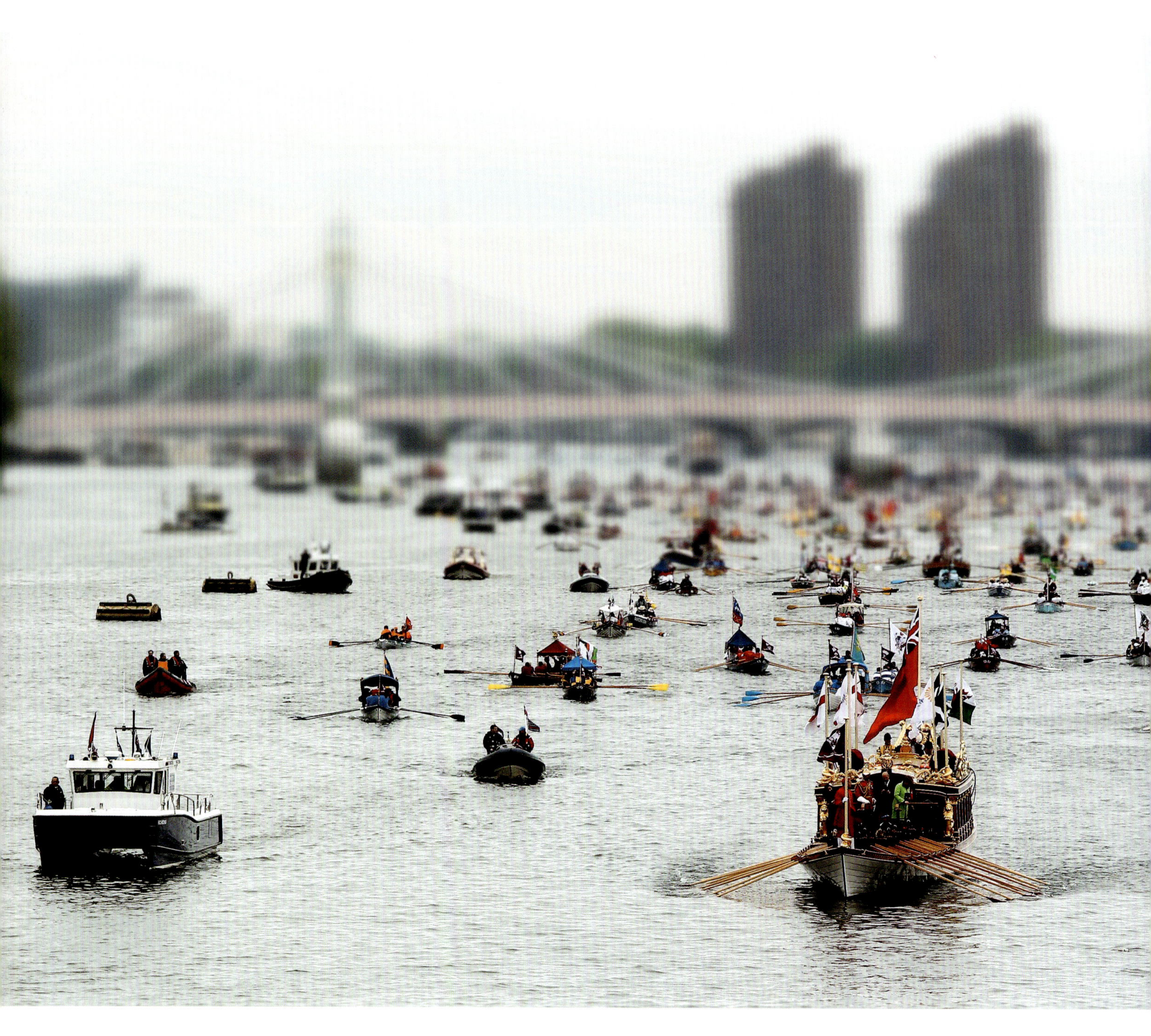

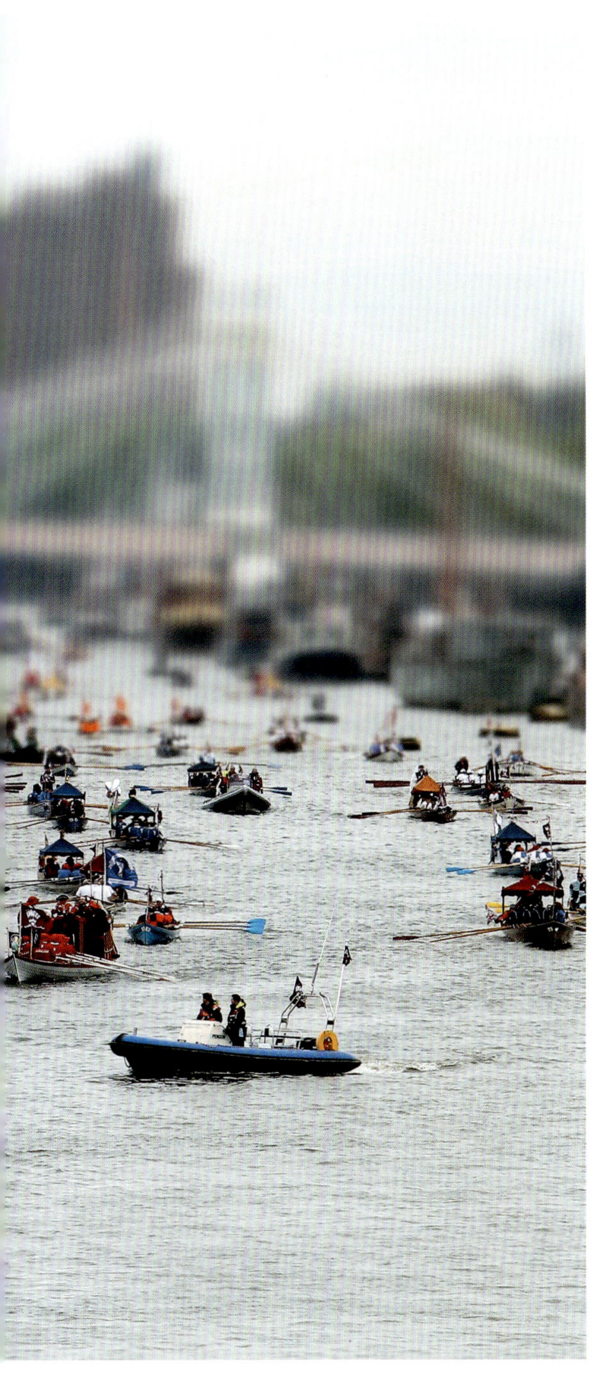

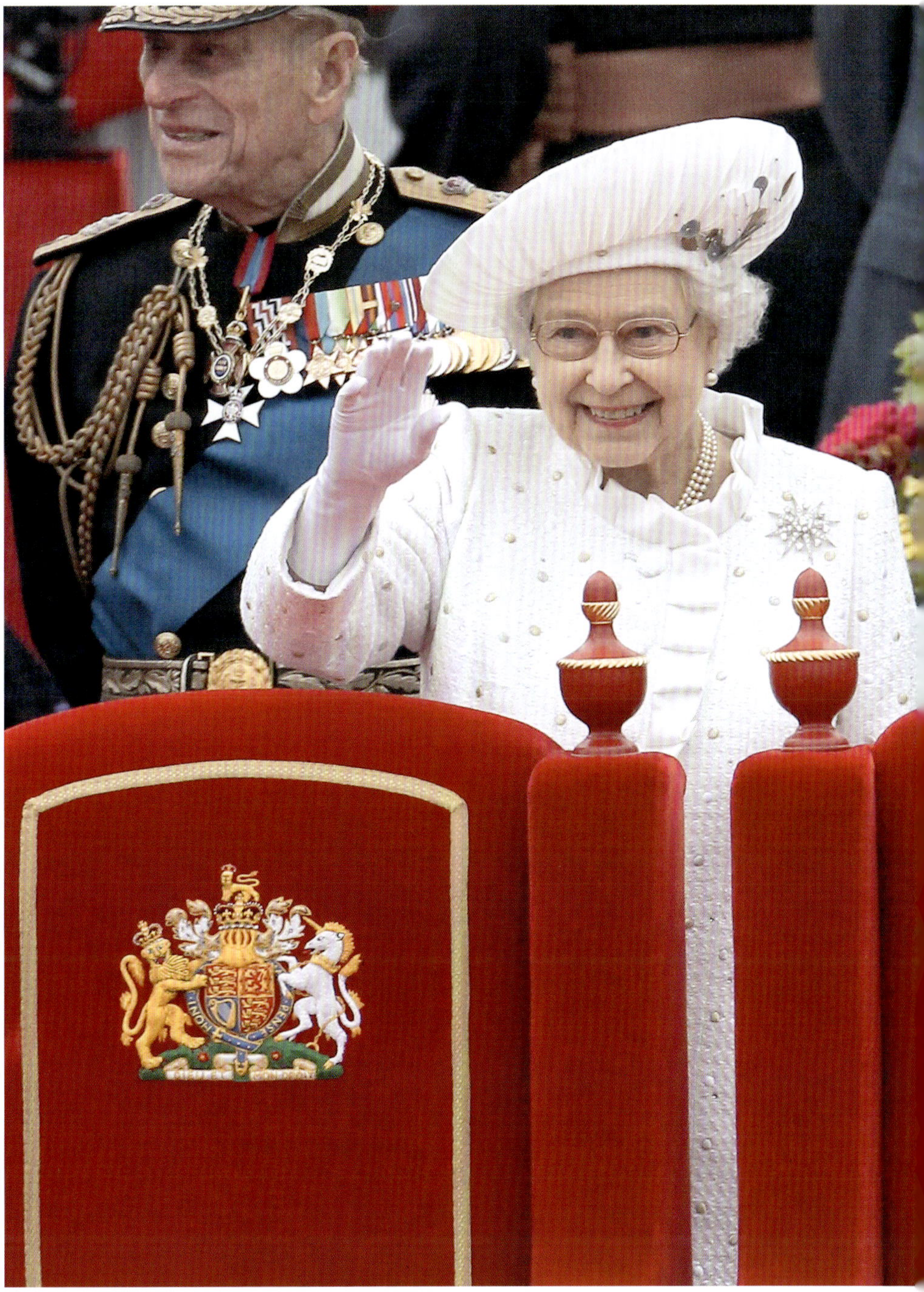

The Thames Diamond Jubilee Pageant took place on June 3, 2012. Nearly one thousand boats sailed on the River Thames in London as part of the celebration of the Diamond Jubilee of Queen Elizabeth II. I was photographing the nautical extravaganza from Chelsea Bridge, a bridge that, coincidentally, my great-grandfather, George Topham Forrest (chief architect of the London Country Council), designed. I photographed looking west toward Albert Bridge. The event started off in fairly dry weather, but the heavens opened shortly after the boats passed my position. Spectators and photographers farther upriver got a drenching of epic proportions!

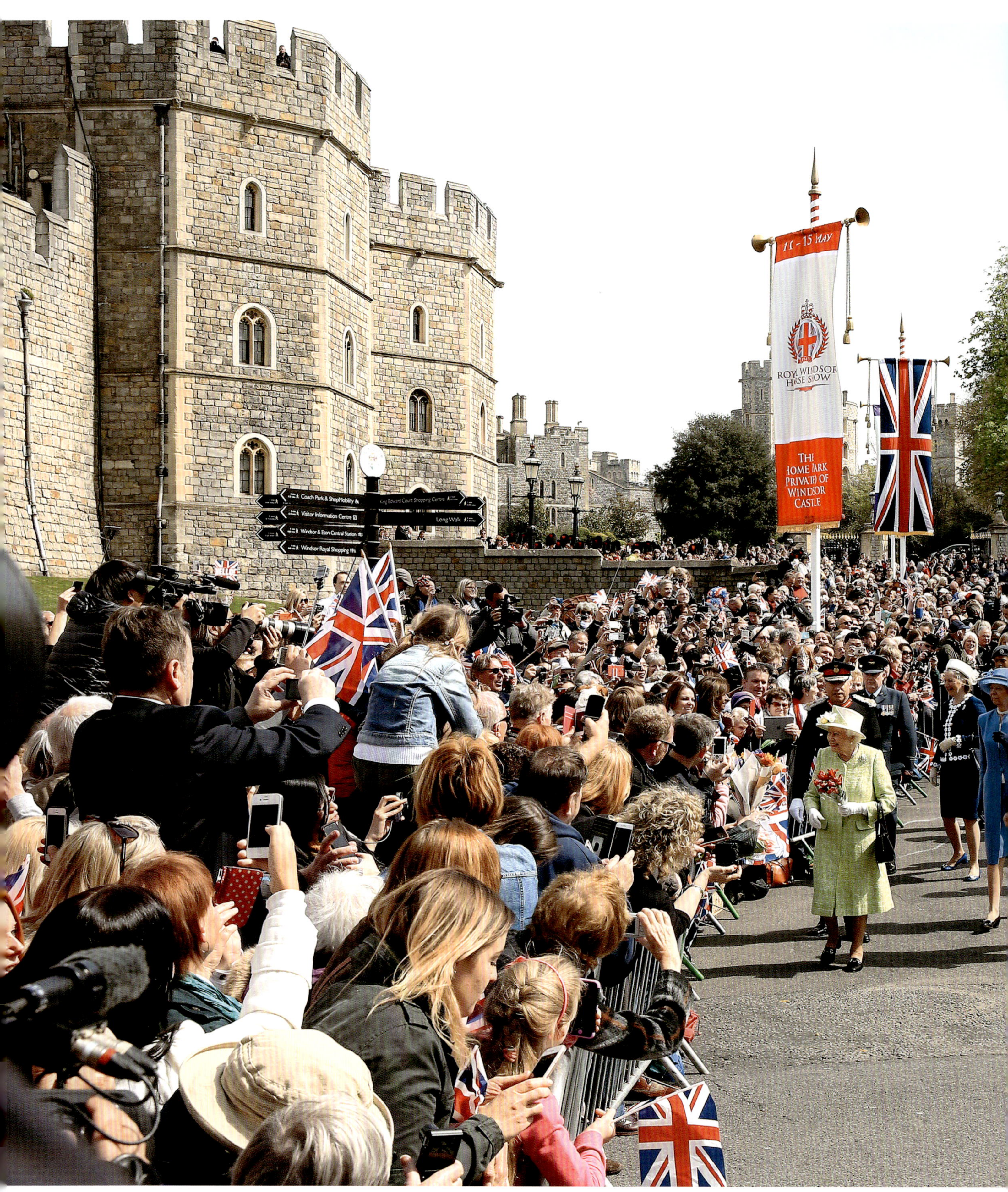
Coach Park & ShopMobility
Visitor Information Centre
Windsor & Eton Central Station
Windsor Royal Shopping
King Edward Court Shopping Centre
Long Walk
15 MAY
1943
WINDSOR
SHOW
HOME
OF
WINDSOR

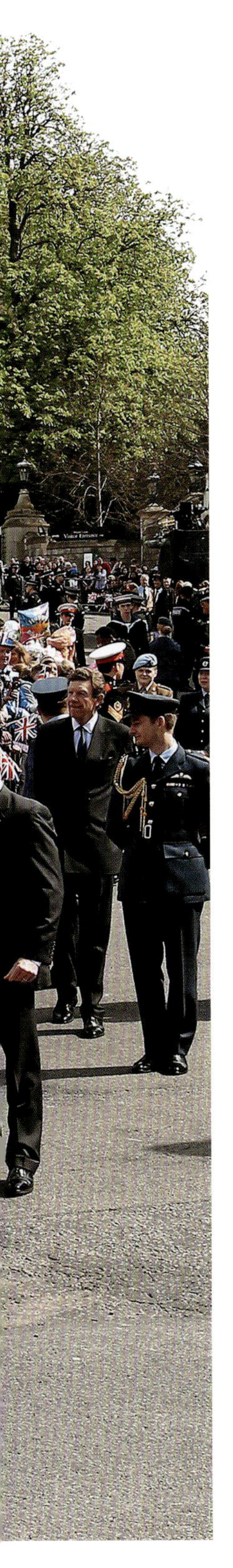

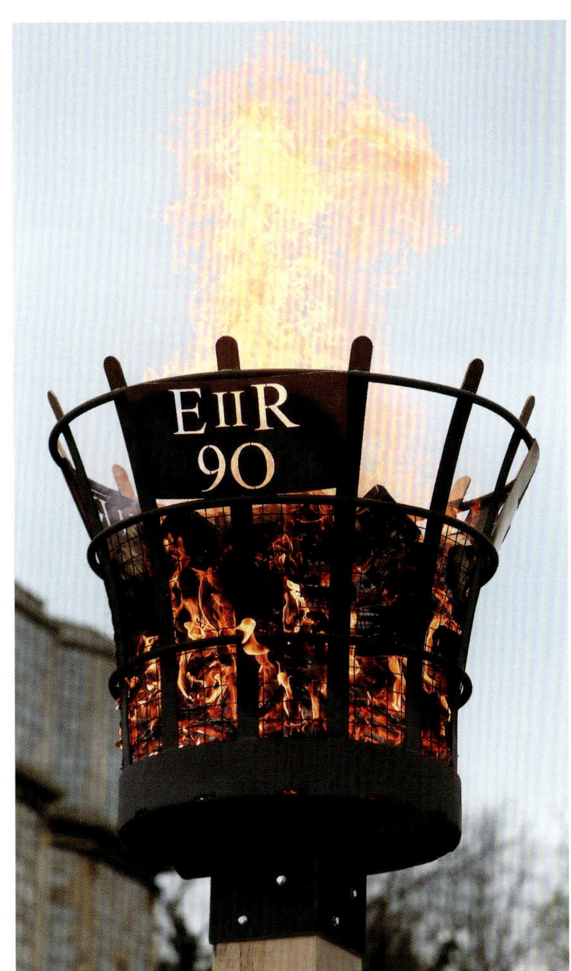

The Queen's ninetieth birthday, on April 21, 2016, was a cause for celebration for the entire nation. The spring sun shone at Windsor Castle as huge crowds (opposite) gathered outside. More than 900 beacons (left) were lit across the country and overseas to celebrate. On May 15, 2016 a gala spectacular featuring more than nine hundred horses was put on in Windsor Great Park to honour Her Majesty, who remained stalwart during a gun salute in her honour (below).

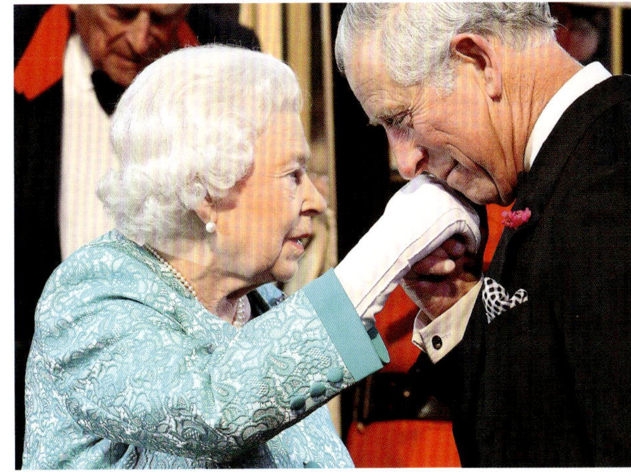

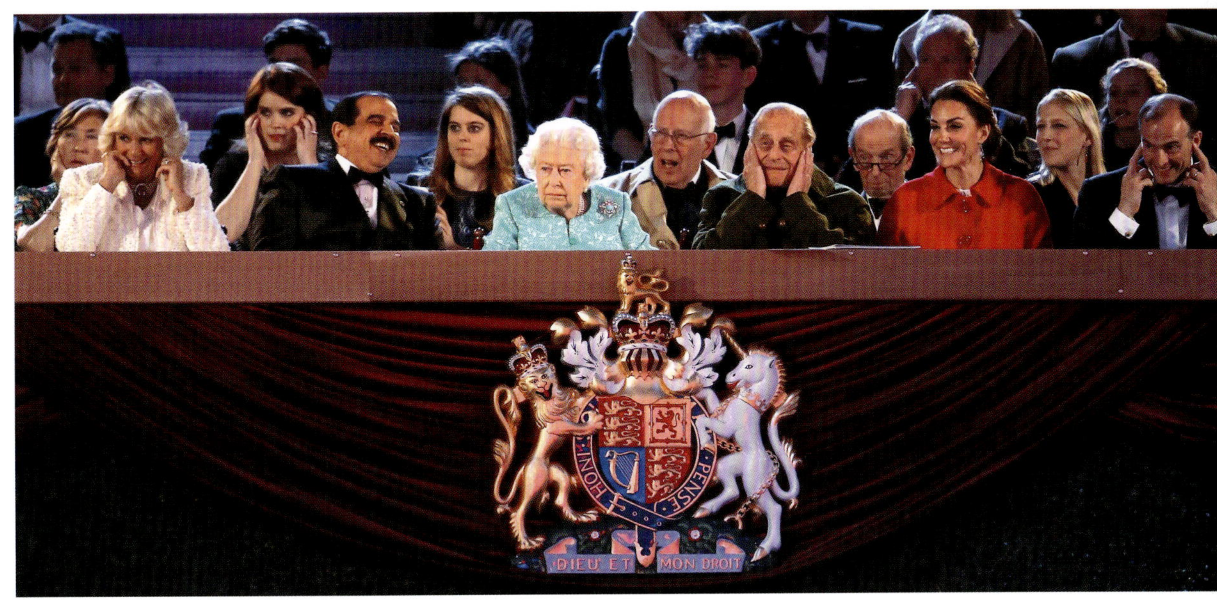

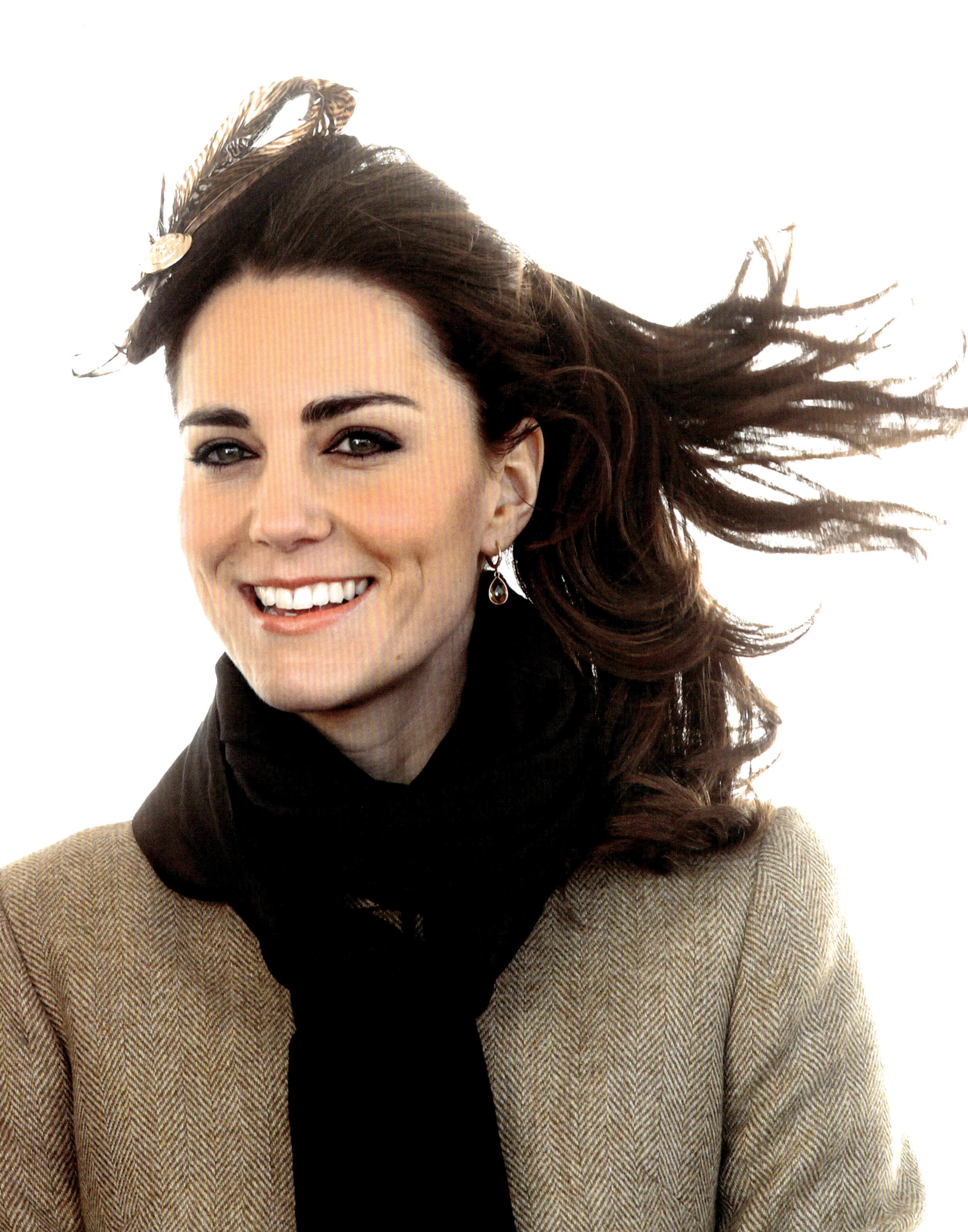

Opposite Not long after their official engagement announcement, Kate Middleton (as she was then known), and Prince William visited a lifeboat station in North Wales. This was Middleton's first public appearance as an official future member of the royal family. At a windy Trearddur Bay lifeboat station, a new inshore lifeboat was named the *Hereford Endeavour*.

This page Meghan Markle made her first public appearance after her engagement to Prince Harry in Nottingham on December 1, 2017. Excited crowds turned out to catch a glimpse of Prince Harry's new bride-to-be. Here Markle is waving at a woman from Toronto, the city where as an actress she filmed *Suits*.

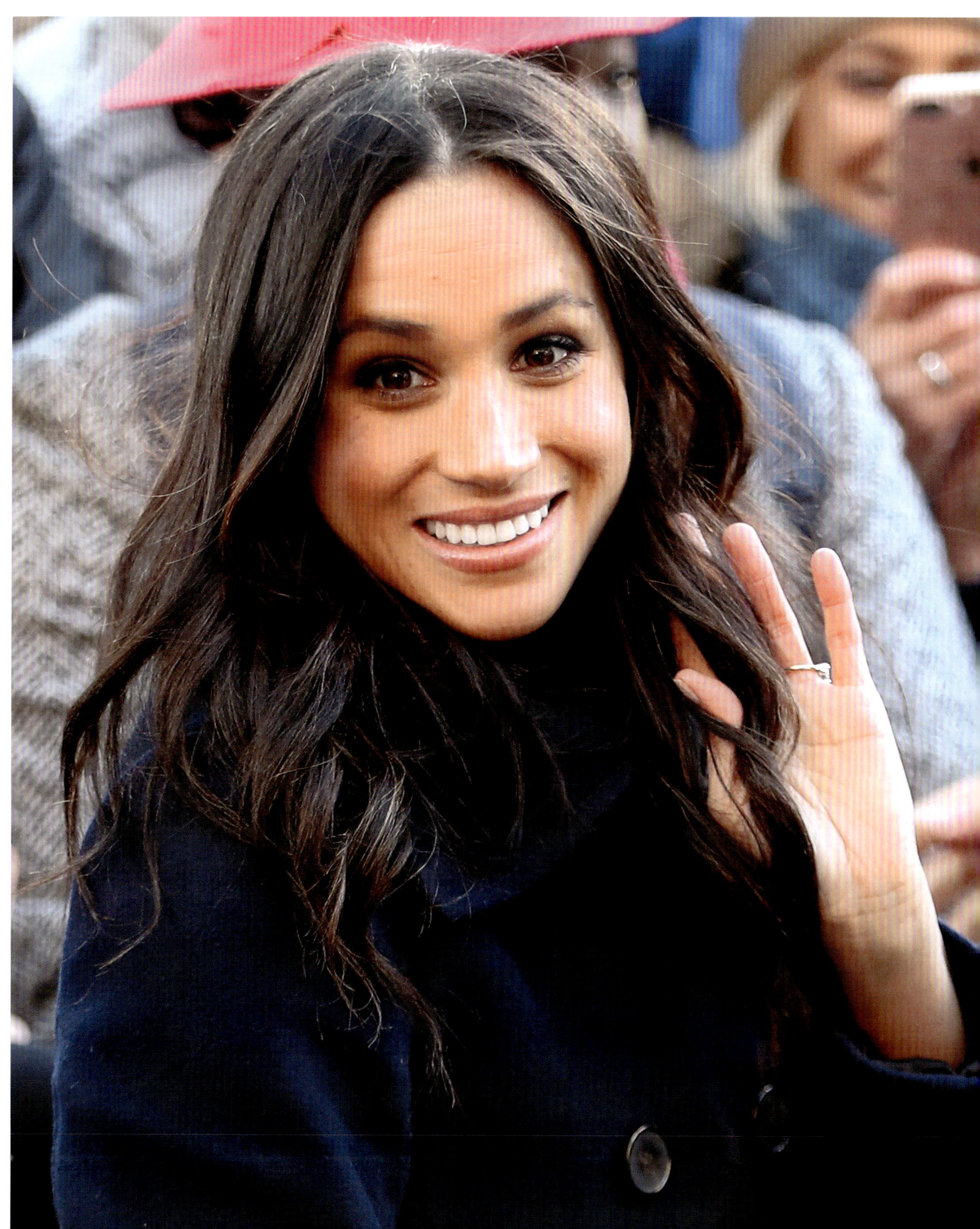

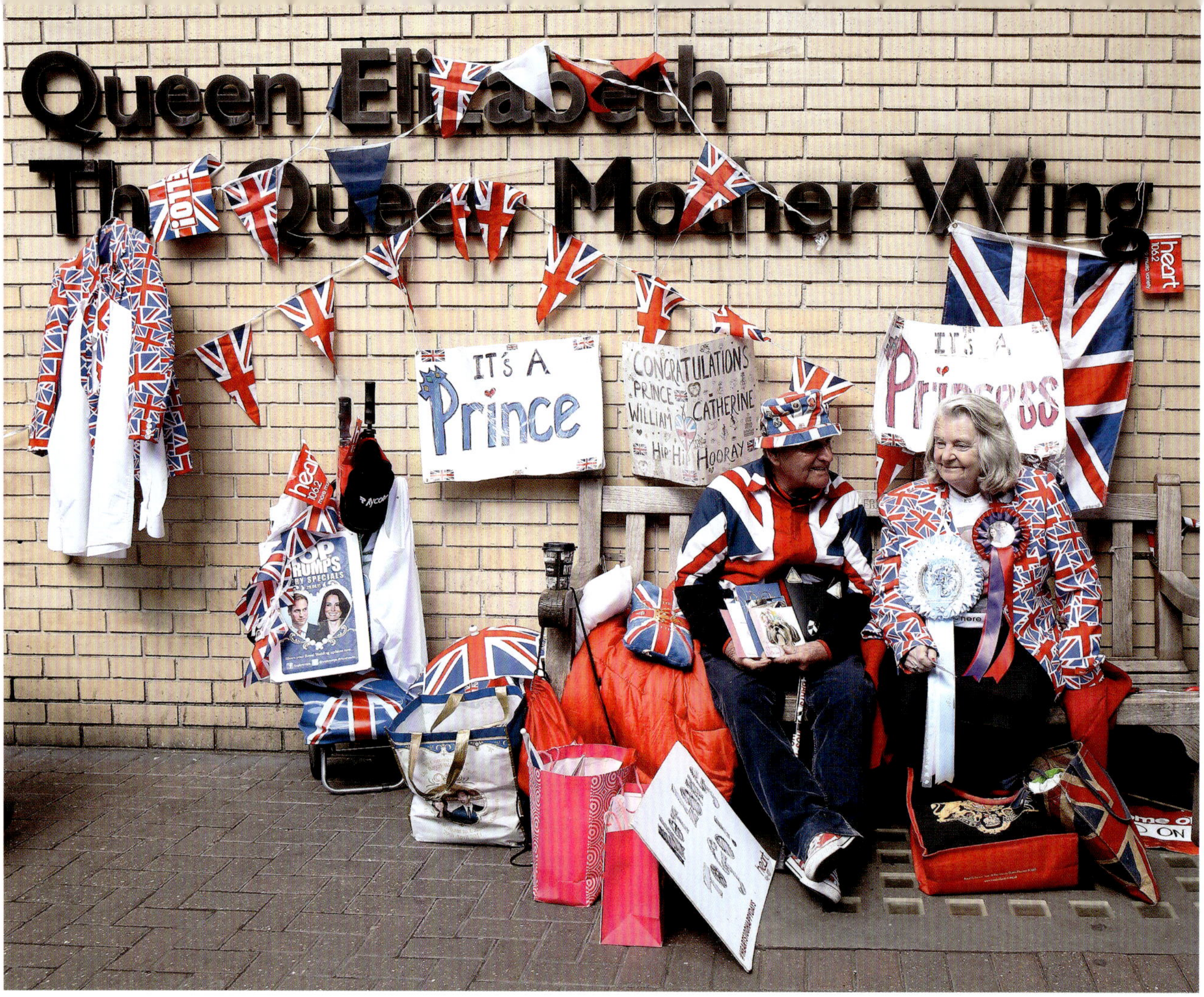

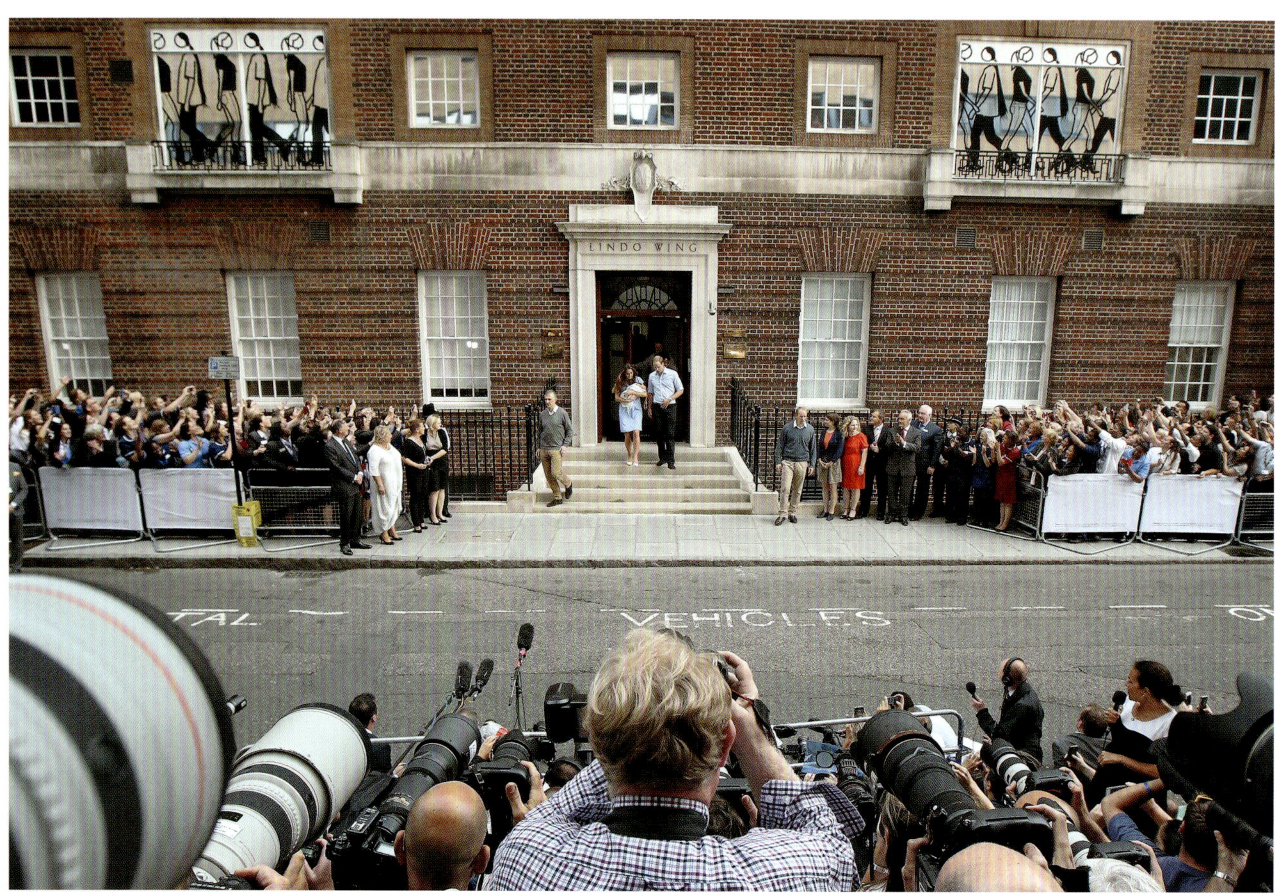
LINDO WING
VEHICLES

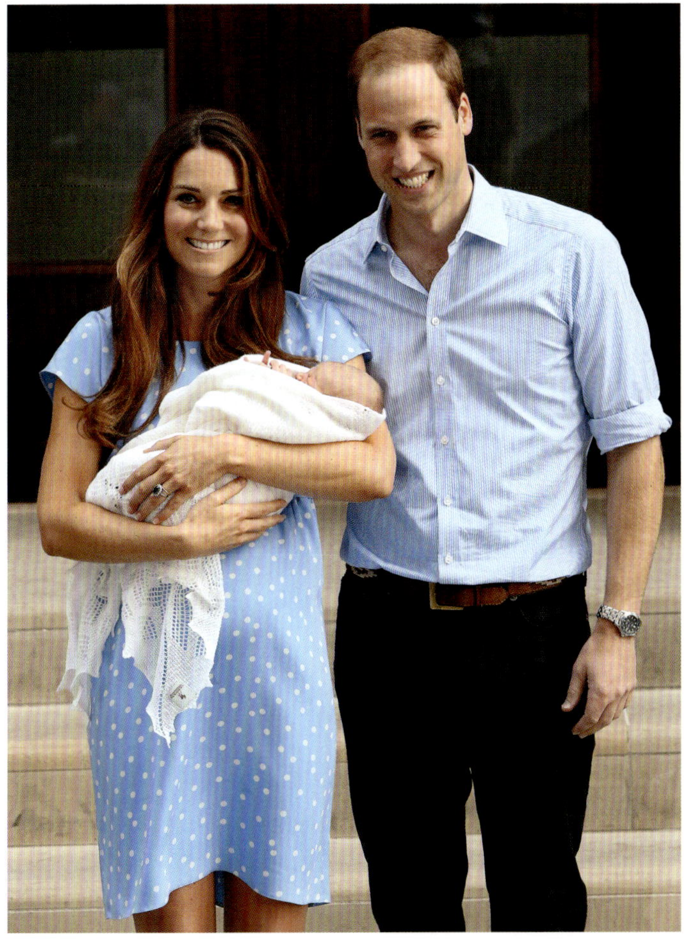

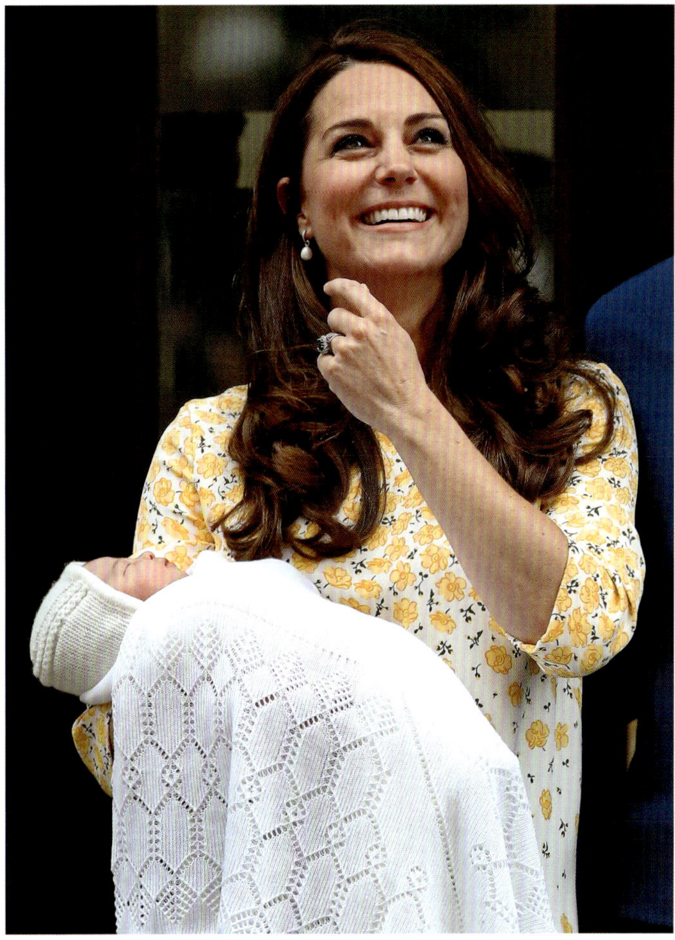

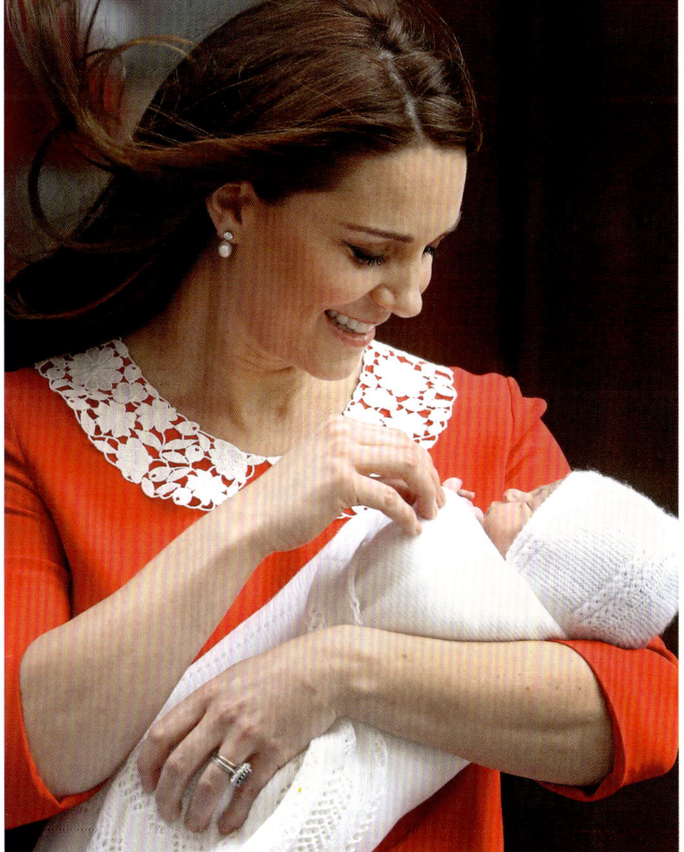

The birth of a new royal prince or princess is always an uplifting time for the country, and as the world's media descends on the Lindo Wing and focuses their lenses on the nondescript brown swing doors, a great feeling of excitement and anticipation takes hold.

Opposite, above Royalists Terry Hut and Margaret Tyler continue to wait for a new royal baby outside the Lindo Wing of St. Mary's Hospital as fans eagerly anticipate the birth of a new royal addition on April 30, 2015.

Opposite, below The Duke and Duchess of Cambridge depart the Lindo Wing with their newborn son Prince George of Cambridge on July 23, 2013.

This page The Duke and Duchess of Cambridge pose on the hospital steps with their newborn children: Prince George (top, left); Princess Charlotte (top, right); and Prince Louis (below).

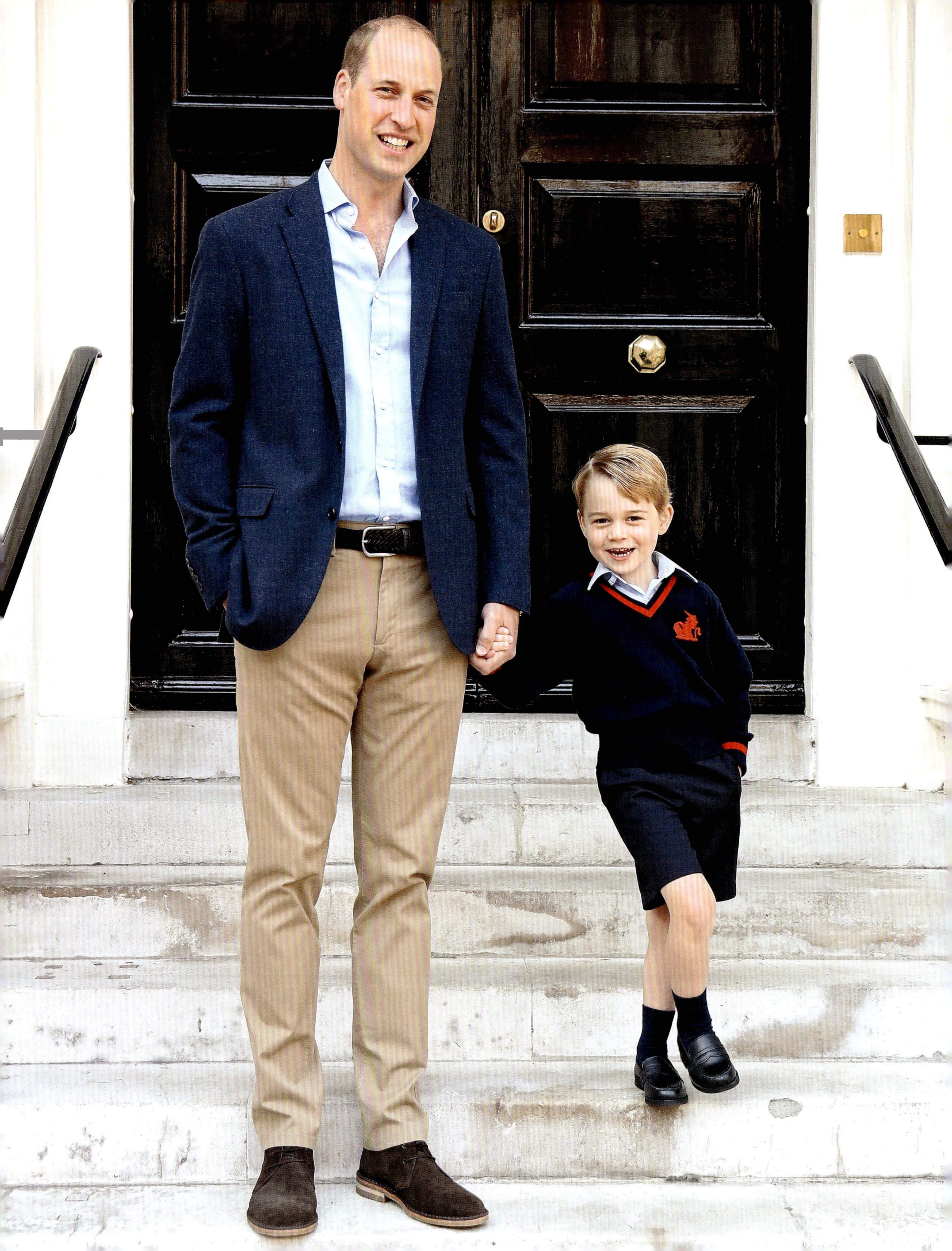

Opposite This picture was taken at Kensington Palace shortly before Prince George left for his first day of school at Thomas's Battersea. Prince George had a cheeky smile on his face as he posed for the traditional first-day-of-school picture.

Right November 16, 2010 started off with a mundane photo shoot in South London, but after the exciting announcement that Prince William and Kate Middleton were engaged, I found myself that afternoon in the state apartments of St. James's Palace capturing this historic image.

Below It was an honour for a portrait I took of Prince George to be released by Kensington Palace to celebrate his fourth birthday on July 22, 2017. The young royal certainly injected some fun into the photo shoot!

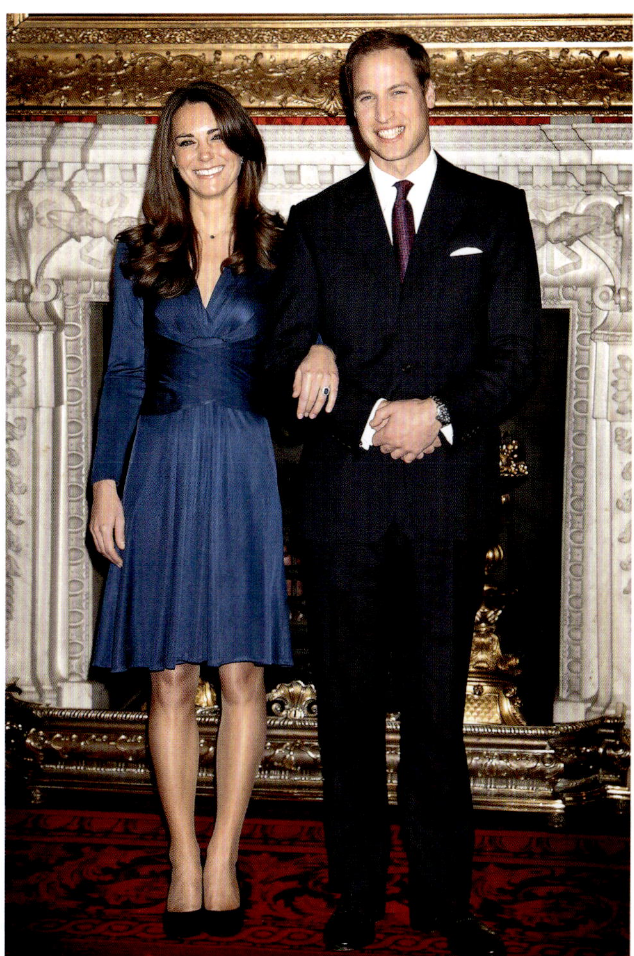

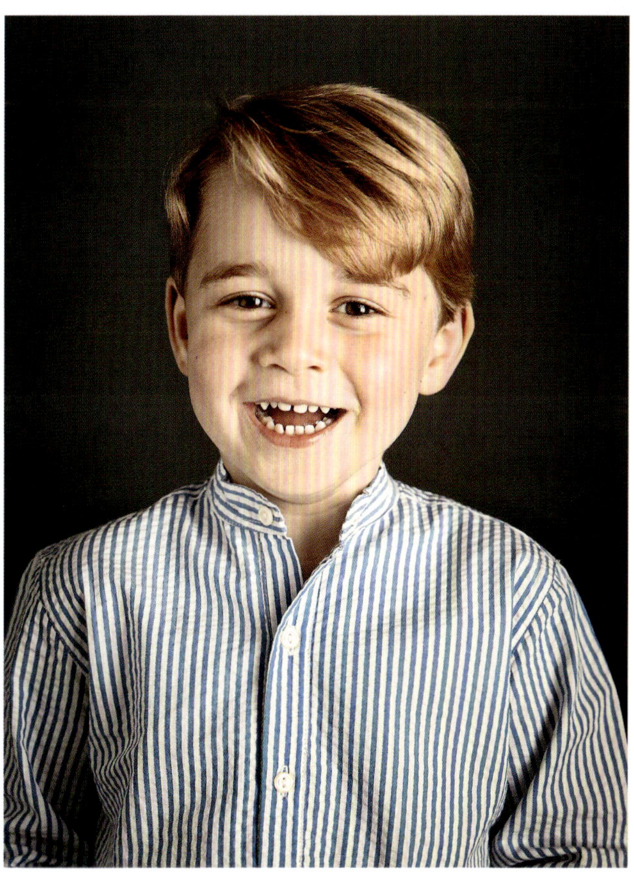

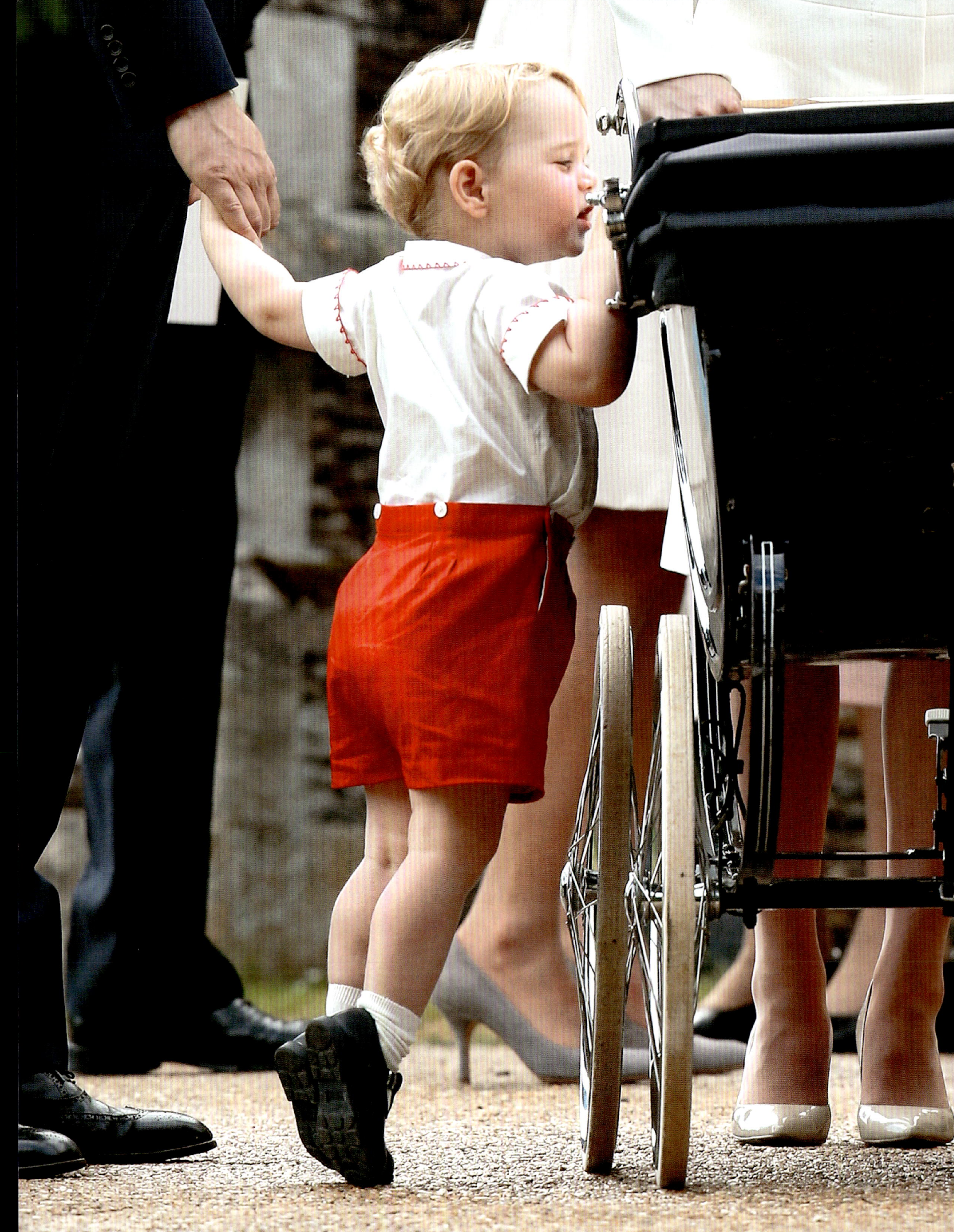

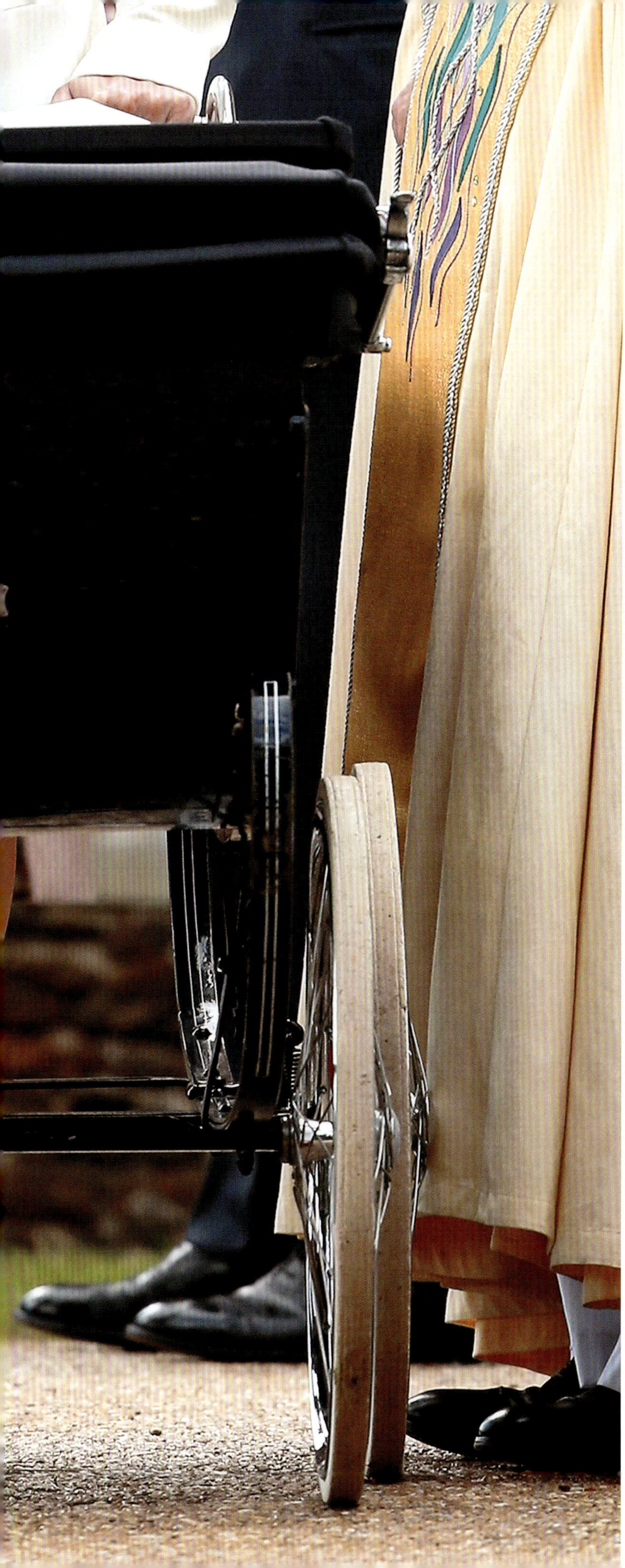

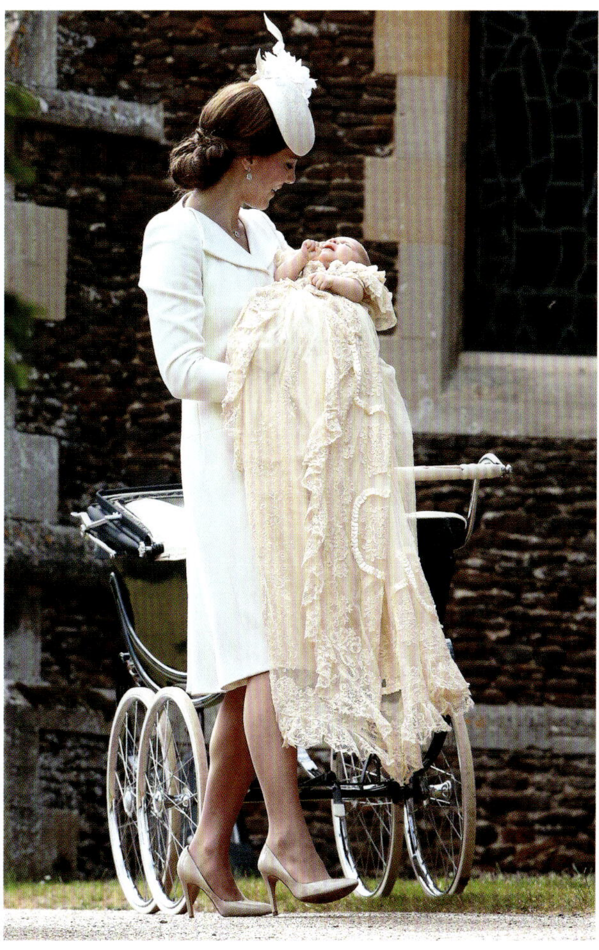

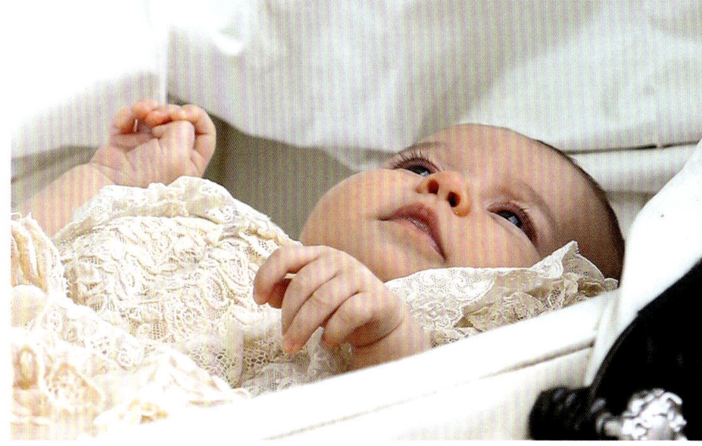

Opposite Prince George stands on tiptoes outside of St. Mary Magdalene Church in Sandringham, Norfolk to get a glimpse of his little sister on her christening day. This was one of those lovely unexpected and candid moments you can't script. Princess Charlotte was the seventh royal baby to be christened in the Honiton lace and white satin gown first used at the christening of Viscount Severn in 2008. The outfit is a replica of the intricate lace and satin christening gown made for Queen Victoria's eldest daughter and used for all royal baptisms until that of Lady Louise Windsor in 2004.

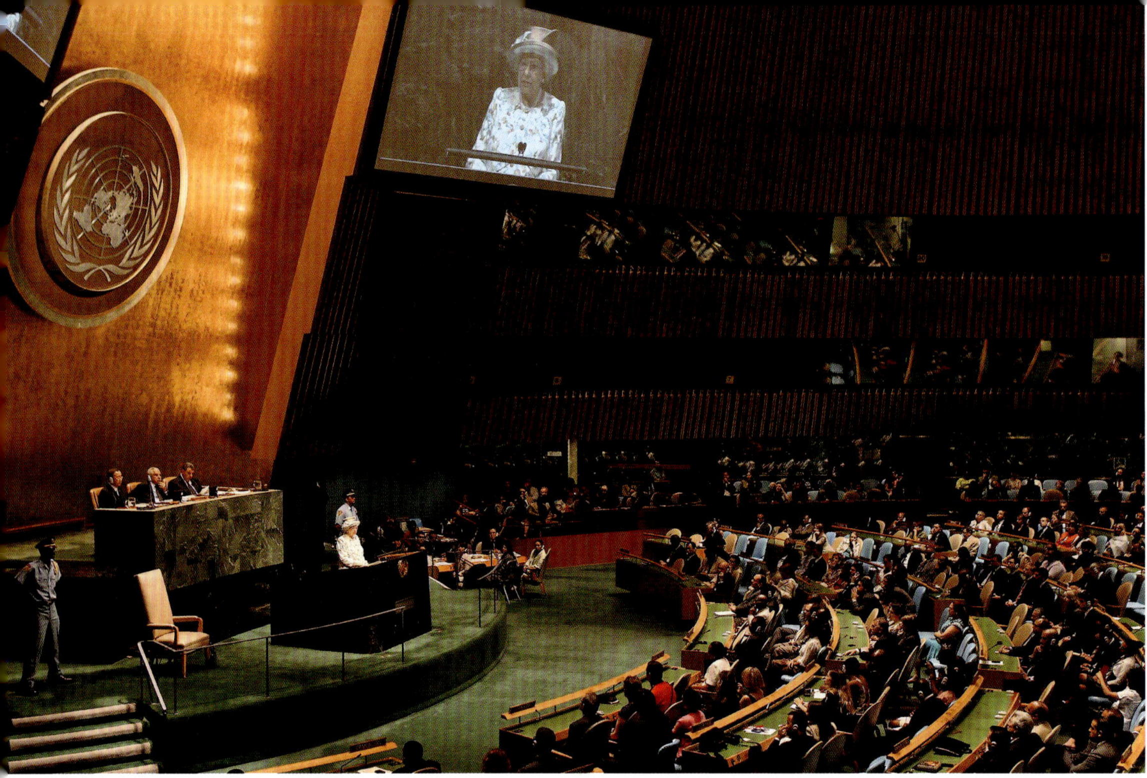

Above The Queen addressing the United Nations assembly at the organization's headquarters in New York in 2010 after completing an eight-day tour of Canada. The Queen had previously addressed the assemby in 1957.

Below On October 24, 2014, the Queen sent her first tweet. Released through the @BritishMonarchy account it stated, "It is a pleasure to open the Information Age exhibition today at the @ScienceMuseum and I hope people will enjoy visiting. Elizabeth R."

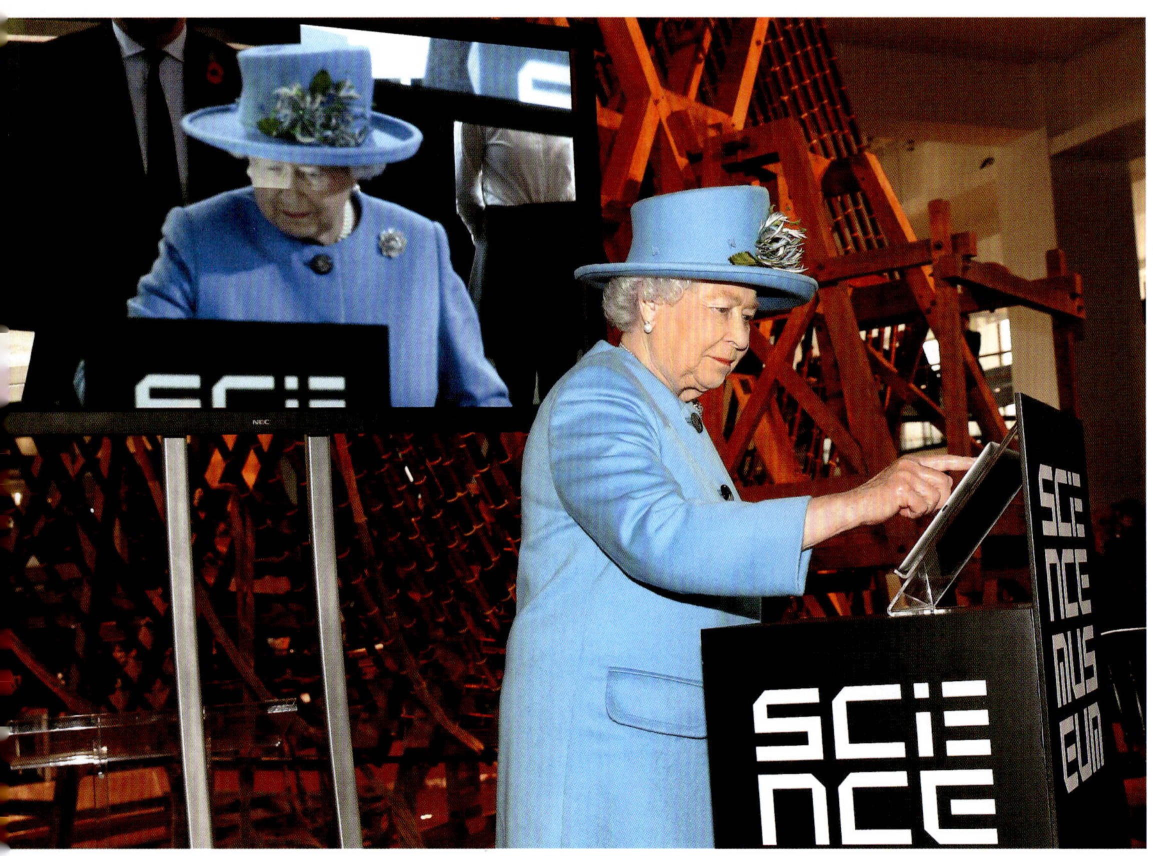

Opposite On September 9, 2015, Her Majesty Queen Elizabeth II became the longest reigning monarch in British history, overtaking her great-great-grandmother Queen Victoria's record by one day. The Queen had at that point reigned for a total of sixty-three years and 217 days. Keeping things characteristically low-key, she spent the day in Tweedbank, Scotland, where she opened the new Borders Railway.

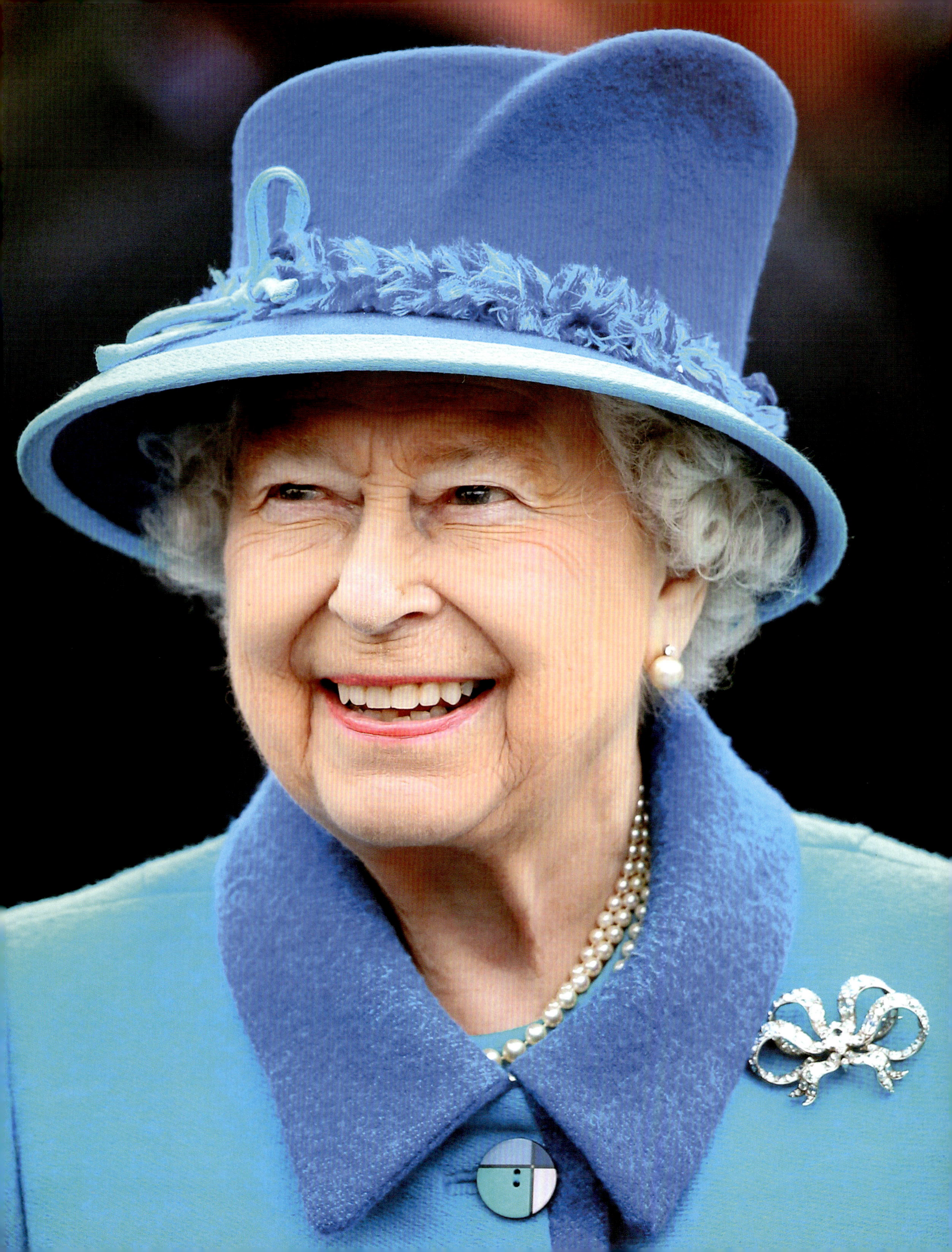

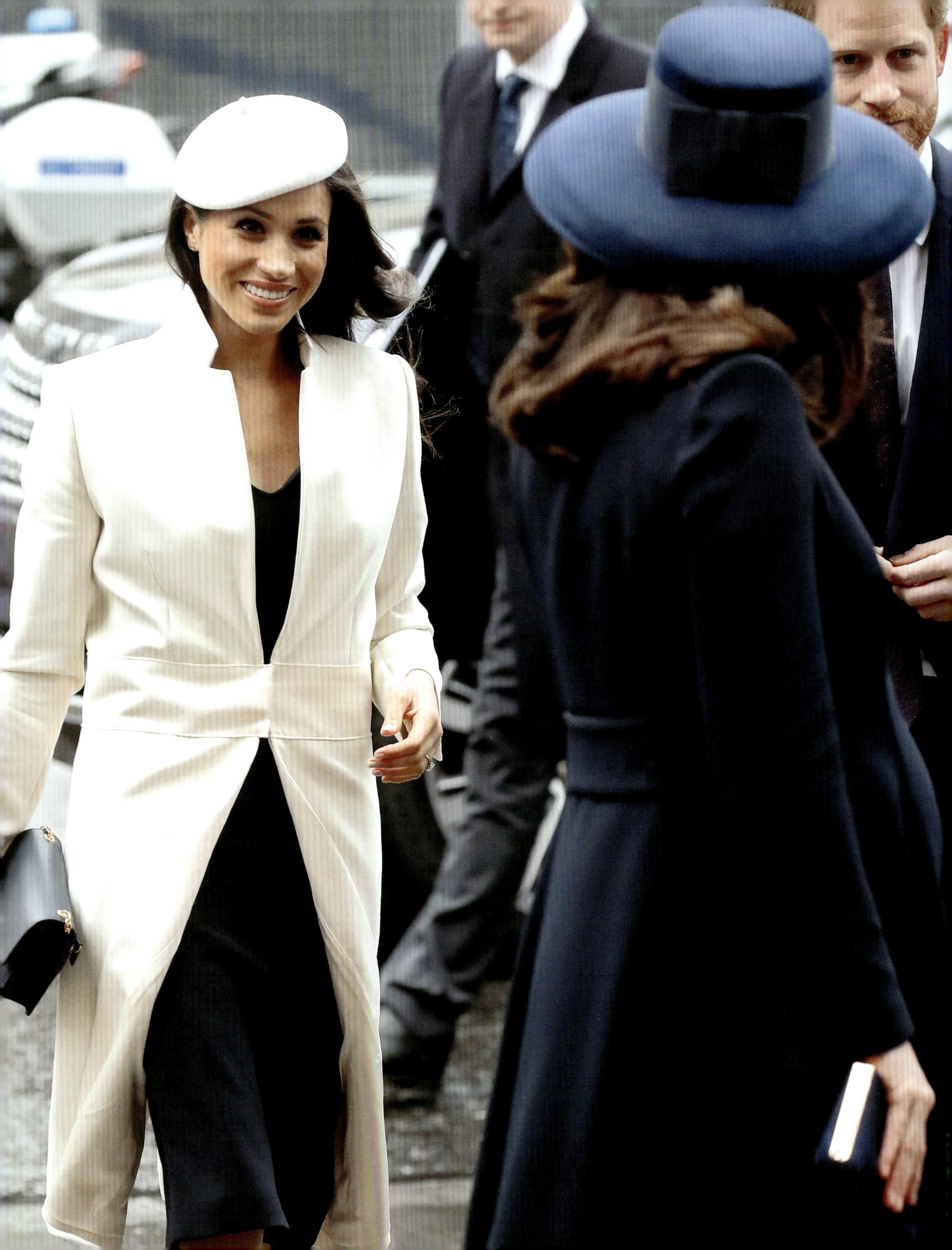

Opposite Meghan Markle smiles at the Duchess of Cambridge as they attend a Commonwealth Day service at Westminster Abbey.

Right A very happy couple at their engagement photo-call in the gardens of Kensington Palace on November 27, 2017. A bleak winter Monday in London was brightened up by the announcement from Kensington Palace that Prince Harry and Meghan Markle were engaged to be married.

Below Prince Harry and Meghan Markle's visit to Cardiff in Wales was delayed by a technical problem with their train. Schoolchildren sang songs as they eagerly anticipated the royal arrival. When the couple finally appeared, more than an hour behind schedule, they chatted to as many of the children as possible. At one point Markle wrote a note for lucky ten-year-old Caitlin Clarke from Marlborough Primary School.

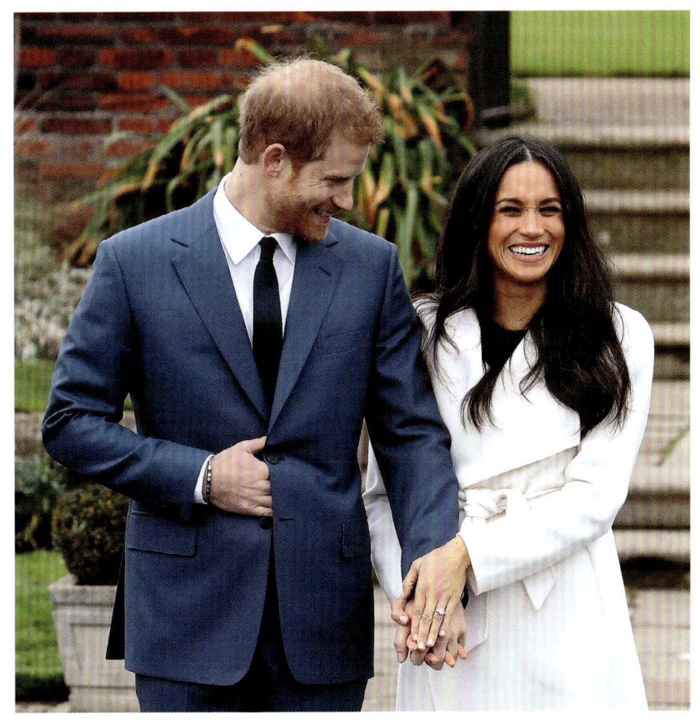

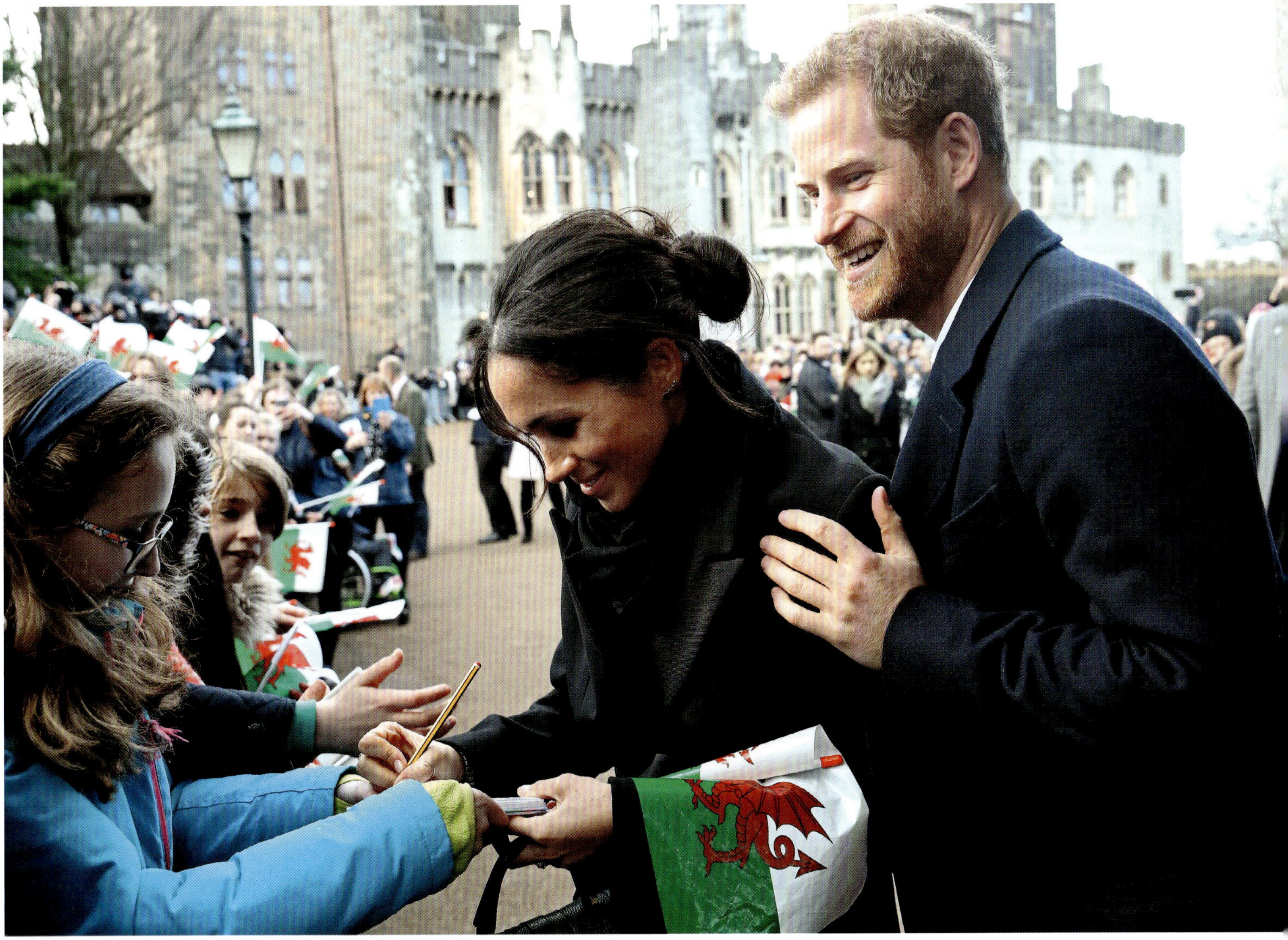

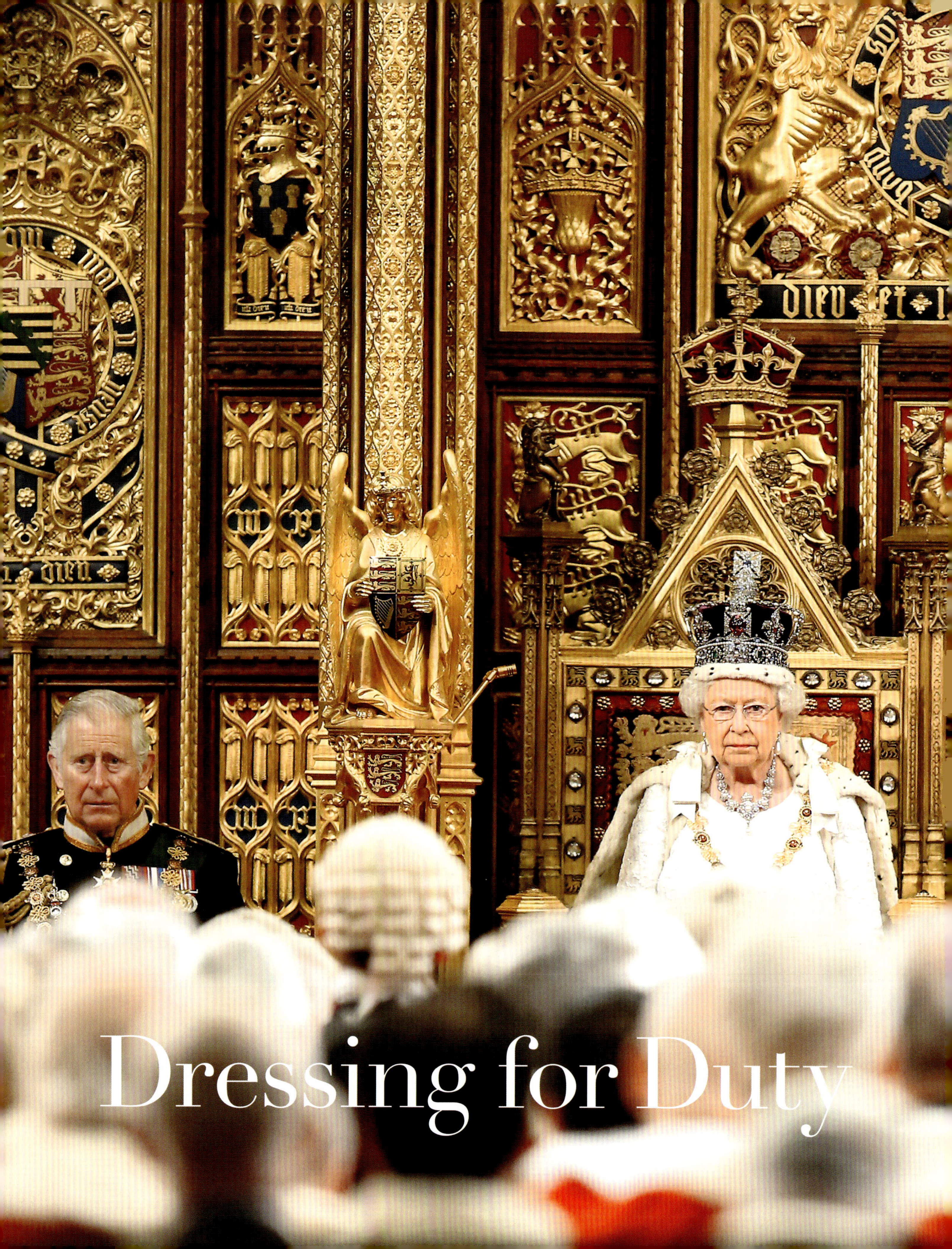

Dressing for Duty

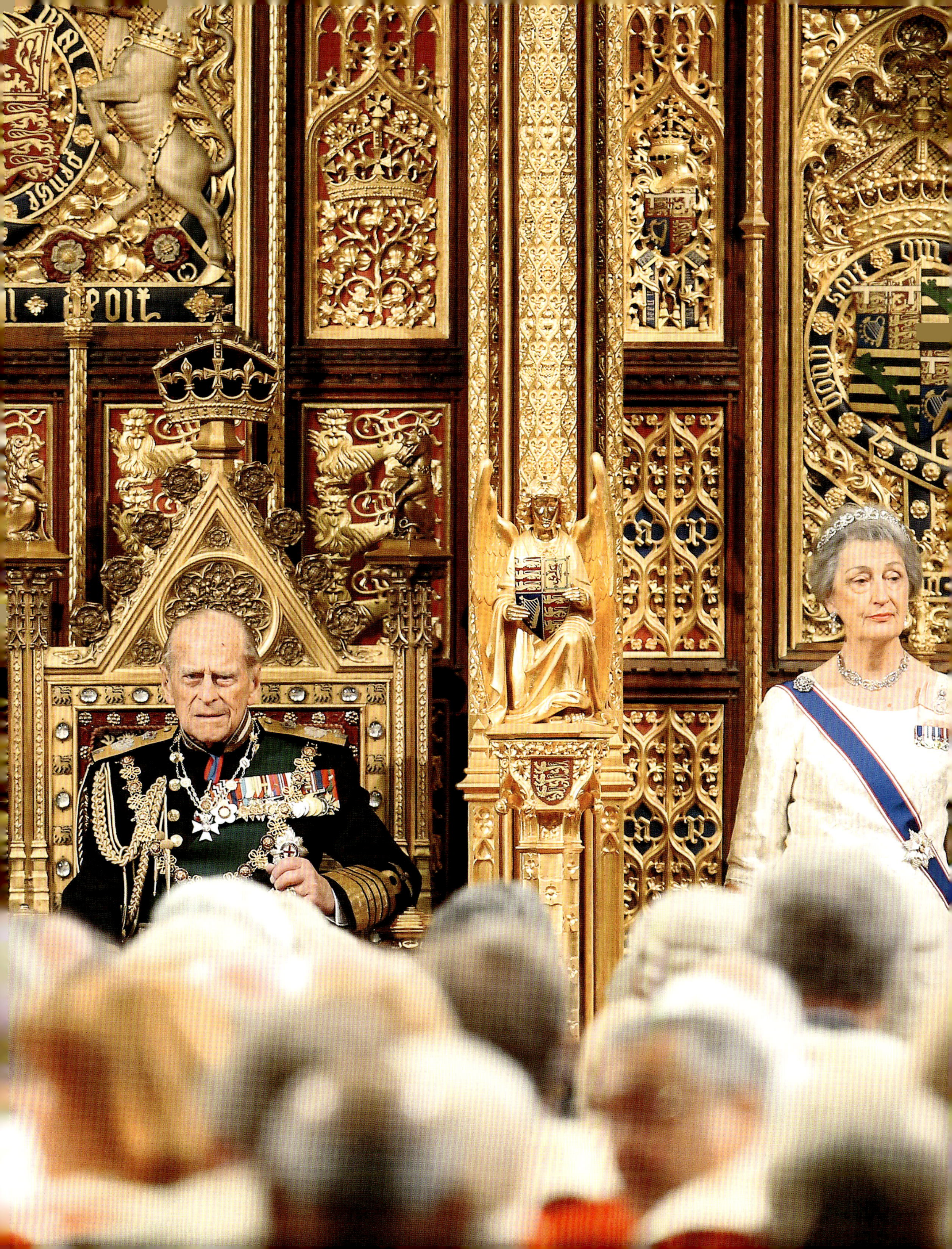

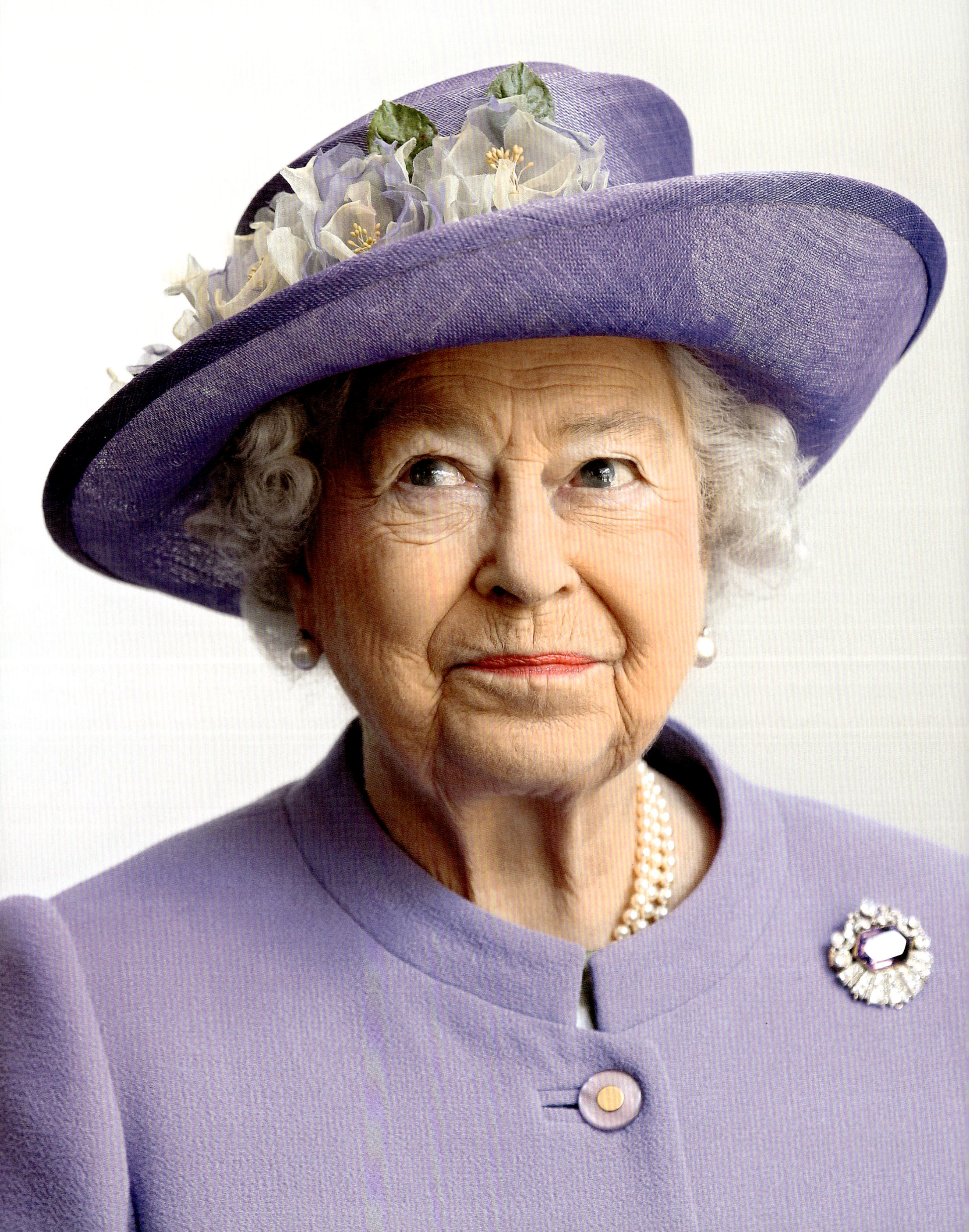

To dress like a royal is to wear clothes that are steeped in tradition and history one day and to dress like a sportsman or movie icon the next. To have the enthusiasm and diplomacy to try on local garb when offered on royal tour and emerge in a stunning tiara and gown in the evening. To be frugal one day and then exude glamour the next. Clothes that suit the weather, be it hot or cold, humid or dry, wet or windy. Clothes that reflect religious sensitivity at holy sites around the world. Hats, hats, and more hats! There is a hat for every occasion, from a top hat at Ascot to a hard hat for abseiling. A statement hat can set the tone for an event—and make things tricky for a photographer, throwing an extra set of challenges into the mix. The modern royals find themselves in any number of different situations and their clothing needs to reflect that. Clothes put out messages, sometimes quite literally, through their colours and design features. The Queen is a fashion icon—entire books can and have been written on her style alone.

Clothes are the first visual reference when a royal appears on duty. No doubt first impressions count and much has been made of the fashion of the younger royals. However, clothing is much more than just fashion for the royal family. Traditions that have survived for centuries dictate and form their day-to-day dressing strategies. Quite often these hark back to historic moments that both serve as reference points for royal family members and remind the rest of us of their enduring legacy. Clothing is also ethically sourced and brand checked. Due diligence is conducted with regard to everything royals wear. Managing a royal tour wardrobe is complex. The garments are packed, prepared, and unloaded with military precision. Many outfits are "recycled"—worn again and again over the decades but maintain a freshness. It is a testament to the timeless style of the royals that they rarely appear out of fashion. The public's curiosity about royal fashion sometimes reaches fever pitch and it is the photographer's job to capture both the full length and the detail, the glamour and the sparkle.

Preceding pages The Queen (wearing the Imperial State Crown) and the Duke of Edinburgh look across at peers in the House of Lords ahead of the Queen's Speech at the State Opening of Parliament, which formally marks the beginning of a parliamentary session.

Opposite A portrait of the Queen captured during a visit to a new maternity ward at Lister Hospital in Stevenage, England.

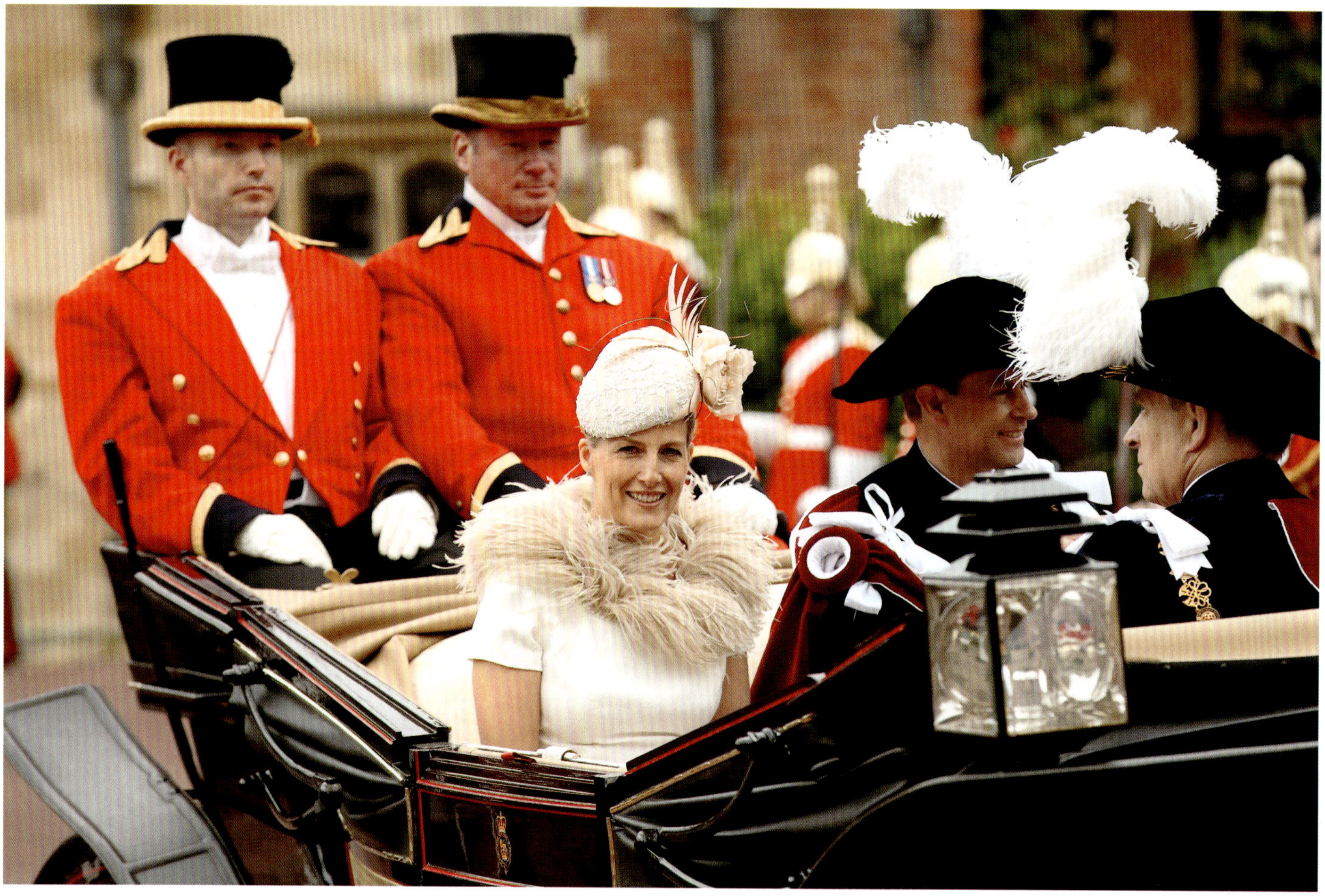

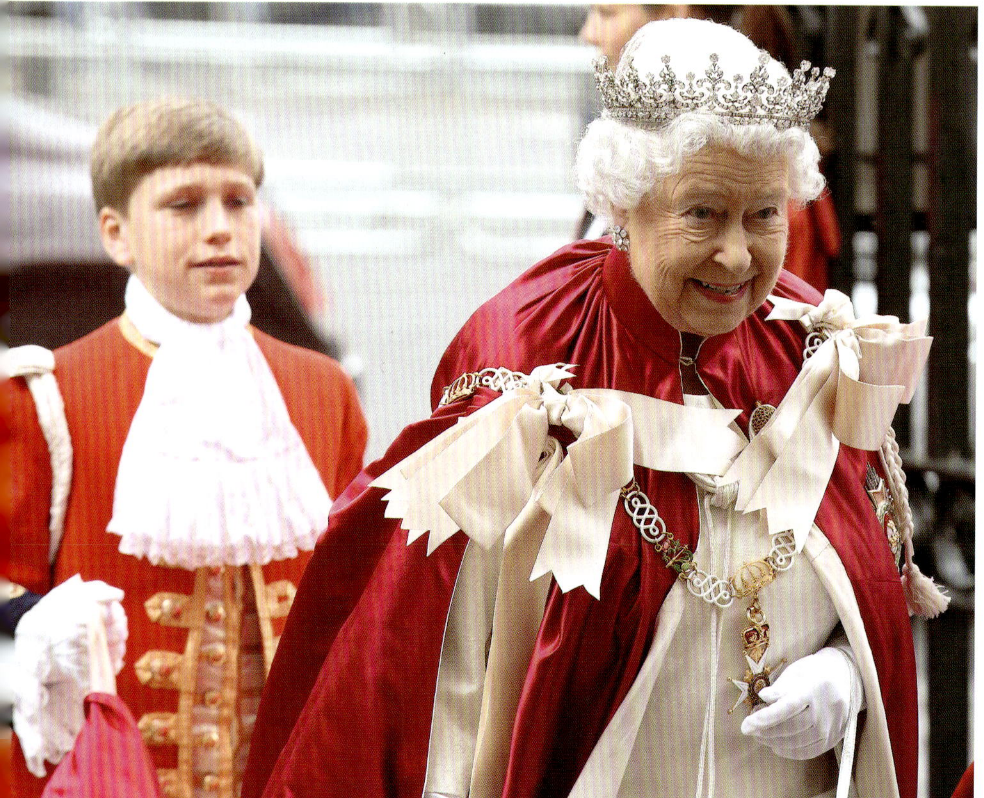

Above The Countess of Wessex and Earl of Wessex travel by carriage from St. George's Chapel in Windsor Castle after the Order of the Garter ceremony.

Left The Queen attends the service of the Order of the Bath at Westminster Abbey, an order of chivalry founded by George I in 1725. The name derives from the medieval ceremony for appointing a knight, which involved bathing as a symbol of purification.

Right The Queen at the Order of the Garter ceremony at St. George's Chapel in Windsor Castle.

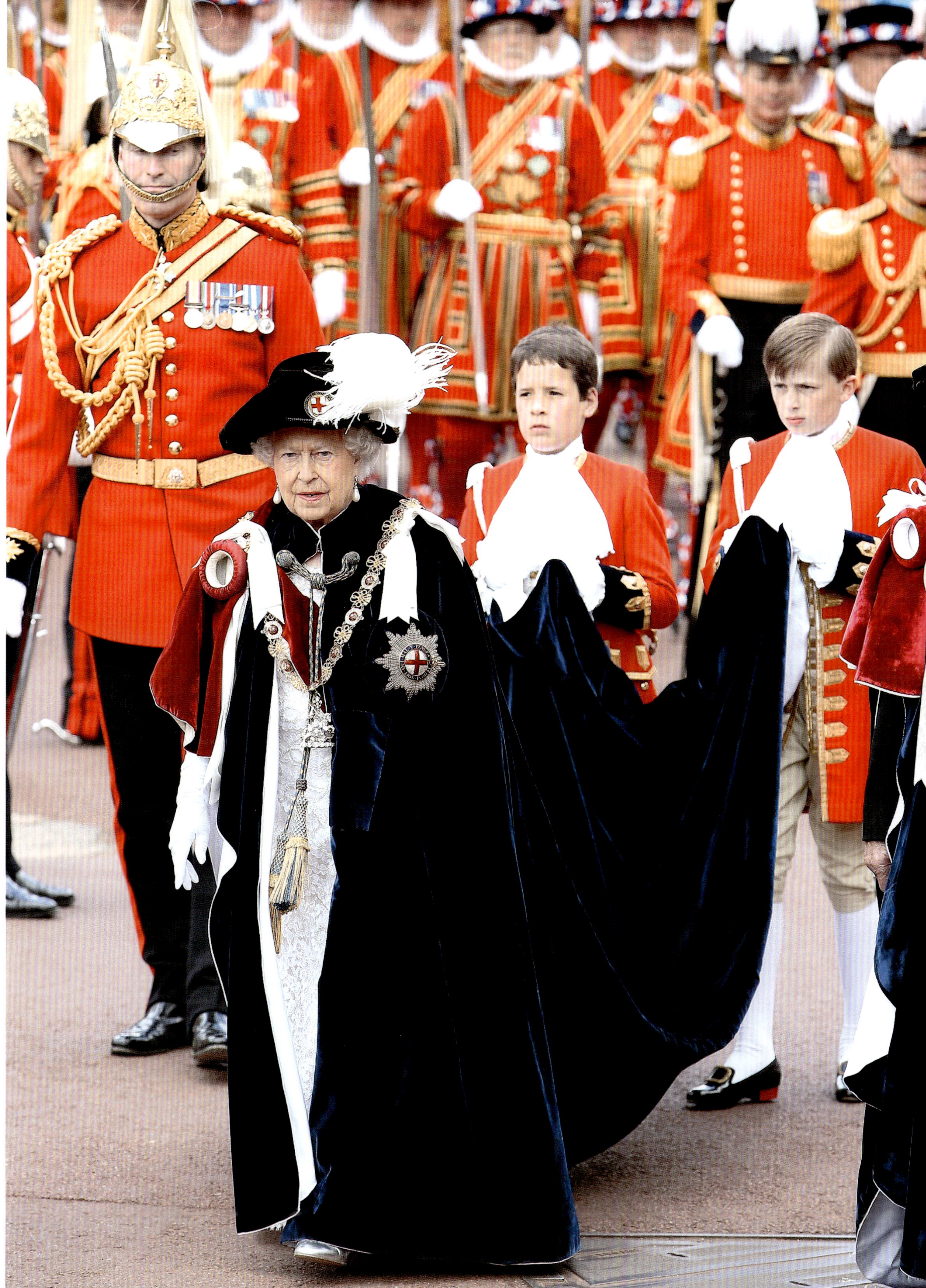

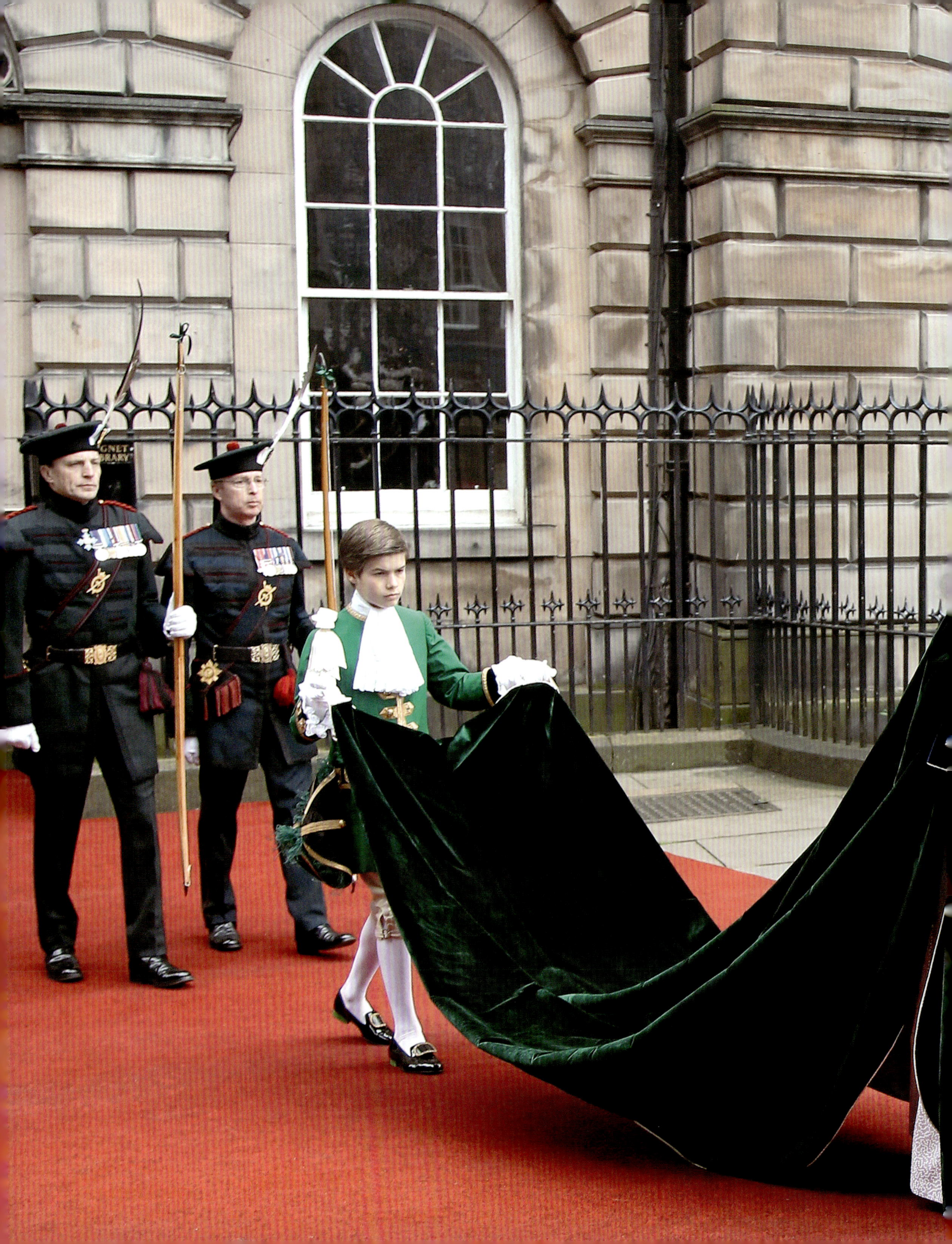

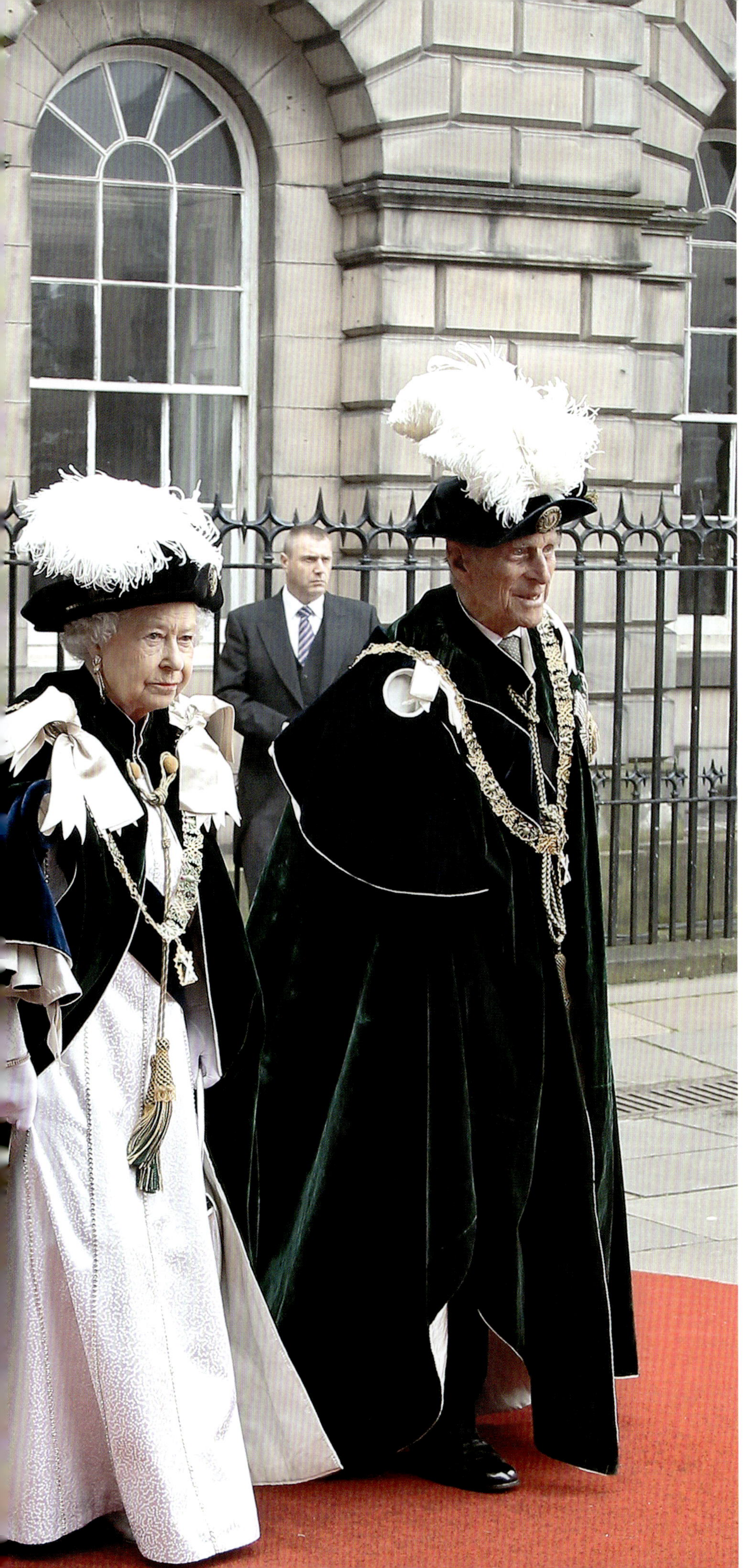

The Queen leaves St. Giles' Cathedral in Edinburgh after the Order of the Thistle ceremony. The Order of the Thistle is the highest order of chivalry in Scotland. This image was taken on the day the Duke of Cambridge, known in Scotland as the Earl of Strathearn, was appointed as a Royal Knight of the Thistle in a ceremony that dates back to its revival by King James VII of Scotland (James II of England and Ireland) in 1687.

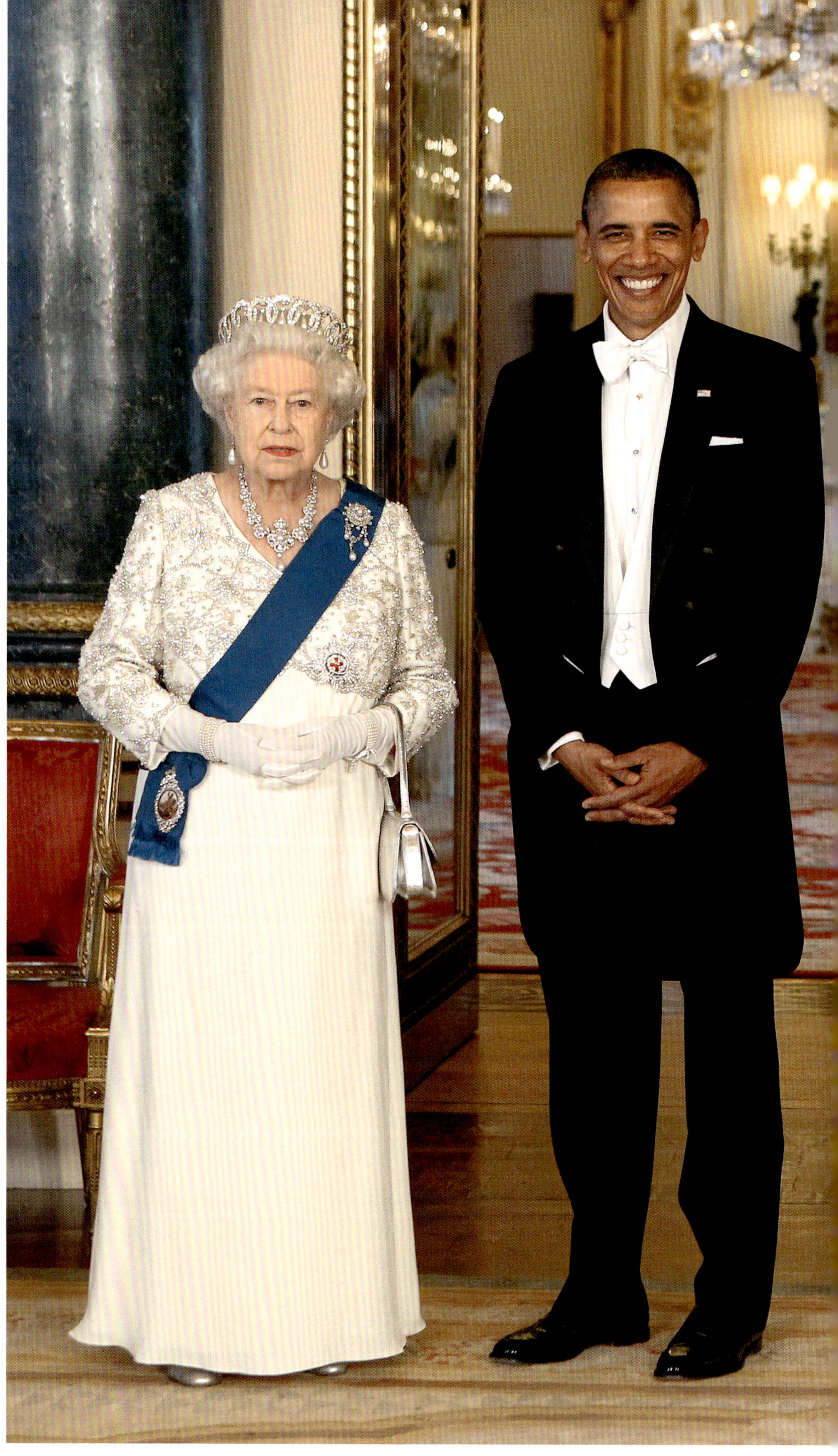

The Queen poses with former U.S. President Barack Obama, his wife, Michelle Obama, and the Duke of Edinburgh in the music room of Buckingham Palace ahead of a state banquet. The forty-fourth president of the United States and his wife were in the United Kingdom for a two-day state visit.

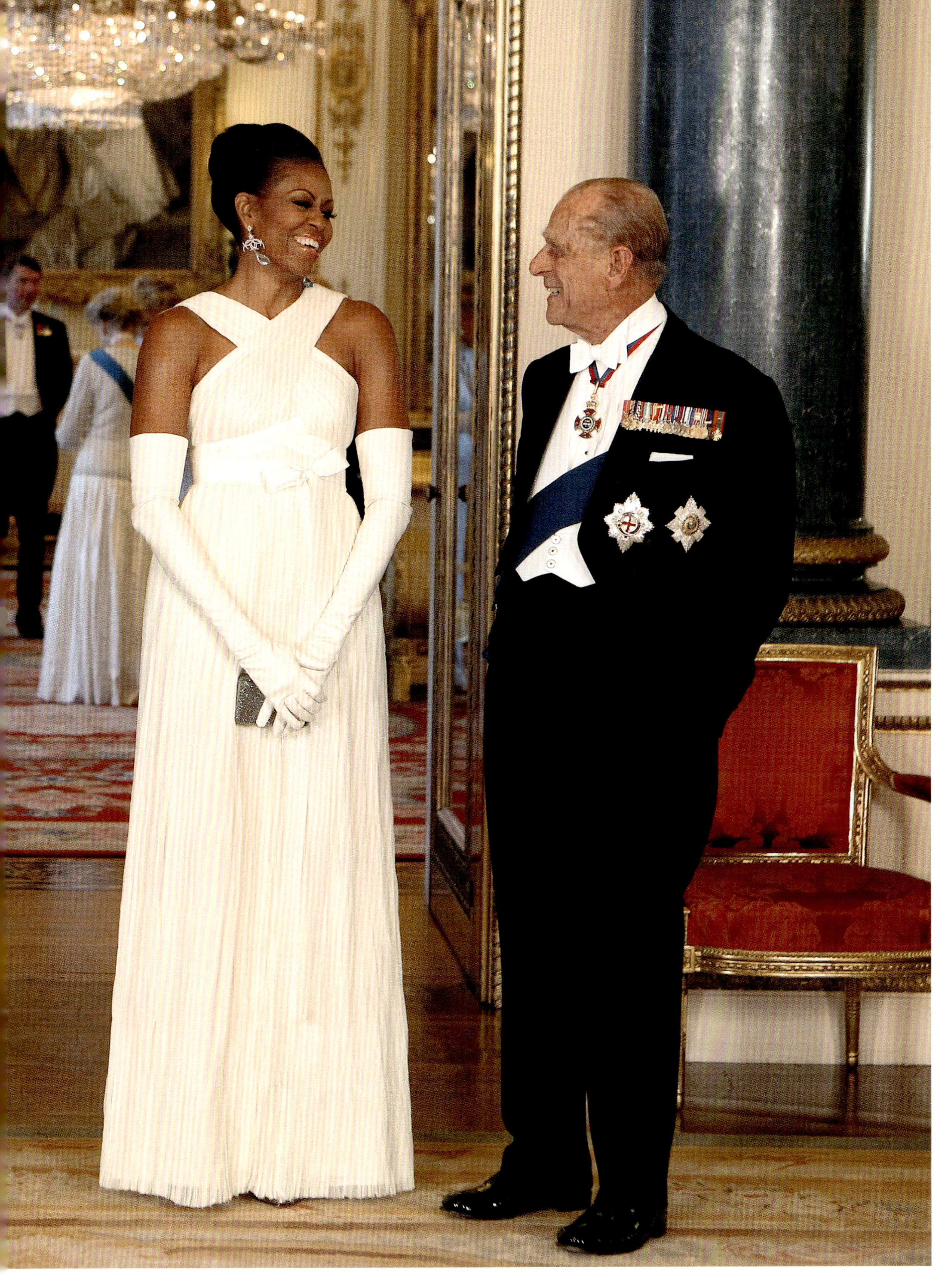

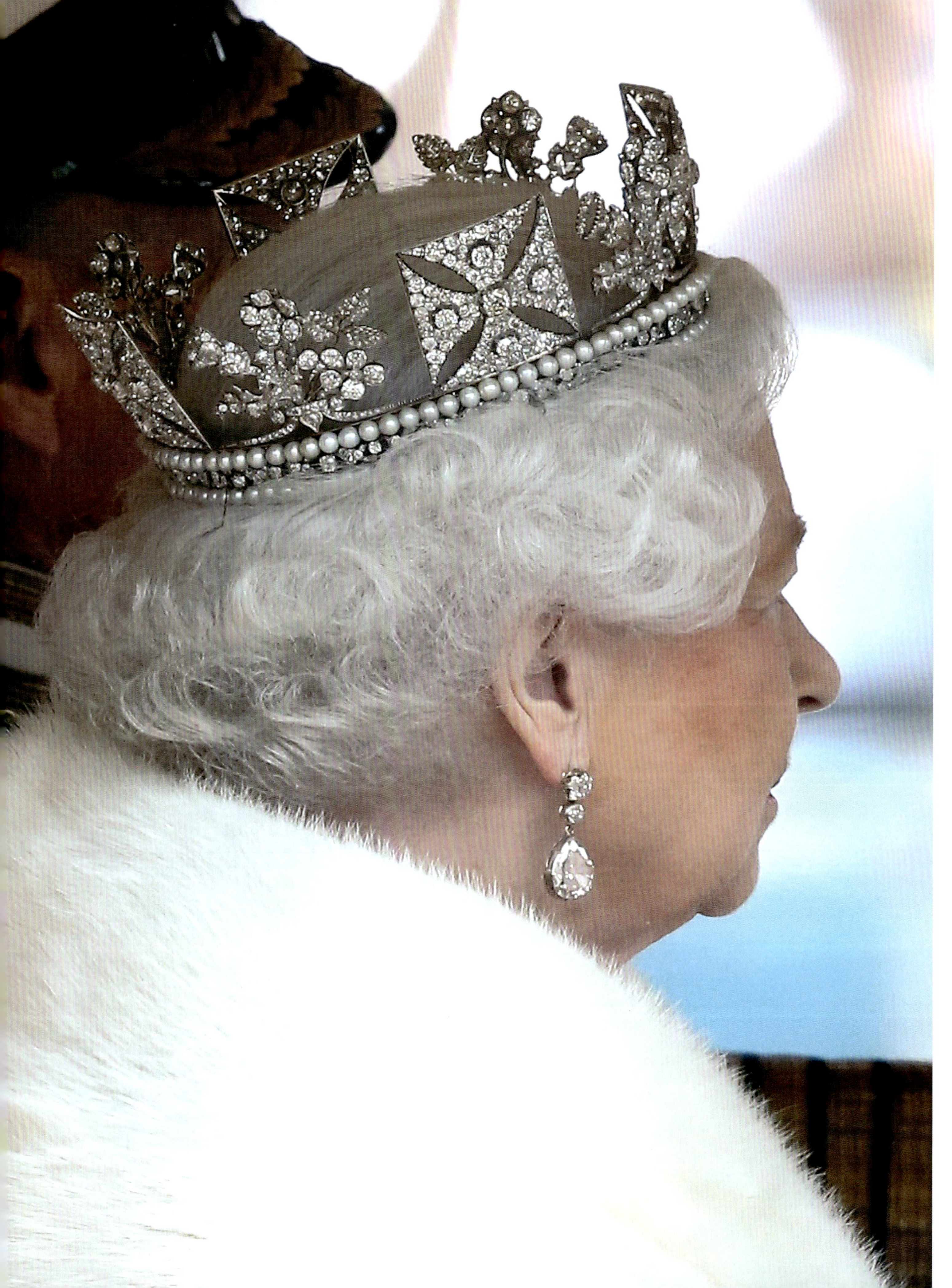

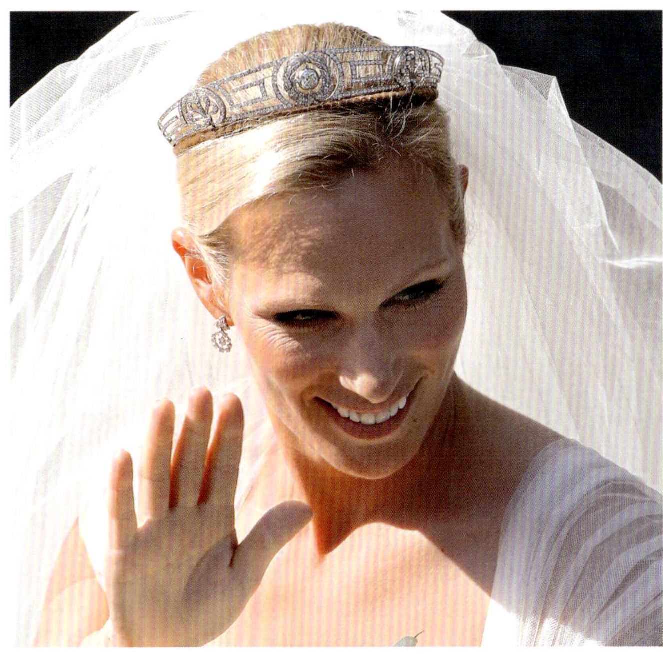

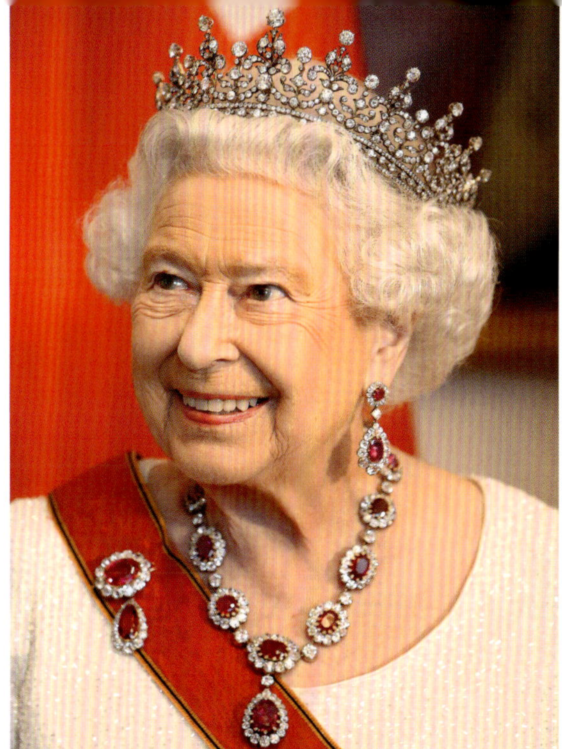

There is no stronger representation of royalty than the image of a crown or tiara. In the days of the modern monarchy, we catch a glimpse of these priceless pieces of history only on rare occasions.

Opposite The Queen wears the George IV State Diadem as she travels by carriage to the State Opening of Parliament in the Diamond Jubilee state coach.

This page, clockwise from top left On July 30, 2011, the day of her wedding in Edinburgh, Zara Phillips wears the Meander Tiara from the collection of her mother, Princess Anne. The Queen wears the Girls of Great Britain and Ireland Tiara during a state banquet at the Schloss Bellevue Palace in Berlin. The Greville Tiara—popular with the Queen Mother and made by Boucheron in 1921—is seen here on the Duchess of Cornwall during the Commonwealth Heads of Government meeting opening ceremony in Colombo, Sri Lanka. The Duchess of Gloucester arrives at the Guildhall in London for a banquet on the second official day of the president of India's state visit, wearing the Honeysuckle Tiara.

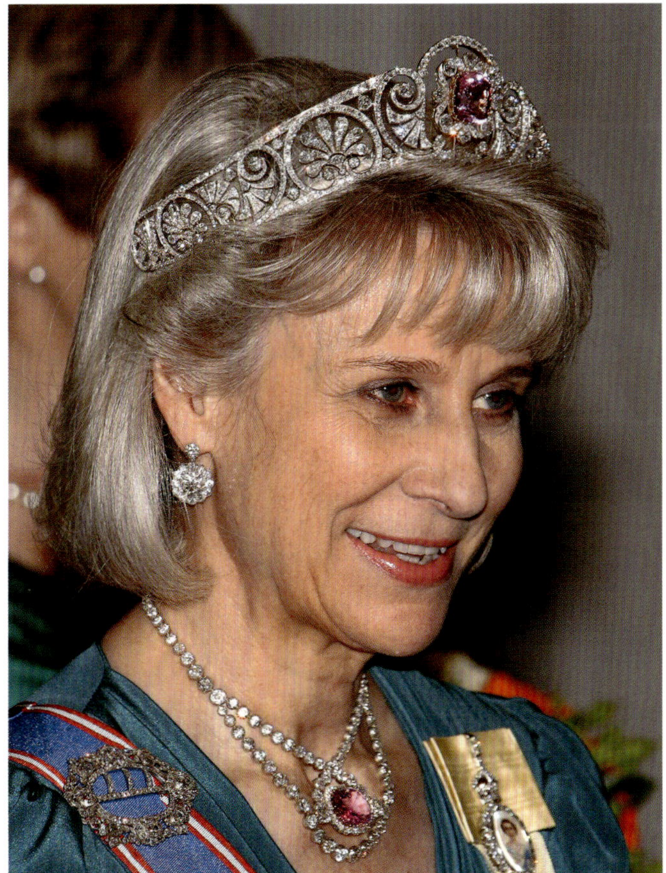

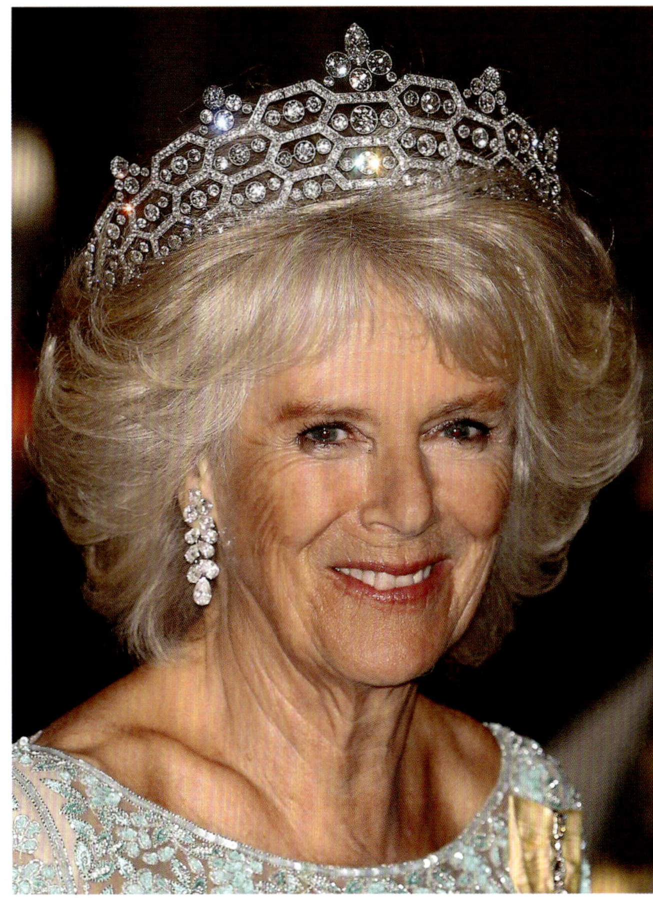

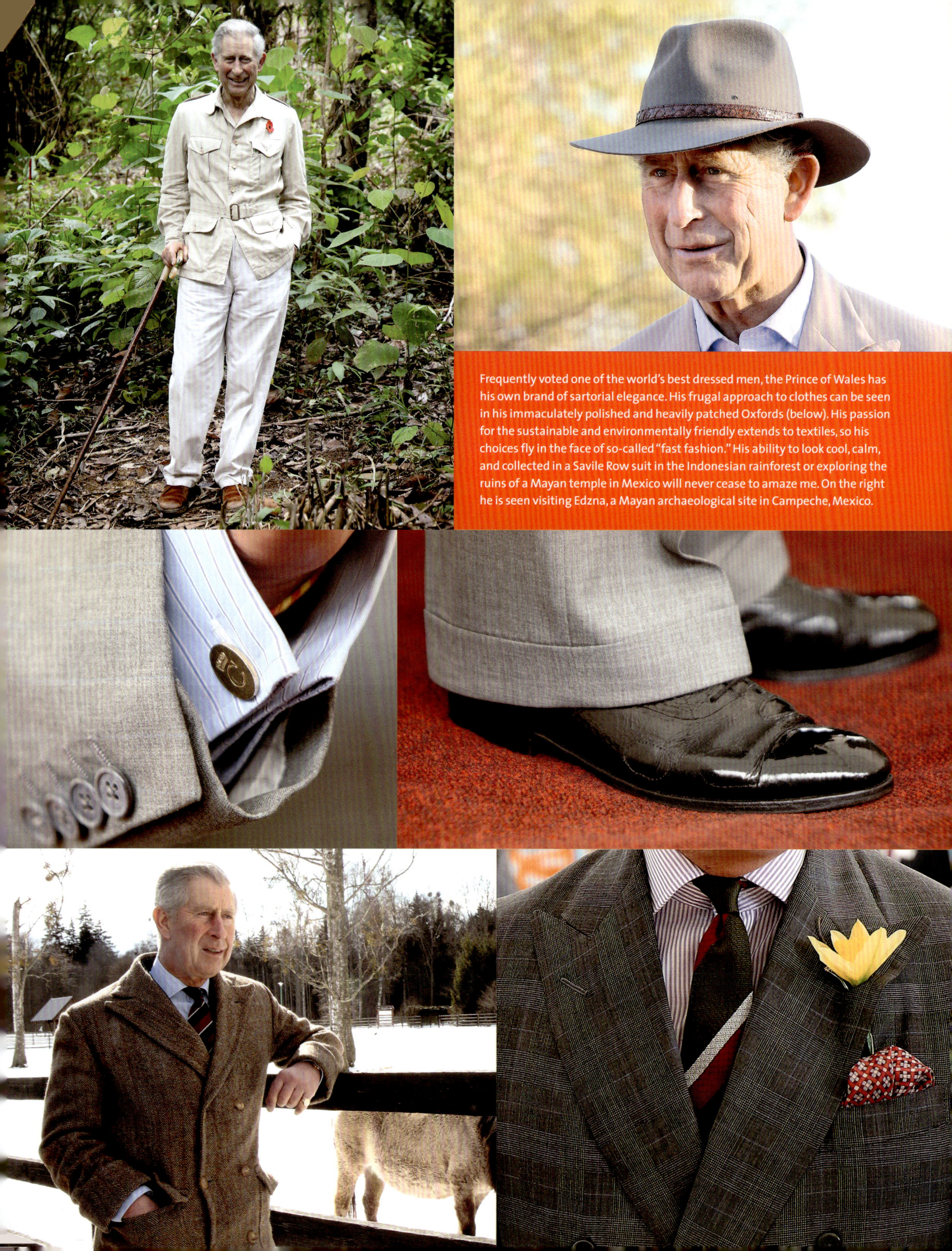

Frequently voted one of the world's best dressed men, the Prince of Wales has his own brand of sartorial elegance. His frugal approach to clothes can be seen in his immaculately polished and heavily patched Oxfords (below). His passion for the sustainable and environmentally friendly extends to textiles, so his choices fly in the face of so-called "fast fashion." His ability to look cool, calm, and collected in a Savile Row suit in the Indonesian rainforest or exploring the ruins of a Mayan temple in Mexico will never cease to amaze me. On the right he is seen visiting Edzna, a Mayan archaeological site in Campeche, Mexico.

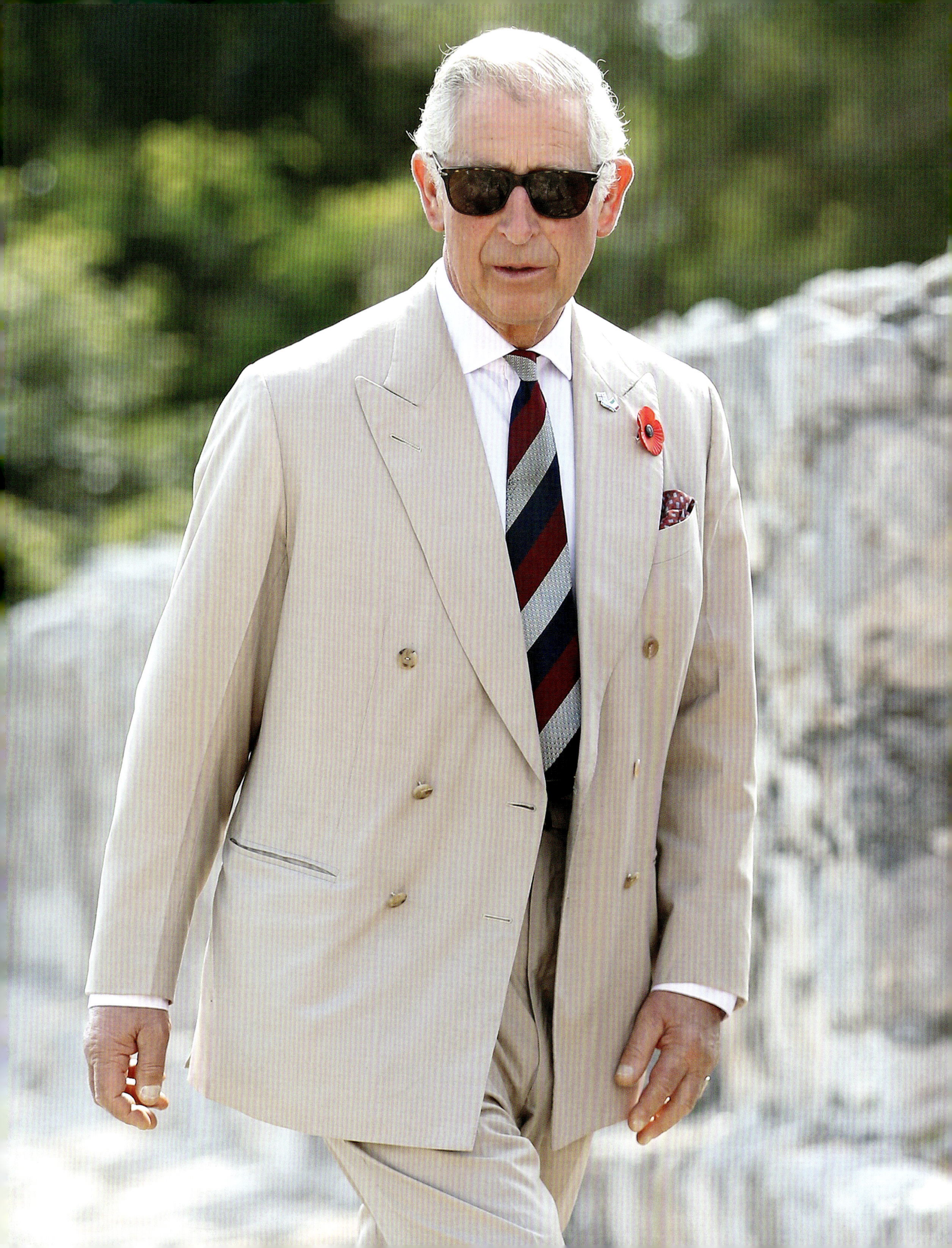

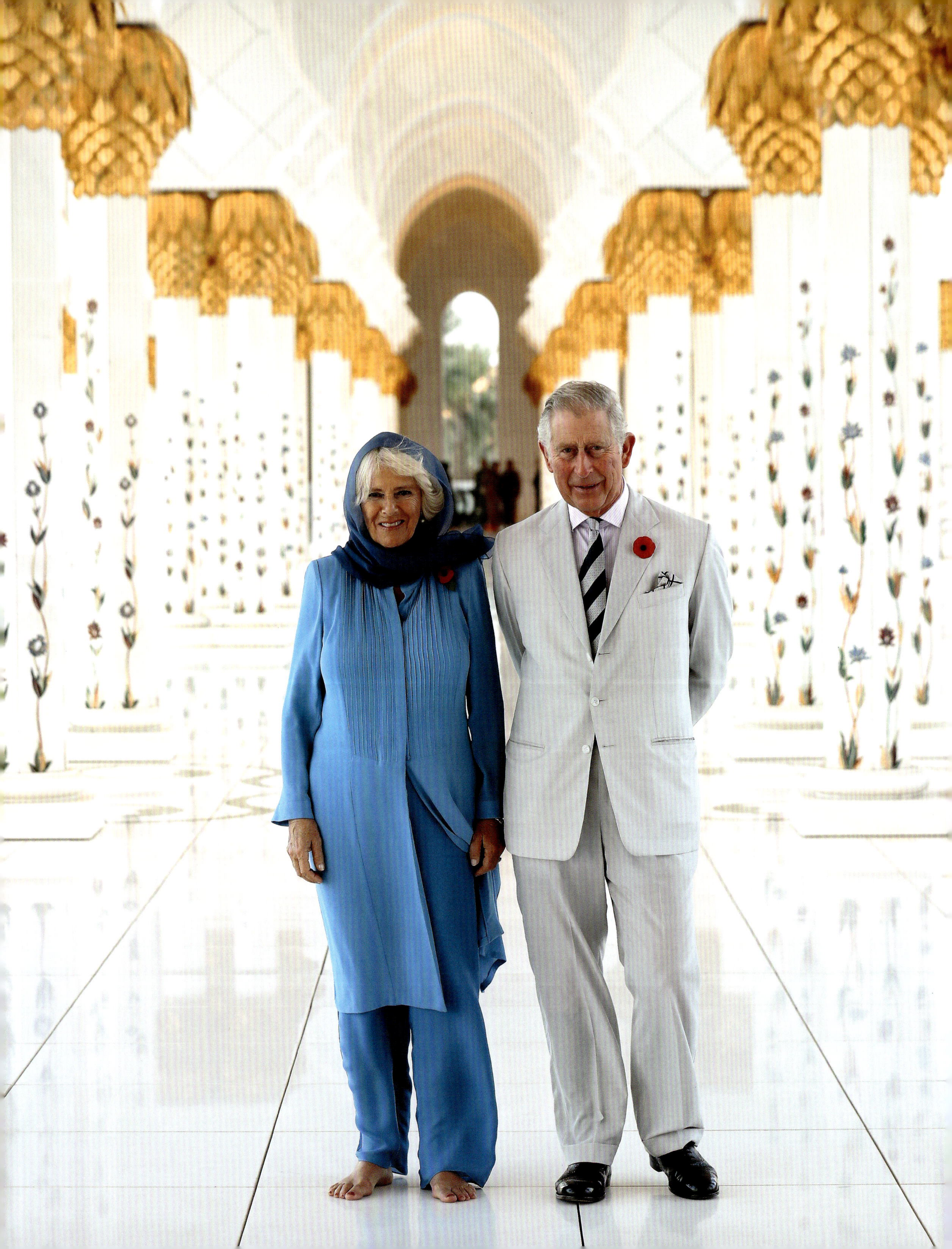

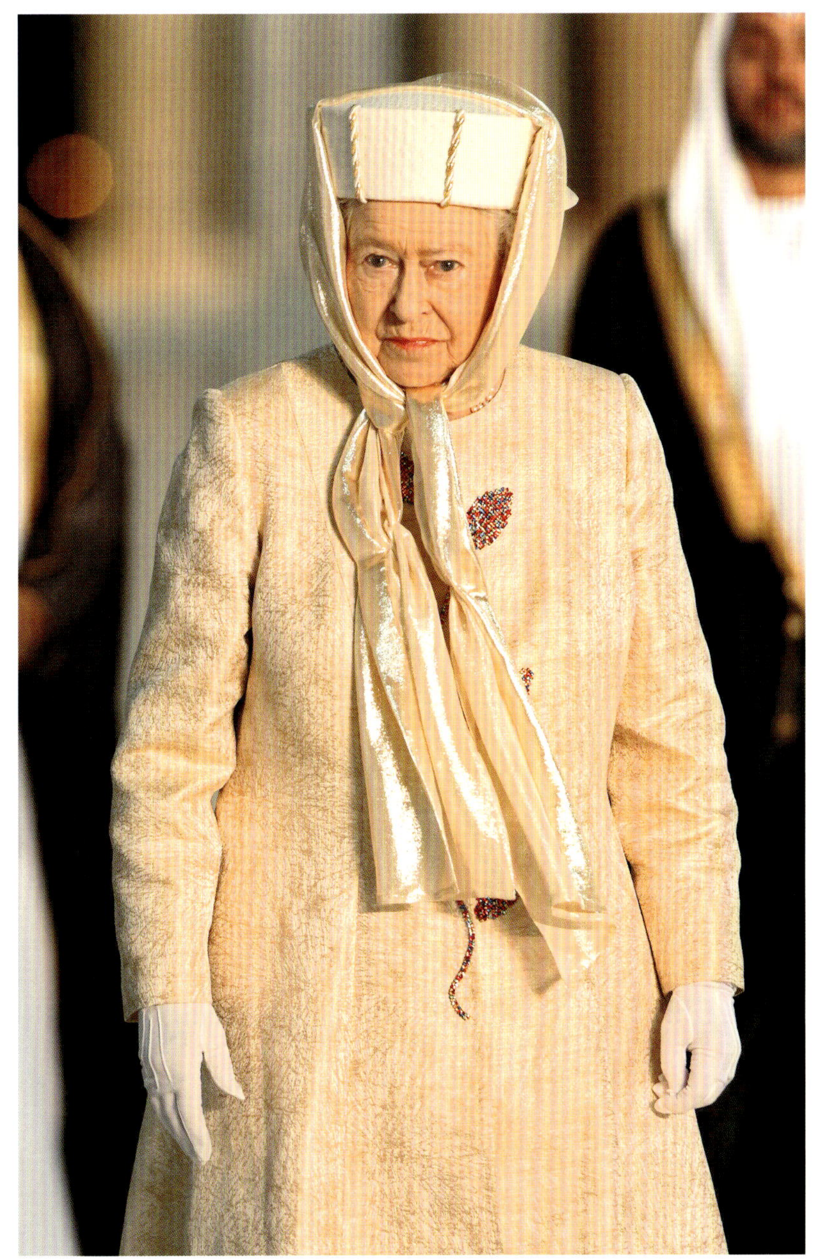

Cultural sensitivity is a key consideration when assembling the royal tour wardrobe.

Opposite A shoeless Duchess of Cornwall poses with the Prince of Wales as they visit the Sheikh Zayed Grand Mosque on the first day of a royal tour of the United Arab Emirates.

Above The Queen visits the Sheikh Zayed Grand Mosque in Abu Dhabi, United Arab Emirates.

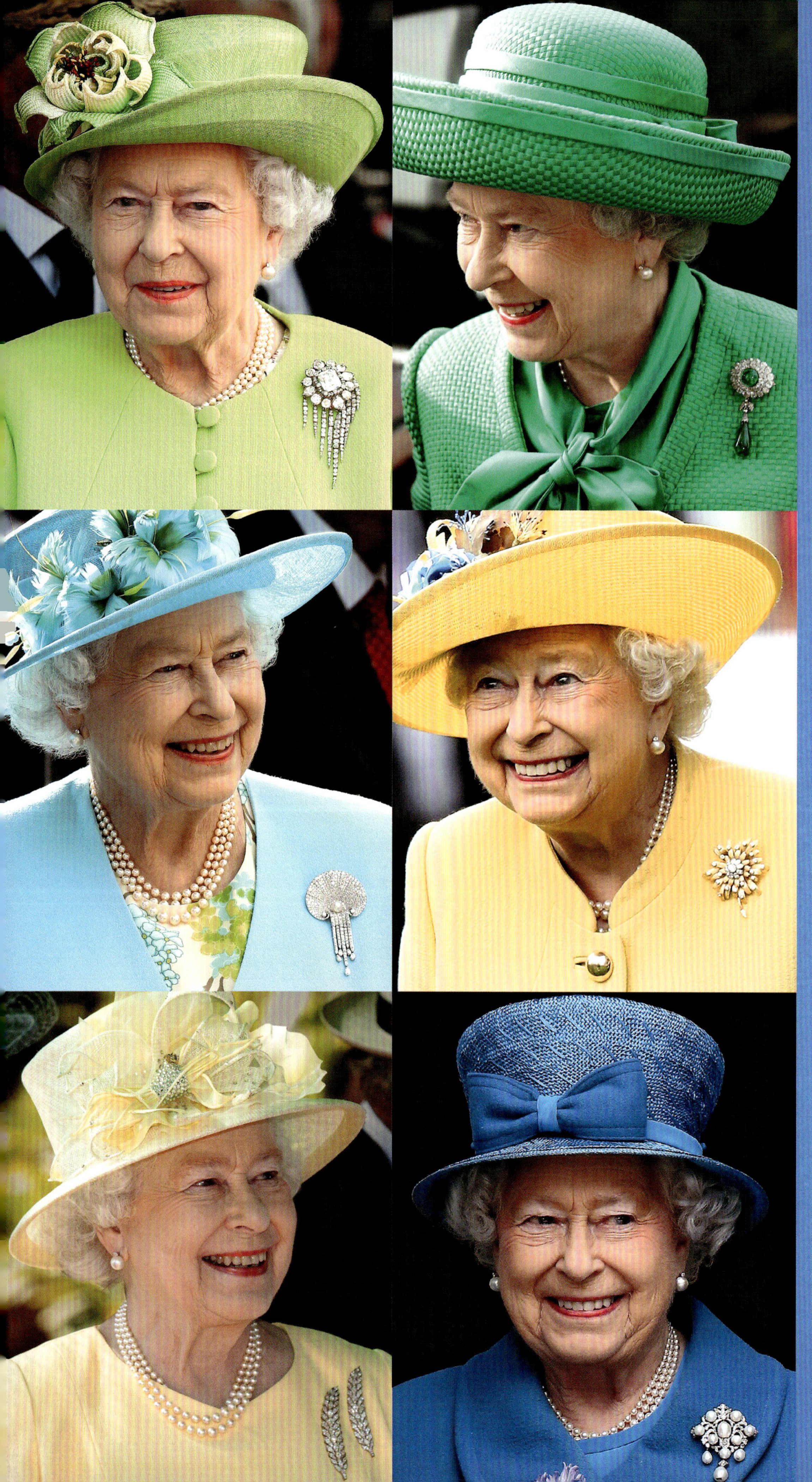

Colour and hats are two mainstays of the Queen's wardrobe. However, a selection from the priceless collection of brooches she has inherited or acquired during her reign often makes her stand out with a bit of sparkle.

Opposite The monarch laughs as she visits the Kennington Centre of the Prince's Trust in London wearing the Prince Albert's Sapphire brooch. The visit marked the fortieth anniversary of the charitable foundation. It was started by the Prince of Wales in support of young people.

A selection of the Queen's brooches, **clockwise from top left**, Queen Victoria's Fringe brooch. Round Cambridge Emerald brooch. Frosted Sunflower brooch. Queen Victoria's 11 Pearl brooch. Queen Victoria's Wheat-Ears brooch. The Queen Mother's Shell brooch.

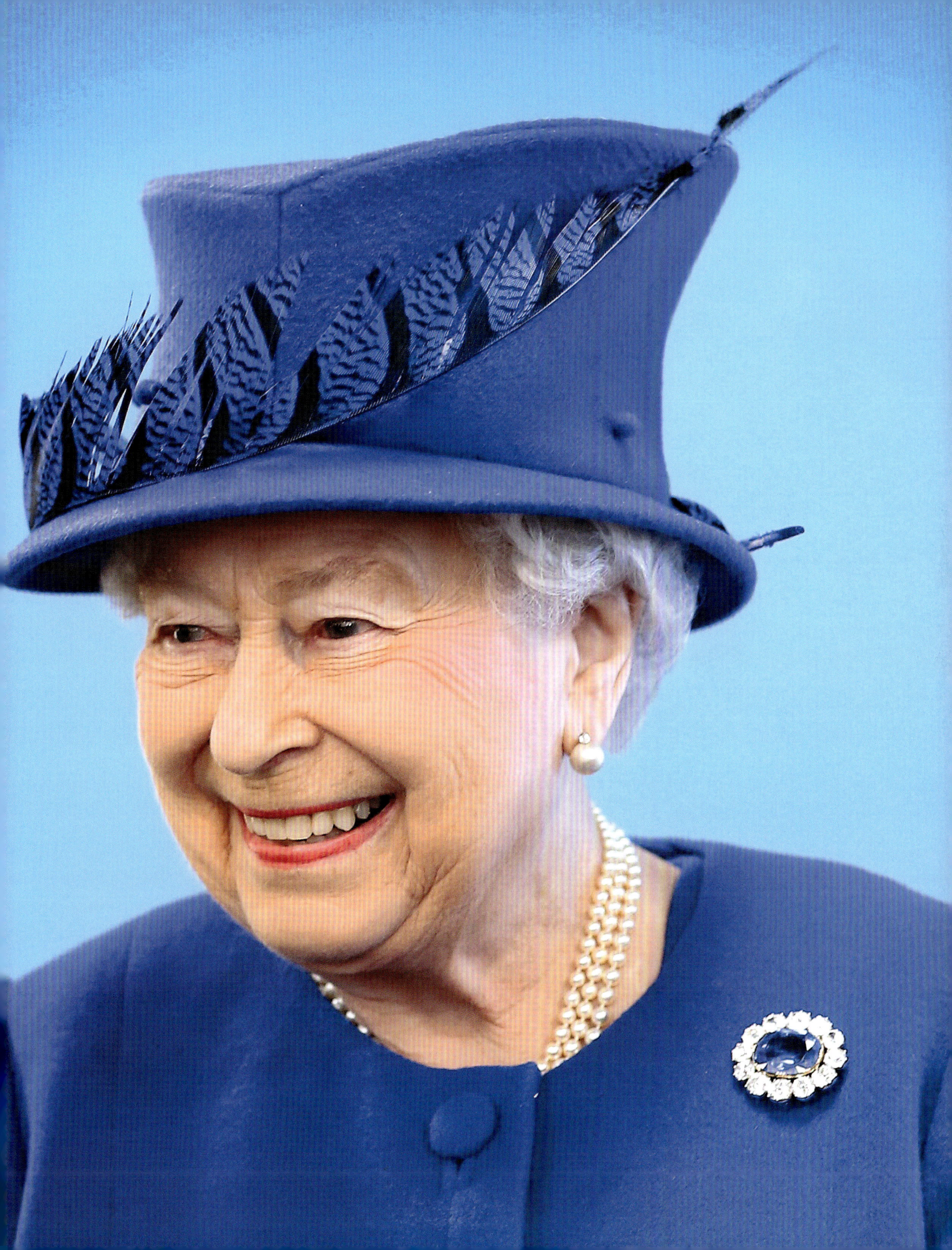

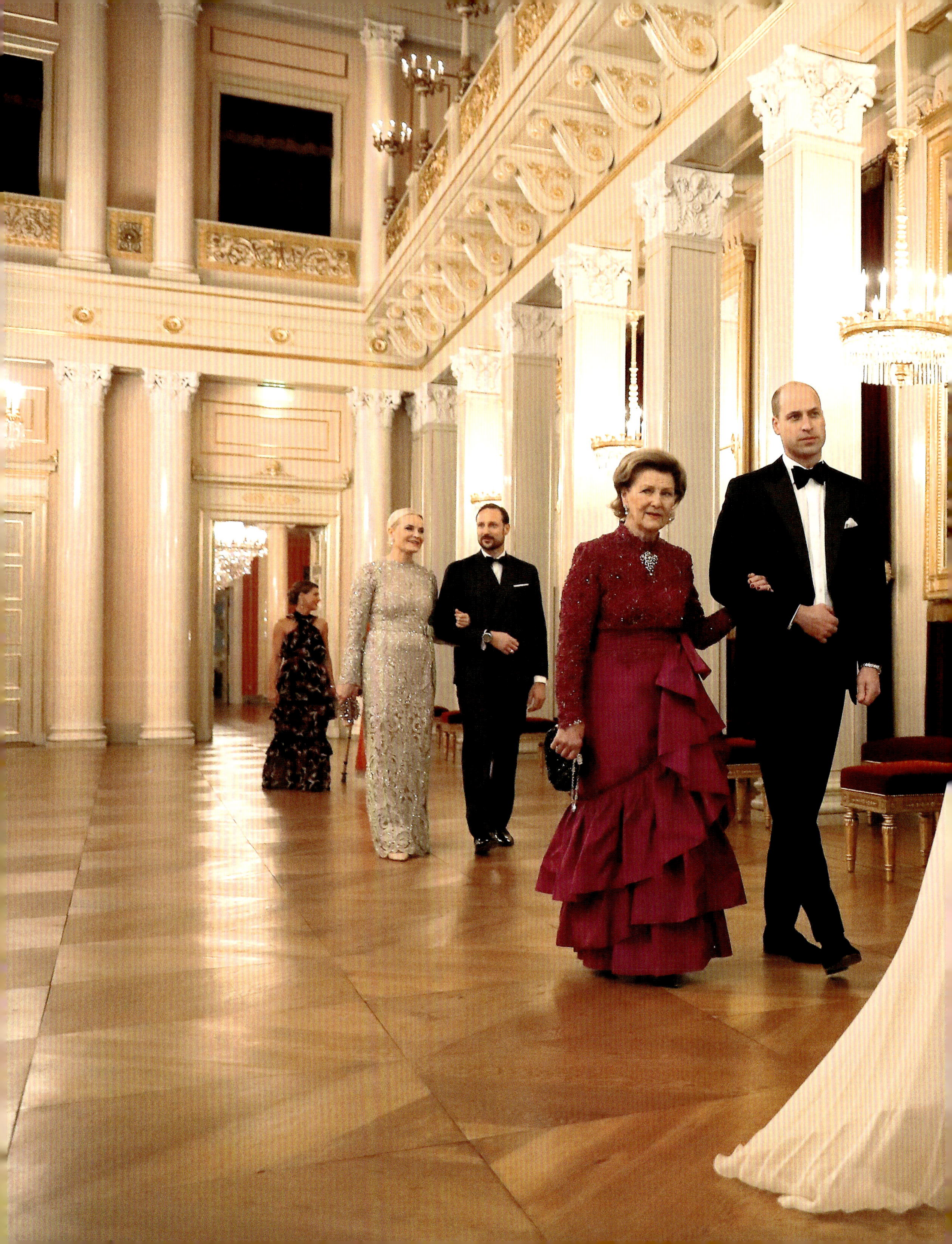

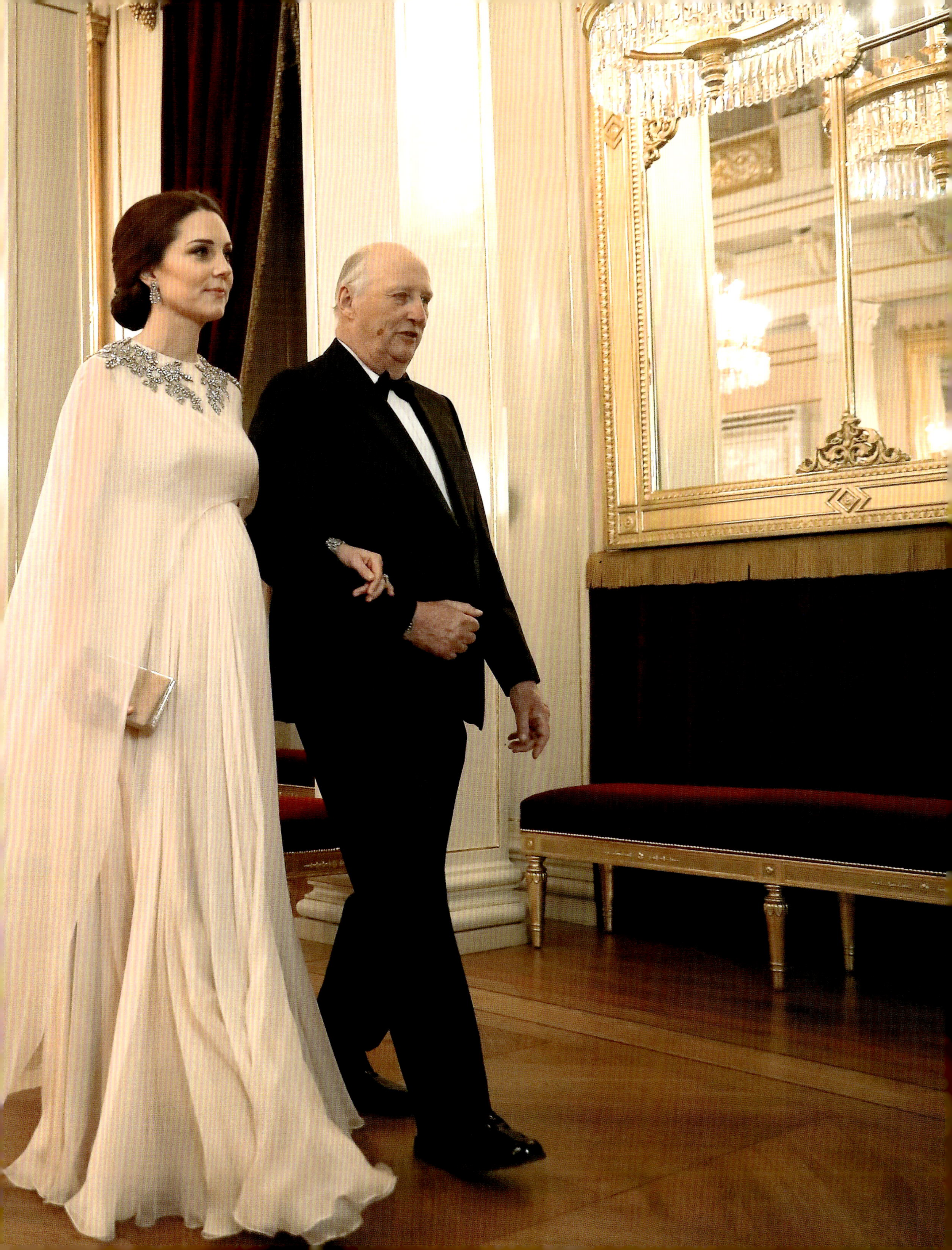

British designers form the backbone of any royal tour wardrobe and the Duchess of Cambridge certainly has some favourite designers.

Clockwise from top left The Duchess of Cambridge attends the 70th British Academy Film Awards (BAFTA) at the Royal Albert Hall in Alexander McQueen. Arriving at Gardens by the Bay wearing Alexander McQueen during a tour of the Far East. Wearing Erdem and arriving at the 100 Women in Hedge Funds Gala Dinner at the Victoria and Albert Museum. Wearing Beulah the Duchess of Cambridge visits Assyakirin Mosque in Kuala Lumpur, Malaysia. Arriving to present medals to members of the Irish Guards in Windsor, England, in Alexander McQueen.

Opposite The Duchess of Cambridge arriving in Jenny Packham for a concert at the Royal Albert Hall (left) and for a Bollywood Inspired Charity Gala in Mumbai at the Taj Mahal Palace Hotel (right).

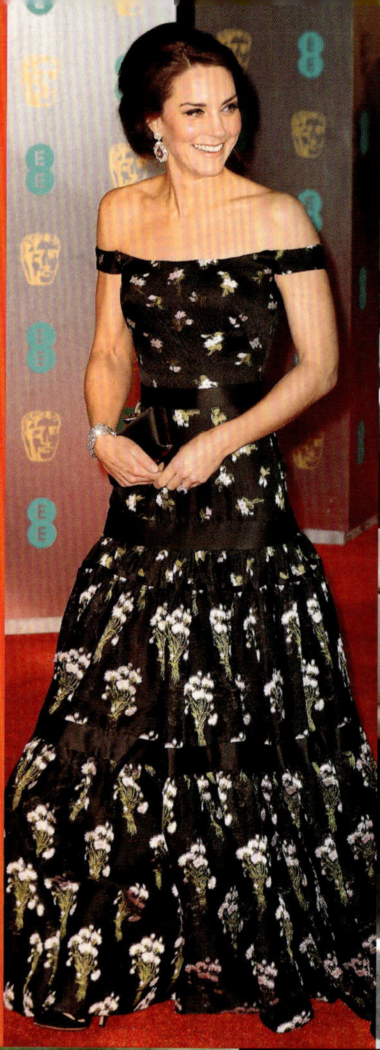

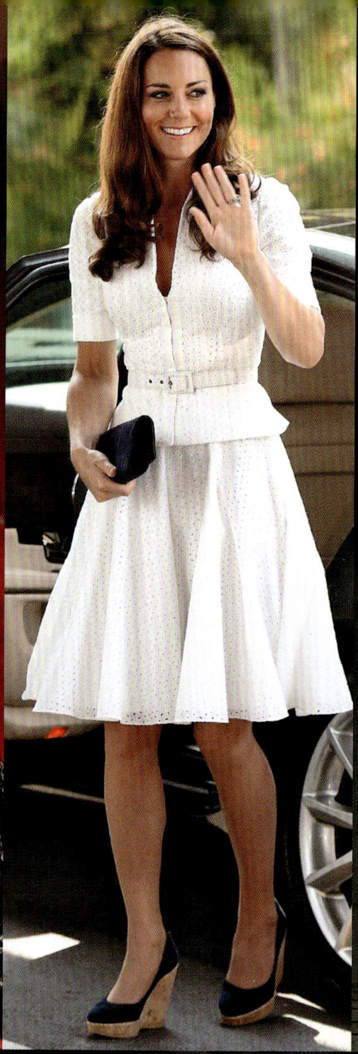

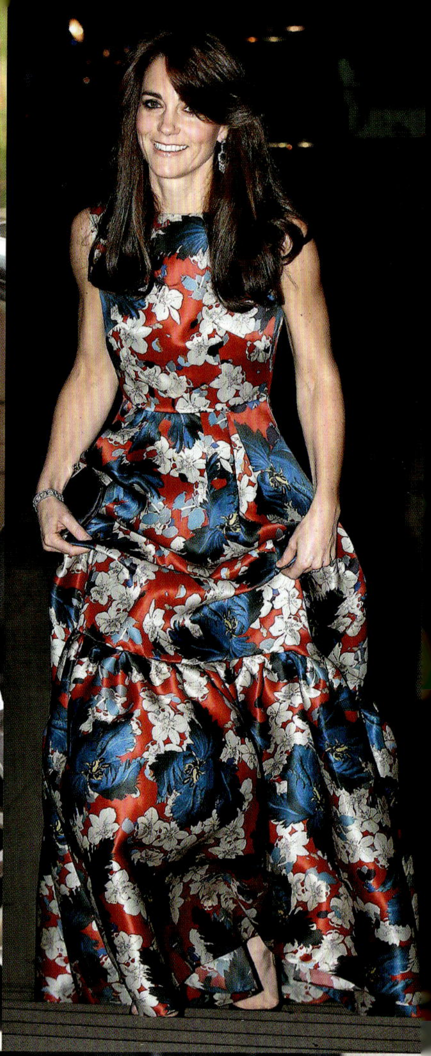

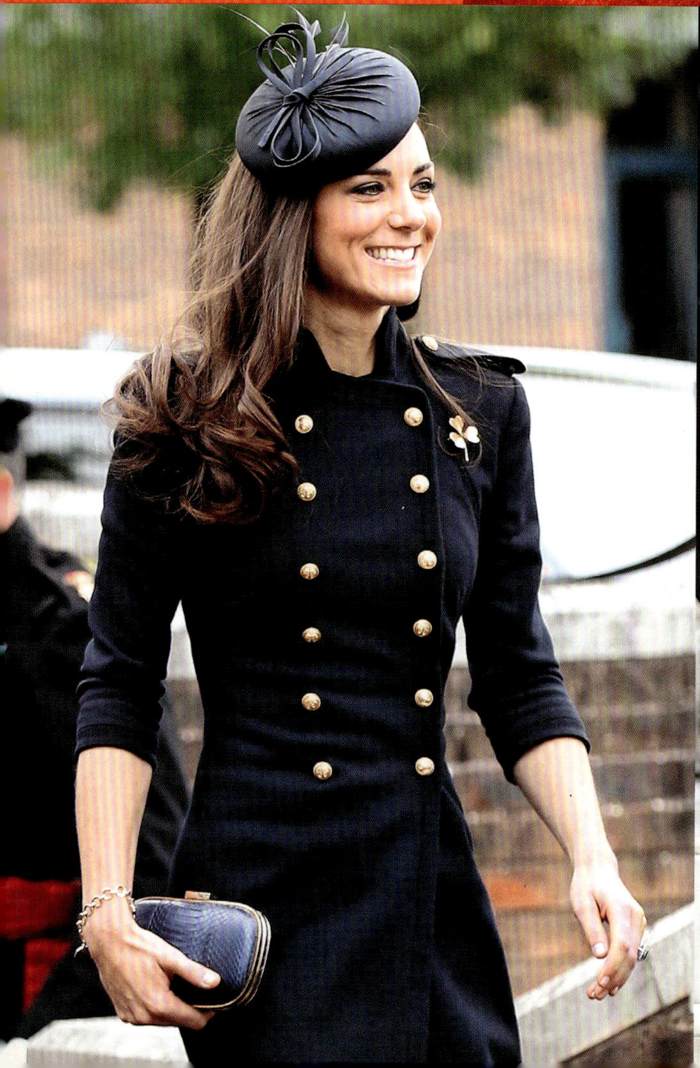

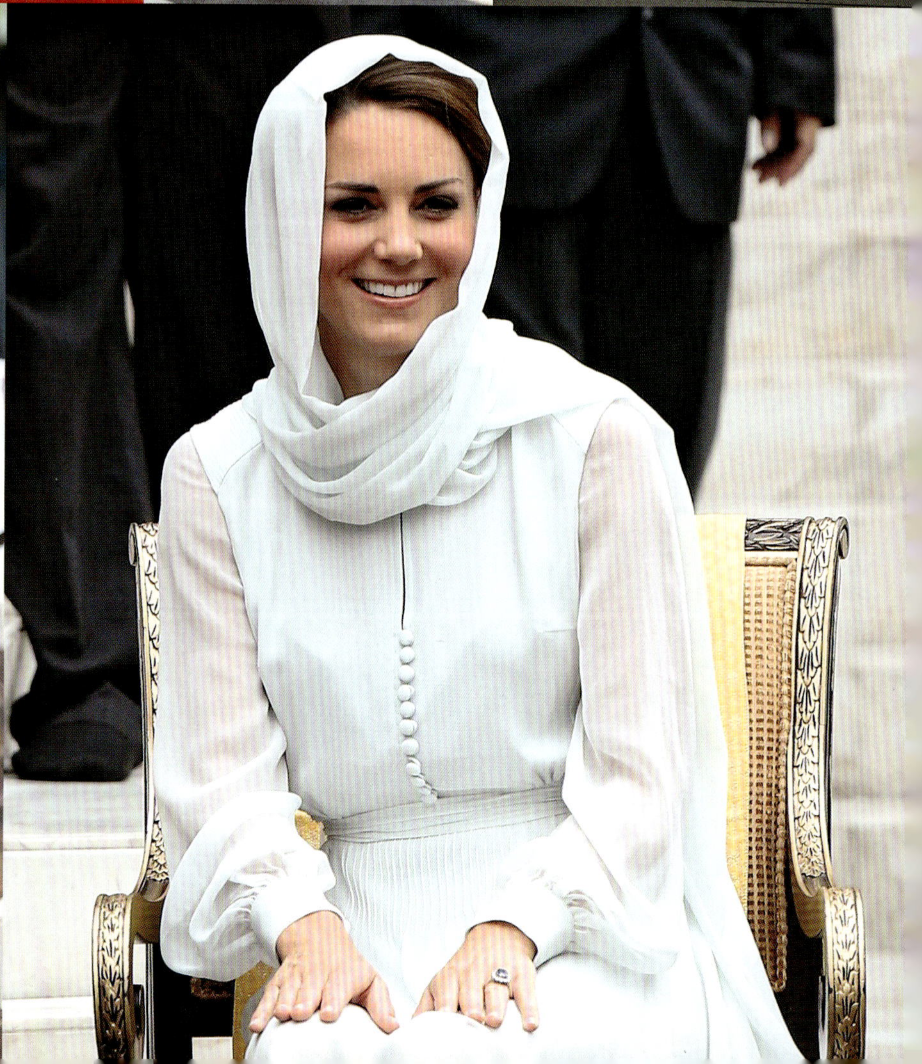

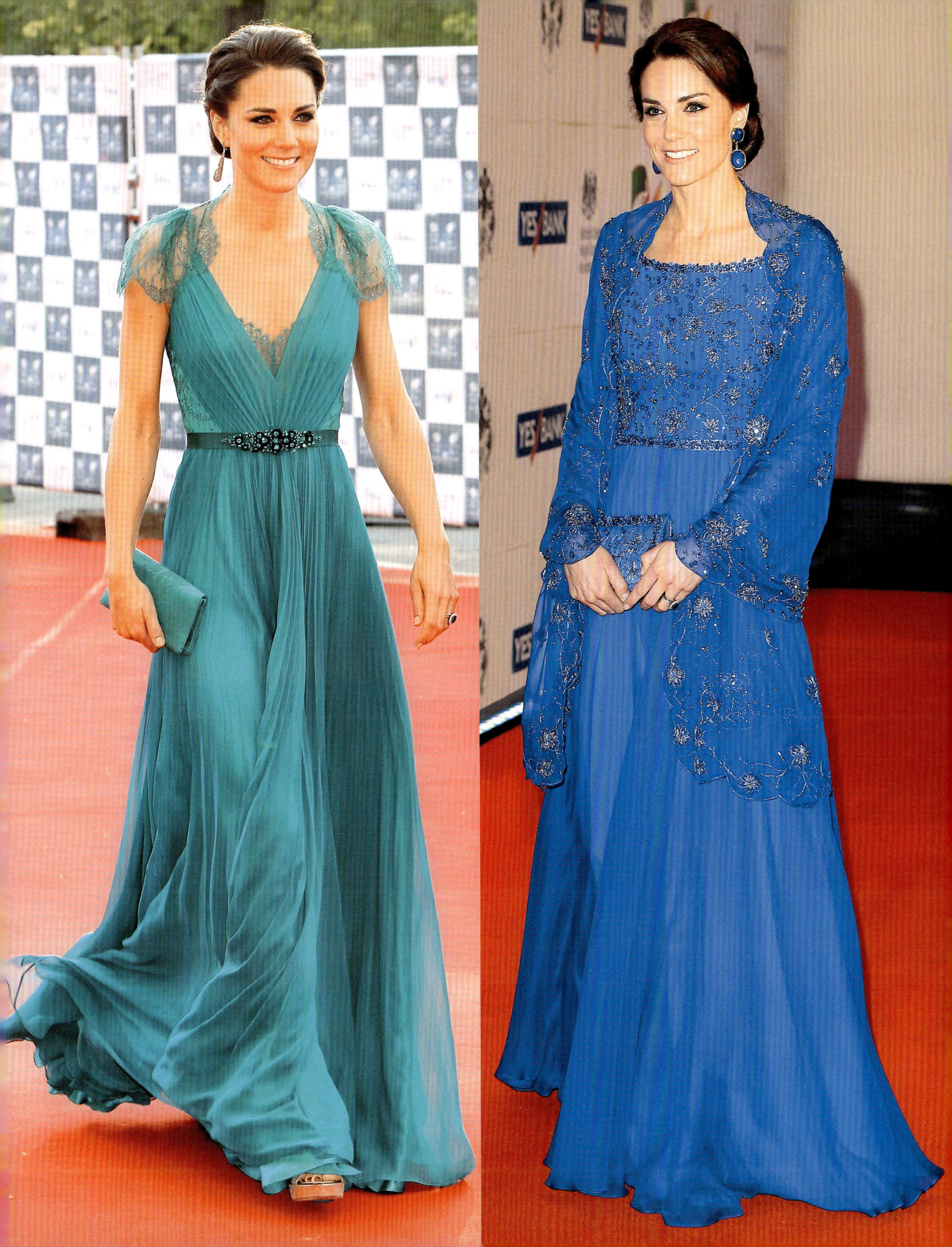
YES BANK

Pages 102–3 Wearing a gown by Alexander McQueen, the Duchess of Cambridge is escorted into a banquet by King Harald V of Norway whilst the Duke of Cambridge is escorted by Queen Sonja of Norway at the Norwegian Royal Palace in Oslo on the third day of a 2018 tour.

Opposite The Queen's love of bright colours and matching outfits is well known. Her unique style makes her easy to spot so that everyone has a chance to see her, even if it is just a glimpse of her hat from the depths of the crowd. Here, Her Majesty is cheered by crowds of children as she arrives at Nine Springs Park in Yeovil, England. The Queen and the Duke of Edinburgh were visiting the southwest of England as part of their Diamond Jubilee tour of the country in 2012.

Pages 110–11 Attention to detail is everything for the Queen—from hats to handbags.

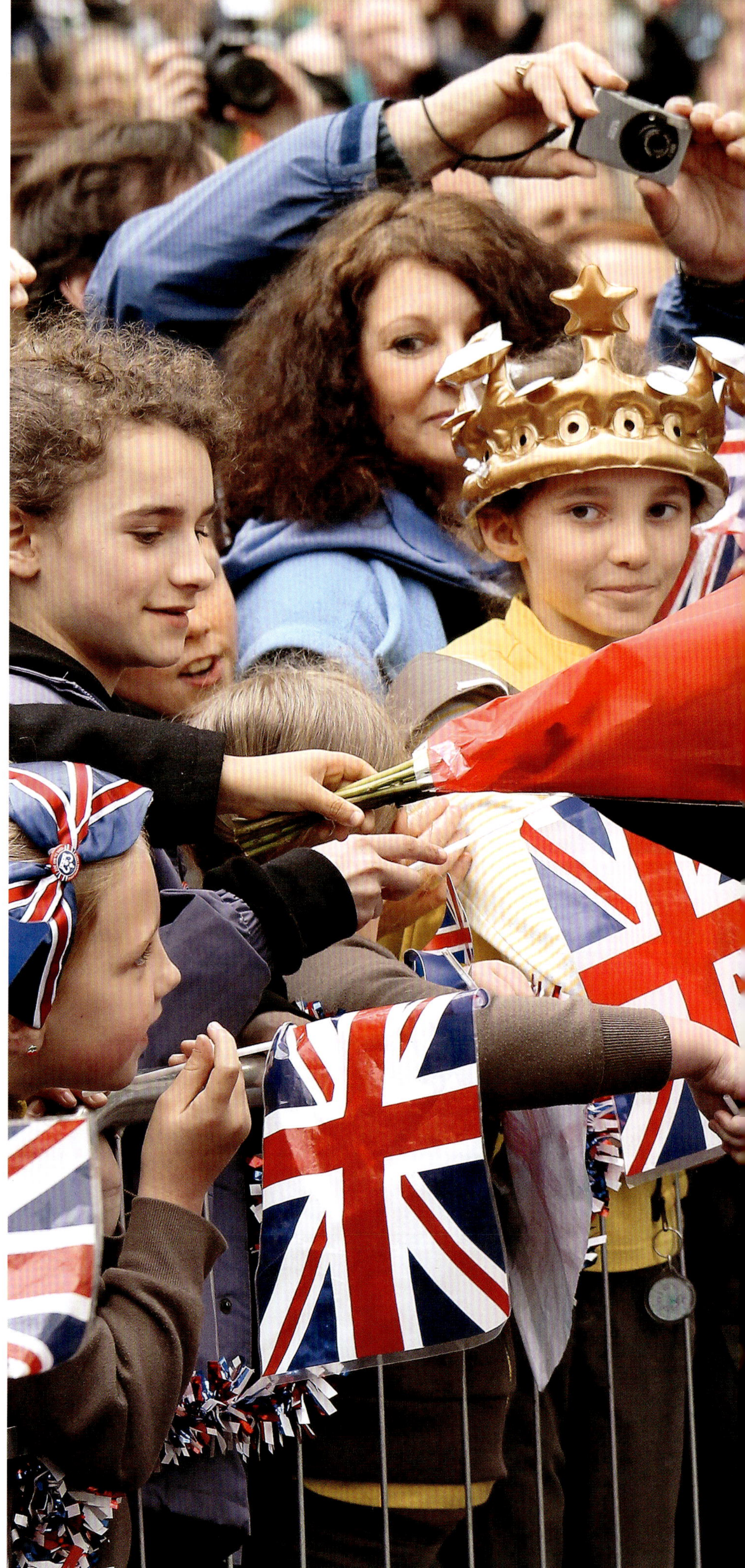

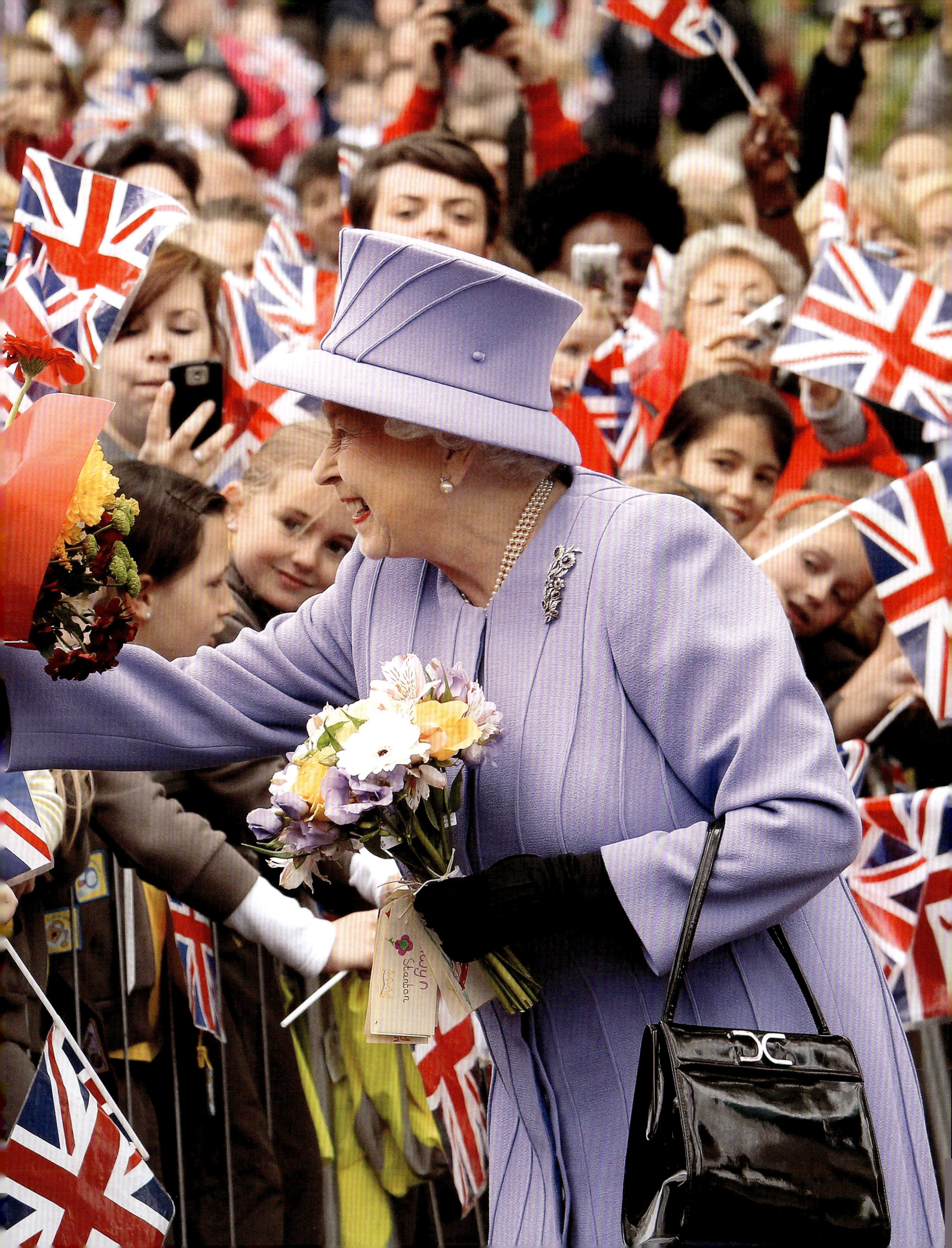

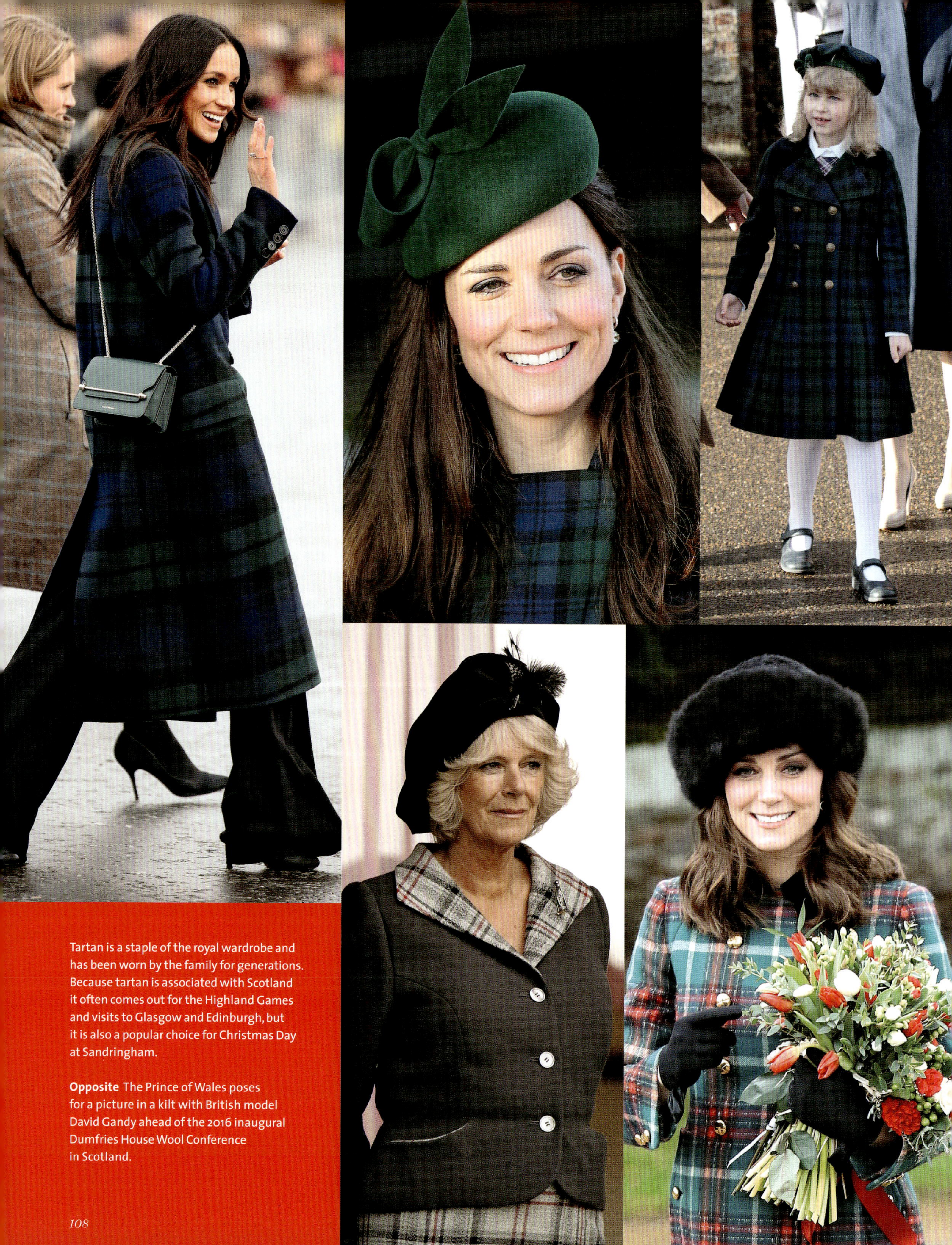

Tartan is a staple of the royal wardrobe and has been worn by the family for generations. Because tartan is associated with Scotland it often comes out for the Highland Games and visits to Glasgow and Edinburgh, but it is also a popular choice for Christmas Day at Sandringham.

Opposite The Prince of Wales poses for a picture in a kilt with British model David Gandy ahead of the 2016 inaugural Dumfries House Wool Conference in Scotland.

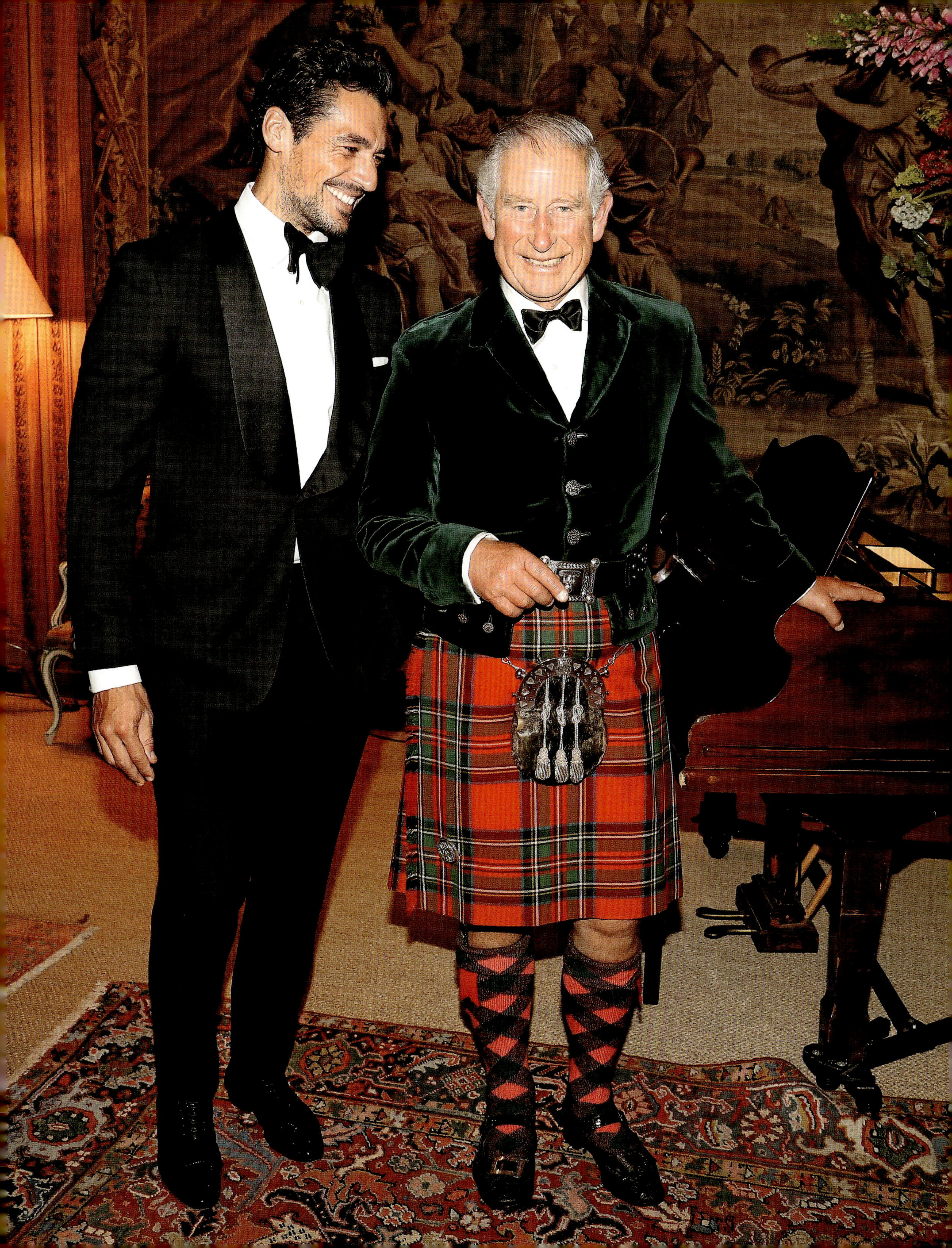

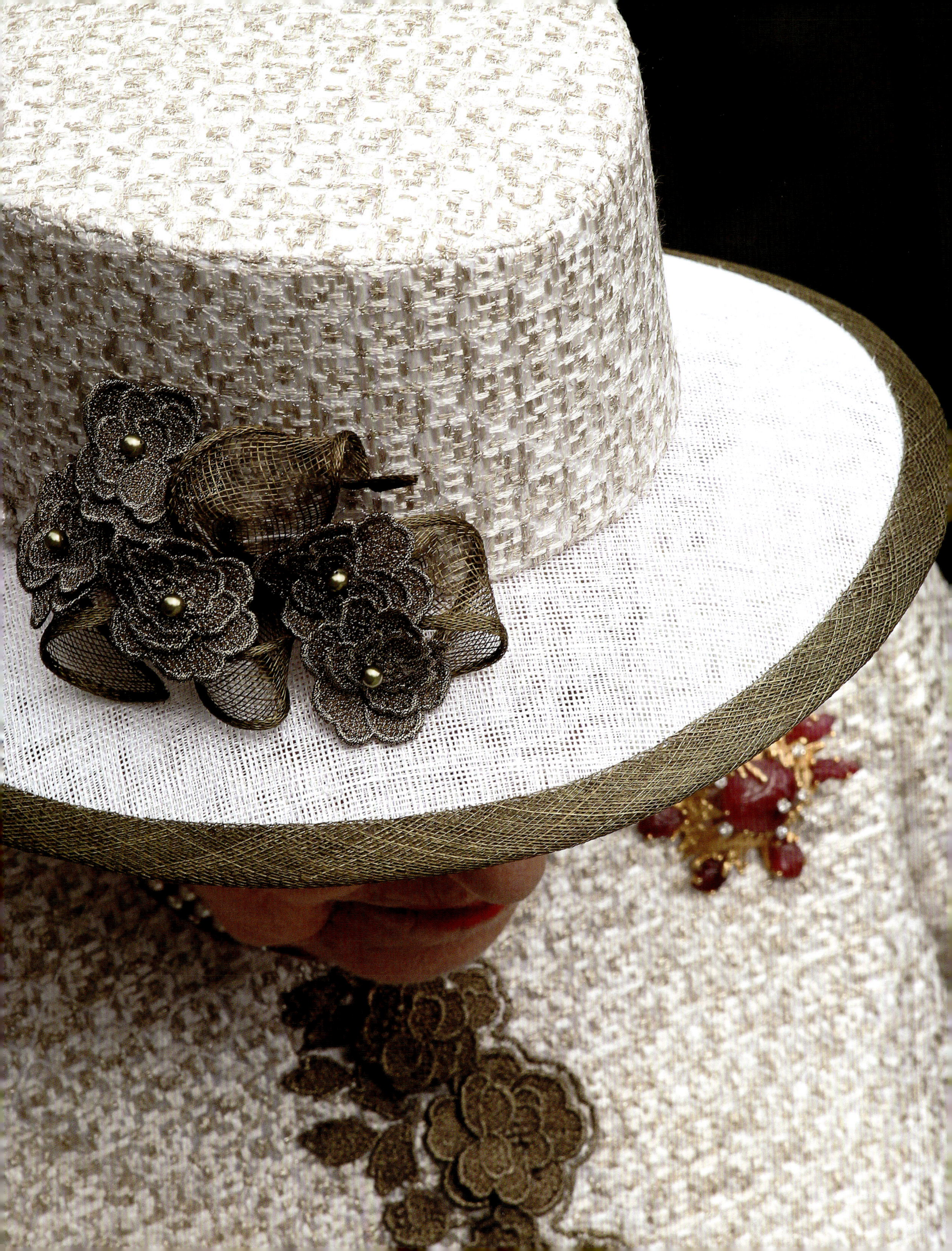

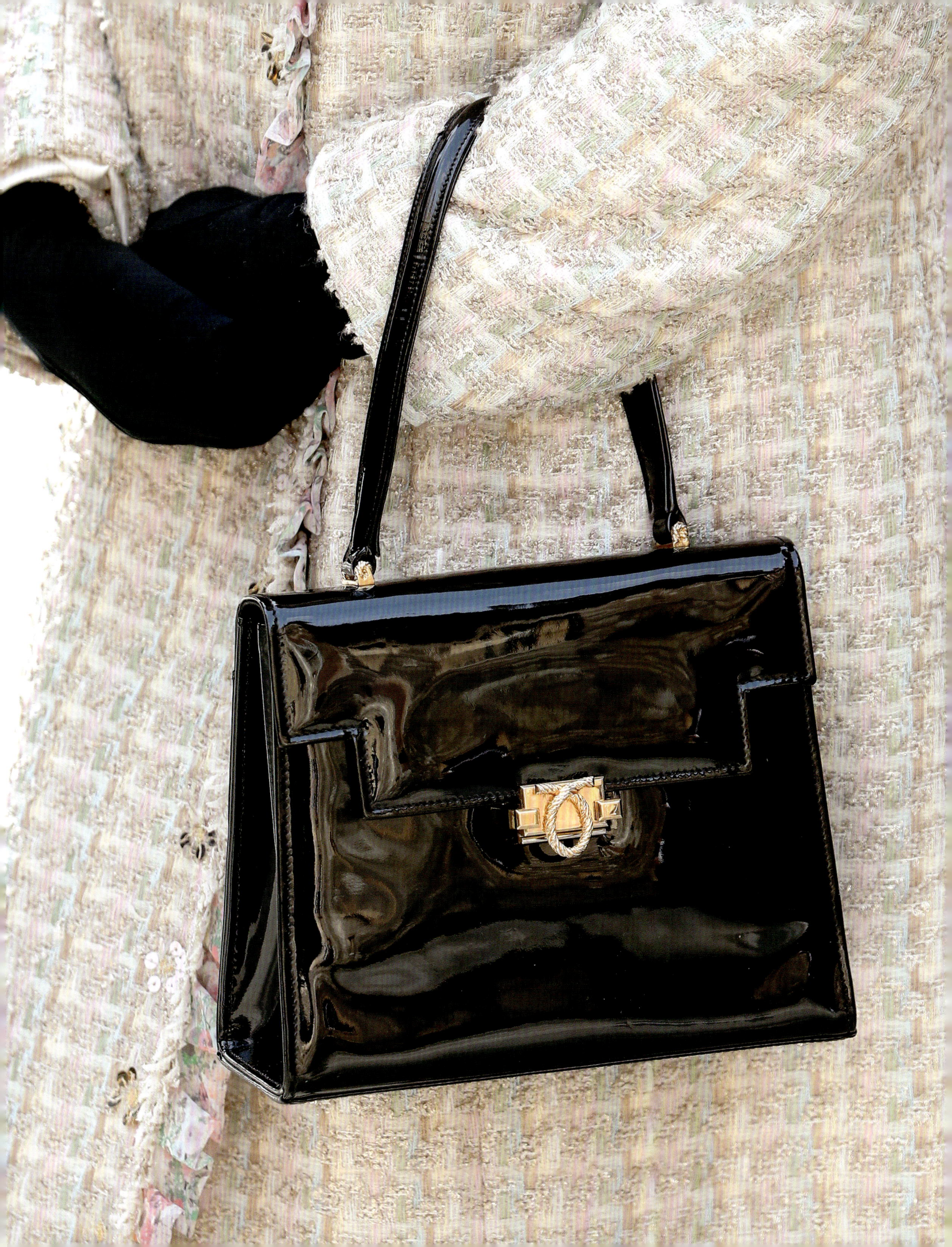

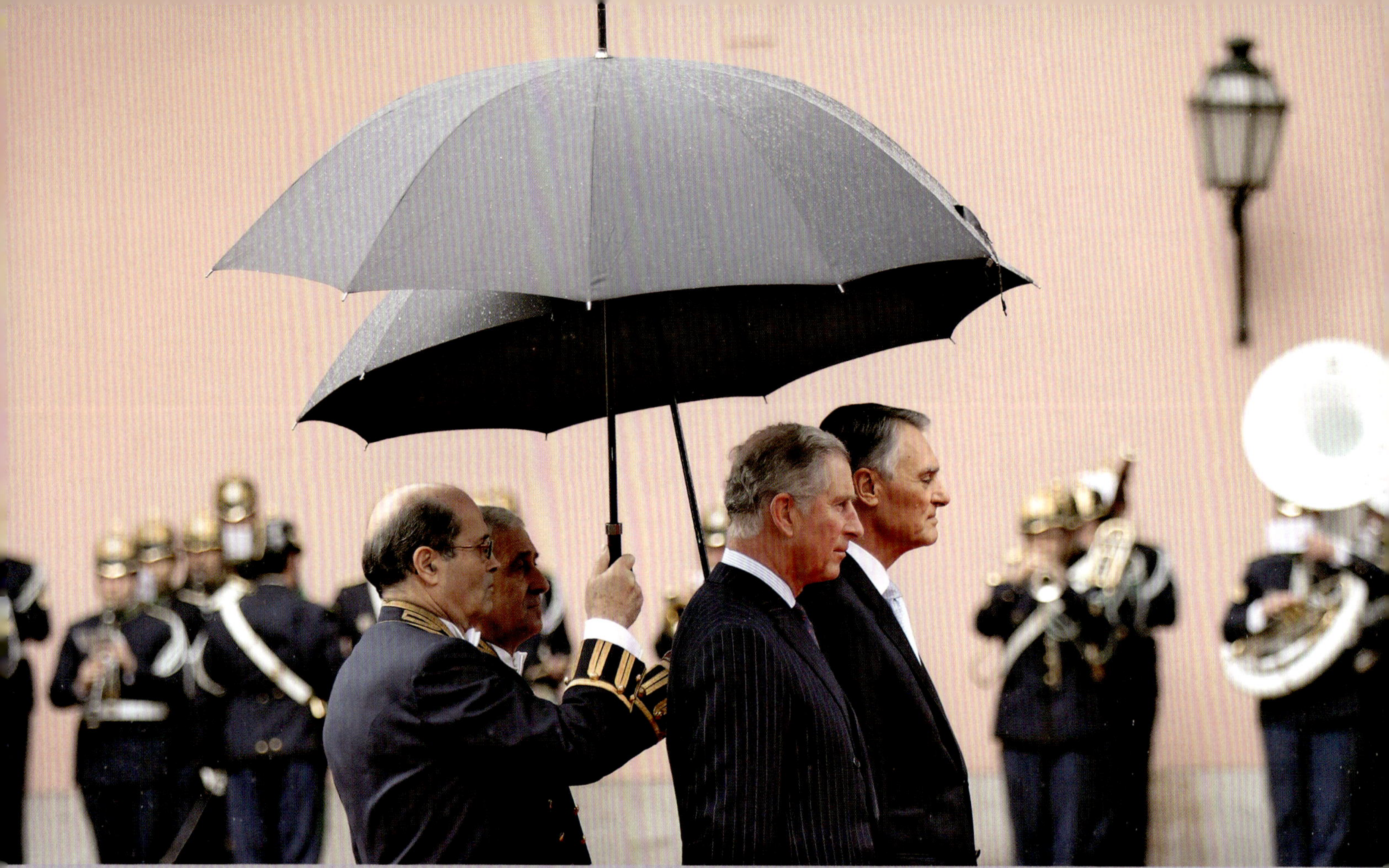

The show must always go on for the royals, wherever they are and whatever the weather. Consequently, a trusty umbrella forms an integral part of the royal fashion armoury and is regularly deployed in our British climate! For a photographer, an umbrella is often an obstacle to a good image, as it throws shadow over a subject's face, but occasionally an umbrella makes the shot a little bit special.

Opposite The best of British summertime as the Duchess of Cambridge emerges from Kensington Palace to visit the Sunken Garden in a deluge.

Above Prince Charles, Prince of Wales, and Aníbal Cavaco Silva, president of Portugal, shelter under an umbrella at Belém Palace in Lisbon in 2011, day one of a two-day visit to the country.

Below, left A well-coordinated Queen at Ascot.

Below, right The Duchess of Cornwall laughs as her neighbour suffers an umbrella malfunction during V-E Day sixty-fifth anniversary tributes at the Cenotaph in Whitehall.

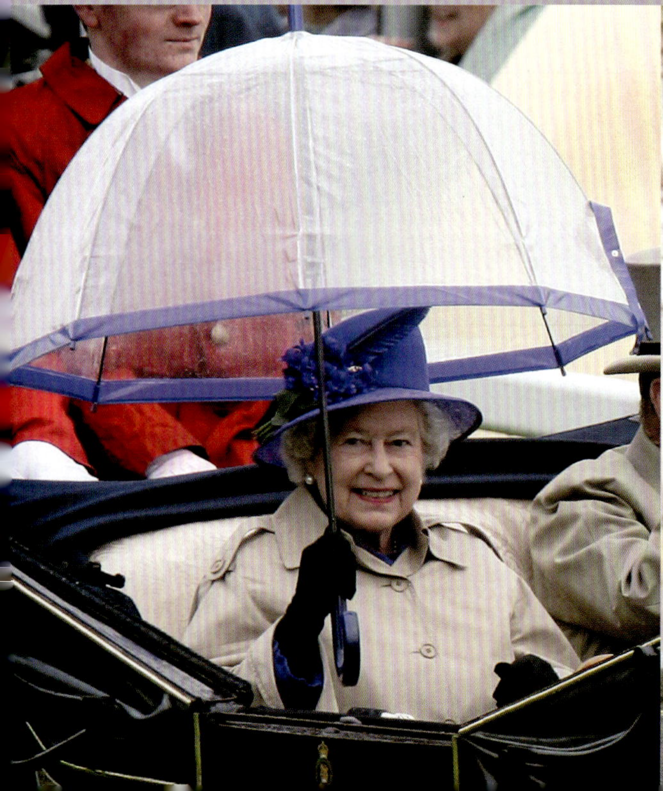

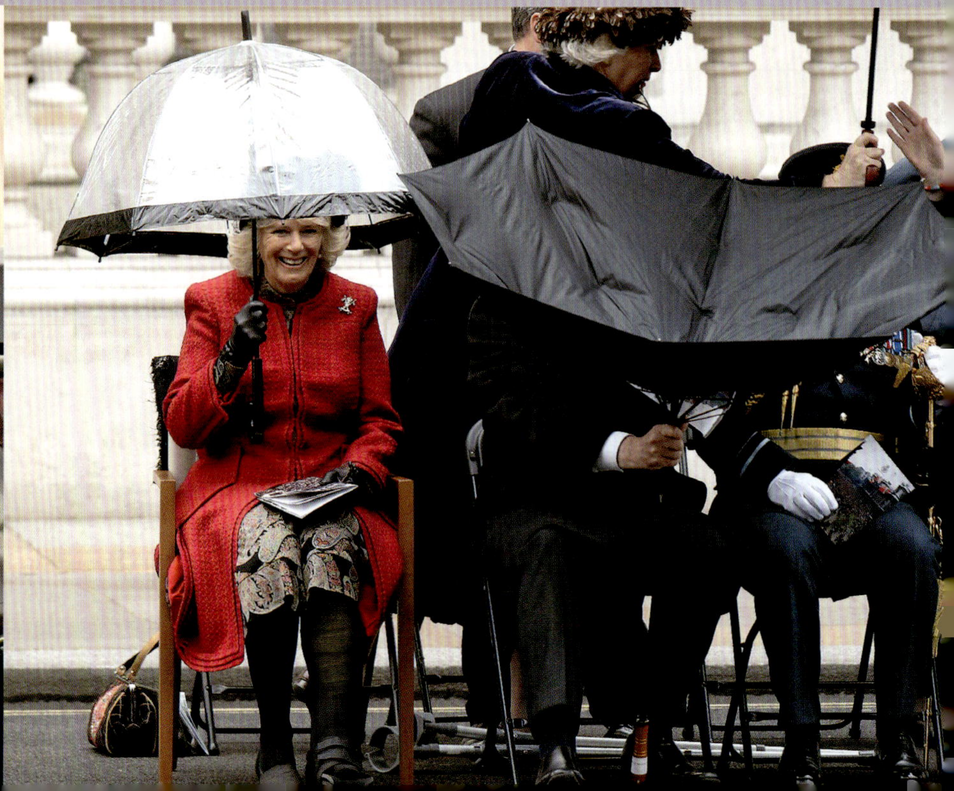

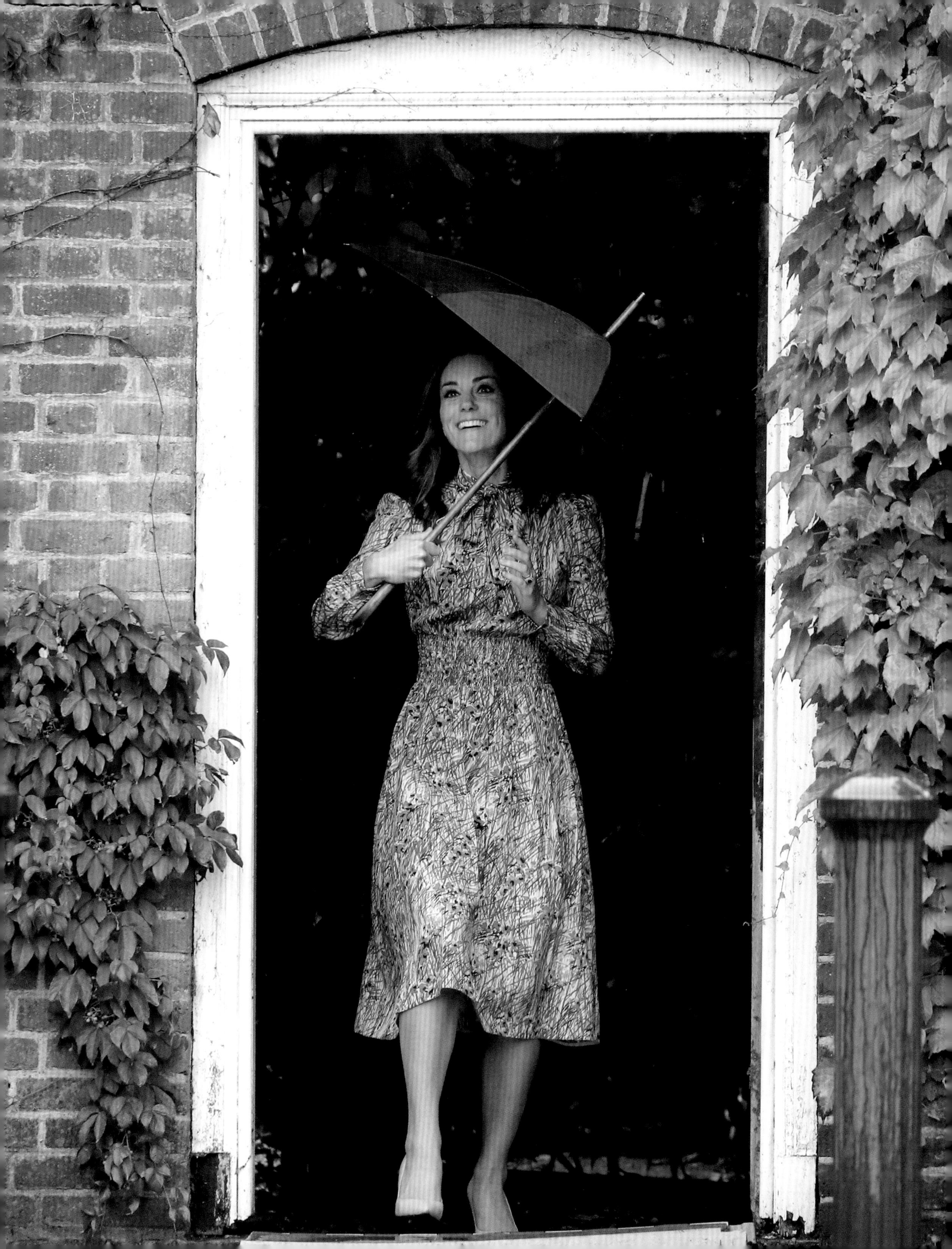

For the Love of Horses

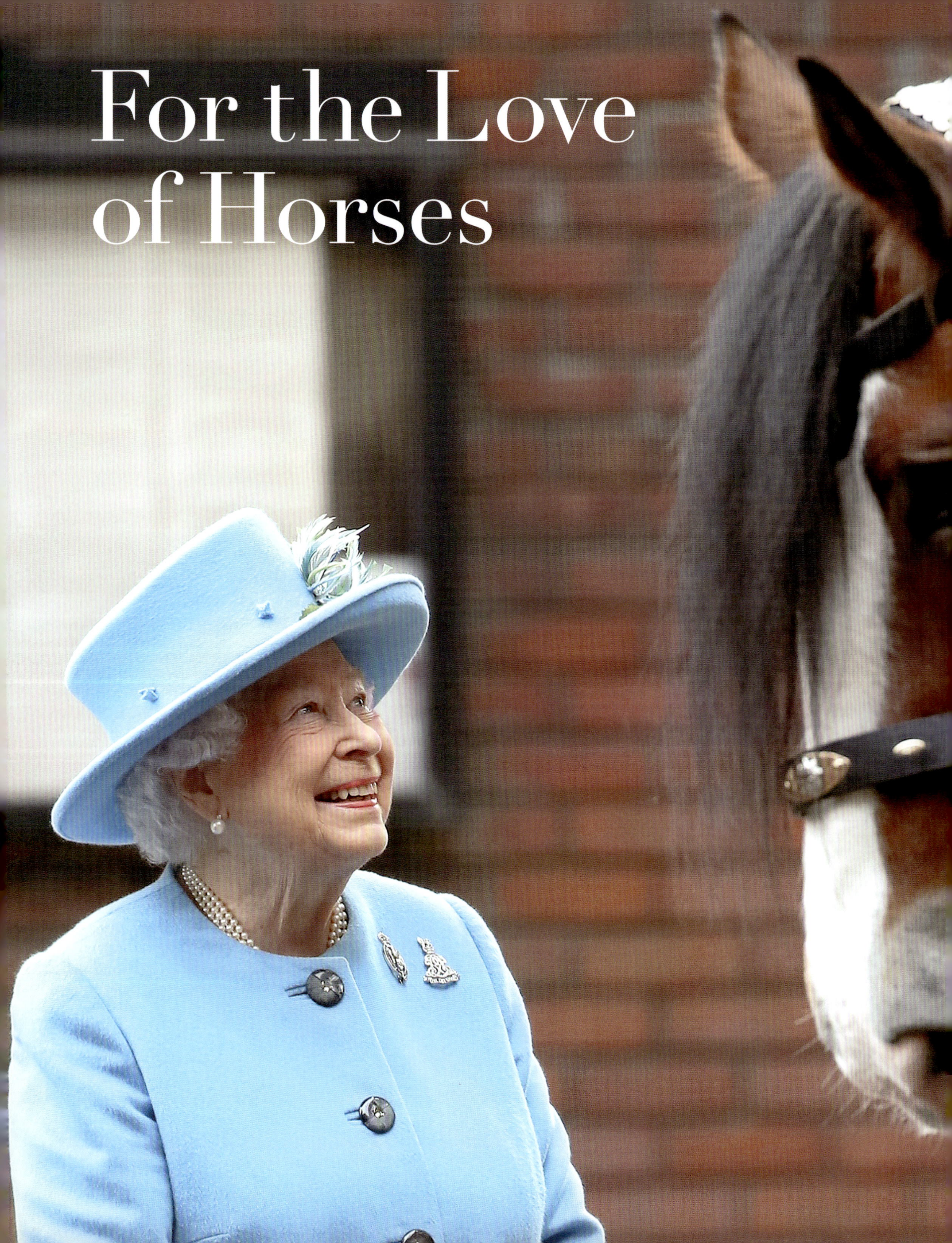

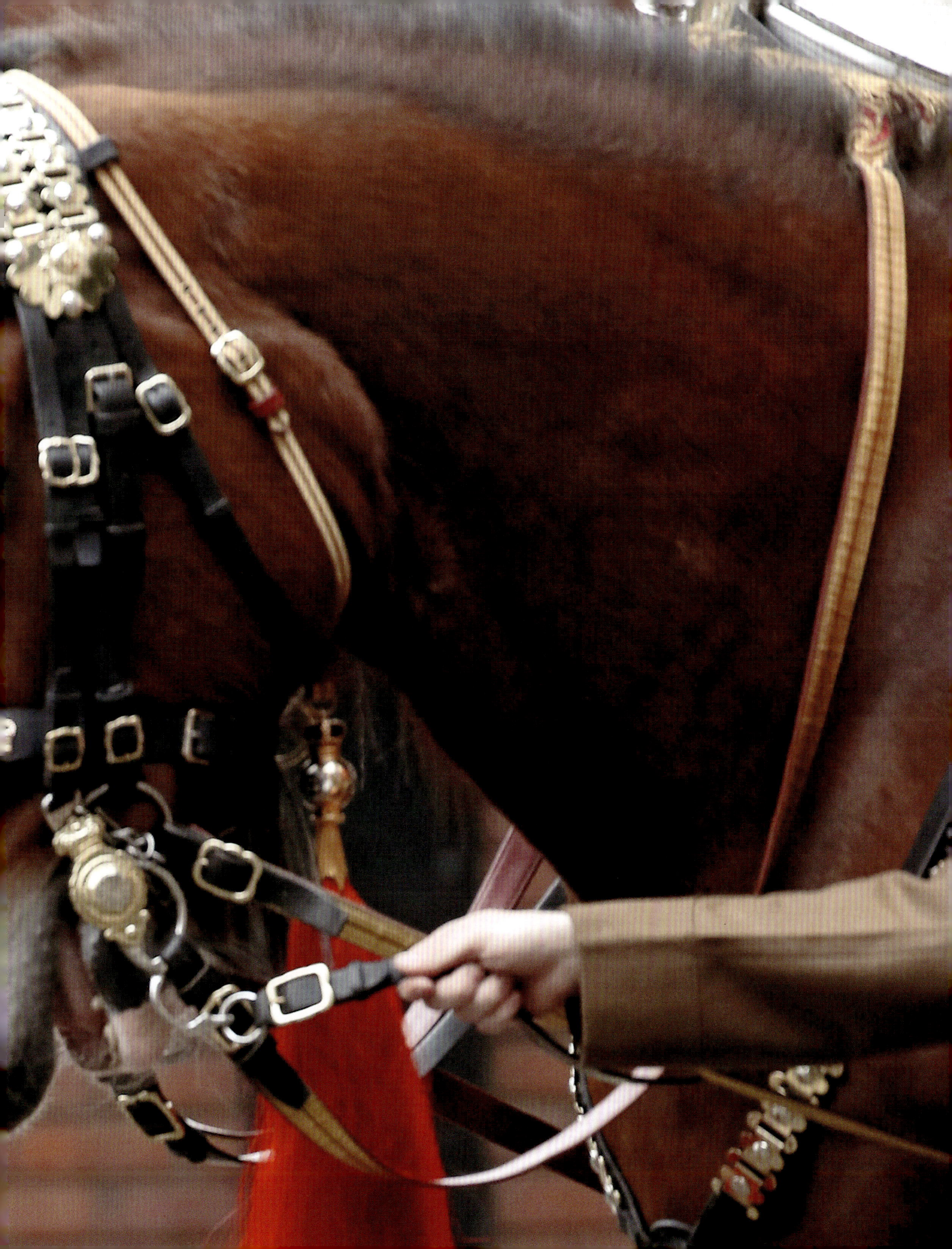

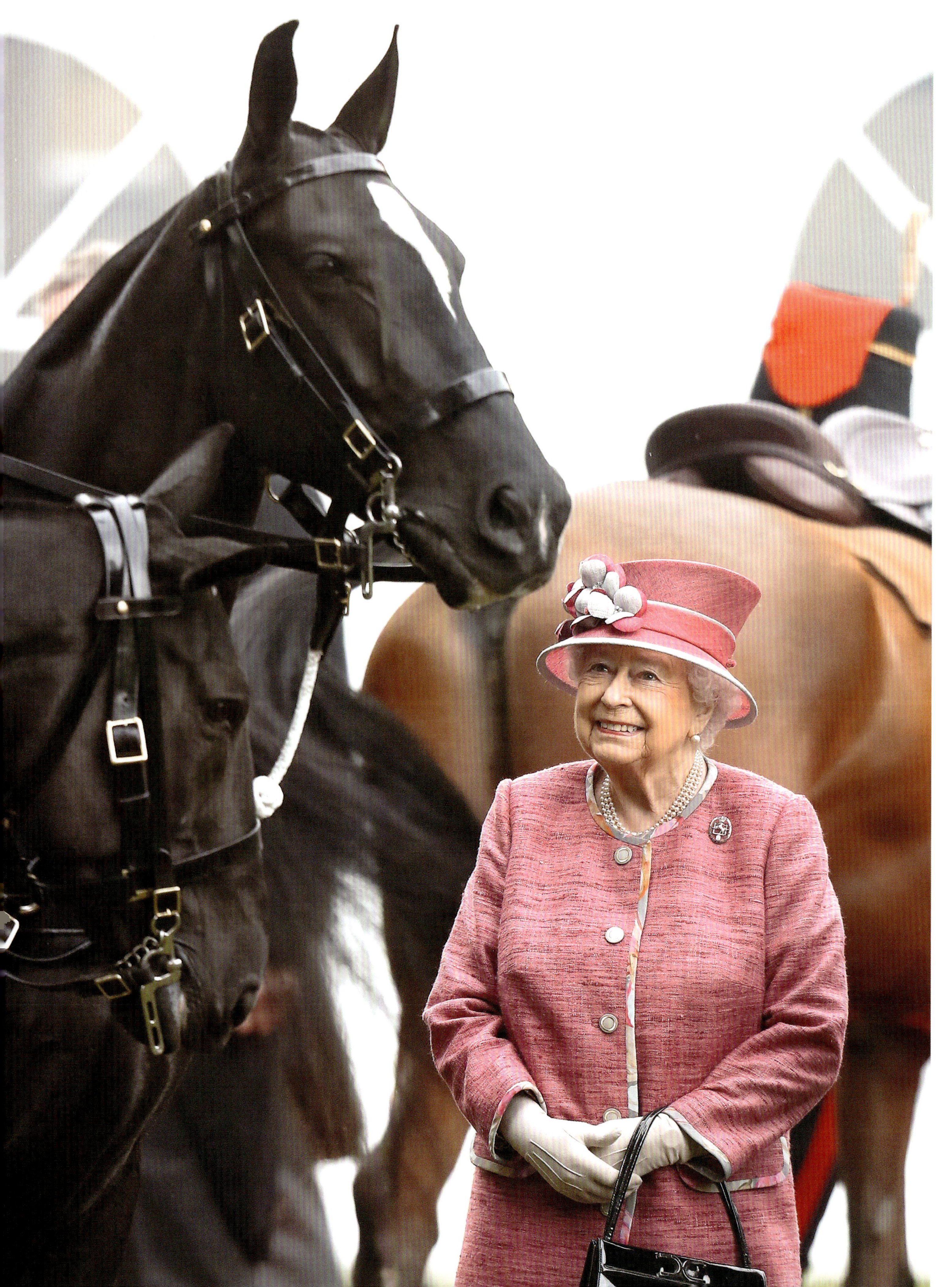

Horses form such a crucial part of life in today's royal family that it seemed only right a chapter should be dedicated to them. They play a ceremonial role at events such as Trooping the Colour, the Garter Ceremony, and the State Opening of Parliament. Carriage riding, eventing, and polo are all pastimes involving horses that members of the royal family perform at an incredibly high level. Zara Tindall became the first royal Olympic medal winner and was poignantly presented the silver medal by her mother, Princess Anne, during the 2012 London Olympics. Princess Anne, the only other royal to have competed in the Olympic Games, took part in the 1976 games in Montreal, missing out on a medal. Clearly a passion for horses runs in the blood. The Queen relishes anything horse-related, from enthusiastically watching the racing at Ascot to reviewing the King's Troop. When her horse Estimate charged to victory in the Ascot Gold Cup, she became the first reigning monarch in the over two-hundred-year history of the race to win the coveted award. The public cheered her horse with memorable and patriotic enthusiasm, and the look on her face as she was handed the trophy was one of pure happiness.

Formality and sporting events aside, there can be nothing more evocative than images of Princes William and Harry galloping across the Lesothan mountaintops in South Africa during a charity visit a few years ago. Both accomplished horsemen and wearing traditional Lesothan blankets, the setting these two brothers found themselves in was a million miles away from the formality and pomp of their ceremonial duties at Trooping the Colour.

The Queen's passion for anything equine extends to their training and wellbeing. It was a special afternoon when I was given the opportunity to photograph the Duchess of Cornwall and the Queen being given a private demonstration by the legendary horse whisperer Monty Roberts at the Royal Mews. Roberts was the inspiration for the eponymous 1998 film starring Robert Redford and has become globally famous due to his innovative training techniques. The Queen is a huge fan of Roberts' work and it was evident by the warm welcome he was given at the palace.

Preceding pages The Queen meets the Household Cavalry's drum horse Perseus during a visit to the Household Cavalry Mounted Regiment at Hyde Park Barracks, home to the Blues and Royals and Life Guards who provide the Queen's mounted escort.

Opposite Reviewing the King's Troop Royal Horse Artillery on its seventieth anniversary in Hyde Park in 2017.

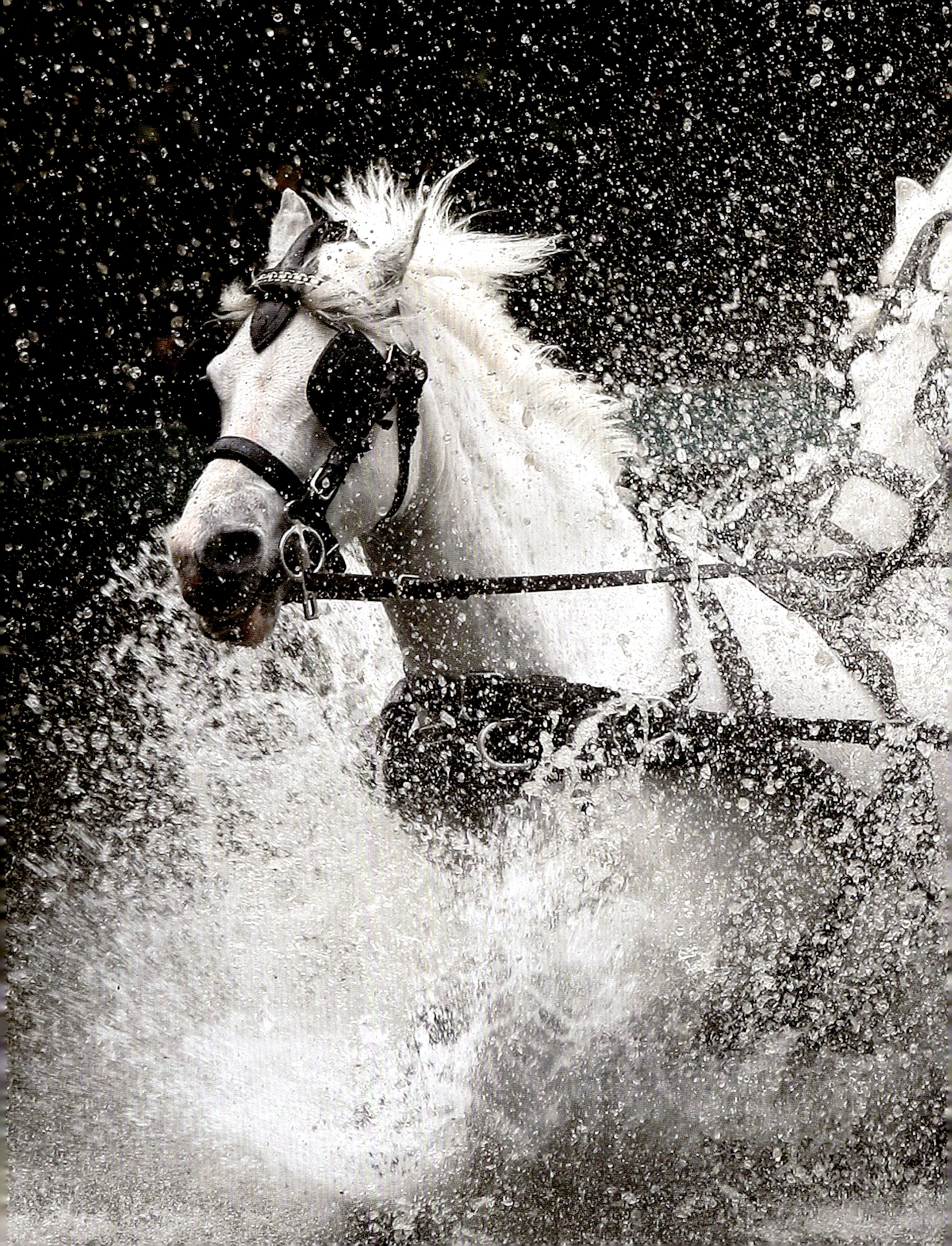

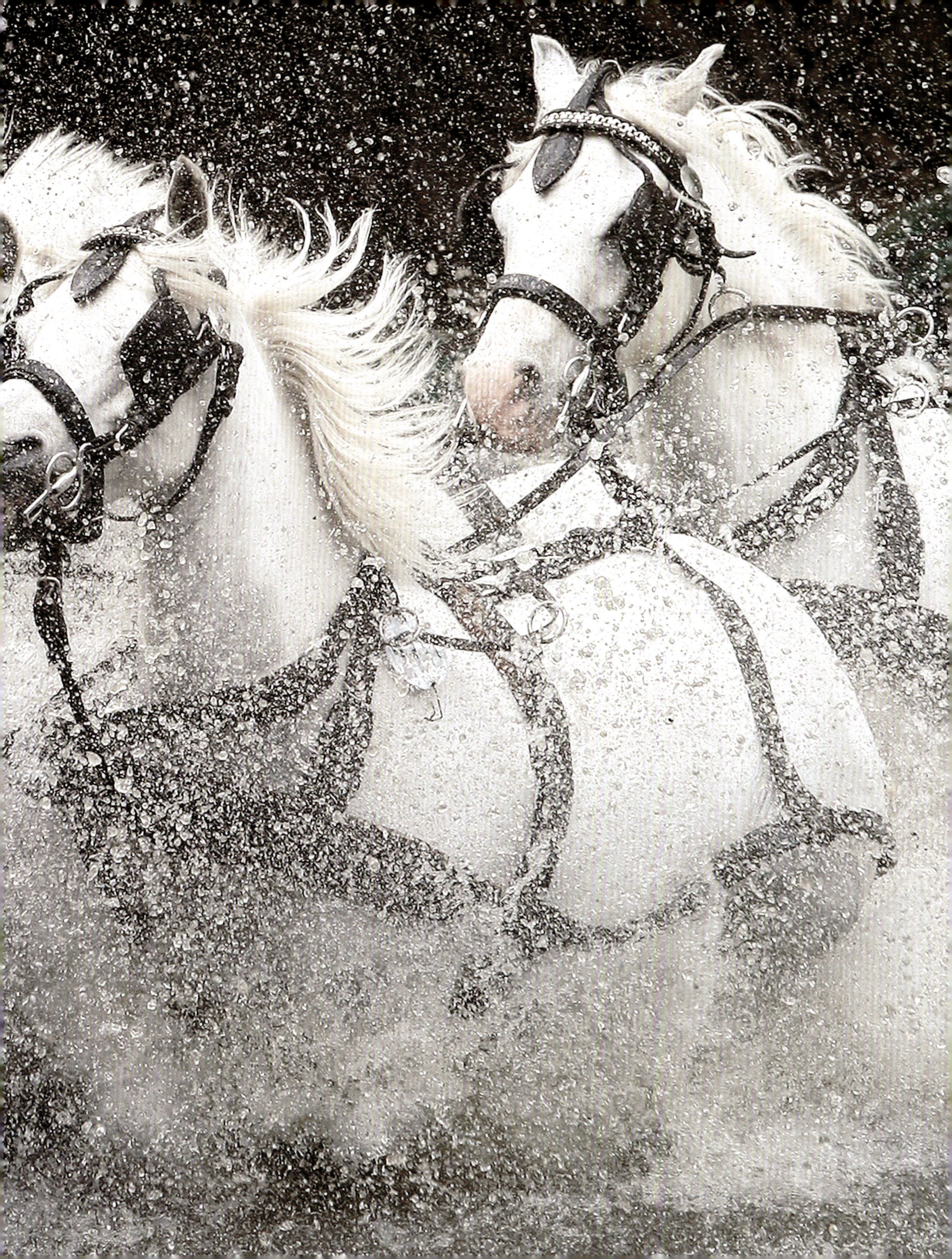

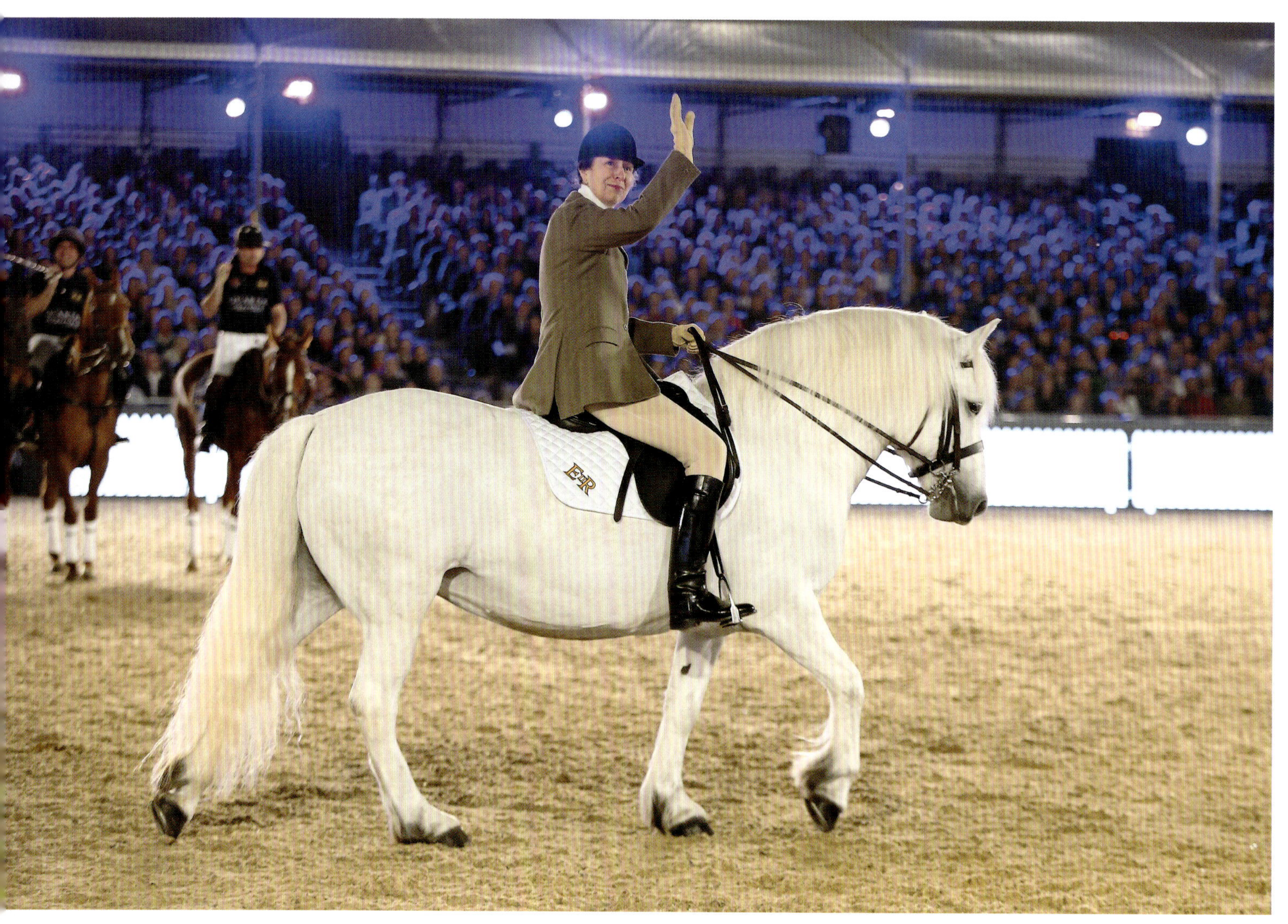

Preceding pages Horses charge the river section of the obstacle course at the Royal Windsor Horse Show as part of the carriage riding competition.

Above Princess Anne waves to her mother, the Queen, on the final night of the Queen's ninetieth birthday celebrations during a gala event in Windsor Great Park on May 15, 2016.

Opposite Zara Phillips (now Zara Tindall) poses for a photograph with her horse Toytown at Burghley Horse Trials. Phillips went on to have great success with Toytown, who was officially retired from competition on the final day of the 2011 Festival of British Eventing at Gatcombe Park.

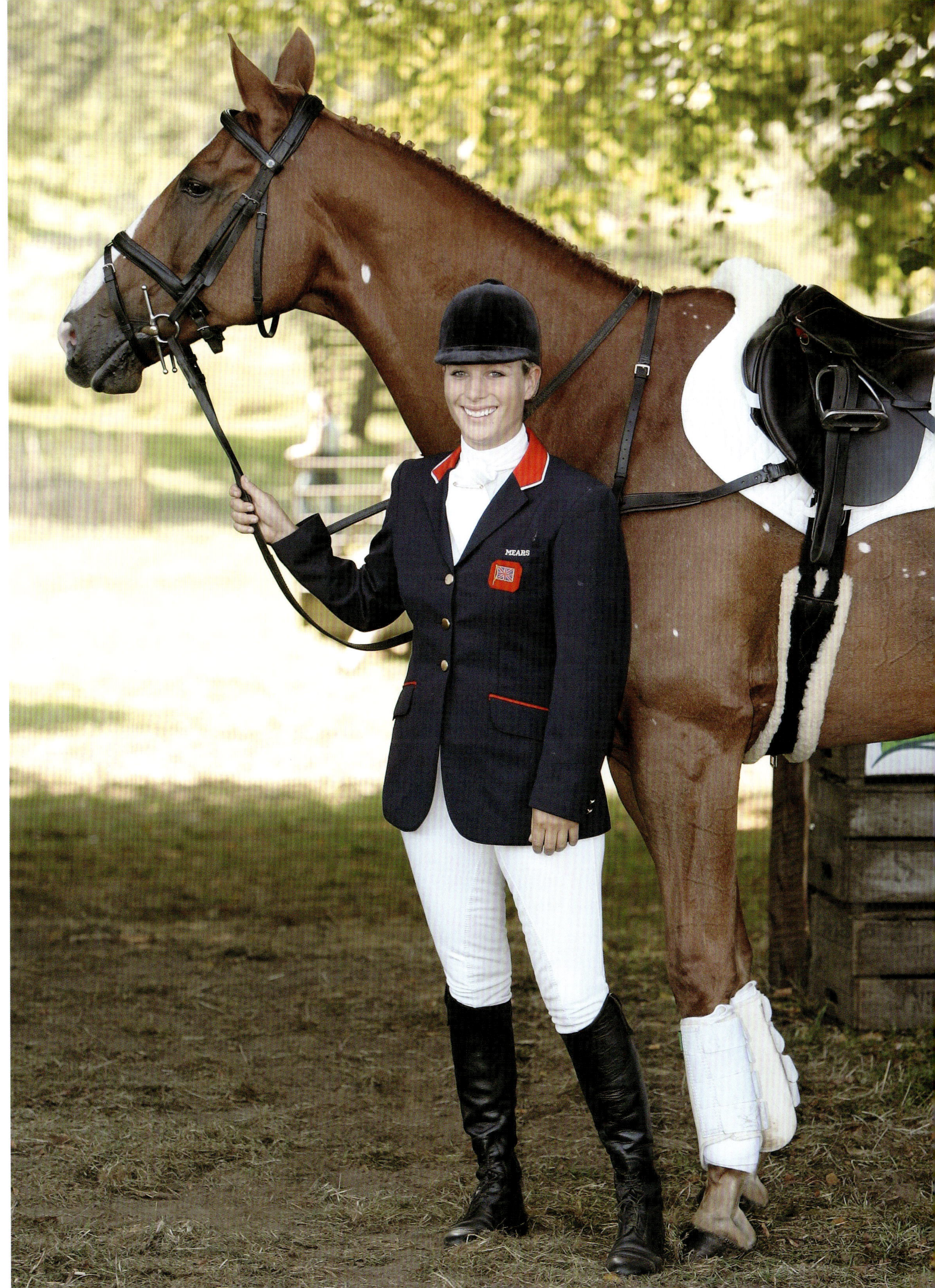
MEARS

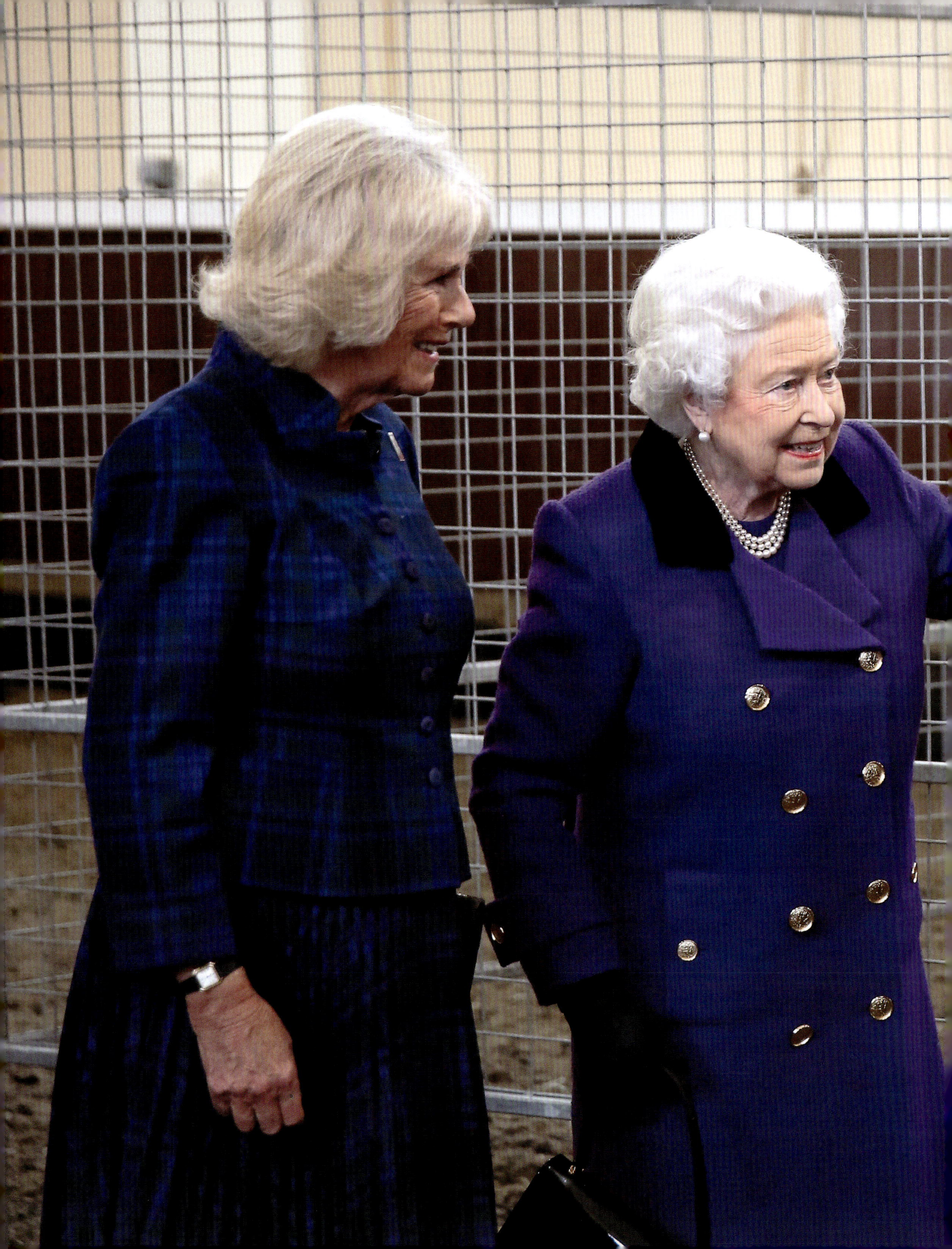

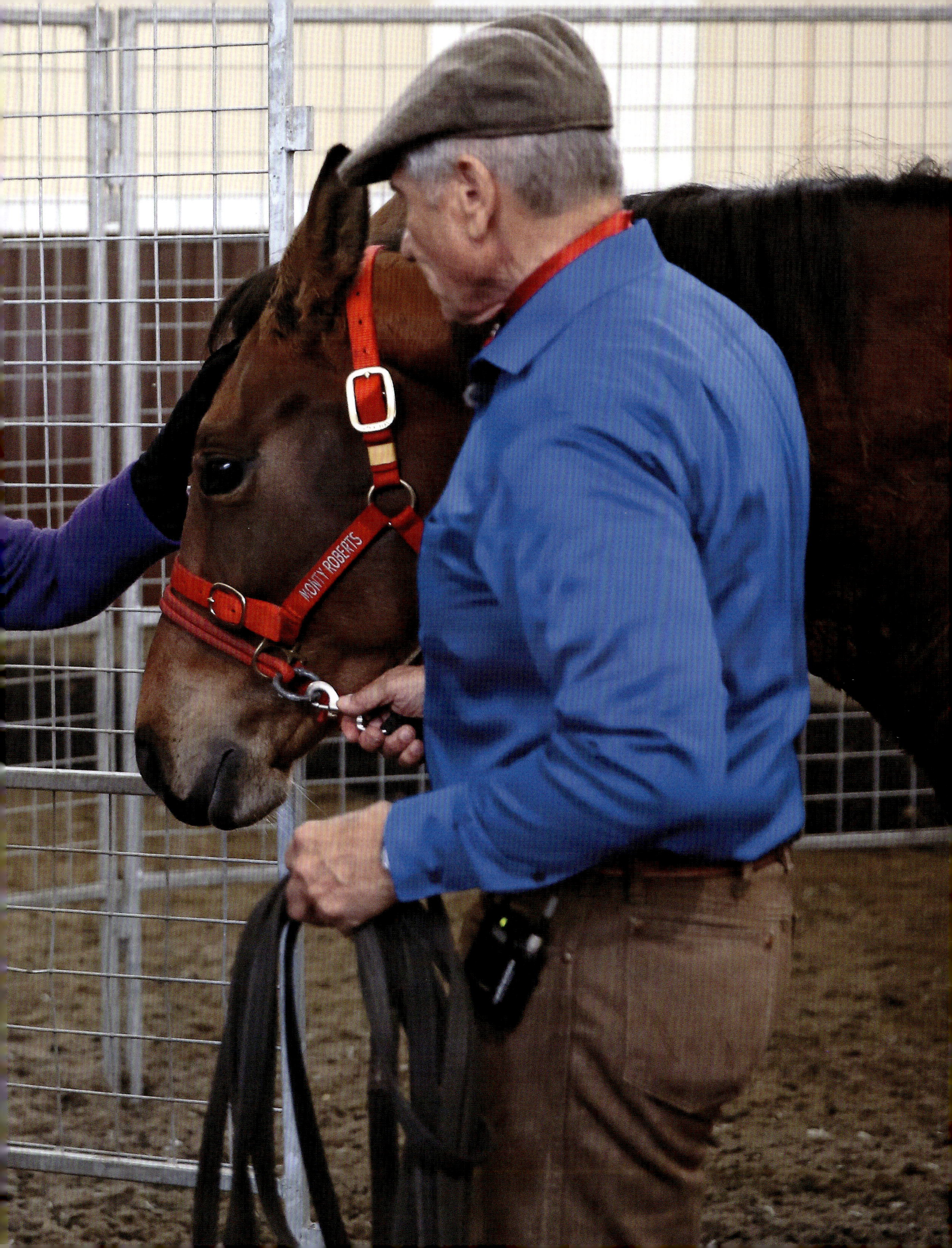
MONTY ROBERTS

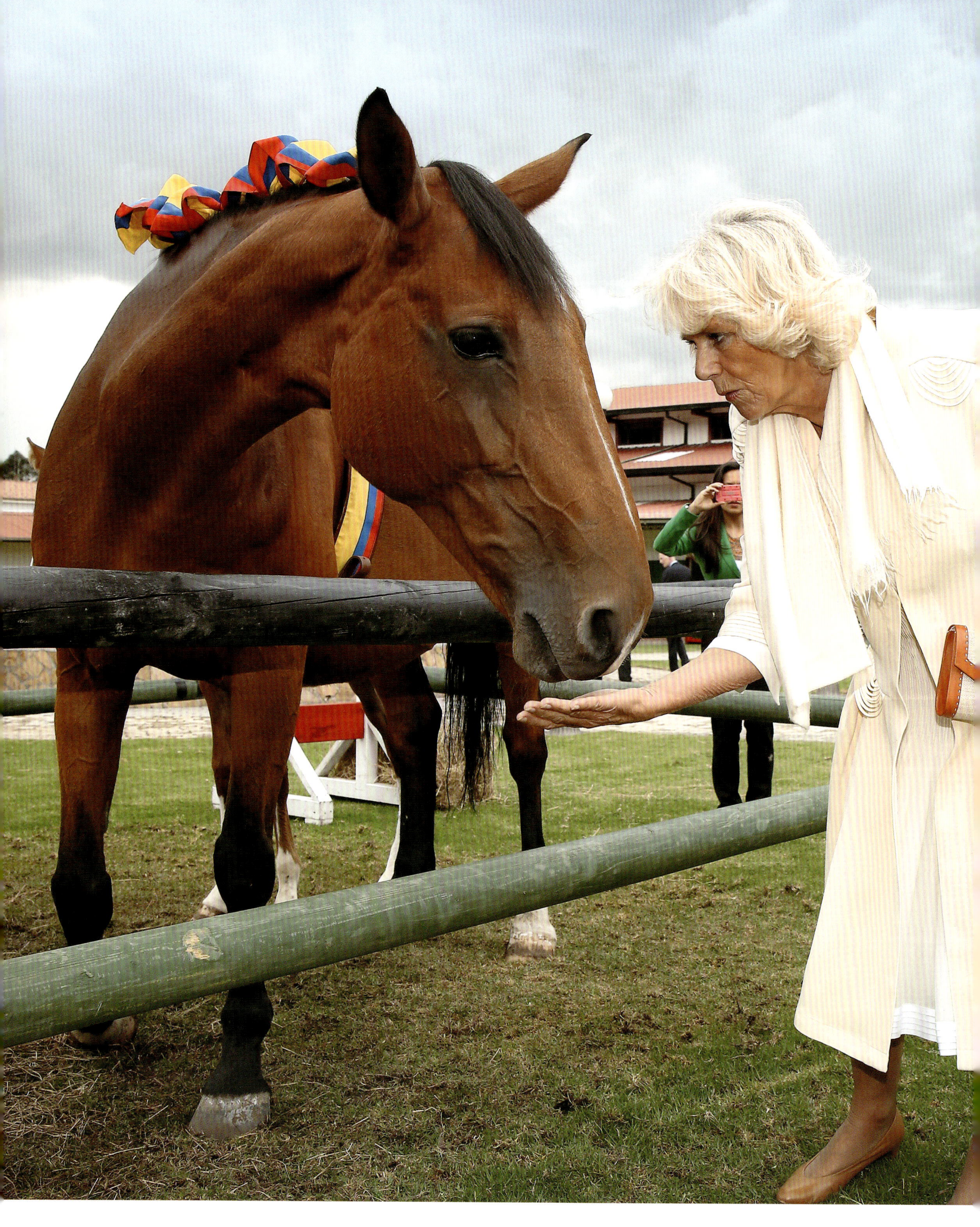

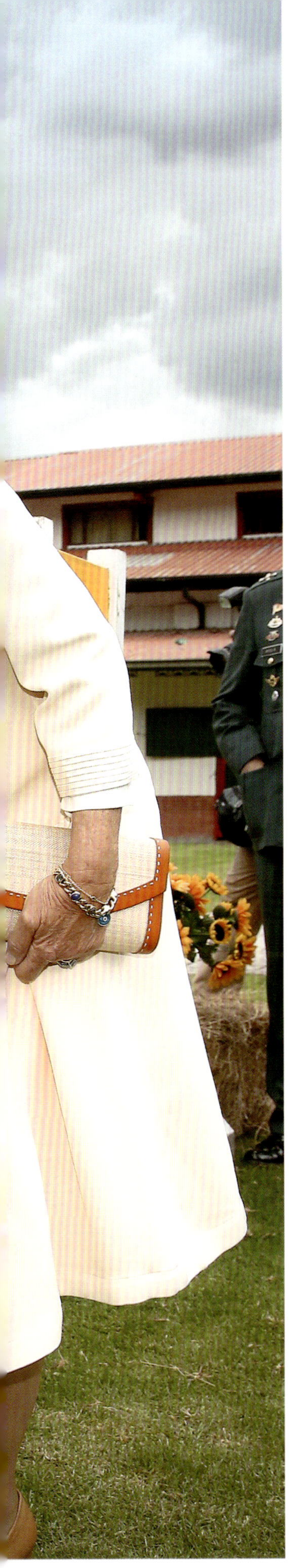

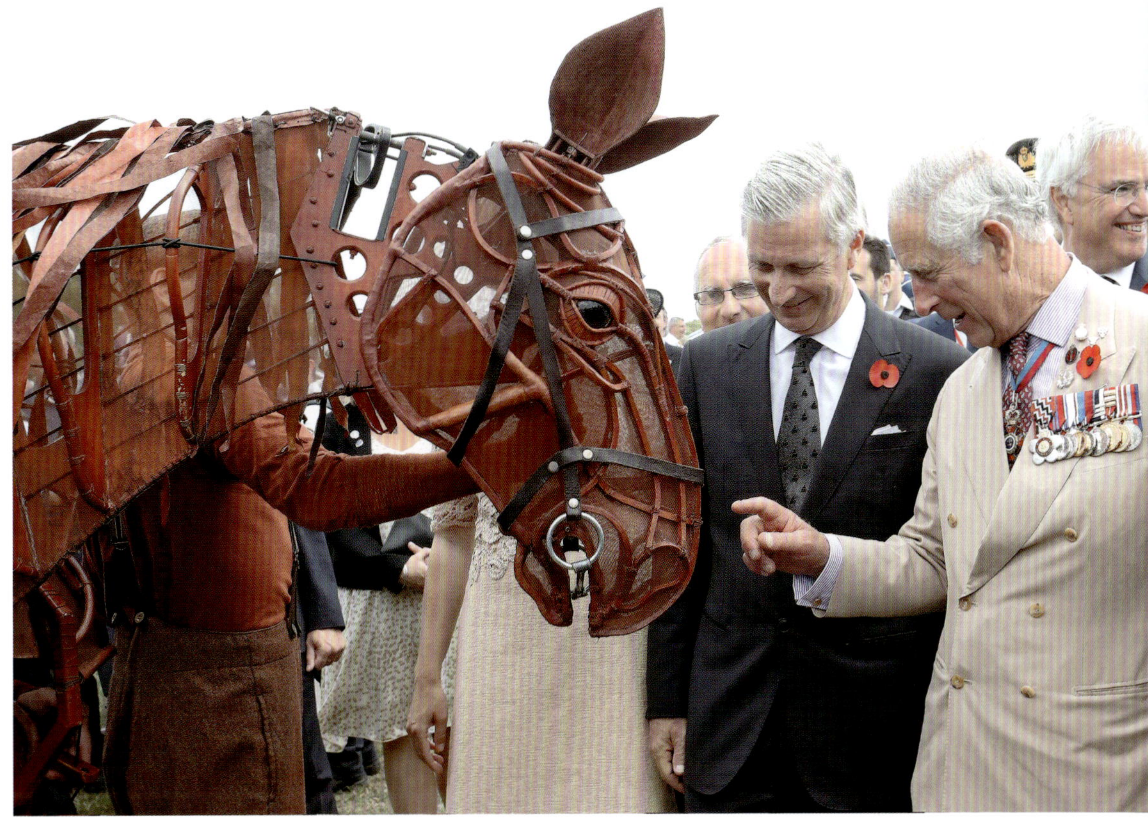

Preceding pages Camilla, Duchess of Cornwall, and the Queen attend a horse-whispering demonstration by Brooke global ambassador and legendary horse whisperer Monty Roberts at the Royal Mews, Buckingham Palace.

Opposite The Duchess of Cornwall meets horses at the Escuela de Caballería of the Colombian military in Bogotá. In 2014 the Prince of Wales and Duchess of Cornwall were on a four-day visit to Colombia as part of a royal tour that also took them to Mexico.

Above King Philippe of Belgium and Prince Charles, with War Horse during their visit to Passchendaele Memorial Park near Ypres, Belgium to meet families and descendants of those who fought and fell during the war.

Following pages Detail of the saddle of a member of the Queen's Life Guard at Trooping the Colour.

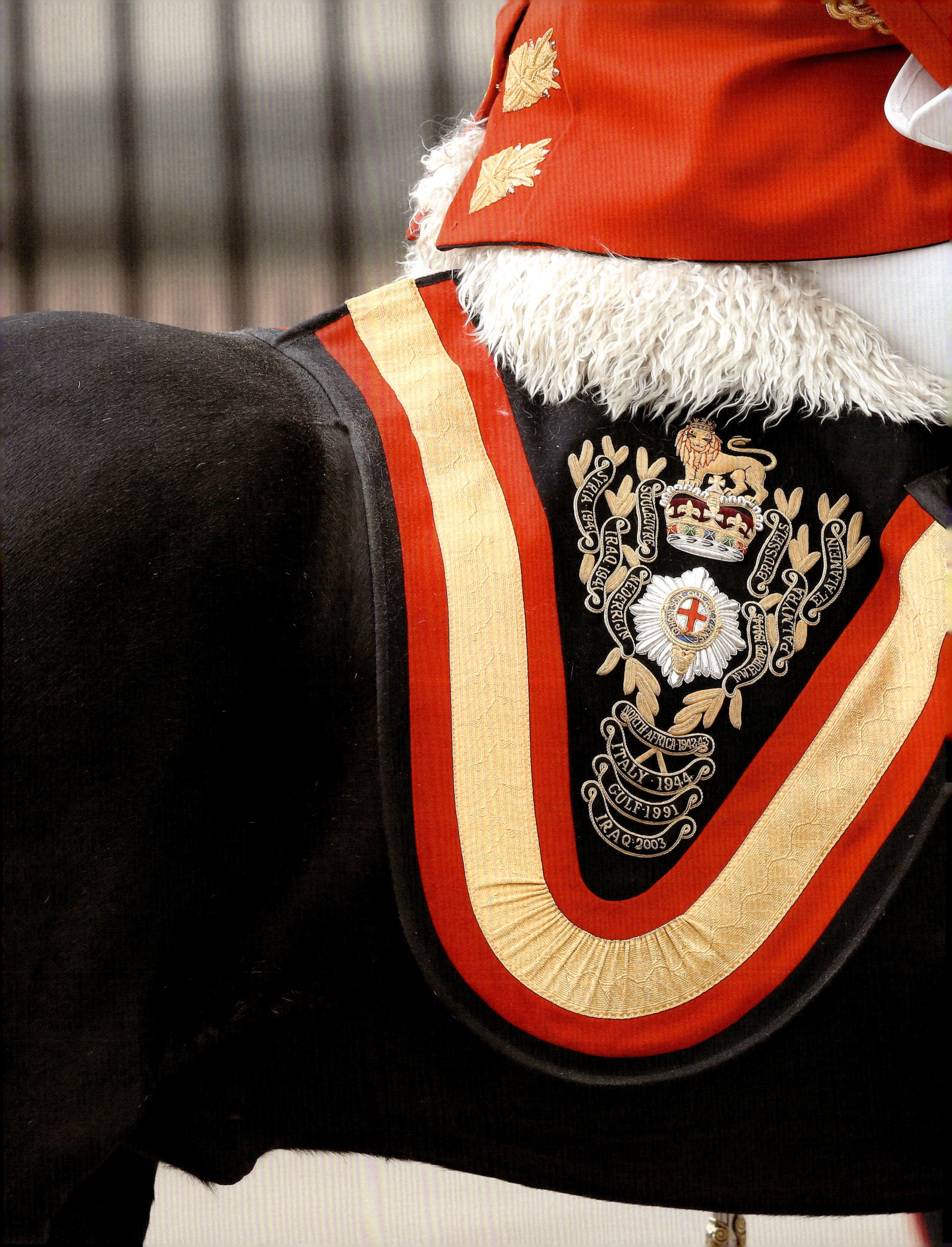
SYRIA 1941
SOULEUVRE
IRAQ 1941
NEDERRIJN
BRUSSELS
EL ALAMEIN
PALMYRA
N.W. EUROPE 1944-45
NORTH AFRICA 1942-43
ITALY 1944
GULF 1991
IRAQ 2003

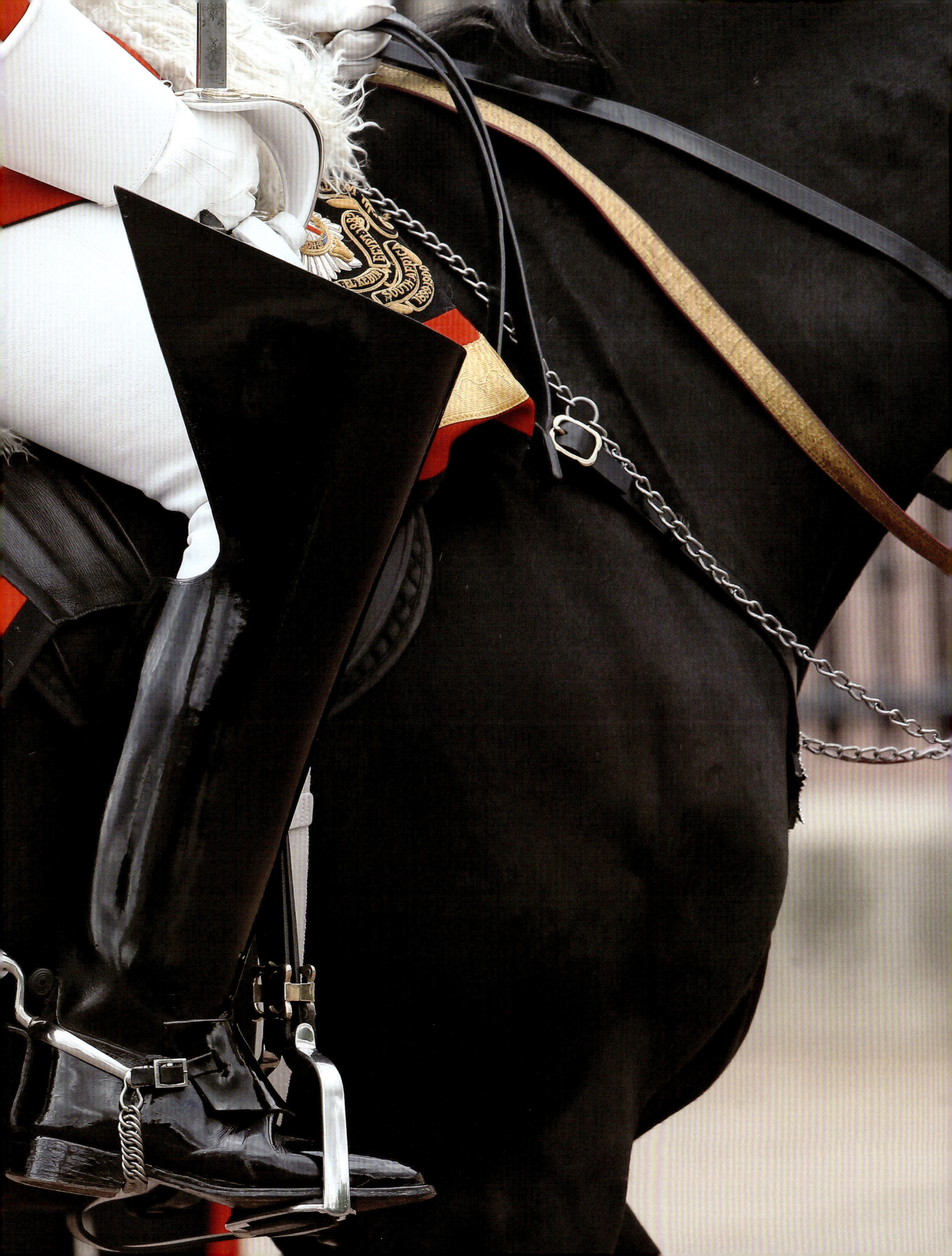
SOUTH AFRICA
1899-1900

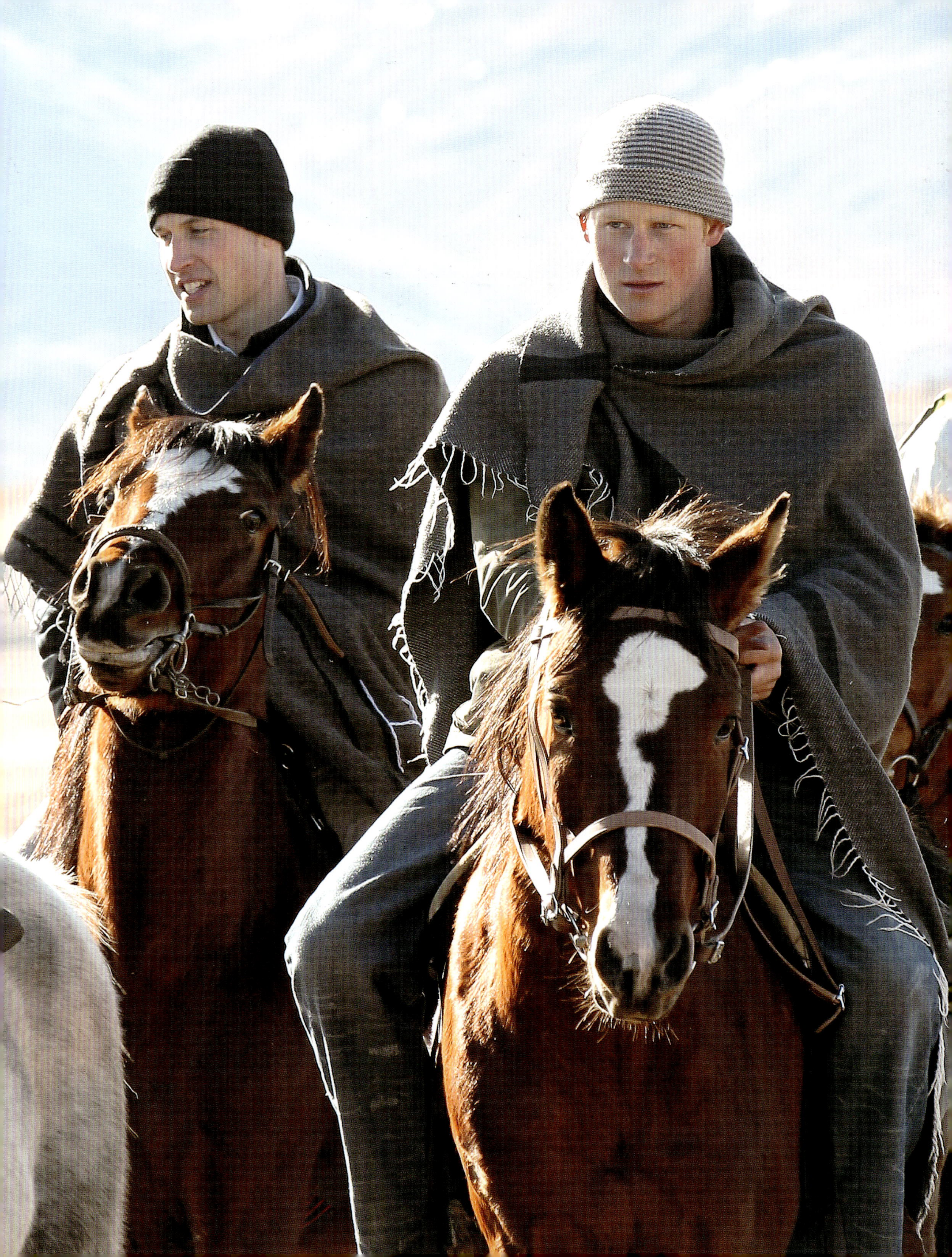

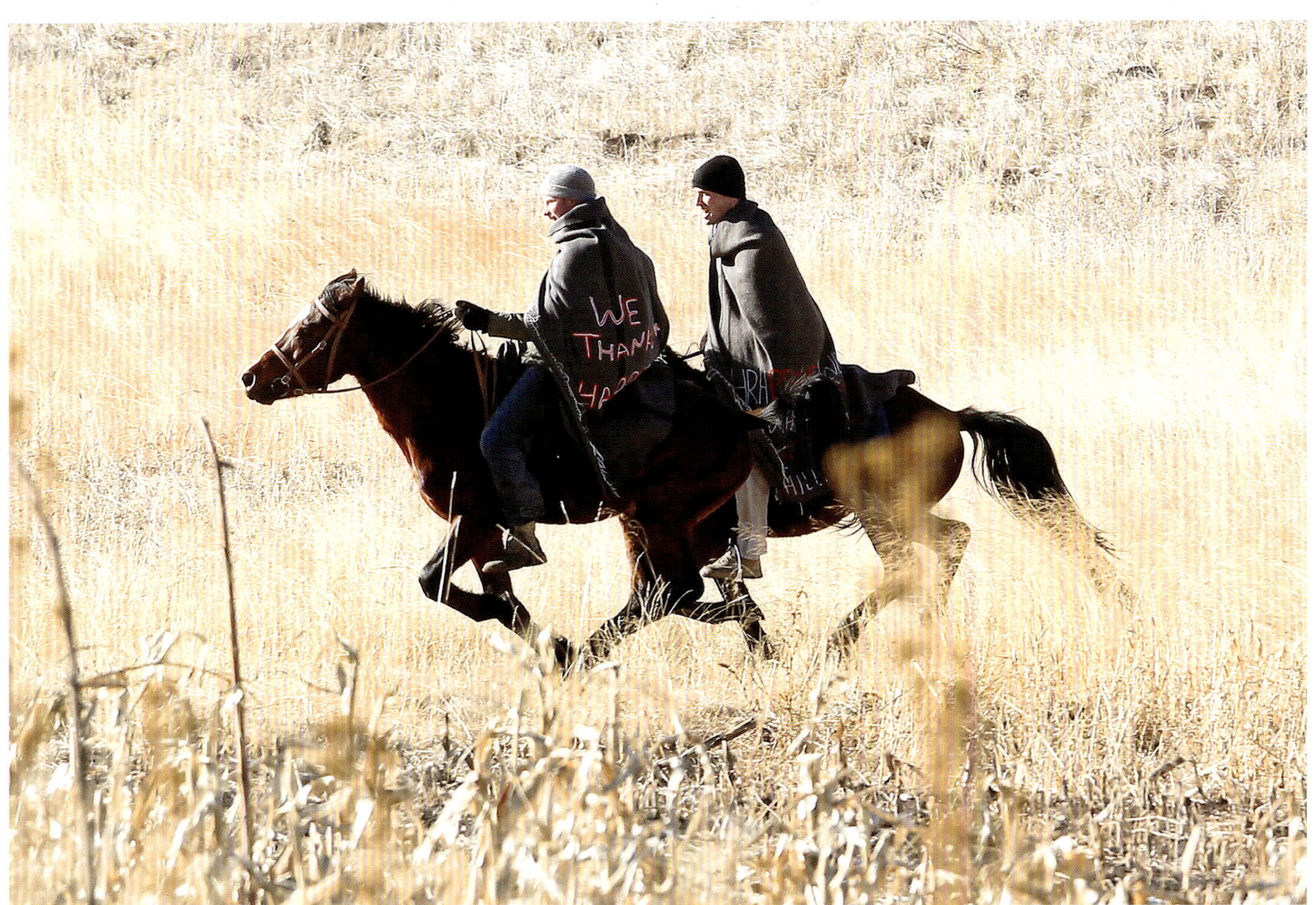

Opposite and this page Prince Harry and Prince William ride across the plains of the African mountain kingdom of Lesotho during a charity visit. Both princes were visiting the landlocked African country to see the work of Prince Harry's charity Sentebale. They were fresh from a visit to Botswana, where they witnessed the work done by Tusk Trust, the umbrella conservation charity for which the Duke of Cambridge is patron.

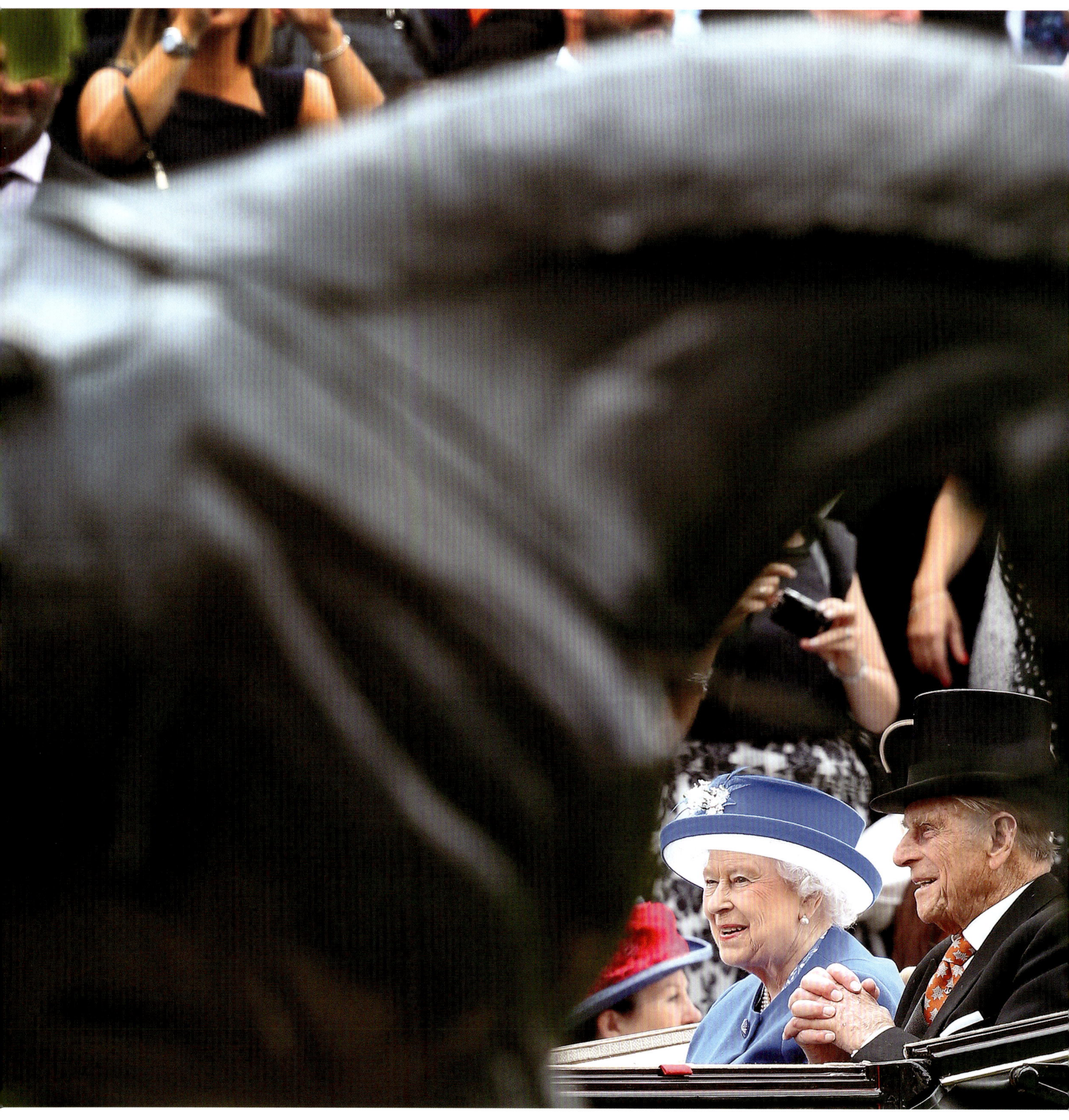

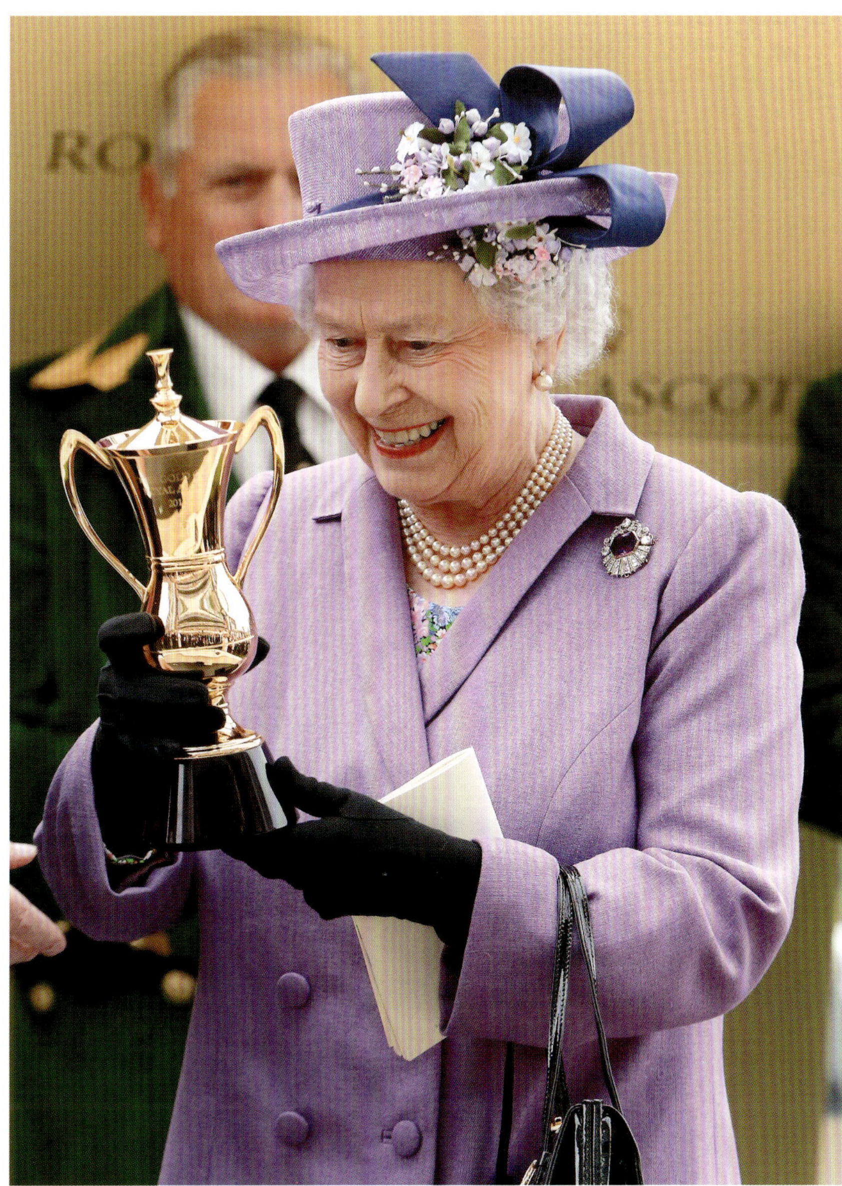

Opposite The Queen and the Duke of Edinburgh are seen through a statue of the legendary racehorse Frankel as they arrive at the parade on the second day of Royal Ascot in 2015.

Above It was a special moment for the Ascot crowd, and for the Queen when, in 2013, she became the first reigning monarch to win the prestigious race in its 207-year history. Here the Queen is presented with the Gold Cup, won by her horse Estimate on Ladies Day.

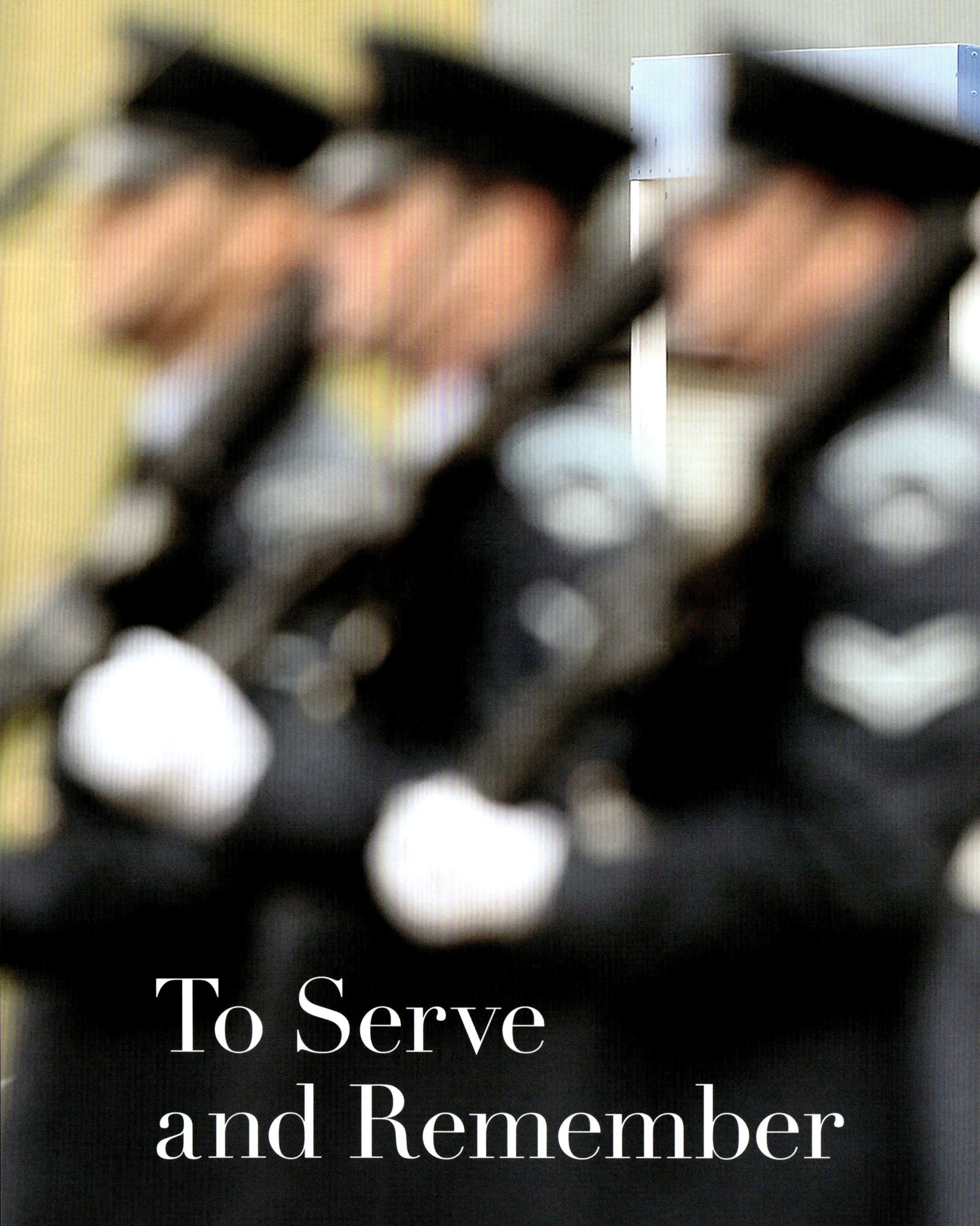

To Serve and Remember

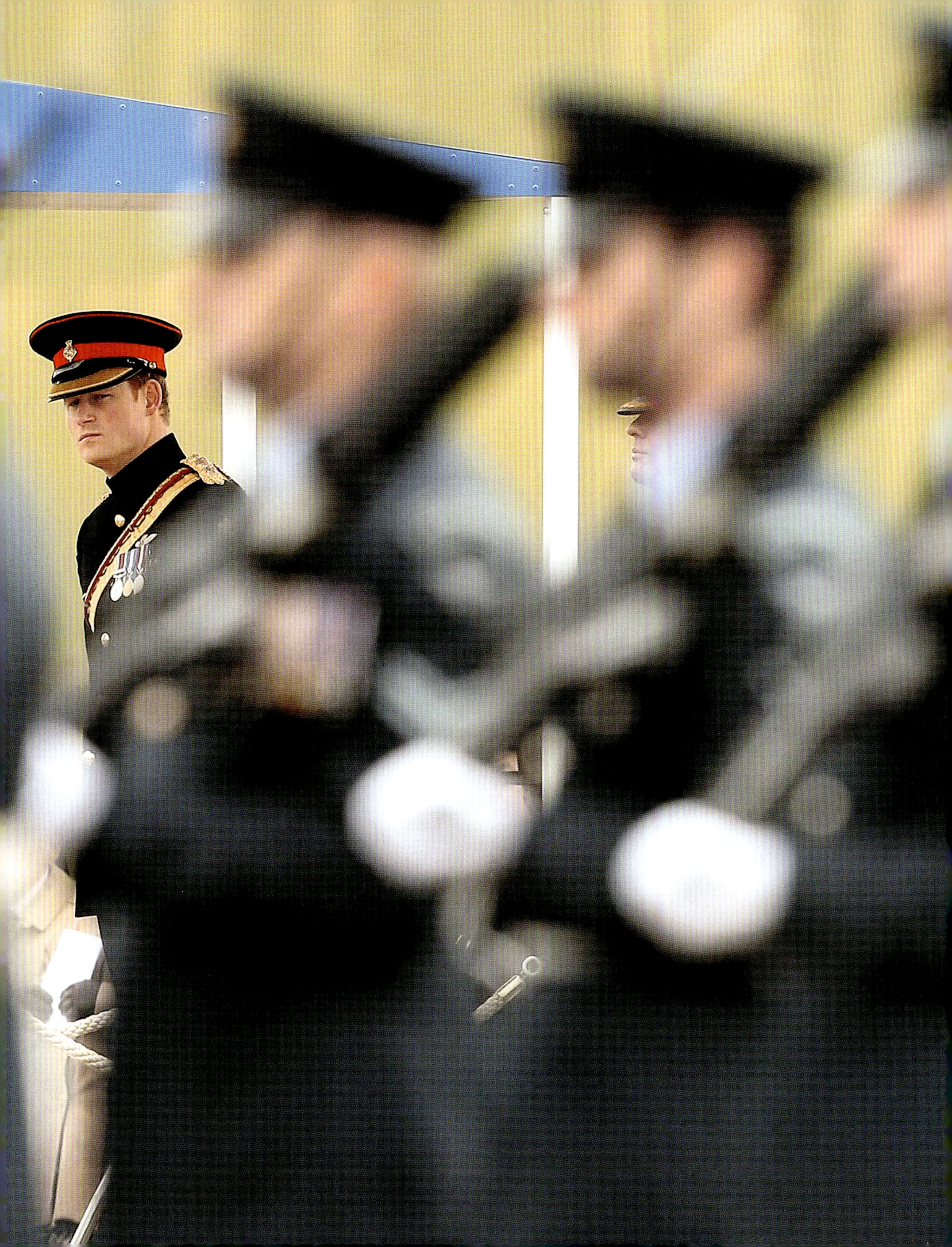

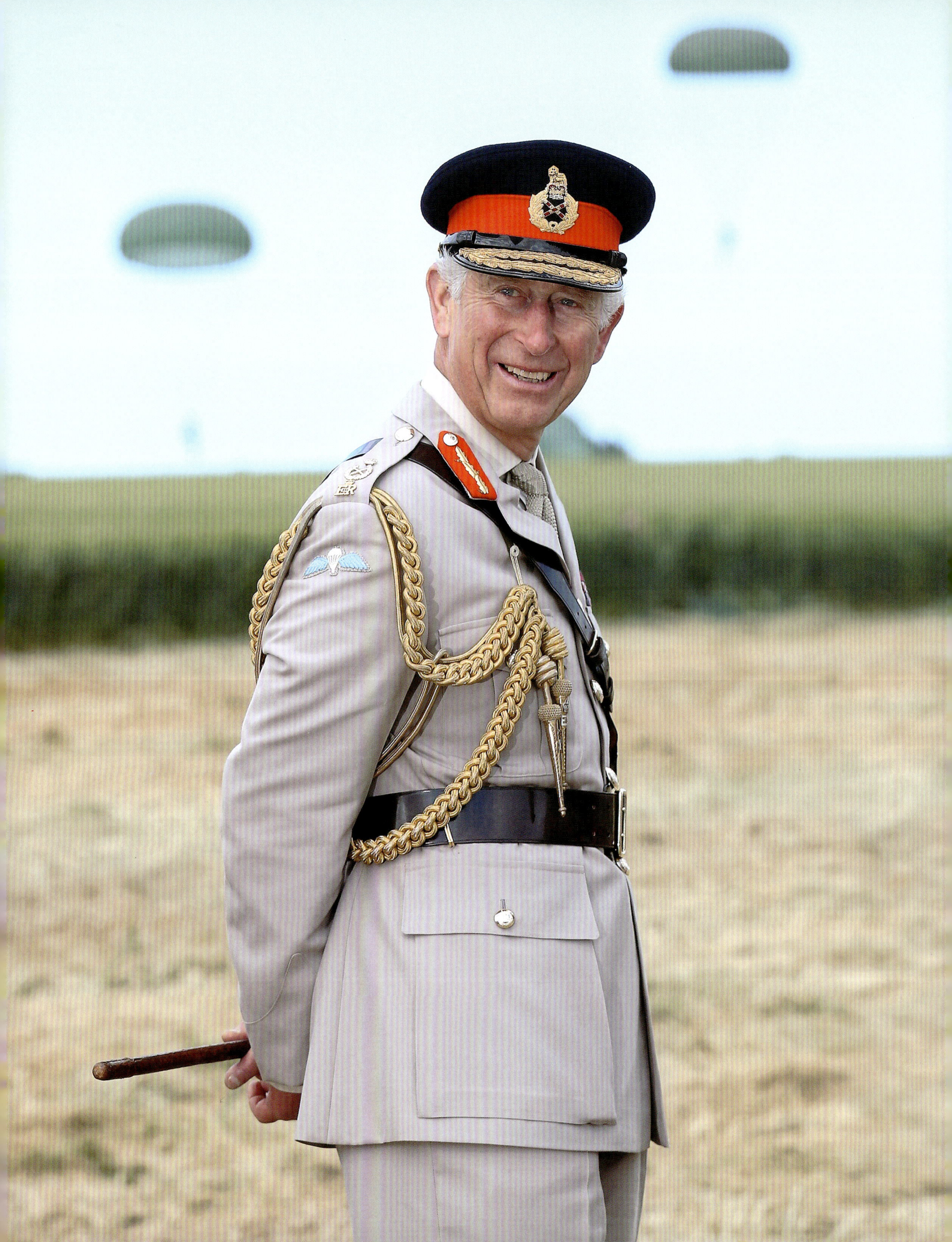

Great Britain's armed forces and the royal family are irreversibly intertwined. Generations of royals have served, and they continue to act, as emotional and ceremonial figureheads for all aspects of the British defence forces. The Queen, as sovereign, is ultimate head of the British Armed Forces, and all serving members pledge their allegiance in a process known as attestation.

The Prince of Wales, the Duke of York, and many in the generations before them have led by example. Prince Charles served as an Air Vice-marshal in the Royal Air Force and Rear Admiral in the navy. In 1976, he retired after seven years of active service. In addition to his earned military ranks, Prince Charles is the honorary Colonel-in-Chief of seventeen regiments of the armed services. Prince Andrew, Duke of York, holds the honorary rank of Vice-admiral in the Royal Navy and saw active service in the Falklands War as a helicopter pilot. Prince Philip, Duke of Edinburgh, served in the Royal Navy and holds numerous honorary appointments, including Lord High Admiral of the Royal Navy.

In recent times it has become clear how much serving their country has meant to both Prince Harry and the Duke of Cambridge. The discipline, adventure, and opportunity to take on new and exciting challenges have been integral to their development. The rapport developed with their fellow soldiers through their service has clearly had a huge impact on them. I have personally seen this through the passion that Prince Harry puts into the Invictus Games. The respect he commands from the competitors and organisers alike is plain to see. His military service gives him a level of validity that could be achieved in no other way. Visiting the Warrior Games in Colorado in 2013 ignited a passion in him to help injured servicemen, like those he had seen so brutally affected during his time in Afghanistan, navigate the complex rehabilitation process. After, as he put it, "stealing this idea," he developed the inaugural Invictus Games in London—a success that has given rise to the Invictus Games in Orlando, Toronto, and Australia. I have photographed this event behind the scenes since the beginning and have witnessed the blood, sweat, and tears that have gone into the organisation since 2014 when the first event was held at the Queen Elizabeth Olympic Park in London. The warm response and relaxed camaraderie Prince Harry enjoys with the competitors makes it abundantly clear that this event has come into its own, something that has benefited a generation of wounded warriors.

Preceding pages Prince Harry, Honorary Air Commandant, attends the Number 26 Squadron Royal Air Force Regiment Standard Parade at Royal Air Force Honington in Bury St. Edmunds.

Opposite The Prince of Wales watches a parachute jump just outside Rainville in northern France. The following day, June 6, 2014, was the seventieth anniversary of the D-Day landings.

Right Detail of a cake designed and made by David Duncan and featuring the Queen for the commissioning ceremony of the Royal Navy aircraft carrier *HMS Queen Elizabeth* at the naval base in Portsmouth. *HMS Queen Elizabeth* is the largest warship ever built for the Royal Navy.

Below Prince William training with the Royal Navy at Britannia Royal Naval College in Dartmouth. The Prince was spending two months with the Royal Navy on an attachment designed to familiarize him with its capabilities and working conditions.

Opposite Clive Robertson, a diver in the Royal Engineers, salutes the Queen from a water tank at the centenary of the Corps of Royal Engineers at Brompton Barracks in Chatham, England.

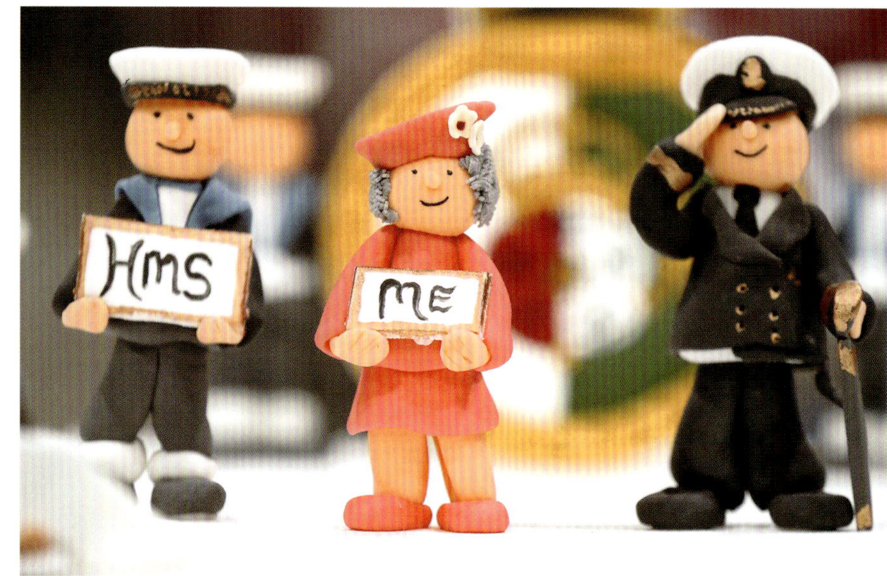

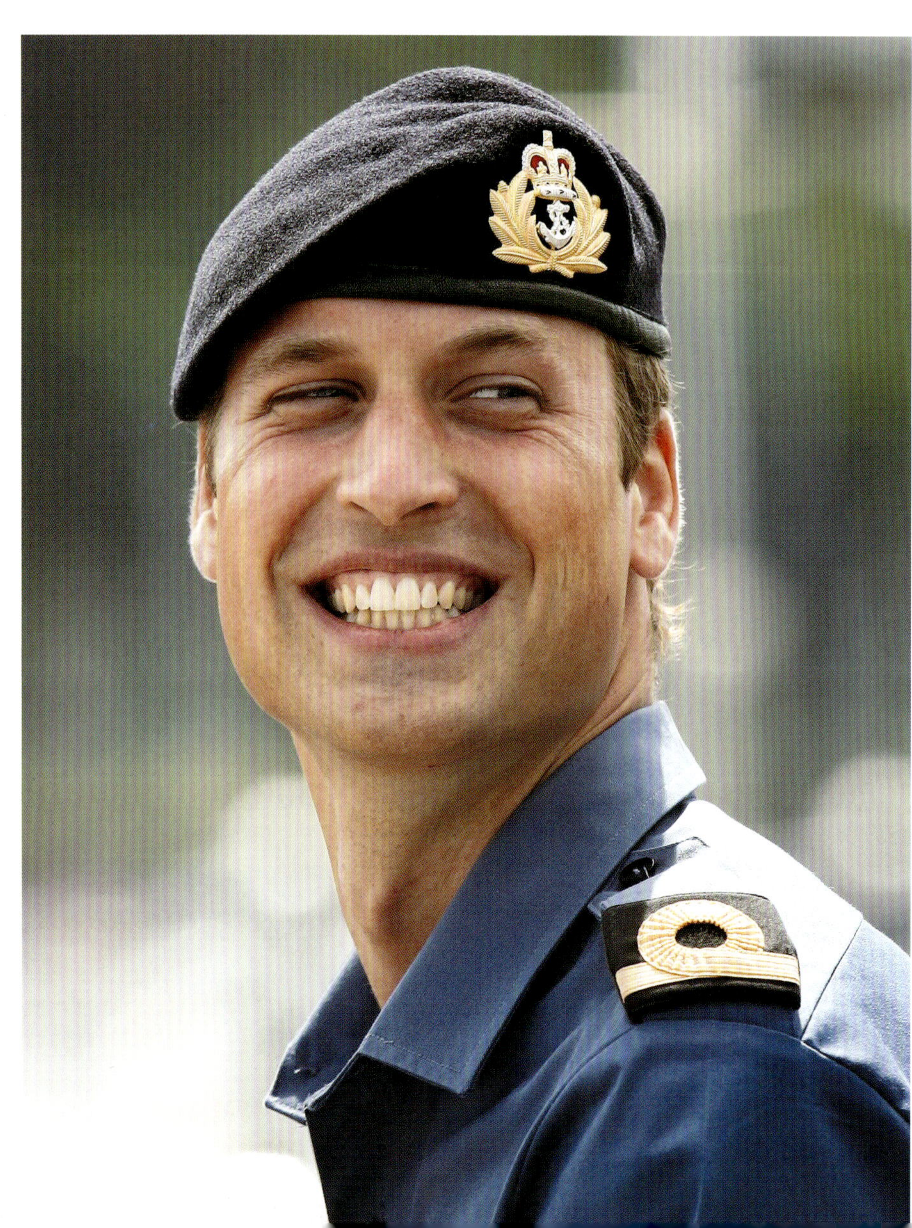

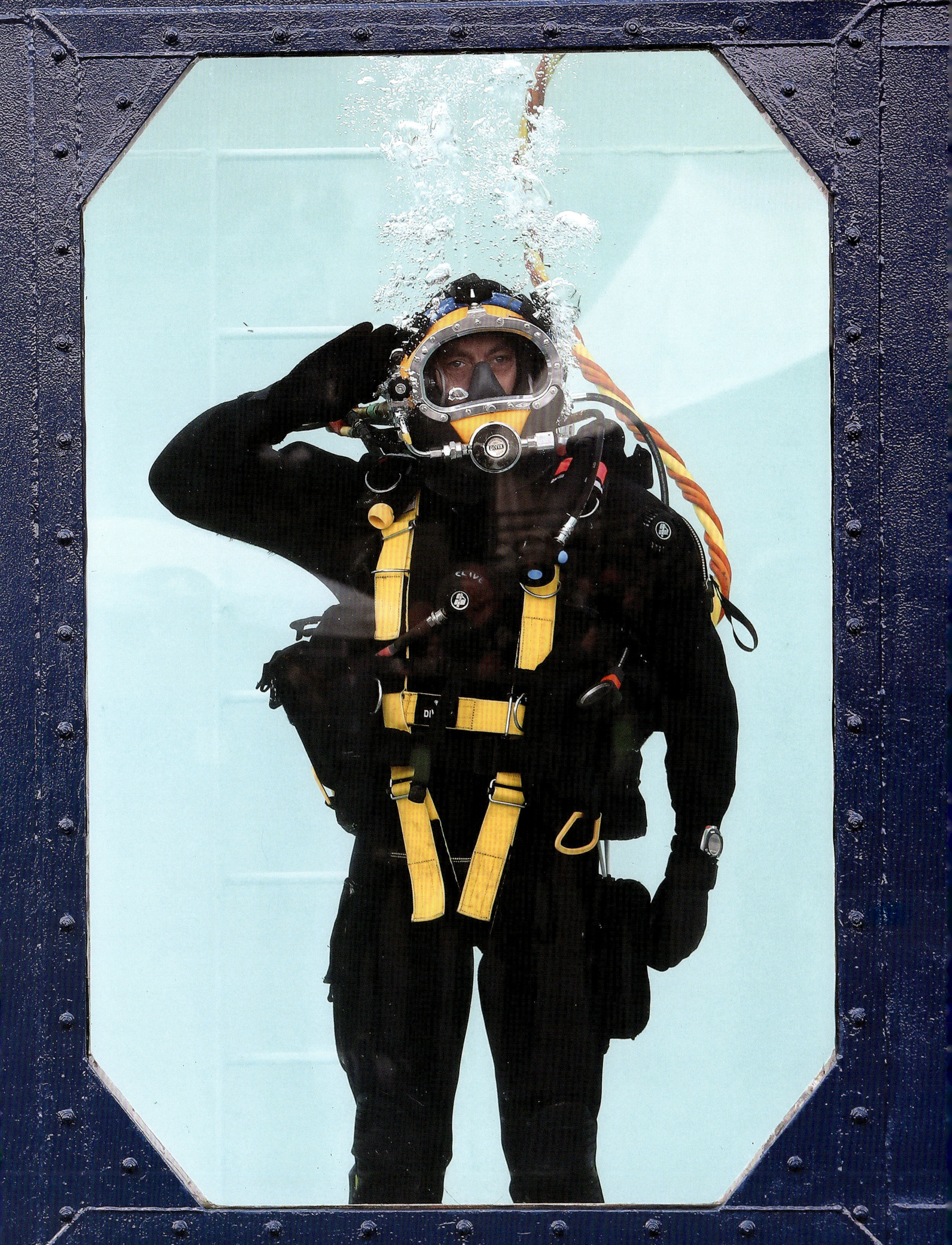

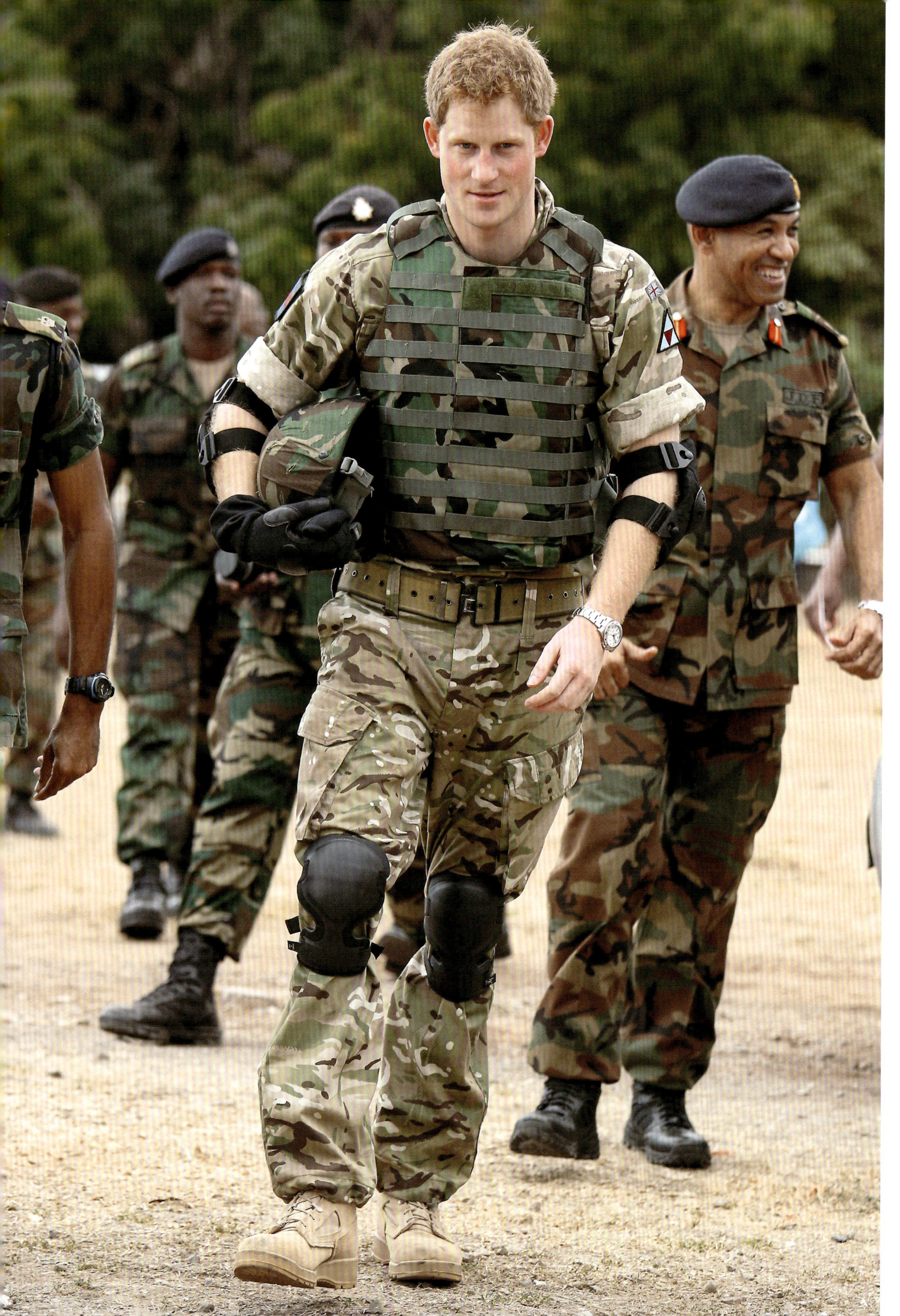

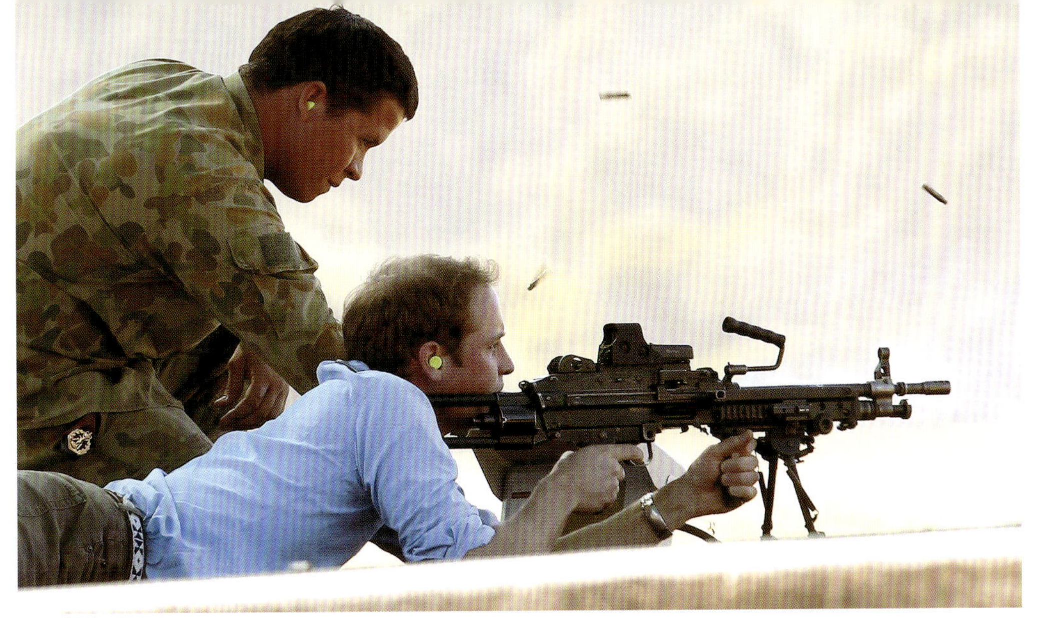

Opposite Prince Harry heads to the range at Up-Park Camp in Kingston, Jamaica in 2017. The Prince was in Jamaica as part of a Diamond Jubilee tour. He also represented the Queen in Belize, the Bahamas, and Brazil.

Above Prince William fires an F89 Minimi machine gun at Holsworthy Army Barracks in Sydney on the second day of a visit to Australia in 2010. This was the first official solo overseas visit for Prince William.

Middle Prince Harry shares a joke with cadets as he visits West Point, a military academy in New York.

Below Prince Charles and Prince William walk back to the Royal Air Force Search and Rescue Force base. Prince William had just shown his father around his rescue helicopter at RAF Valley in Anglesey, North Wales. He served nearly five years as a Royal Air Force rescue pilot before joining the East Anglian Air Ambulance in March 2015.

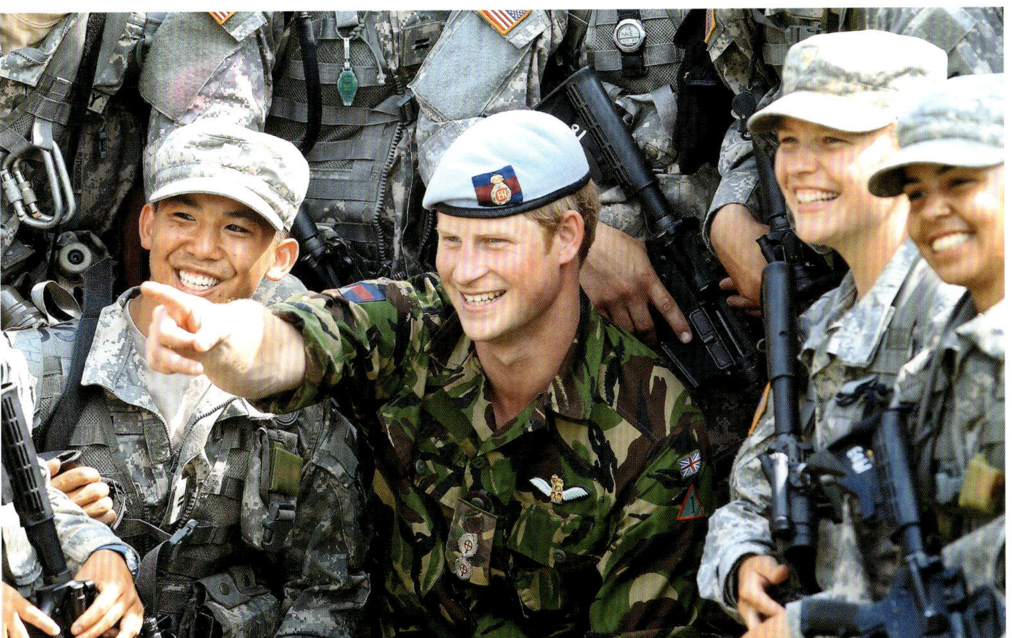

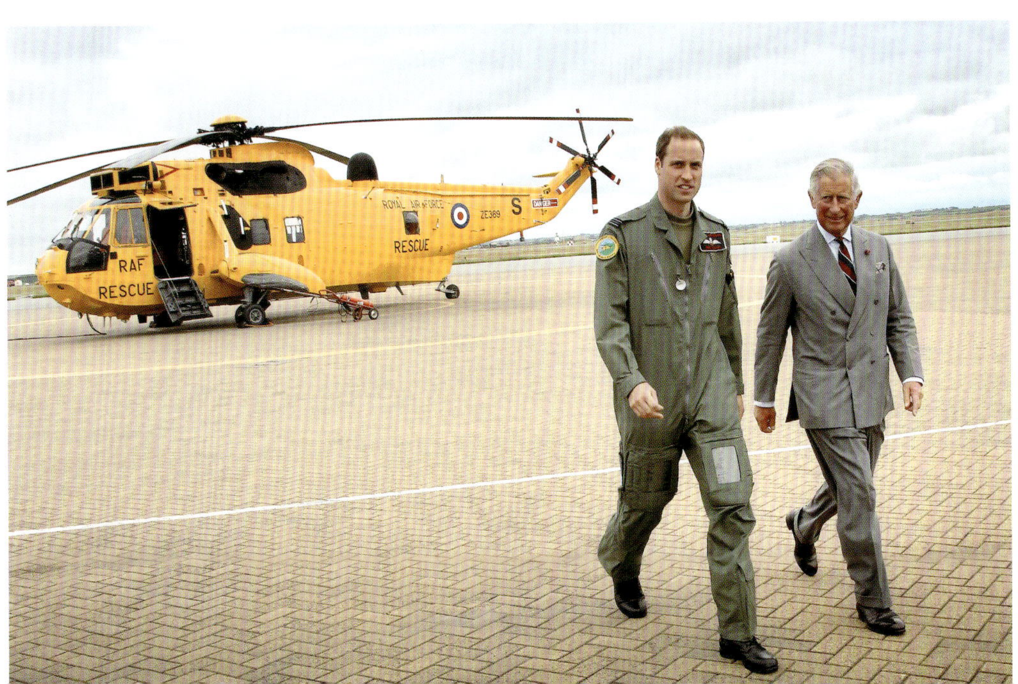

Following pages Detail of the uniform of Prince Charles, Colonel-in-Chief of the Parachute Regiment, as he meets veterans near Pegasus Bridge during D-Day commemorations in Rainville, France in 2014. On the right, Prince Harry's medals at the unveiling of the Bastion Memorial at the National Memorial Arboretum in Staffordshire. The first is an Afghanistan campaign medal, awarded in 2008 to mark his service on the frontline in Helmand Province, second from the left is the Queen's Golden Jubilee Medal, and on the far right is the Queen's Diamond Jubilee Medal.

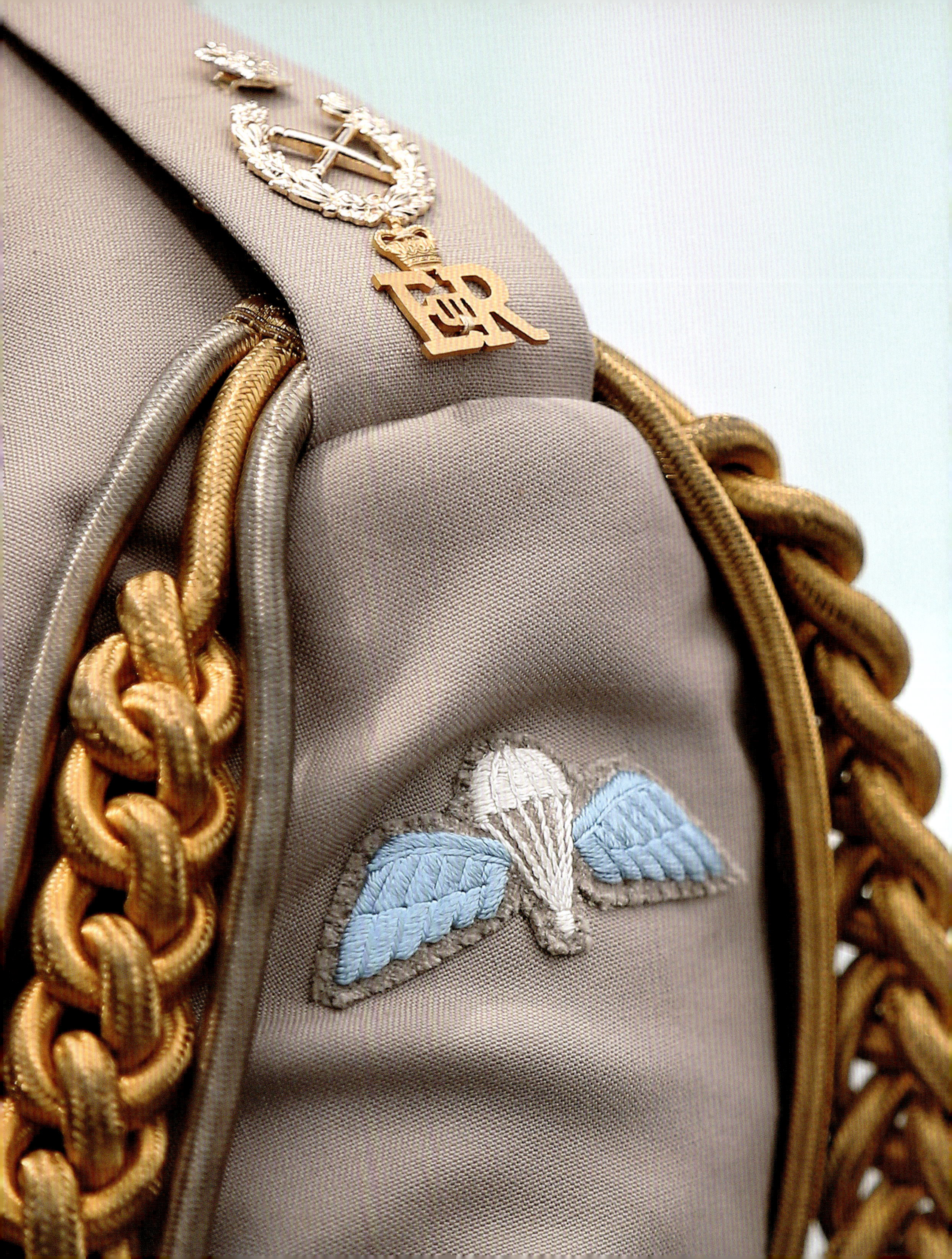

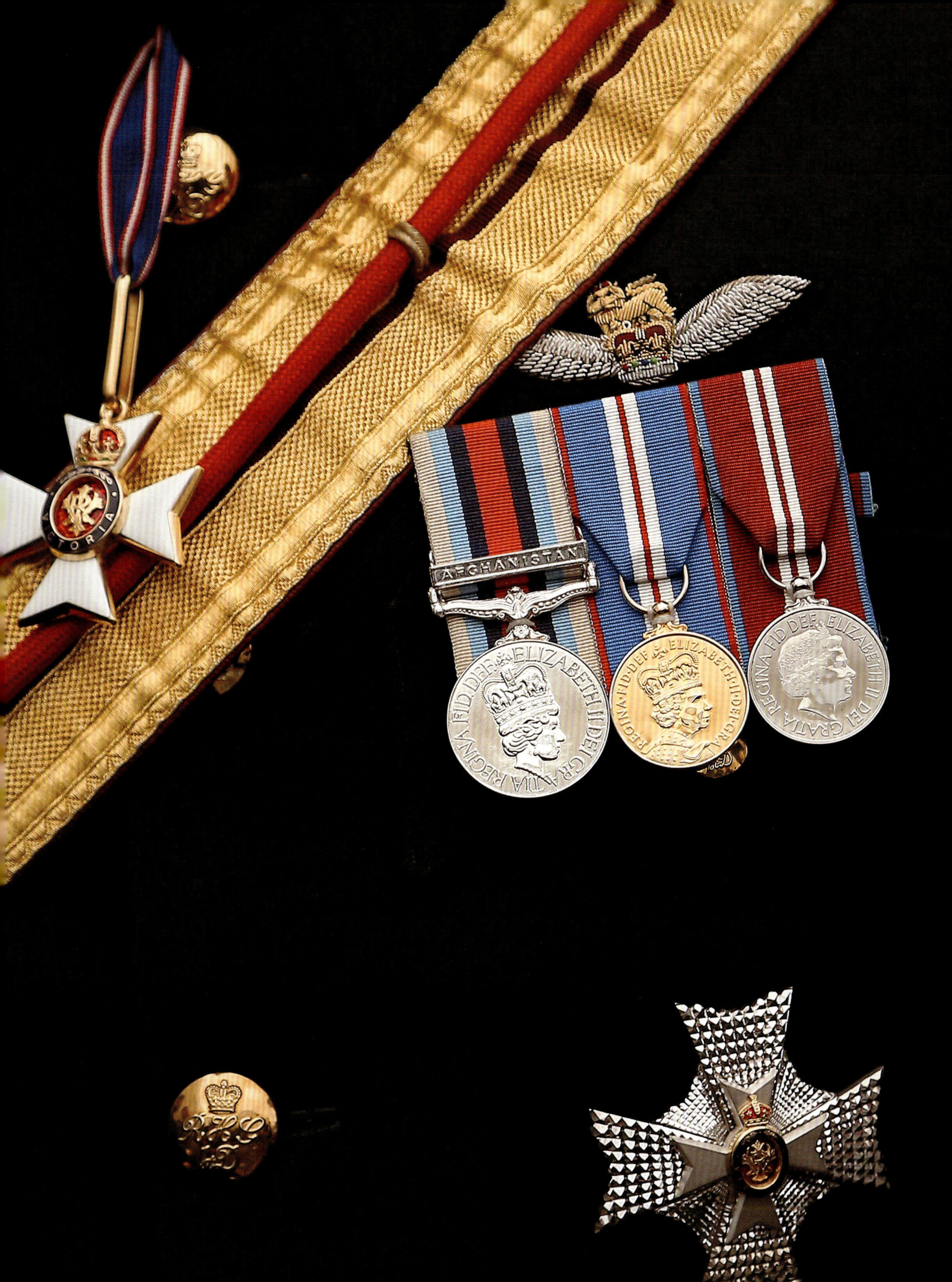
VICTORIA
AFGHANISTAN
ELIZABETH II DEI GRATIA REGINA FID DEF
ELIZABETH II DEI GRA REGINA FID DEF
ELIZABETH II DEI GRATIA REGINA FID DEF

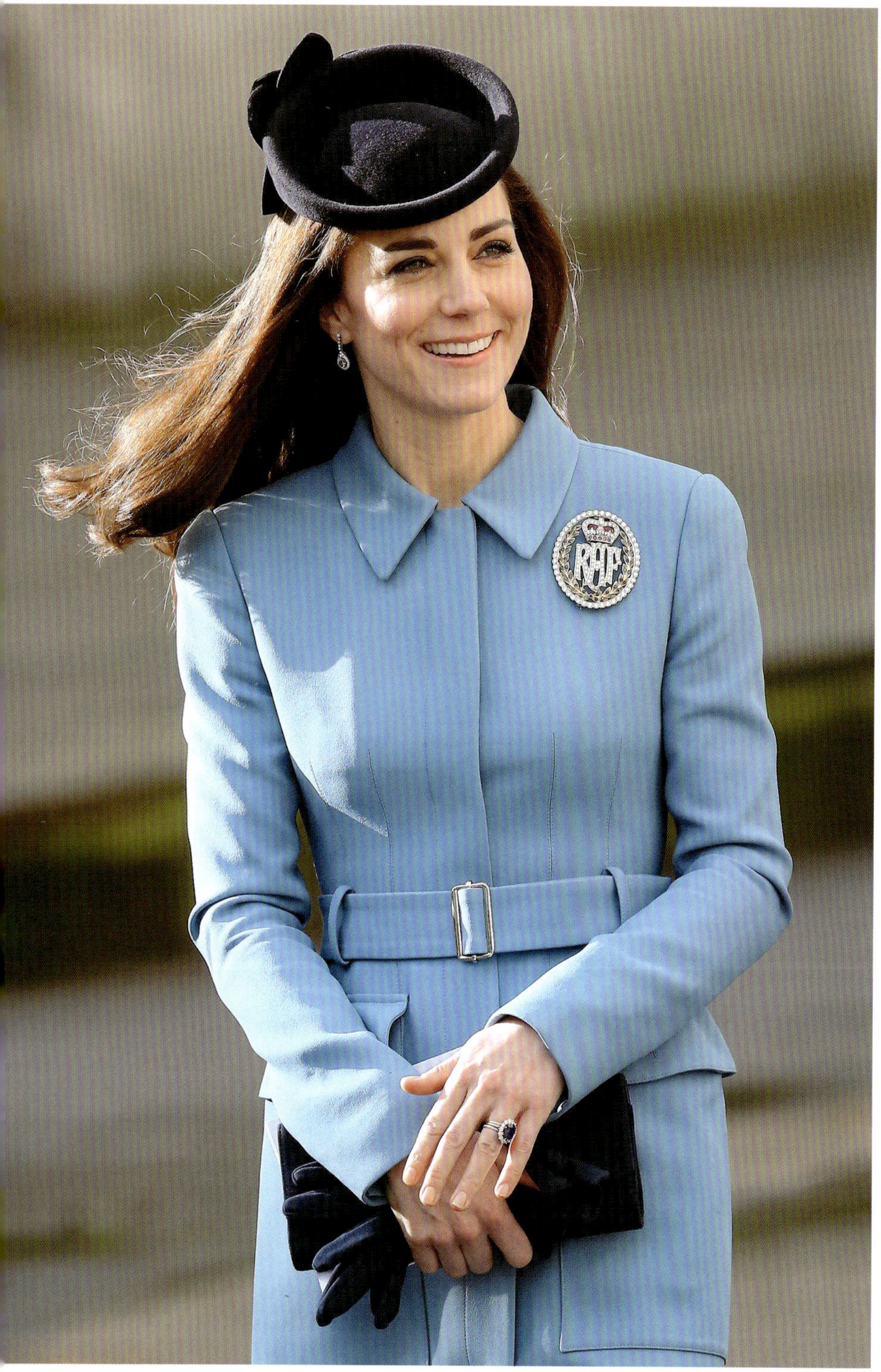

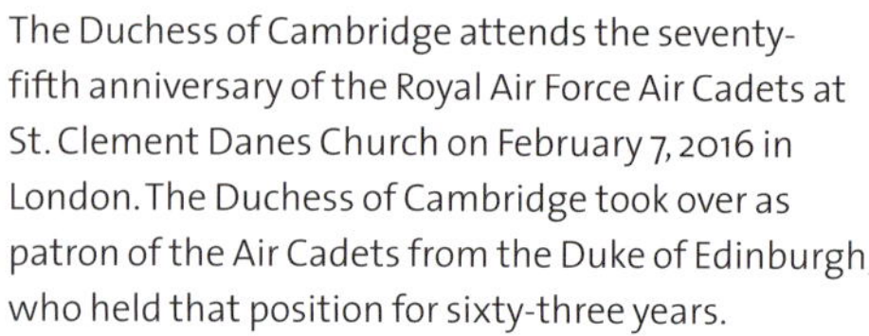

The Duchess of Cambridge attends the seventy-fifth anniversary of the Royal Air Force Air Cadets at St. Clement Danes Church on February 7, 2016 in London. The Duchess of Cambridge took over as patron of the Air Cadets from the Duke of Edinburgh, who held that position for sixty-three years.

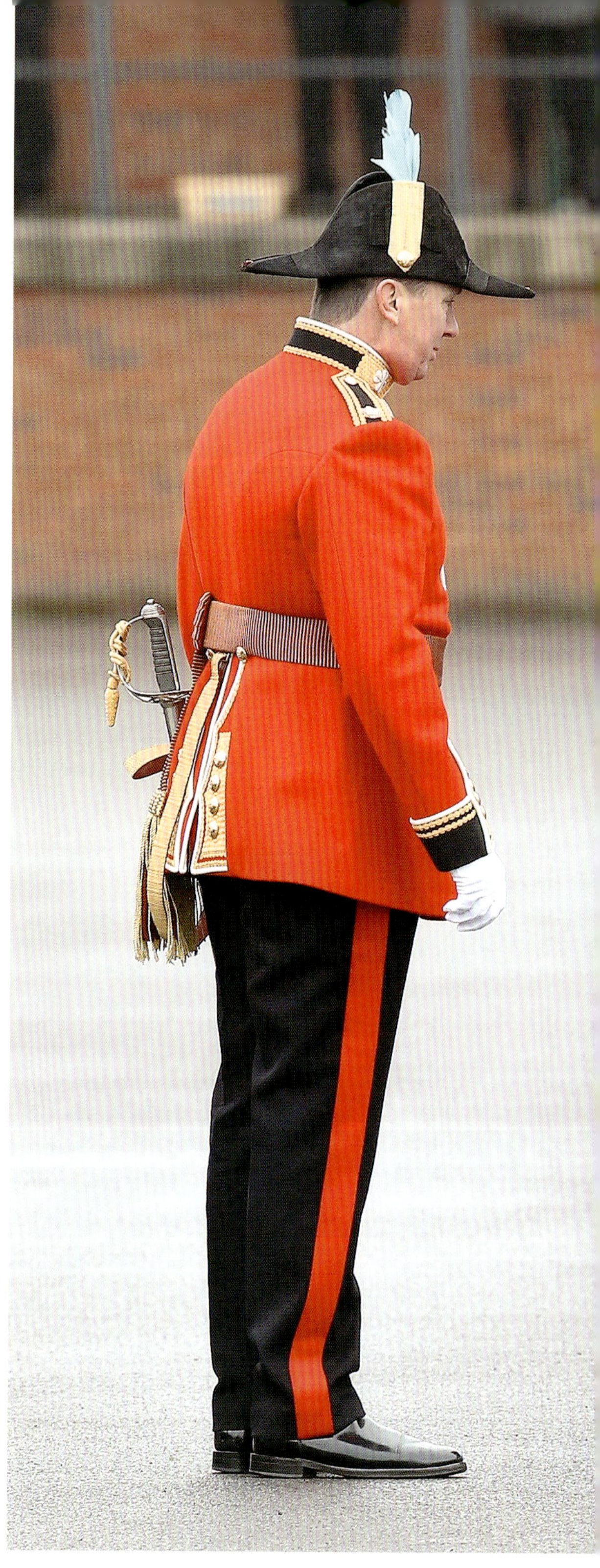

An Irish wolfhound called Domhnall, the regimental Mascot of the Irish Guards, is presented with a shamrock by the Duchess of Cambridge as she takes part in a St. Patrick's Day parade at Aldershot Barracks.

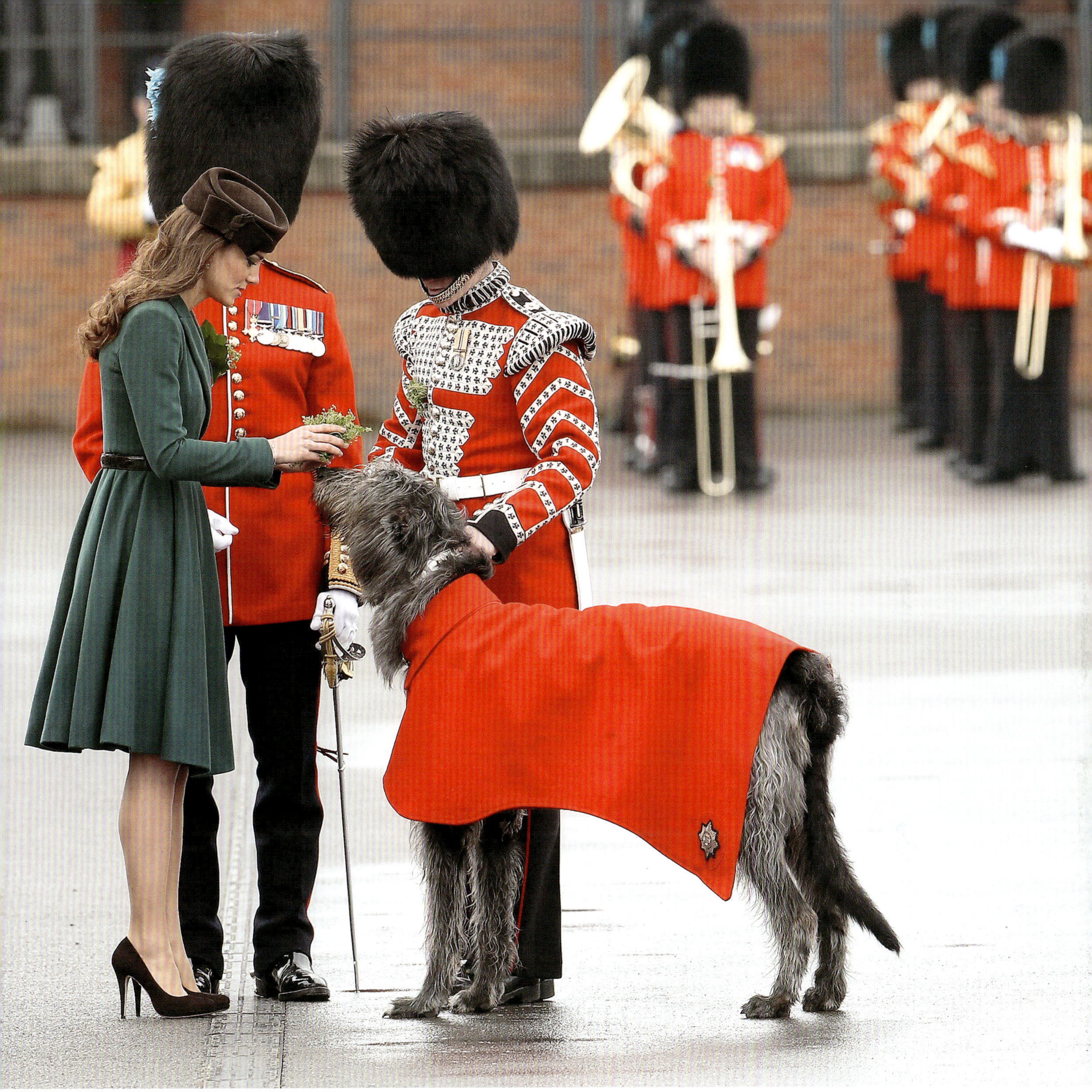

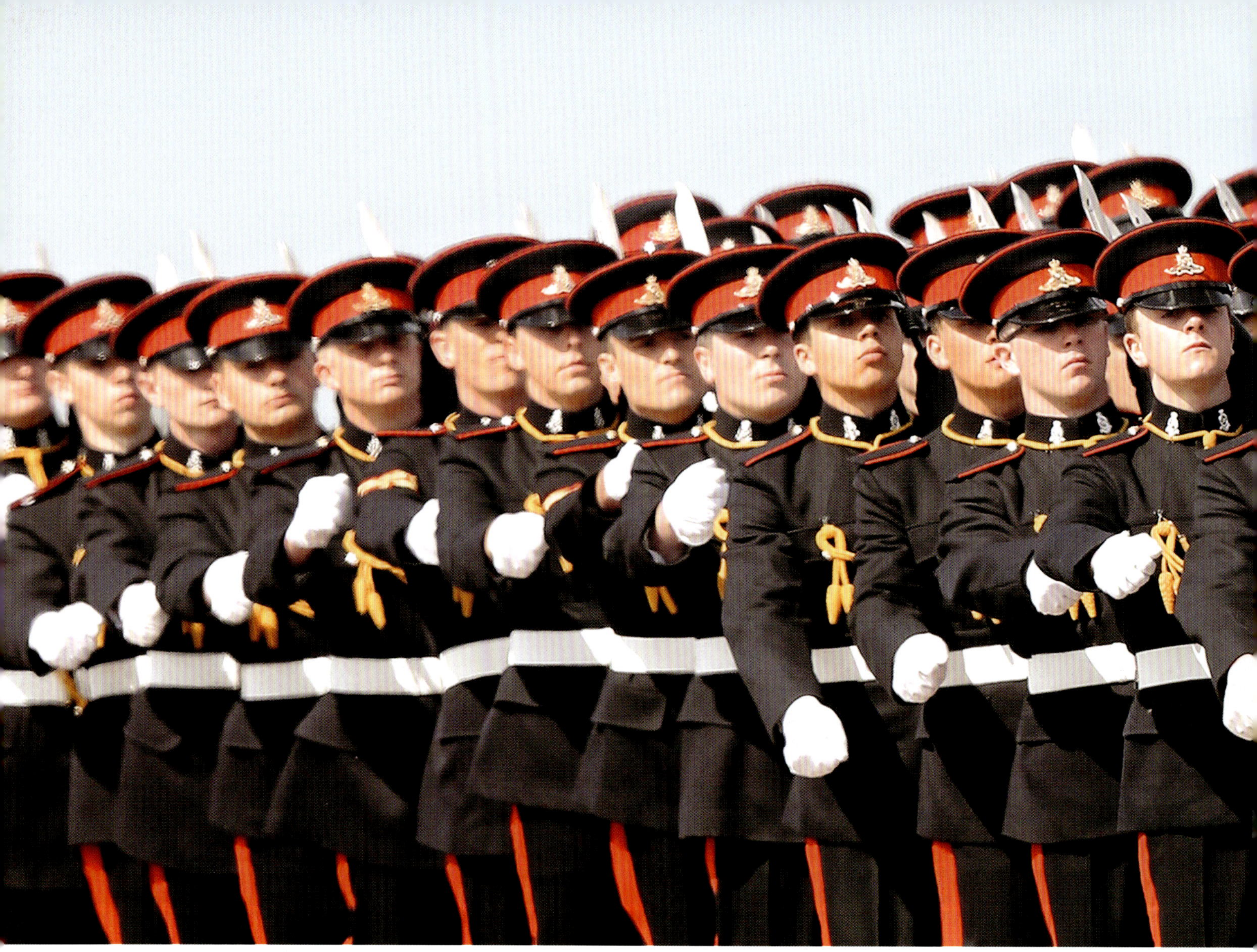

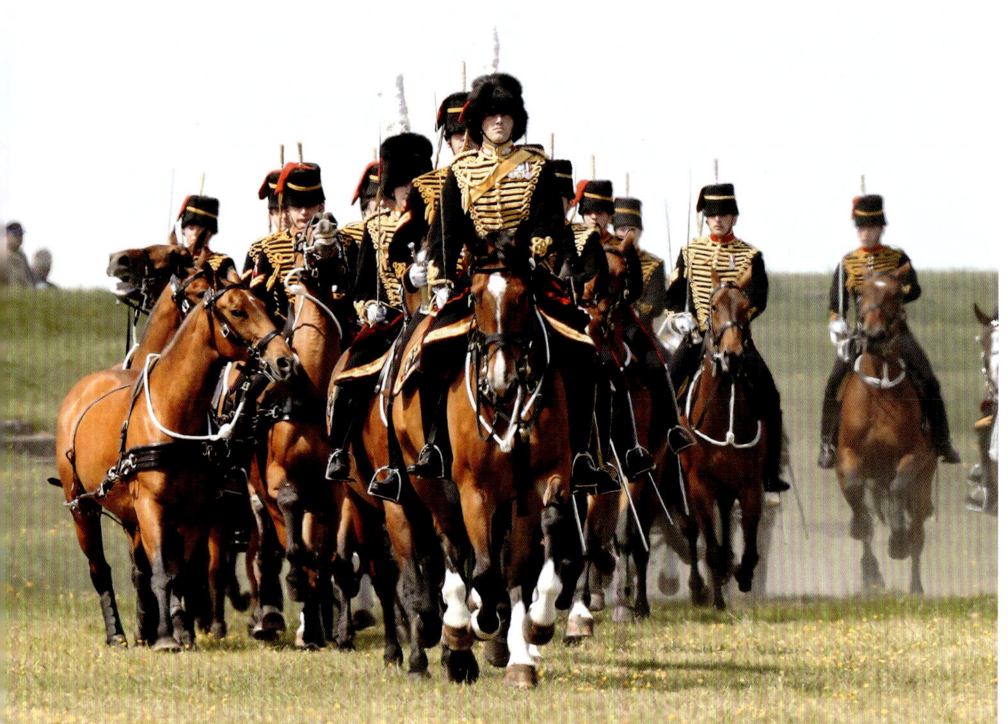

Above and left Royal Regiment of Artillery troops take part in a royal review on the occasion of their tercentenary in 2016 at Knighton Down in Larkhill. The Queen has been Captain-General of the Royal Regiment of Artillery since February 6, 1952.

Opposite Alongside Lieutenant-General Sir Mark Mans and Lieutenant Colonel Sean Cunniff, the Queen reviews the parade of the Corps of Royal Engineers at Brompton Barracks from the back of her customised Range Rover Vogue as she marks the group's centenary on October 13, 2016 in Chatham.

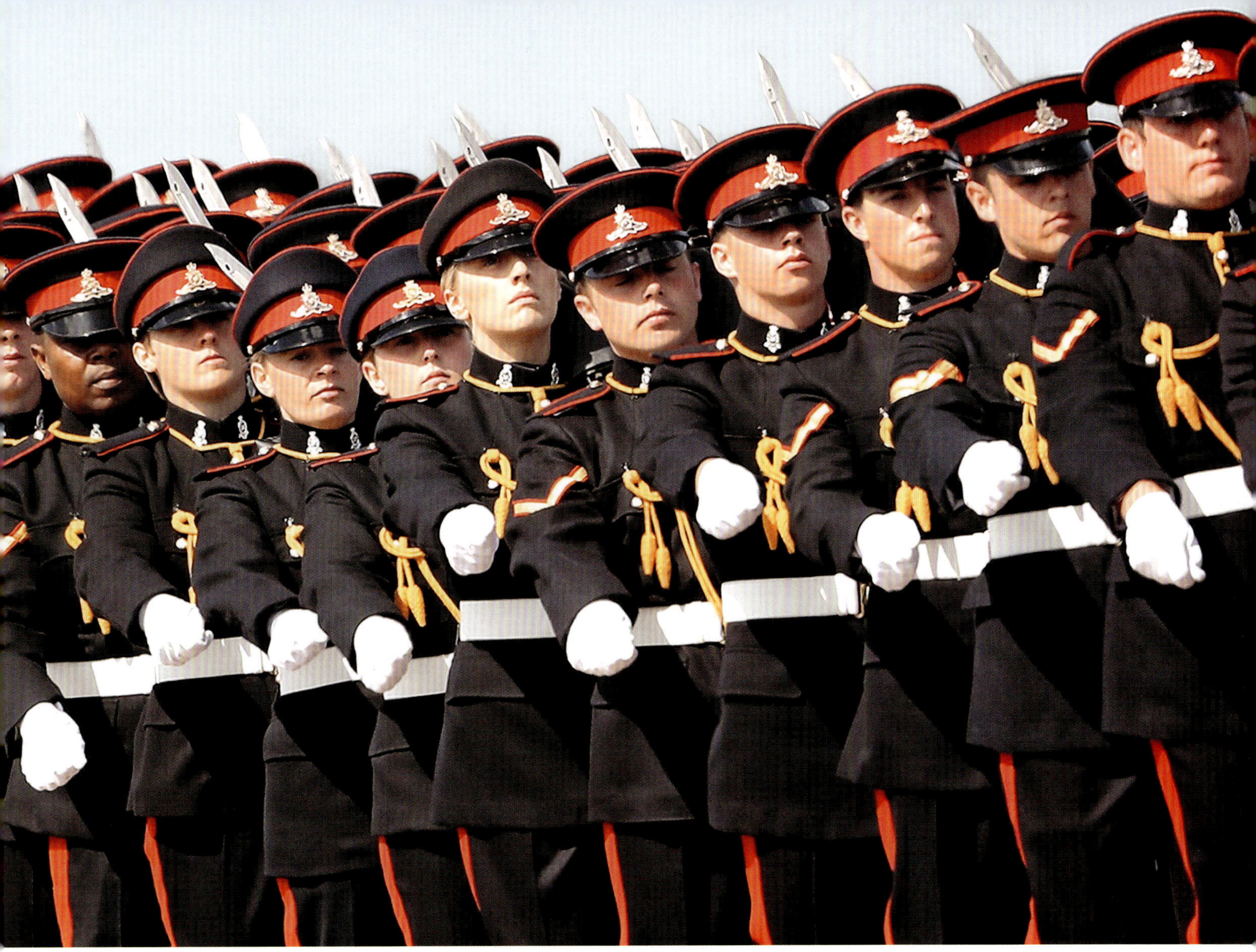

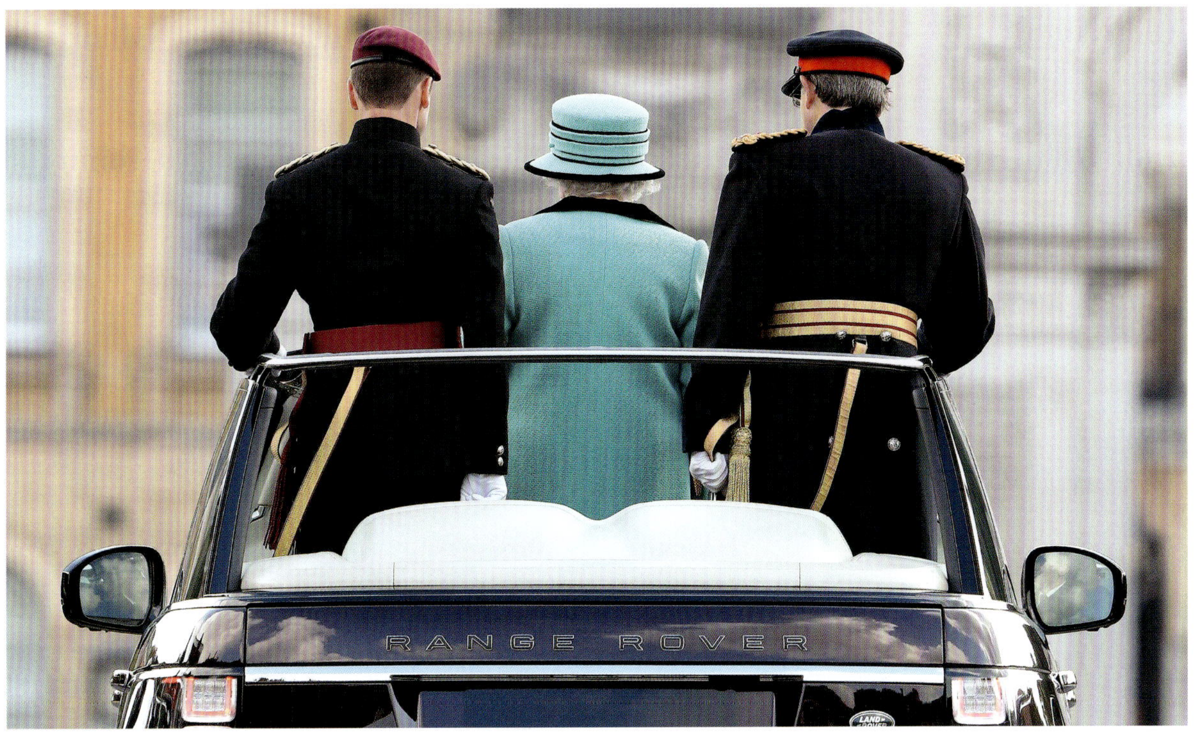
RANGE ROVER

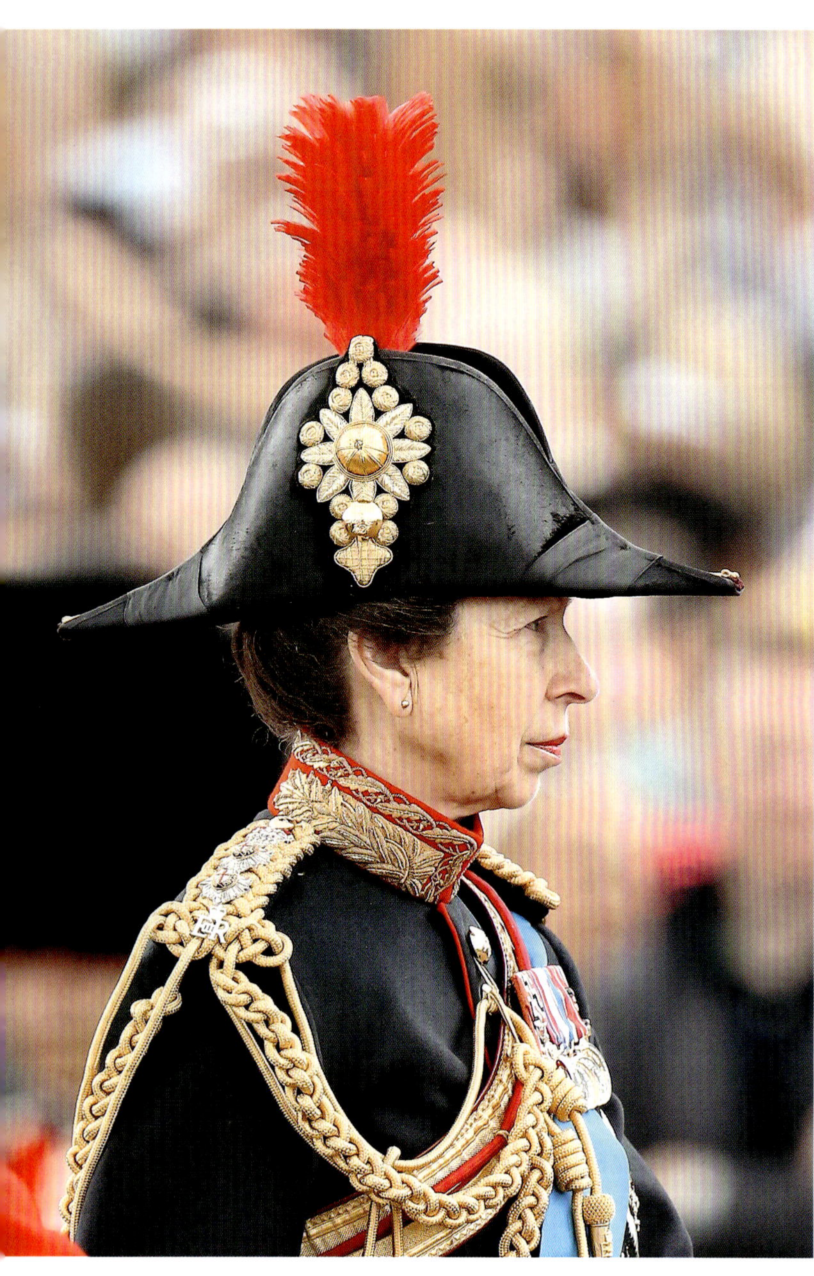

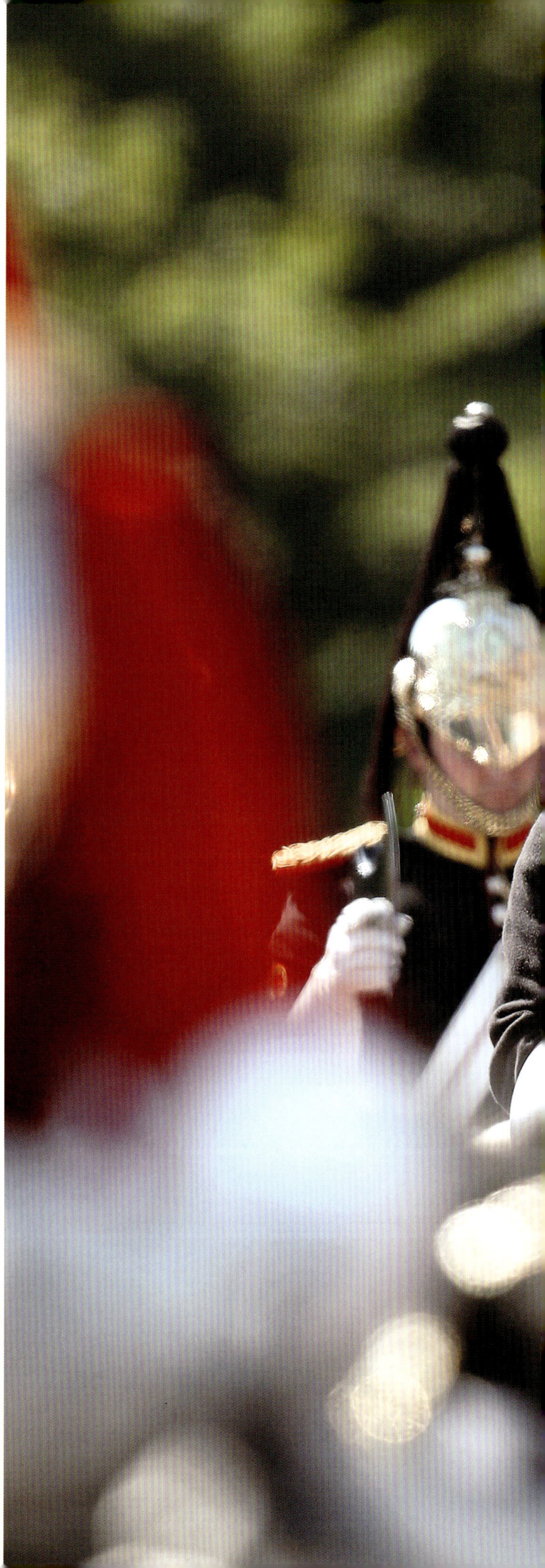

Above The Princess Royal (on horseback) takes part in the annual Trooping the Colour ceremony on Horse Guards Parade in London. Princess Anne holds a number of honorary appointments in the armed forces of numerous Commonwealth countries.

Opposite Troops advance down the Mall during the Trooping the Colour parade.

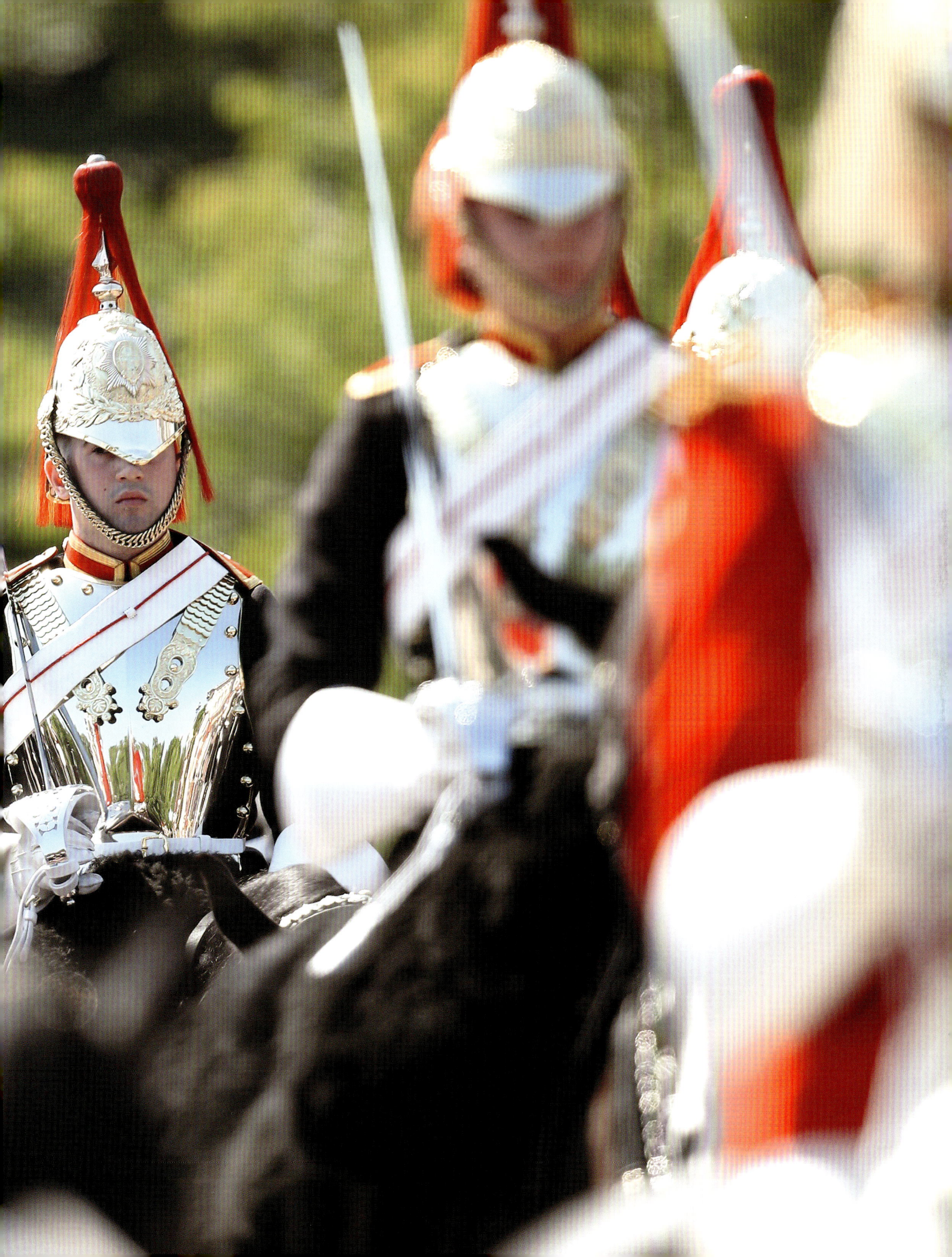

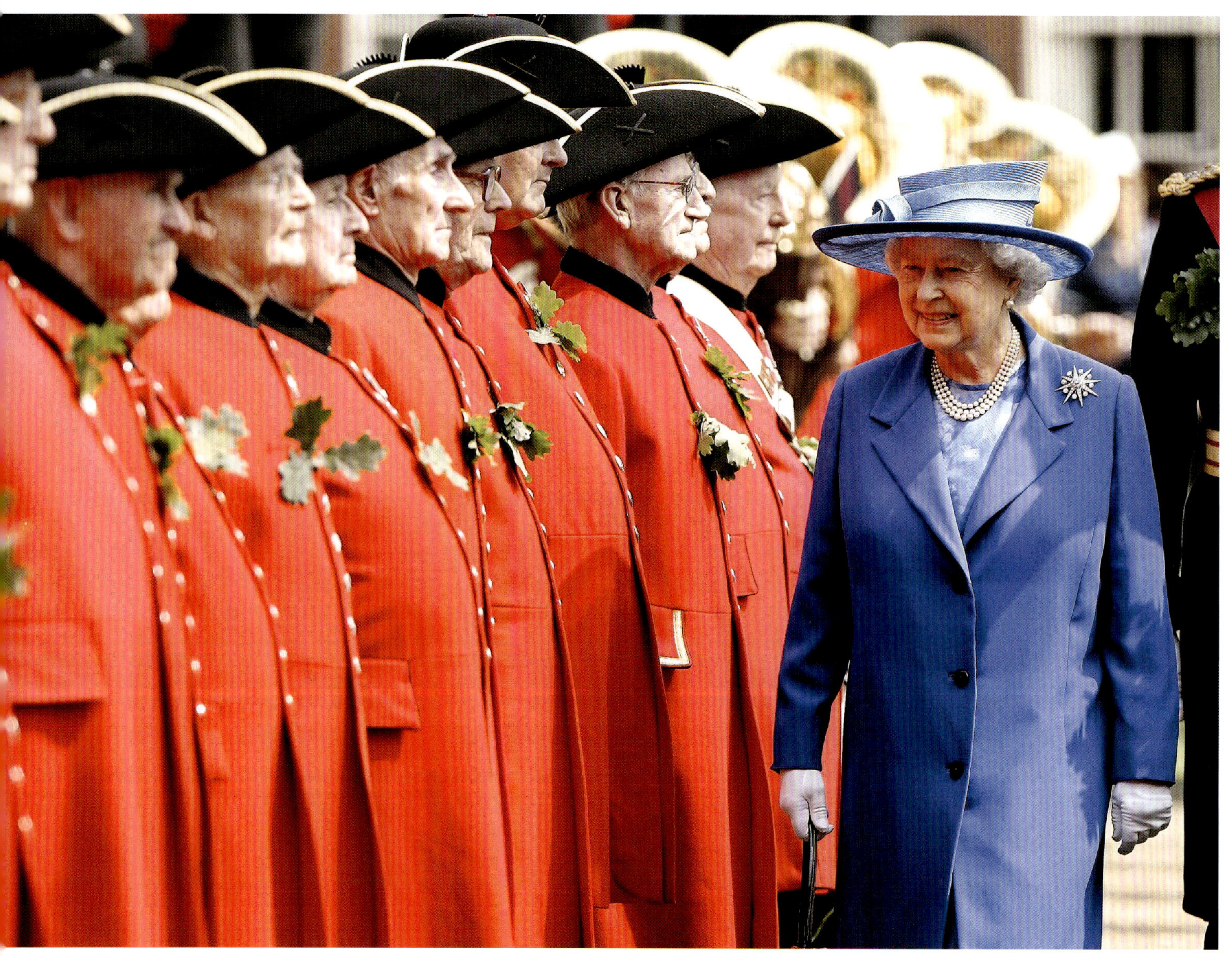

Above Remembering and rewarding those who have served remains an important role of the royal family. The Queen inspects Chelsea Pensioners on Founder's Day at the Royal Hospital Chelsea in London, founded by King Charles II in 1682 as a home for old and infirm soldiers. On Founder's Day, pensioners wear oak leaves on their lapels to commemorate King Charles's escape from the Roundheads. The king hid in an oak tree to evade them.

Opposite The Prince of Wales meets veterans with New Zealand prime minister John Key after an Armistice Day commemoration at the Auckland War Memorial in New Zealand.

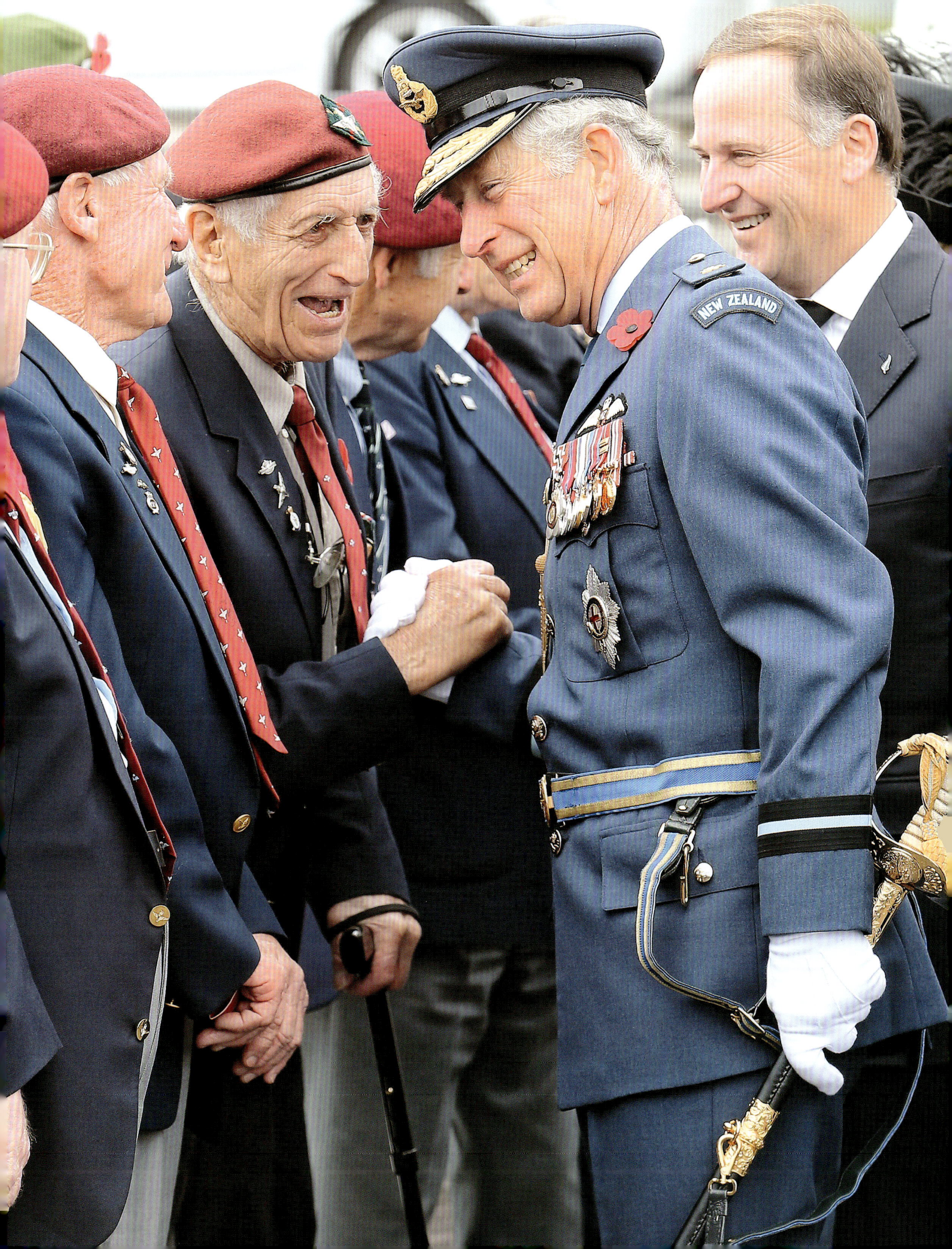
NEW ZEALAND

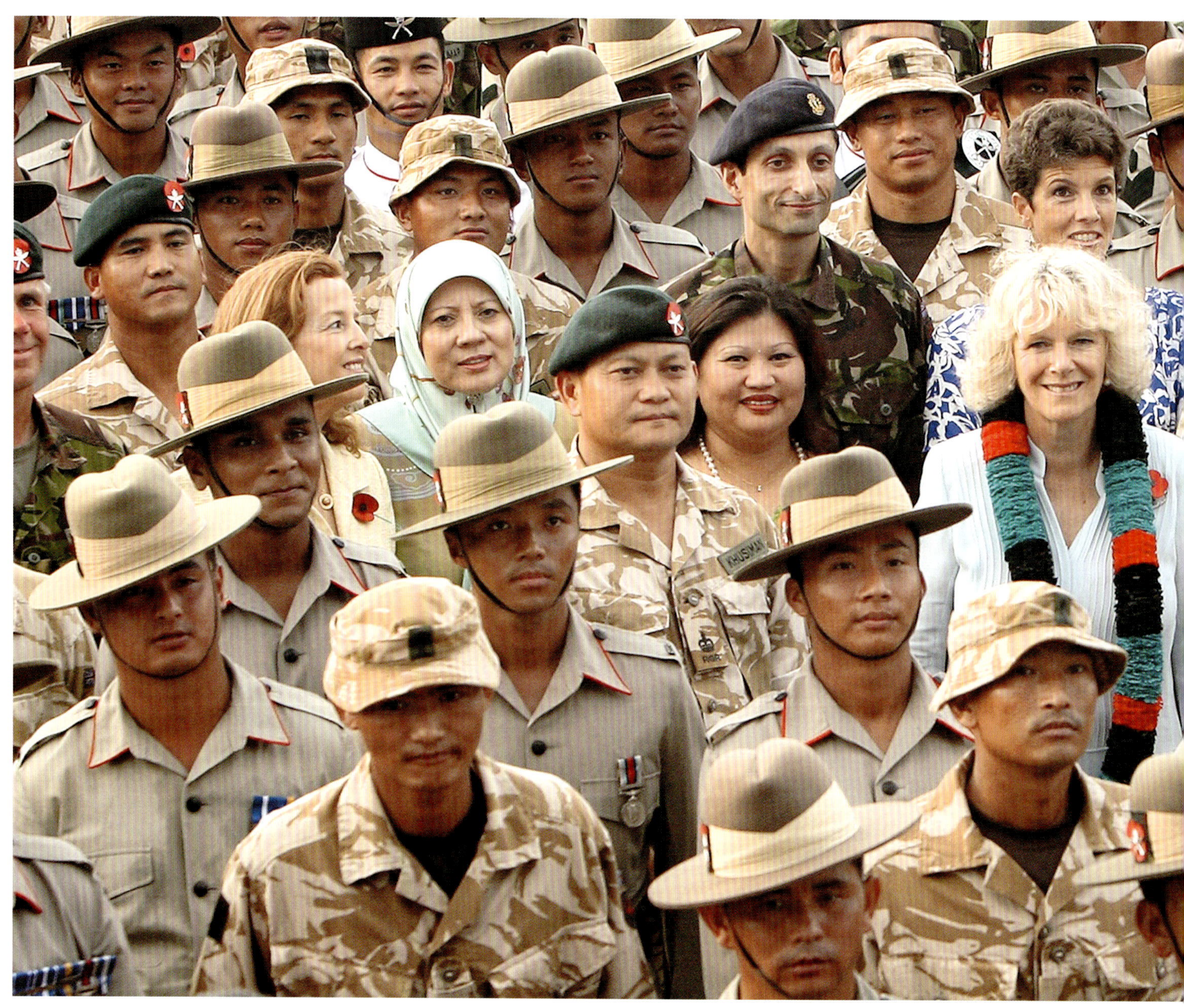

The Duchess of Cornwall and Prince of Wales pose for a photograph with Gurkhas in Bandar Seri Begawan, Brunei, in 2008, after being presented with garlands at the British garrison. The Prince and Duchess were in Brunei as part of a ten-day tour of East Asia that also took them to Japan and Indonesia.

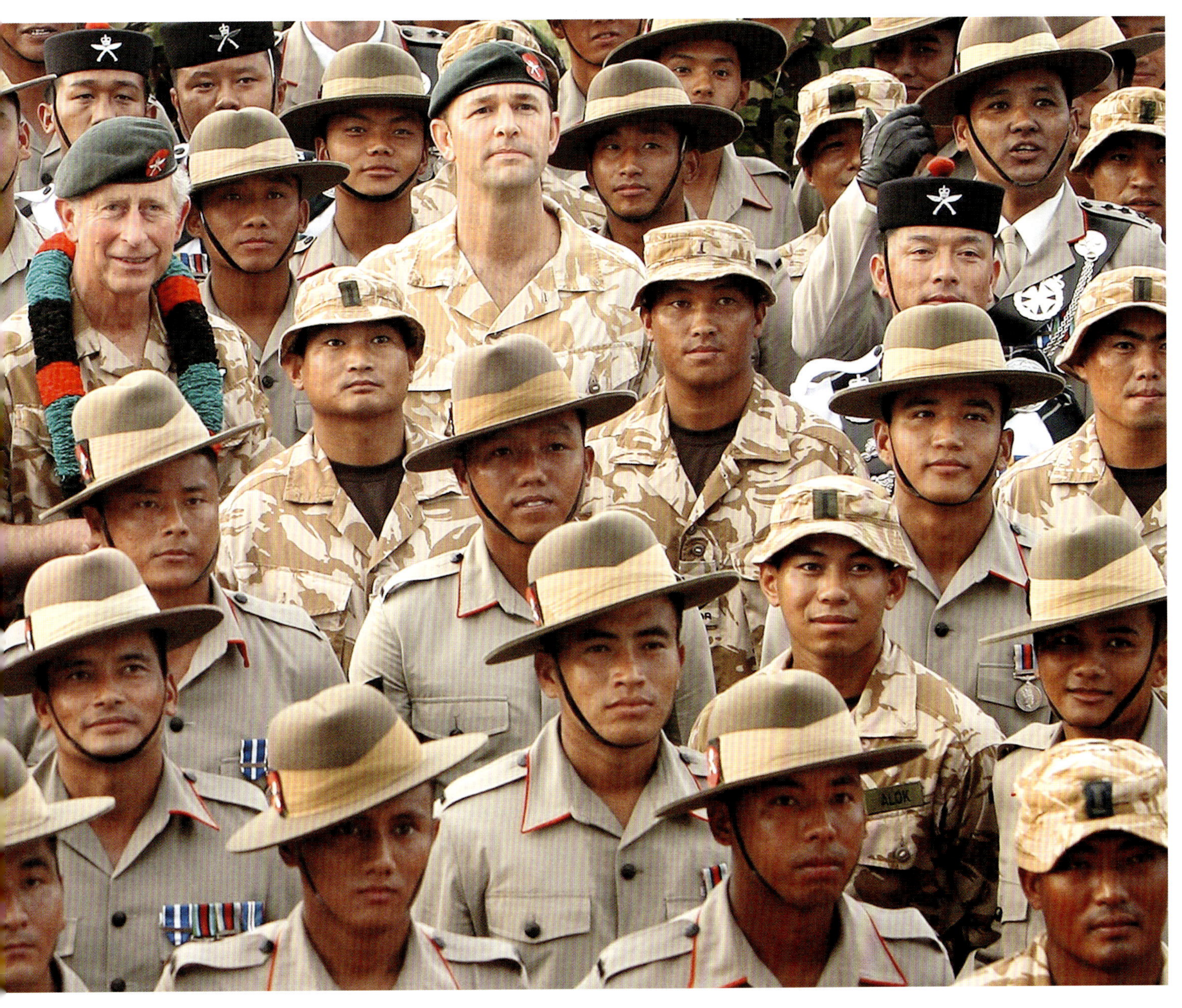
ALOK

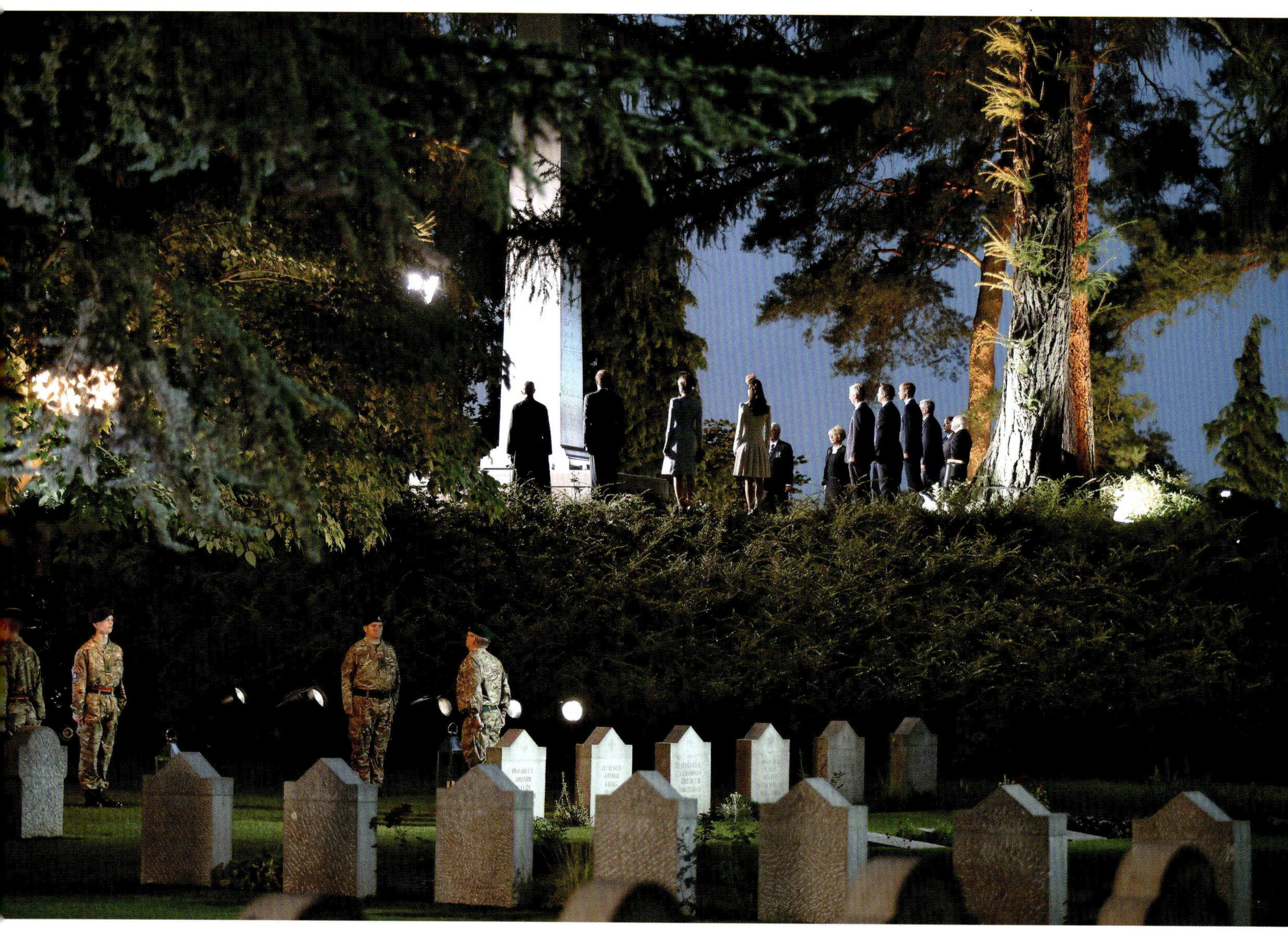

This page The Duke and Duchess of Cambridge pay their respects during an evening service at St. Symphorien Military Cemetery in Mons, Belgium, on August 4, 2014. The day marked the 100th anniversary of Great Britain declaring war on Germany.

Opposite A cross rests within the Menin Gate Memorial to the Missing in Ypres, Belgium next to the names of 50,000 lost soldiers. On the evening of July 30, 2017, the Duke and Duchess of Cambridge attended the Last Post ceremony, which has taken place every night since 1928. The royal couple's 2017 visit marked the centenary of the Battle of Passchendaele, also known as the Third Battle of Ypres.

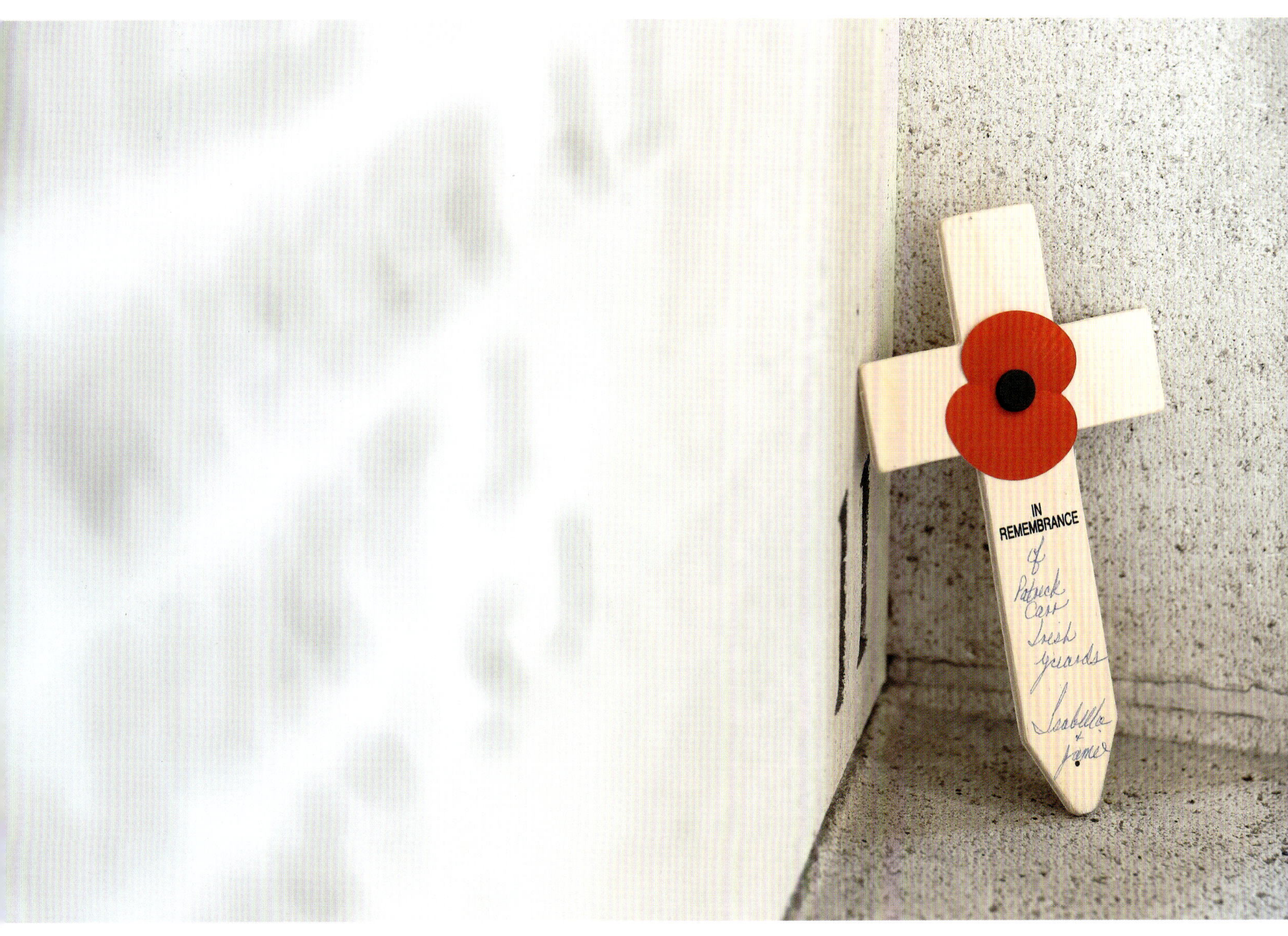

Following pages The Duchess of Cambridge glances back as she leaves Kranji War Cemetery in Singapore on day three of her 2012 Diamond Jubilee tour of the Far East. Singapore was the first stop on a tour that also took the royals to Malaysia, the Solomon Islands, and the tiny Pacific island of Tuvalu.

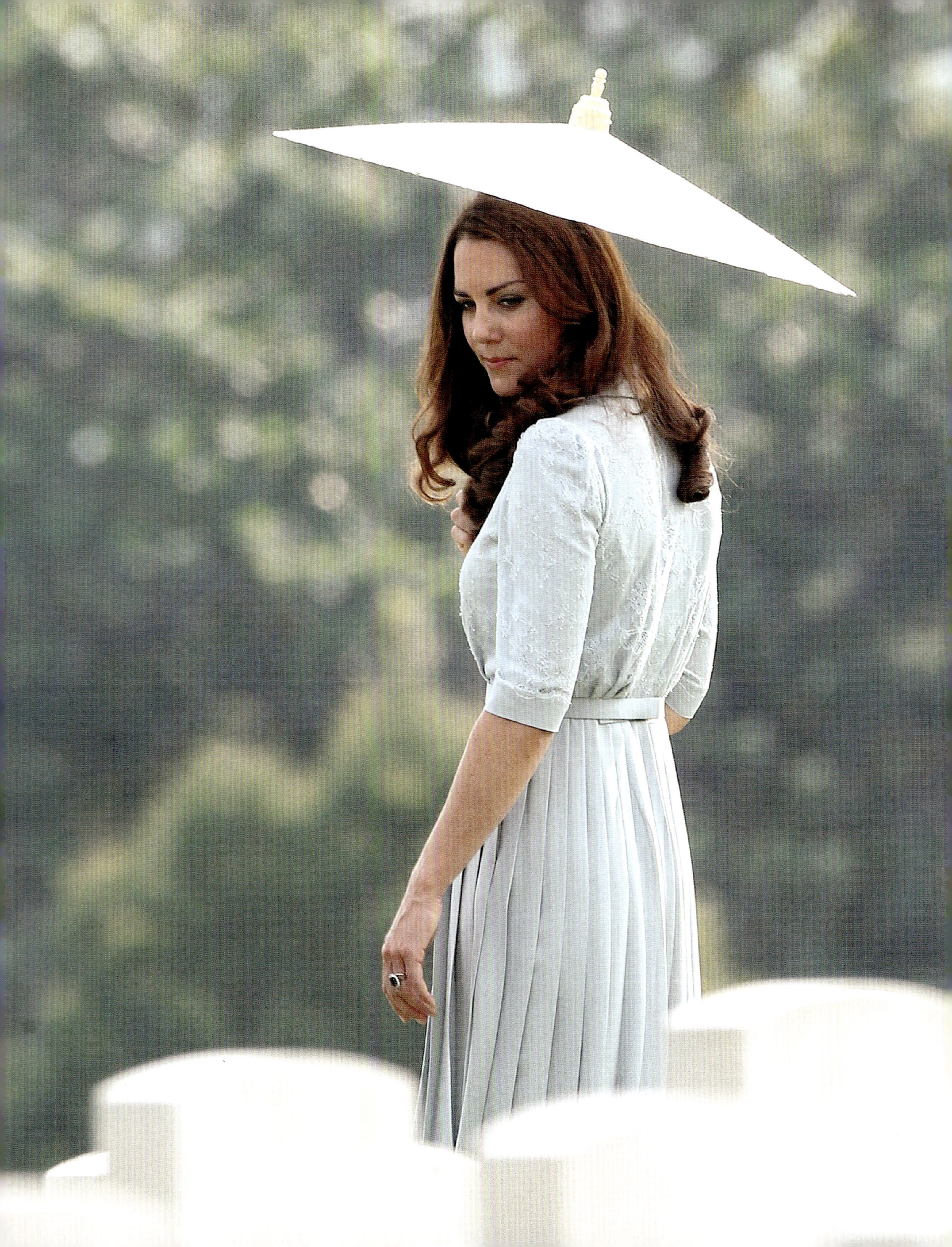

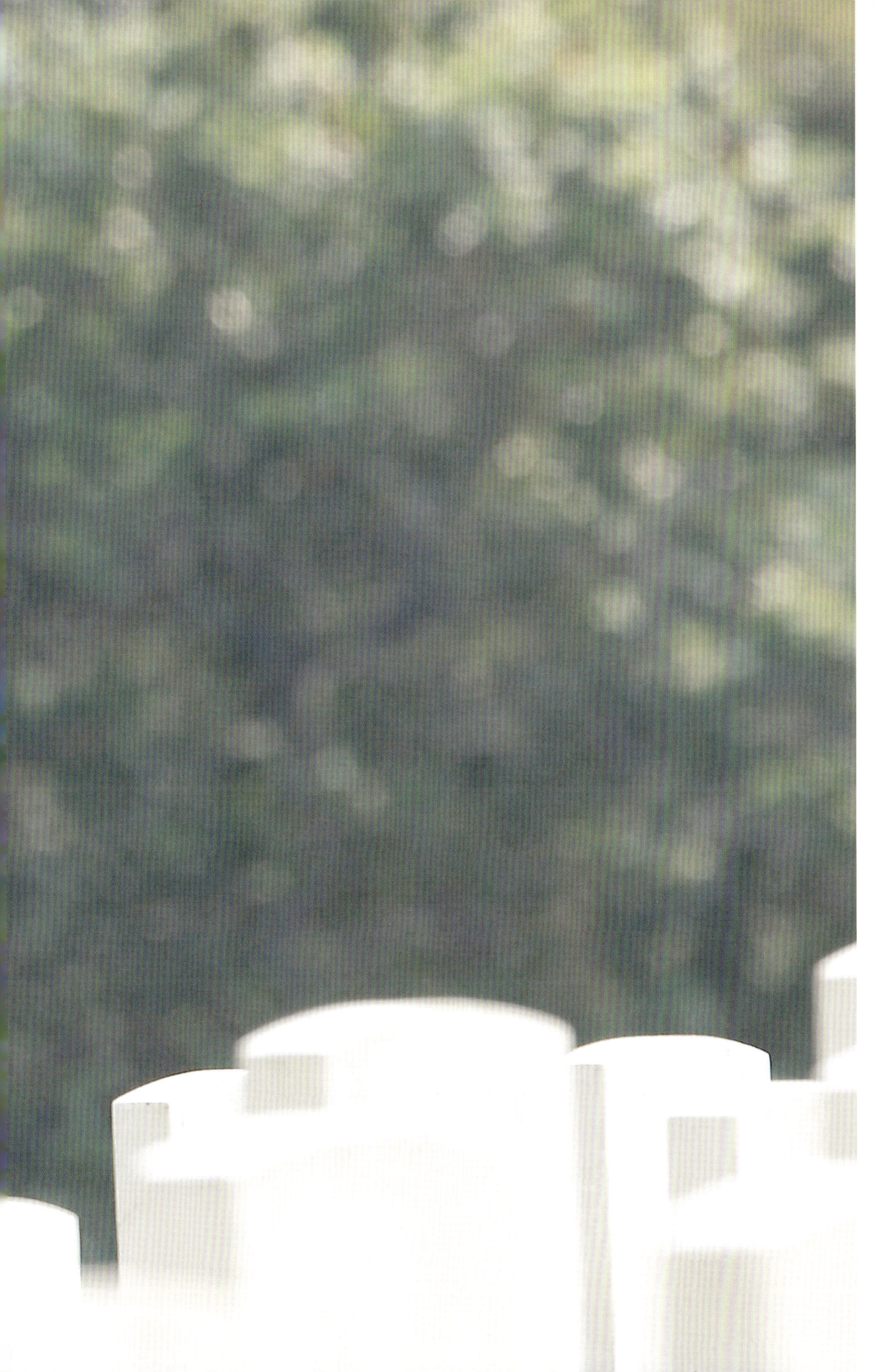

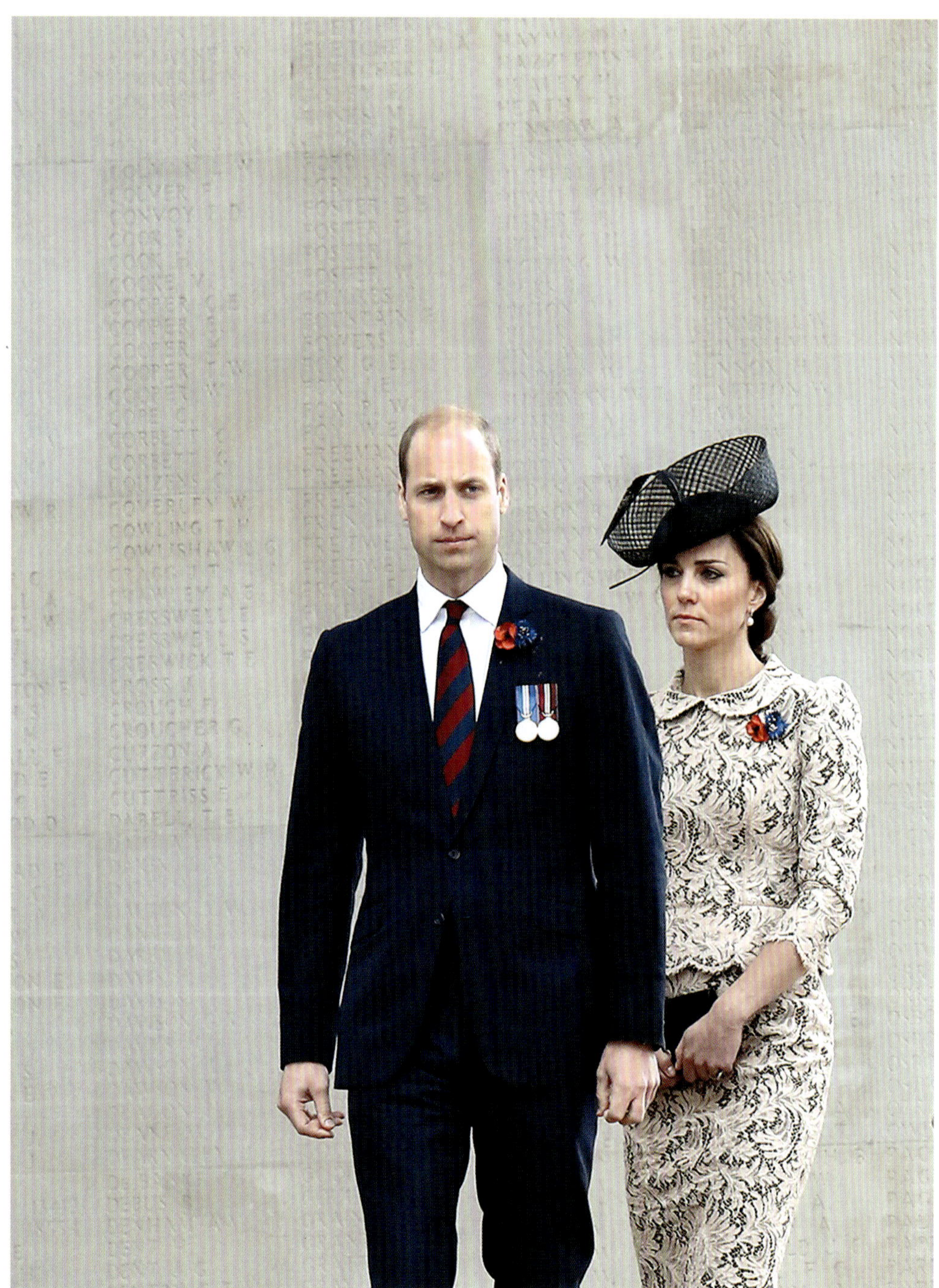

The Duke and Duchess of Cambridge walk past engraved names of the missing on the Thiepval Memorial to the Missing of the Somme in France on July 1, 2016. That day marked exactly 100 years since the beginning of the bloodiest battle of the First World War, the Battle of the Somme.

Opposite The Queen visits *Blood Swept Lands and Seas of Red*, an evolving art installation at the Tower of London in 2014. Volunteers planted 888,246 ceramic poppies in the moat. Each poppy represented a British or colonial fatality in the First World War. The last poppy was planted on November 11, 2014. This powerful and moving installation captivated the nation and attracted record numbers of visitors.

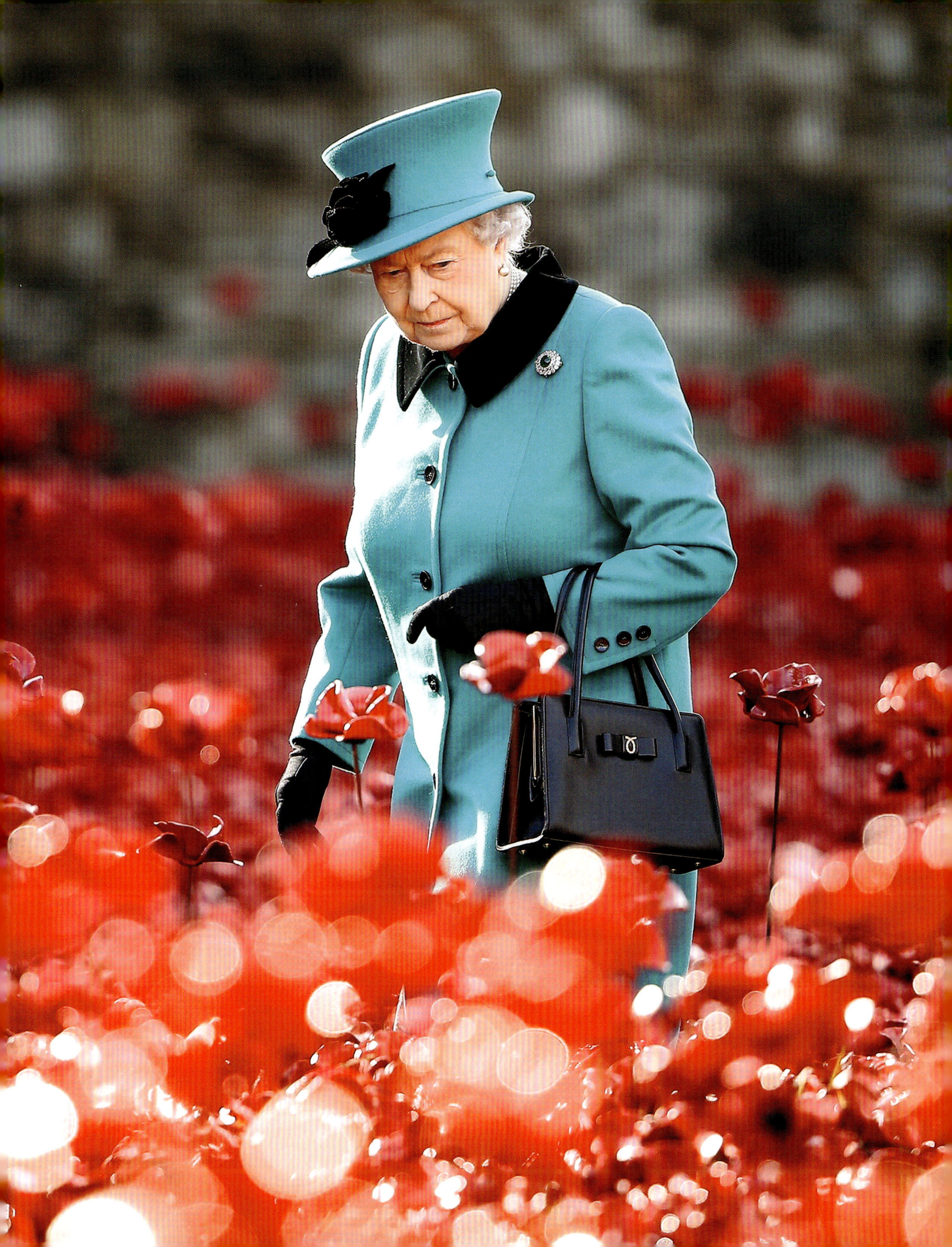

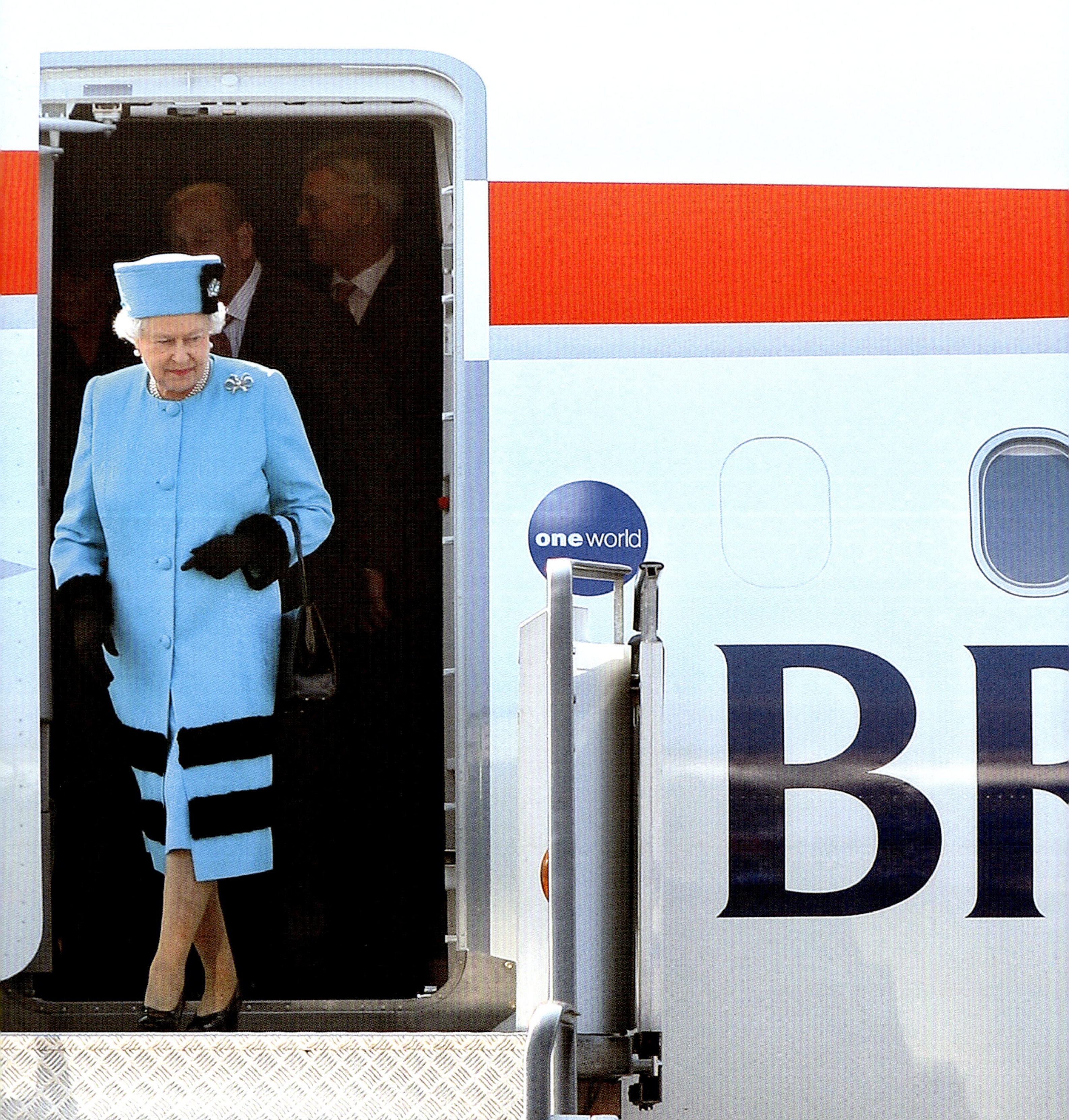
oneworld
BR

The Art of Royal Travel

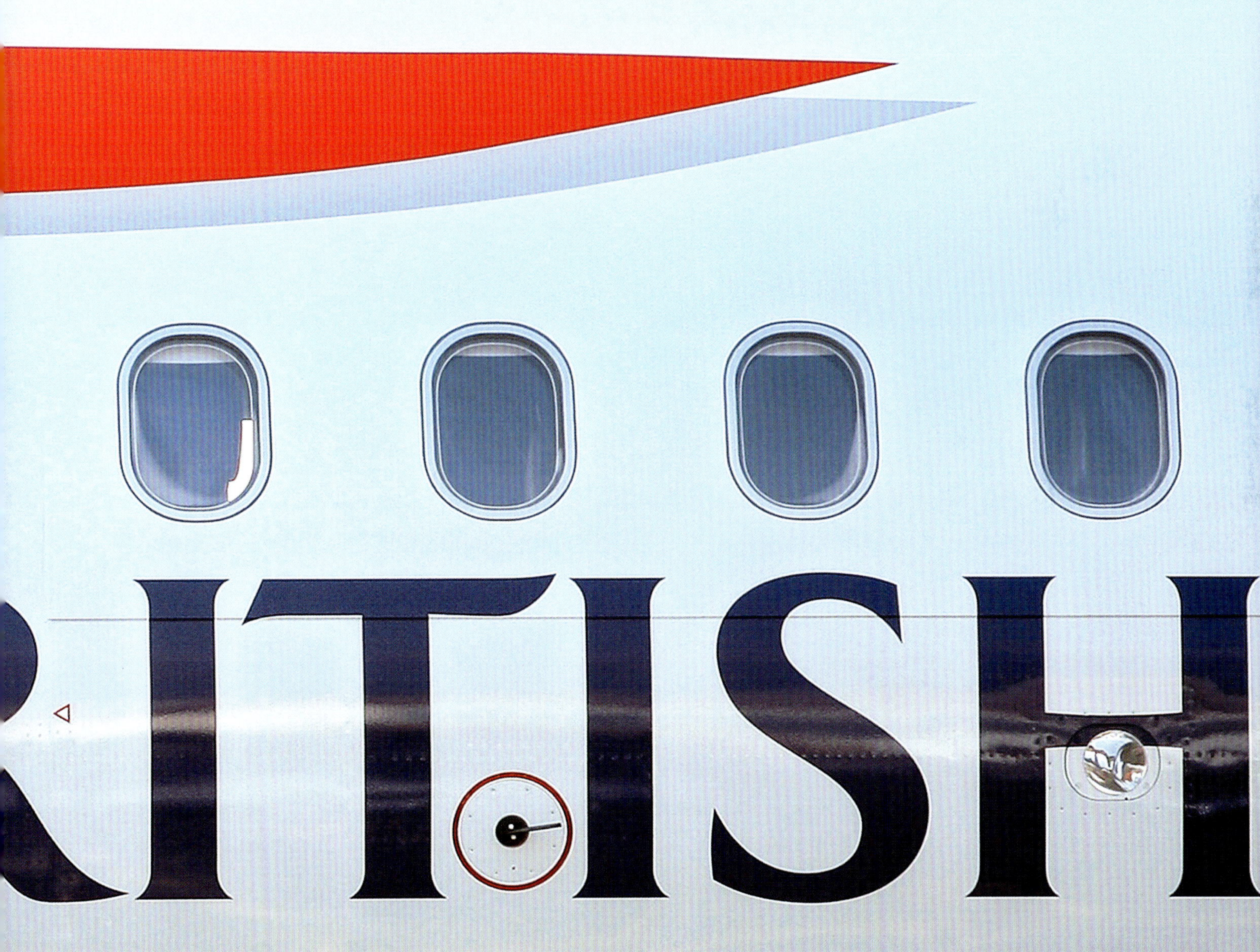

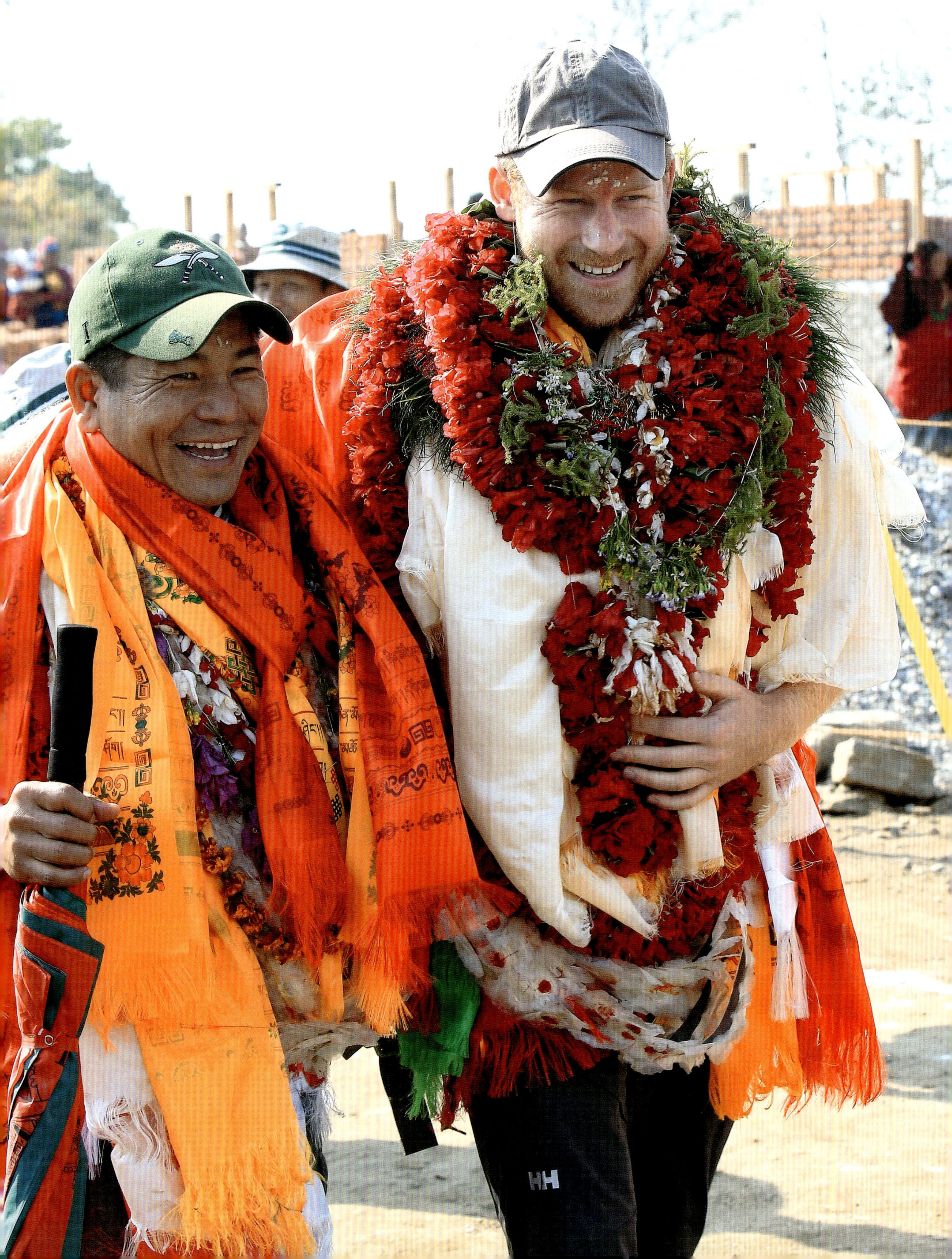
HH

Travel is part of the very essence of the royal family. The Queen once said, "I have to be seen to be believed." The need to get out there and be seen means travel is an integral part of royal life. The royal tour is one of the things that gives the British royal family their unique ability to act as ambassadors for the United Kingdom around the world. In the early days of Queen Elizabeth's reign, royal tours would last for months at a time. These days a tour rarely lasts longer than ten days, but these trips are an important facet of the royal family's public relations strategy. A high-profile royal tour can take their message to places it would not otherwise reach. In these days of Instagram and Twitter, the impact of seeing someone in "real life" can't be overstated. The images from these tours define their success and establish how they are perceived back home and globally. It is my role as a photographer to document these and I relish the challenges and privilege that such a position entails.

Over the last fifteen years I have travelled to all four corners of the globe with the British royal family visiting over a hundred countries and have just acquired my fifth passport. From the earthquake zones of Pakistan to the Galápagos Islands, Papua New Guinea, Mexico, Sierra Leone, Indonesia, India, and Japan. I've been to Durbar festivals in Nigeria and the jungles of Borneo with the Prince of Wales and Duchess of Cornwall. I have visited the Forbidden City in China, New Zealand, and Vietnam with the Duke of Cambridge, and the Caribbean Islands, Brazil, and South Africa with Prince Harry. I have photographed the Prince of Wales dancing the samba in the favelas of Brazil, the Duchess of Cambridge playing cricket in a maxi-dress in Mumbai, and Prince Harry taking part in a volleyball match on the beaches of Brazil. Regular visits are made to Commonwealth countries where Queen Elizabeth reigns as monarch, such as Canada, New Zealand, and Australia. More recently, the younger royals have even embarked on Brexit-related visits to European destinations. The royal tour is a rite of passage for younger royals, an opportunity to embrace the privilege of their roles and take their messages to a wider audience. Royal tours test their diplomatic skills to the limit whilst providing the opportunity to tailor schedules to reflect their passions and charitable concerns. Covering these trips as a photographer can be a madcap rollercoaster at times, involving everything from overzealous drivers speeding in convoys to the logistics of negotiating airport check-ins with heavy photography equipment. They are consistently both the highlights and by far the biggest challenges of each photographic year.

Preceding pages The Queen steps off a British Airways plane at Jože Pučnik Airport in Ljubljana for a two-day visit to Slovenia. This was the monarch's first trip to the former communist country.

Opposite Festooned in garlands, Prince Harry treks into the Himalayan village of Okhari with Major Prakash Gurung. Gurung served in Afghanistan at the same time as Prince Harry and was Gurkha Orderly Officer for the Queen at Buckingham Palace.

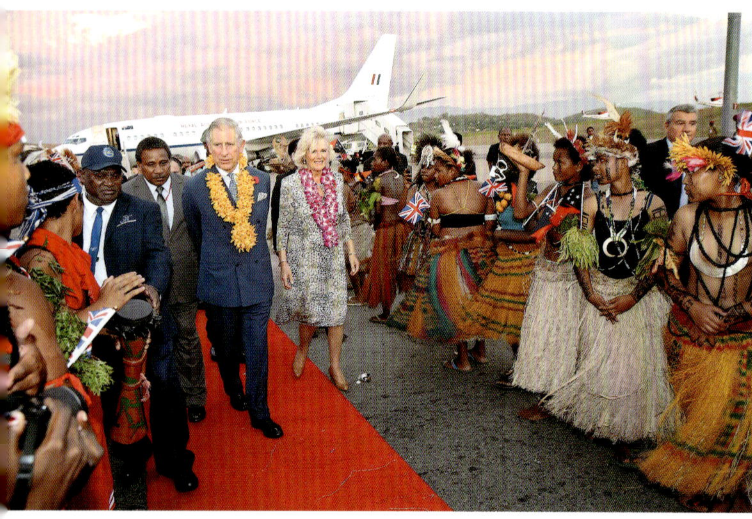

Above The Prince of Wales and Duchess of Cornwall arrive at Jacksons International Airport in Port Moresby, Papua New Guinea. The couple were on the first leg of a Diamond Jubilee tour that also included stops in Australia and New Zealand.

Below On a tour of the Middle East, the Prince of Wales performs a traditional sword dance with local Omanis at Nizwa Fort.

Opposite Taking in the views and the wildlife, the Prince of Wales and the Duchess of Cornwall walk along the beach on North Seymour Island during their visit to the Galápagos. This was the final day of an epic 2009 South American tour of Chile, Brazil, and Ecuador.

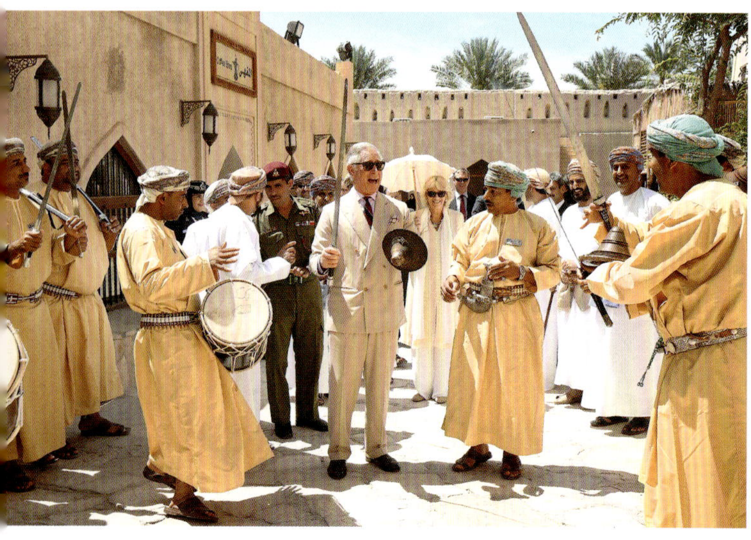

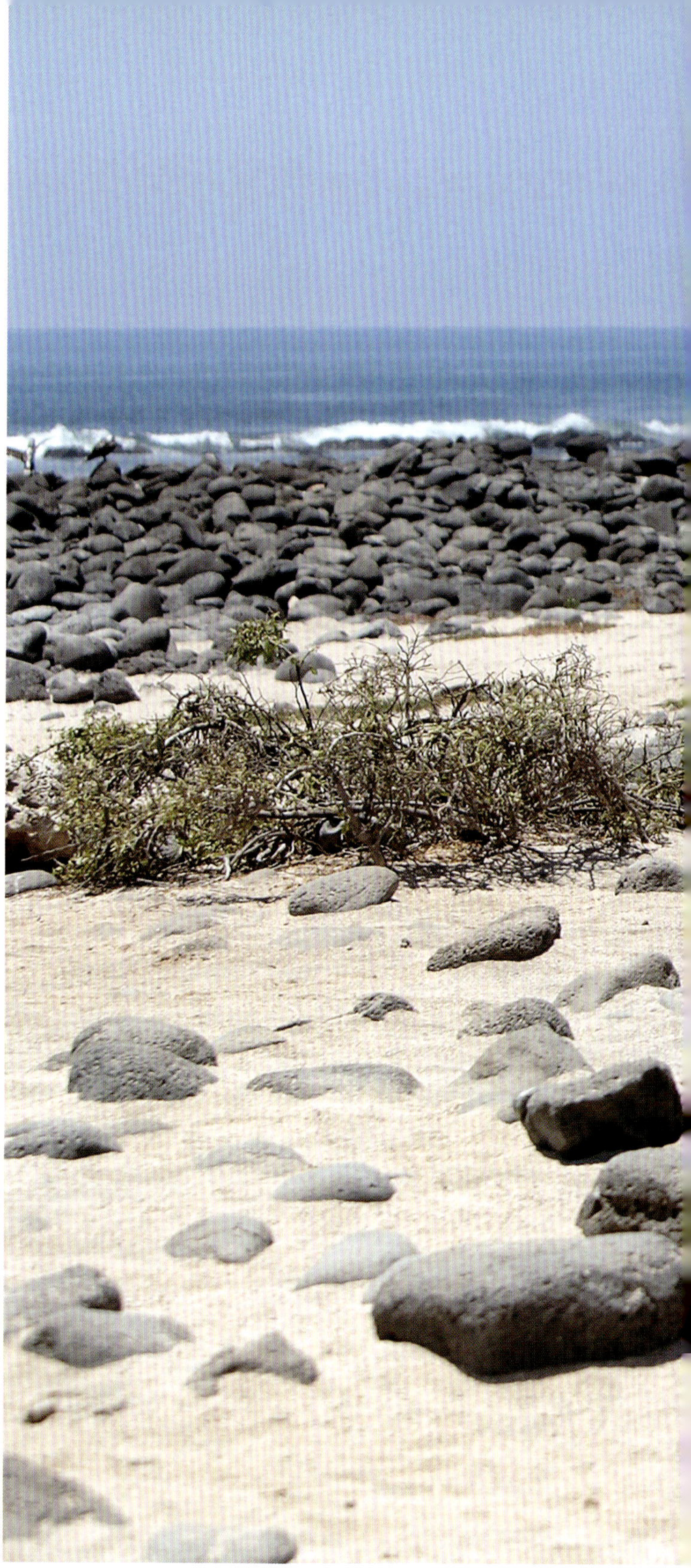

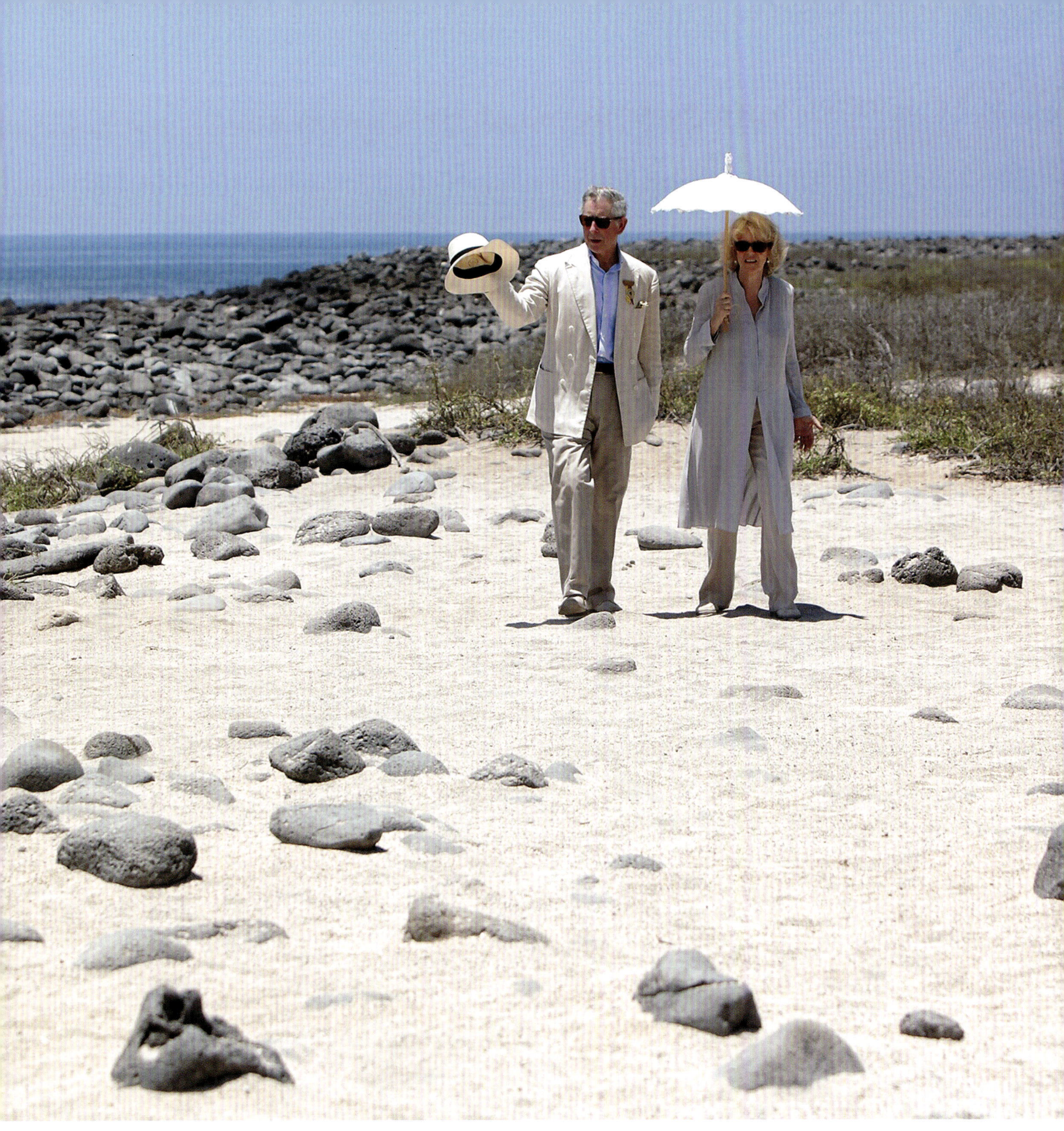

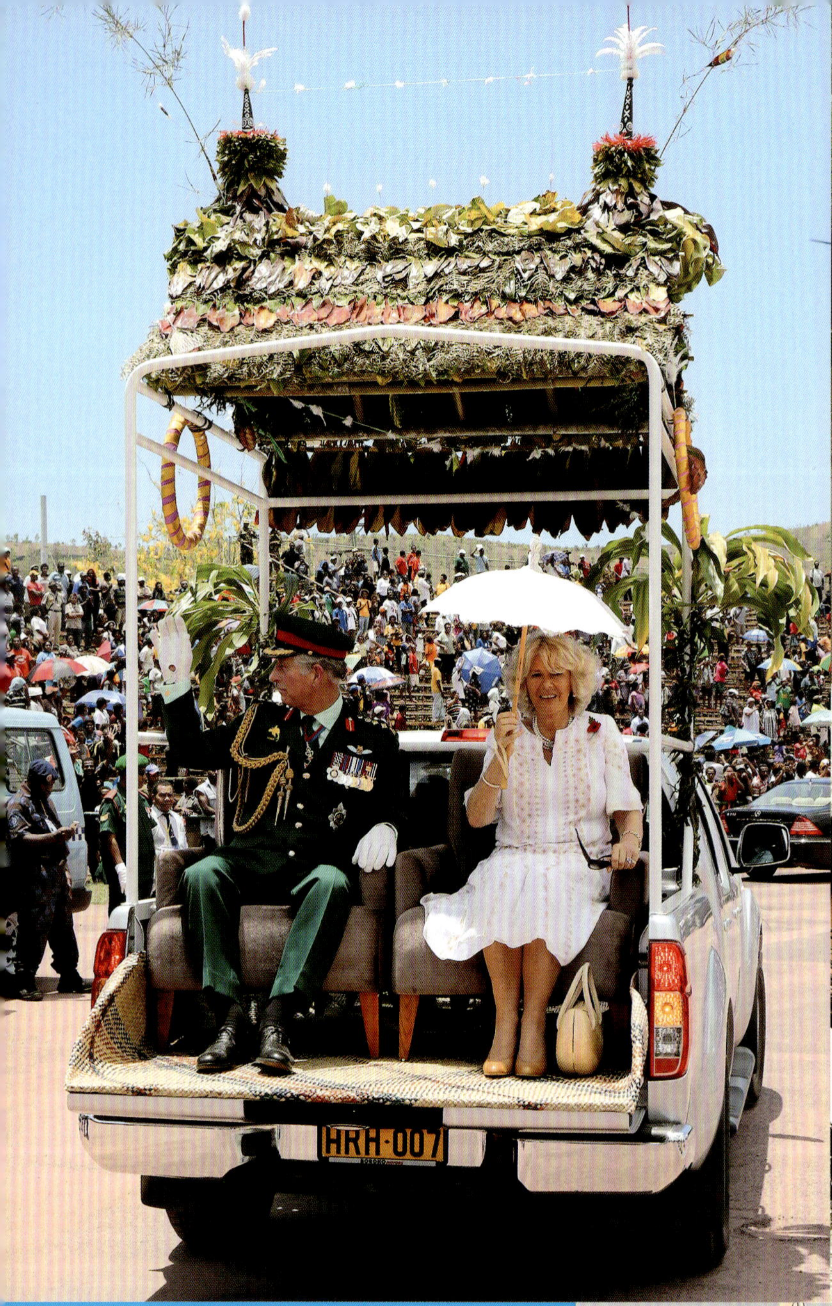

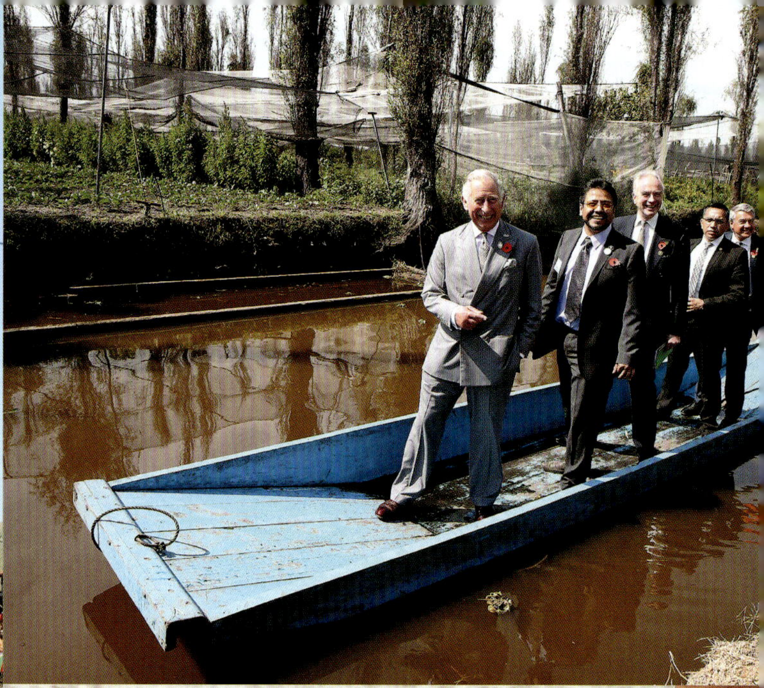

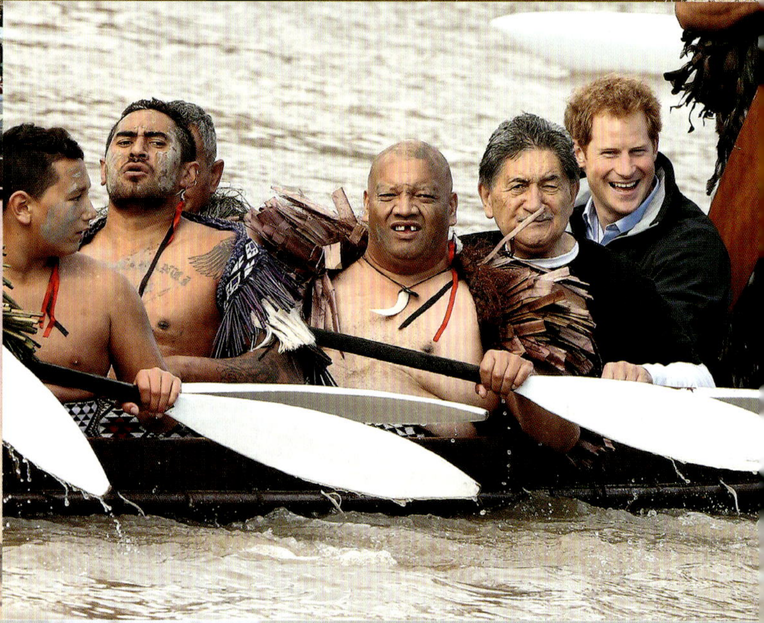

Travel on royal tours can be colourful and surprising, as the royals are frequently invited to move around in traditional modes of transport.

Top, left The Prince of Wales and Duchess of Cornwall in Papua New Guinea (note the numberplate!); **top, middle** the Prince of Wales on a punt as he visits a *chinampa*, or floating farm, just outside Mexico City; **centre** Prince Harry on a Maori war canoe in New Zealand; **below** the Duchess of Cambridge on a traditional canoe in Tuvanipupu in the South Pacific (with a papier-mâché shark in hot pursuit).

Opposite The Duke and Duchess of Cambridge on arrival at Honiara, Guadalcanal, in the Solomon Islands in 2012.

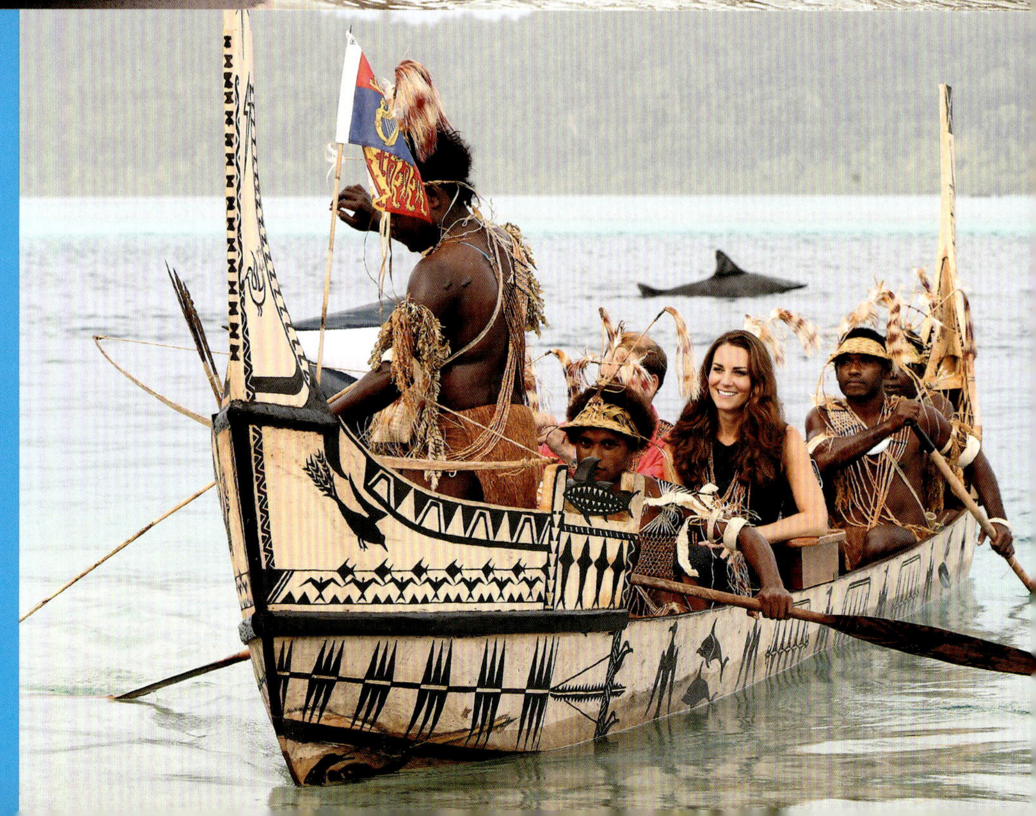

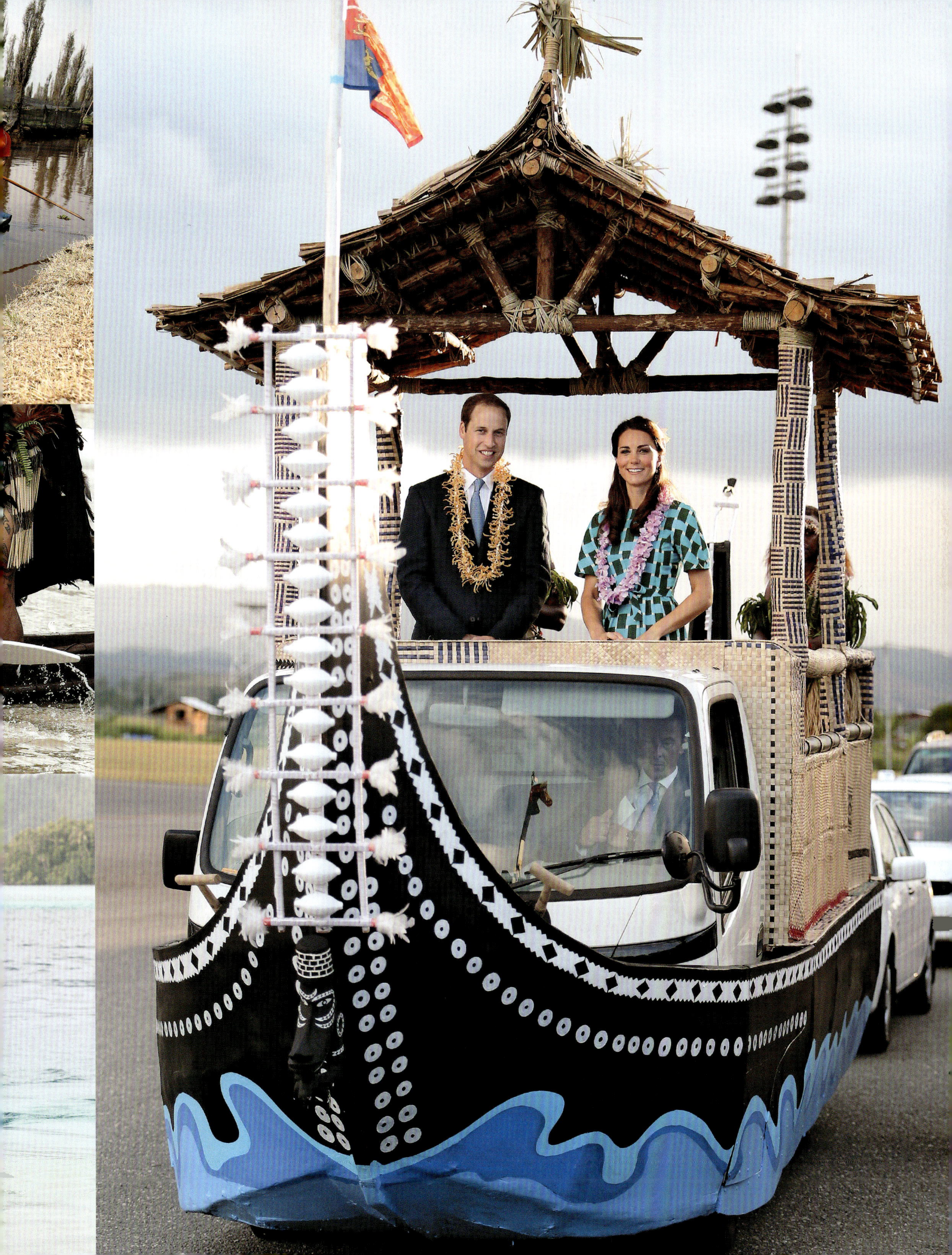

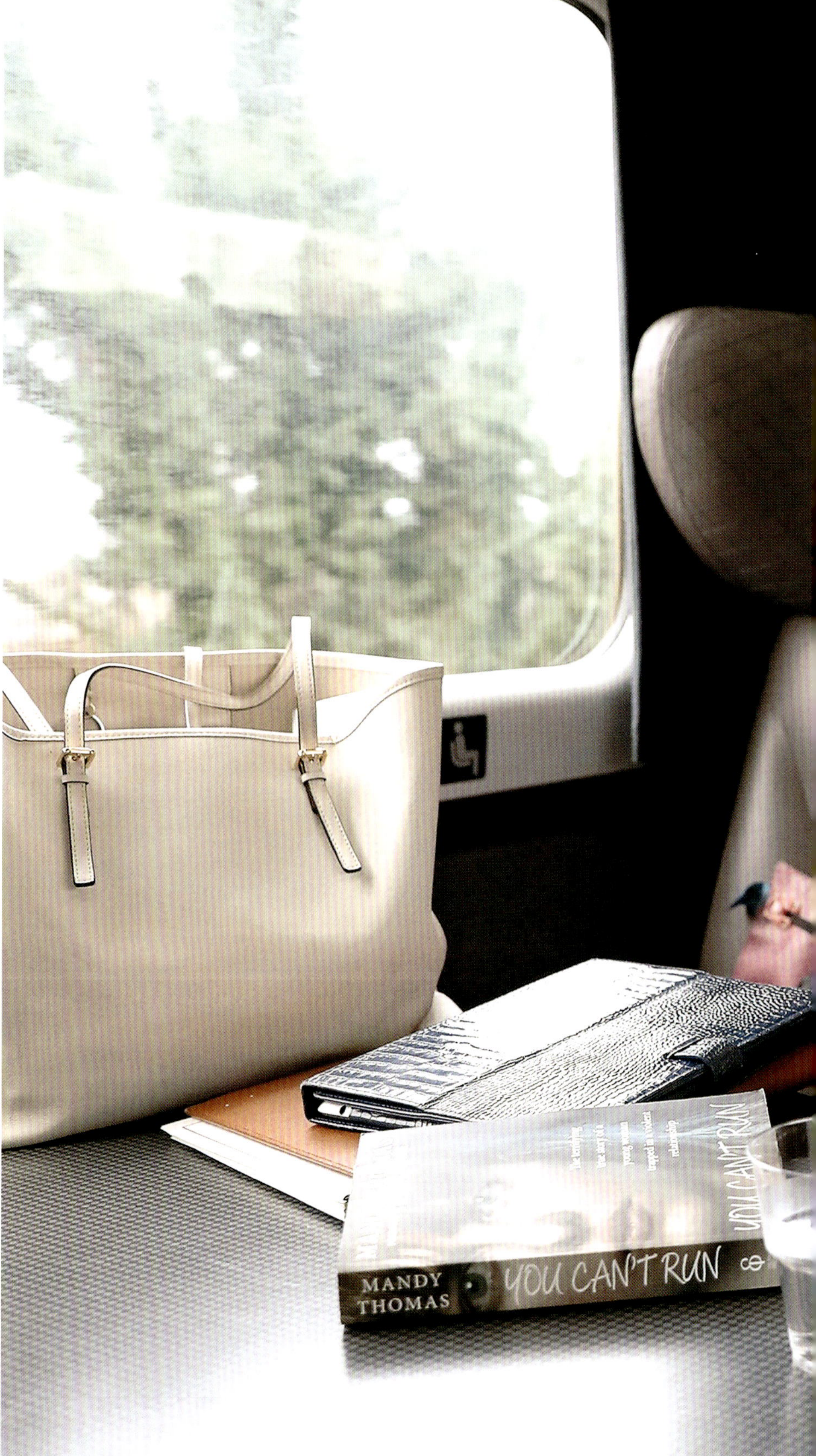

Opposite Domestic travel is a considerable part of royal life and the modern royal spends much of the year crisscrossing the United Kingdom by plane, train, and automobile. The Duchess of Cornwall works on her notes as she travels back to Clarence House from a day of engagements in Bristol.

Following pages Local children are caught in the down-draught of the royal helicopter as it lands in Sark during a visit by the Prince of Wales and the Duchess of Cornwall. One of the Channel Islands, Sark sits off the coast of Normandy, France. It is these peripheral, unexpected moments that I most love to capture.

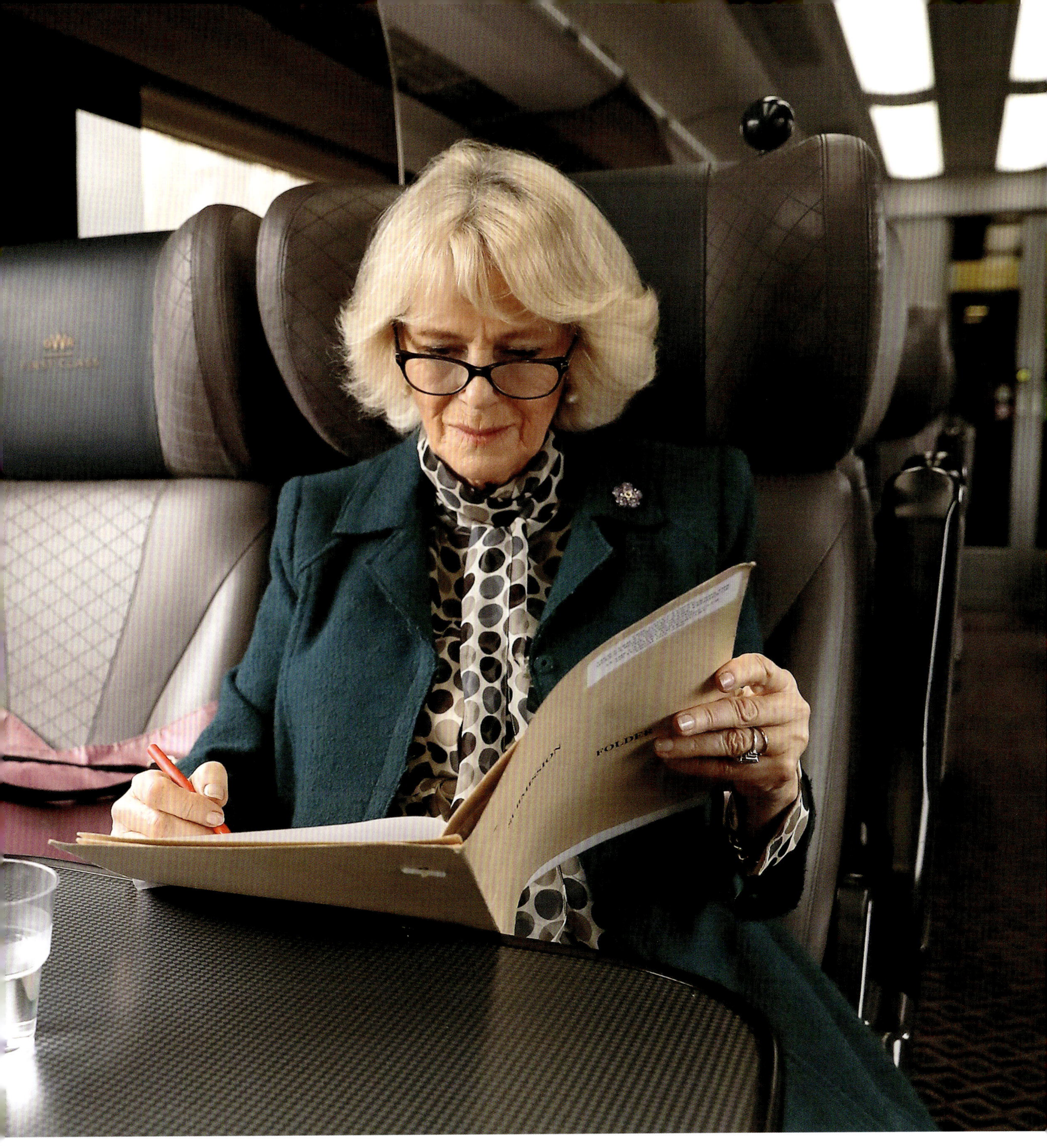

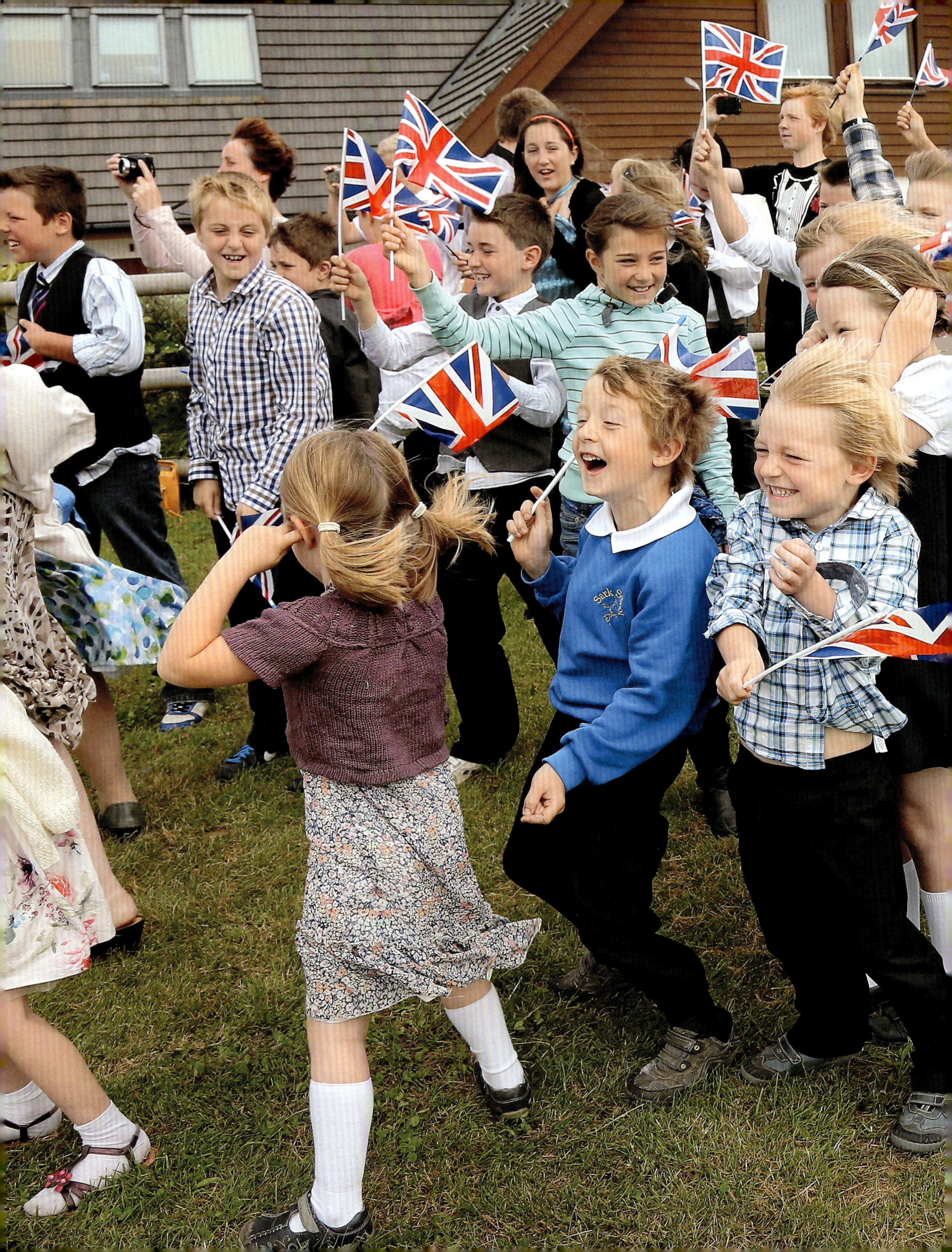
Sark

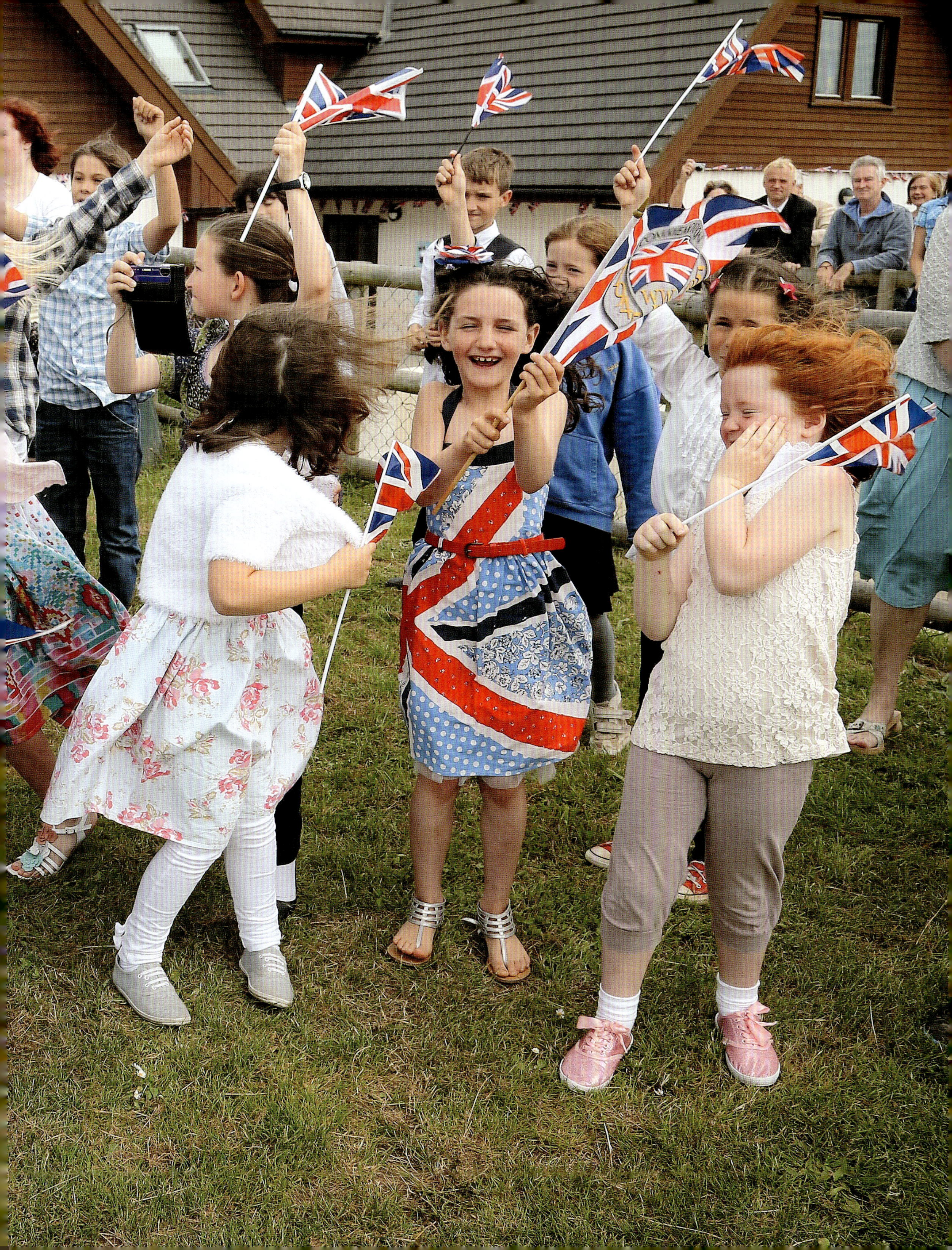

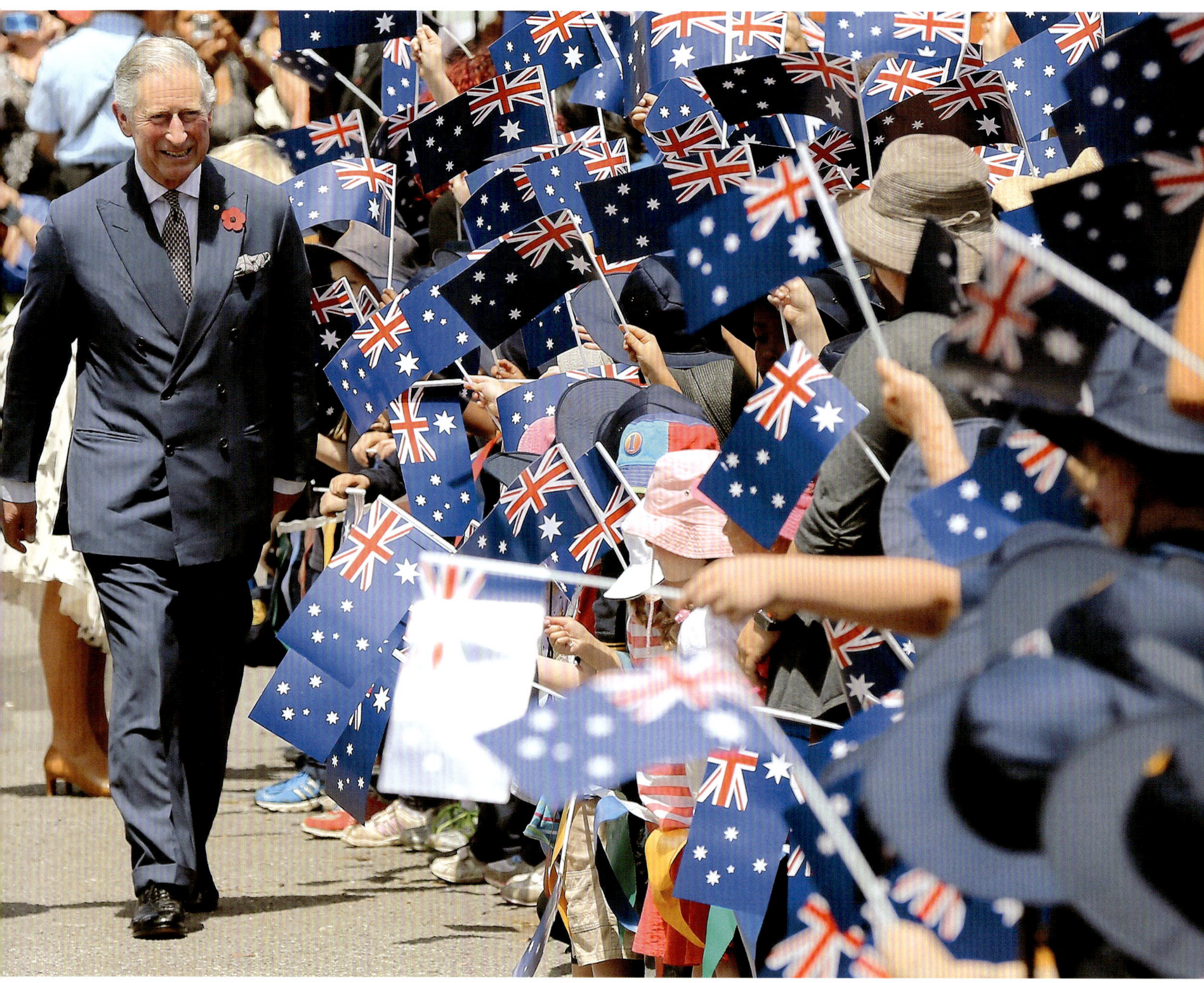

This page Schoolchildren wave Australian flags as Prince Charles visits Kilkenny Primary School in Adelaide, Australia.

Opposite The Duke and Duchess of Cambridge walk around the base of Uluru, or Ayers Rock, in Australia. The royals were on a three-week tour of Australia and New Zealand, their first official trip overseas with their young son Prince George.

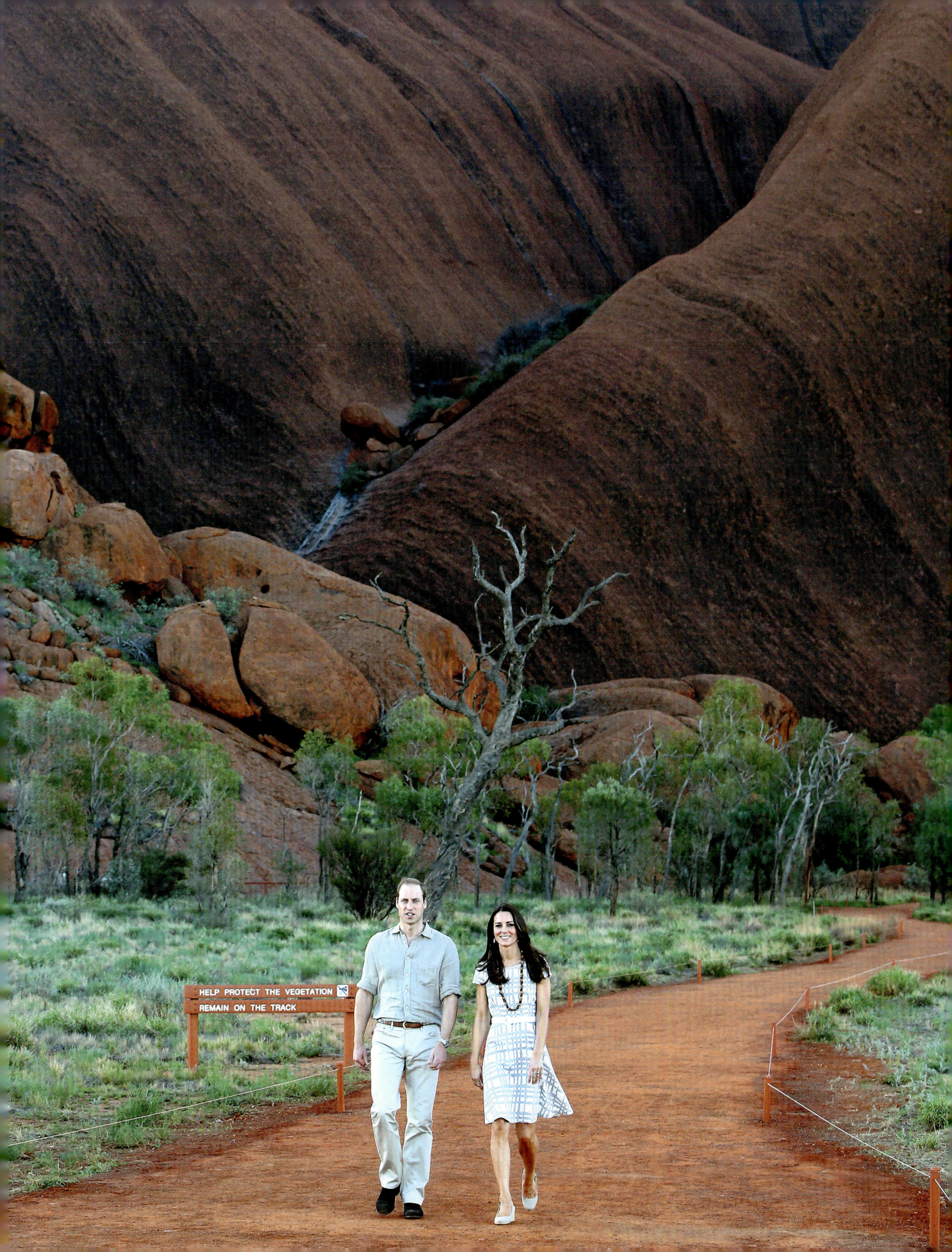
HELP PROTECT THE VEGETATION
REMAIN ON THE TRACK

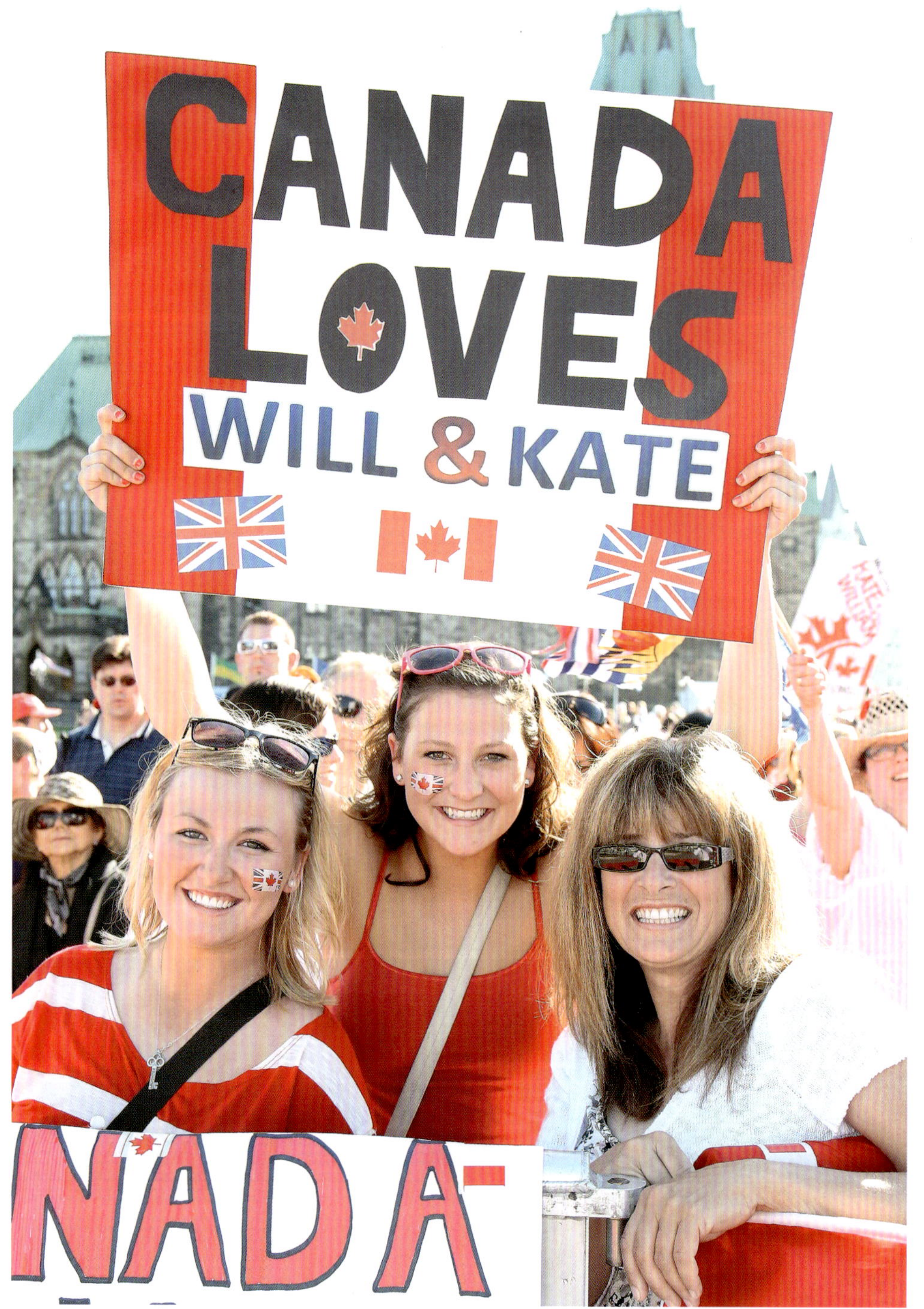

This page Royal fans wait to catch a glimpse of the Duke and Duchess of Cambridge as they arrive at Parliament Hill in Ottawa for Canada Day celebrations on July 1, 2011. The newly married royal couple were on the second day of their first joint overseas tour, and interest in them had reached a fever-pitch off the back of the royal wedding in London. The Canada Day celebrations marked the beginning of a two-week tour across North America that ended in Los Angeles.

Opposite Pressing the button to launch the iconic Calgary Stampede.

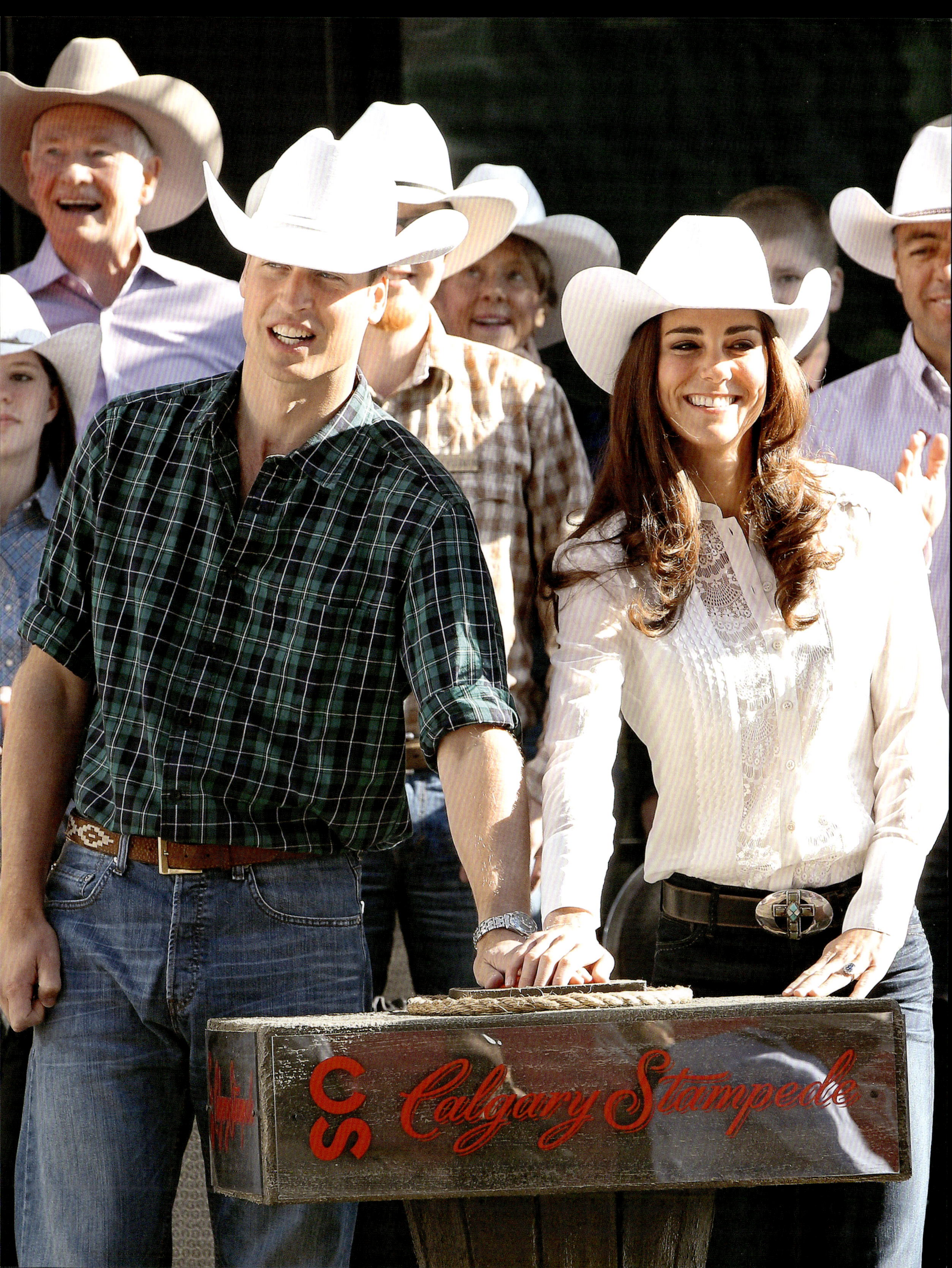
CS
Calgary Stampede

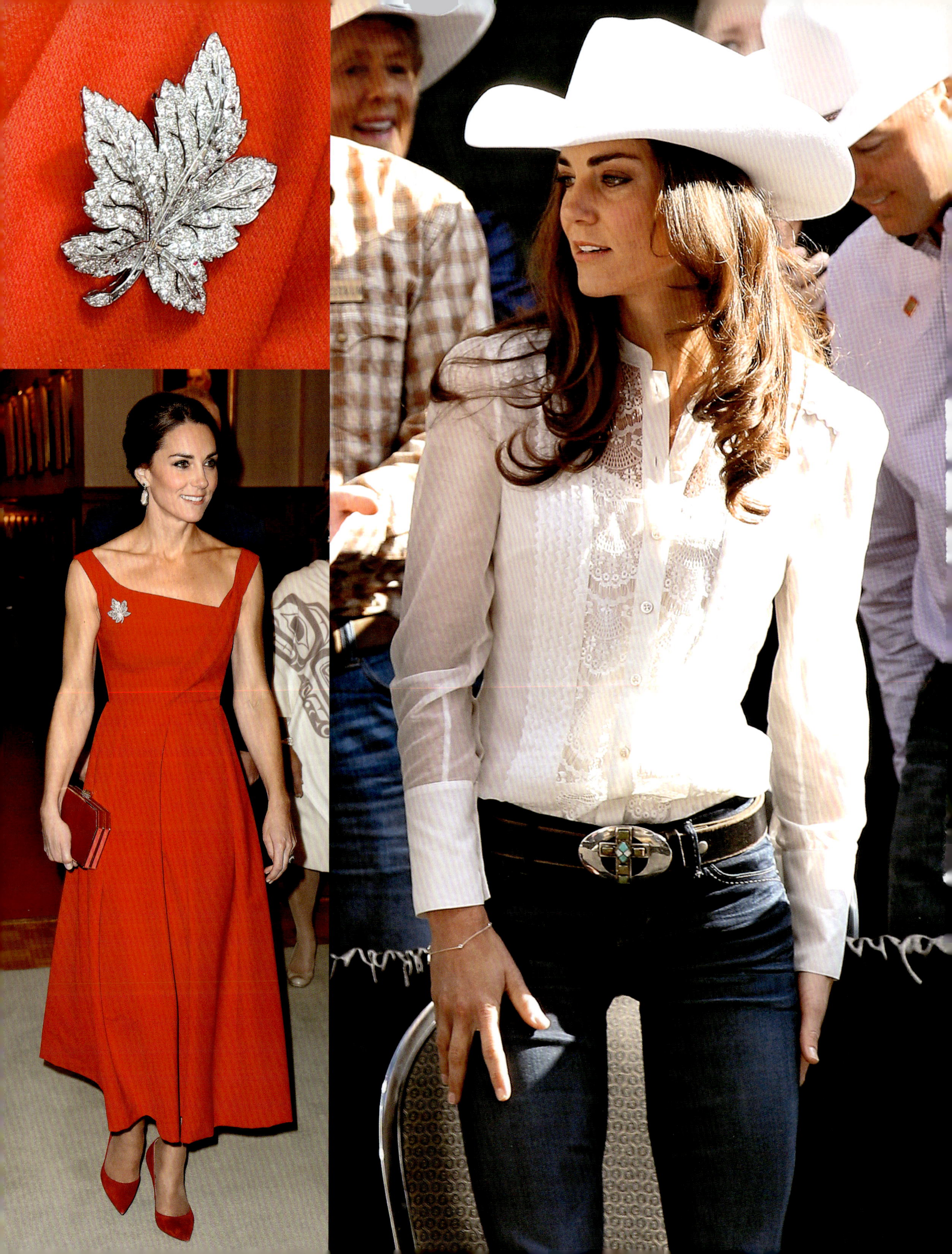

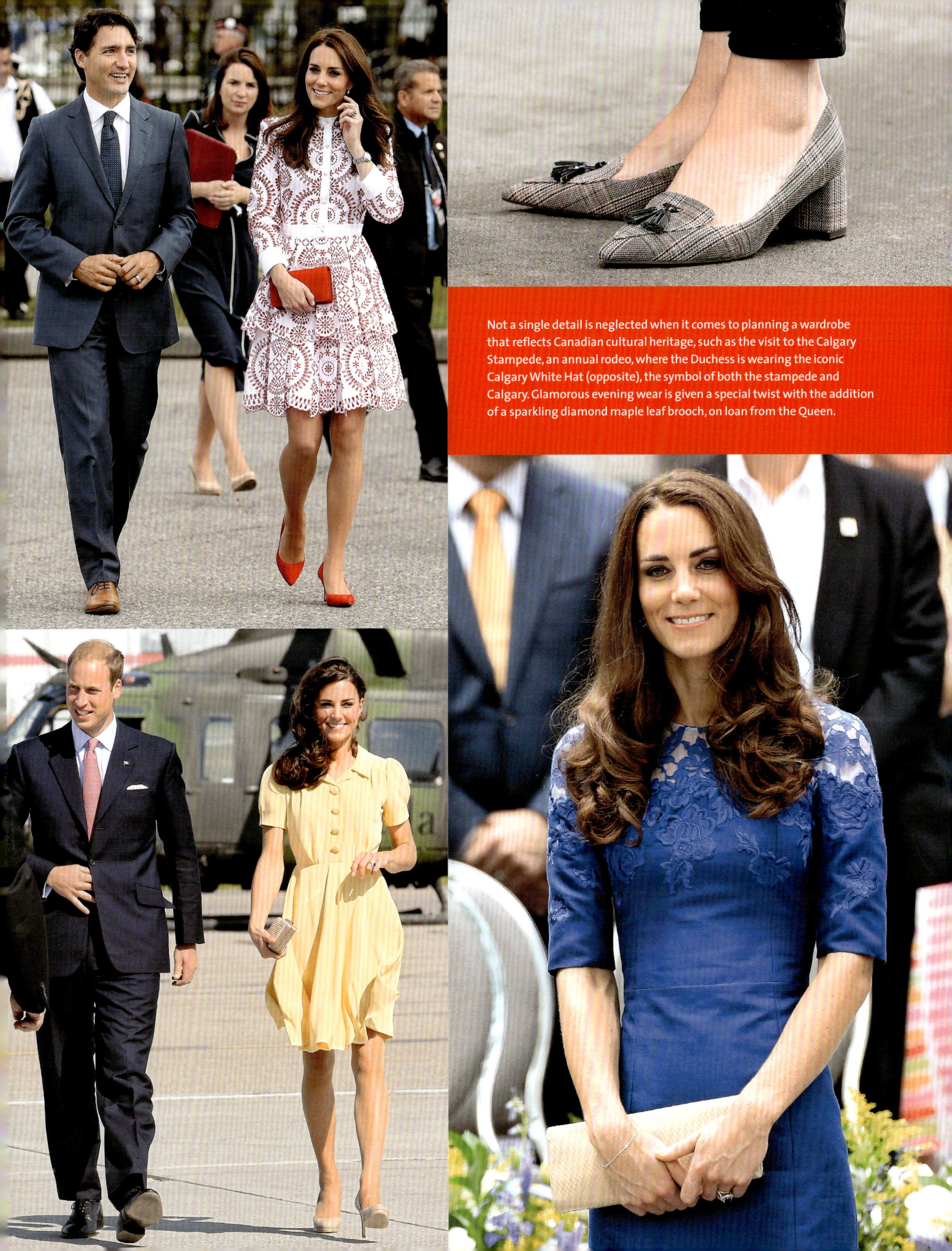

Not a single detail is neglected when it comes to planning a wardrobe that reflects Canadian cultural heritage, such as the visit to the Calgary Stampede, an annual rodeo, where the Duchess is wearing the iconic Calgary White Hat (opposite), the symbol of both the stampede and Calgary. Glamorous evening wear is given a special twist with the addition of a sparkling diamond maple leaf brooch, on loan from the Queen.

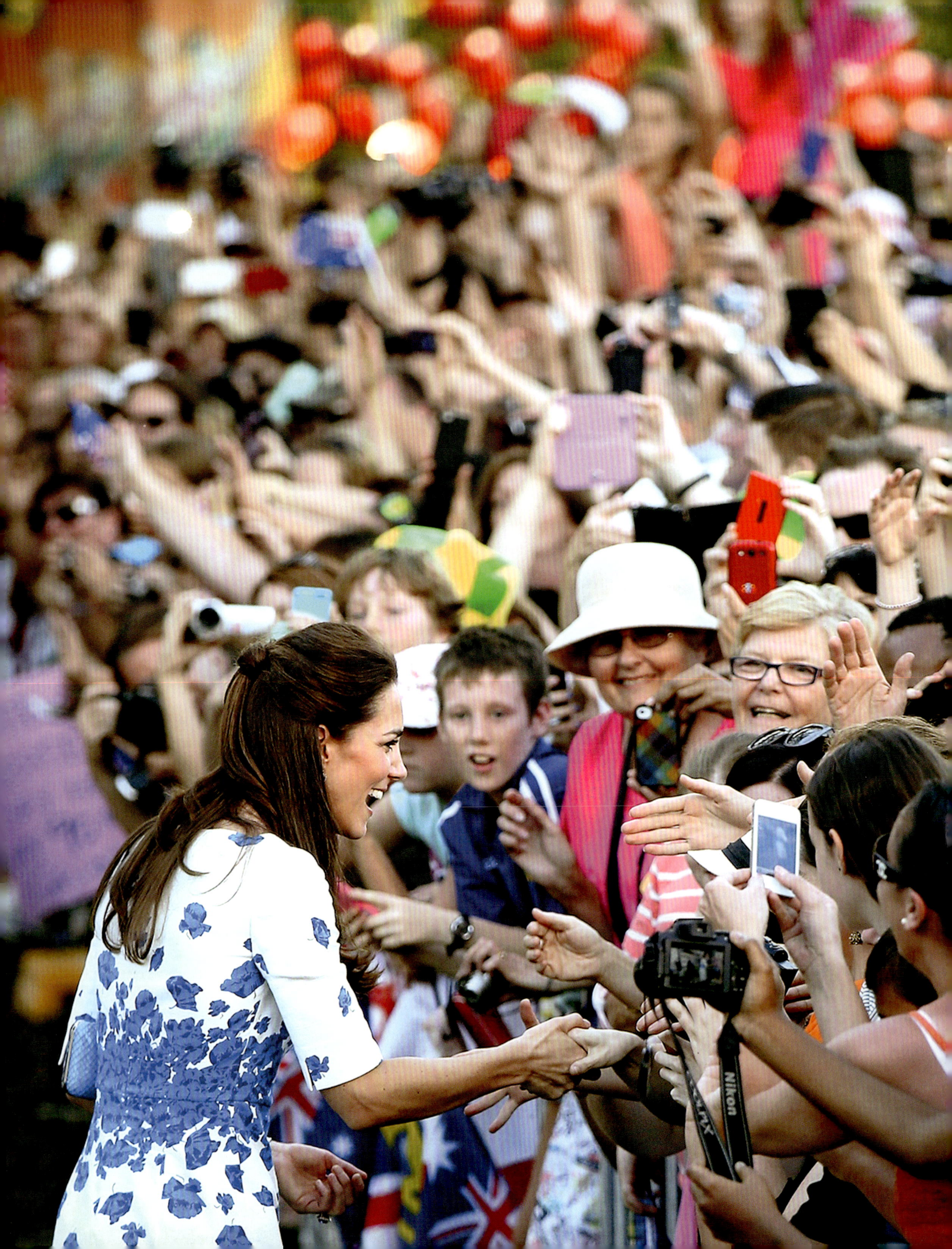
Nikon

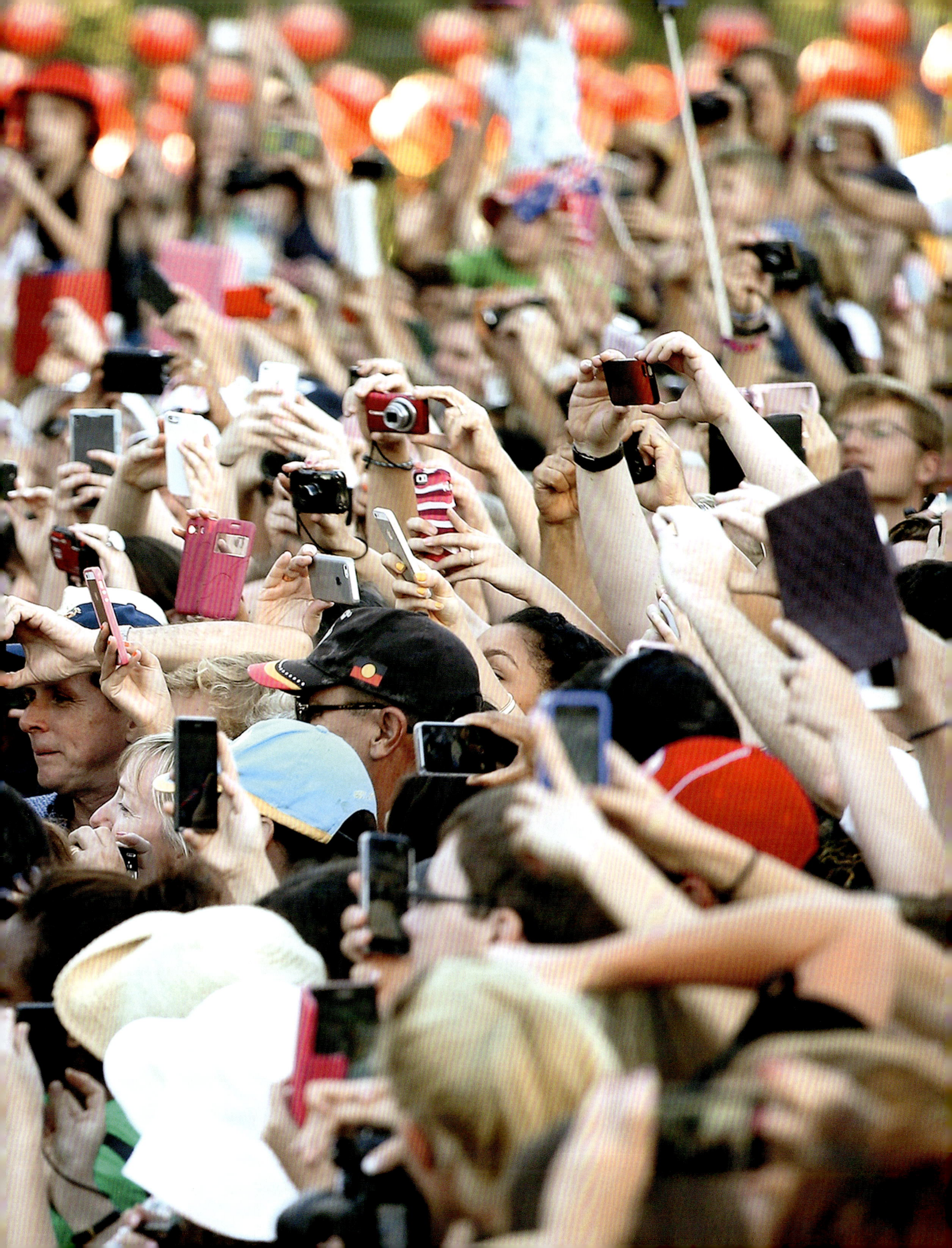

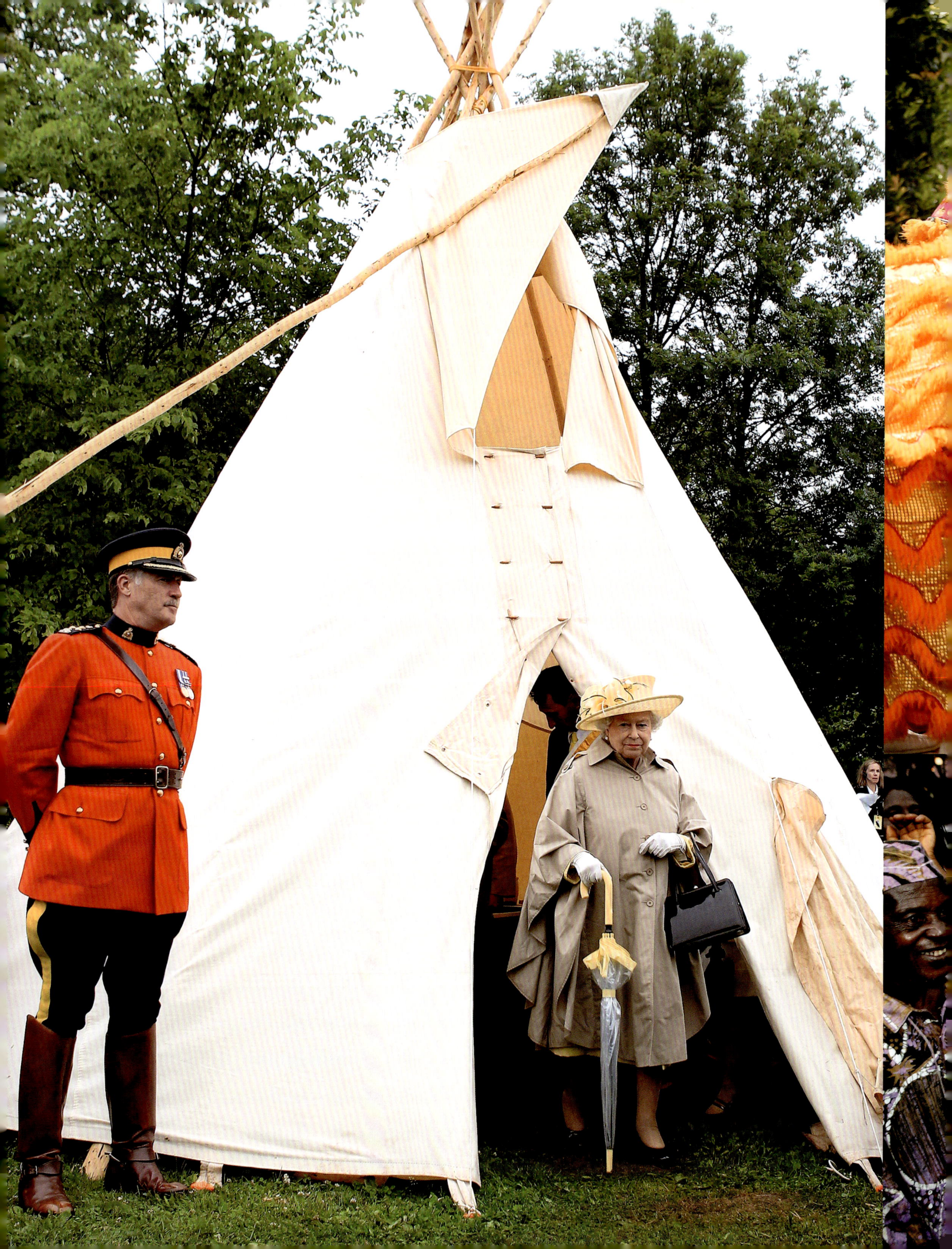

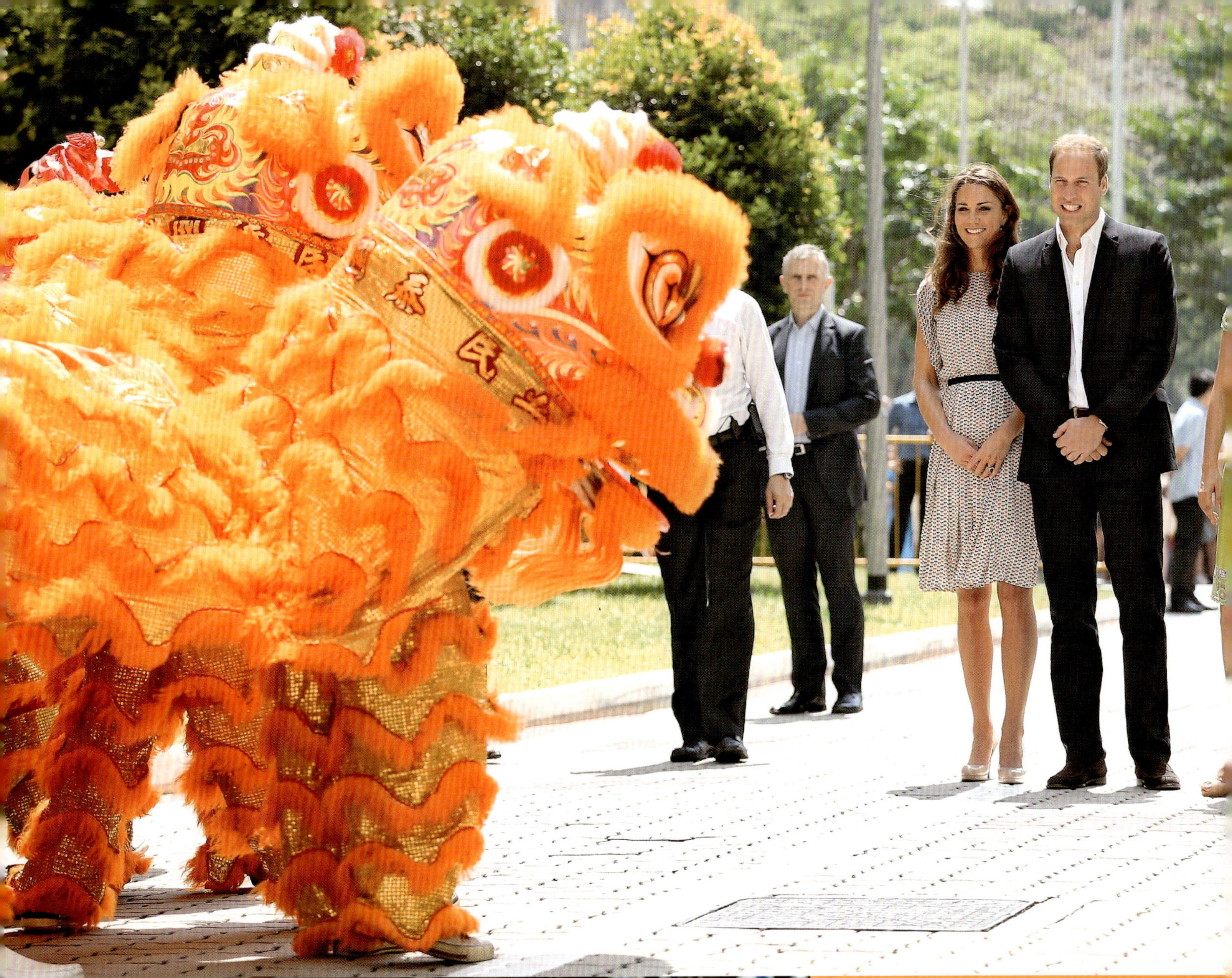

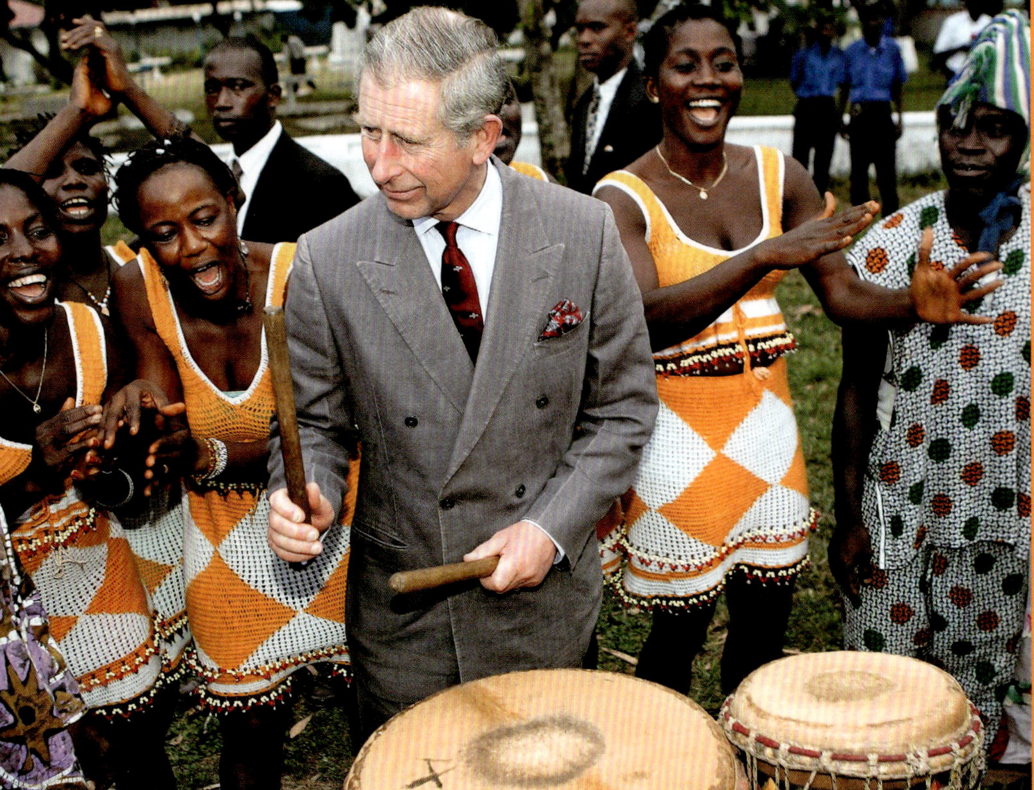

Preceding pages Large crowds cheer and try to catch a glimpse of the Duchess of Cambridge as she meets members of the public on the South Bank in Brisbane, Australia.

Culture and tradition always form the backbone of a tour. Recognising diversity and acknowledging past struggles are important parts of any visit.

Opposite The Queen emerges from a wigwam at a First Nation event on Halifax Common in Canada.

Above The Duke and Duchess of Cambridge are treated to the spectacle of a dancing dragon as they attend a cultural event in Singapore.

Left The Prince of Wales plays the drums with dancers in the Sierra Leone national troupe as he arrives at Freetown Golf Club.

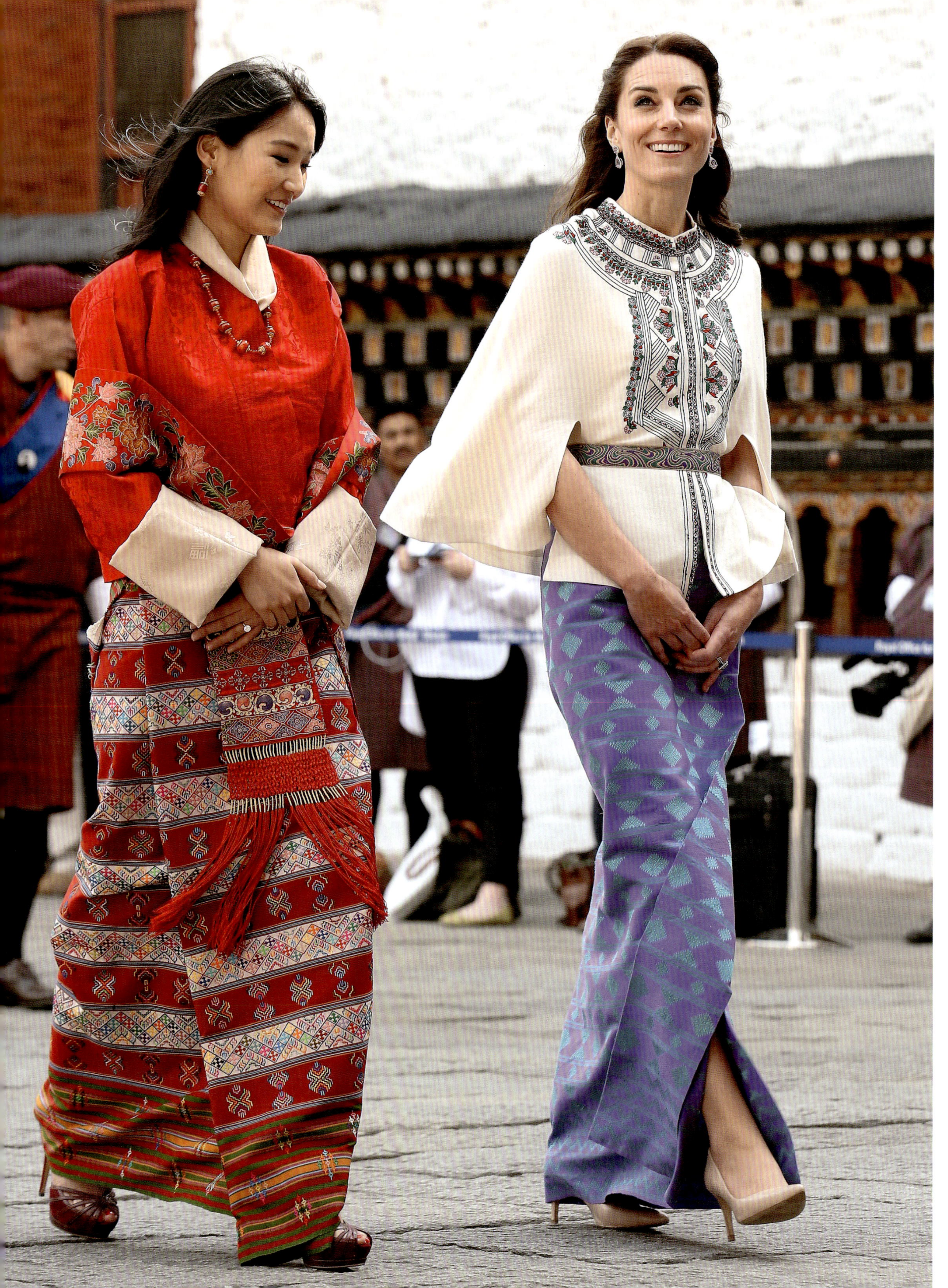

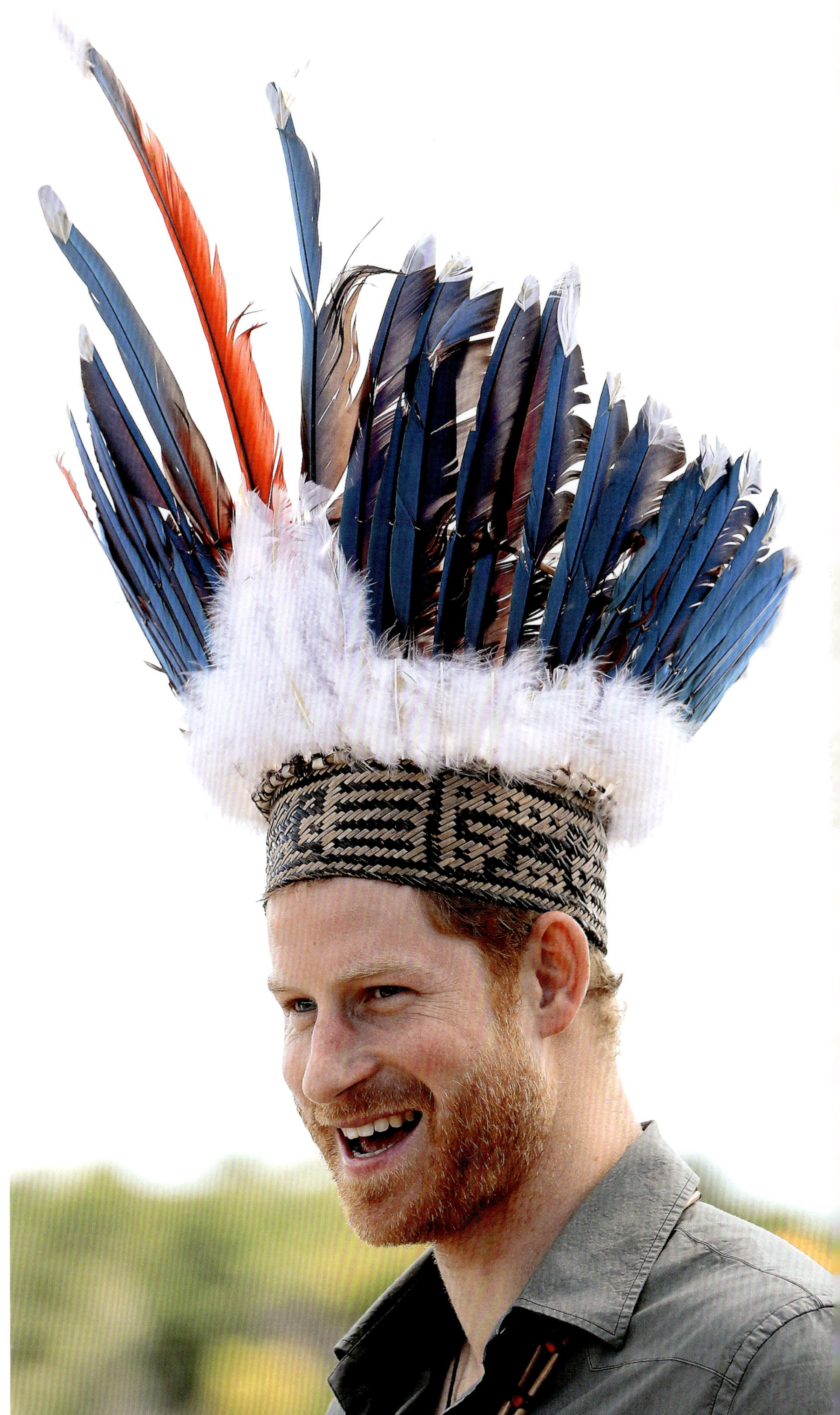

Opposite The Duchess of Cambridge walks with Queen Consort Her Majesty Jetsun Pema Wangchuck in Tashichhoedzong, a Buddhist monastery and fortress on the northern edge of the city of Thimphu on the first day of a two-day visit to Bhutan.

This page Wearing a traditional headdress, Prince Harry visits Surama village in the Guyana hinterland. The Prince of Wales visited the same village sixteen years earlier and donned similar headwear.

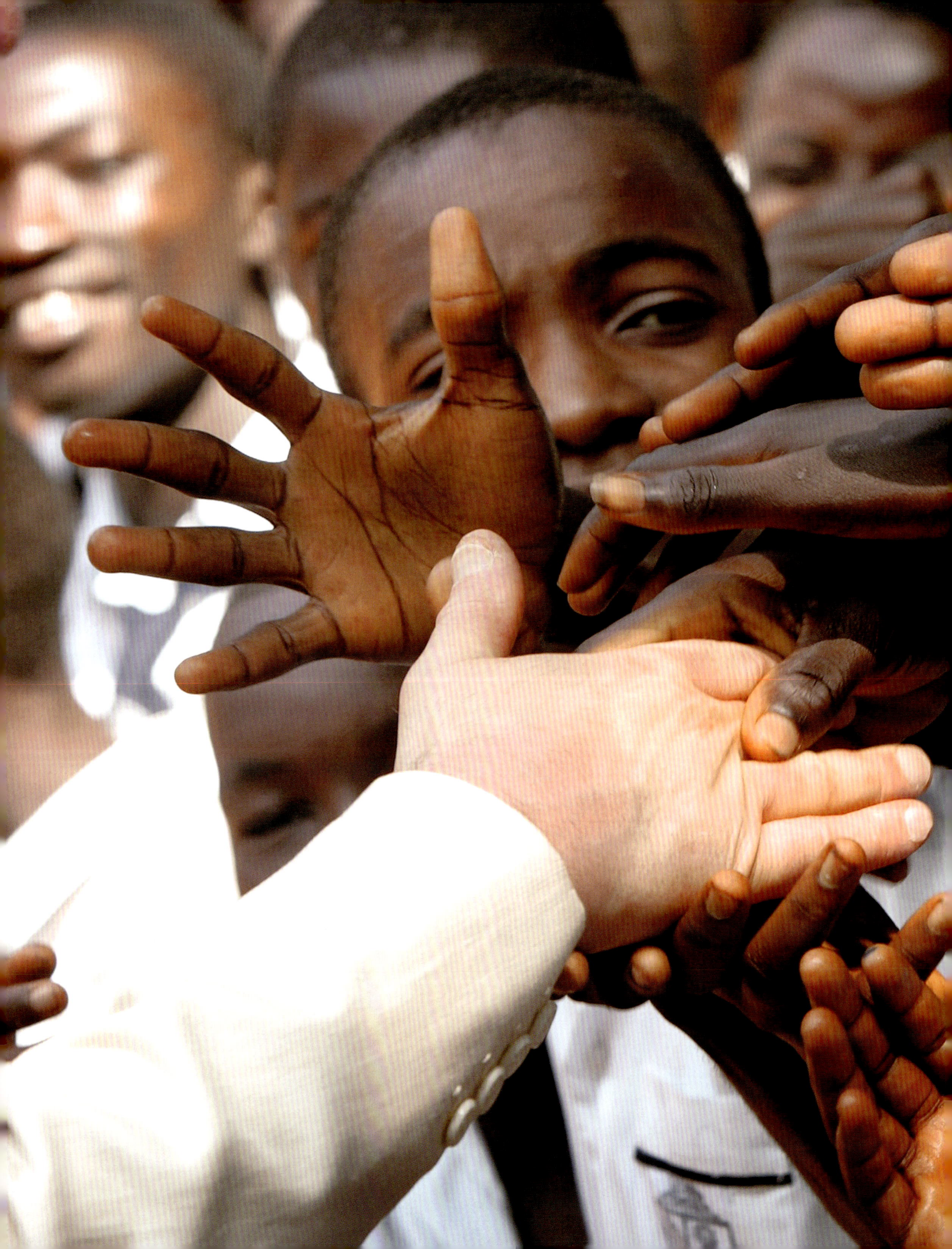

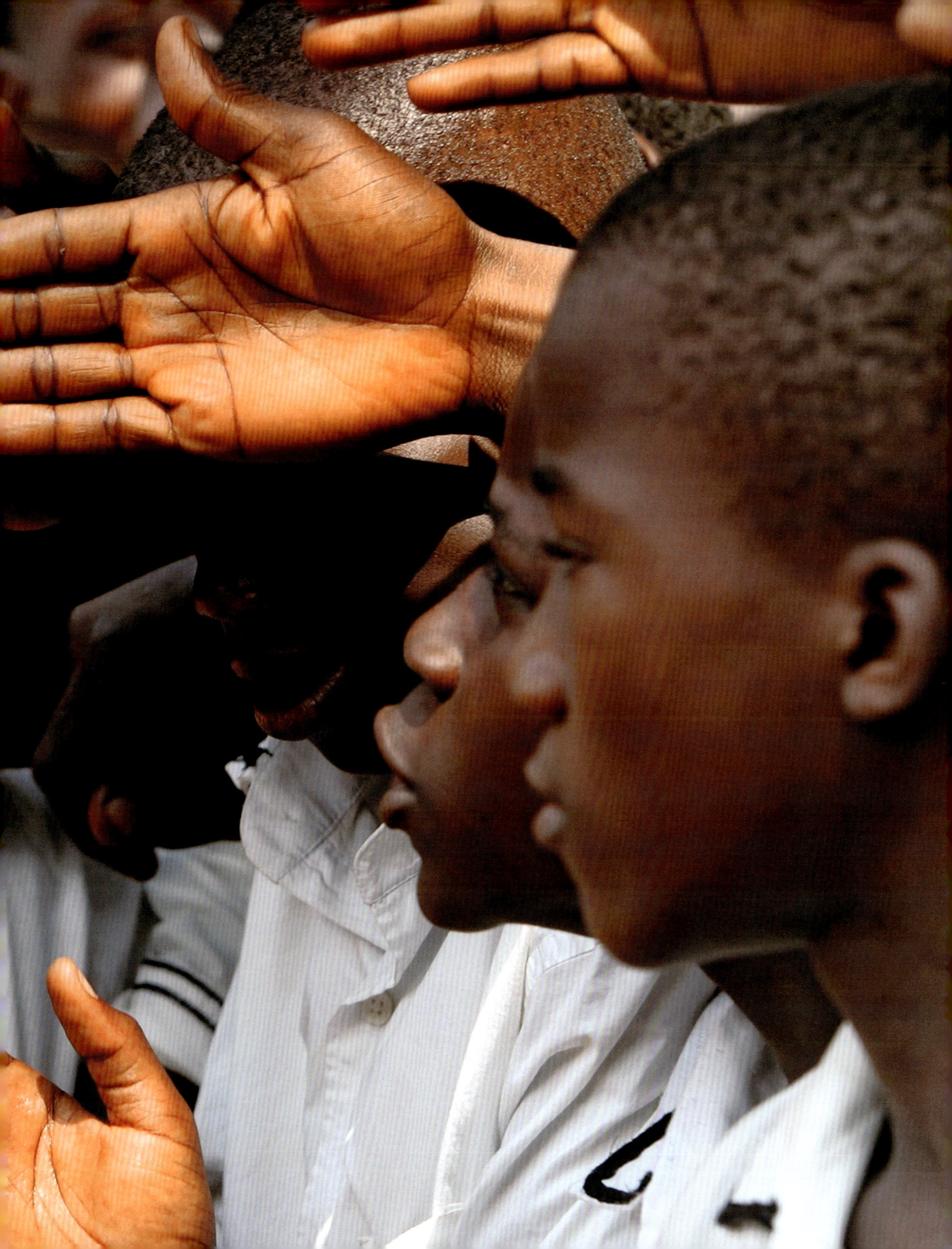

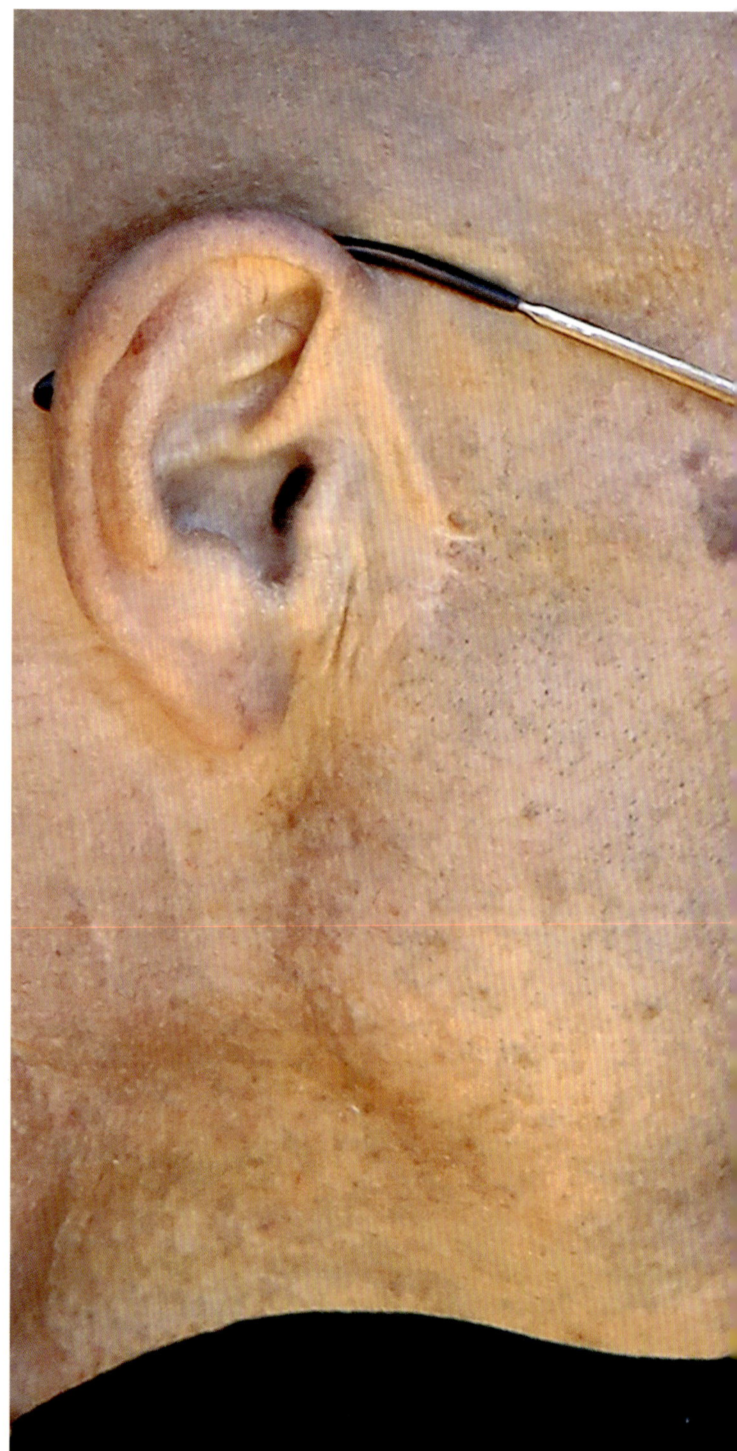

Preceding pages Children reach out to grab the hand of Prince Charles as he meets pupils at Methodist Boys' High School in Kissy near Freetown, Sierra Leone.

Opposite Prince William takes part in the hongi, a traditional Maori greeting, as he arrives at Kapiti Island Nature Reserve on the second day of his visit to New Zealand. This was the first official solo overseas visit for the second in line to the throne.

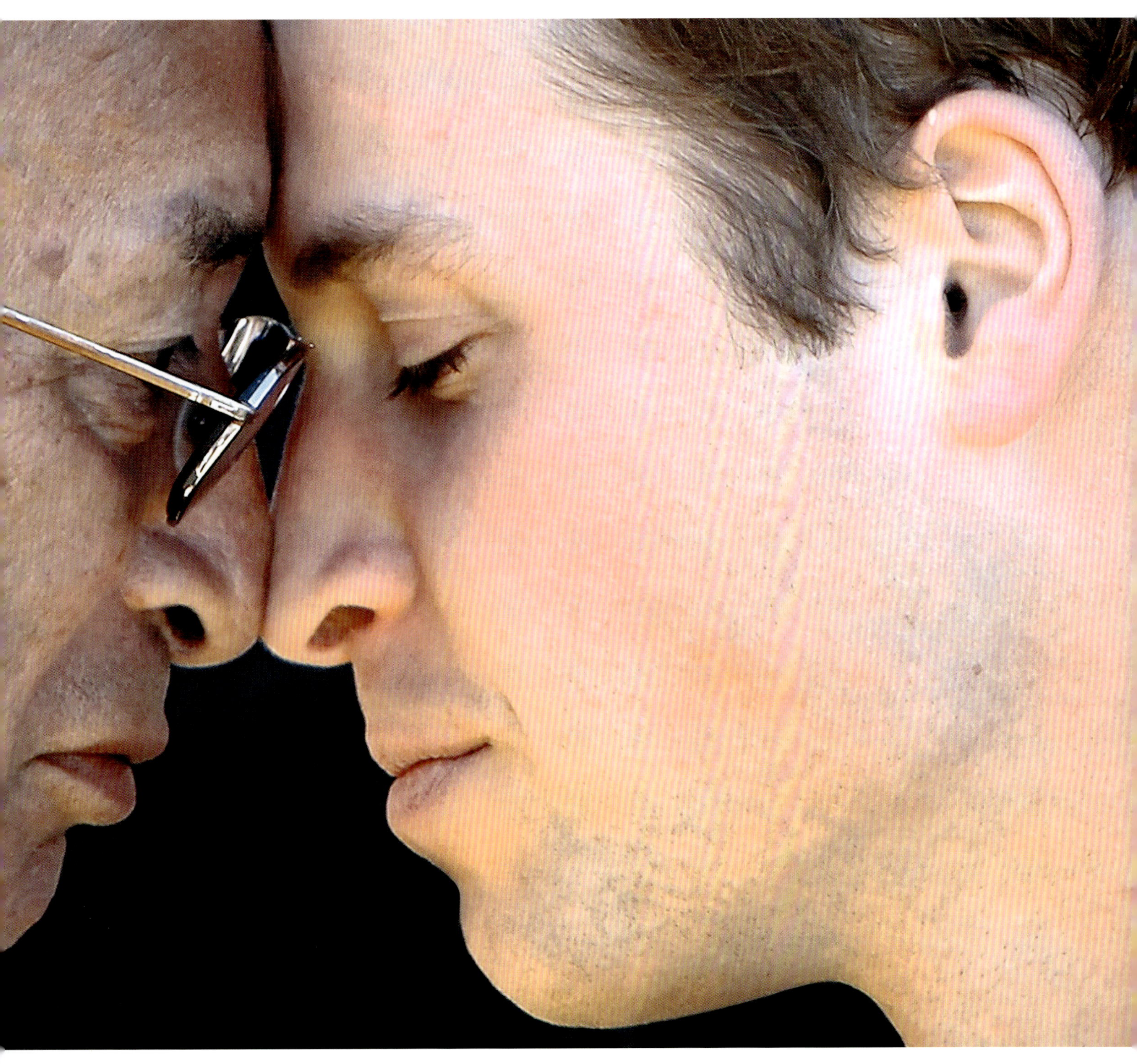

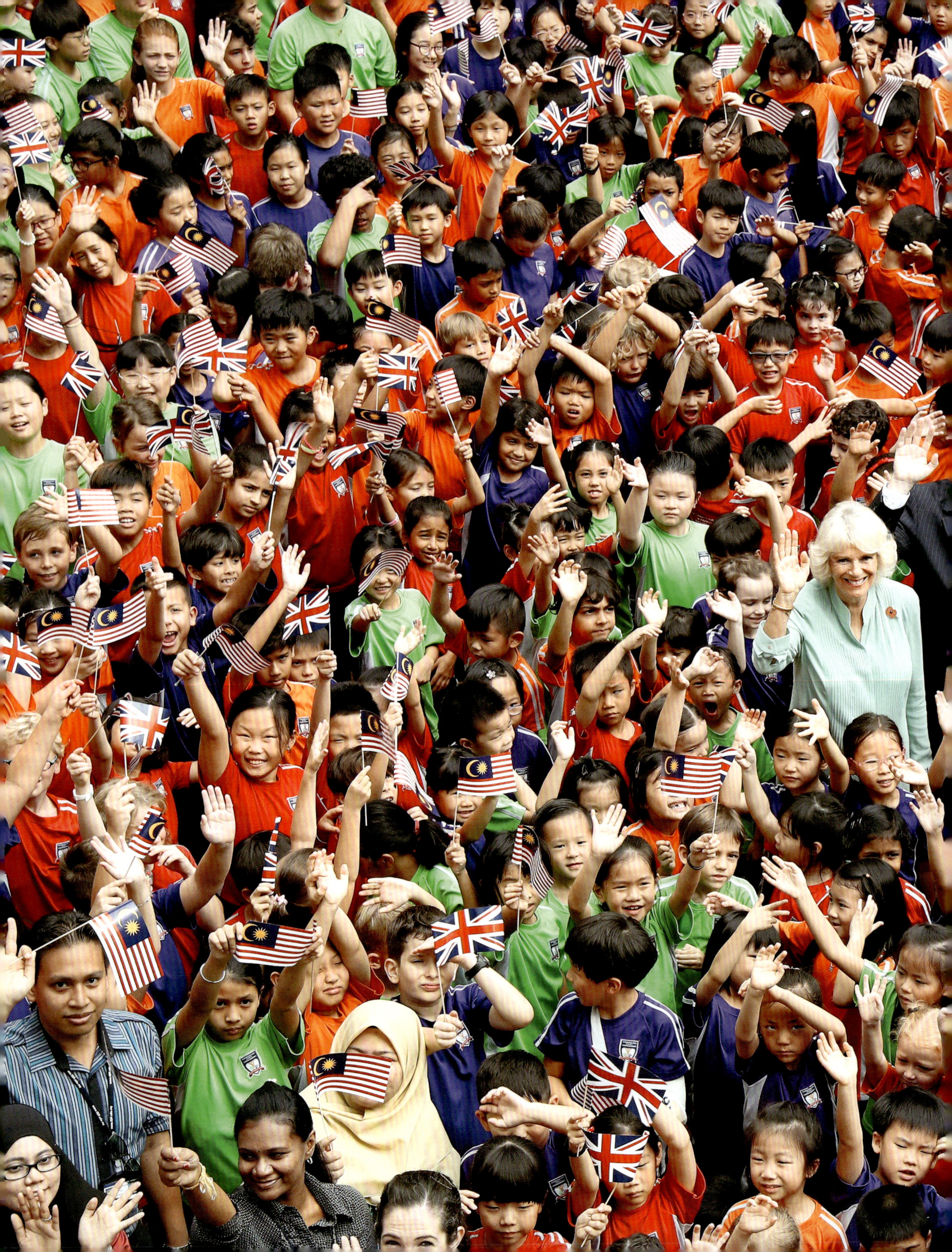

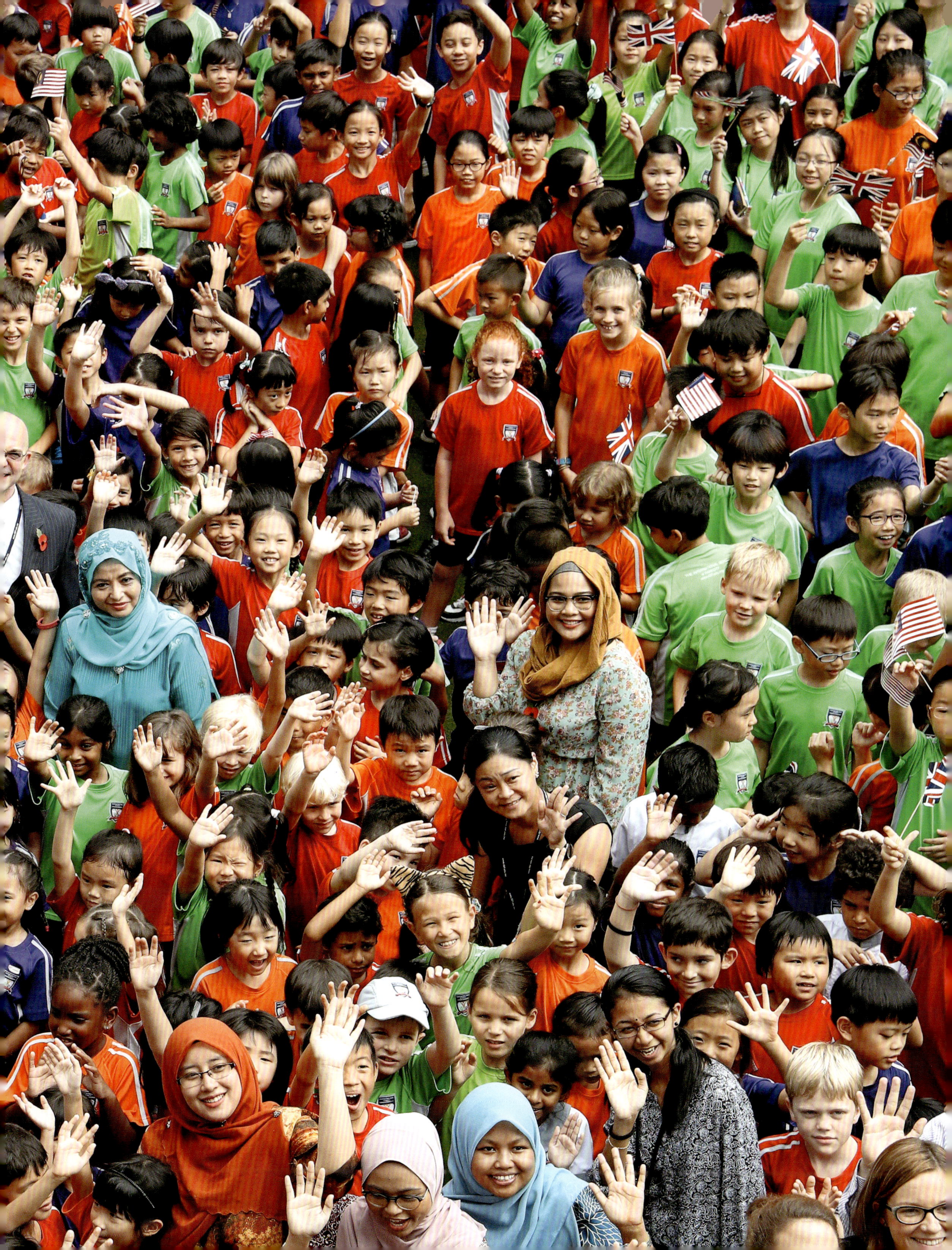

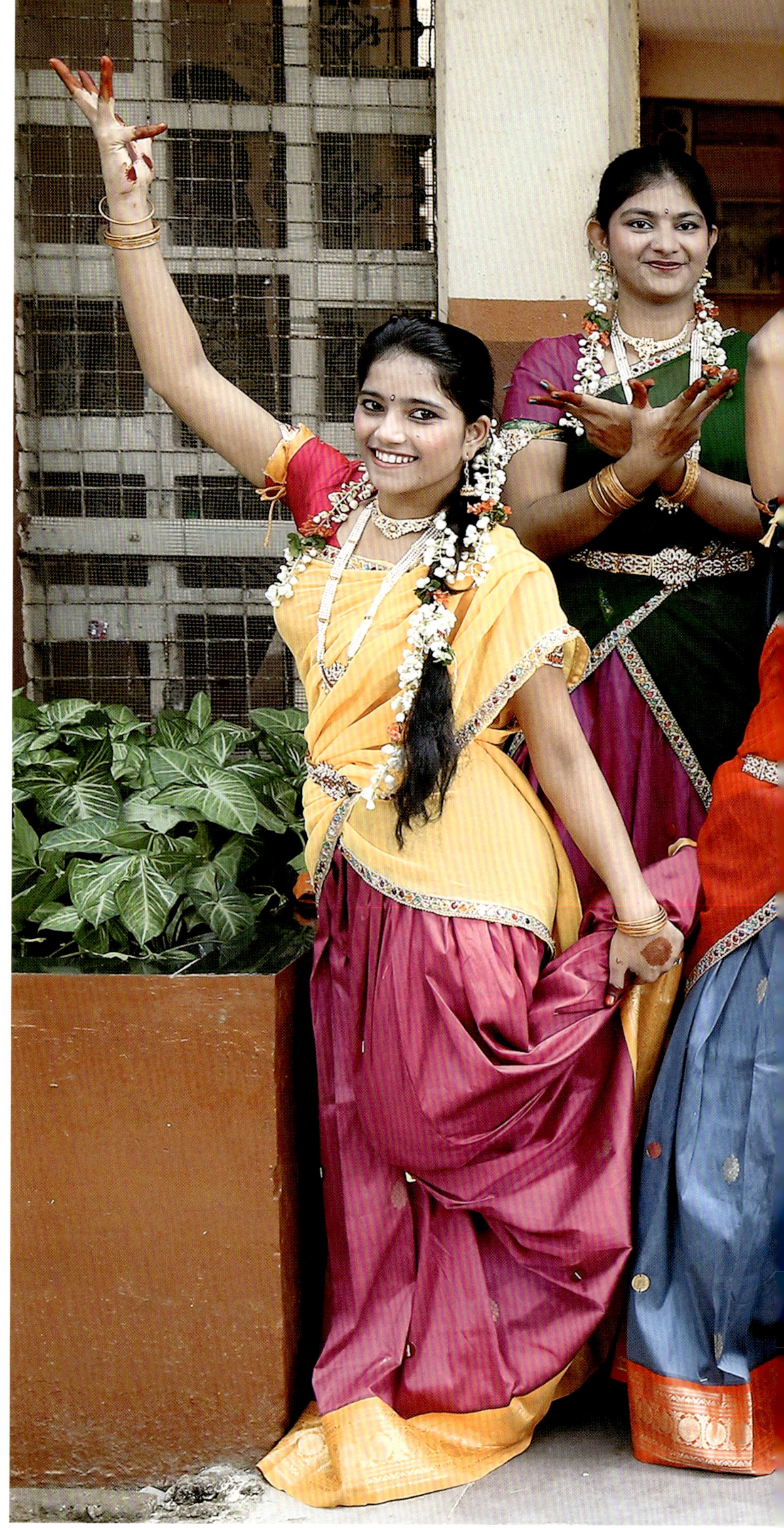

Preceding pages Camilla, Duchess of Cornwall, school principal Andrew Dalton, and Her Majesty Raja Zarith Sofiah, the Queen of Johor, pose for a photograph with students and teachers at the International School at ParkCity in Kuala Lumpur, Malaysia.

This page The Duchess of Cornwall is shown some Indian dance moves in Mumbai by girls from Asha Sadan (which means "House of Hope"), a refuge for children who have been abandoned or abused. Supporting victims of sexual violence is a cause dear to the heart of the Duchess. This was the third official visit the Prince of Wales and the Duchess of Cornwall made to India together. They spent nine days in the country and then headed to Sri Lanka to attend the 2013 commonwealth heads of government meeting.

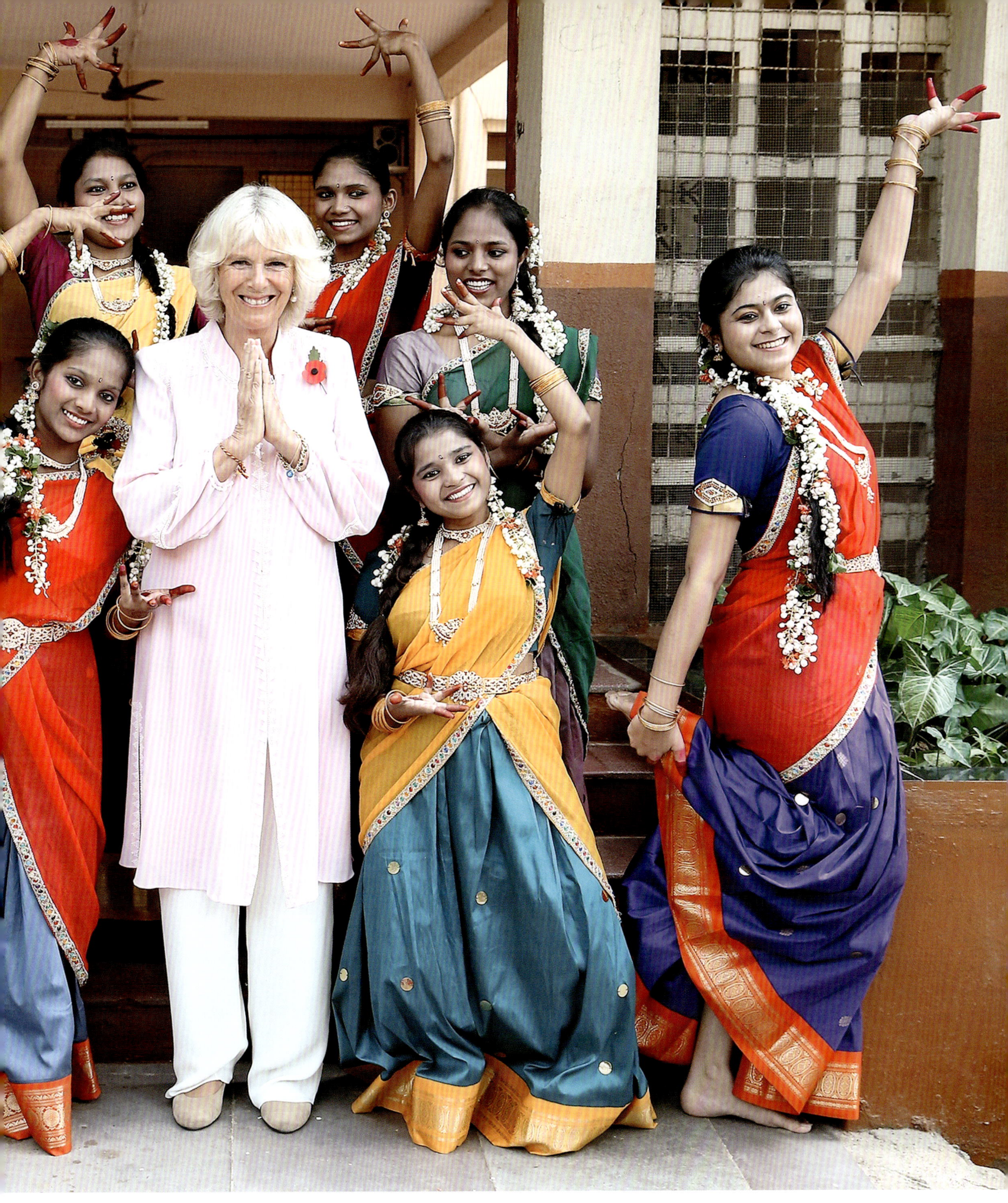

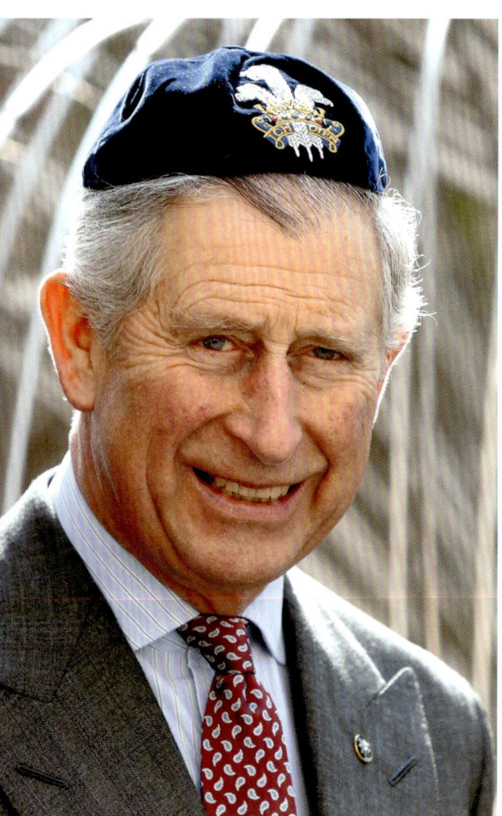

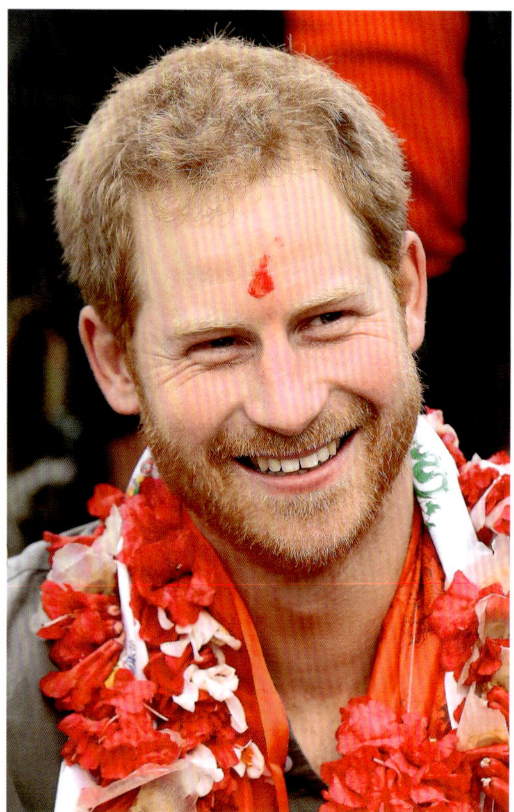

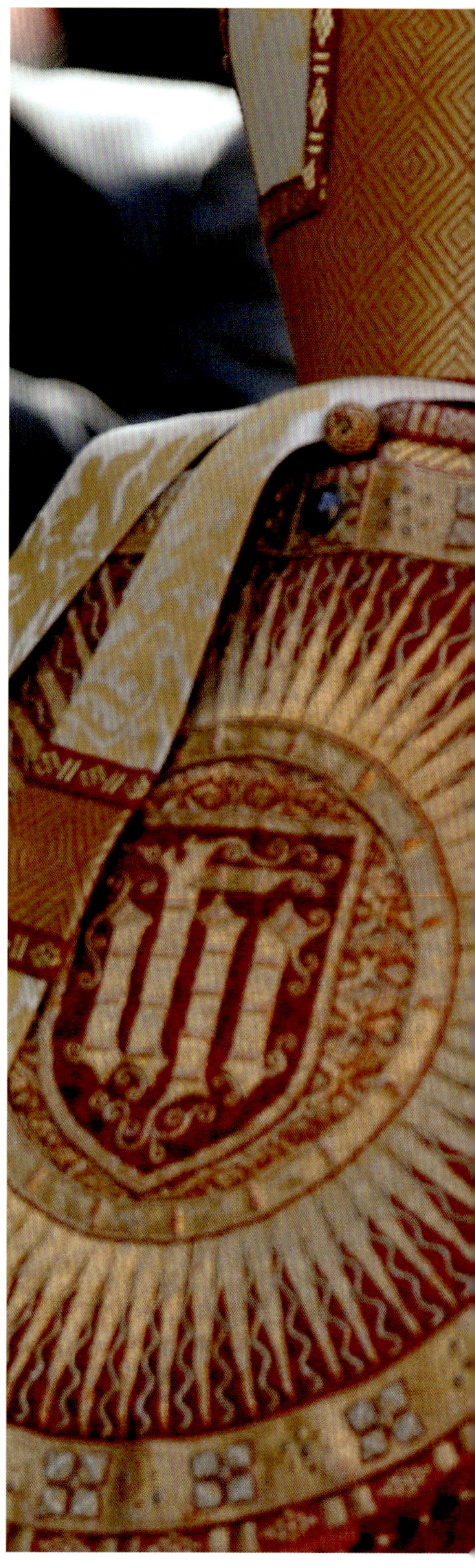

Religious understanding and respect remain important aspects of any royal travel, be it domestic or overseas.

Above Prince Charles visits the Jewish cemetery at the Dohány Street Synagogue in Budapest, Hungary.

Above Prince Harry visits the village of Leorani in the Himalayan foothills on day three of his visit to Nepal.

Opposite The Queen greets John Sentamu, the Archbishop of York, upon arriving for Maundy Thursday service at York Minster.

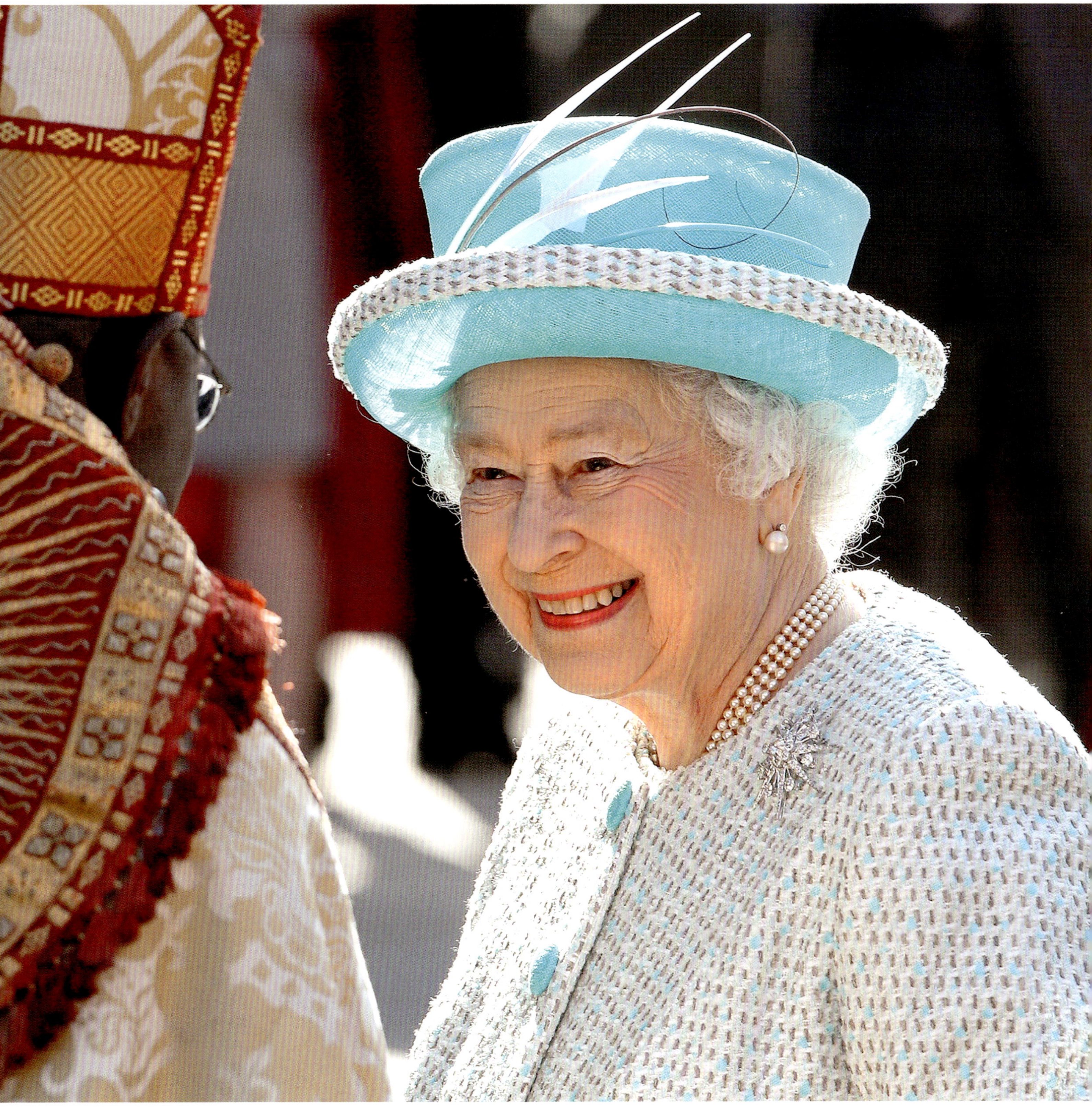

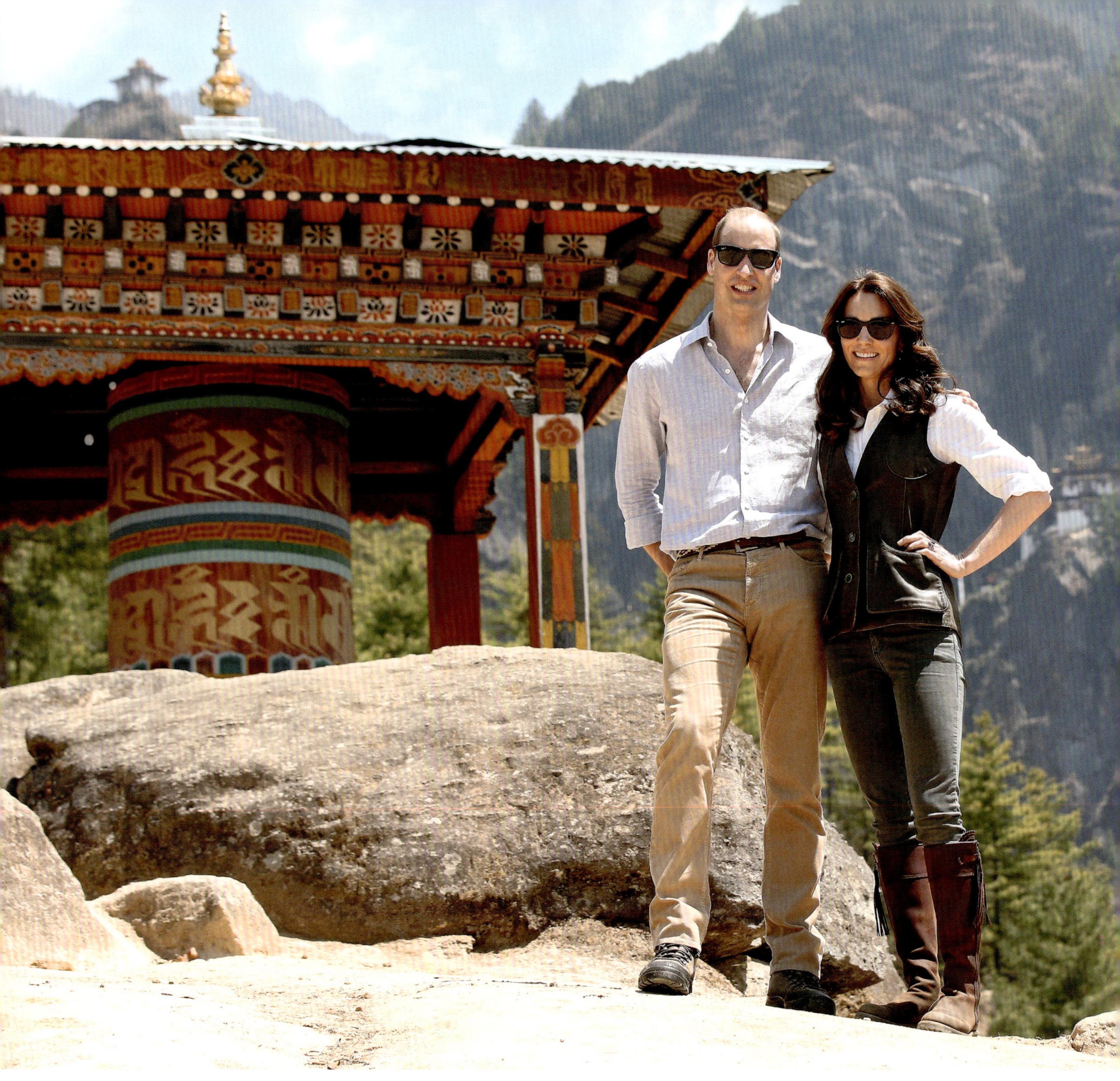

During a visit to Bhutan, the Duke and Duchess of Cambridge pose next to a prayer wheel on the trek up to Tiger's Nest. On the same trip the royal couple visited Mumbai, Delhi, Kaziranga, and Agra in India. Of all the places I have visited to photograph the royal family on tour, Bhutan remains one of the most stunning and special. In a country that measures its Gross National Happiness—alongside the more conventional Gross National Product—the warm welcome and kindness of the people is unmistakable.

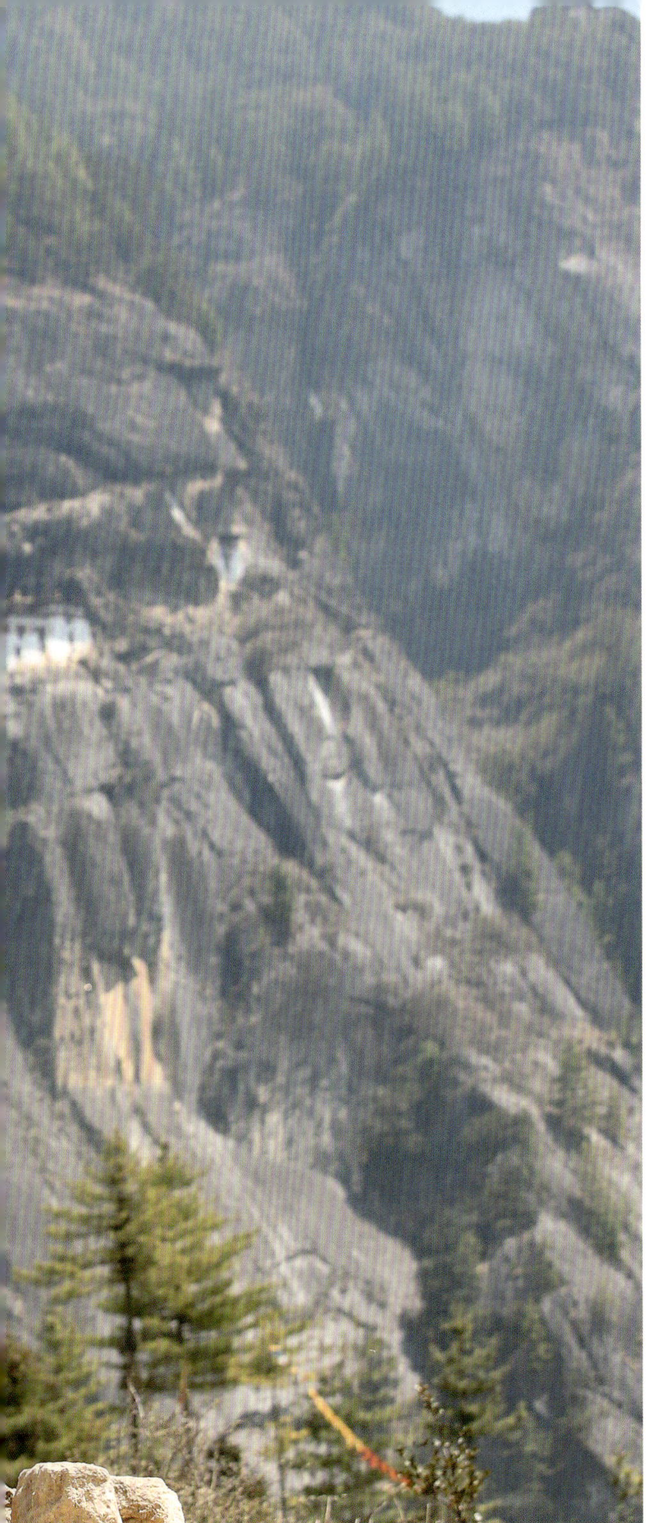

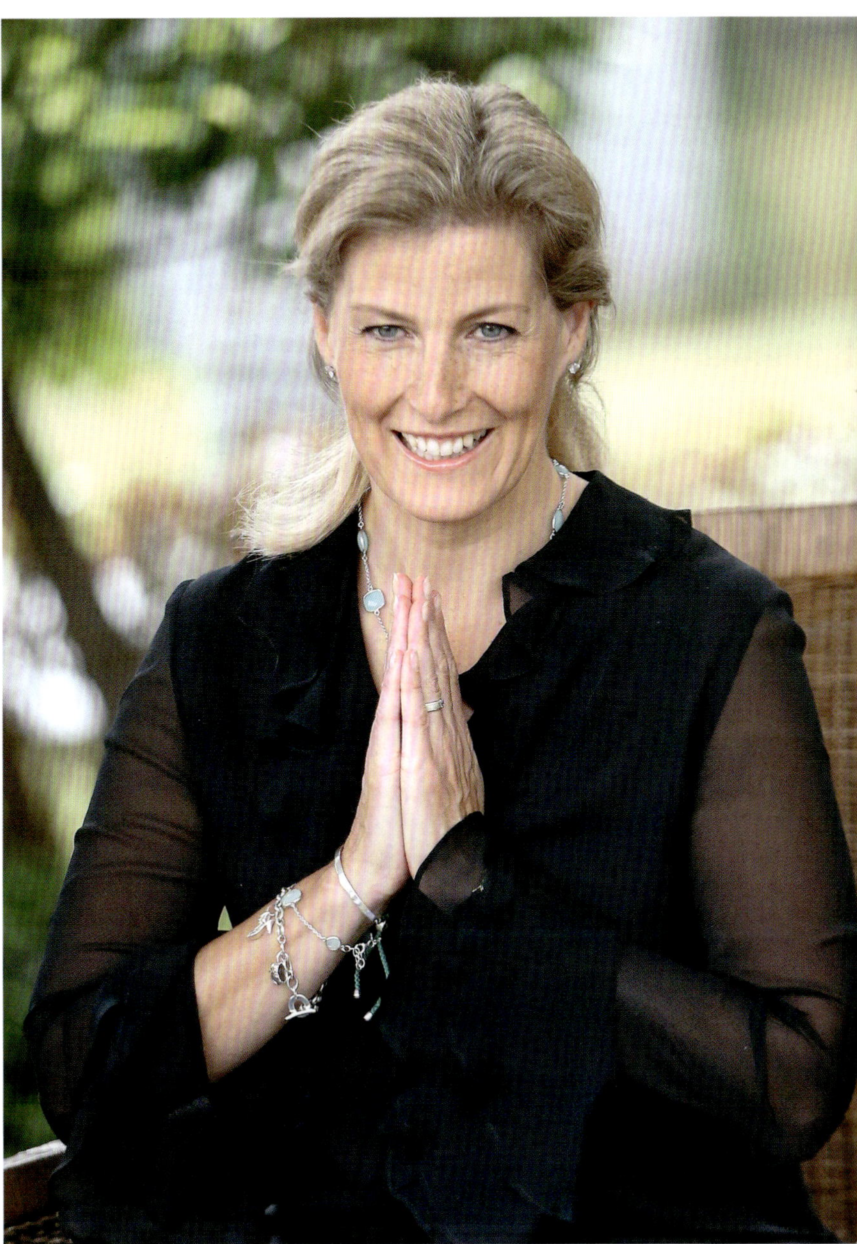

Sophie, Countess of Wessex, in Kolkata, India.

Following pages Prince Harry watches the sun rise after spending the night in the Himalayan village of Leorani on his first official tour of Nepal.

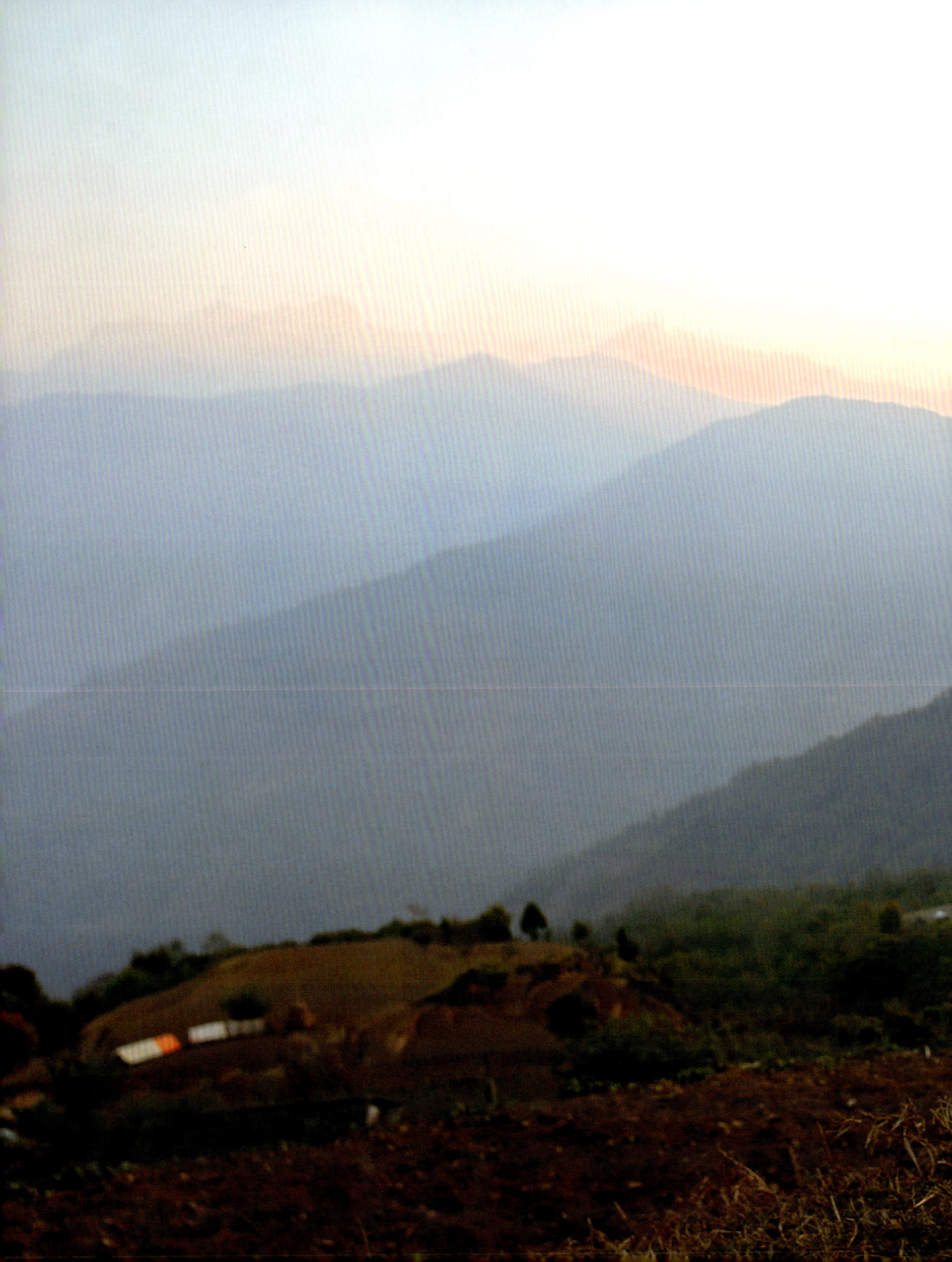

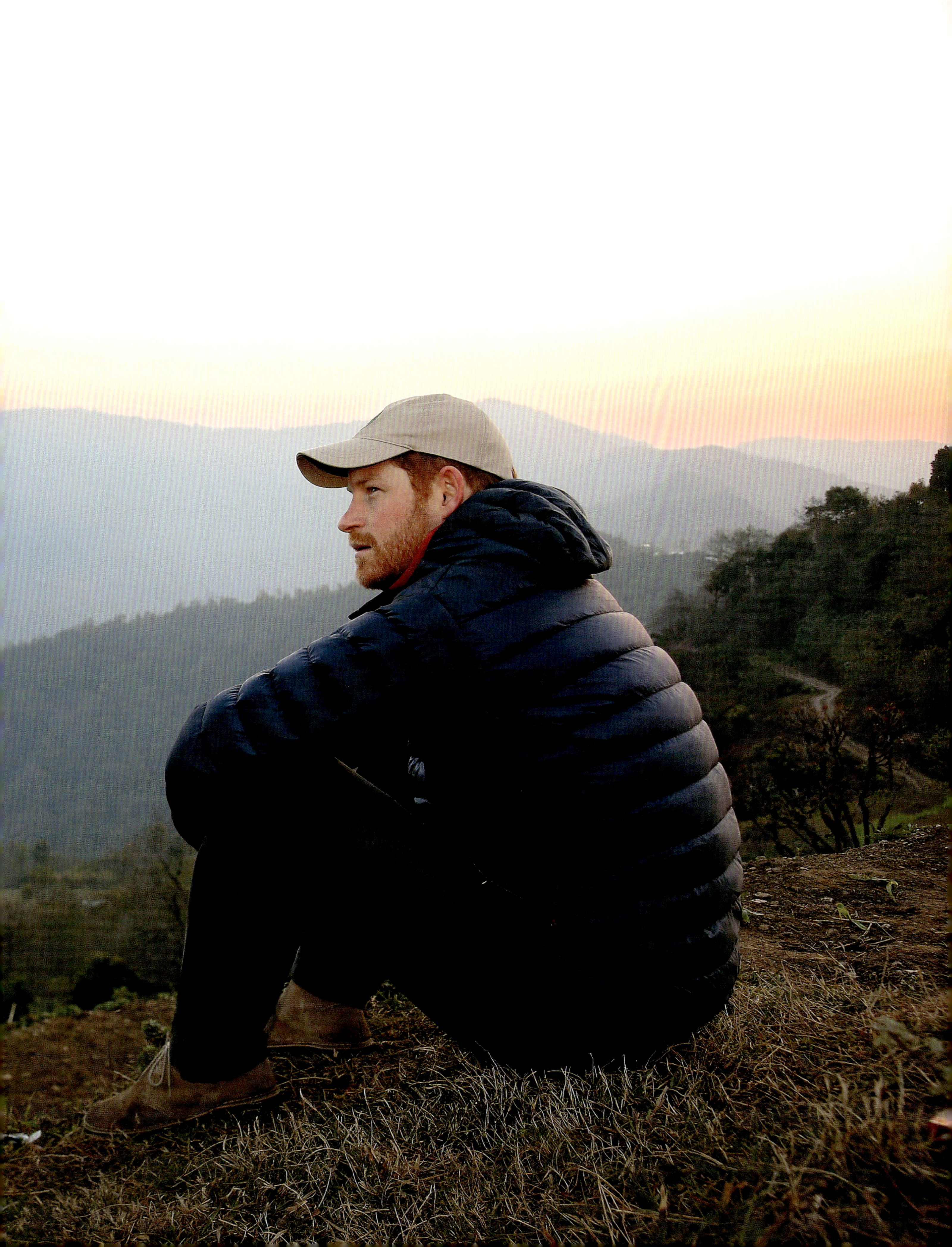

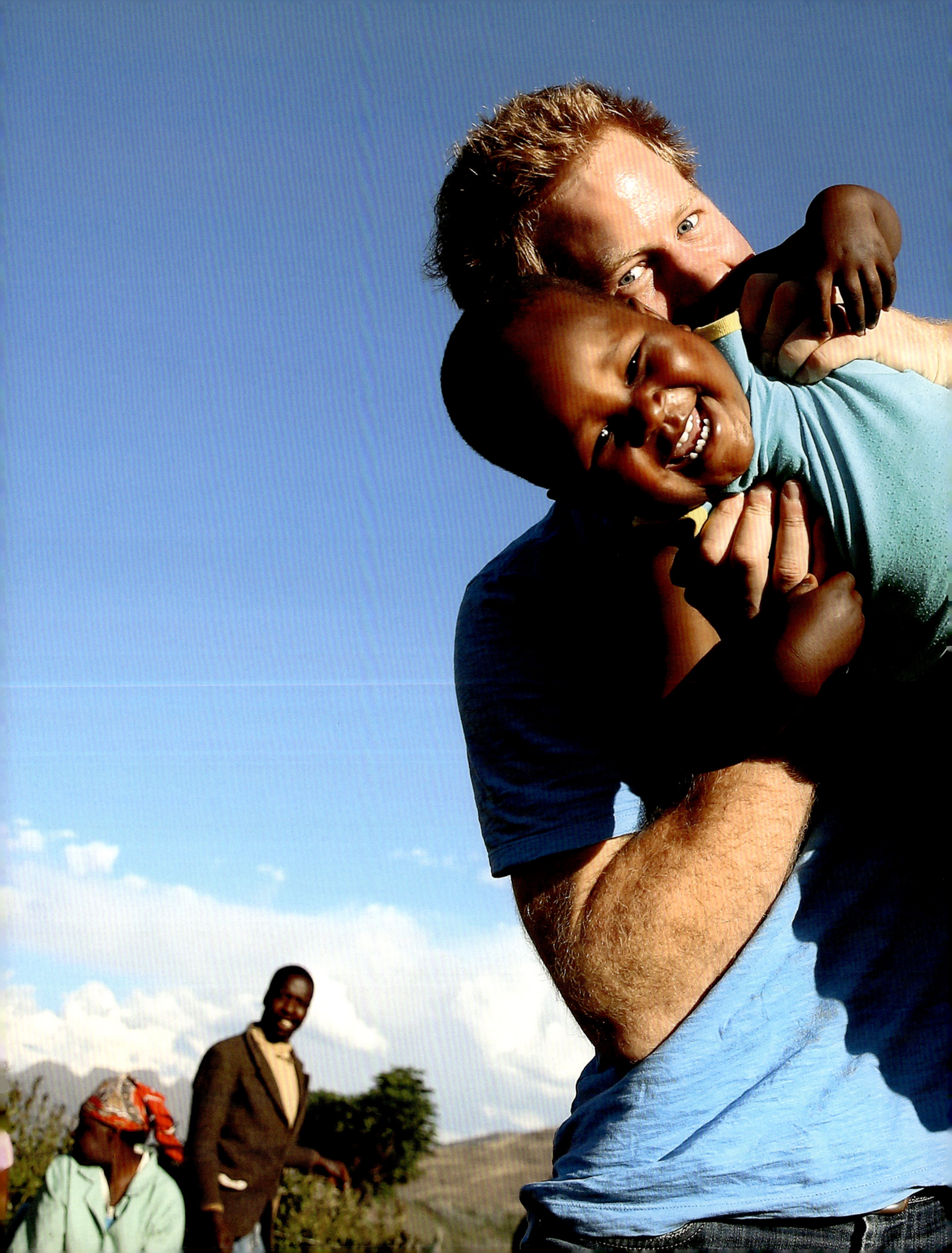

A Passion for Charity

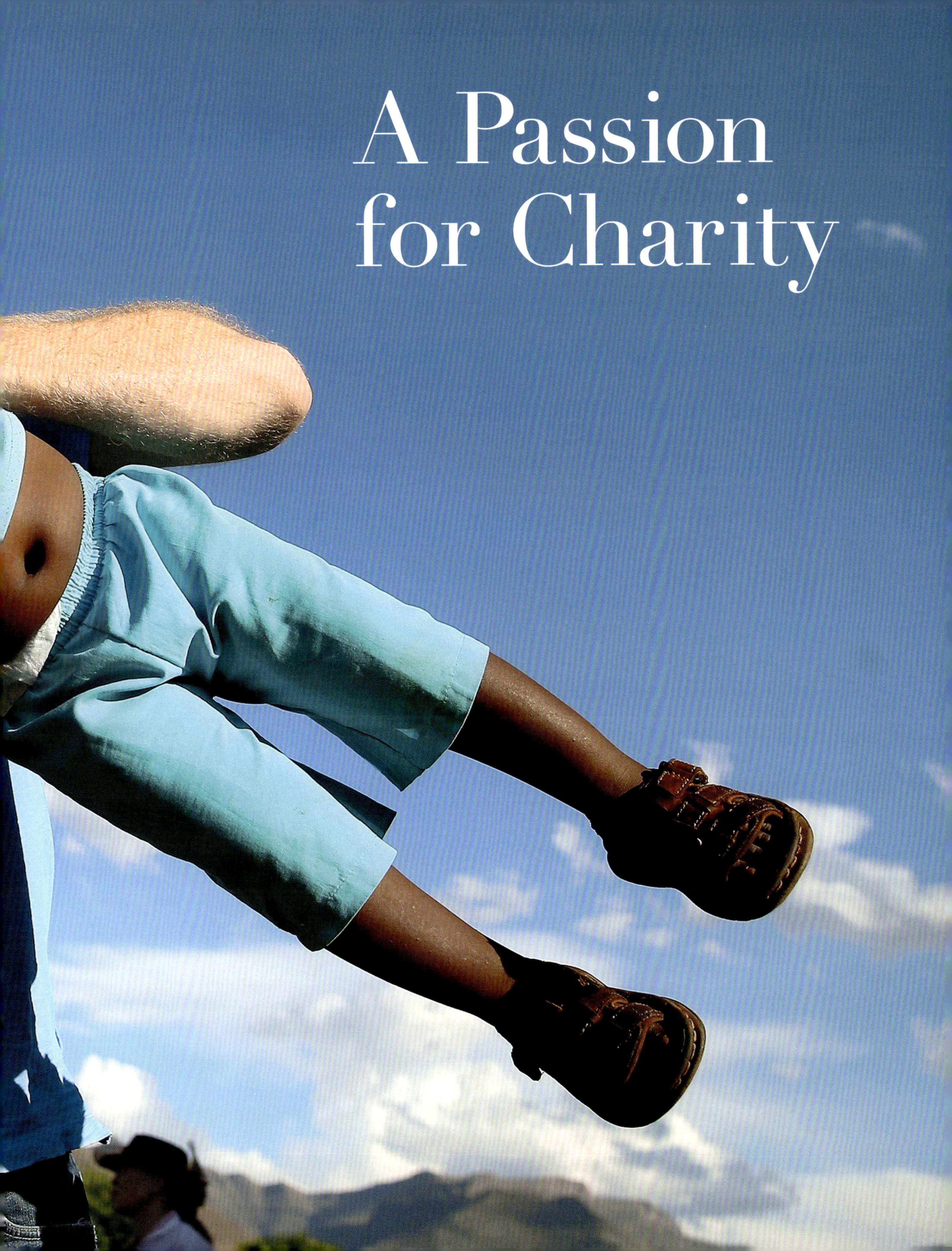

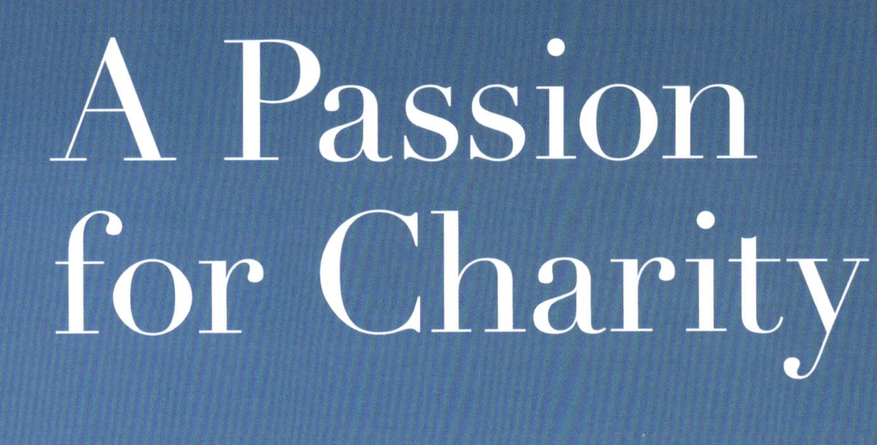

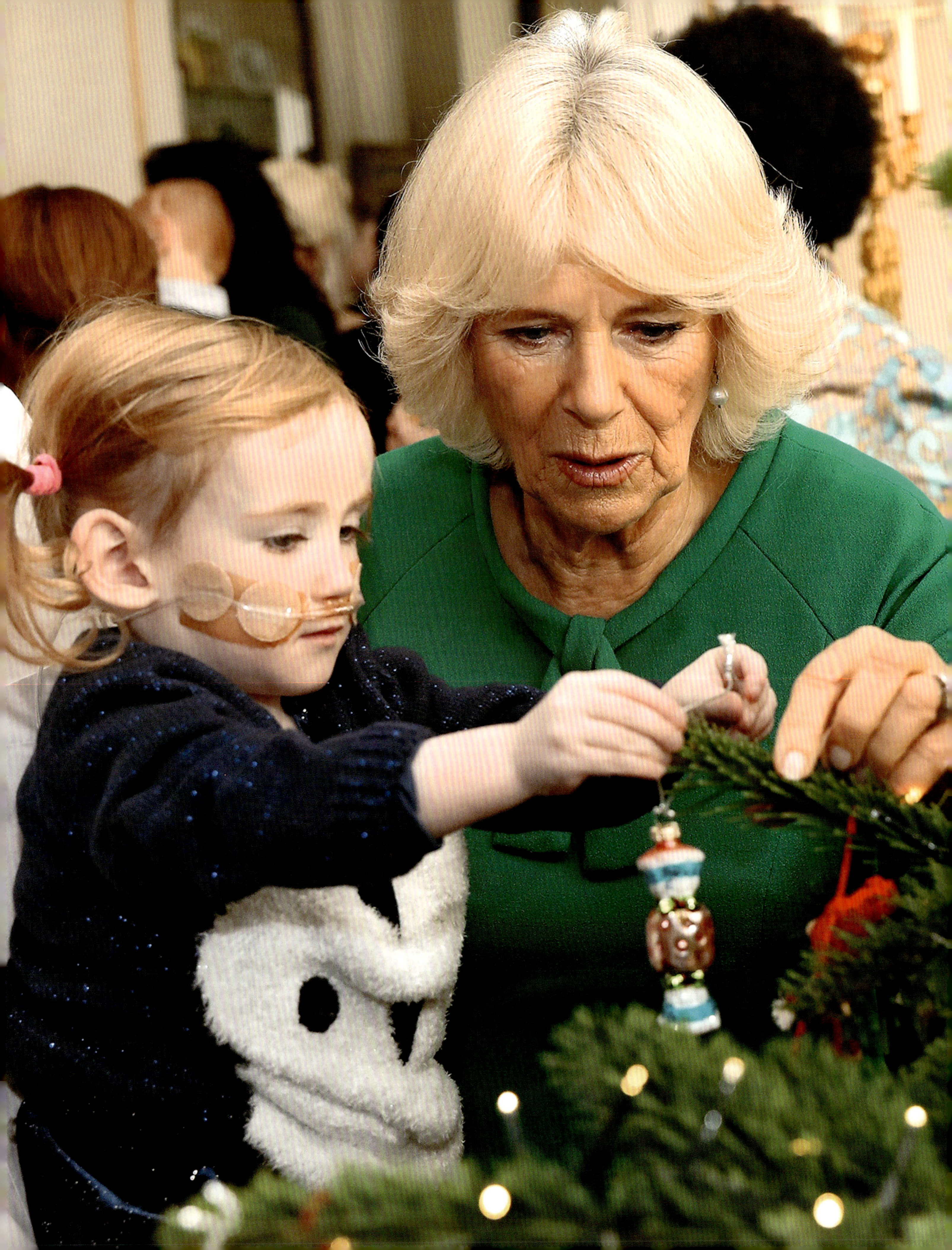

Members of the royal family members have an incredible ability to shine a spotlight on causes close to their hearts and affect change in a positive way. Many of these causes are charitable legacies. We see much of Princess Diana's passion reflected in the work of Prince Harry and the Duke and Duchess of Cambridge. Their work on HIV awareness, landmines, and more recently mental health awareness (including the Heads Together campaign) has been highly successful, much under the umbrella of the Royal Foundation. Squashed in a corner of a very cramped clinic in South London, I photographed Prince Harry taking an HIV test—the first ever taken by a member of the royal family, and a moment that served as a great example of how the young royals are breaking down stigmas and getting their message heard.

Some of my formative memories at school were generated by taking part in the Duke of Edinburgh's Award. Wet and windy hikes in the Brecon Beacons in Wales were just one part of this scheme that encourages young people to develop themselves to the best of their potential. My experiences are by no means unique. Founded in 1956 by the Duke of Edinburgh, the programme has now expanded to more than 144 nations and sees more than 300,000 participants annually. The Prince's Trust, started by the Prince of Wales in 1976, touches the lives of more than 60,000 young people each year by helping them get their lives on track. Seeing the work of these charities and meeting the people whose lives these initiatives have changed make them so much more than just a set of statistics.

Photographing the Duke of Cambridge helping five other Tusk Trust conservationists and rangers roll the largest bull elephant in northern Kenya, so they could collar the animal and protect it from the perils of poachers, I saw the passion, sweat, and commitment to instigating change firsthand. I have been working with Prince Harry's charity Sentebale for many years and have witnessed the changes in its organisational structure that have made it into a modern and dynamic charity. The idea for the organisation developed during Prince Harry's gap year, which he spent in the small, landlocked mountainous kingdom of Lesotho. Sentebale means "forget me not" in the local Sesotho language and was started by Prince Harry and Prince Seeiso of Lesotho in memory of their mothers. It helps vulnerable and HIV-positive children living in this beautiful country amid harsh conditions. Prince Harry's passion for Lesotho is evident the moment he steps off the plane. With recent expansion into Malawi and Botswana, the organisation has increased its reach significantly, and it forms an important part of Prince Harry's charitable portfolio. The Prince was recently appointed President of African Parks, another sign of the magnitude of his love for this continent, as well as his desire to be a force for positive change.

Preceding pages Prince Harry swings a young orphan boy during a visit to Phelisanong Children's Home in Lesotho. The prince was visiting the African kingdom of Lesotho to see the ongoing work of Sentebale, the charity he founded more than ten years ago with Prince Seeiso of Lesotho to support the HIV-positive and vulnerable children of this mountainous landlocked country.

Opposite The Duchess of Cornwall helps two-year-old Violet Webster, who has a hole in her heart, decorate the Clarence House Christmas tree during her annual children's reception supported by the Helen & Douglas House charity. The Duchess is patron of the charity, which provides hospice and palliative care to children and young adults in Oxfordshire and surrounding counties.

Following pages Prince Harry gives a speech on stage at the closing ceremony of the inaugural Invictus Games in London in 2014. This was the culmination of an inspiring week. It was a huge effort for Prince Harry and the team, but the upbeat atmosphere and smiles on the contestants' faces were testament to the success of the project. The games have since taken place in Orlando, Toronto, and, in 2018, Sydney.

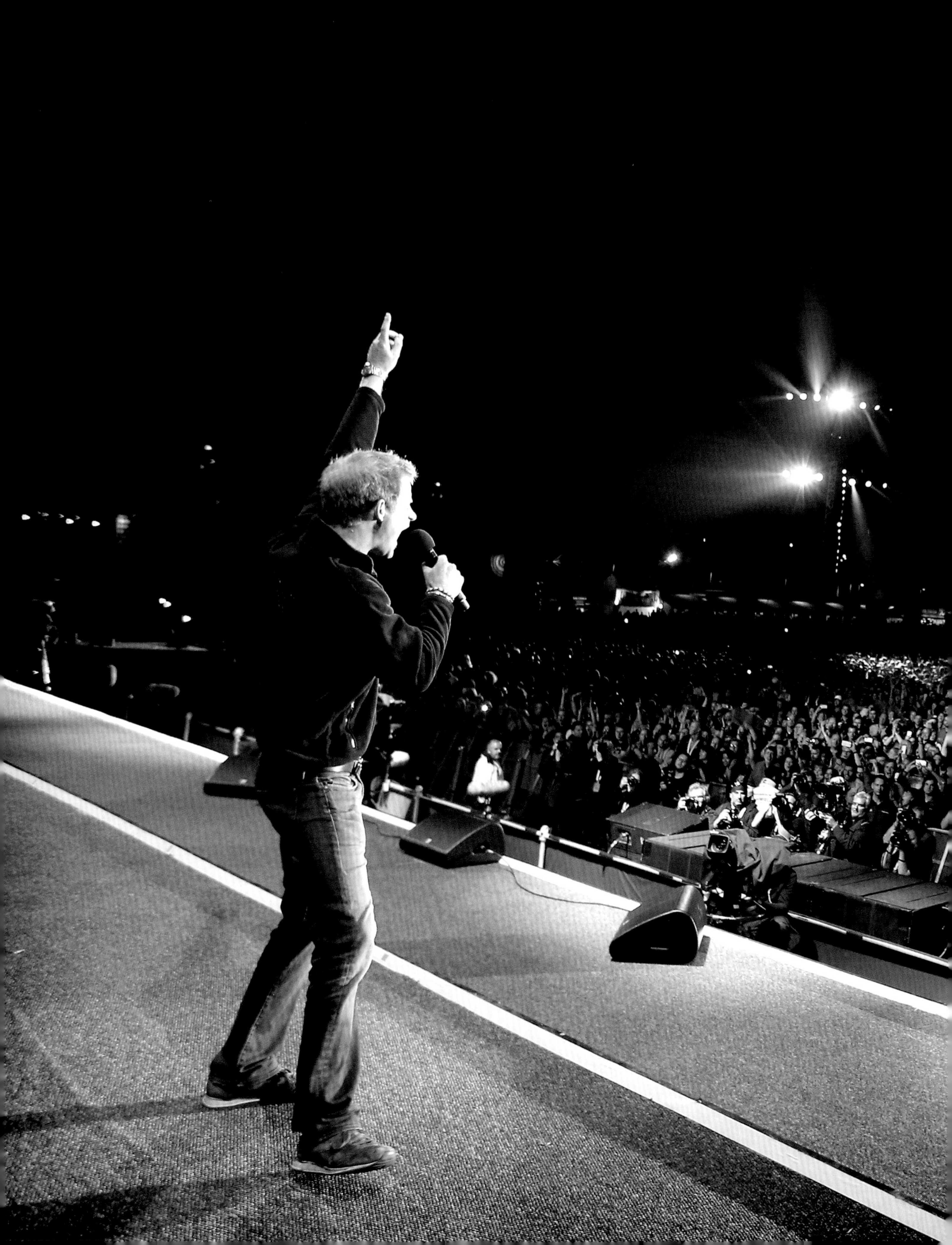

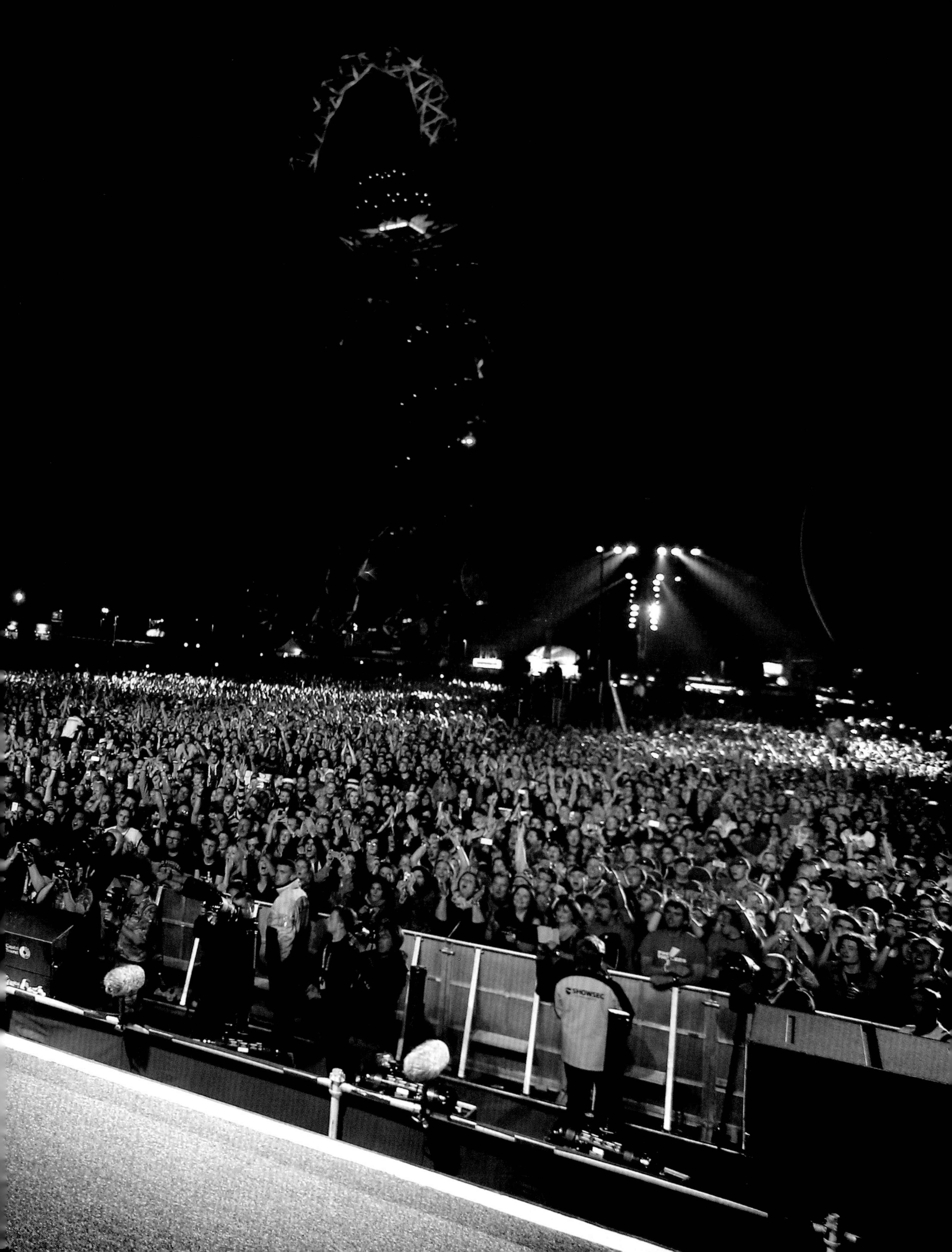
SHOWSEC

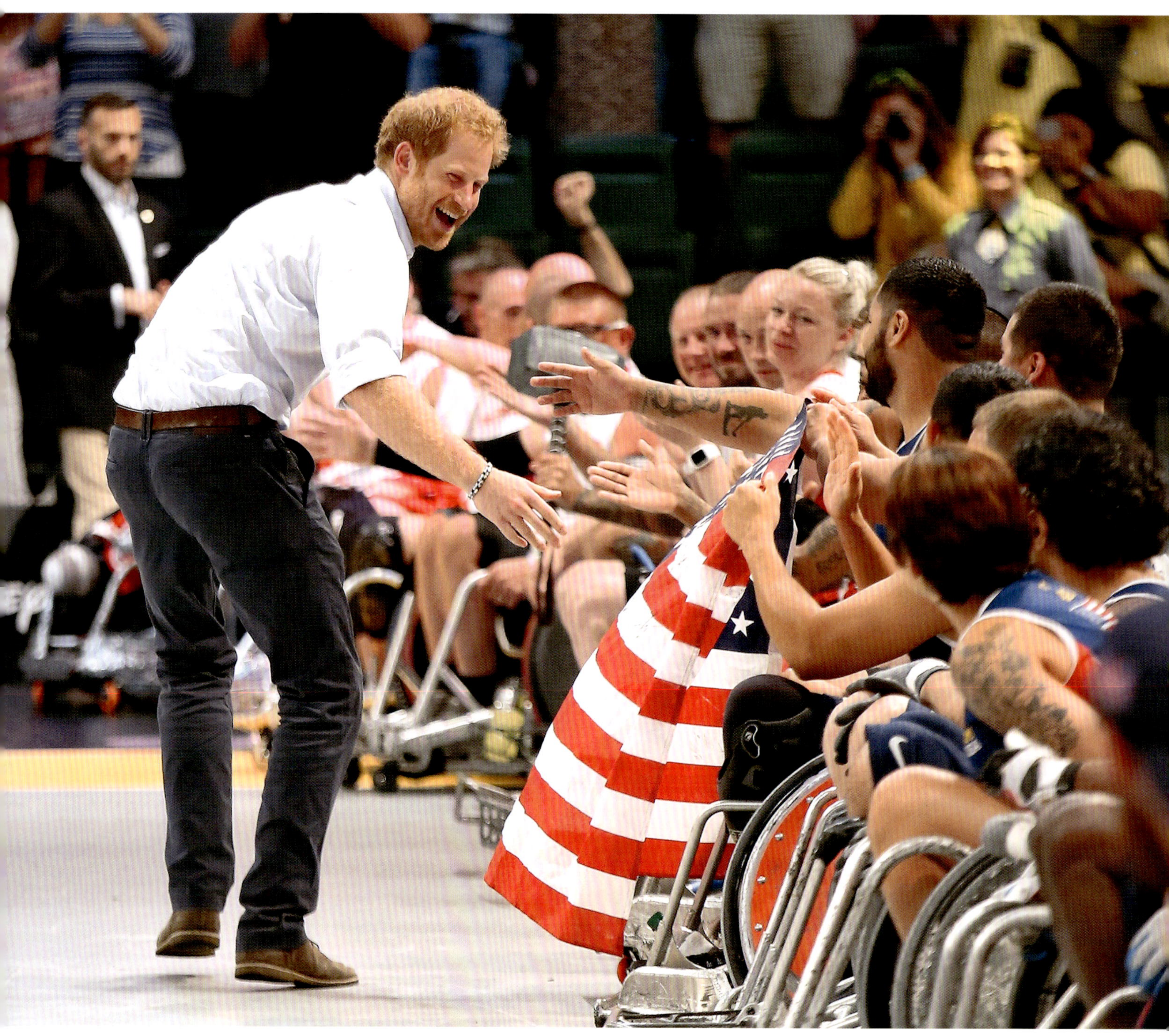

Prince Harry presents medals to the United States wheelchair rugby team after they beat Denmark in the finals at the 2016 Invictus Games in Orlando.

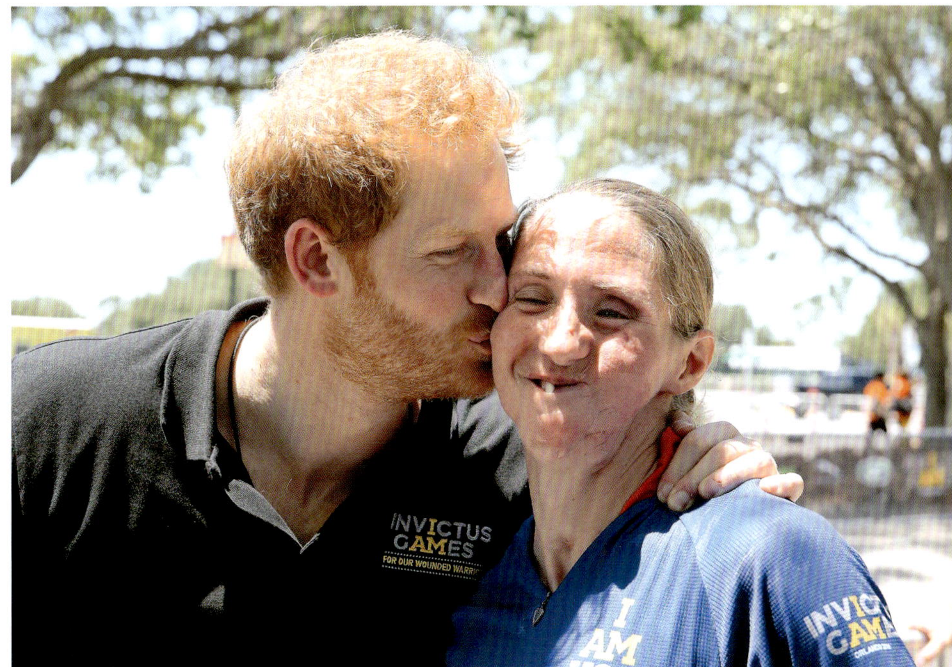

Above Katie Kuiper of the United States team gets a kiss from Prince Harry at the road cycling event during the 2016 Invictus Games in Orlando. This was a lovely moment, and afterwards Kuiper, a staff sargeant who served in Iraq and at Guantánamo Bay Naval Base, spoke about what it meant to her: "I feel invisible a lot of the time because of the way I look. He made me feel special."

Below Prince Harry poses with United Kingdom armed forces medal winners at the track and field events during the 2016 Invictus Games at Orlando's ESPN Wide World of Sports Complex.

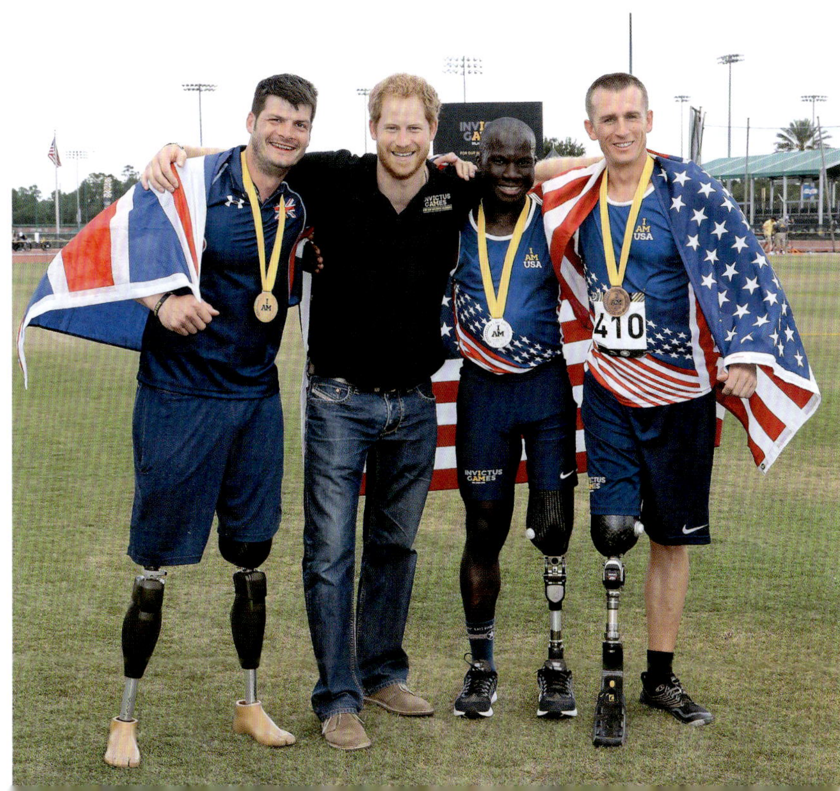

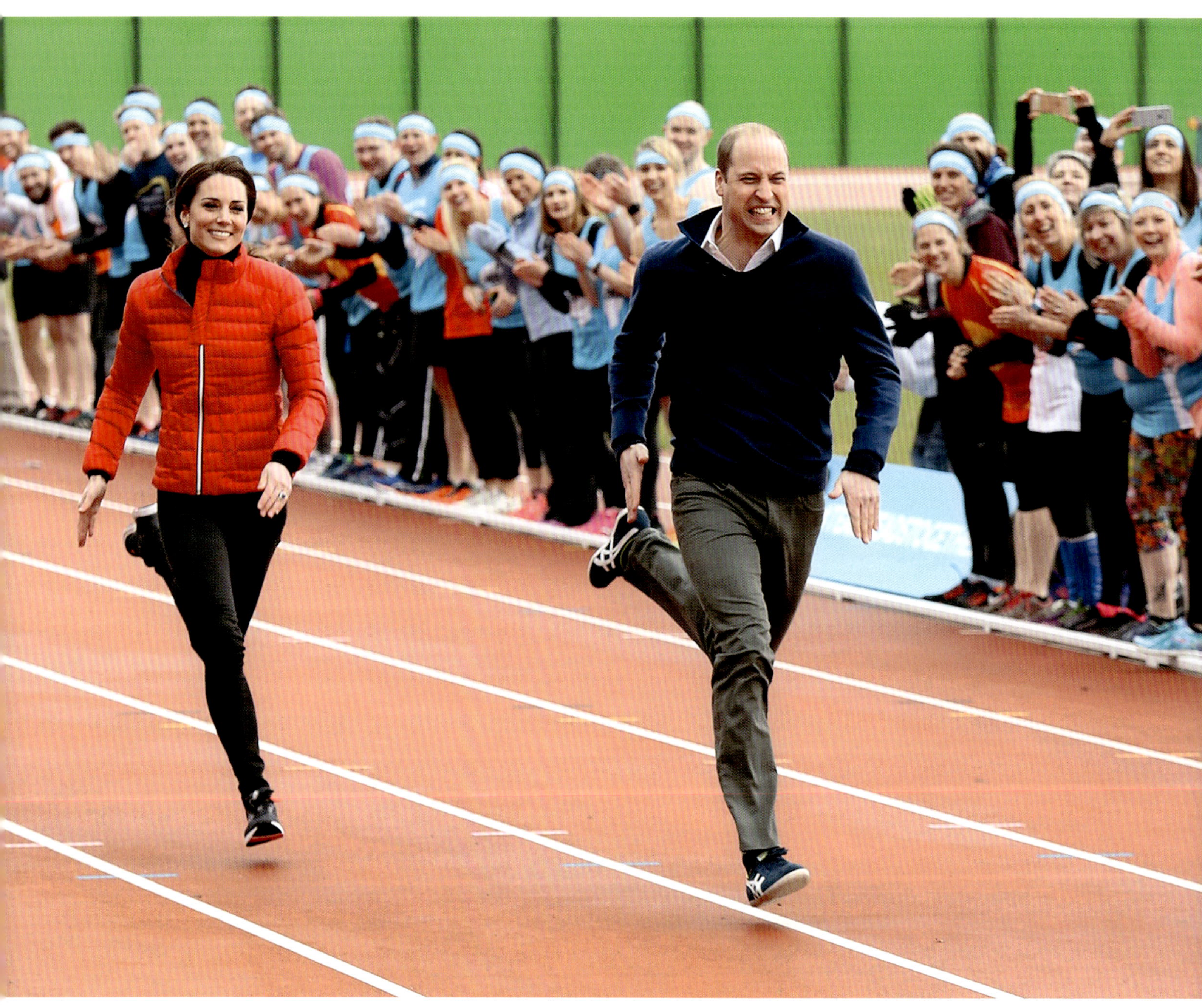

The Duke and Duchess of Cambridge and Prince Harry join Team Heads Together at a London Marathon training day at Queen Elizabeth Olympic Park.

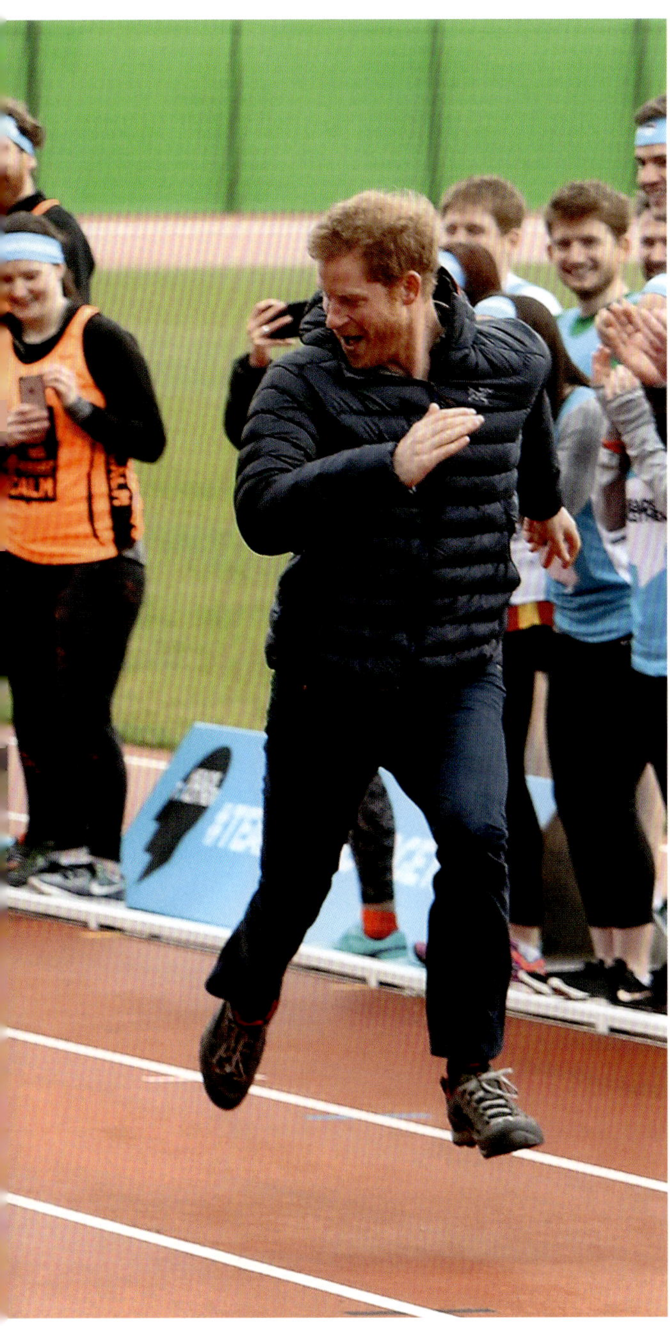

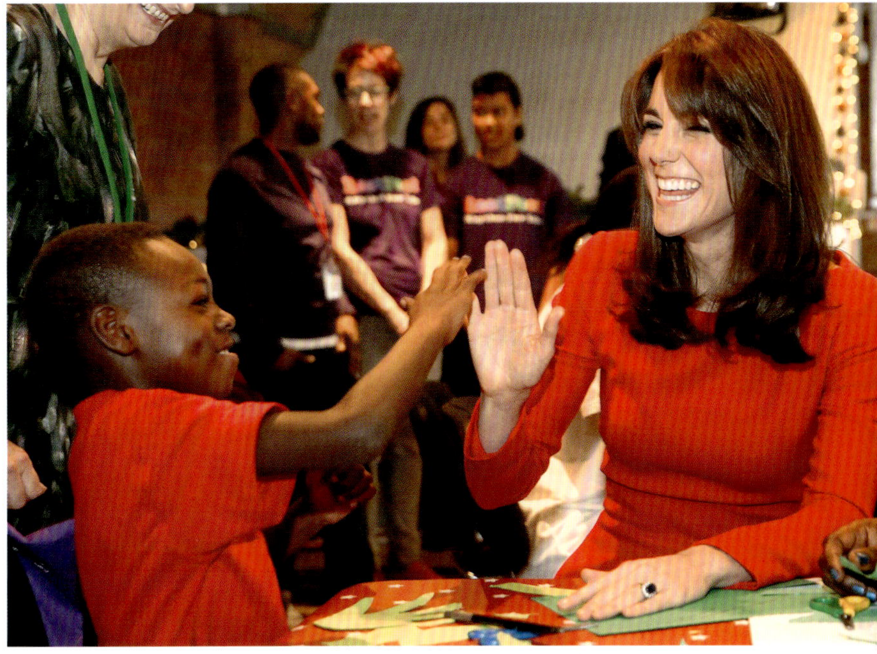

Above The Duchess of Cambridge attends the Family School London Christmas party at the Anna Freud National Centre. During the visit, the Duchess joined groups of families in festive activities designed to help pupils reflect on the positive progress in their social relationships and communication skills.

Right Buy high, sell low! Prince William and Prince Harry take part in multi-billion-pound trades on the BGC Partners trading floor at Canary Wharf on September 11, 2013. Their appearance was part of an annual charity day held in memory of those from the company and others who died in the World Trade Center attacks.

Following pages Camilla, Duchess of Cornwall, is seen with children from the hospice charity Helen & Douglas House during a Christmas party at Clarence House.

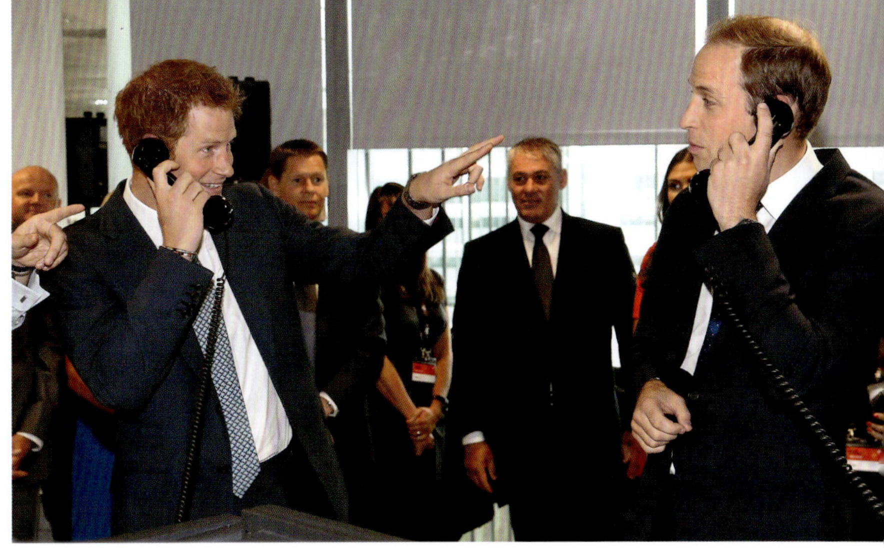

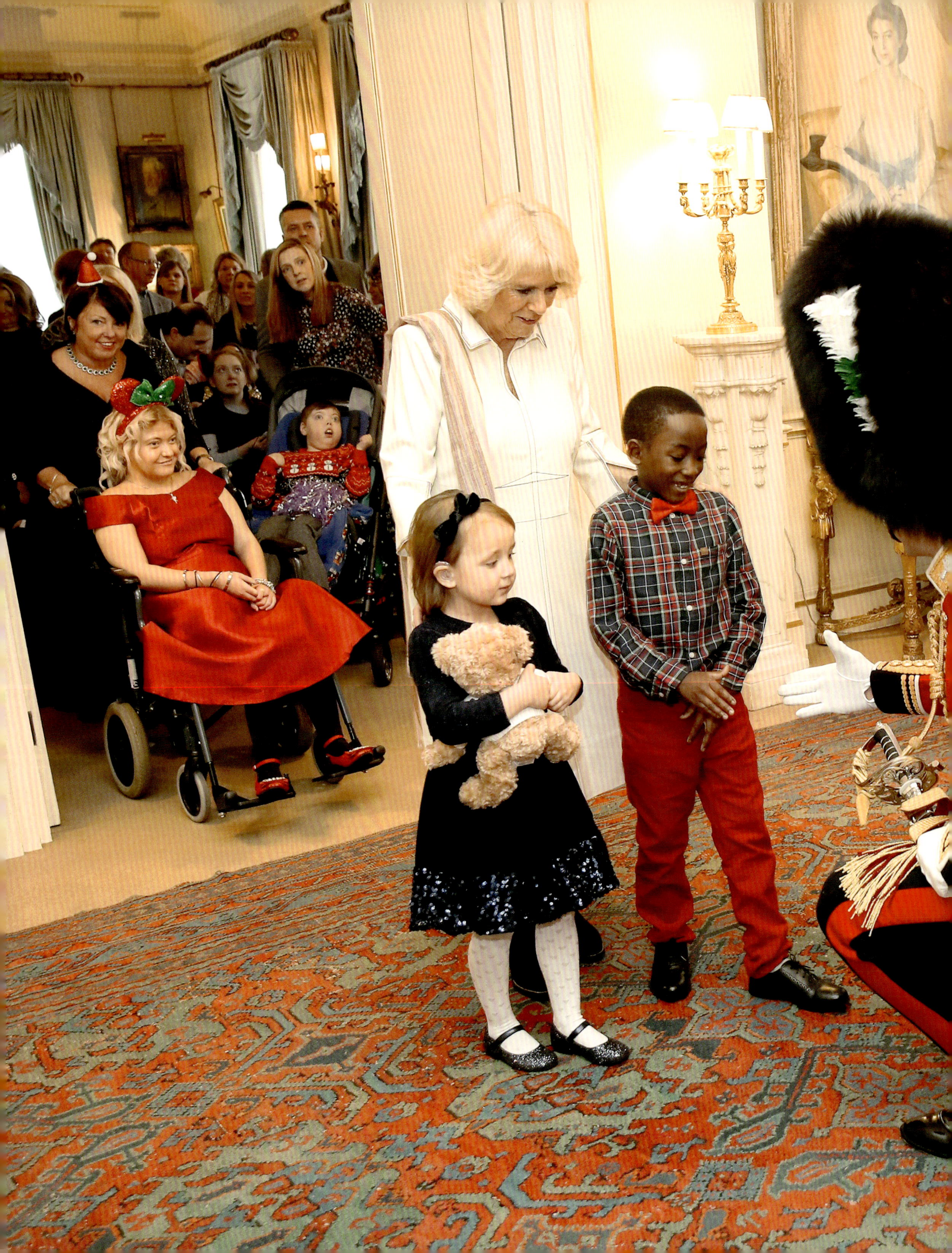

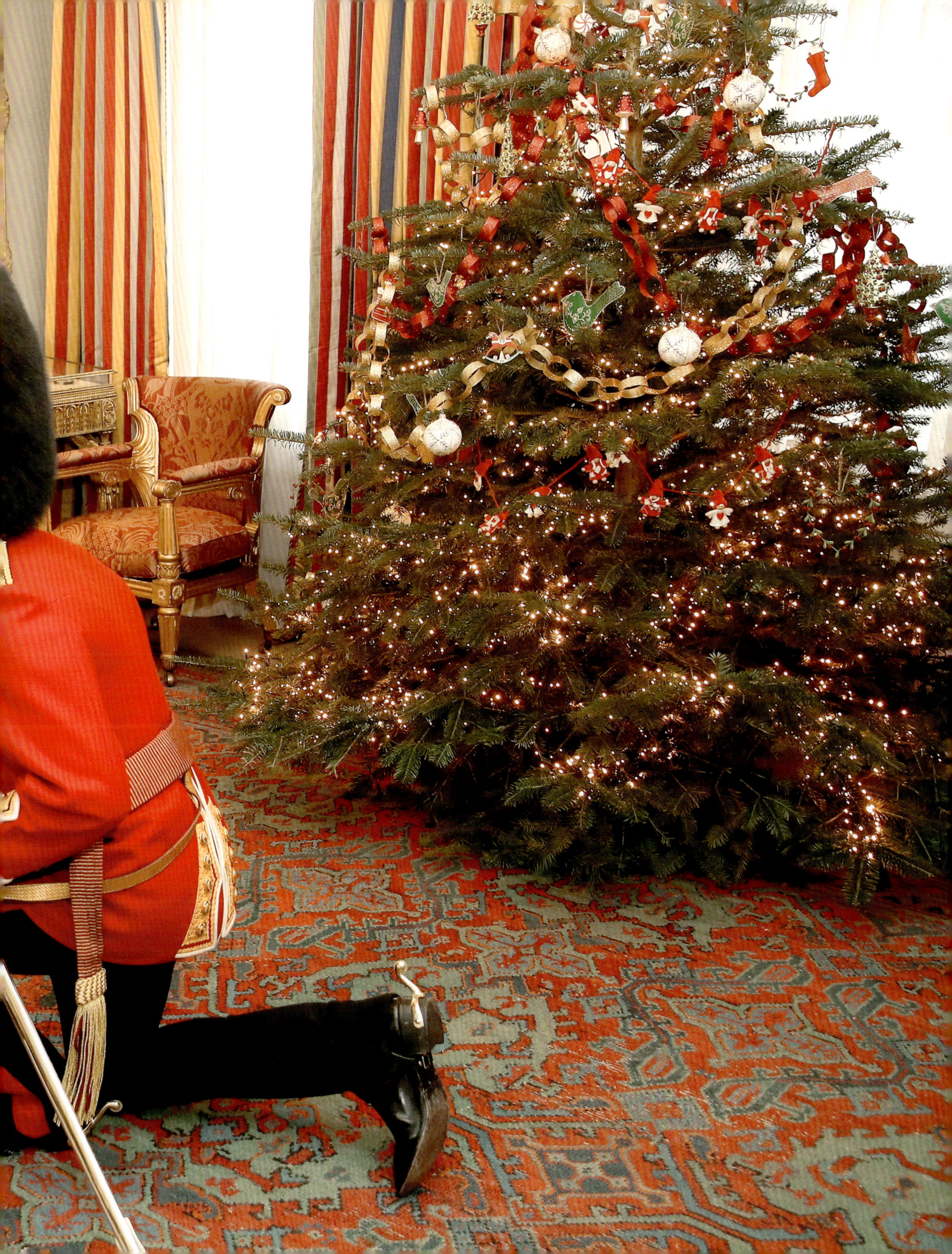

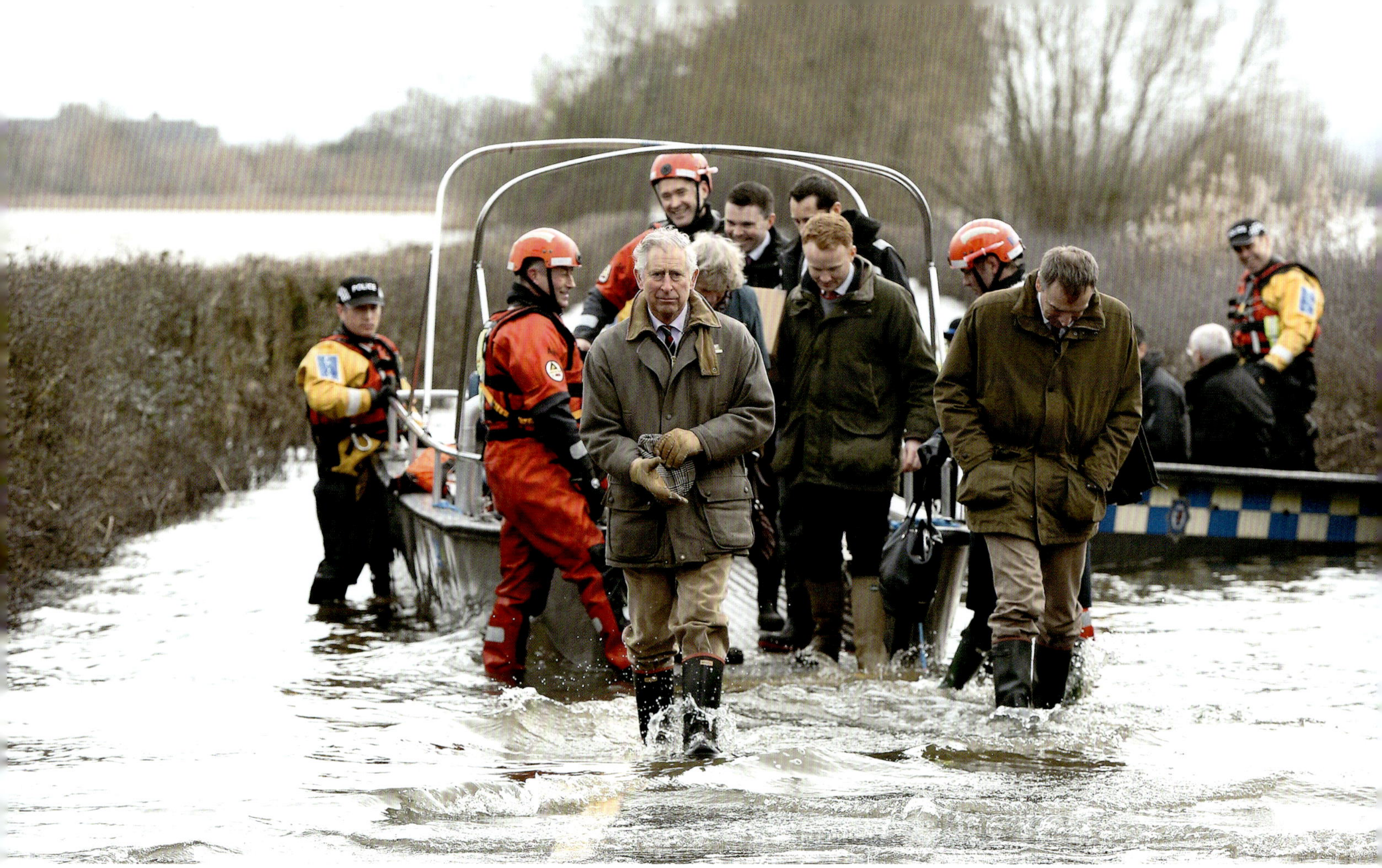

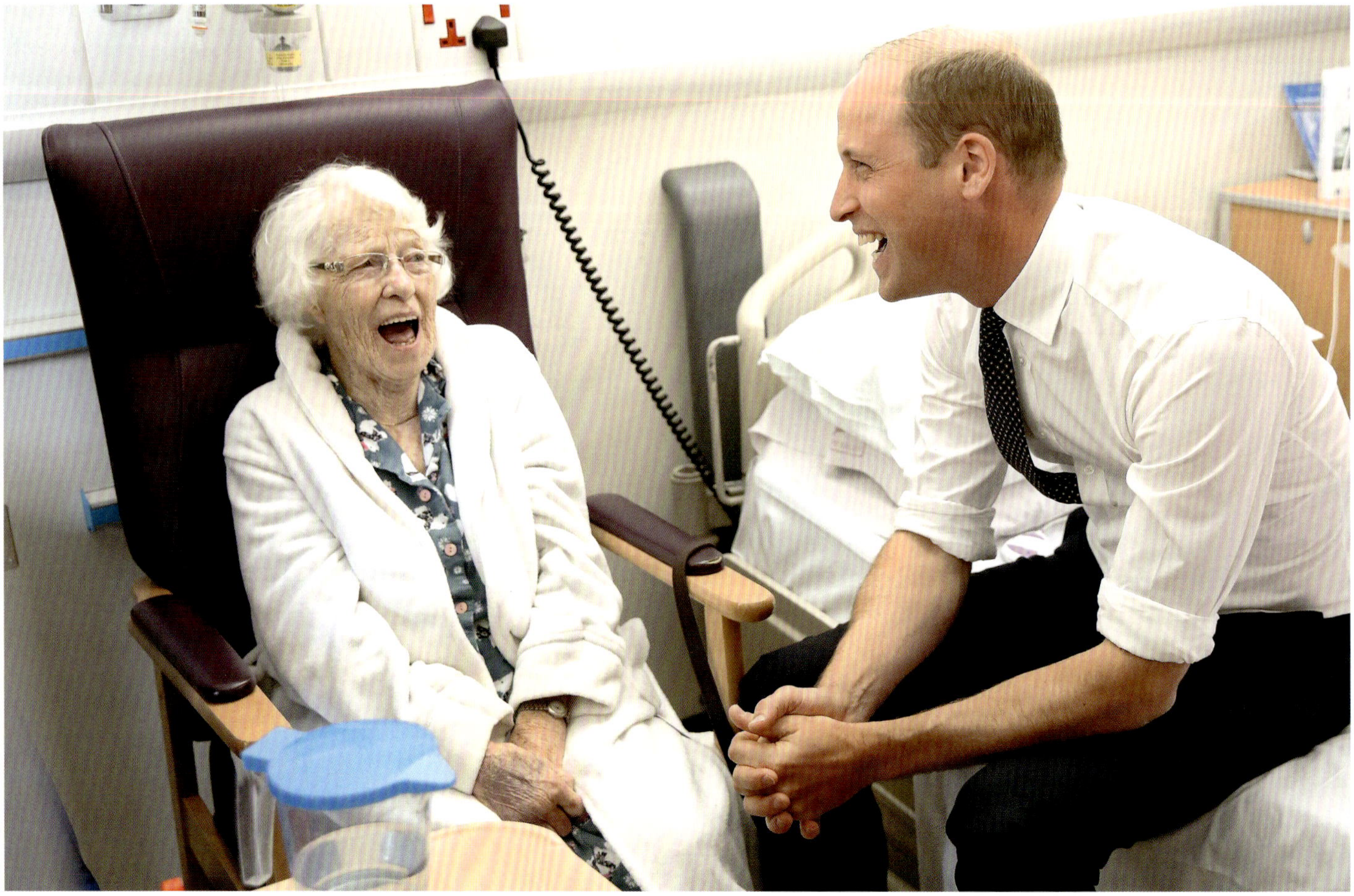

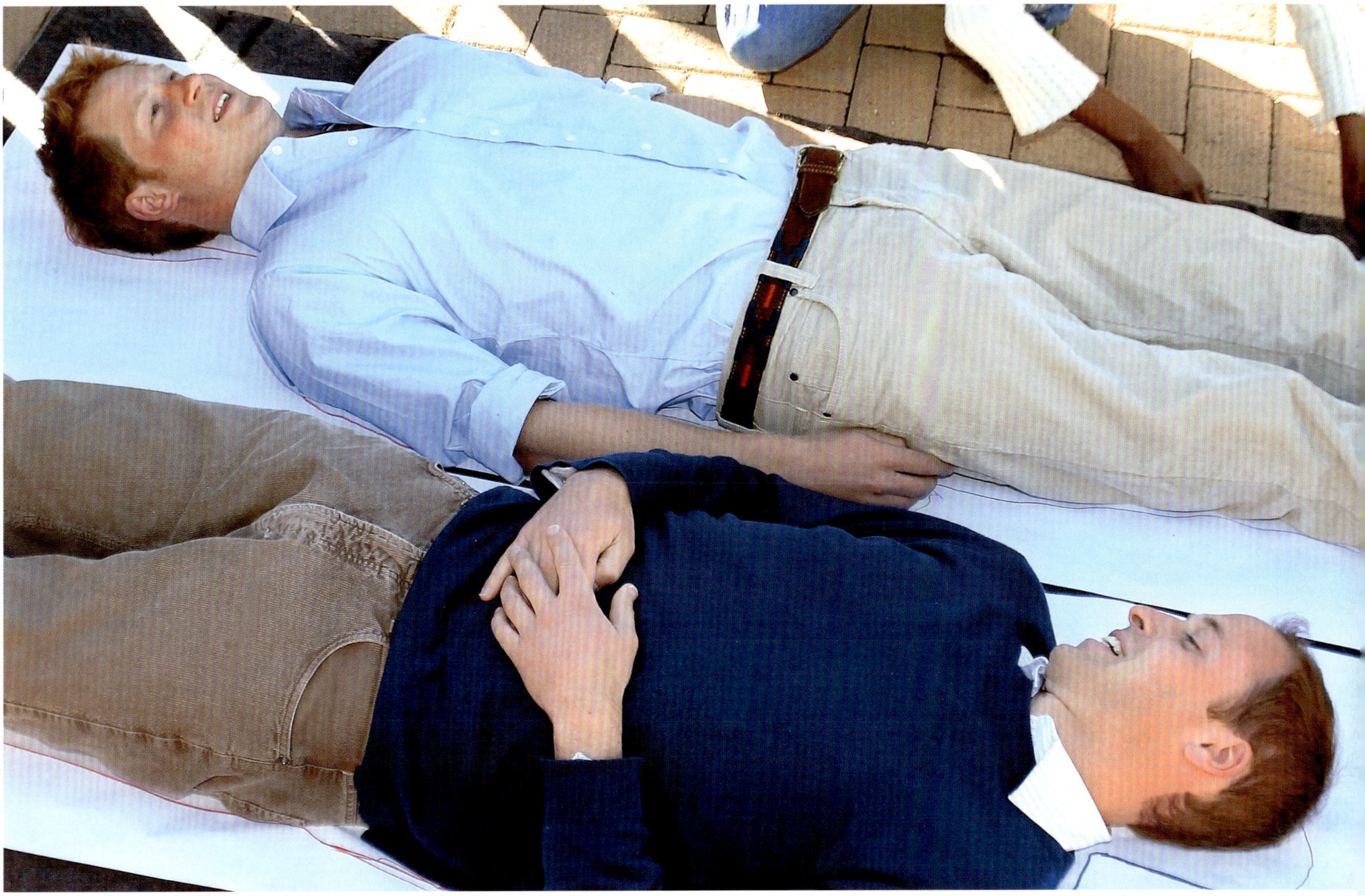

Opposite, top The Prince of Wales disembarks from a police boat in Muchelney as he visits flood-affected parts of Somerset Levels in 2014.

Opposite, bottom The Duke of Cambridge chats with patient Theresa Jones in the frailty unit during a visit to Aintree University Hospital in Liverpool.

Above Prince Harry and Prince William take part in a game with HIV-affected children in the Mamohato Network Club at the palace of King Letsie III in Lesotho. The two brothers were on a joint trip to Africa and visited each other's charities in Botswana and Lesotho.

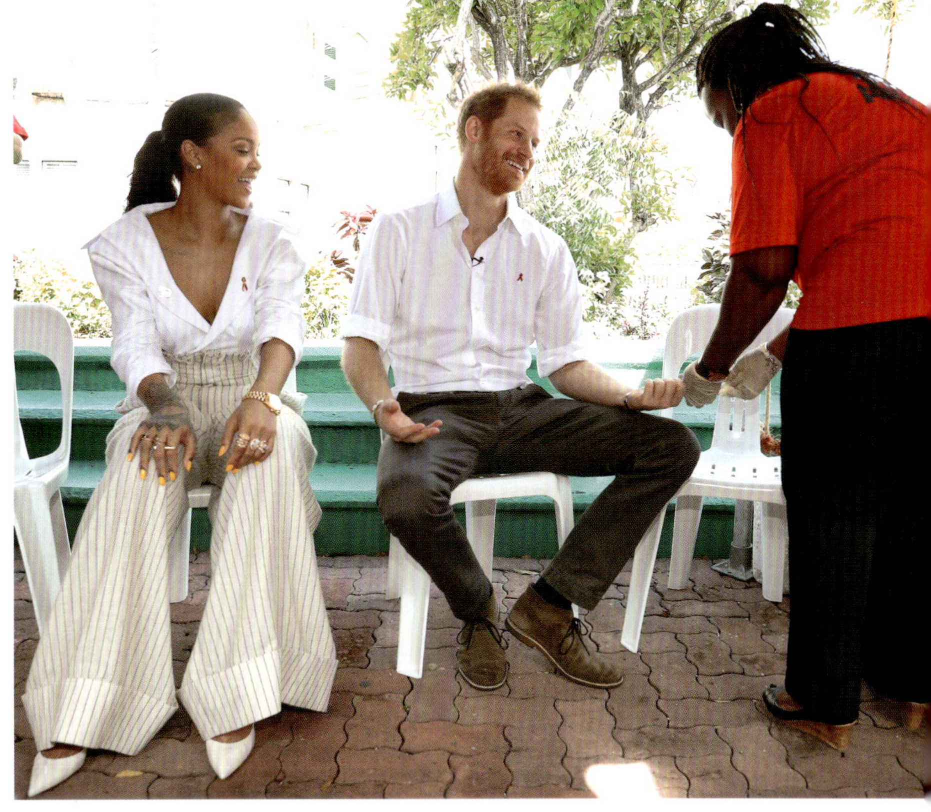

Right Prince Harry takes an HIV test as singer-songwriter Rihanna looks on at Man Aware, an event held by the Barbados National HIV/AIDS Commission in Bridgetown to promote more widespread testing for the public.

Following pages Prince William, royal patron of Tusk Trust and president of United for Wildlife, assists rangers in northern Kenya as they move Matt, a tranquilised bull elephant, whilst a wildlife vet fits the elephant with a new satellite tracking collar to monitor and protect him from poachers. The Duke co-piloted the aircraft during the darting exercise to tranquilise Matt whilst on a private visit to see firsthand some of the conservation work supported by Tusk Trust.

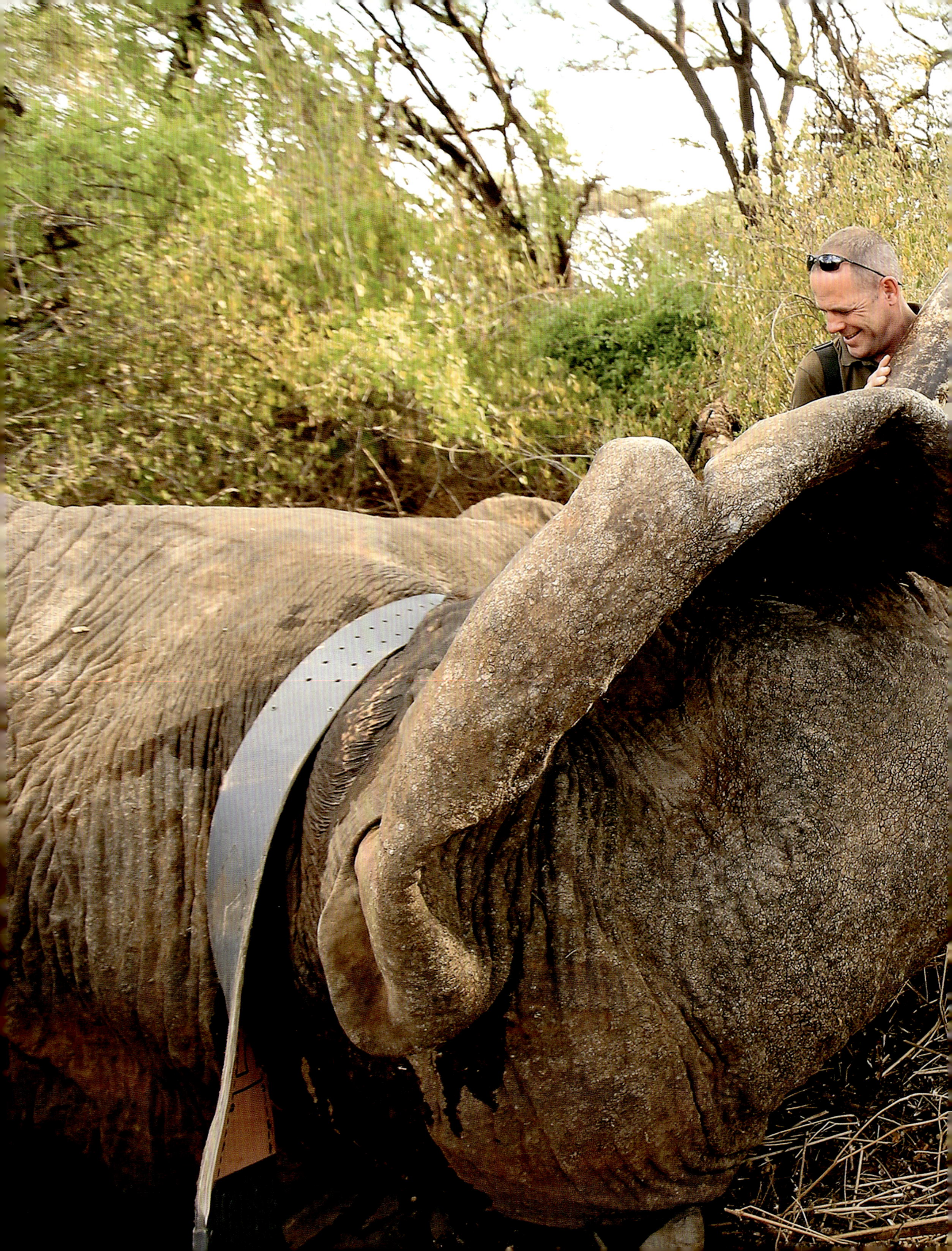

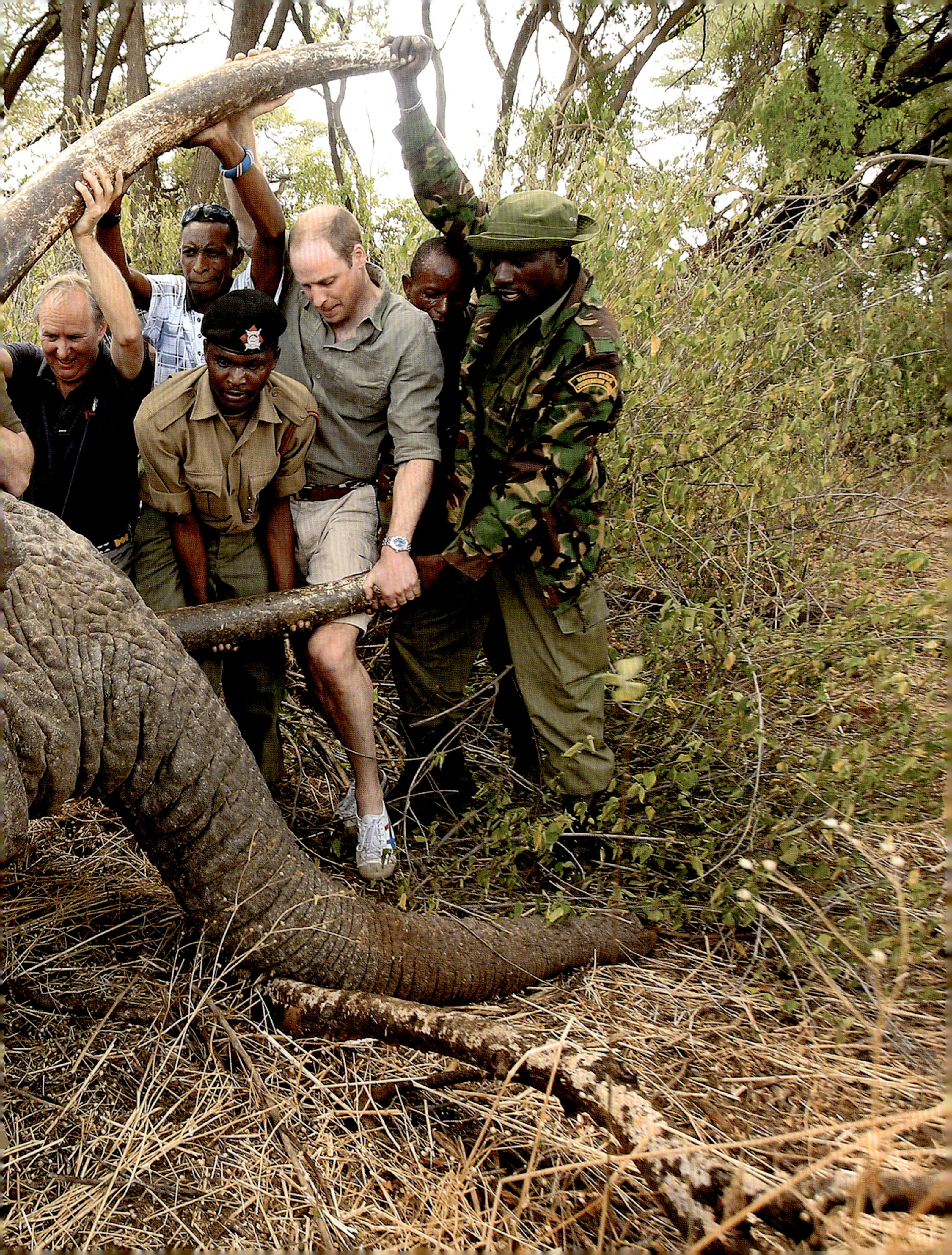

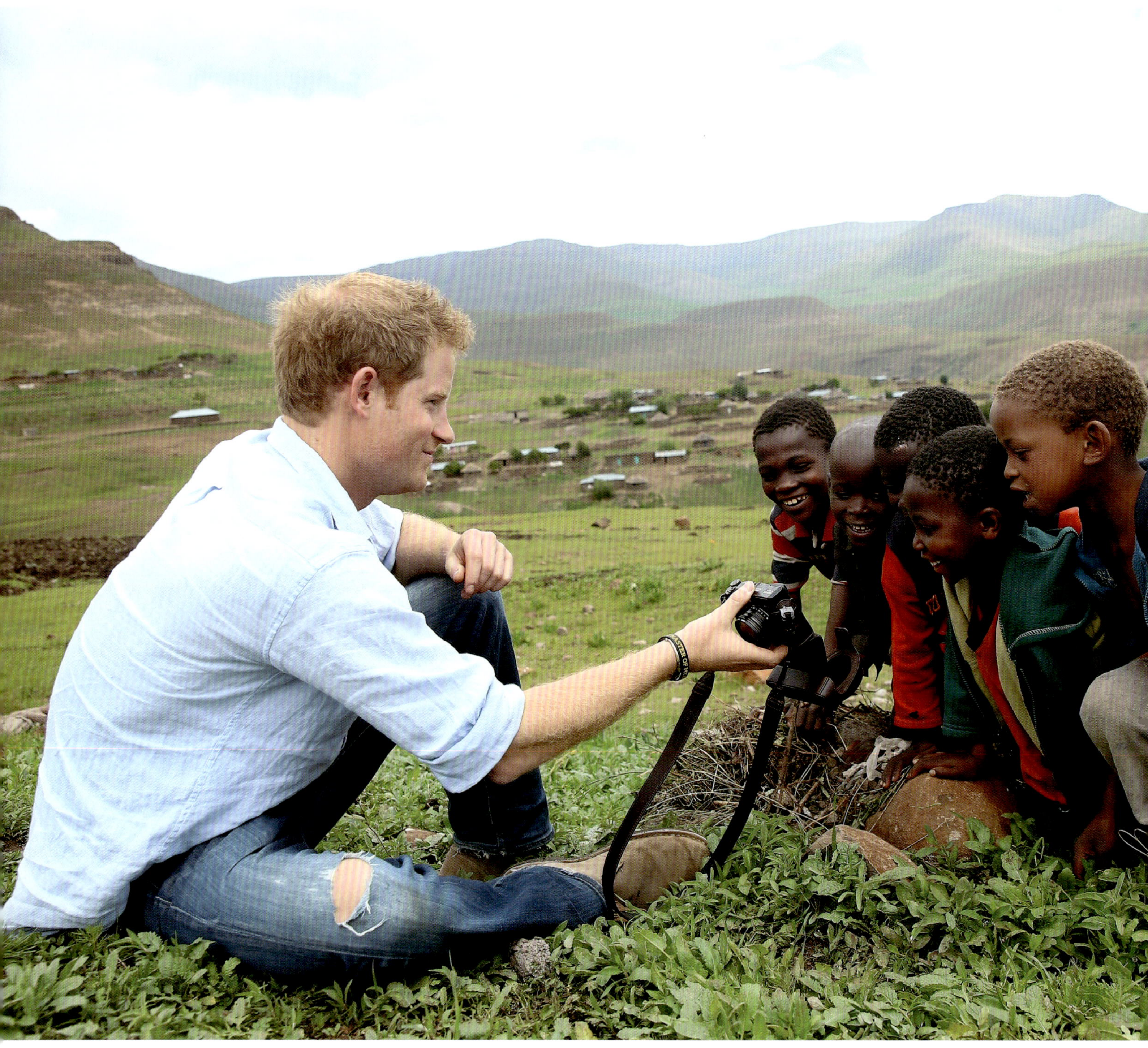

Above Prince Harry shows children a photograph he has taken during a visit to a herd boy night school constructed by Sentebale in the mountainous region of Mokhotlong, Lesotho. Sentebale, which means "forget me not" in the local Sesotho language, is the charity founded by Prince Seeiso of Lesotho and Prince Harry to help the HIV-positive and vulnerable children of Lesotho.

Opposite, top Prince Harry dances with hearing impaired children in a silent dance during a visit to the Kananelo Centre for the Deaf in Lesotho.

Opposite, bottom Prince Harry meets fifteen-year-old orphan Keneuoe and partially sighted children at St. Bernadette's Resource Centre for the Blind, a project supported by his charity, Sentebale, in Maseru, Lesotho.

Following pages The Duchess of Cornwall listens to a storytelling session with author Jeremy Strong and children from St. Augustine's Church of England Primary School at Clarence House to mark the fifteenth anniversary of the national Young Readers Programme. The Duchess supports more than ninety charities as patron or president. Her charity work is varied, but several themes prevail: health; literacy; supporting victims of rape, sexual abuse, and domestic violence; empowering women; food; animals; and heritage and the arts.

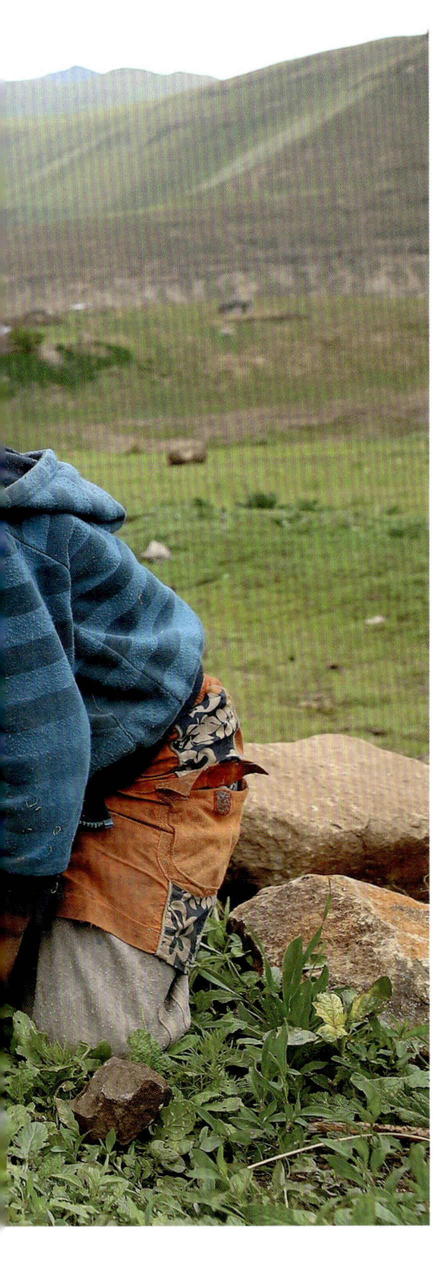

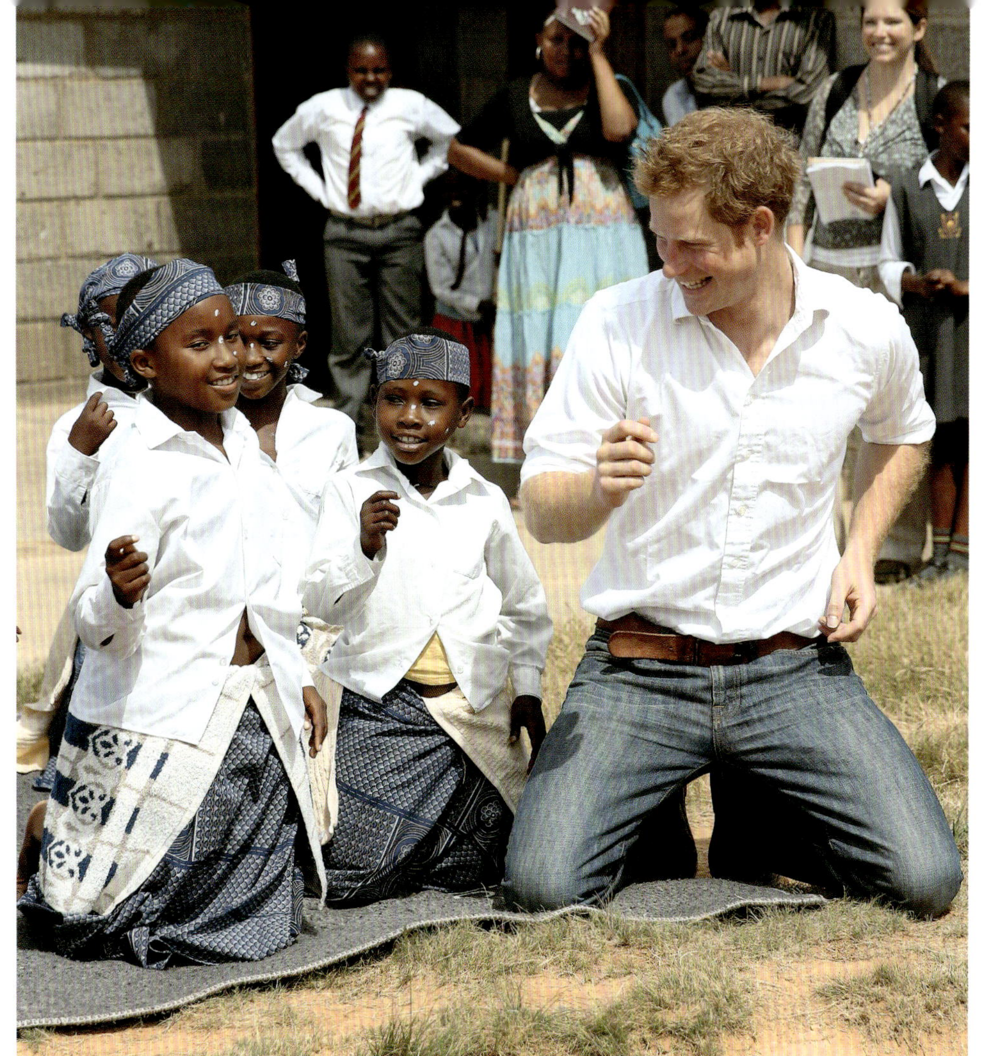

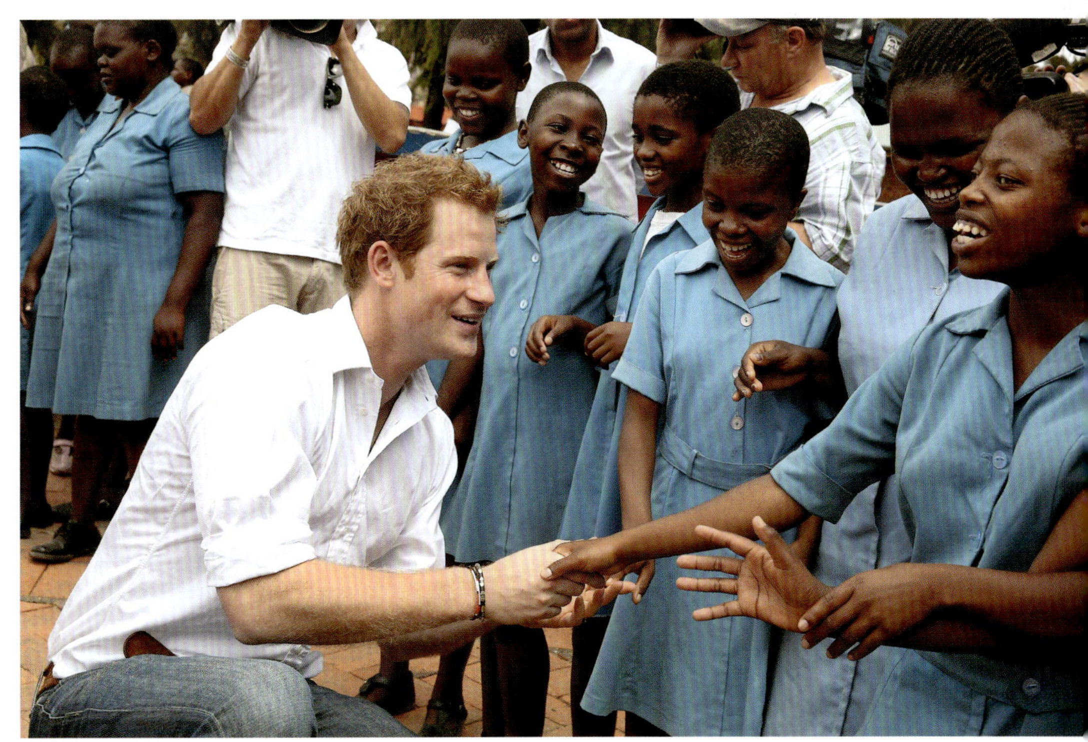

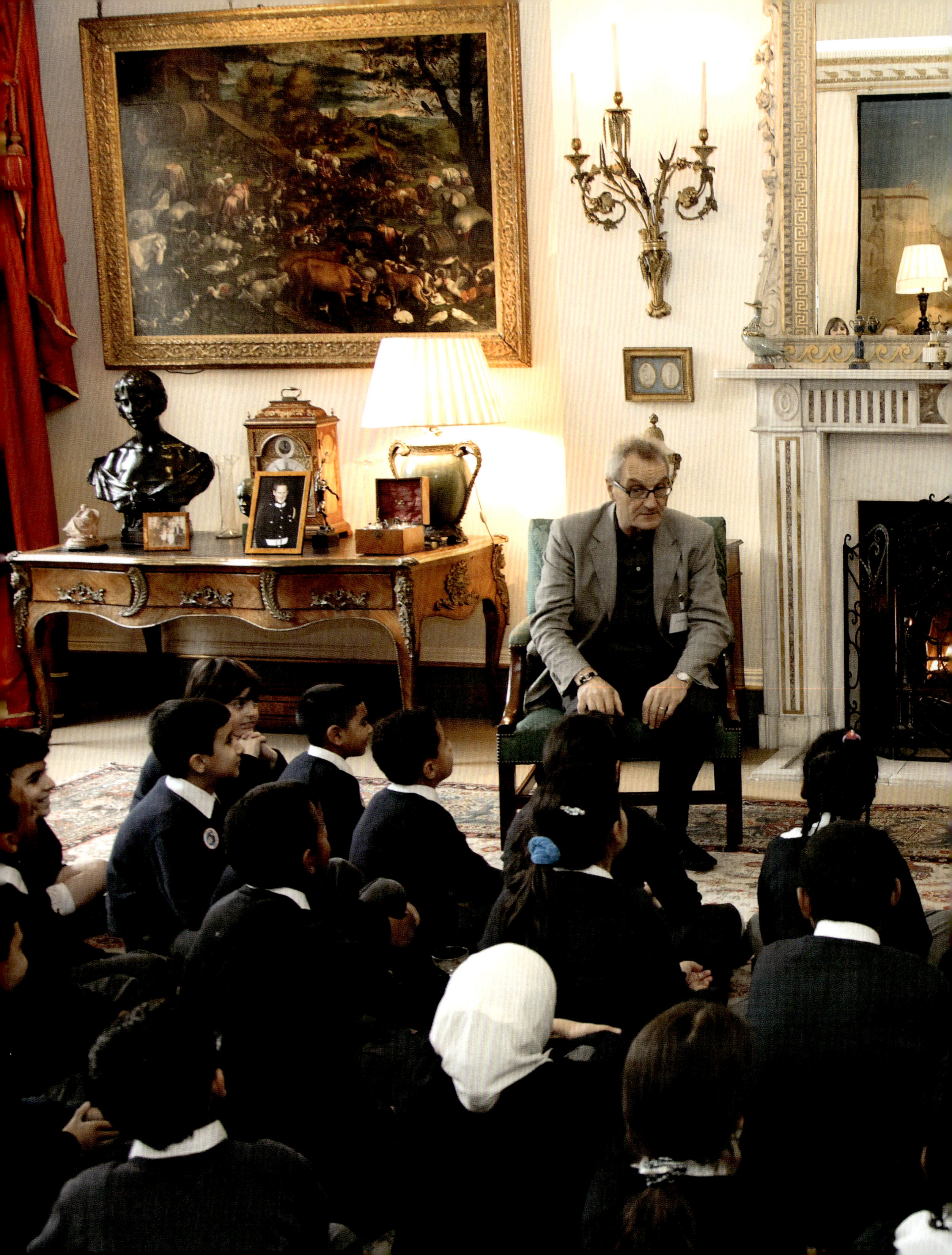

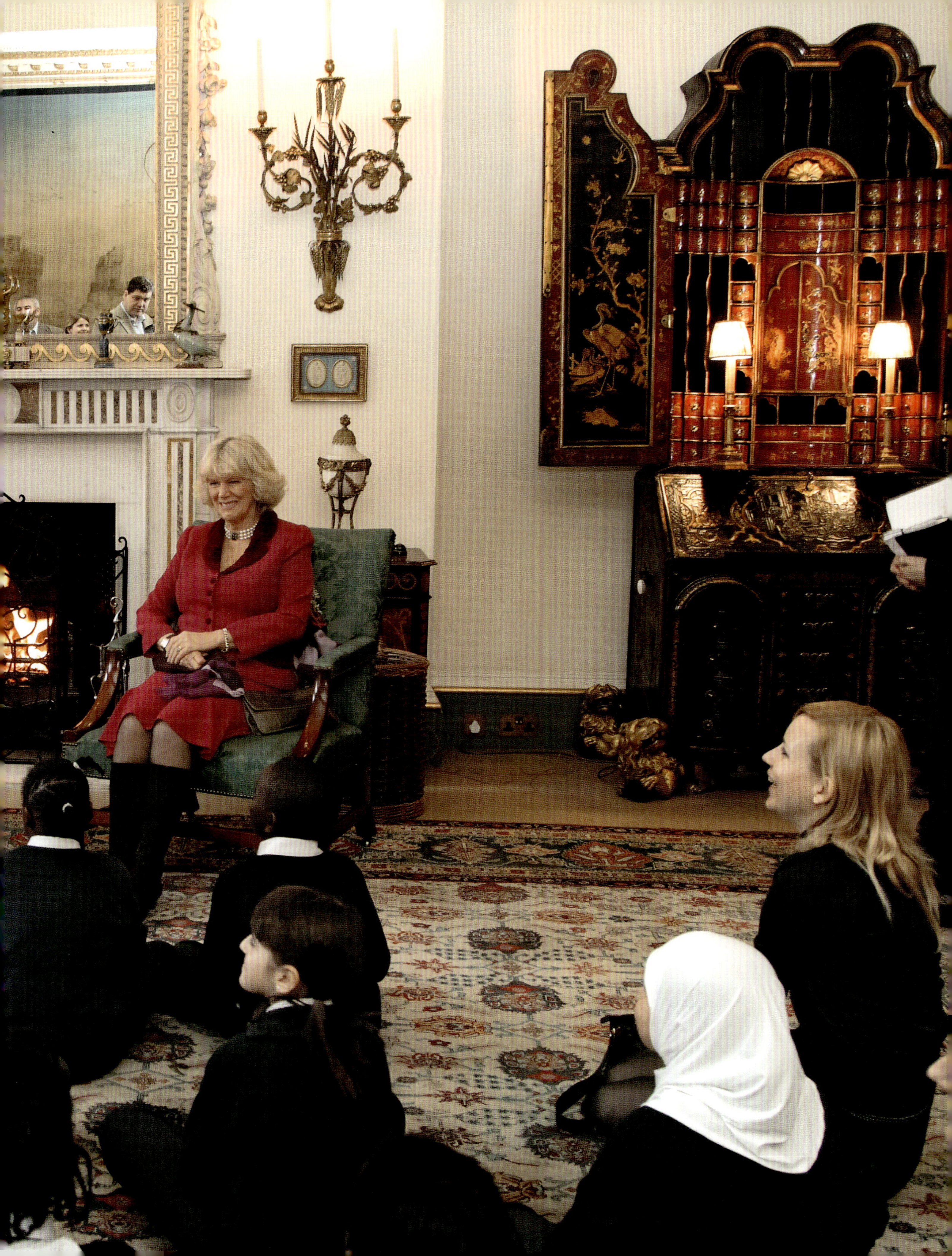

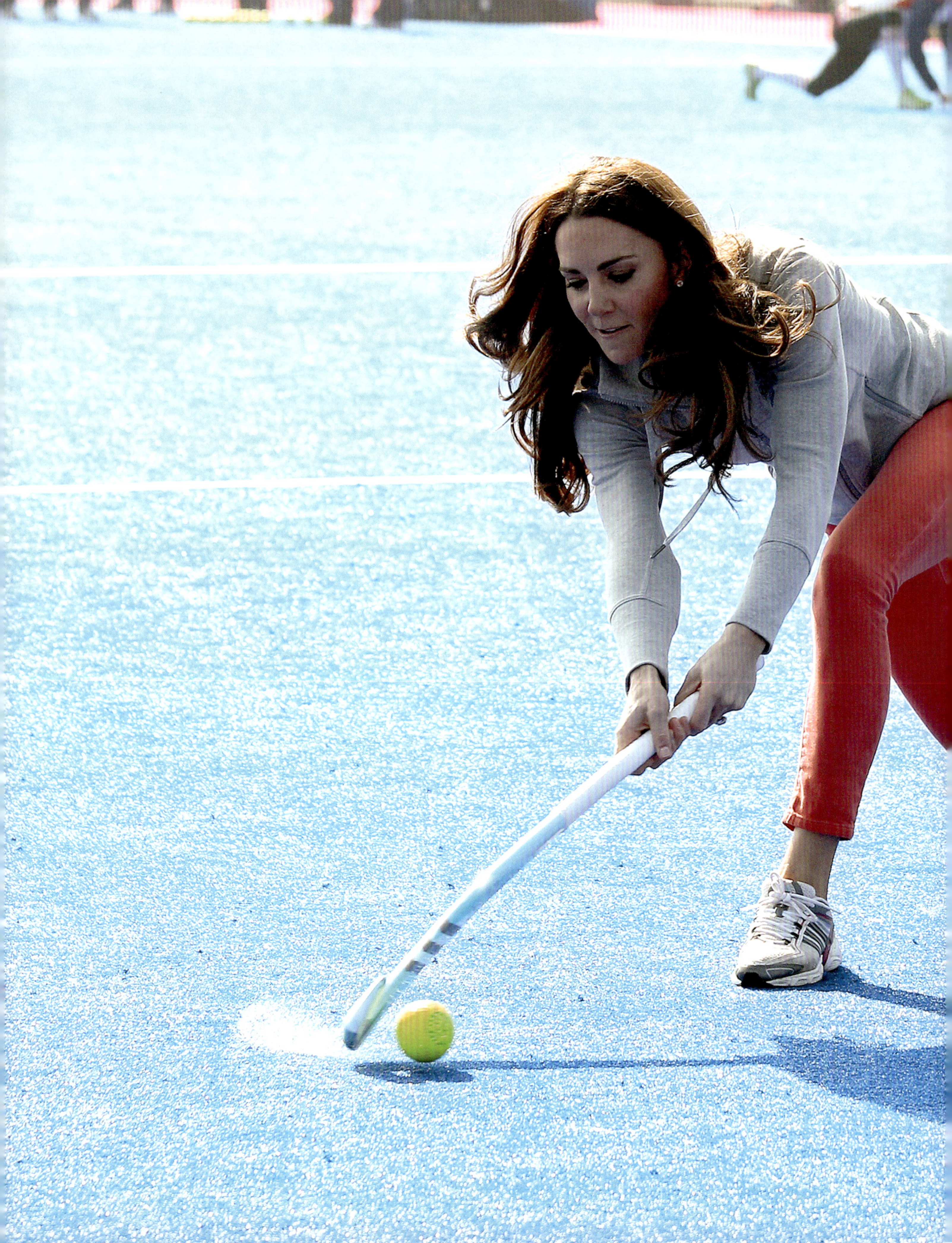

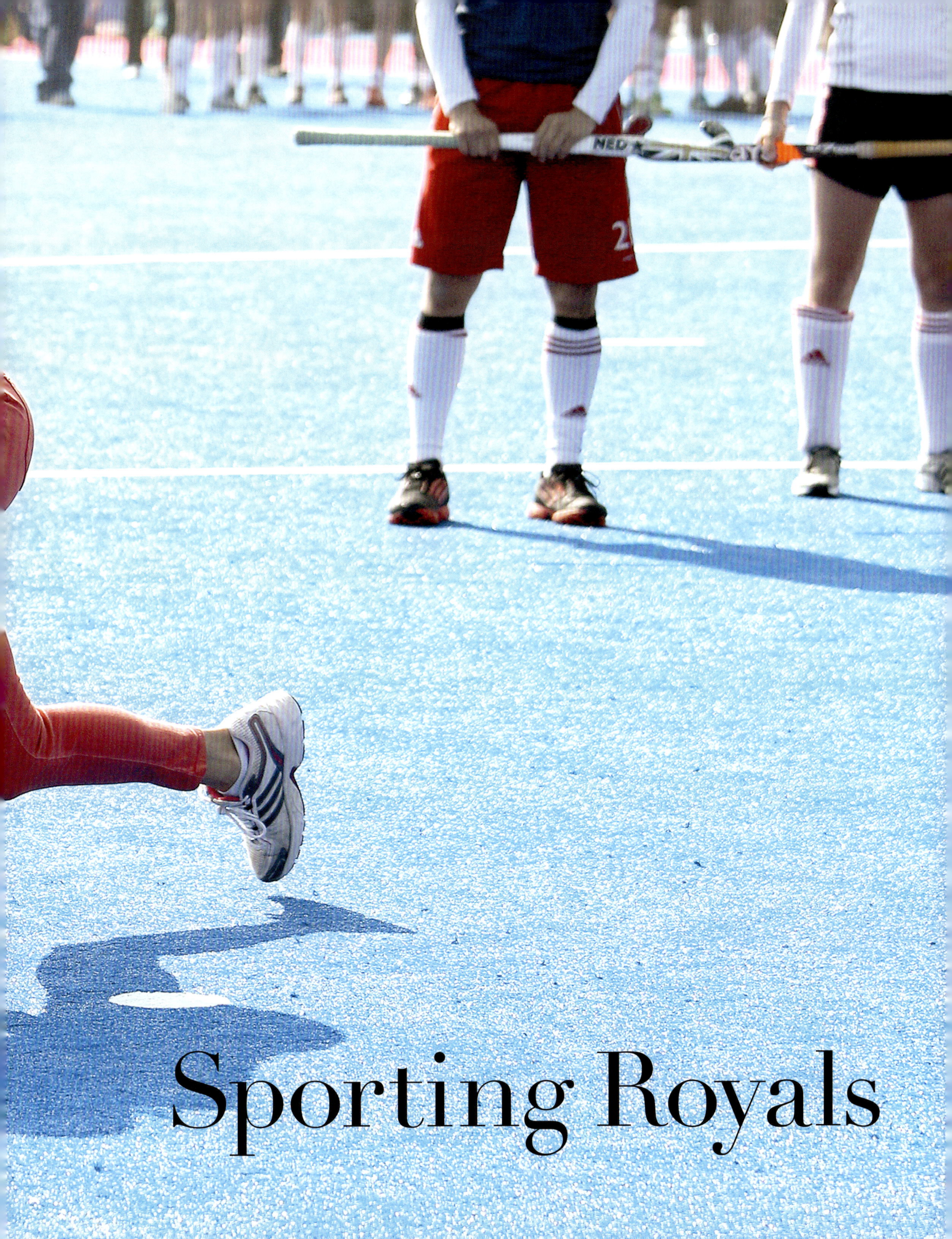

Sporting Royals

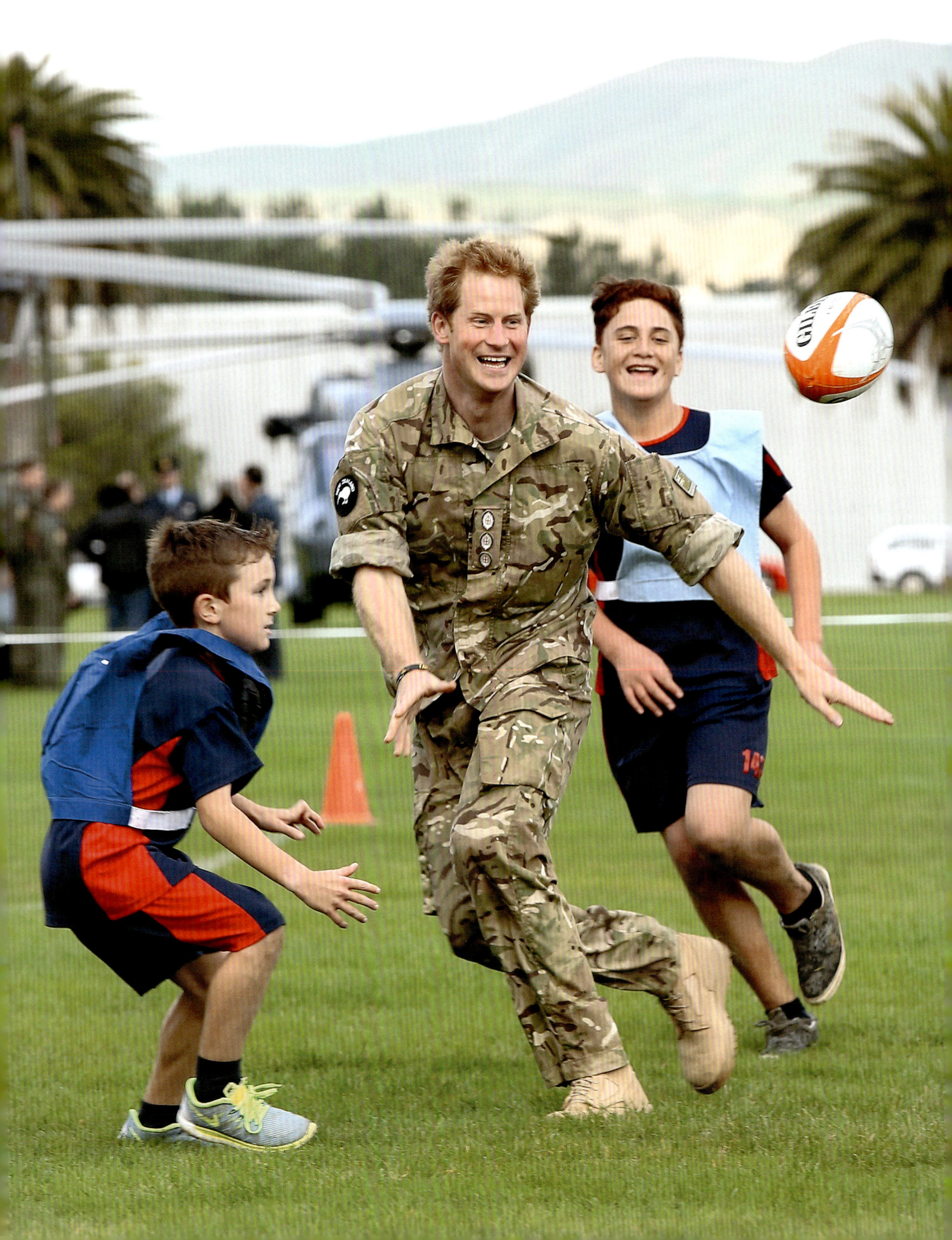

For the royals, sport is a medium to connect, a universal language appreciated and understood by many. It enables them to communicate with young people, as well as people from other cultures who may speak other languages. Sport puts us all at ease and can help get a message across and change lives for the better. Getting stuck into a game of football, cricket, or even table tennis can break down barriers, but above all it nearly always provides great pictures! The younger royals are incredibly accomplished at many of these sports. All excelled in some form of sport at school, and this is evident in their professional lives. From Prince Harry scissor-kicking into goal during a visit to New Zealand to the Duchess of Cambridge whacking a six in cricket whilst wearing a maxi-dress as a bemused Sachin Tendulkar looked on in India. Even the Prince of Wales has been known to shoot some hoops on royal tour, and I once photographed him giving a climbing wall in Jersey a go whilst wearing a double-breasted Savile Row suit. Memorable images indeed. Sport is more than just fun, though; often these strong images transmit an important message.

Sport has long been a key feature in royal life. The royal family's involvement in the 2012 Olympic and Paralympic Games in London was critical to the enduring success of these events. Patronage of groups such as England rugby (Prince Harry), and Welsh rugby (Prince William) provides these organisations with well-known figureheads. I have previously mentioned Princess Anne's involvement in the Olympics but her commitment to the Olympic movement is plain to see, from her competing in the 1976 Montreal Summer Olympic Games to her ongoing dedication to the games today. Zara Tindall won the Eventing World Championship in 2006 and a silver medal in the 2012 London Summer Olympics; she was even named the 2006 BBC Sports Personality of the Year. Prince Charles gave up polo in 2005, but his two sons have continued his legacy, raising millions through charity polo matches in the summer season.

Preceding pages Catherine, Duchess of Cambridge, plays field hockey with the Great Britain hockey team at the Riverside Arena in Queen Elizabeth Olympic Park ahead of the London 2012 Olympic Games.

Opposite During a visit to Linton Military Camp in Palmerston, New Zealand, Prince Harry plays touch rubgy with schoolchildren.

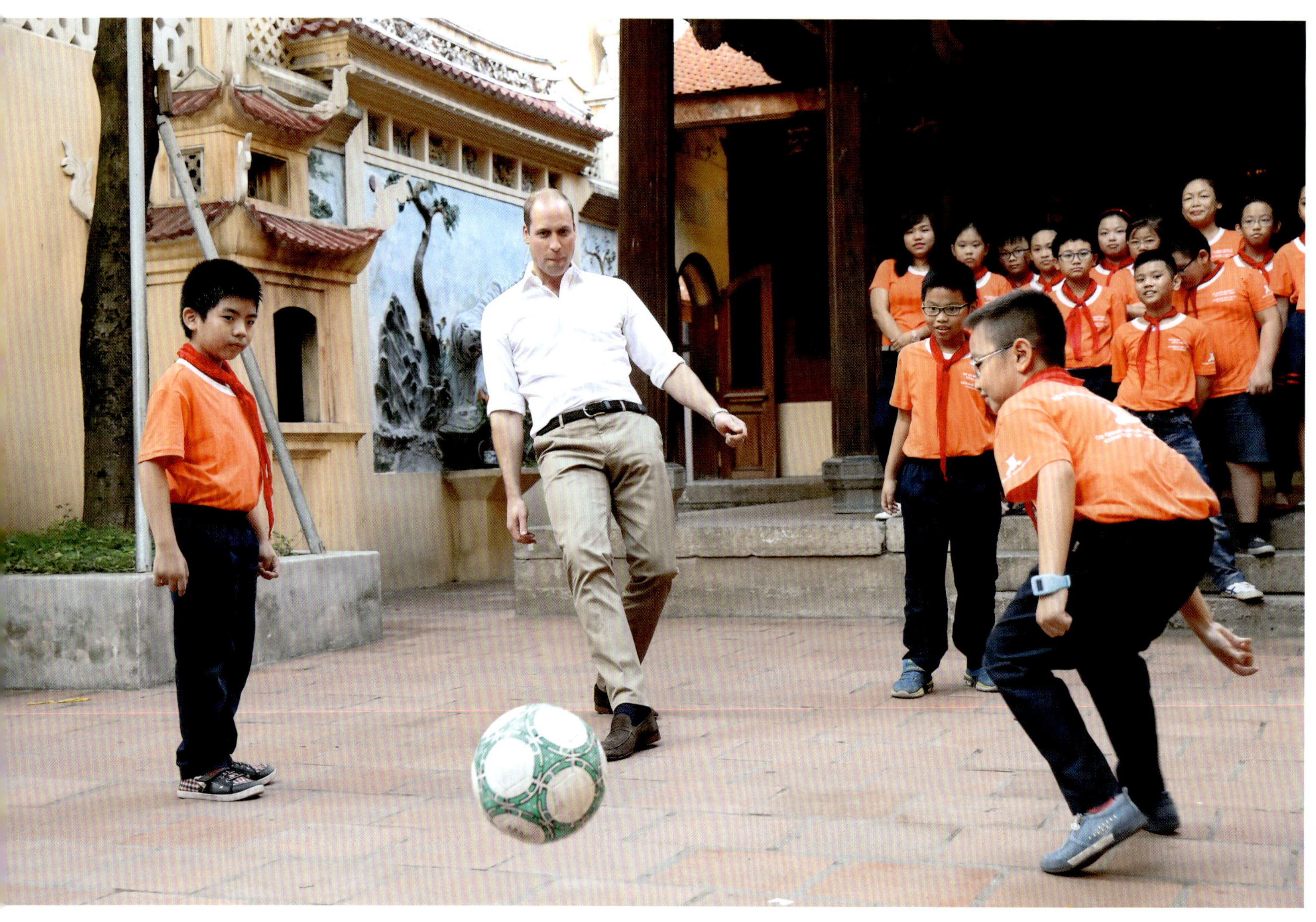

Above During a visit to discuss wildlife conservation initiatives and attend the third international Conference on the Illegal Wildlife Trade, Prince William plays football with schoolchildren in Hanoi, Vietnam.

Opposite The Duchess of Cambridge takes part in sporting activities with children from Magic Bus, a non-governmental organization supporting young Indian children, at Mumbai's iconic recreation ground, the Oval Maidan, on the first day of a royal visit to India and Bhutan.

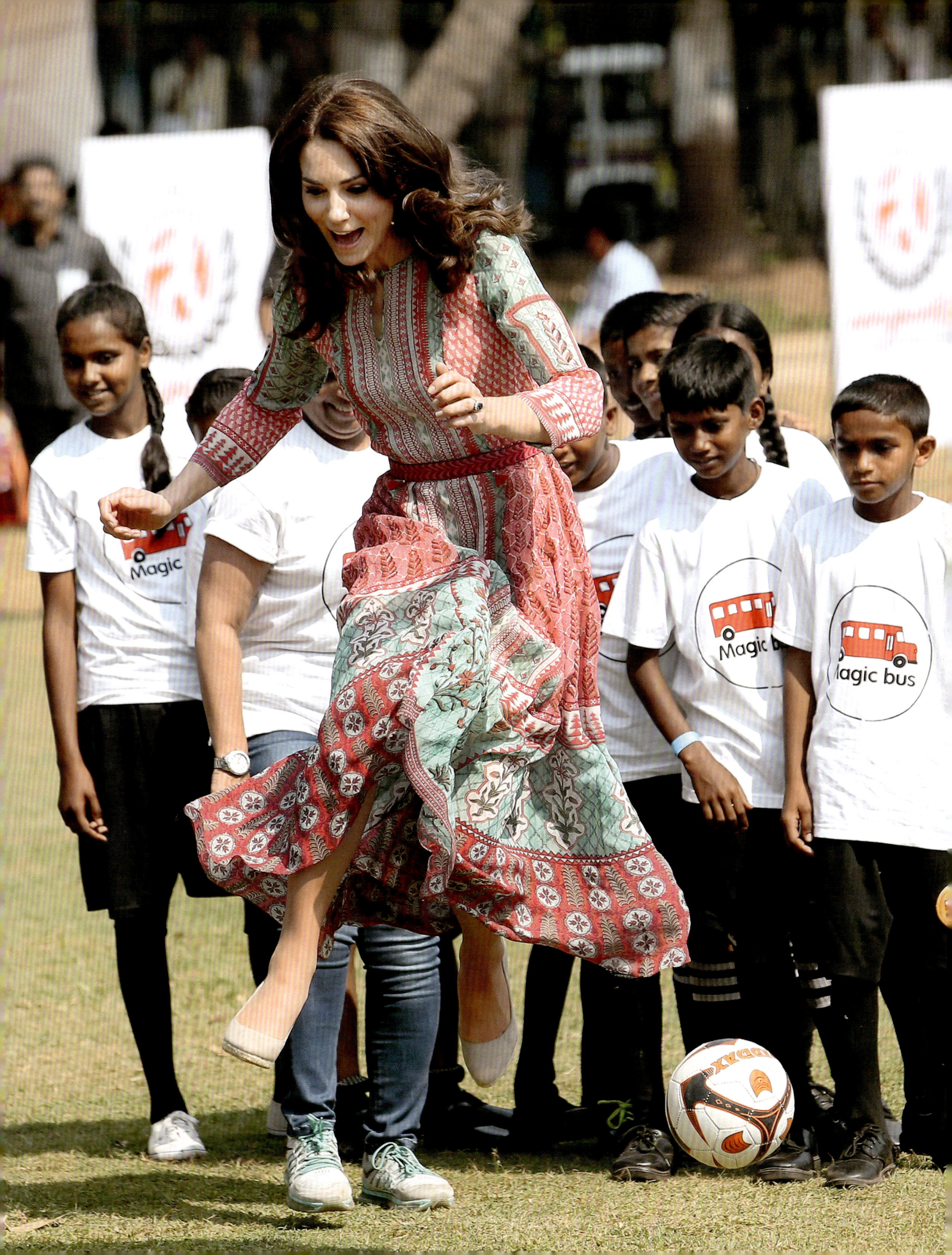
Magic
Magic
bus

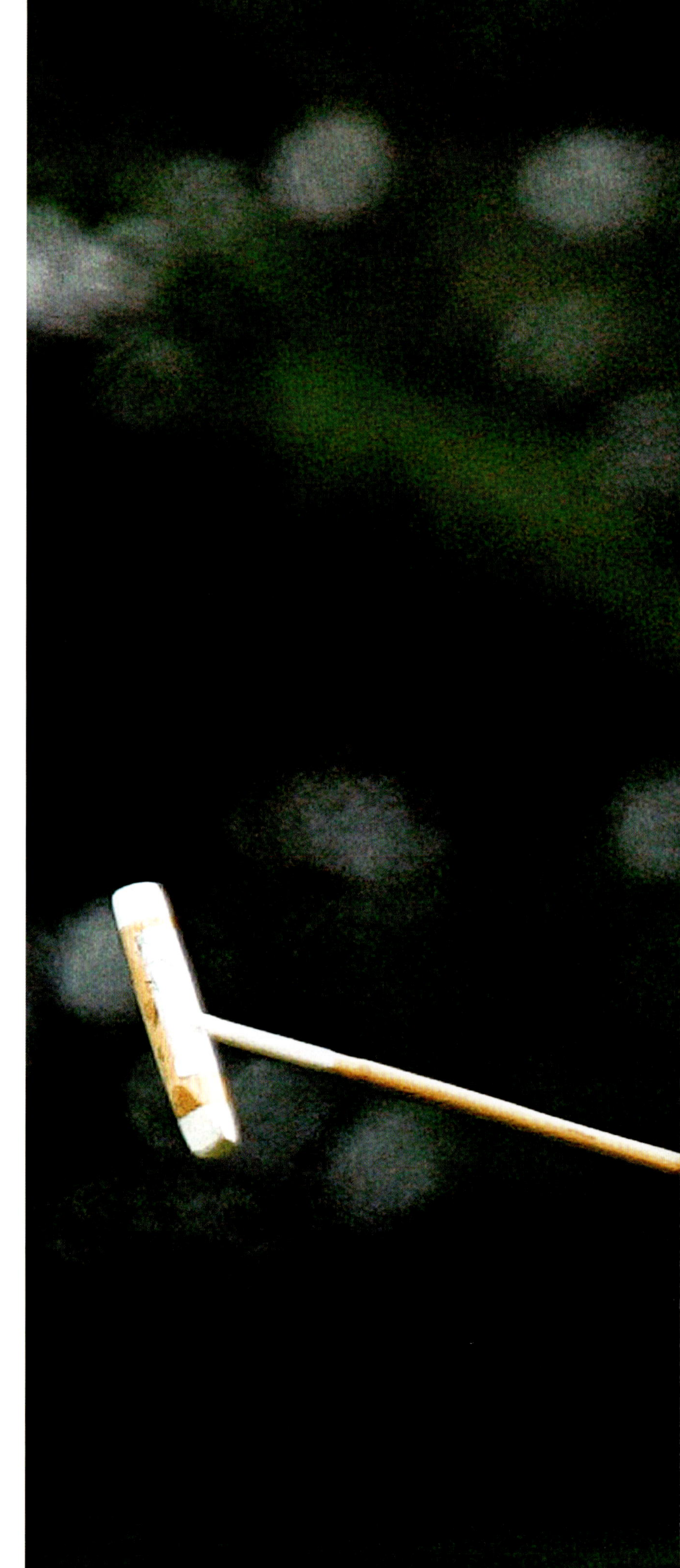

Prince Harry plays polo for the Hunt Staff Benefit Society against American team Virginia State Polo at Cirencester Park Polo Club.

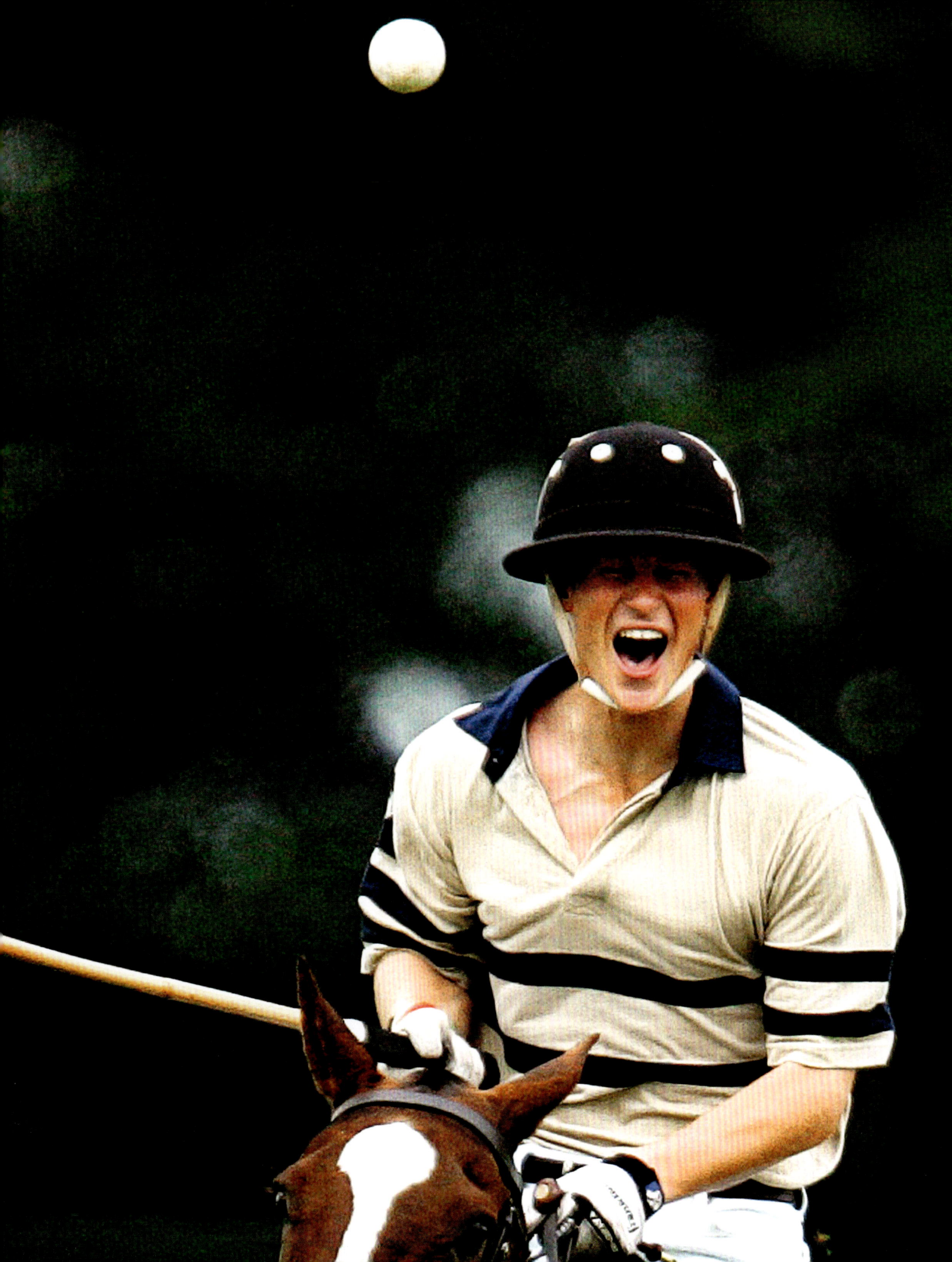

Right Zara Phillips takes part in a novelty bicycle polo match as part of the activities on Rundle Cup day at Tedworth House.

Below Prince Harry plays for team Royal Salute and Prince William plays for team Piaget at the Gigaset Charity Polo Match at Beaufort Polo Club in Tetbury.

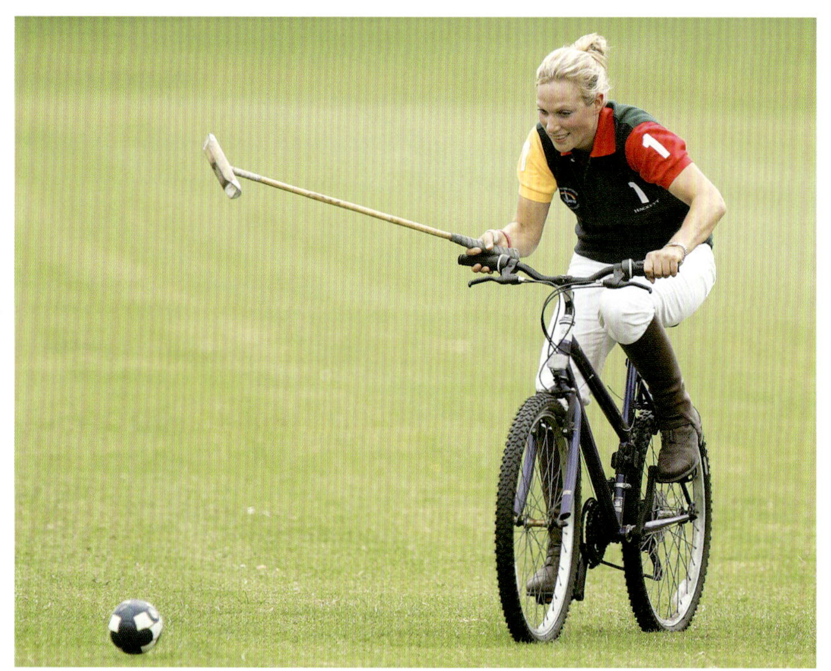

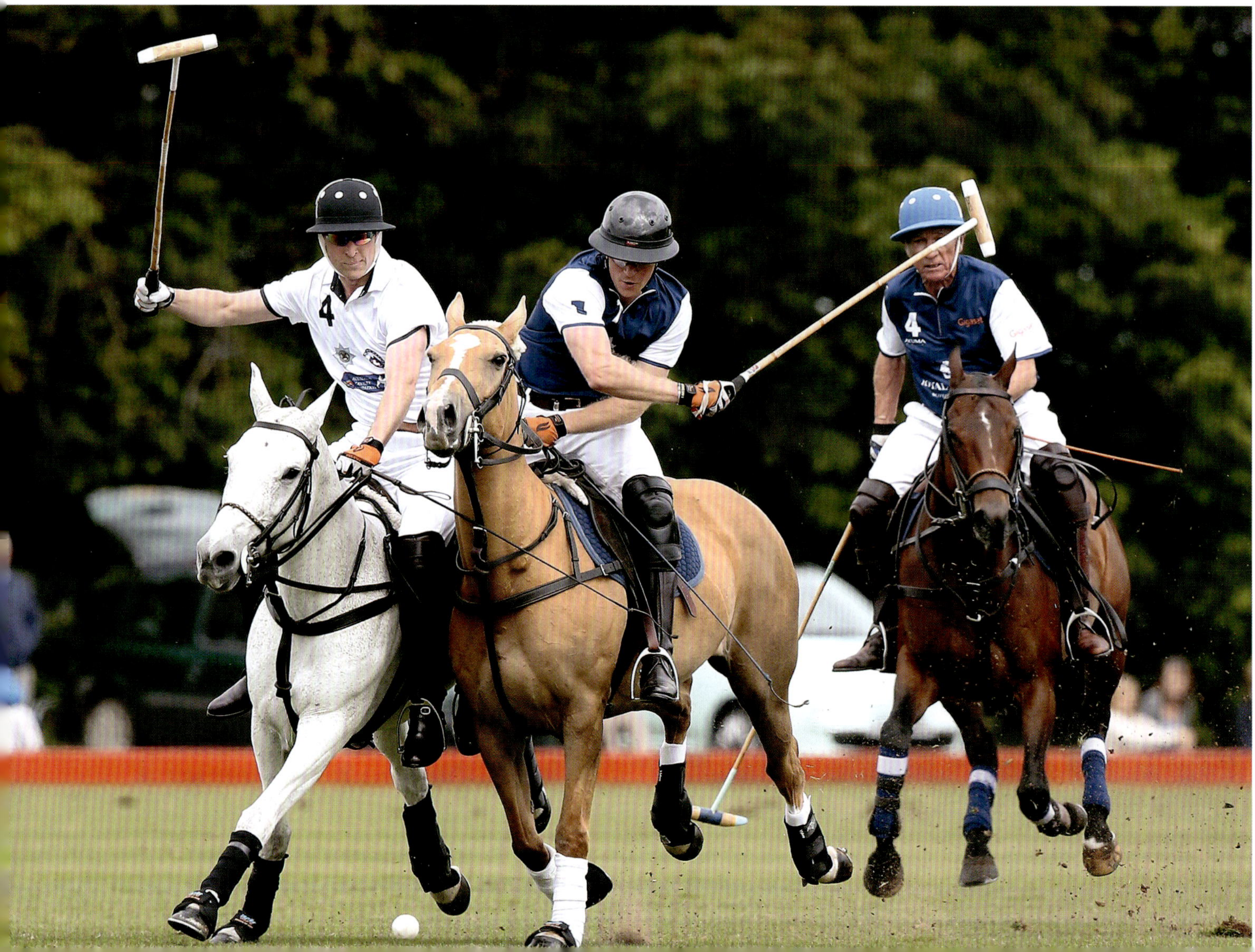

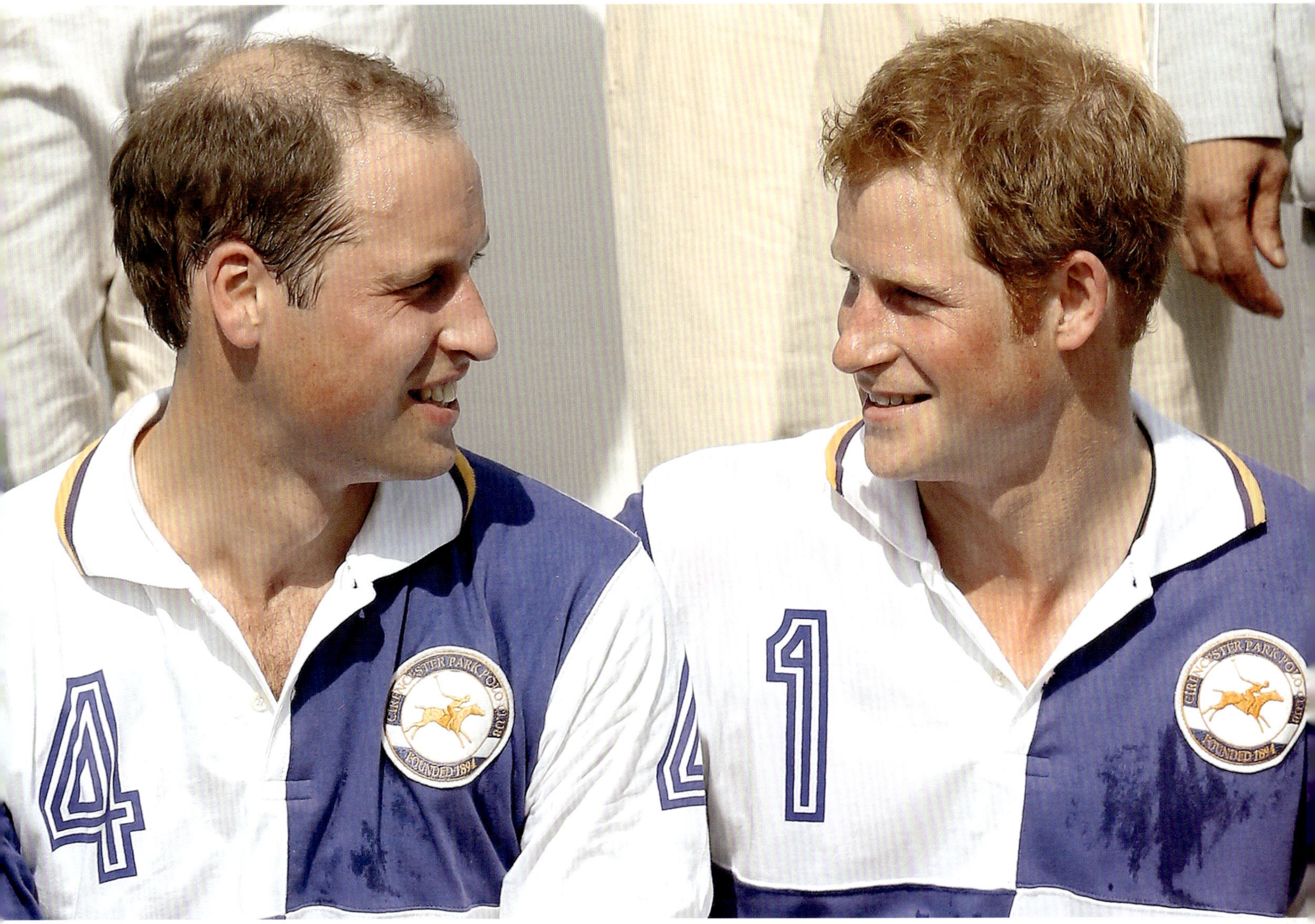

Above Prince William and Prince Harry after competing in the Jerudong Trophy at Cirencester Park Polo Club.

Bottom left Polo sticks at the Cartier International Dubai Polo Challenge at the Desert Palm Resort in Dubai.

Bottom right The Prince of Wales treads in the divots at Cartier International Polo Day at Guards Polo Club in Egham.

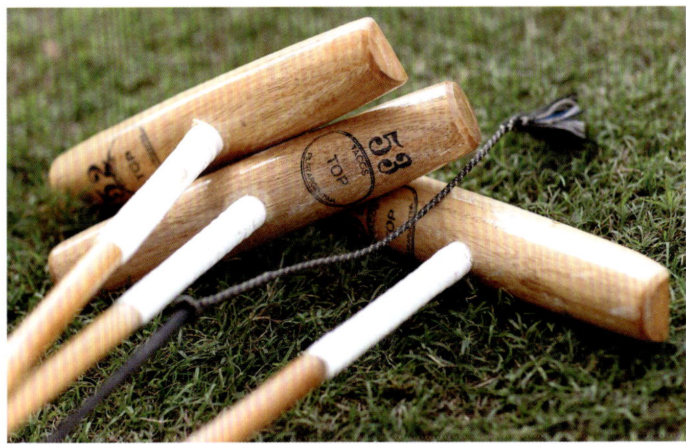

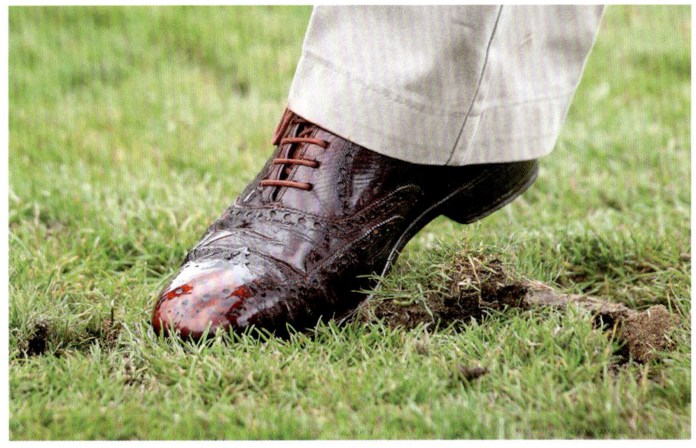

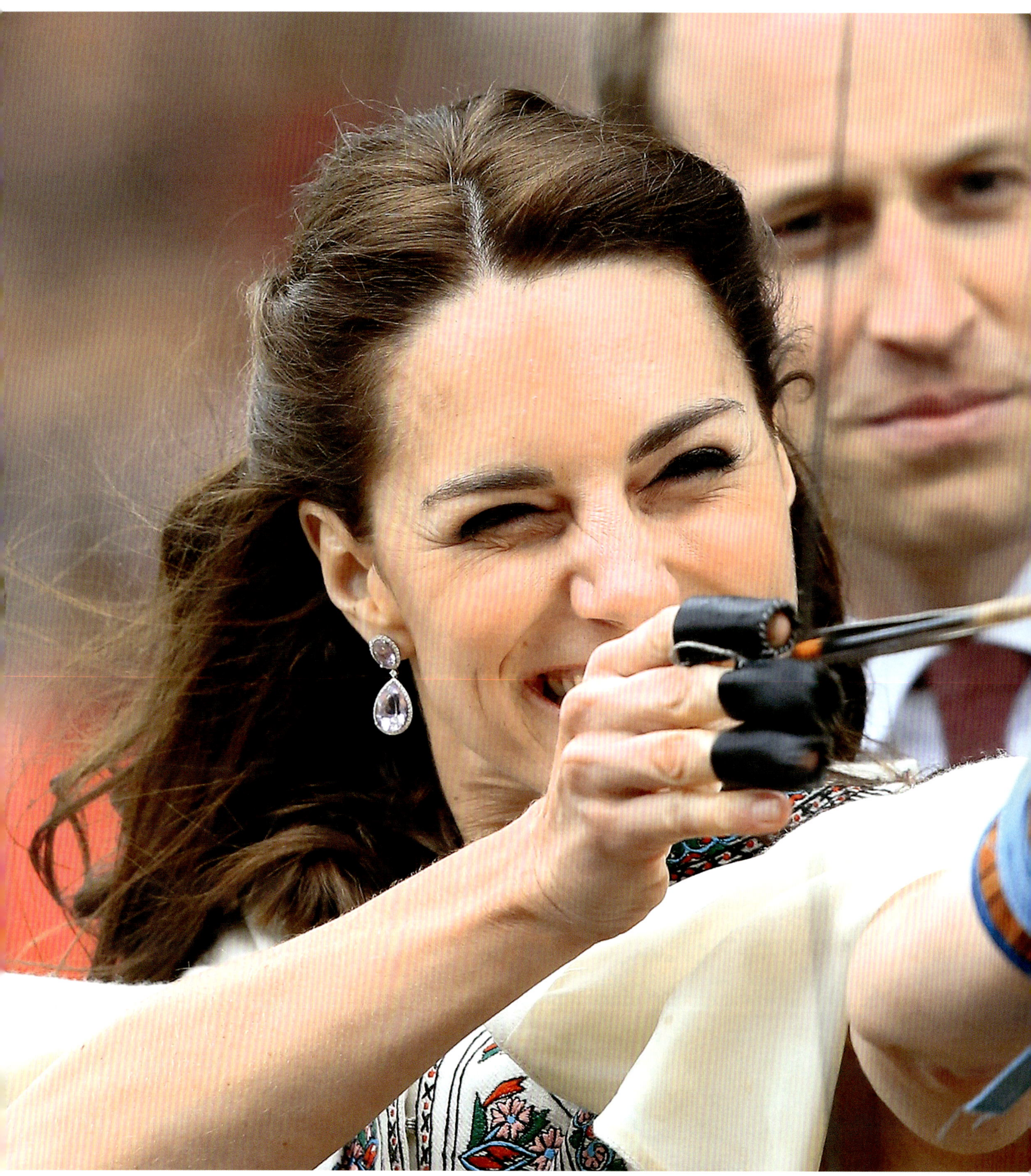

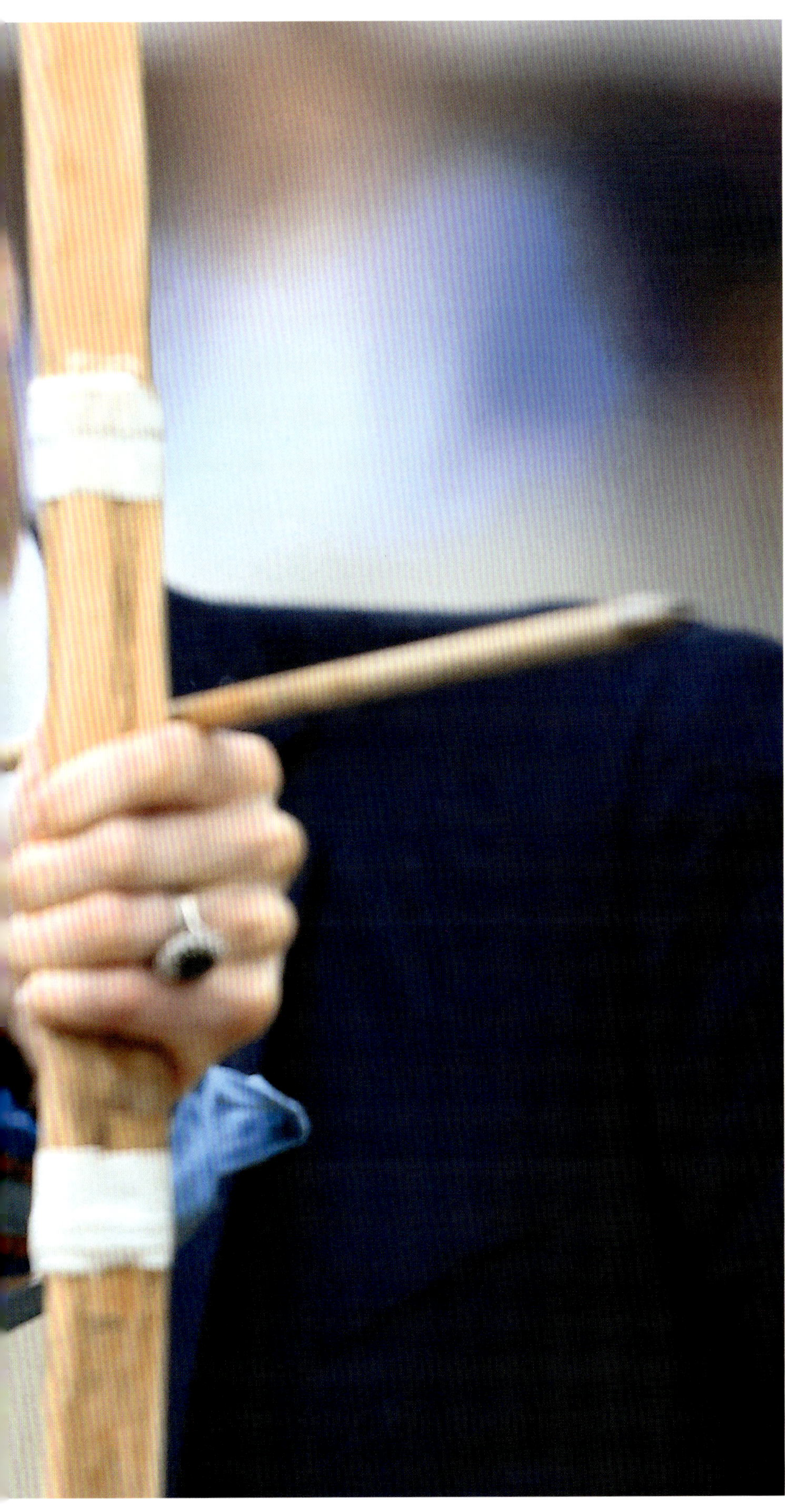

The Duke of Cambridge looks on whilst the Duchess of Cambridge prepares to fire an arrow as they take part in Bhutan's national sport during an archery demonstration on the first day of their visit to the Himalayan mountain kingdom. When it came to her turn the Duchess's concentration was evident, however, in the event the shot drifted slightly wayward of the target!

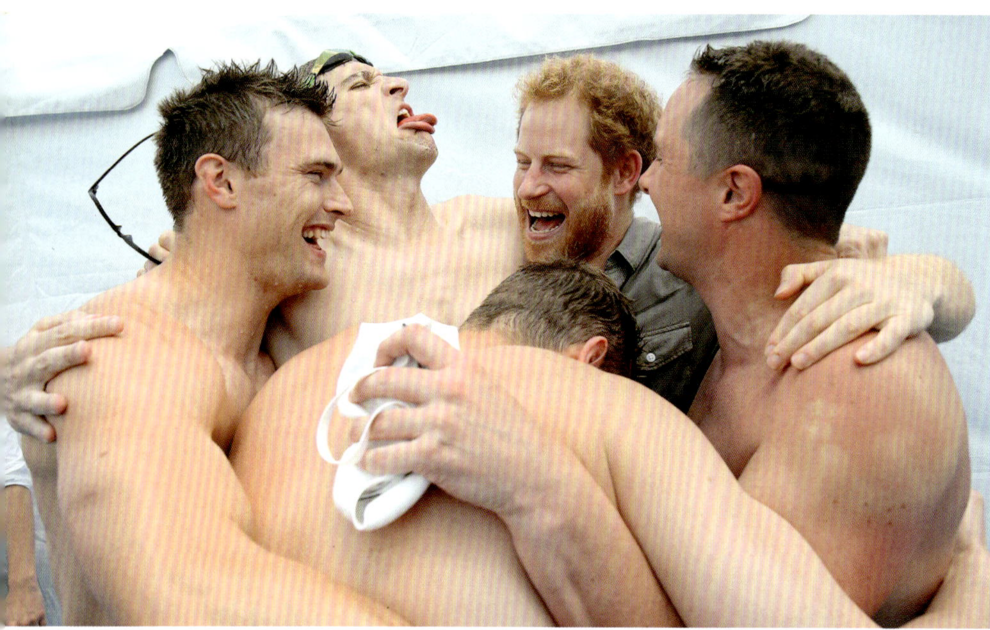

Above Prince Harry celebrates with the United Kingdom Armed Forces four-by-fifty-metre relay team, who won gold in the swimming pool during the 2016 Invictus Games in Orlando, Florida.

Right Prince Harry, patron of the Invictus Games Foundation, and Meghan Markle attend the United Kingdom team trials for the 2018 Invictus Games in Sydney at the University of Bath Sports Training Village.

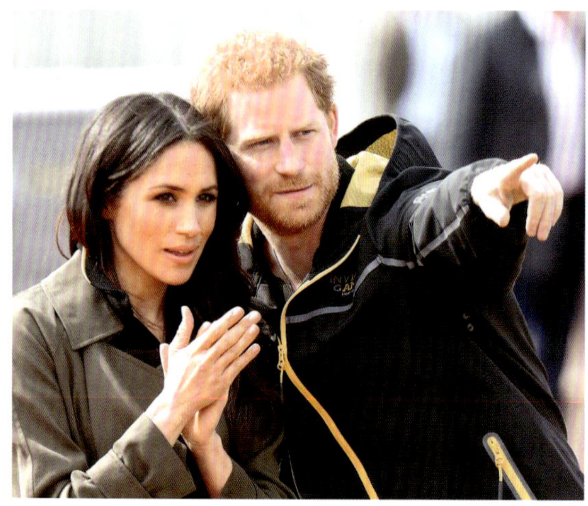

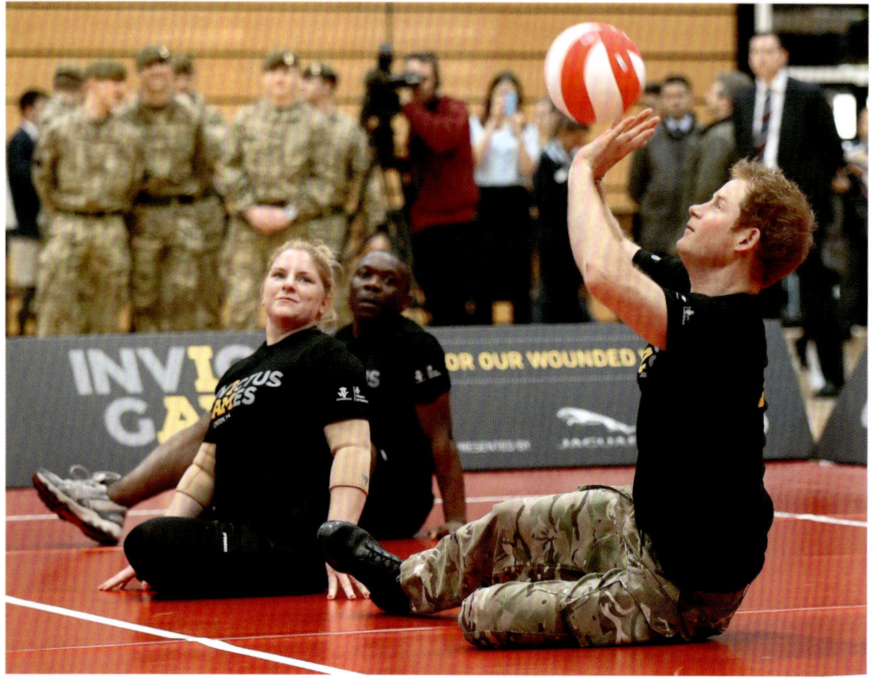

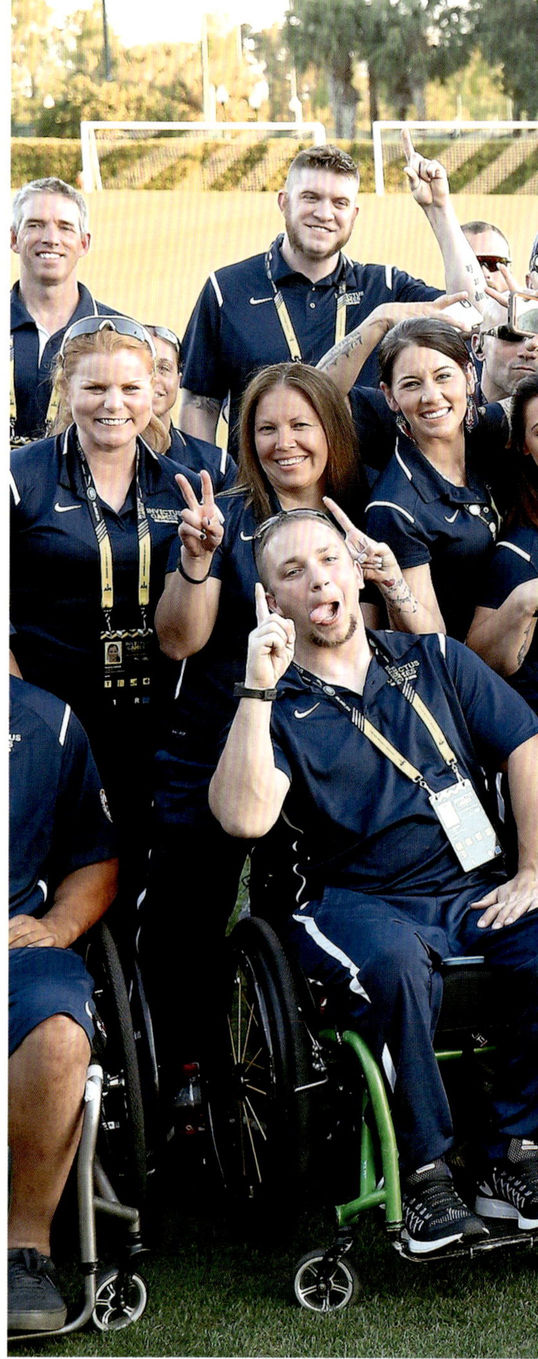

Left Playing sitting volleyball at the Copper Box Arena in Queen Elizabeth Olympic Park during the media launch for the 2014 Invictus Games.

Above Former First Lady Michelle Obama and Prince Harry pose for a photograph with the United States Invictus Games team ahead of the 2016 opening ceremony in Orlando, Florida.

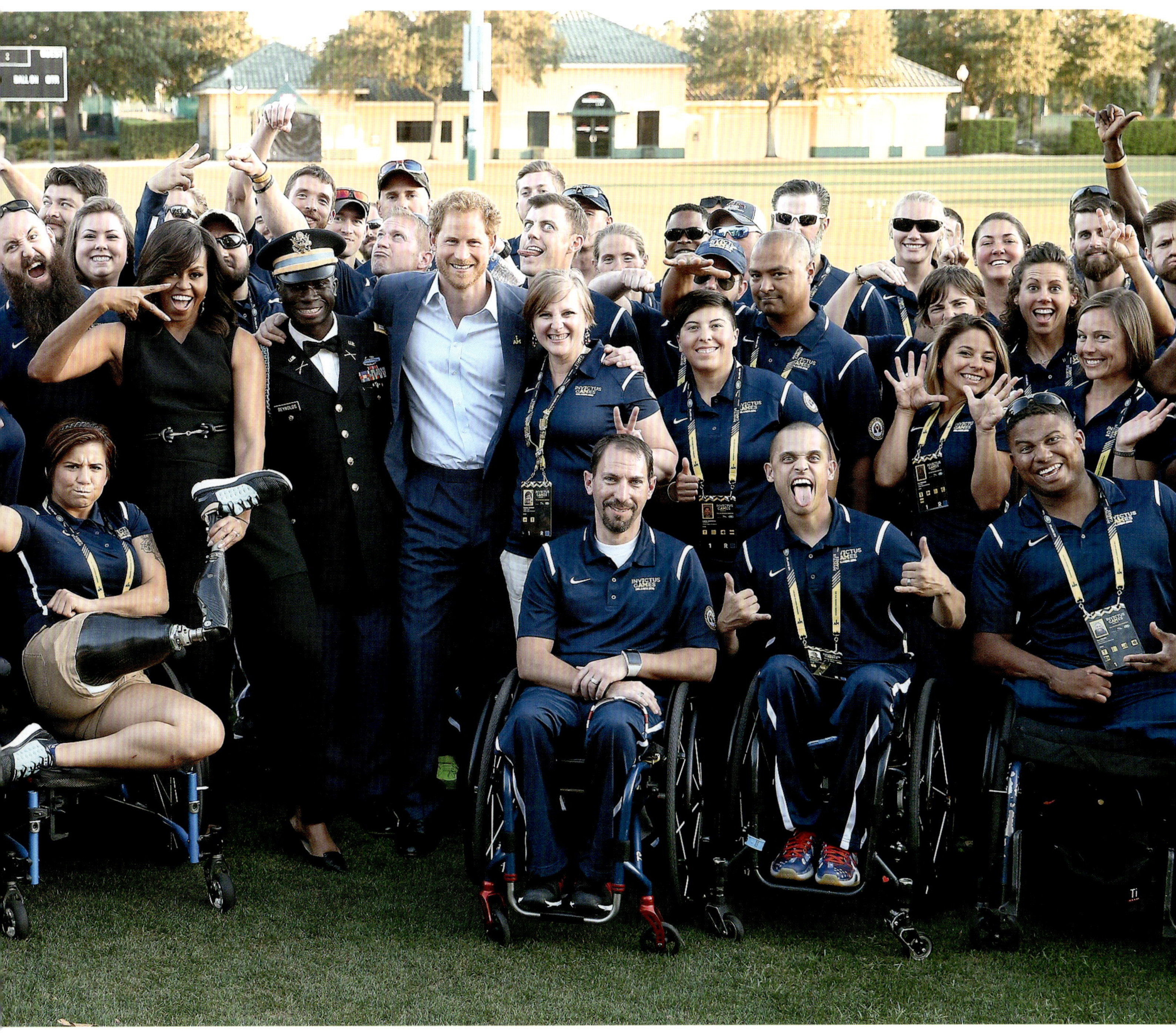
INVICTUS GAMES

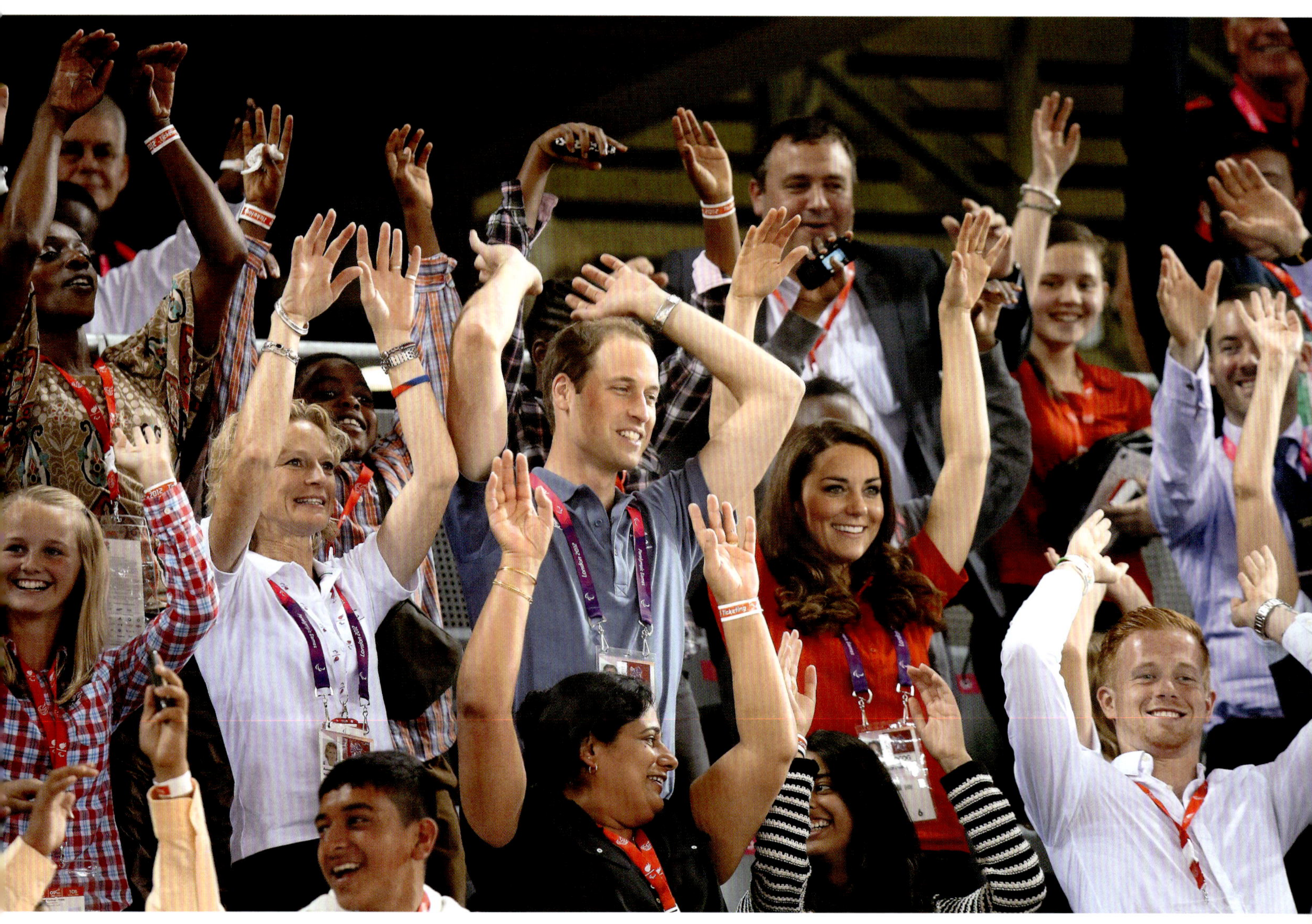

The Duke and Duchess of Cambridge take part in a wave at the velodrome whilst watching track cycling on day one of the London 2012 Paralympic Games. The royals' support of national sporting events, such as the Olympics, Paralympics, and Commonwealth Games, remains a significant part of their ambassadorial role and is clearly something they relish.

Prince Harry joins Jamaican sprinter Usain Bolt in striking his iconic lightning bolt pose at the Usain Bolt Track in Kingston, Jamaica. This was moments after the prince and the charismatic runner raced each other. Prince Harry took a cheeky head start and sprinted over the line, leaving the fastest man in the world trailing in his wake.

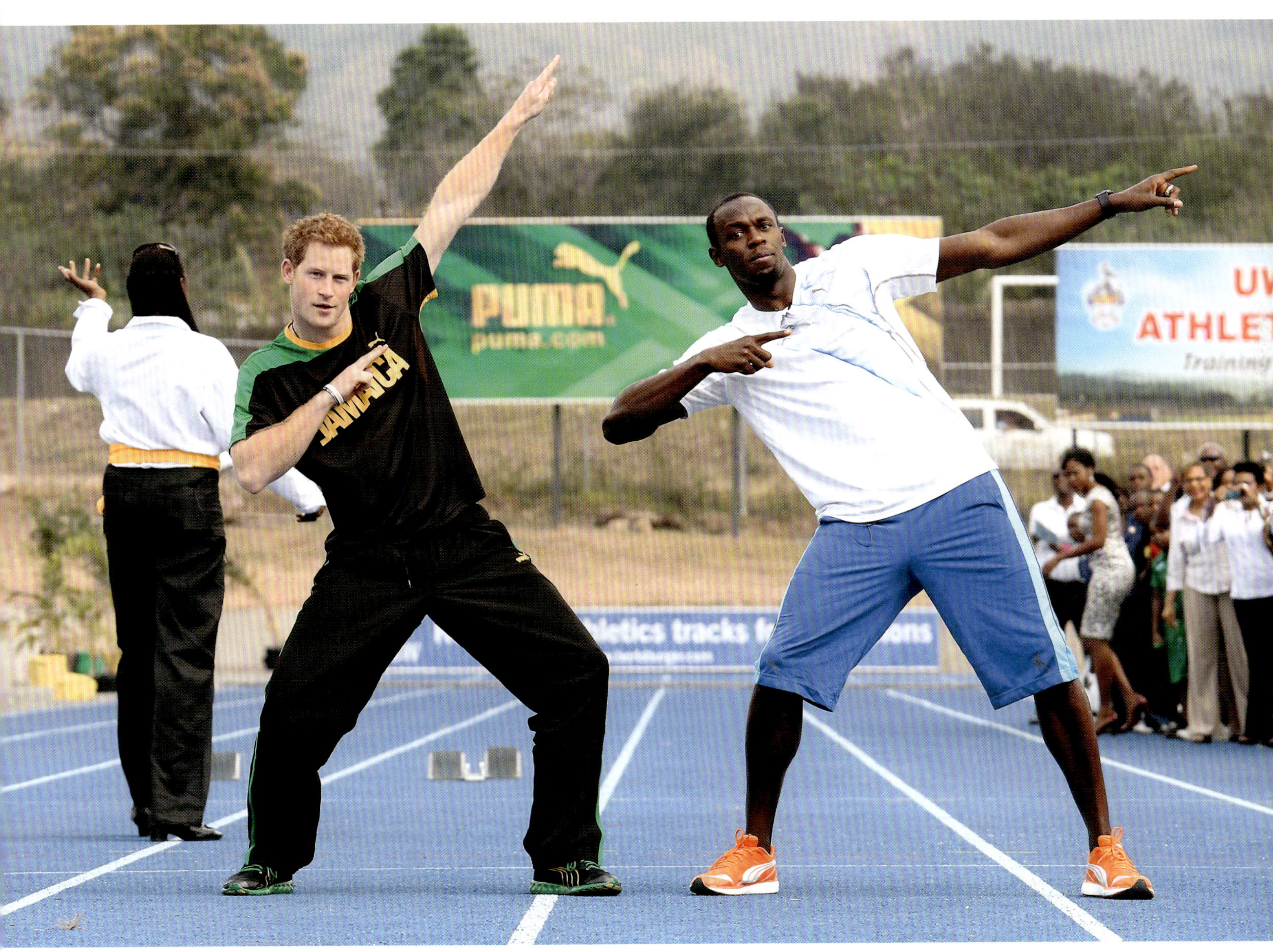

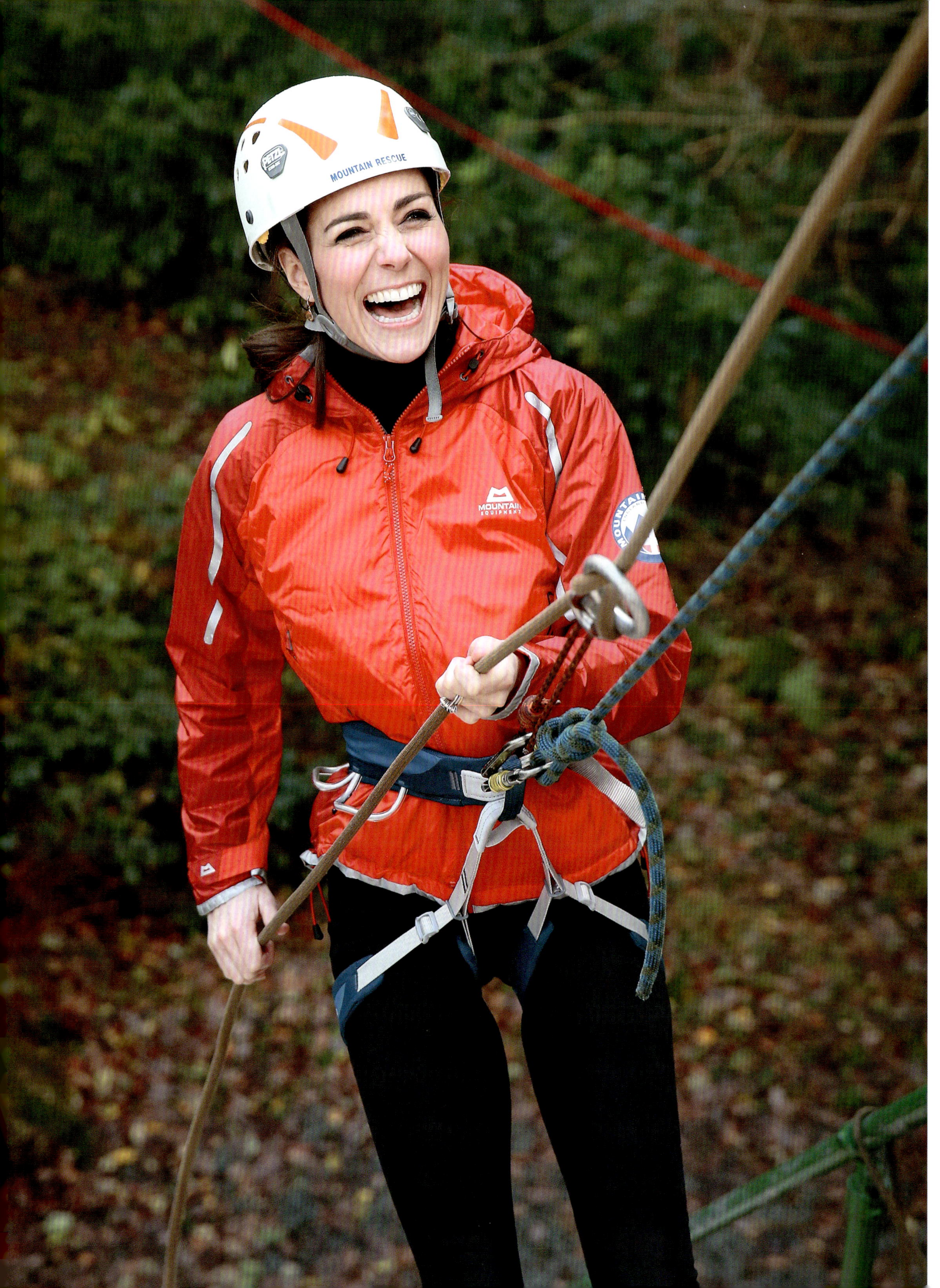
MOUNTAIN RESCUE
MOUNTAIN
EQUIPMENT

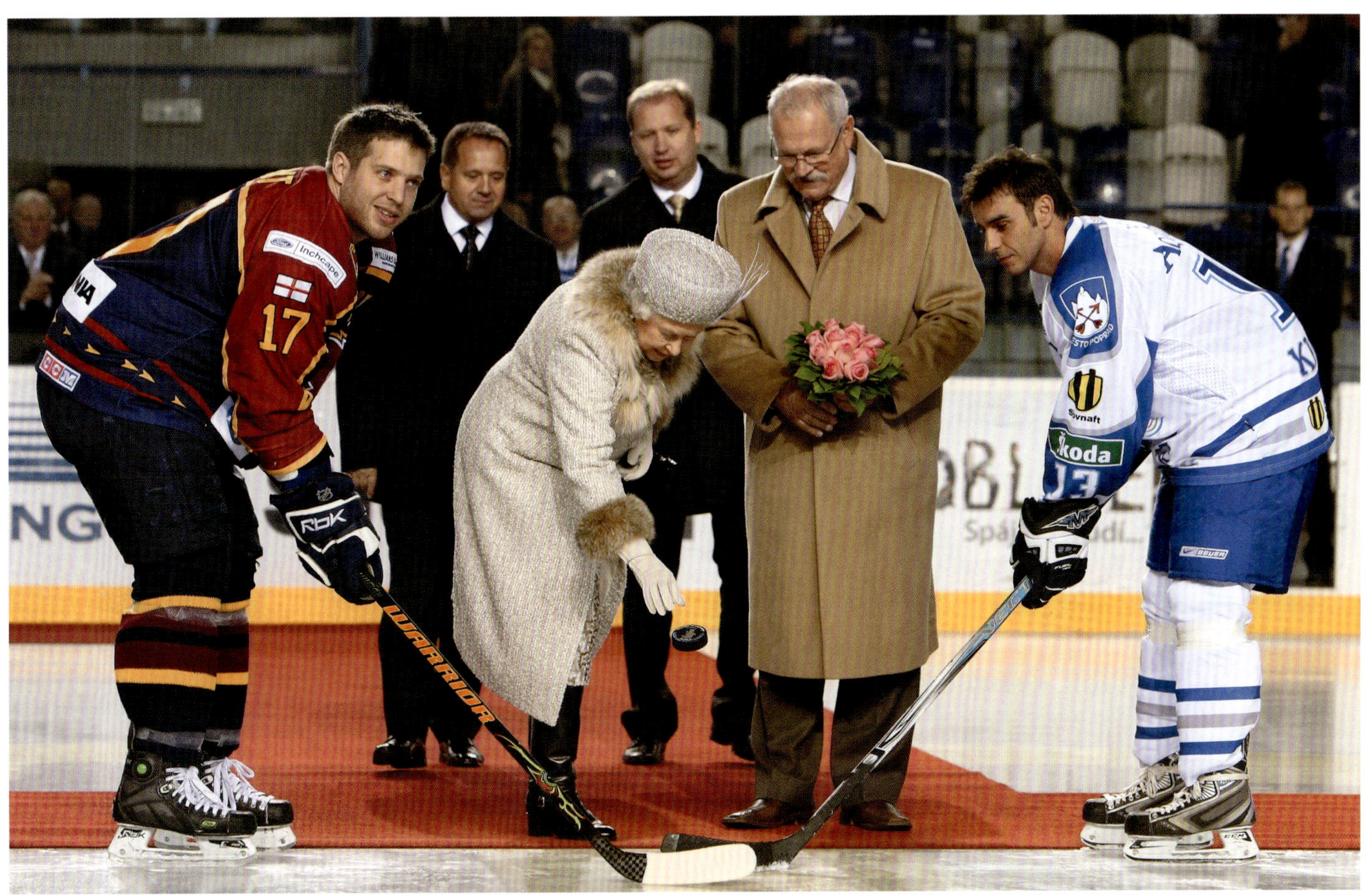

Opposite The Duchess of Cambridge abseils during a visit to the Towers Outdoor Education Centre in Capel Curig, North Wales. Run by the City of Wolverhampton Council, the centre provides adventure activities for children.

Above The Queen throws in the puck to start an ice hockey match between AquaCity Poprad and Guildford Flames at the ice hockey stadium in Bratislava, Slovakia.

Family Ties

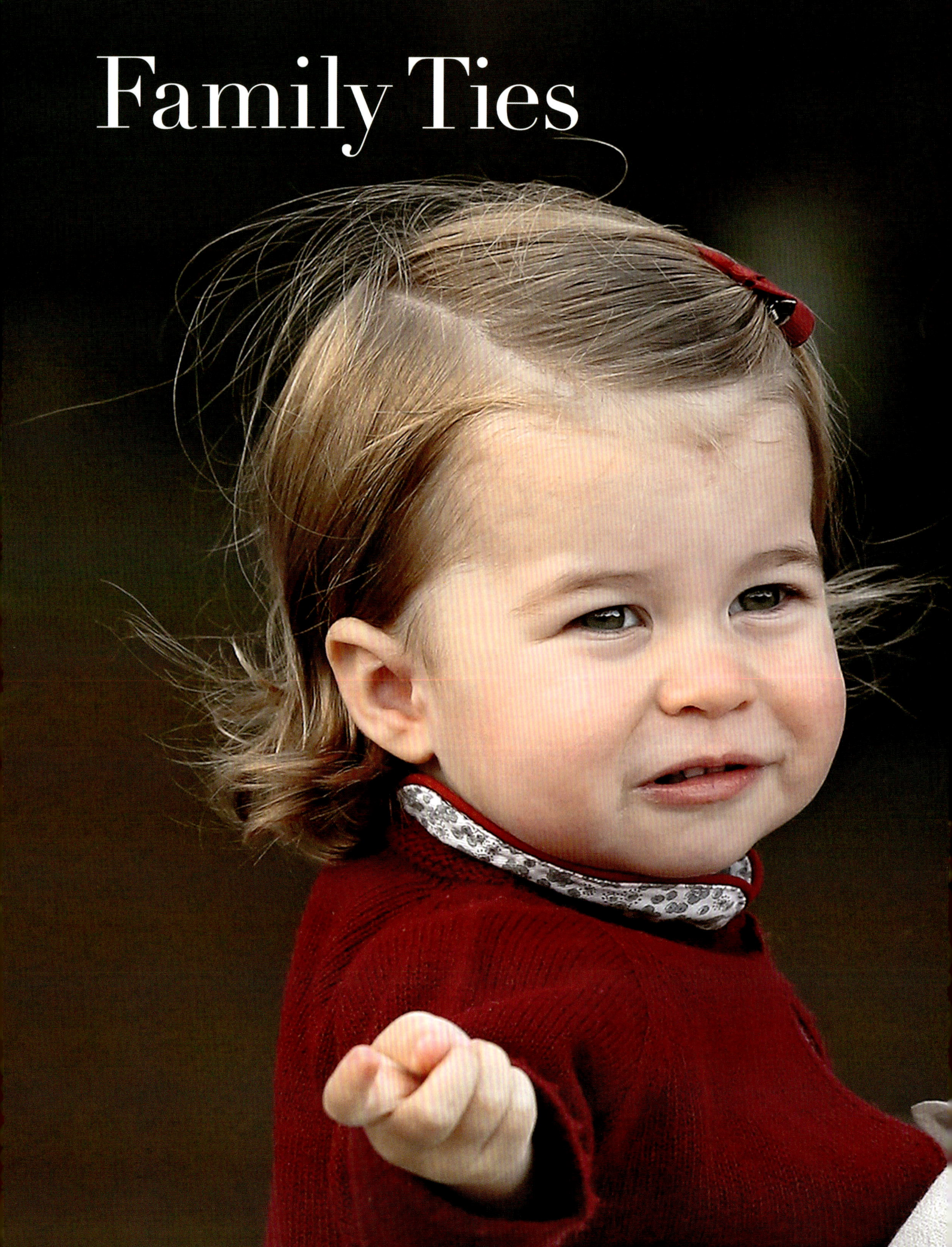

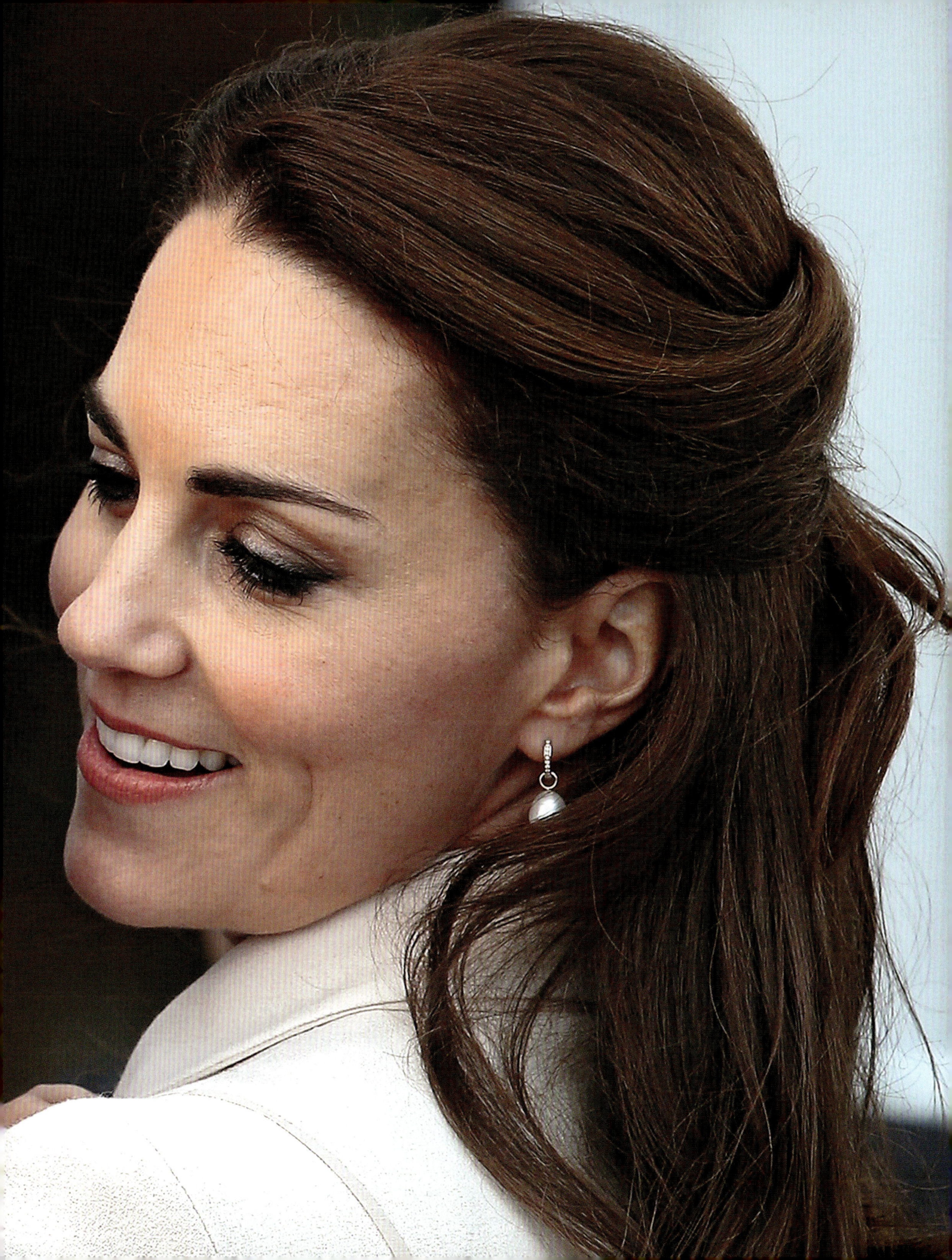

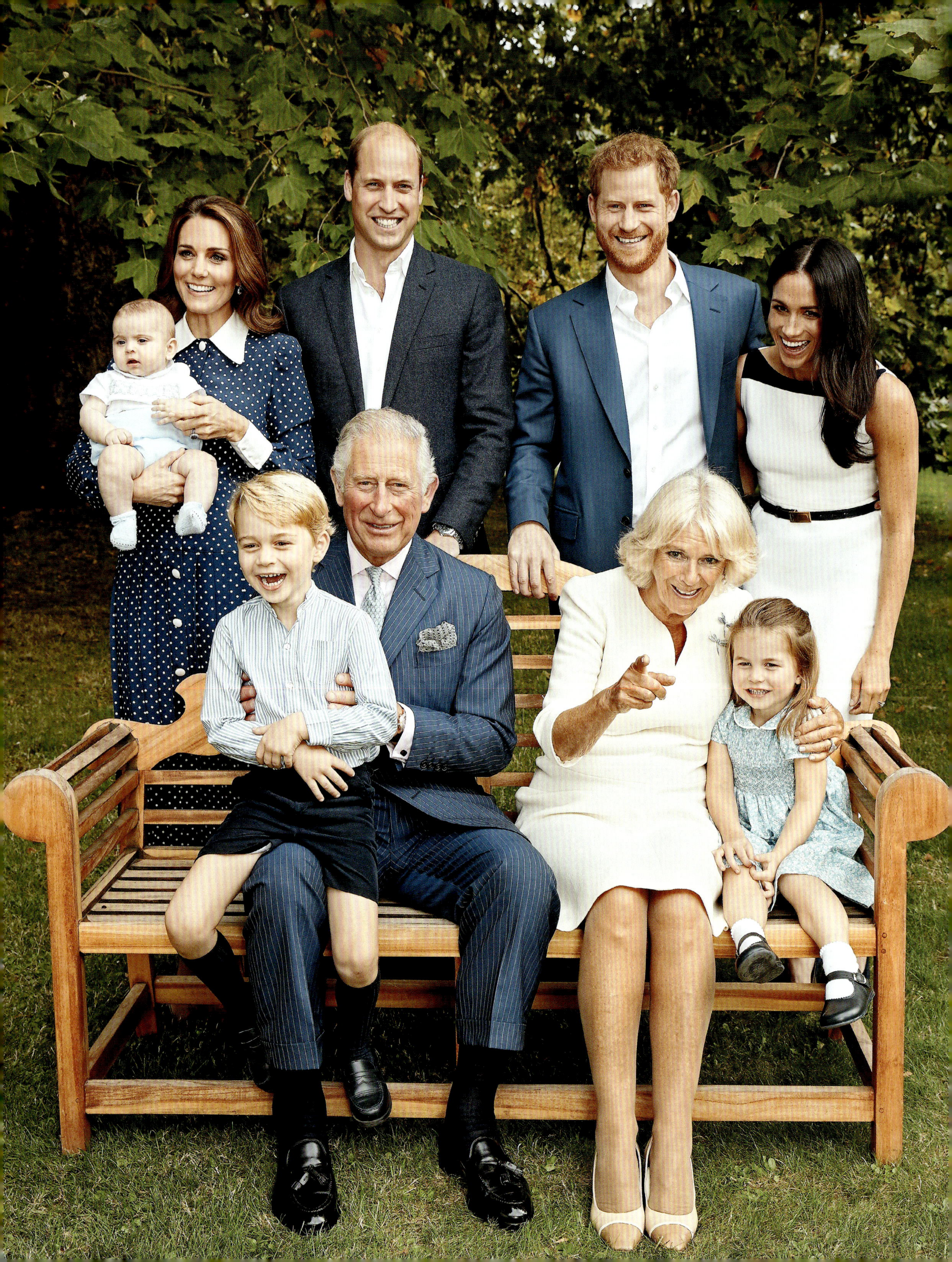

For a royal photographer, whilst it's important to capture the pomp and tradition of life as a modern royal, one of the greatest privileges is having the opportunity to document family moments, not only the historic milestones such as births, christenings, and weddings, but also the quieter and often more fleeting interactions that, despite the titles and responsibilities involved, remind us that above all the people being photographed are mother and son, sister and brother, father and daughter. Many of these "normal" moments, such as a first day of school, are shot solo. Others (the not-so-normal) are shared with crowds of additional photographers and are global media events that garner attention on a worldwide scale. When the domestic and foreign media descended on the Lindo Wing for the births of Prince George, Princess Charlotte and Prince Louis, I was reminded that this is far from a "normal family." In the midst of such mega-media moments, I sometimes find heartwarming situations that leave me smiling behind the camera. Often the family shots are those that give me the most pleasure, as they have a warmth to them that we don't see in photographs of the family members performing their more formal duties.

When Prince George arrived at the Lindo Wing and stepped out of the car to meet his newborn sister for the first time, he was greeted by a vast array of TV cameras and photographers. There was a look of astonishment on his face that prompted a collective "Awww!" from the crowd. In synchrony with his father, the young Prince offered a shy and incredibly sweet wave, while Prince William gave him a reassuring hug. Some of my other favourite shots capture subtle and very personal interactions, such as Prince George commenting on the Queen's hat at Princess Charlotte's christening, or the Queen sharing a joke with her daughter and the ladies of the Women's Institute, or the Prince of Wales in hysterics with his mother at the Highland Games as they watched the tug-o-war.

With new additions to the family, such as recent arrival Meghan Markle, novel and interesting dynamics emerge. It's exciting for me as a photographer to get to know the personality of someone new. Having spent many years capturing images of Prince Harry as a solo royal, it's been great to document his royal duties as he performs them as part of a team with his new wife. Over the many years of doing this job, you build up a knowledge of the nuances and characteristics of all members of the family and how best to photograph them. You become familiar with traits that are reflective of age, title, and position within the family. To document the Queen one day and Prince George the next requires two very different approaches, and it is this variety that keeps royal photography fresh and exciting.

Preceding pages The Duchess of Cambridge and Princess Charlotte leave from Victoria Harbour as they prepare to board a seaplane on the final day of their royal tour of Canada in 2016.

Opposite It was an honor to take this family portrait in September 2018 on the occasion of the Prince of Wales' seventieth birthday. I'd been working on a "behind-the-scenes" project with Prince Charles, capturing him throughout this landmark year, at work and relaxing. This portrait, shot on a lovely autumnal day in the gardens of Clarence House, was without a doubt the standout image of the day.

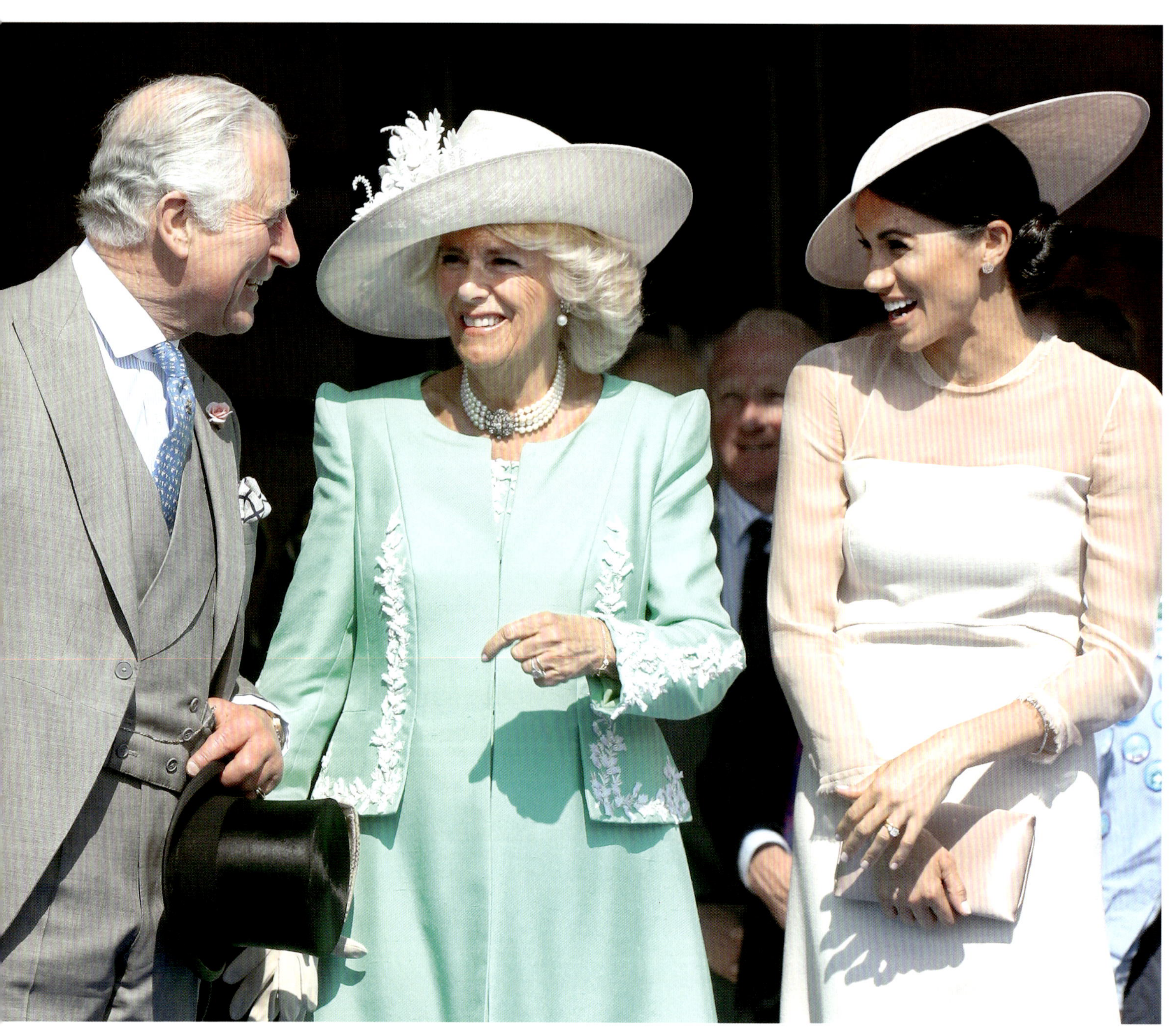

This candid moment between the Prince of Wales, the Duchess of Cornwall, and the recently minted Duchess of Sussex was photographed during her first formal appearance after her wedding to Prince Harry. The occasion was the Prince of Wales' 70th Birthday Patronage Celebration, held in the gardens of Buckingham Palace on May 22, 2018. As Prince Harry gave a speech at the podium the royal trio shared a joke and it was clear that Meghan Markle was now very much part of the family.

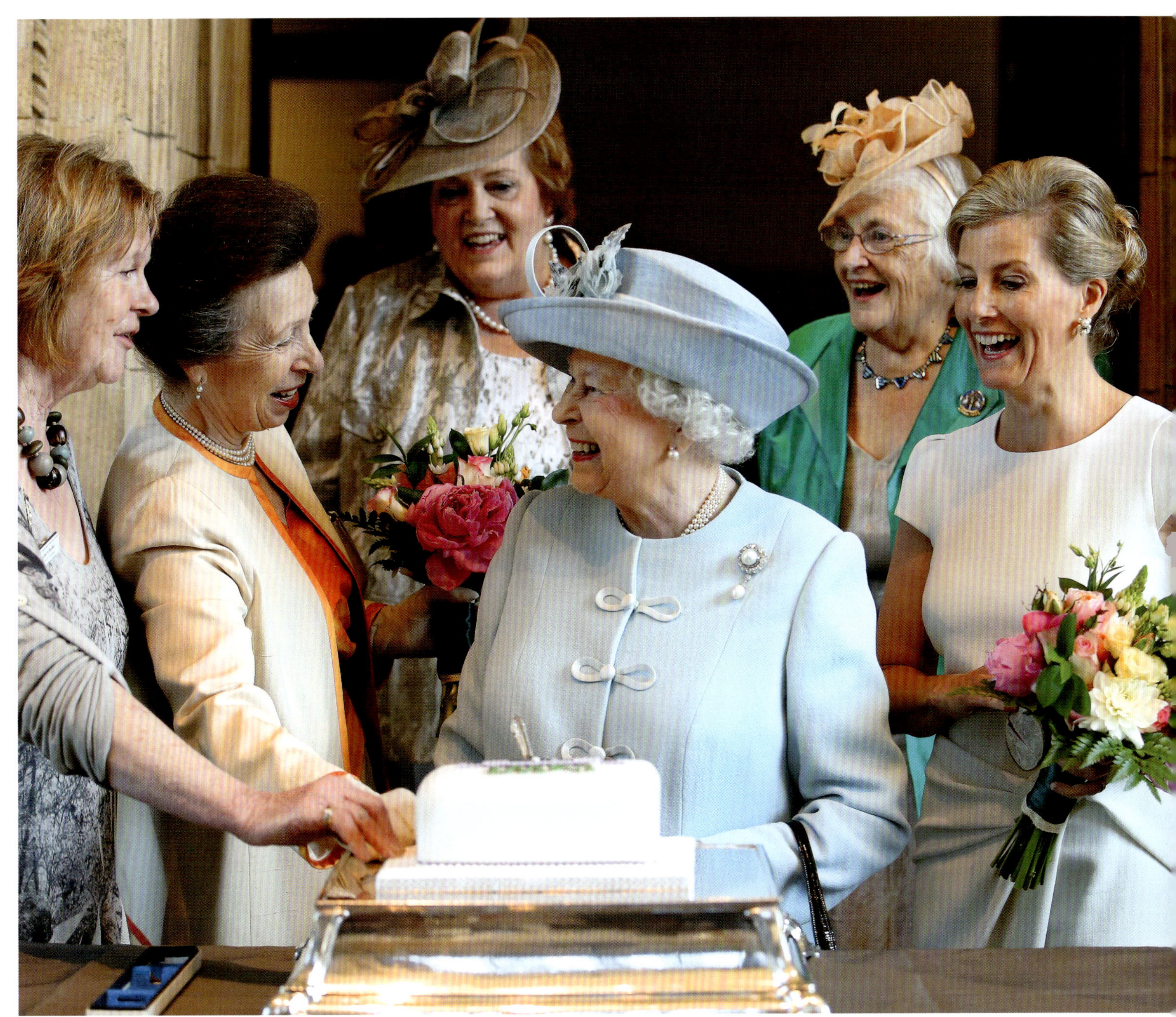

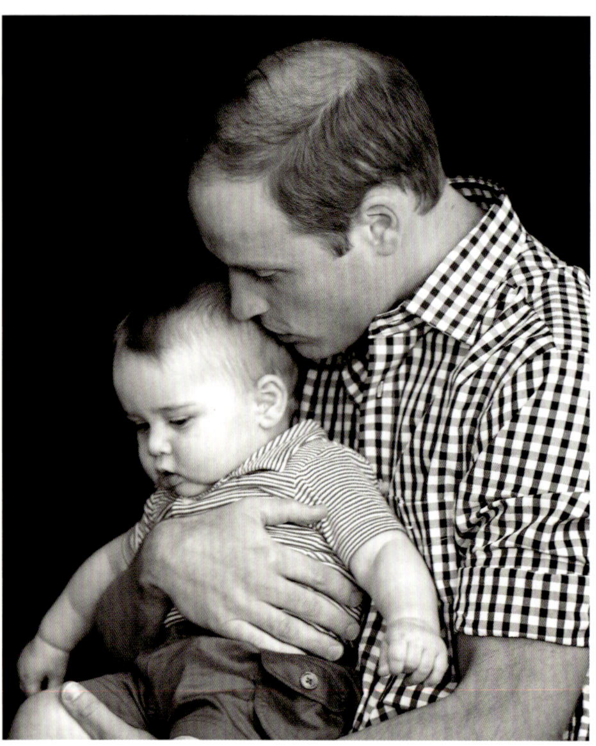

Above The Duke of Cambridge kisses Prince George on the head as they visit the bilby enclosure in Taronga Zoo, Sydney.

Opposite Prince George reaches up to catch bubbles blown by his father during a children's party for military families at Government House in Victoria, Canada.

Following pages Prince Harry, Meghan Markle, the Duchess of Cambridge, and the Duke of Cambridge share a joke as they attend the first annual Royal Foundation Forum in London in 2018.

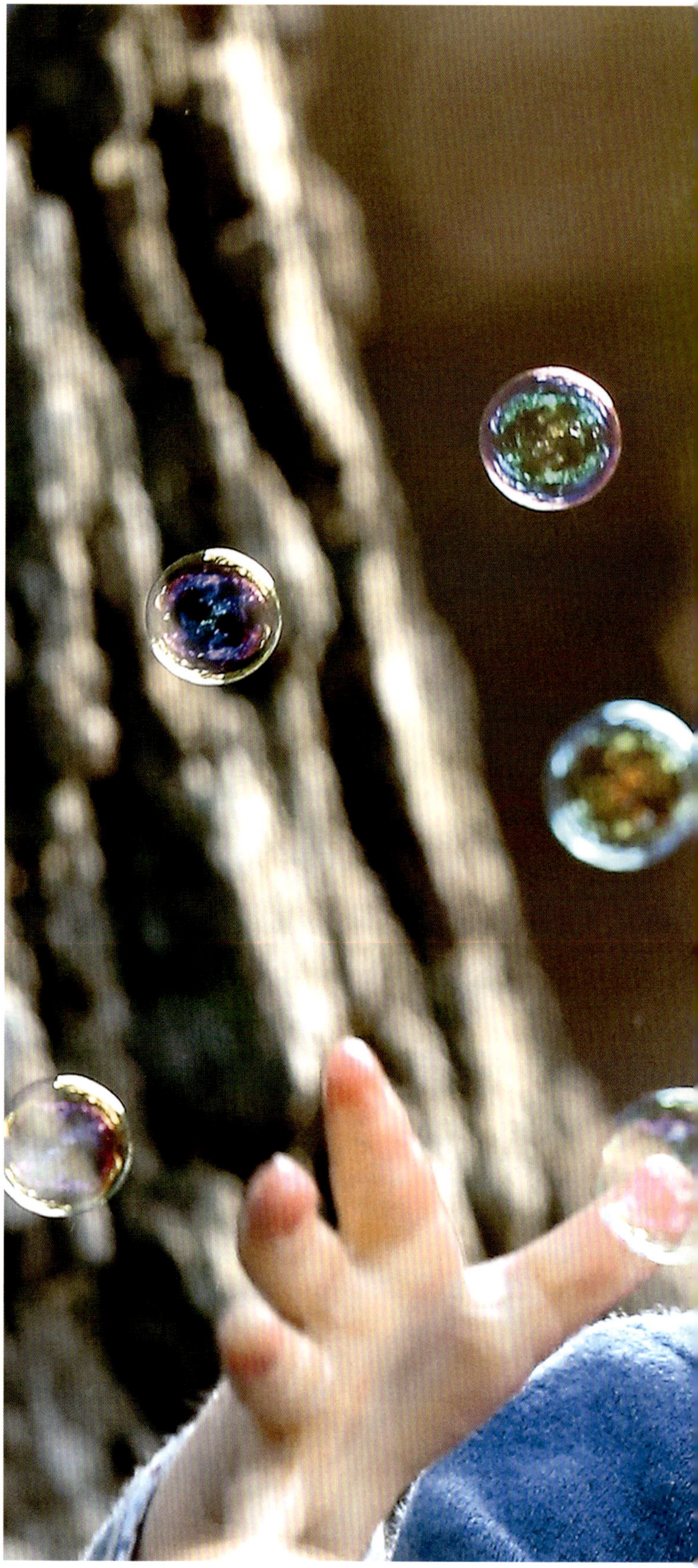

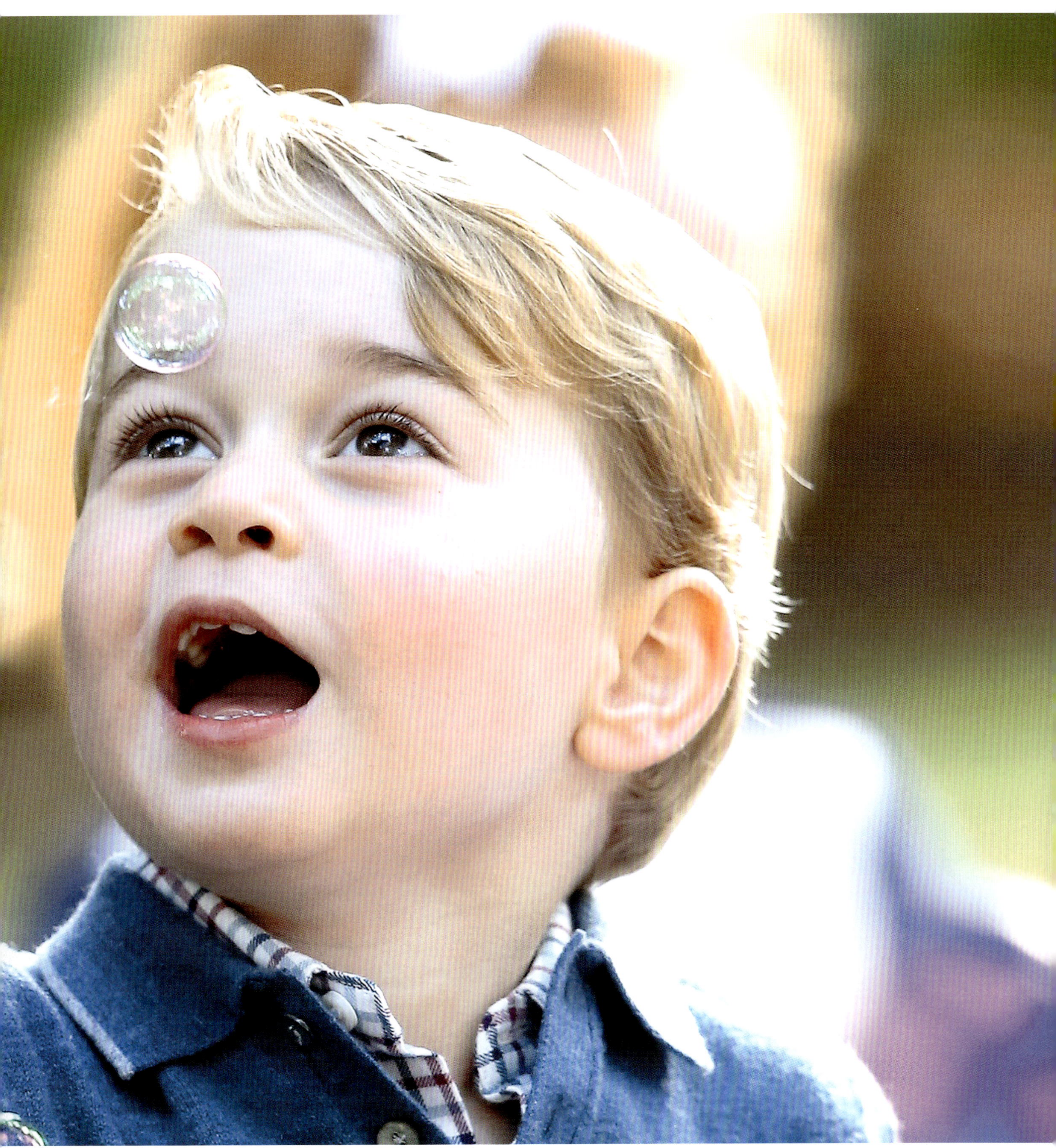

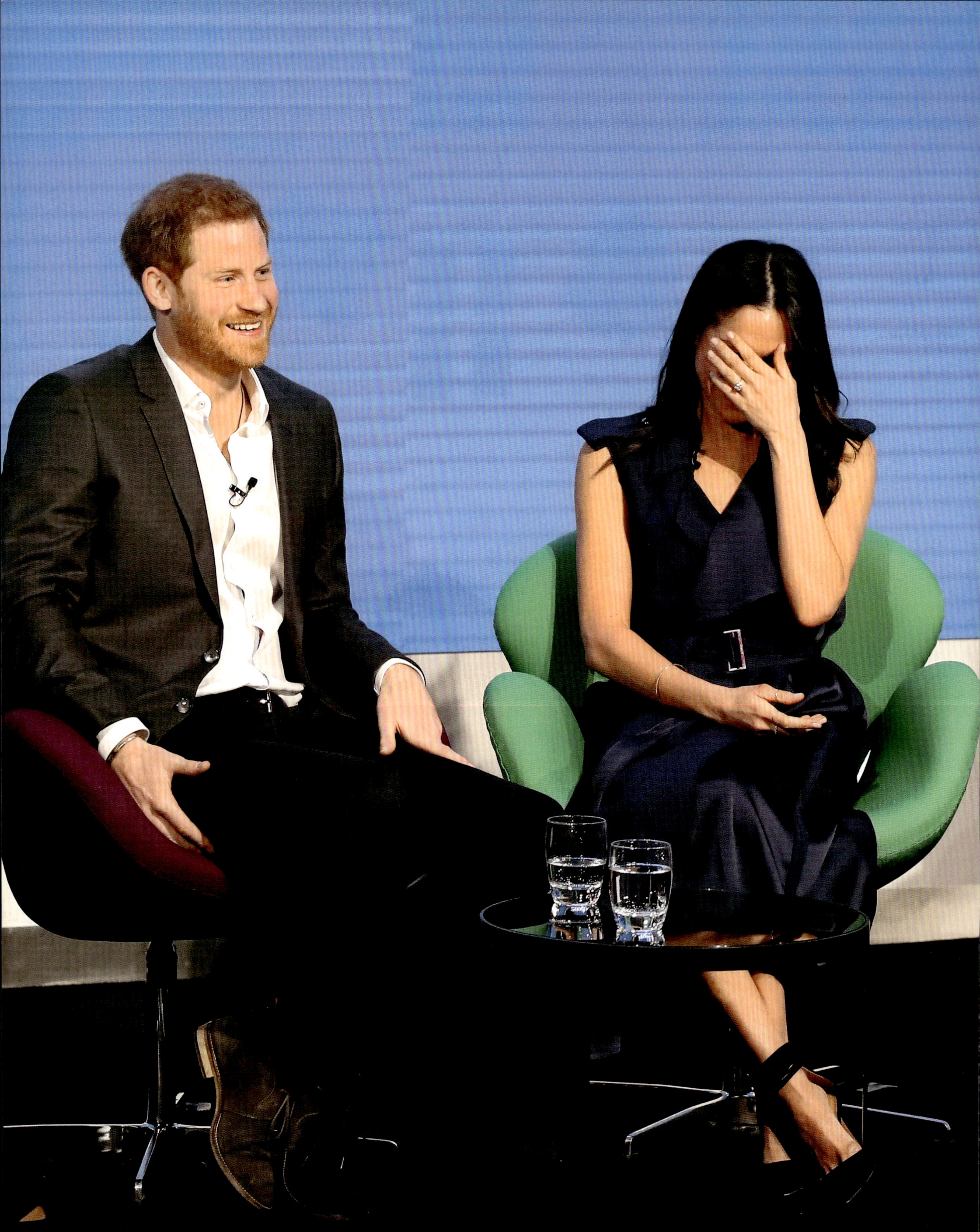

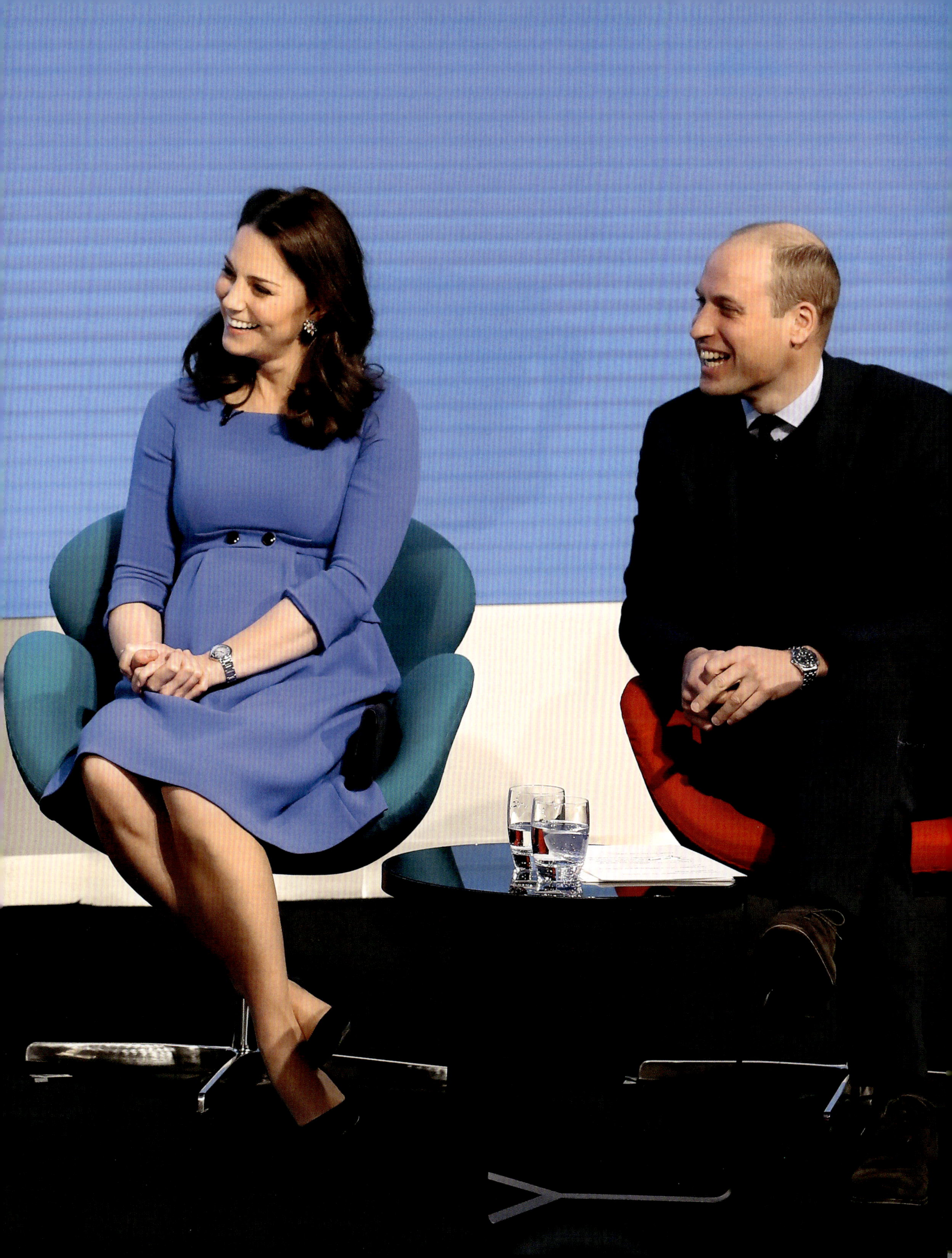

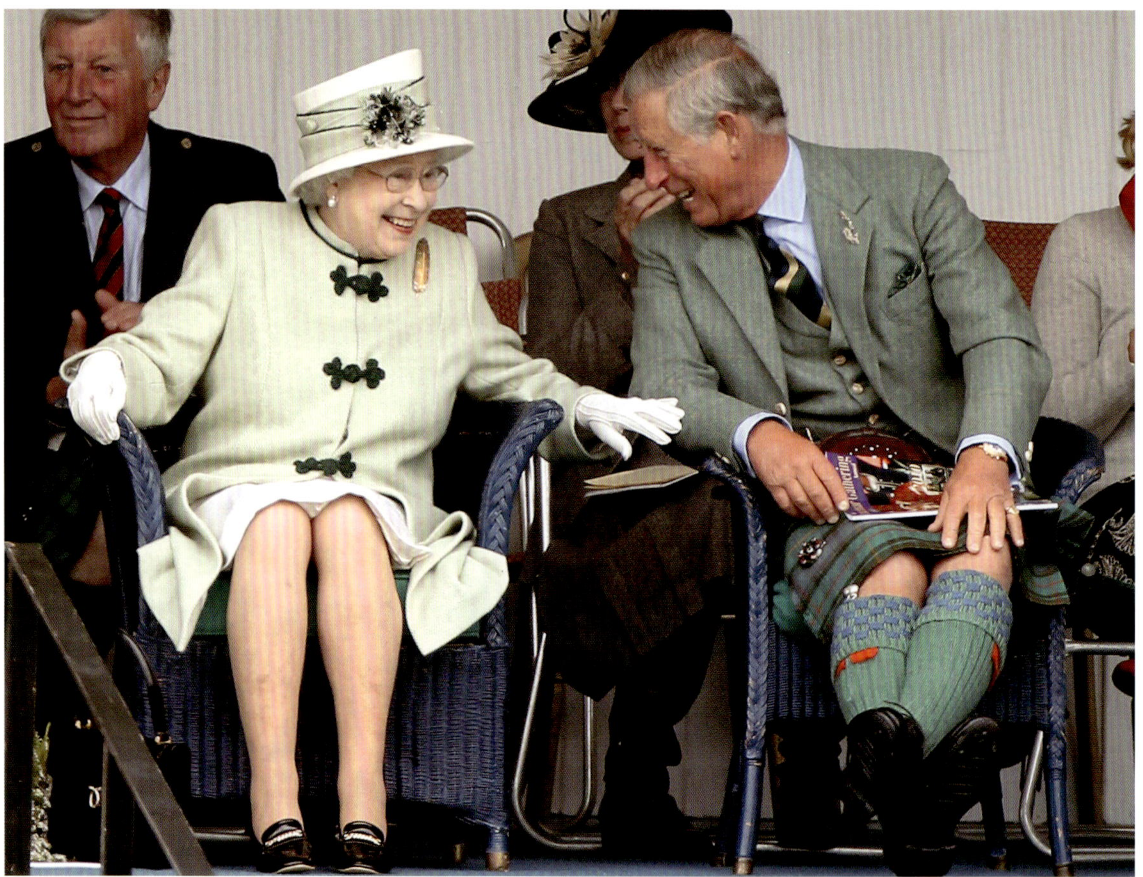

Above The Queen and the Prince of Wales watch the tug-o-war during the Braemar Gathering, also known as the Highland Games, at the Princess Royal and Duke of Fife Memorial Park.

Below The Queen and the Duke of Cambridge chat to each other in the royal box at Royal Albert Hall during the annual Festival of Remembrance.

Opposite Prince George talks to the Queen outside St. Mary Magdalene Church on the Sandringham Estate before the christening of his sister, Princess Charlotte, in 2015

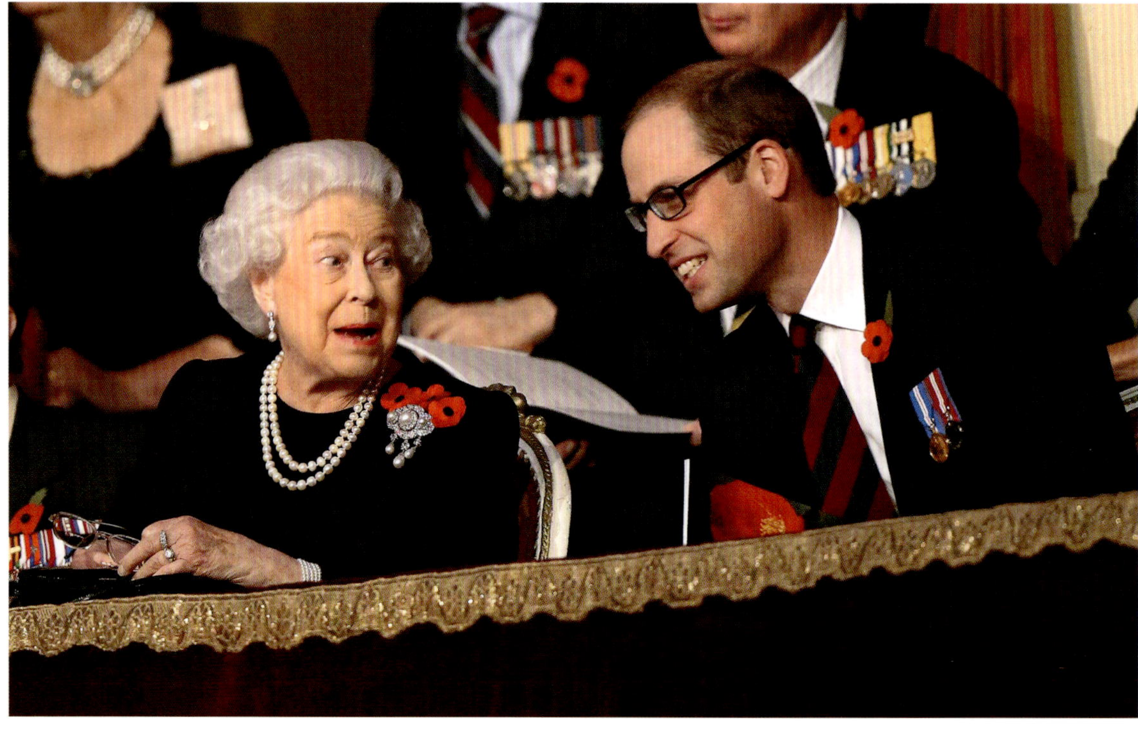

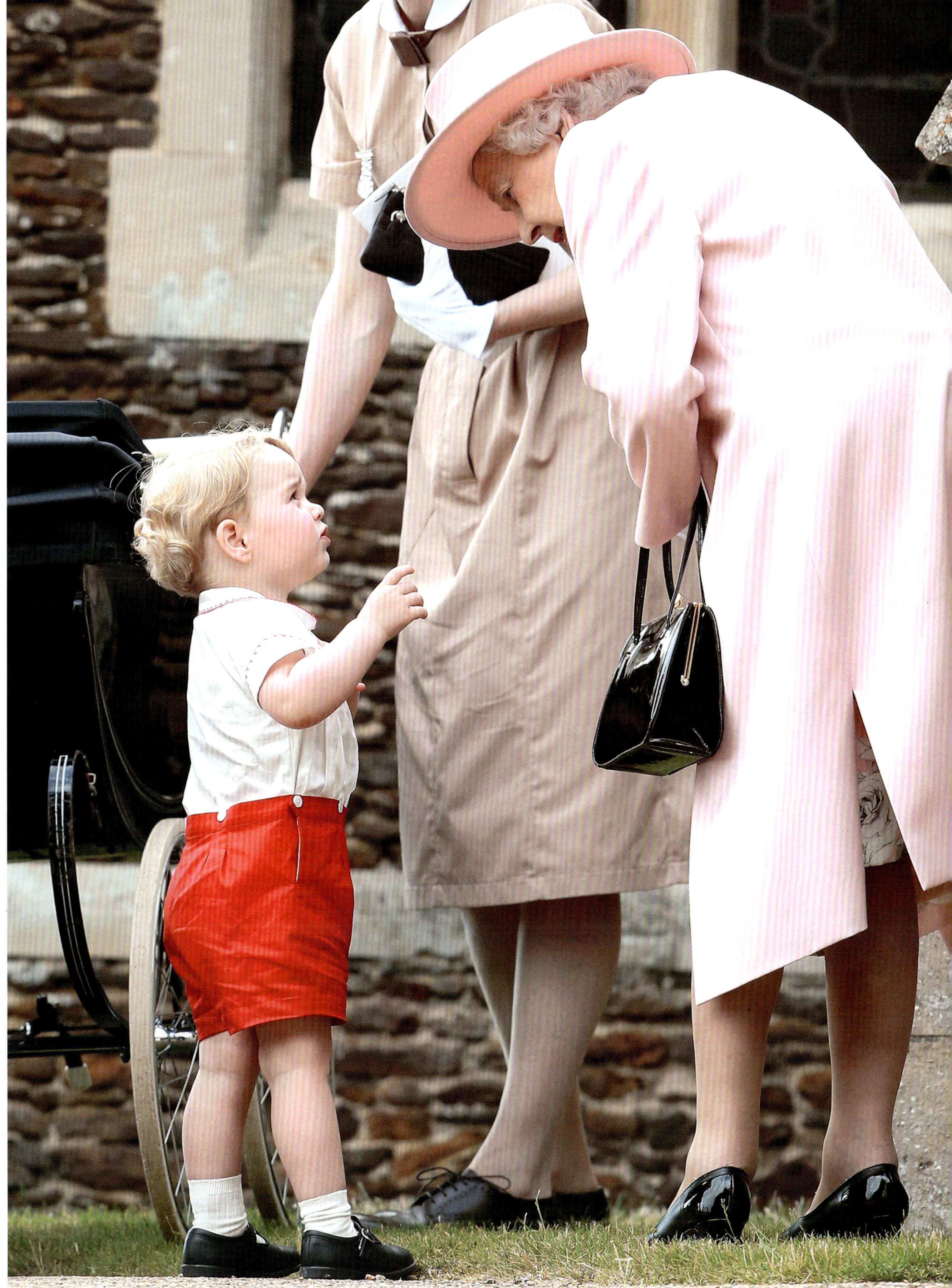

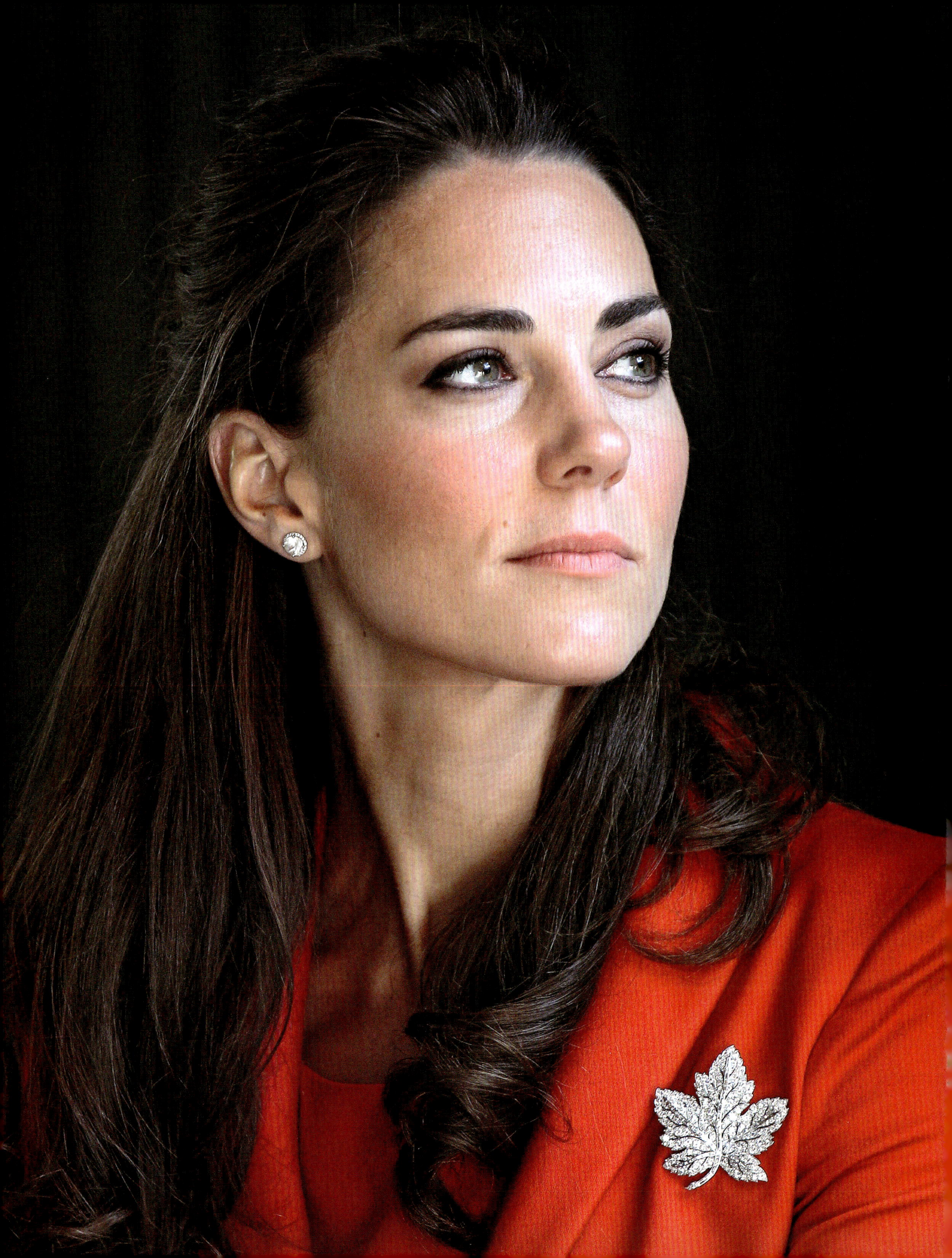

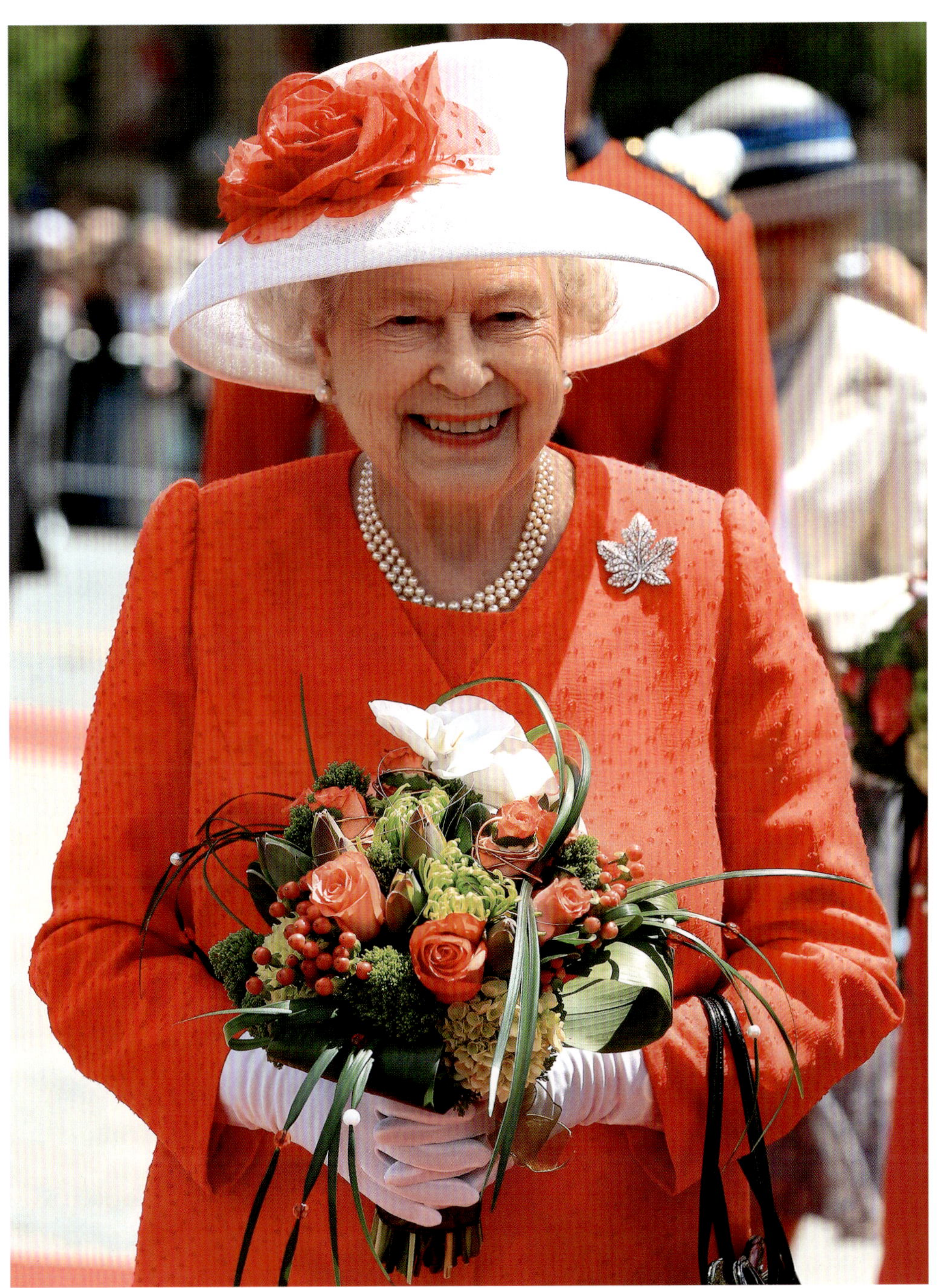

Opposite The Duchess of Cambridge wears a maple leaf diamond brooch as she attends a reception at Calgary Zoo during the 2011 Canada tour. The brooch was loaned to the Duchess for the duration of the tour and demonstrates the role historic jewellery has played in tying together generations of the royal family.

This page The Queen wears the same maple leaf brooch during Canada Day celebrations in Ottawa on July 1, 2010. The brooch was given to her mother, Queen Elizabeth, by George VI on the occasion of their state visit to Canada in 1939.

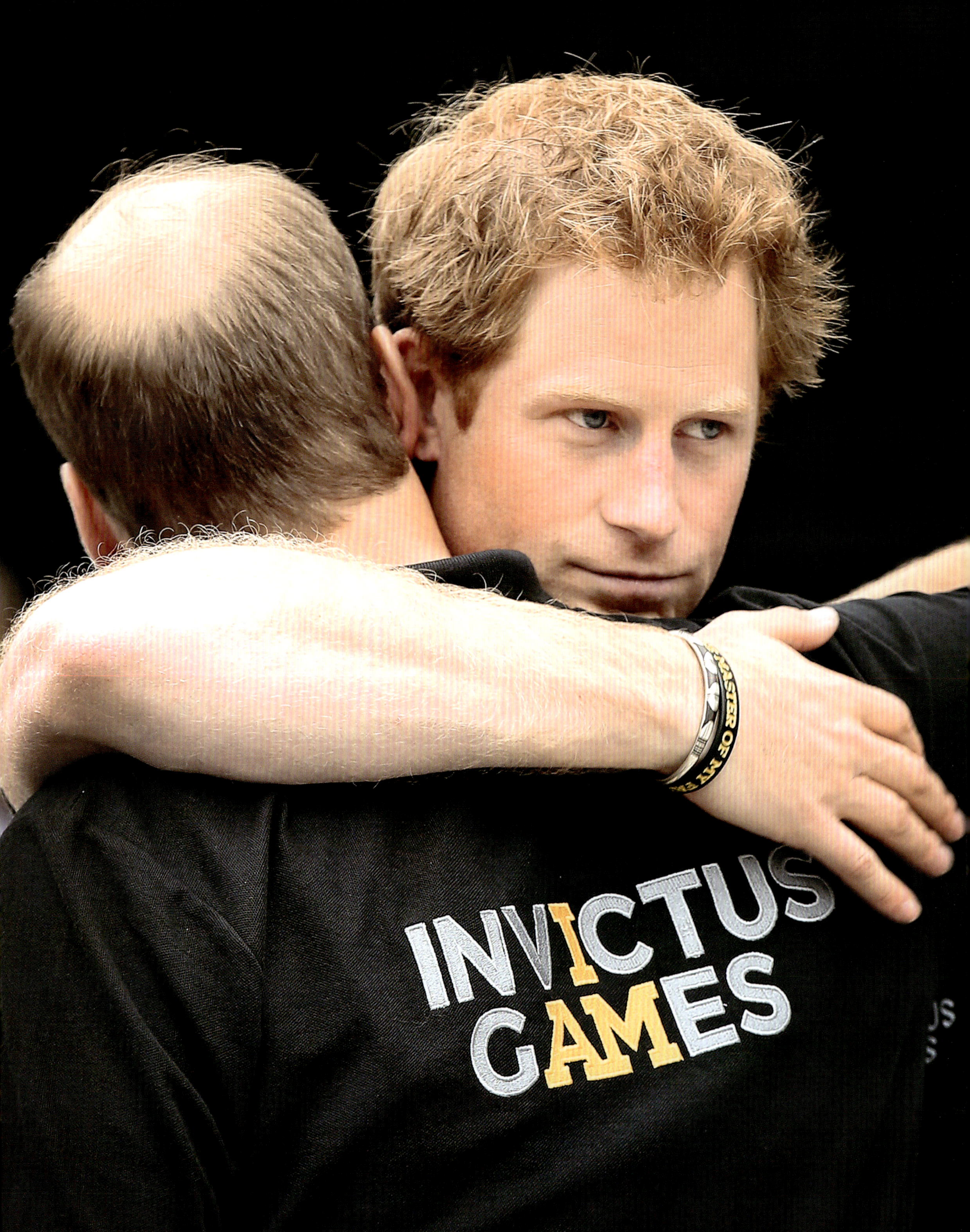
INVICTUS
GAMES

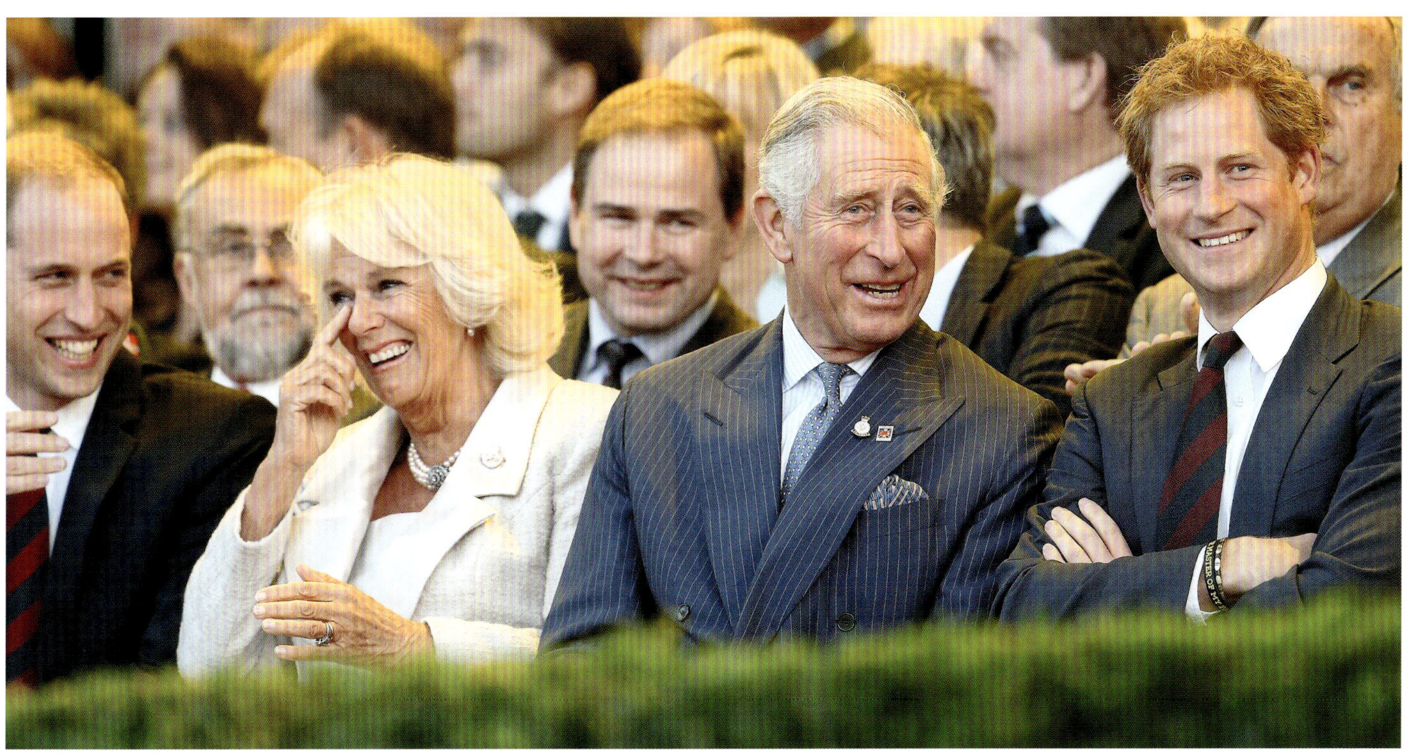

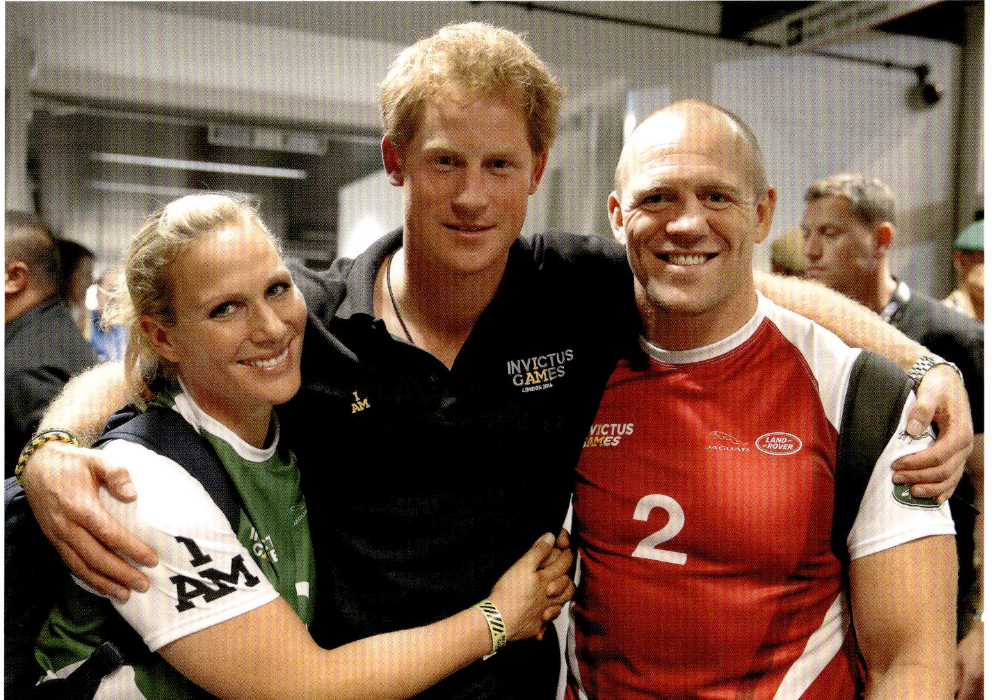

Opposite Prince Harry gives his brother, Prince William, a hug as they leave athletics training at Lee Valley Athletics Centre ahead of the Invictus Games in London.

Above The Duke of Cambridge, the Duchess of Cornwall, the Prince of Wales, and Prince Harry share a joke during the Invictus Games opening ceremony.

Below Prince Harry, Zara Phillips, and Mike Tindall pose for a photograph after competing in an exhibition wheelchair rugby match during the inaugural Invictus Games.

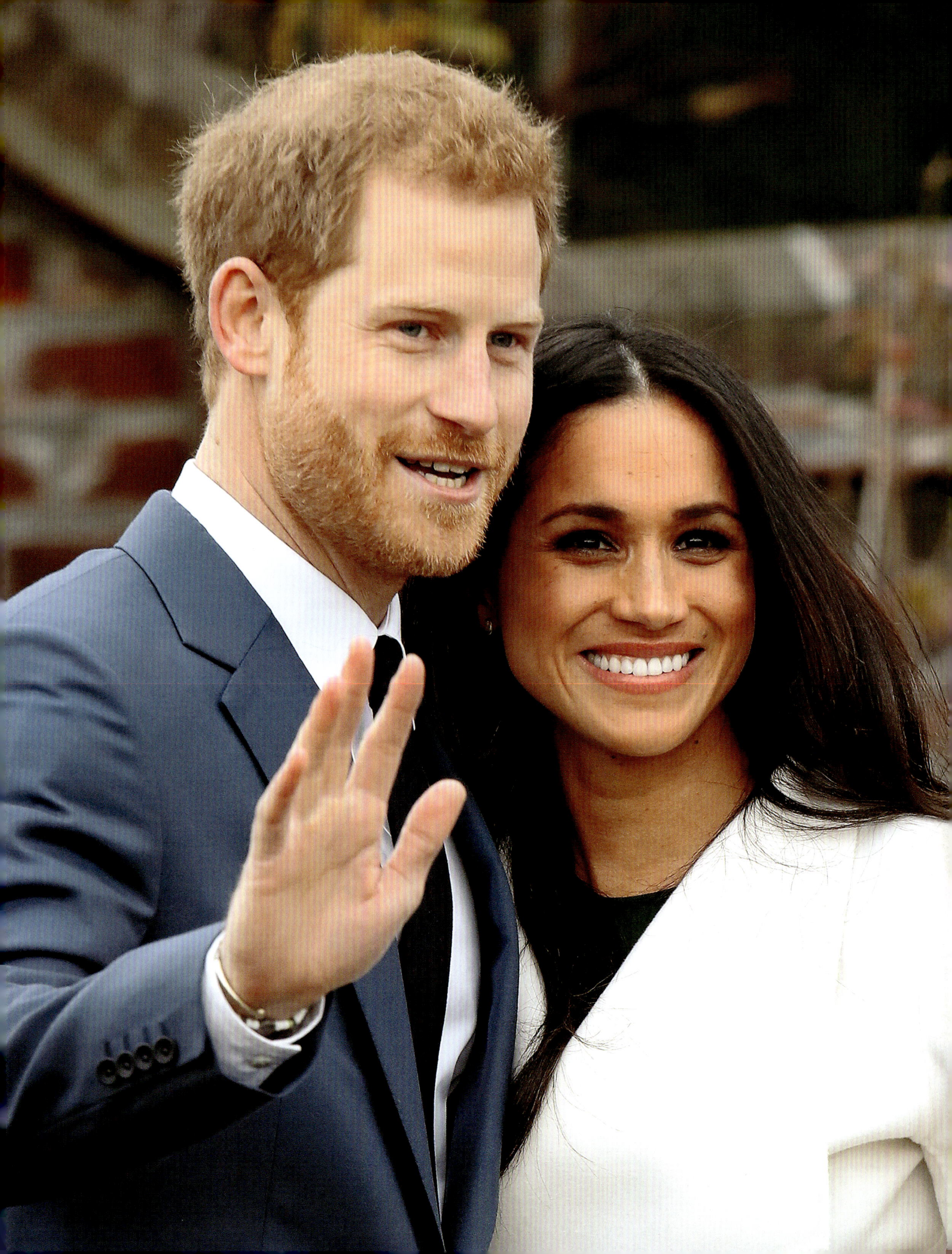

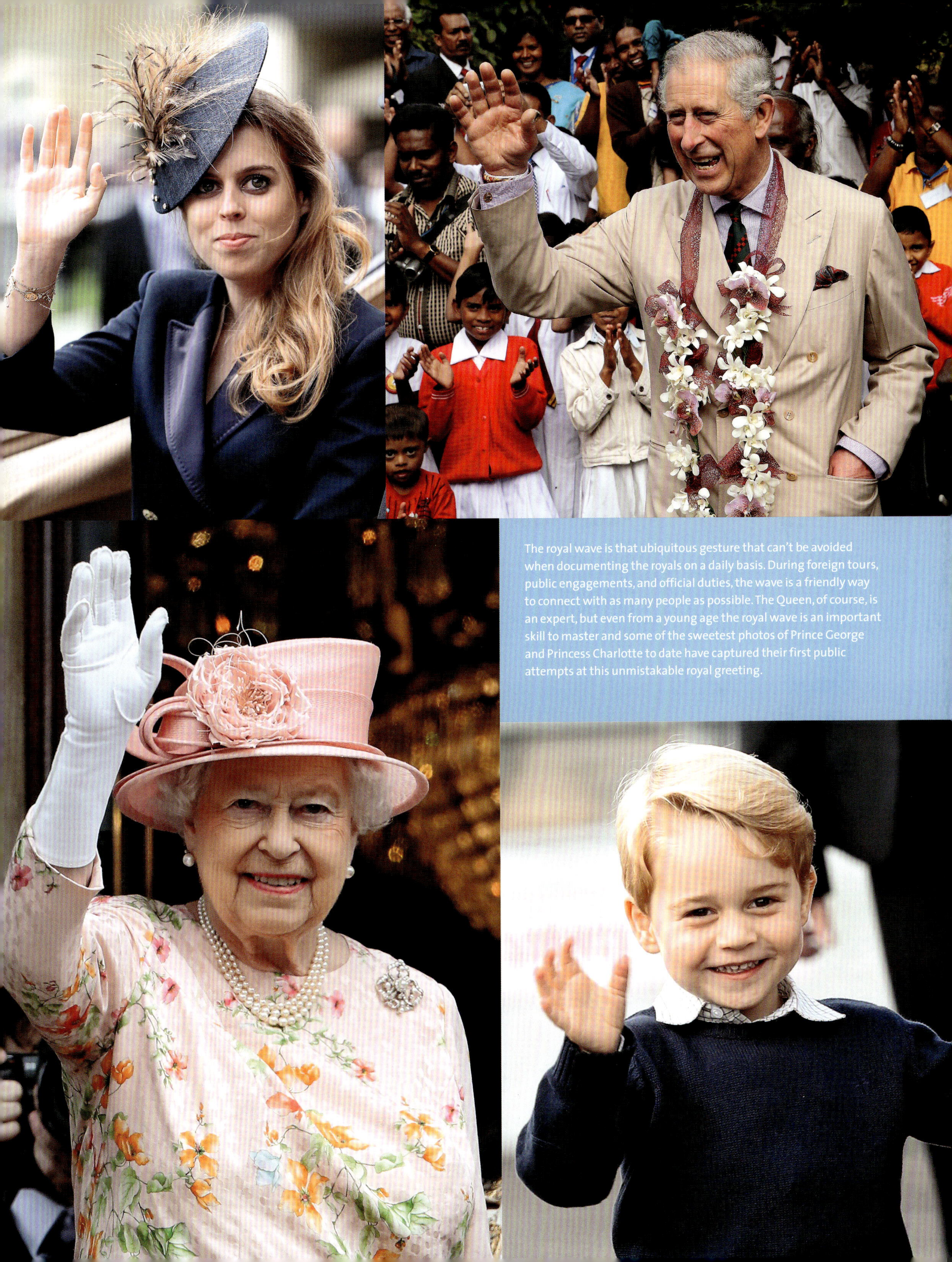

The royal wave is that ubiquitous gesture that can't be avoided when documenting the royals on a daily basis. During foreign tours, public engagements, and official duties, the wave is a friendly way to connect with as many people as possible. The Queen, of course, is an expert, but even from a young age the royal wave is an important skill to master and some of the sweetest photos of Prince George and Princess Charlotte to date have captured their first public attempts at this unmistakable royal greeting.

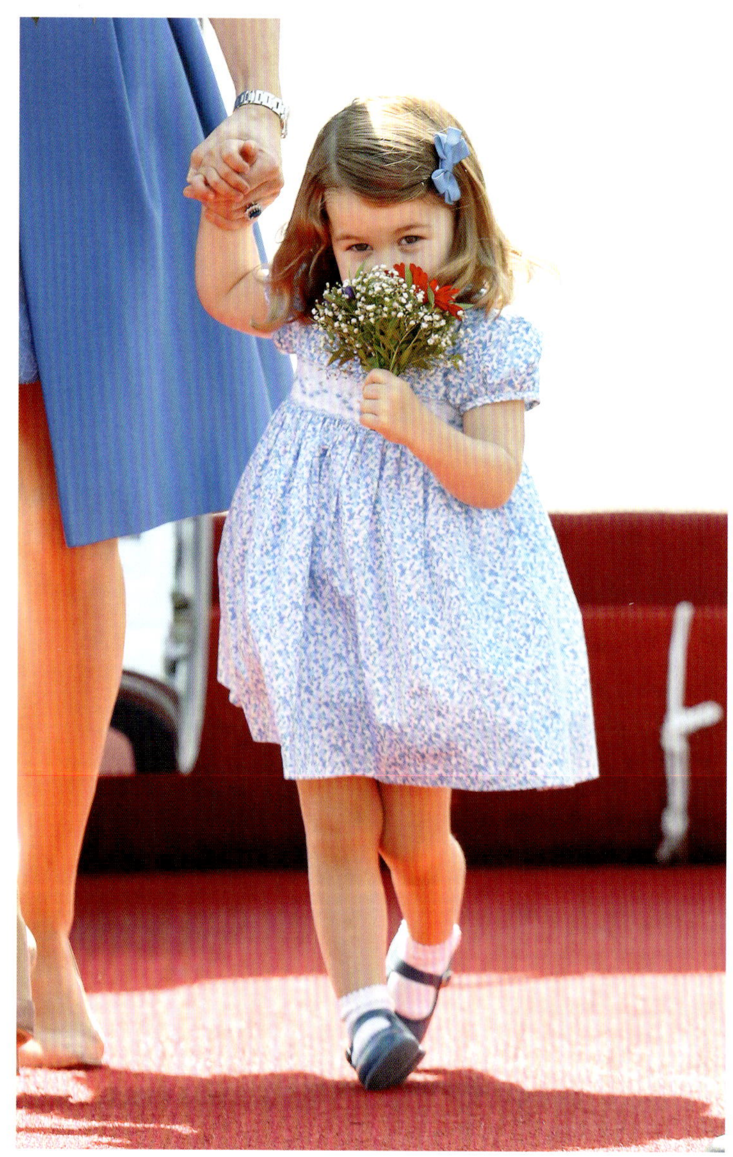

Above Princess Charlotte sniffs a bouquet of flowers presented to her at Berlin Tegel Airport when she arrived with her family on an official visit to Poland and Germany.

Opposite The Cambridge family boards a seaplane in Victoria Harbour on the final day of their royal tour of Canada in 2016.

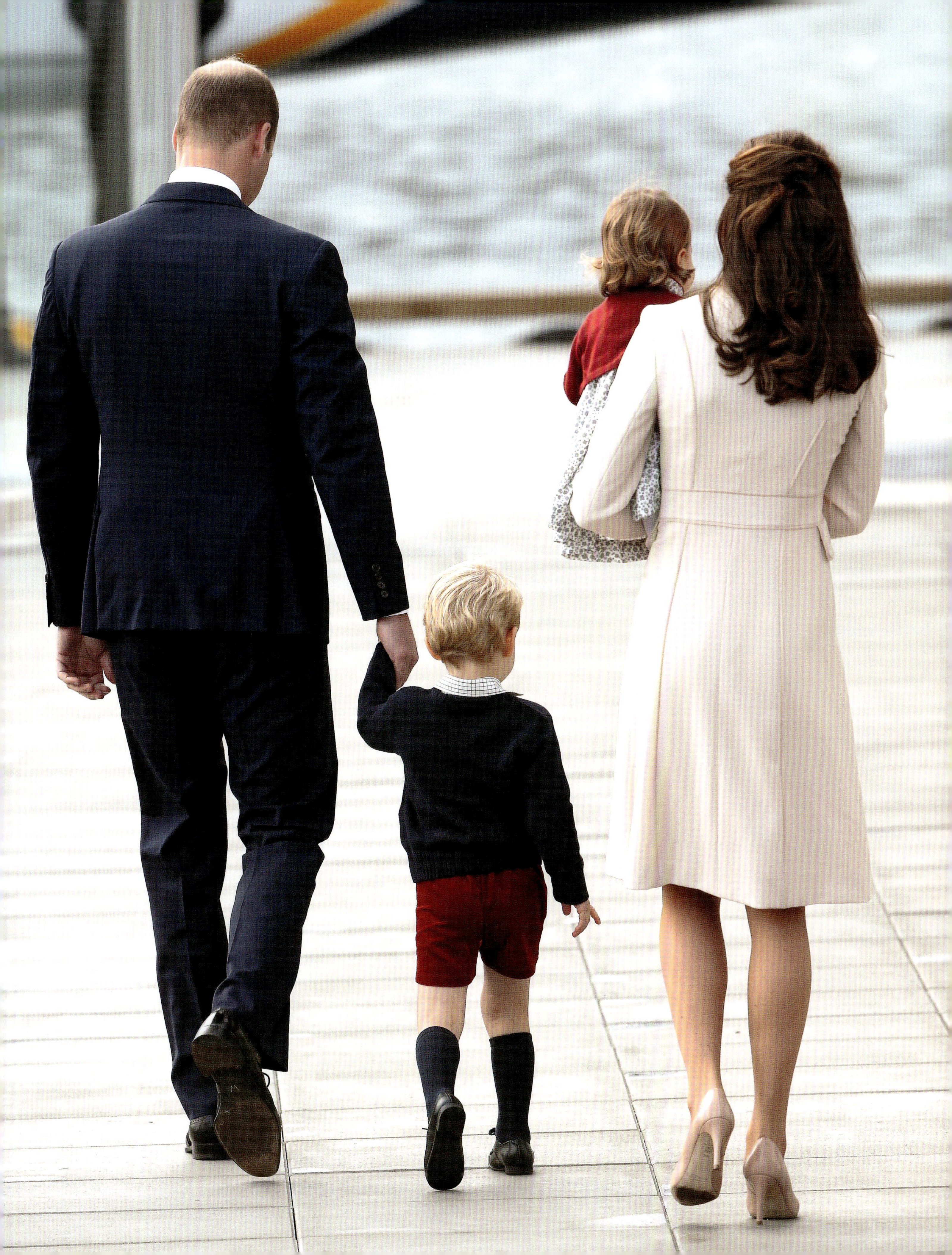

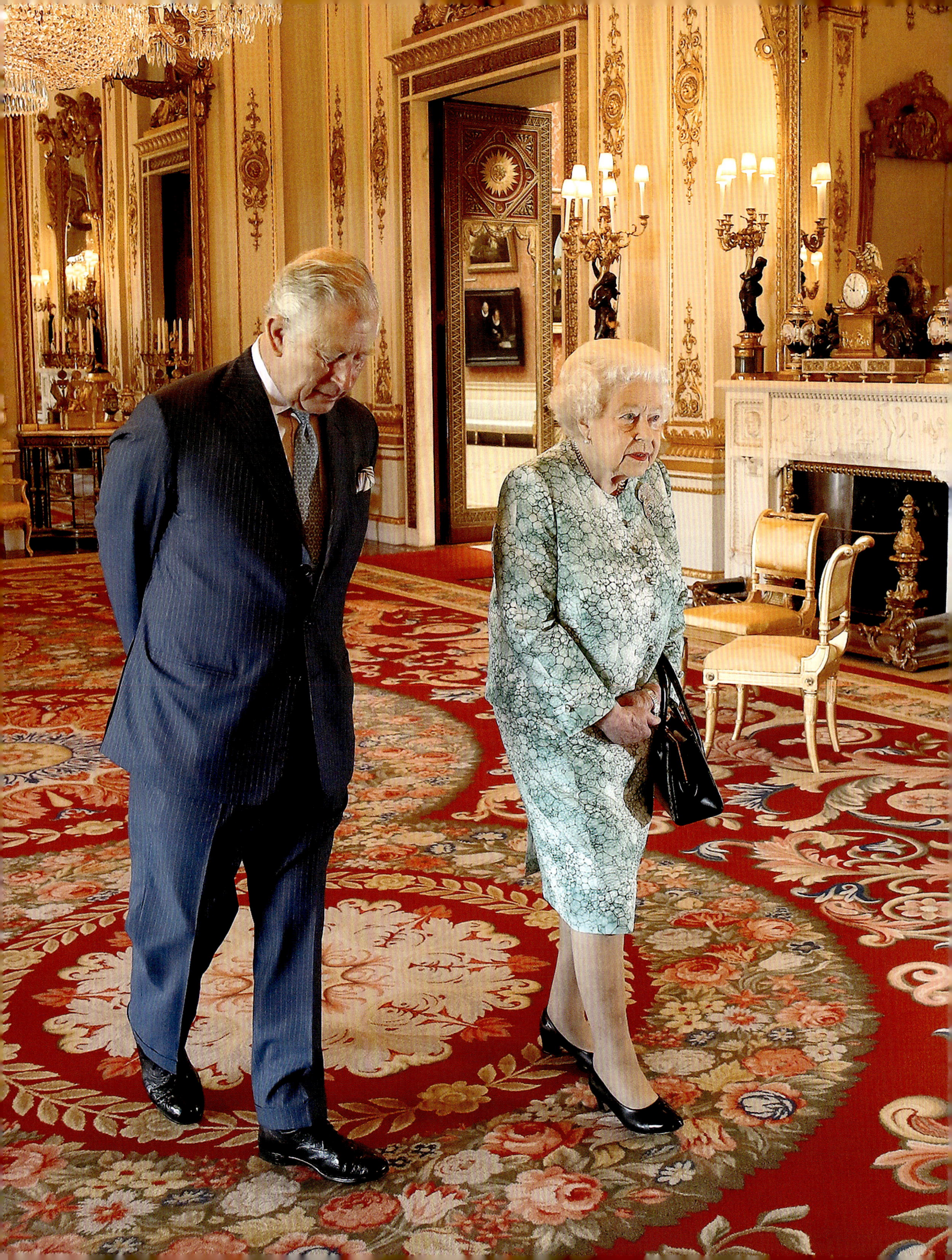

Acknowledgments

A huge amount of work has gone into this book from a number of amazing and dedicated people, and for that I am incredibly grateful.

Firstly, I would like to thank the team at Rizzoli: Giulia Di Filippo for her expert guidance, Ray Watkins for her experienced eye, and Charles Miers for his enthusiasm for the initial concept all those many months ago.

Special thanks to the inspiring team at Getty Images for their support over the years, primarily Lisa Marie Rae, whose patience and project management skills have been invaluable. Ken Mainardis and Lee Martin for their work behind the scenes on making this project happen, as well as Anthony Holland Parkin for pitching in with his expertise. Vicky Dearman, Edward Smith, and the team who keep the well-oiled cogs of the machine moving on a daily basis. The picture desk editors at Getty Images—across all time zones in New York, Los Angeles, and, of course, London—who work tirelessly to deliver images to our clients around the world. Over recent years our UK field-editing team—Caroline Ryan, Brian Dayle, and Rosie Hussein—for enabling us to get those shots to clients as quickly and as beautifully as possible. Jonathan Klein, Dawn Airey, Mark Getty, Adrian Murrell, Hugh Pinney, and Georges De Keerle for giving me ample opportunity and advice early on in my career. Whoever I am speaking to and wherever I am in the world I have always been proud to say I work with such a talented team of photographers and for a company that values the importance of visual storytelling and embodies a genuine and deep passion for pictures.

I am grateful to Jeff Vickers, Ambassador for the Royal Photographic Society, who sparked the idea for this book and offered up his deep wisdom and experience throughout the process, and to his lovely wife, Barbara, for all the ginger tea!

A profound thank-you to Michael Pritchard and the Royal Photographic Society. It is an honour to be associated with an organisation with such history and pedigree.

My sincere thanks must also go to the communications teams at Clarence House, Buckingham Palace, and Kensington Palace, especially Sally Osman and Julian Payne for their advice and time. All the press officers I have worked with over the years and travelled countless miles with on "tour buses," convoys, planes, trains, and automobiles for their good humour "in the field"—you know who you are. The team at Sentebale, Invictus Games, and all the lovely people at Tusk Trust. The privilege of being able to capture images that hopefully make a difference in these areas remains one of the most special aspects of my job.

Finally, immense gratitude to my parents, Sue and Nick, for providing me with an insightful education and encouraging me to follow my own path in life throughout the uncertain early days of forging a career as a photographer. To Bill Archer for his wise words and encouragement. Above all else, my greatest thanks goes to my amazing wife, Natasha, for always pushing me to try new ideas and for putting up with all those last-minute trips and numerous weekends away from home—I am eternally grateful.

Chris Jackson

Queen Elizabeth and Prince Charles walk through the ballroom of Buckingham Palace ahead of the formal opening of the Commonwealth Heads of Government Meeting in April 2018. During the opening remarks the Queen spelled out her "sincere wish" that Prince Charles continue her legacy as the next Head of the Commonwealth. The following day a unanimous vote elected Prince Charles as her successor.

First published in the United States of America in 2018 by
Rizzoli International Publications, Inc.
300 Park Avenue South
New York, NY 10010
www.rizzoliusa.com

Designed by Raymonde Watkins

2019 2020 2021 2022 / 10 9 8 7 6 5 4

Distributed in the U.S. trade by Random House, New York

Printed in China

ISBN-13: 978-0-8478-6428-7

Library of Congress Catalog Control Number: 2018939588

Front cover: A very Modern Monarchy watches the flypast on the balcony of Buckingham Palace during Trooping the Colour on June 9, 2018 in London. The parade marks the official birthday of the Queen, even though her actual birthday is on April 21st. This year was the Duchess of Sussex's first appearance on the balcony with the royal family.
Back cover: (top row) Prince Charles and Camilla, Duchess of Cornwall, on the balcony of Buckingham Palace during Trooping the Colour in 2015; the Duchess of Cambridge on royal tour in Norway; Prince Harry with a young boy during a visit to a child education centre in Semonkong, Lesotho; (middle row) The Queen on her way to tour the Mildmay Centre for AIDS in Uganda; Prince Charles with a dancer in traditional attire after a performance at the cultural museum in Kochi, India. (bottom row) Meghan Markle greets a fan as she departs the 2018 Commonwealth Day service at Westminster Abbey. Princesses Eugenie and Beatrice at Ascot Racecourse.
Back flap: Photograph by Claus Andersen/Getty Images for the Invictus Games Foundation.

Front endpaper: Students from Royal Holloway, University of London capture the Queen and the Duke of Edinburgh as they pass by.
Back endpaper: Troops march in time during the Colonel's Review, a traditional rehearsal for the Queen's official birthday parade.

p. 1: The Queen's signature in the visitors' book of the Royal College of Physicians.
p. 2: The Queen walks past a Union Jack flag during a visit to Sherborne Abbey.
pp. 4–5: Guests gather in the gardens of Buckingham Palace during a garden party hosted by the Queen.
pp. 6–7: Prince Charles holds a bald eagle called Zephyr, the mascot of the Army Air Corps, during a visit to the 132nd Sandringham Flower Show.
pp. 8–9: The Queen takes part in the naming ceremony for the P&O Cruises vessel *Britannia* at Ocean Cruise Terminal in Southampton.
pp. 10–11: Troops prepare for an official welcome ceremony for the president of Singapore on Horse Guards Parade.
p. 12: The Duke and Duchess of Cambridge look through the iconic railway clock at the Musée d'Orsay in Paris.
Right: Detail of the Prince of Wales' school history notebook, from a 2008 exhibition at Windsor Castle in celebration of his sixtieth birthday.

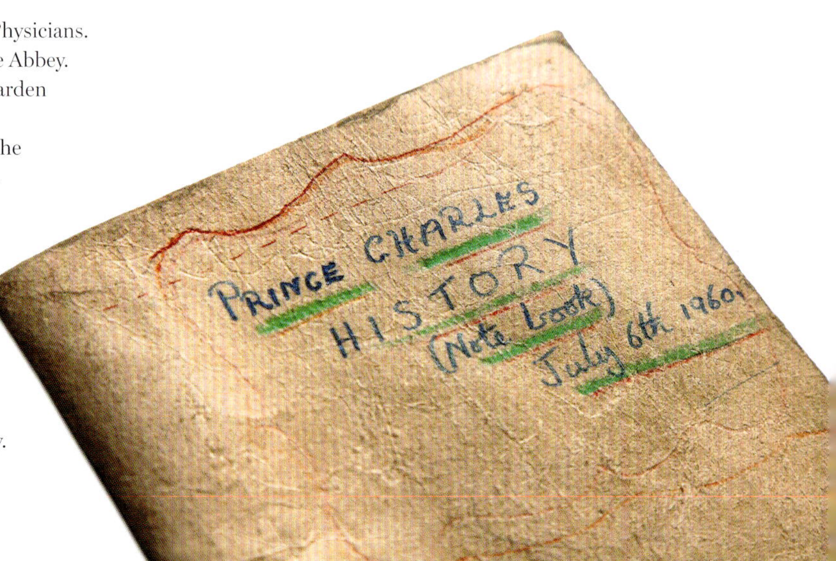

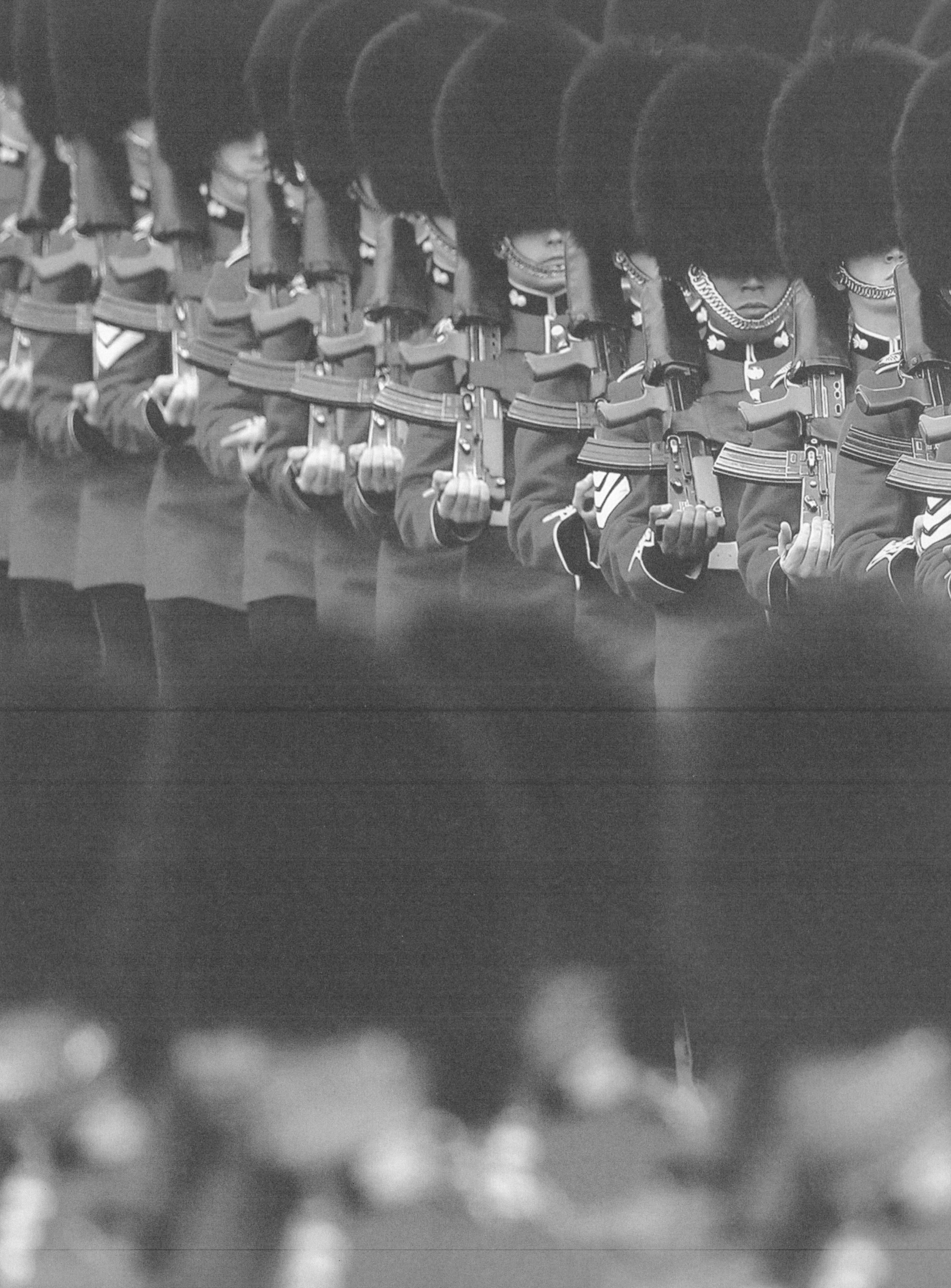